PEARSON CUSTOM LIBRARY
Selections from Mercury Reader

D1487092

Edited by
Todd Barry, Jon Brammer,
Frederick Knowles, Andrew Marvin and
Joseph Selvaggio

General Editors

Janice Neuleib
Illinois State University

Kathleen Shine Cain
Merrimack College

Stephen Ruffus
Salt Lake Community College

Table of Contents

Readings Alphabetical by Author

Starting
an Argument

Starting
an Argument

Often, people associate the word *argument* with winning, as in "winning the argument" or "losing the argument." For this reason, when taking a course on argument, they hope to learn how to argue better because they want to win and they don't like to lose.

The word *argue*, though, originates from the Latin word, *arguere*, which means to "make clear." The ability to make your ideas clear and support them with good evidence is the essence of successful argumentation, not winning or losing. In fact, the vast majority of arguments don't determine who wins or who loses. Instead, most arguments involve people striving to reach a common understanding or consensus.

1 How argument has changed recently

Arguing Today

The way people argue has been changing during your lifetime. Not long ago, argument primarily relied on a person's ability to *persuade* others to agree with a particular point. These kinds of arguments were typically one directional: A writer or speaker would argue for a specific position, and the readers or audience would

FIGURE 1 Arguing in Networks Is Crucial to Your Success
Arguing effectively today means being able to persuade and participate in ongoing conversations.

decide whether they agreed with it. These one-directional arguments happened in essays, editorials, political speeches, closing arguments, advertisements, and business proposals. The ability to make these kinds of arguments is still important, but now arguments are much more complex and dynamic.

Today, we live in a world in which arguments are multidirectional. Arguments flow in real time through networks such as e-mail, Facebook, Twitter, Reddit, YouTube, blogs, chat rooms, conference calls, and video conferencing, as well as virtual and in-person meetings. Mobile phones and electronic networks allow us to stay in constant communication, so you will be expected to work effectively with others in teams while participating in ongoing conversations (Figure 1). These real-time arguments flow, evolve, and shift directions, so you need to stay light on your feet. You need to know how to manage the flow of conversations and generate new ideas as events are happening.

In college, your professors will expect you to learn and interact with others through these kinds of networks. College courses are becoming increasingly collaborative and team-centered. Likewise, in your career, you will also need to work in these kinds of networks. Today, employers consistently report that they are looking for people who know how to work in teams and who communicate effectively. Your ability to argue in person and through a variety of media will help you succeed in today's networked workplaces. Meanwhile, as a citizen, you need to engage in the important conversations happening all around you. That's what arguing today is about.

2 Two approaches to argument: the generative approach (power with) and persuasive approach (power over)

Generative Arguments and Persuasive Arguments

To help you succeed in college, in your career, and as a citizen, this text will teach you two fundamental approaches to argument: the *generative approach* and the *persuasive approach*.

Generative Approach (Power With)

Generative arguments are conversations that happen within groups, teams, or networks, both large and small. In generative arguments, people discuss issues, generate new ideas, share experiences, and strive toward consensus in an open-ended way. These kinds of arguments include discussions, team projects, negotiations, brainstorming sessions, planning meetings, and social networking. They happen in meeting rooms, in cafes, through e-mail or blogs, on Facebook or Twitter, and other places where people gather to talk about issues. Generative arguments are sometimes called "power with" arguments because the people involved are working together to build a mutual understanding and sort out their differences.

Persuasive Approach (Power Over)

Persuasive arguments happen when an individual, a team, or an organization is trying to influence other people to believe something or take specific actions. Persuasive arguments include advertisements, opinion essays, legal cases, political speeches, sales pitches, business proposals, recommendation reports, and sermons. These arguments happen in political events, news websites, law courts, legislatures, corporate boardrooms, and on television. They are sometimes called "power over" arguments because the writer or speaker is attempting to exert power over others with words and images.

These two approaches are basically two ends of the same argument spectrum (Figure 2). In any argument, you will need to use both generative and persuasive strategies to achieve your purpose.

However, you might also find it helpful to view generative arguments and persuasive arguments as different, because they pursue different goals:

- In a generative argument, you and others are sharing opinions and information in an open-ended way, striving toward consensus. You're having a conversation because your minds aren't made up yet. Your common goal is to reach an understanding on the issue being discussed.

- When making a persuasive argument, you have mostly decided what you believe and what you want to do. You are trying to persuade others to agree with your opinions. You want to win them over to your side.

When you get into an argument, you first need to figure out whether you are in a generative (*power with*) or persuasive (*power over*) situation (Figure 3). This decision will help you figure out the best way to argue in that particular moment.[1]

---

[1] This division is an ancient one, but William Covino created this vocabulary for distinguishing between the "generative" approach and "arresting" approach in his book *Magic, Rhetoric, and Literacy* (1994).

FIGURE 2

Two Types of Argument: Generative and Persuasive
Almost all arguments fall somewhere between having a generative conversation and trying to win people over with persuasion.

FIGURE 3 Arguing in Generative and Persuasive Ways
Generative arguments tend to happen in groups or teams, where people are striving toward consensus. Persuasive arguments usually involve one person or a team trying to influence others to think or act a particular way.

Throughout this text, you will learn how to argue in both generative and persuasive ways. Specifically, you will learn how to use generative argument strategies to be successful in conversations and work more effectively in groups and teams. Then you will learn how to persuade others by using good reasoning, establishing your authority on a topic, and making effective use of emotions.

3 How to start inventing an argument by identifying the five elements of the rhetorical situation: topic, angle, purpose, audience, and context

Starting an Argument

All right, let's say you're in an argument or you're getting ready for one. Where should you start? You should begin by answering five basic questions:

Topic: *What exactly am I arguing about?*

Angle: *What new perspective can I bring to this issue?*

Purpose: *What am I trying to achieve?*

Audience: *Who is reading or listening to my argument?*

Context: *How will place, time, and medium shape my argument?*

Experts in argument call these five elements the "rhetorical situation." These elements give you a starting place for *inventing* your argument. They help you figure out what you are arguing about and what you are trying to achieve (Figure 4). Let's look at these elements individually.

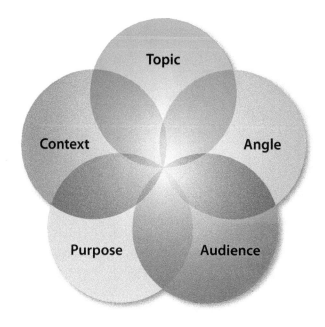

FIGURE 4 The Five Elements of the Rhetorical Situation
When you are preparing for an argument, you should consider these five elements.

Topic: What Exactly Am I Arguing About?

Your first task is to figure out what exactly you are arguing about. In college and the workplace, your professors and supervisors will usually assign you topics to write or speak about. If you are able to pick your own topic, make sure it's something that interests you.

Once you figure out your topic, you should explore it and narrow the topic down to something you can handle in a brief argument.

Exploring Your Topic

To explore your topic, you should begin with some prewriting, such as freewriting, making a brainstorming list, or creating a concept map. Prewriting will help you figure out what you already know about the issue.

> **Freewriting**—Spend about five minutes writing everything you know about your topic. Don't stop to correct or change anything. Just keep typing or writing. Sometimes it helps to not look at the screen as you are typing. You might even turn off or darken your screen so you can write without revising. Then, when you turn on your screen, you will find that you have written quite a bit about your topic already.

> **Brainstorming List**—Put your topic at the top of your screen or piece of paper. Then, for about three minutes, make a list of everything you know about that topic. Keep typing or writing everything that comes to mind and don't cross out or delete anything.

> **Concept Map**—Write your topic in the center of a piece of paper or your screen. Circle it. Then, for about three minutes, write down everything you can think of on your sheet or screen. Circle each item and connect them to other items.

Figure 5 shows how you might use a concept map or a brainstorming list to explore the same topic (minimum age for drinking alcohol). Whether you prefer freewriting, brainstorming, or mapping depends on you. All three of these invention tools are useful for getting your ideas out on your screen or a piece of paper.

Narrowing Your Topic

After freewriting, brainstorming, or drawing a concept map, you should look for ways to narrow your topic. Underline or put stars next to the few items that seem most interesting to you in your freewrite, brainstorming list, or concept map. Then spend a few minutes creating a second freewrite, brainstorming list, or concept map around those starred issues.

A second pre-writing activity is the secret to finding a great topic. It will help you focus your topic to an issue you can handle in a college-length paper or presentation. Similarly, in the workplace, narrowing your topic will help you pinpoint exactly what your supervisors or clients need to know about the issue.

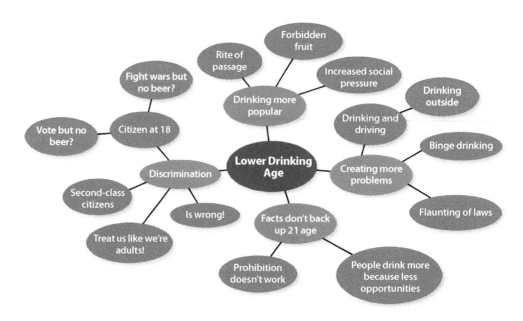

Brainstorm: Minimum Age for Alcohol

- Full citizen at 18
- Drinking and driving
- Alcoholism
- Drinking in high school
- Binge drinking increasing
- Prohibition doesn't work
- Discrimination is wrong
- Force drinking outside
- Canada's drinking age is 18
- People drink and drive more!
- Bars and homes are safer
- Age 21 makes alcohol more desirable
- We're adults. Treat us that way.

- Forbidden fruit
- Fight in wars but not have beer?
- Alcohol and illegal drugs not same
- Drinking in controlled environments
- People learn to break laws
- Flaunting of laws sets bad precedent
- Would be less social pressure to drink
- Statistics don't back up 21 age limit
- Drinking becomes a rite of passage
- Makes drinking an underground activity
- College presidents support lower drinking age
- Much advertising pitched at college students
- Drink too much when you have it
- Other countries have lower age limits

FIGURE 5
Concept Mapping and Brainstorming
Concept maps and brainstorming lists are good ways to narrow your topic.

Angle: What New Perspective Can I Bring to This Issue?

Mistakenly, people often assume they need to find a *new* topic. They waste hours looking for something "new" that they can write an argument about. Truth is, new topics are rare because almost all topics have been argued about before. However—and this is important—you can always find new *angles* on existing topics.

A new angle is a fresh perspective that allows you to see an established topic in a new light. To find your angle, answer the following two questions:

What has happened recently that makes this topic especially interesting or important *right now*?

What new perspective can I personally bring to this topic?

What Has Happened Recently?

For example, the topic of underage drinking has been around for decades, so it's not a new topic. If you want to write about this topic, you should first ask yourself, "What's new about this topic that makes it interesting or important right now?" Here are a few possible answers:

Possible Angle 1: The recent fad of combining energy drinks and alcohol is increasing the number of people who are binge drinking, because the caffeine makes people feel more sober than they are.

Possible Angle 2: Binge drinking has become entrenched in some parts of the 18- to 20-year-old culture because my generation has now grown up with the 21-year minimum age limit. College students are still drinking alcohol, but they have changed their drinking practices to skirt and even rebel against the law. Binge drinking is one of those changes.

Possible Angle 3: Last Saturday, two underage college students drowned in Tennessee because they were drinking near a river when a flash flood happened. They were drinking in this remote area because it's an "illegal" activity even though the product is legal.

Possible Angle 4: In August, the government reported that binge drinking among 18- to 20-year-olds has actually increased over the three decades since the 21-year minimum age law passed.

Each of these new angles puts this "old" topic in a new light. They all refer to something that happened recently, which makes this topic interesting or important.

What Has Happened to Me Personally with This Topic?

You can also find a new angle by reflecting on your own experiences with an issue. Has something happened to you that caused you to change your mind or see your topic from a new perspective? You could use your own experiences as a basis for discussing your topic in a new and interesting way. For example,

Possible Angle 1: Within 48 hours of stepping onto this campus, I was offered my first beer even though I was only 18 years old. That night, I went to my first college party, where people were binge drinking. Needless to say, the 21-year-old minimum age was not a deterrent. To be honest, nobody even thought about it. What I thought I learned that night was that some laws could be ignored by college students. That was a bad lesson to learn.

Possible Angle 2: Mike Hampton was a kid who grew up with me in Franklin, Georgia. We didn't hang out together much, but we played football and had mutual friends.

He liked to party a bit more than me, but I did my share. Last month, Mike was out drinking with his college roommates. He ran a stop sign at a rural intersection and smashed into another car, killing one person and injuring two others. Mike's now out of jail on bail, awaiting trial for vehicular homicide. Since then, I keep thinking about how that could have been me. An age limit hadn't kept Mike from driving drunk, and it hadn't kept those people from getting hurt. Surely, I keep thinking, there must be a better way to stop young people from drinking and driving.

Here's a hint: Even if your professor asks you to write about a traditional college essay topic, you should look for new angles on that topic. Don't just offer the same predictable response to the assignment prompt. That's what the others in your class will do. Your argument will stand out if you respond to the assigned topic in a way that reflects current issues or your own experiences.

The same is true in the workplace. The innovators and entrepreneurs are the people who are always looking for new angles or perspectives on existing problems. Completely new products and services are rare, but there are always new ways to innovate on existing products and services. Your colleagues and supervisors will appreciate your efforts to be creative and solve problems in new ways.

Purpose: What Am I Trying to Achieve?

Your purpose is what you want your argument to accomplish. Any time you make an argument, you should have a clear sense of *why* you are arguing and *what* you want to achieve. You should be able to state your purpose in one sentence.

Writing a Purpose Statement

Your purpose needs to be focused, and it needs to be clear about what you are trying to do. For example, an initial purpose statement might be something like, "I'm trying to get the drinking age reduced from 21 to 18 years old." That may be your long-term goal, but is that *really* the purpose of the argument? Could a single argument really accomplish that? No, of course not.

You need to focus your purpose statement on something that could be actually achieved. It's fine to start with a broad purpose statement, but then you need to sharpen it. For example,

Broad Purpose Statement: In this paper, I am arguing that the minimum drinking age should be reduced from 21 to 18 years old.

More Focused Purpose Statement: In this paper, I am arguing that the minimum drinking age does not decrease incidents of binge drinking or drunk driving; therefore, it is an unnecessary law.

Even More Focused: In this paper, I am arguing that the rights of adult citizens between the ages of 18 and 21 are being infringed upon by a minimum drinking age law that does not decrease incidents of binge drinking or drunk driving; therefore, as full citizens who are being discriminated against, we should work toward overturning this unnecessary law.

The "Even More Focused" purpose statement is a bit long, but it sets an achievable and specific purpose for the argument.

Try to boil your purpose statement down to one sentence. This will help you keep your argument narrow enough to be handled in a college-length paper.

Audience: Who Is Reading or Listening to My Argument?

Your audience includes the people who are discussing an issue with you or reading or listening to your argument. Obviously, different people will react to your argument in different ways. Think about your audience's needs, values, and attitudes (Figure 6). Doing so will help you select information that is most important to them and present it in ways that they will find most helpful or persuasive.

FIGURE 6 Analyzing Your Audience
Each audience is different and will respond to your ideas in a different way. Before writing or speaking, you should analyze their needs, values, and attitudes.

What Do They Need?

Make a list of the information your audience *needs* in order to understand your topic, make a decision, or take action. Meanwhile, think about which of these "needs" will motivate them. At a basic level, people need material things like food, security, health, money, and shelter. At a more complex level, they need immaterial things like friendship, respect, self-esteem, confidence, dignity, and love.

What Do They Value?

Make a list of your audience's values and the things they value. In other words, try to figure out what your audience values and where those values come from. On a social level, their values might be based on their experiences, personalities, faiths, social expectations, or cultures. On a personal level, one person might value creativity while someone else values predictability. Another person prefers an emotional attachment to an issue, while someone else prefers a logical approach. Making a list of your audience's social and personal values will help you determine how to appeal to them.

What Is Their Attitude?

Try to figure out your audience's attitude toward you and your topic. Are they positive, wary, hopeful, careful, concerned, skeptical, or excited about what you have to say? If they have a positive attitude toward you and your topic, you will probably find it easier to reach consensus or persuade them. But if they have a negative attitude toward your topic or you, you are going to need to work around their negative attitude to present your ideas in ways that appeal to them.

This thorough audience analysis might seem like additional work, but it really only takes a few minutes. You can even use Internet search engines like Google, Bing, or Yahoo to help you learn more about your audience and their needs, values, and attitudes.

Context: How Will the Place, Time, and Medium Shape This Argument?

The context is the place, time, and medium in which your argument will be accessed by your audience. An argument that works in one place and time might not work in a different place and time. Likewise, an argument that works in one medium, such as a website, a blog, paper document, or podcast, might not work as well in another medium.

You need to shape your argument to the context in which your audience will experience it. Here are some factors to consider:

What Is the Physical Context?

Think about the physical places in which people will most likely read or hear your argument. Are they at home or in a meeting? Are they in a café or in a classroom? Could they be reading on a bus or airplane? Each of these physical contexts would require adjustments to the content, organization, style, and design of the argument.

How Does the Medium Affect the Message?

Today, most arguments happen in electronic media, not on paper. Obviously, an argument uploaded to YouTube will have a different effect on the audience than a traditional 1-inch-margin, double-spaced college essay (Figure 7). Each medium has its strengths and weaknesses, so you should find out how the medium you choose will influence how your audience interprets and understands your argument.

What Is the Economic Context?

Think about how monetary concerns and other financial issues impact your audience's decision making. Even the best ideas won't be accepted if there isn't money or resources to put them into action. So consider the costs involved with your ideas.

What Is the Political Context?

Consider the ways in which your argument changes the political landscape on a personal level. When people make decisions, their choices affect their relationships with others in both positive and negative ways. Even the best ideas won't be accepted if they dramatically alter a person's relationships in an overly negative way.

FIGURE 7 The Choice of Medium Will Affect Your Argument Using a medium like YouTube will change the nature of your argument and the ways your audience reacts to it.

As with audience analysis, this deep thinking about your argument's context probably seems like extra work. But it only takes a couple minutes to identify the contextual forces that shape how your audience thinks about your topic or makes decisions. You want to make sure you are aware of all the factors that might influence the direction of the argument and how people react to what you are arguing.

Developing Your Main Claim (Working Thesis)

4 Strategies for developing a main claim or working thesis

The heart of an argument is its *main claim*, which usually begins as a *working thesis*. Once you have figured out your topic, angle, purpose, audience, and context, you can begin to develop the working thesis that will guide your research. There are four major types of thesis statements for an argument:

Generative Thesis—A generative thesis statement tells your audience, "Here's what I believe right now, but I'm open to hearing what others believe and modifying my views." A generative thesis usually highlights the common values, beliefs, and experiences that will help people reach a common understanding or consensus. For example,

> **Working Thesis:** As college students, we see first hand the negative consequences of the under-21 age restriction on alcohol consumption. By working with legislators, administrators, the public, and other students, we can work toward developing a solution to this problem.

Highlights common values and experiences

Stresses a willingness to consider different ideas

Working Thesis: Human-caused climate change is something that will impact our generation, but we need to keep an open mind about the many pathways available to achieving sustainability.

These generative thesis statements are seeking common understanding and consensus with the audience.

Persuasive Thesis—A persuasive thesis statement tells your audience, "Here's what I believe, and I'm going to try to persuade you to believe it, too." A persuasive thesis presents an argumentative claim that the readers or audience can choose to agree or disagree with. This kind of thesis typically has two parts, an *assertion* and *support*.

Assertion

Support

Working Thesis: Politicians won't lower the drinking age as long as students stay silent; therefore, we need to become much more active in the political system by registering to vote, getting our message out there, and rallying for laws that benefit us.

Assertion

Support

Working Thesis: In this proposal, we argue that Knapp University should convert completely to sustainable energy sources and end its dependence on fossil fuels. That way, we can do our share to minimize human-caused climate change while making Knapp into a forward-thinking, elite university that attracts top faculty and students.

An effective persuasion thesis needs to be *reasonable*, meaning at least two defensible sides are available and your audience should feel able to agree or disagree with your claim.

Question Thesis—In some arguments, you might want to hold off stating your thesis until the conclusion, especially if you are making a controversial argument or your audience might be resistant to your views. In these situations, you might pose your thesis as a question:

Working Thesis: Is the current under-21 drinking age reducing the amount of alcohol that young people consume, or is it really causing more harm than good?

Working Thesis: Would the benefits of converting to sustainable energy sources be worth the costs for Knapp University?

If you use a question thesis in your introduction, you need to include a generative or persuasive thesis statement in the conclusion of your argument. For example, the following thesis statements could appear in the conclusion.

Concluding Thesis: The current under-21 drinking age causes more harm than good, so it is vital that we work toward changing laws and attitudes in ways that promote a lower age and a healthier relationship between young people and alcohol.

Concluding Thesis: The costs of fossil-fuel energy will soon rise dramatically, so a conversion to sustainable energy, though seemingly expensive now, will eventually save Knapp University a great amount of money and make it more competitive for top faculty and students.

These kinds of concluding thesis statements answer in a definitive way the thesis questions that were posed in the introduction.

Implied Thesis—In some kinds of arguments, you may choose to not state your thesis explicitly. An implied thesis lets the readers or audience figure out the meaning of your argument for themselves. This kind of thesis is especially common in a narrative argument, because you want the audience to figure out the meaning of your story without explicitly telling them.

An implied thesis can be tricky, though, so you should use this kind of thesis only in special situations. After all, if you don't explicitly state a thesis in your argument, your audience could interpret what you write or say in ways you didn't expect. So, if you choose to use an implied thesis, you need to make sure the main point of your argument comes through clearly for the audience, even though you aren't stating that main point directly.

Using Genres to Argue Effectively

In this text, you will also learn how to use *genres* to argue clearly and compellingly. You may have learned how to use genres in a previous writing or public speaking course. If so, in this text you will learn a new "genre set" that is especially useful for developing arguments.

If the concept of genres is new to you, you are about to learn a very useful tool for writing and speaking. Genres are helpful for generating, organizing, editing, and designing arguments. Knowing how to use genres will save you time while helping you write and speak more effectively in almost any situation.

What Is a Genre?

That's not an easy question to answer. Traditionally, the concept of genres has been used to sort literary texts into categories (e.g., novels, poems, dramas, comedies, tragedies, biographies, epics). Genres can be used to sort other things like movies (e.g., horror, romantic comedy, buddy flick, science fiction), video games (e.g., shooter, adventure, role-playing, racing, strategy, trivia), or music (e.g., hip-hop, country, bluegrass, heavy metal, jazz, classical).

More recently, though, genres have been used to understand how people use familiar patterns to communicate in recurring situations. For example, a movie review is a common argument genre. Let's imagine you are looking for reviews of a recently released movie on Rotten Tomatoes (rottentomatoes.com). Before you begin reading a review, you already have expectations about its content, organization, style, and design. Both you and the review writer is already familiar with the movie review genre, so you are both able to use this genre to make meaning together.

In other words, a movie review is a genre because it is a familiar social pattern that occurs over and over. You, as the reader, know what to expect. If one of the reviewers decides to ignore the genre, you're going to be confused or annoyed. For instance, let's say one of the reviewers on Rotten Tomatoes spends most of her time

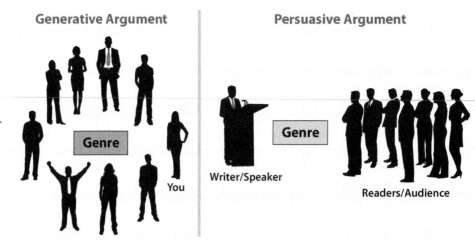

Generative Argument

Persuasive Argument

Genre

Genre

You

Writer/Speaker

Readers/Audience

FIGURE 8 Genre as a Place Where People Make Meaning Together People make meaning together with genres. Therefore, genres need to be flexible to fit the needs of various situations and people.

complaining about her "dull" weekend while offering only a few comments about the movie she was supposed to be reviewing. You're going to be irritated. She just wasted your time because she didn't use the genre properly.

Genres are more than organizational structures. They do provide helpful patterns for organizing arguments, but they also offer much more. Instead, genres should be understood as *meeting places where people make meaning together* (Figure 8). You, as a writer or speaker, supply the words and images that support your argument. Meanwhile, your audience is responsible for interpreting those words and images to figure out your meaning. The genre is a familiar space in which you and your audience create this common understanding together.

OK, Got It. So, What Is a Genre?

Here's a bottom-line definition of genre: *Genres reflect recurring social activities and the ways people in communities and cultures get things done.* Genres help you make choices about the following:

- the information you should include in your argument

- how the information in your argument should be organized

- what style would be appropriate for your argument

- how the argument should look

- what medium would work best for the argument

You already use genres every day. They are the familiar patterns you use when you communicate with others, whether you are talking on the phone, ordering coffee at a café, or debating politics with your friends. Even more than that, though, genres

What do you need to do?	Try this genre.
Describe a person, object, place, or event from a specific perspective.	Description
Compare two or more similar people, places, or objects.	Comparison
Explain what caused something else to happen.	Causal Analysis
Use images and graphics to explain something.	Visual Essay
Tell a story that argues a point.	Narrative
Review or critique something.	Review
Express an opinion on a current event.	Commentary
Evaluate or review someone or something.	Evaluation
Challenge an argument made by someone else.	Refutation
Propose a new idea, product, or plan.	Proposal
Research an issue and explain my findings.	Research Paper or Report

FIGURE 9
Figuring Out the Appropriate Genre
The best genre for your paper or presentation depends on what you need to do.

also reflect the common values, practices, beliefs, and expectations of the groups and cultures to which you belong.

So, when you need to write or present an argument, you should first figure out which genre would be best for achieving your purpose and getting your message across to your audience. Once you figure out which genre is appropriate, writing your paper or creating your presentation becomes much easier. Similarly, when you are analyzing or responding to someone else's argument, you should figure out which genre the writer or speaker is using. Once you recognize the genre, you can better understand, challenge, or respond to that person's argument.

Choosing the Best Argument Genre

Choosing the right genre for an argument depends on what you are trying to achieve. Figure 9 lists the most common argument genres you will use in college, the workplace, and public life.

When you know your purpose, you can then figure out which genre or genres would be appropriate for that kind of argument. Keep in mind, though, that more than one genre might be available to help you accomplish your goals. So you should consider a couple possible genres before settling on one that will work.

Fortunately, your professors and supervisors will usually signal to you which genre they want you to use.

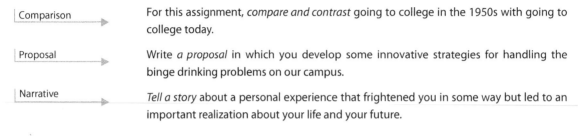

Comparison — For this assignment, *compare and contrast* going to college in the 1950s with going to college today.

Proposal — Write *a proposal* in which you develop some innovative strategies for handling the binge drinking problems on our campus.

Narrative — *Tell a story* about a personal experience that frightened you in some way but led to an important realization about your life and your future.

Your professors won't always name a specific genre, but if you look closely at the assignment sheet, you will usually find that the assignment itself will signal which argument genre you need to use. Similarly, at your job, your supervisor may or may not signal the genre that he or she wants you to use:

Causal analysis — I need you to figure out what's *causing* the sudden rise in applications for government-funded lunches in our school district.

Evaluation — Your task this week is to *evaluate* which industrial robot is best for spot-welding the bodies of our tractors.

Again, if you look closely at what your supervisor is asking you to do, you can usually figure out which genre will help you get the project done.

 **5** How genres are used to invent, organize, draft, design, and edit arguments

Using Genres and the Five Elements of the Rhetorical Situation

We threw quite a bit at you in this chapter, so let's wrap up with a simple takeaway. You need to learn how to argue in both generative and persuasive situations. The five elements of the rhetorical situation will help you figure out your topic, angle, purpose, audience, and context. Then choosing the right genre will help you invent your ideas, organize them, create the appropriate style, design your argument, and pick the best medium.

This is one of those "work smarter, not harder" kinds of situations. You are going to save time and argue more effectively if you spend a few minutes thinking about the elements of the rhetorical situation, developing a working thesis, and choosing the appropriate genre.

Yes, this kind of preparation takes time, and your time is valuable. Try out what you learned in this chapter. You will find that the ten minutes you spend preparing to argue will save you a great amount of time and effort, because you won't waste your time going down dead ends. Meanwhile, this kind of preparation will make you a much more effective writer and presenter, which will help you succeed in your classes and your career. The extra time you spend on preparation will be worth it.

Are you ready to get going right now? Here are some basic ideas to help you prepare for an argument:

1	There are two approaches to argument: *generative arguments* (power with) and *persuasive arguments* (power over).
2	The differences between these approaches to argument are not clear cut. Persuasive arguments sometimes happen in groups, and generative arguments can be persuasive.
3	Generative arguments happen when people discuss issues and strive toward *consensus* in groups. People work together to build common ground and decide what to do.
4	Persuasive arguments happen when one side is trying to convince others to take action or believe something.
5	The five elements of the rhetorical situation include topic, angle, purpose, audience, and context.
6	Genres reflect recurring social activities and ways people in communities and cultures get things done.
7	A genre is a place where people—both the writer/speaker and the audience—meet to make meaning together.
8	Genres help you make choices about the information you should include, how that information should be organized, what style would be appropriate, and how the document or presentation should look.
9	In most cases, your professors or supervisors will signal directly or indirectly which genre would be suitable for an assignment.
10	Genres and the five elements of the rhetorical situation work together in both generative and persuasive arguments to help you develop an effective argument.

TEN THINGS YOU NEED TO KNOW

1. With your group, look over the list of genres that are included in Figure 9. Ask each member of your group to choose one of these genres and find three examples of that genre. The Internet is a good place to start searching, but you will also find examples in newspapers, magazines, and other print sources. Then have each member compare and contrast the three examples, explaining their content, organization, style, and design.

2. Ask each member of your group to find an example of a document or presentation that was *not* appropriate for its audience or context. How did the writer or speaker misunderstand his or her audience? What were some of the problems created by this misunderstanding? How, if possible, could the writer or speaker have adjusted the argument to fit this audience?

3. Think of two advertising campaigns aimed at college students, one effective and one ineffective, that you have seen on television or on the Internet. How did the effective advertising campaign target you or people like you in a persuasive way? Did the advertising agency properly anticipate your needs, values, and attitude? Why did the ineffective campaign fail? What did the advertisers not understand about people like you that led them to design an ineffective campaign?

1. Choose a contentious issue that is in the news right now. Write one page in which you describe how people could use a generative approach to talk about this contentious issue. Then write one page that describes how someone might use a persuasive approach to influence the opinions of others. Write a reflection in which you talk about the differences and similarities between these two approaches to argument.

2. Make a list of five topics that interest you personally. Then come up with a new angle for each of these five topics. Your new angle should refer to something that has happened recently or a personal experience that gives you a unique insight into this topic. Choose the best topic and narrow it down to something very specific. Then develop a thesis statement that would give you the basis of an interesting argument. Hand in your thesis statement with notes to your professor.

3. Choose a topic that interests you. Come up with a new angle on this topic. Then develop a thesis statement that you could support or prove. Look through the table of genres in Figure 9. Which genres on this list could be used to make an argument that supports your thesis statement? Why do you believe some genres would work better than others? Now choose a genre that would not be appropriate for your topic. Why would this genre not work well? In a brief e-mail to your instructor, explain why you believe some genres would work better than others to help you make the argument you have in mind.

Credits

Credits are listed in order of appearance.

Photo Credits

Digital Vision/Photodisc/Getty Images; (bl), Blend Images/Alamy; (bm), Maridav/Fotolia; (br), Monkey Business/Fotolia; (tl), Radius Images/Alamy; (tml), PhotoEdit/Alamy; (tmr), Iain Masterton/Alamy; (tr), PSL Images/Alamy; (bl), William Perugini/Shutterstock; (br), Pressmaster/Shutterstock; (l), Monkey Business/Fotolia; (r), Wavebreakmedia Ltd UC1/Alamy

Text Credits

Screen.Capture, "21 Is It Time to Lower the Drinking Age?" Used by permission from Reason.com and Reason TV.

Persuasive
Arguments

From Chapter 3 of *Argument Today with Readings*, First Edition. Richard Johnson-Sheehan and Charles Paine. Copyright © 2015 by Pearson Education, Inc. All rights reserved.

Persuasive
Arguments

The purpose of a persuasive argument is to influence the beliefs of others and motivate them to do what you think should be done. Aristotle, the ancient Greek philosopher, offered one of the first known definitions of rhetoric (and argument) when he wrote,

> Rhetoric is an ability in each particular case to see the available means of persuasion.[1]

In this definition, you can see the essence of a persuasive argument. To persuade others, you first need to *envision* or *imagine* the available paths for winning them over to your side. Then you need to choose one or more paths and use your abilities to write, speak, and design to convince them that you know the best way forward.

Persuasive arguments are sometimes called "power-over" arguments. When trying to persuade others, you are trying to exert power over them. You are trying to change their minds or influence them to take a specific action. Persuasive arguments are not bullying or trying to "win at all costs." Quite the opposite. To be persuasive, you need to listen carefully to all sides of an issue and respond fairly to any reasonable alternatives. You need to be flexible, adjusting your argument as you gain more information and hear other sides of the issue.

---

[1] This definition is a variation found in George Kennedy's translation of Aristotle's *On Rhetoric,* 2nd ed. Oxford: Oxford, UP, 2007, p. 37.

Persuasive arguments *feel* like arguments. There are usually two or more sides, and people disagree about what to believe and what to do. Your audience understands that you are trying to persuade them to believe or do something. Your job as the writer or speaker is to state your claims clearly and give your audience good reasons and evidence to see things your way (Figure 1).

The ability to persuade others will be vital to your success in college, your career, and your life as a citizen. In advanced college courses, you will often be asked by professors to argue for or against specific views. In the workplace, you will need to persuade your supervisors, coworkers, and clients that you have good ideas and know the best way forward. And, as a citizen of a democracy, you will need to take a stand for what you believe.

FIGURE 1 Persuasive Arguments
Persuasive arguments involve a speaker or writer trying to convince others to believe or do something specific.

Strategies for Successful Persuasive Arguments

1 How persuasive arguments are used to influence others to change their minds or take action

When you make a *persuasive argument*, you are in a position of power. You "have the floor" or you are holding the attention of the audience. There are five main strategies you can use to argue persuasively:

Strategy 1: State a reasonable and specific claim (your thesis).

Strategy 2: Support your claim with reasoning, authority, and emotion.

Strategy 3: Support your claim with existing evidence.

Strategy 4: Use commonplaces to structure your argument.

Strategy 5: Avoid fallacious arguments.

In any persuasive argument, you will use a combination of these strategies to build a convincing argument.

2 Five strategies for developing successful persuasive arguments

Strategy 1: State a Reasonable and Specific Claim (Your Thesis)

Using a persuasive thesis is one of the surest ways to cue your audience that you are making a persuasive argument. Your thesis is the moment in your argument at which you are going to tell your audience exactly what you are trying to prove. A good persuasive thesis signals to your audience that you will be asking them to decide whether they agree or disagree with your claim.

A version of your thesis will typically appear in two places in your persuasive argument:

Introduction—State the claim you are trying to prove, or you will ask a key question that you intend to answer.

Conclusion—Restate your thesis with more emphasis. This concluding thesis statement drives home your main claim for the audience.

Here are a few examples of persuasive thesis statements:

Thesis statement: The death penalty is necessary because execution is still the only way to ensure that the worst criminals will never walk free and won't be able to harm others.

Thesis statement: The 2012 remake of *Red Dawn* is one of the worst action movies of all time because of its farfetched plot, unconvincing characters, and blatant xenophobia.

Sometimes the best way to express your thesis is with a thesis question in your argument's introduction and a thesis statement in your conclusion.

Thesis question (in the introduction): Has cheating on exams become so common that college students no longer view cheating as dishonest or unethical?

Thesis statement (in the conclusion): As I have shown in this report, students still believe cheating is dishonest, but the pressure to do well on exams sometimes causes them to put their ethics aside.

Thesis Question (in the introduction): Shakespeare's *Hamlet* has been remade in just about every imaginable way, so is it possible for the Millennium Theater to give this old classic new life?

Thesis Statement (in the conclusion): The Millennium Theater's production of Hamlet uses contemporary political themes and stunning imagery to put an exciting new spin on Shakespeare's *Hamlet*.

An effective thesis question opens the door by identifying an issue to be investigated. Then the thesis statement in the conclusion closes the door by stating your final response to that issue.

A Reasonable Thesis: Choosing Sides

Your thesis is reasonable if your audience is able to agree or disagree with it in a logical way. In other words, at least two defensible sides to the issue need to be available.

A reasonable thesis tends to exist somewhere between personal judgments and proven facts (Figure 2). After all, statements based on proven facts, such as "The Earth is a round planet" or "The Battle of Hastings happened in 1066 ADE," are not really worth arguing about. If we stopped to quarrel about every proven fact, our arguments would soon become trifling and meaningless. Likewise, matters of personal taste, such as "I hate cold weather!" or "Cold pizza is my favorite breakfast food," are also not worth arguing about because people are entitled to their personal likes and dislikes.

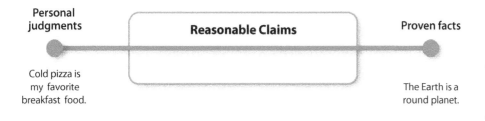

FIGURE 2 The Region of Reasonable Claims An effective persuasive argument begins with a reasonable claim. These claims lie in the region between personal judgments and proven facts.

Can you still argue about proven facts or matters of personal taste? Sure. In a sense, you can argue about anything. Some people still argue that the Earth is flat, and your friends might be skeptical that you really like cold pizza for breakfast. You could argue about these topics just for fun, but it's unlikely you would argue about these topics in a serious way.

Therefore, your first task is to state a reasonable claim that you will try to persuade your readers to accept as probably true. For example, here are three claims that take three opposing sides of an issue (other sides are possible as well).

Thesis 1: If we can educate American consumers about the immorality and unsustainability of the palm-oil industry, they will be less likely to buy these products, which will reduce the exploitation of Indonesians and reduce the amount of deforestation.

Thesis 2: While it's true that the palm-oil industry exploits Indonesians and causes massive deforestation, anything that reduces American consumption of palm oil will only make matters worse for the Indonesians by depriving them of employment.

Thesis 3: We must enact federal laws that severely limit the use of palm oil in American food and cosmetic products because American consumers care more about price and convenience than about ethics or saving the planet.

While these claims reflect the personal opinions of the writers, they turn those opinions into reasonable claims. All three sides want to persuade you, the reader, that they are *probably* right.

To test whether your thesis is reasonable, try to come up with at least one opposing thesis statement that disagrees with it. If someone might reasonably support this opposing thesis, then your thesis is addressing an issue worthy of an argument.

A Specific Thesis: Focusing Your Argument

Your persuasive thesis also needs to be specific, meaning it is focused enough for you to prove it in the space and time you have available.

The Roman orator Cicero believed that every argumentative claim could be viewed as hinging on a main question, or *issue*. He suggested that there are four kinds of issues that people argue about:

- Definition: What is it?

- Causation: Why did it happen?

- Evaluation: How good or bad is it?

- Recommendation: What should be done about it?

Typically, one of these four issues will be the main focus of your argument (Figure 3). For example, let's say you want to defend an American citizen's right to bear arms while developing some sensible guidelines about the kinds of weaponry people can own. The first version of your thesis might be something like the following:

Rough thesis statement: United States citizens should have the right to bear arms.

This rough thesis statement is way too broad, but it's a start. Let's use Cicero's four issues to focus it. Ask yourself whether your argument is based on an issue of *definition, causation, evaluation,* or *recommendation*. Then narrow your thesis statement by focusing on one of these issues:

Definition thesis: A clearer definition of the Second Amendment is needed because most people agree that some kinds of arms, such as rifles and shotguns, should be allowed, while almost all of us agree that other kinds of arms, such as grenades, machine guns, howitzers, and chemical weapons, don't belong in the hands of citizens.

Causation thesis: Politically motivated gun laws take weapons out of the hands of law-abiding people who want to protect themselves and their homes while ensuring that only criminals and gang members have access to weapons.

Evaluation thesis: The failure of the 1994 Federal Assault Weapons Ban demonstrated that these kinds of sweeping gun laws don't really keep semiautomatic firearms off the streets because such laws are easily subverted or undermined.

Recommendation thesis: My recommendation is that we put the emphasis on gun owners, not guns, by creating a licensing system that reinforces safety, responsible gun ownership, and earned access to more powerful forms of weaponry.

Each of these thesis statements focuses the argument a different way. Which one is most persuasive? That depends on your argument's topic, angle, purpose, audience, and context of use. You might find it helpful to write a thesis statement that fits each of these four issues. Then choose the one that seems the most persuasive.

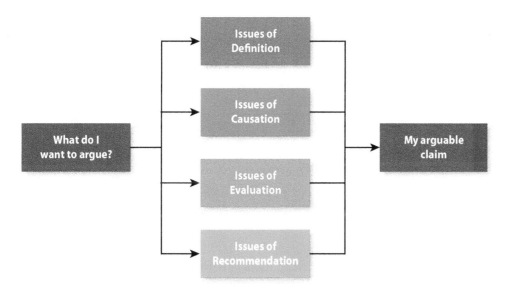

FIGURE 3

Developing a Specific Thesis
First, figure out what you want to argue. Then sharpen your claim by figuring out which type of argument you are making. The result will be a much more focused thesis statement.

Strategy 2: Use Appeals to Reason, Authority, and Emotion (*Logos*, *Ethos*, and *Pathos*)

After you finish crafting a reasonable and specific thesis, you should start thinking about how you will support your claim. Aristotle suggested that three kinds of "invented" proofs could be used to support argumentative claims:

Reasoning *(logos)*—using logical statements and examples to reason with your audience

Authority *(ethos)*—using your reputation or the authority of others to demonstrate to your audience that you are knowledgeable, fair, and practical

Emotion *(pathos)*—using emotional appeals to influence your audience to sympathize with your cause or reject another point of view

You may have been told that an argument should rely exclusively on solid reasoning while avoiding appeals to authority or emotion. That's not true. Almost all persuasive arguments rely on a combination of reasoning, authority, and emotion to persuade people to believe or do something (Figure 4).

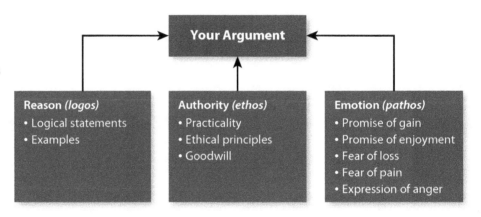

FIGURE 4
Supporting Claims with Reason, Authority, and Emotion
Three kinds of appeals can be used to support a claim: appeals to reason, to authority, or to emotion.

These three proofs, which are commonly known by the Greek terms *logos, ethos,* and *pathos,* are called "invented" proofs because they depend on you, the writer or speaker, to create or invent them. In other words, these proofs didn't exist before you or someone else came up with them. As such, they are different from already existing evidence, such as proven facts, artifacts, physical evidence, data, contracts, photographs, testimonials, and so on. (You will learn about using these noninvented proofs later in this chapter.)

Using Reason (*Logos*): Employing Logical Statements and Examples

When you appeal to reason, you are trying to convince your audience that your claim is based on logic and common sense. There are two kinds of reasoning: logical statements and examples.

Logical Statements

When using logical statements, you should use the beliefs, evidence, and facts that your audience already accepts to build your claims.

Logical Pattern	Example
If...then. "If you believe X, then you should also believe Y."	If you agree that biodiversity is essential for the survival of humanity, then you should support the ratification of the Biodiversity Convention.
Either...or. "Either you believe X or Y; you can't logically believe both."	Either you believe that *both* abortion and the death penalty are immoral, or you are not truly prolife.
Cause and effect. "X causes Y" or "Y is caused by X."	The teen-girl media actively peddle the "boyfriend story," which teaches young women that their happiness ultimately depends upon their attractiveness to boys.
Costs and benefits. "The benefits A, B, and C show that X is worth the costs."	Because online learning enhances interactions among students and affords greater flexibility for working students, colleges should invest in online learning despite the significant start-up costs.
Better and worse. "Y is better than X" or "Y is worse than X."	The *Halo* video game franchise is showing its age, but its rich storyline still makes it superior to the more simplistic *Call of Duty* series.
Possible and impossible. "If X is/is not possible, then Y (which is easier/harder by comparison) is/is not possible."	If we could put a human being on the moon at a time when the handheld calculator hadn't yet been invented, then surely we should be able to put humans on the surface of Mars with today's computers and biomedical advances.
Opposites. "If A is X, then its opposite B is Y."	If civil political discourse generally leads to responsible governance, then uncivil and combative political discourse generally leads to irresponsible governance.

Examples

Using examples is also an effective way to support your arguments with real or realistic cases or illustrations.

Type of Example	Illustration
Historical examples	For example, on September 11, 2001, terrorists took advantage of our free society to launch a devastating attack.
Personal experiences	Last summer, I witnessed other employees at the restaurant picking up dropped food from the floor and serving it to customers because they were afraid the manager would yell at them for falling behind.
Facts and data	Data from the 2012 election revealed that that Hispanics are now a rapidly growing 10 percent of the voters; therefore, they can no longer be ignored or abused by candidates who want to win ("Election" 23).
Patterns of experiences	In every national election since 1996, people have reported less resistance to the decriminalization of marijuana, and we see no reason for that trend to change (Ramirez 87).
Quotes and opinions of experts	Dr. Shirley Hampton, a presidential historian at Rutgers University, says, "Eisenhower is often viewed as a popular President who didn't do much, but he actually exerted great influence on the rapidly-changing American society of the 1950s" (54).

In-text citations should be used to signal the source for each fact.

Note: Keep in mind that each of these examples relies on preexisting facts. If those facts were taken from another source, then the original source and the page numbers should be cited.

Authority (*Ethos*): Establishing Credibility

People tend to be persuaded by individuals they trust. If your audience trusts you and your sources, you will speak with more authority and your argument will be more persuasive (Figure 5). If they don't trust you or your sources, reasoning alone will not win them over to your side.

FIGURE 5
Authority through Reputation
Celebrities are often used to promote causes because their credibility with the public is already established. If you're not a celebrity or expert, you will need to work harder to establish your authority with the audience.

You can build or strengthen your authority by showing your audience that you are practical, follow ethical principles, and are a person of goodwill.

Practicality

Being practical means putting an emphasis on solving problems, being resourceful, and getting things done.

Keep it simple—People prefer straightforward solutions that they can understand. Avoid giving them long lectures or spinning out complicated theories that explain the issue. Instead, put the emphasis on taking action and keeping things as simple as possible.

Be resourceful—Try to be as resourceful as possible, and show that you are willing to endure some hardship yourself. Being practical means being mindful of costs and the sacrifices people will need to make if they agree to your argument.

Know your stuff—Demonstrate through your sources that you have researched the topic thoroughly and know the facts and major issues accurately and in depth.

Accept disagreement—You should acknowledge that reasonable people can disagree about the issue. Being practical involves being realistic about what is possible, not idealistic about what should happen in a perfect world.

Ethical Principles

Demonstrate that you are arguing for an outcome that meets a consistent set of ethical principles.

Know your rights (and the rights of others)—When appropriate, use established constitutional rights or human rights to back up your claims. You can turn to documents like the U.S. Constitution or the United Nations Universal Declaration of Human Rights to support your positions.

Find the laws that fit your argument—Refer to local, state, or national laws that support your argument. You can also appeal to any rules or bylaws that govern your university or the organizations you belong to.

Be utilitarian—Utilitarianism means doing what is best for the majority of people. In some cases, you might find it helpful to argue that your position is better because it is beneficial to the most people. Keep in mind, though, that the rights and interests of the minority should also be protected.

Show that you care—The ethics of care stresses that rigid ethical standards can be especially harmful to vulnerable people. In situations that involve people at risk, compassion or understanding might be needed when rigid laws or practices can cause undue harm.

With some audiences and contexts, you might also demonstrate that your position is consistent ethically with your own and your readers' religious beliefs or cultural values.

Goodwill

Goodwill involves being helpful, friendly, and cooperative. It means you are showing that you care for your audience and others.

Understand your audience's needs—Demonstrate that you have your audience's needs in mind, not just your own. Of course, you are likely arguing for something that benefits you. That's a given. Show your readers or listeners that you understand and care about their needs, too.

Stress the benefits to others—Explain to your audience how your approach will be beneficial to them or someone they care about. They should be able to see that the benefits of your approach outweigh the costs.

Show how your position is a win-win—Point out how everyone benefits from your approach. In other words, demonstrate that all sides will be better off if everyone agrees with your position. Don't, however, give the impression that they will win and you will lose. People tend not to believe writers or speakers who seem overly willing to accept a loss.

Arguments that rely on *ethos* often use a combination of appeals to practicality, ethical principles, and good will.

Emotion (*Pathos*): Preparing Your Audience to Make a Decision

Using emotions to persuade your audience is appropriate if the feelings you draw upon are suitable for your subject and your audience. Aristotle wrote that emotions were appropriate if they helped *prepare* the audience to make a decision. However, he pointed out that emotional appeals are inappropriate if used merely to manipulate and warp the audience's judgment.

As you develop your argument, think about the positive and negative emotions that are associated with your topic.

Positive Emotions

Using positive emotions is the best way to motivate your audience to do something they are inclined to do already.

Promise of gain—Demonstrate to your audience that agreeing with your position will help people gain things they need or want, such as trust, time, money, love, advancement, reputation, comfort, popularity, health, beauty, or convenience.

Promise of enjoyment—Show your audience that accepting your position will lead to more personal satisfaction, including joy, anticipation, surprise, pleasure, leisure, or freedom.

Negative Emotions

Like it or not, people can be motivated by fear or anger, especially when they are reluctant to do something. You should be very careful about overusing negative emotions in your arguments, though, because people who are afraid or anxious often end up being more defensive and more hesitant to make a decision or take action.

> **Fear of loss**—Suggest that the alternative to your position might cause the loss of things your audience values, such as time, money, love, security, freedom, reputation, popularity, health, or beauty.

> **Fear of pain**—Hint that the alternative to your position might cause feelings of pain, sadness, frustration, humiliation, embarrassment, loneliness, regret, shame, vulnerability, or worry.

> **Expressions of anger or disgust**—Demonstrate that you share your audience's feelings of anger or disgust about a particular event or situation.

You should avoid threatening or attempting to frighten your readers, because people tend to reject bullying or scare tactics. Instead, use positive emotions as much as you can, because these emotions will build a sense of goodwill in your readers (Figure 6). Generally, people like to feel good and believe that agreeing with you will bring them gains, enjoyment, and happiness.

FIGURE 6 Using Emotions in an Argument Animals are often used to add an emotional element to advertisements. The American Society for the Prevention of Cruelty to Animals (ASPCA) used this photo on the homepage of its Web site to remind people about the importance of the organization's mission.

Combining All Three Appeals

Aristotle's three-appeals system of using reasoning (*logos*), credibility (*ethos*), and emotion (*pathos*) offers a useful way of inventing proofs for your arguments. This three-part system will help you invent your own argument or analyze an argument written by someone else. Most arguments use a combination of all three kinds of appeals.

When inventing your argument, you might find it helpful to draw three columns on a sheet of paper. Put "Reasoning," "Authority," and "Emotions" at the top of these columns. Then spend some time listing out possible proofs from all three areas that will help you create a balanced argument. The strongest arguments typically draw proofs from all three kinds of appeals.

Usually, an argument focuses more on one of the three kinds of proofs (*logos, ethos, pathos*) than the other two. For example a scientific argument may depend more on reasoning (*logos*), while appeals to authority (*ethos*) and emotion (*pathos*) play secondary and supportive roles.

Strategy 3: Support Your Claim with Existing Evidence

The basis of a good argument is solid evidence, usually gathered from doing research. The evidence for your argument should include factual information that already exists, such as proven facts, physical evidence, artifacts, data, contracts, photographs, and other material items. Evidence can also include testimonials and quotes from witnesses or authoritative sources.

In later chapters, you will learn some helpful research methods for collecting electronic, print, and empirical evidence about your topic. For now, let's talk about how to determine what kinds of evidence will be helpful to your argument.

The STAR Approach to Evaluating Evidence

Some researchers use the STAR acronym (sufficient, typical, accurate, and reliable) to help them determine whether they have gathered adequate and appropriate support for their argument.[2]

Sufficient—Do you have enough evidence to support your argument? If you are relying on only one or two sources, then the answer is probably "no." You need to collect a variety and an adequate number of sources. The types and number of sources you will need depend on your argument's subject and your audience. A controversial subject or a skeptical audience will require more evidence than a noncontroversial subject or favorable audience.

Typical—Are you able to find similar kinds of evidence in a variety of sources? If a source seems to be offering evidence that contradicts what other sources are saying, you should take a closer look at how the information was gathered or why its conclusion contradicts other sources. It's always possible that the majority is wrong, but usually sources are more reliable when they are saying what other sources are saying.

---

[2]This approach is adapted from Richard Fulkerson's STAR approach in *Teaching the Argument in Writing* (NCTE, 1996).

Accurate—Did the author of the source use trustworthy methods to gather the information? If the author's methods are unsound or questionable, then the information is probably not accurate. And, if authors don't explain their information-gathering methods at all, then you should be highly skeptical of their so-called evidence.

Reliable—Is the organization or author who wrote the information someone you can trust? Neutral sources are usually the most reliable because they aren't trying to profit from the information. If organizations or authors have something to gain, then you should be more skeptical about the information they are providing. Above all, follow the money. If someone will gain financially from others agreeing with him or her, then you should question whether the source is reliable.

In later chapters, you will learn how to "triangulate" sources to help you determine whether your evidence is sufficient, typical, accurate, and reliable. The STAR approach is best used as a way to double-check whether you have gathered the evidence you need to support your argument and persuade your audience.

Images as Evidence

You have often been told to "show, don't just tell." In today's visual society, the ability to argue with images is more important than ever. As you collect information for your argument, you should also be searching for images that will help you explain your subject and support your argument (Figure 7).

FIGURE 7
Images as Evidence
Images should add something beyond mere decoration. They can drive home a point by intensifying emotions or making your point memorable.

Choose images that reinforce your words. Images should be more than "eye candy" or "decorations" for your argument. They should improve understanding, provoke interest, or arouse curiosity. They could stress an important point by evoking emotional responses that stay in your reader's memory. Images can also clarify an issue or even express a unique point that is difficult to make in writing (Figure 8). Finally, they can provide alternative access points for readers to skip around through your document or search for specific kinds of information.

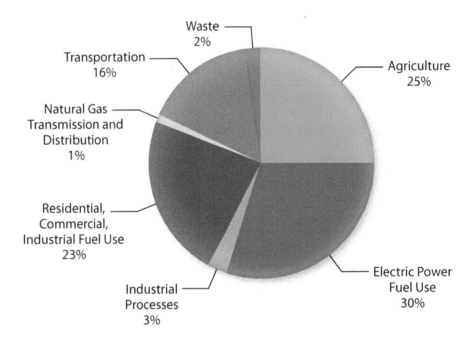

FIGURE 8 2010 Iowa Gross Greenhouse Gas Emissions Charts like this one (or graphs and illustrations) present information in alternative ways that clarify what you have written with words. *Source:* Iowa Department of Natural Resources

In later chapters, you will learn more about how to create and use images that support your arguments.

Strategy 4: Use Commonplaces to Structure Your Case

More than two thousand years ago, ancient Greek and Roman orators identified a variety of *commonplaces*—strategies or "moves"—that writers and speakers could use to structure their arguments. These patterns can help you present information in logical and efficient ways, especially at the sentence and paragraph levels.

There are two types of commonplaces: *asserting* commonplaces and *responding* commonplaces. The table in Figure 9 summarizes these types of commonplaces.

Asserting Commonplaces	Responding Commonplaces
Definition	Better and worse
Negation	Qualification
Two sides	Rephrasing the opposition position
Comparison and contrast	Counterstatement
Classification	Refutation
Cause and effect	Concession and absorption
Division	
Narration	
Proposal	

FIGURE 9
Asserting and Responding Commonplaces Commonplaces can be used to assert new ideas or respond to potential criticisms or questions.

Asserting Commonplaces

You should use asserting commonplaces when you are stating something you believe is true. Here are the most commonly used asserting commonplaces:

Definition *(X is...)*
When defining a word or term, you should state the class to which it belongs and the features that distinguish it from that class:

A _____ is a _____ that has _____ and _____ .

Negation *(X is not...)*
A negation is similar to a definition, except a negation defines something by stating what it is not.

A _____ is not a _____ , because it has _____ and

_____ .

Two Sides *(X can be viewed two ways: A or B)*
In some arguments, you might find it helpful to divide the issue into two sides.

There are two ways to look at this issue: _____ or _____ .

People tend to respond to this situation in one of two ways. They either

_____ or they _____ .

Comparison and Contrast *(X is similar to/different from Y)*
Comparing and contrasting two things is a good way to help people understand something new or unique.

_____ is similar to _____, because they both have _____ and _____ .

However, _____ is different from _____, because it doesn't have _____ and _____ .

Cause and Effect *(X causes Y, or Y is caused by X)*
Identifying causes is a good way to explain why something happened. A cause-and-effect statement is an effective way to argue that an issue addressed now will have positive or negative effects in the future:

_____ was caused by _____ and _____ .

If we do _____, then it will cause _____ and _____ to happen.

Classification *(X can be sorted into Y number of groups)*
Classification means sorting people or items into groups. Classification can be especially helpful when you are trying to discuss a complex issue or something that involves many different kinds of people or things.

_____ can be divided into _____ types: _____ , _____ , and _____ .

By paying attention to how they respond to _____differently, we can sort _____ into the following groups: _____, _____, and _____ .

Division *(X can be divided into Y parts)*
You can also examine or describe something in more depth by first dividing it into its major parts.

_____ has _____ major parts, which include _____ , _____ , and _____ .

Then you can divide each major part into minor parts.

Its major part _____ can then be further divided into smaller parts, including _____ , _____ , and _____ .

Narration *(X happened, so they decided to do Y)*
The narration commonplace uses a miniature story or anecdote to support part of your argument.

One time, _____ happened, and we needed to do _____ .

Our experience with _____ was similar to the time when _____

happened and they needed to _____ .

Proposal *(X is a problem, so we should do Y)*
A proposal statement usually identifies the problem and then offers a solution to that problem.

_____ is happening, so our best way forward is to do _____ .

In order to achieve _____ , we will first need to address the problems

with _____ .

Responding Commonplaces

You can use responding commonplaces to counteract or neutralize real or anticipated objections to your argument.

Better and Worse *(X is better than Y)*
When two or more options are available, you should argue that yours is better or that others are worse.

We believe _____ is the better way to go, because it has advantages

like _____ , _____ , and _____ .

Other options may look attractive in some ways, but they would be worse be-

cause they would lead to _____ , _____ , and _____ .

Qualification *(X might not be true when Y happens)*
No solution or plan is perfect, so you should point out any limitations to your audience. That way, you can anticipate and perhaps neutralize criticisms from opponents.

One limitation of our approach is _____ , but we feel the advantages outweigh this minor problem.

It is possible that _____ could happen, but that's unlikely when you

consider _____ , _____ , and _____ .

Rephrasing the Opposing Position *(The other side believes X, Y, and Z)*
When responding to an opponent, you should first rephrase their position in your own words. That way, you can avoid sounding defensive when you argue for your views and against theirs.

Here's what the other side really wants you to believe: _____,

_____, and _____.

Just so we are clear about what _____ believe, they seem to be

saying _____ .

Counterstatement *(X might be true in rare cases, but Y is also almost always true)*
More than likely, the opposing side has some points that are valid. You should identify where you agree with them and then extend their argument in the direction you want to go.

The other side is correct when they argue that _____ , and we believe

the proper way to handle the situation is to _____.

We agree on many points, including _____ and _____;

therefore, we think the best way forward is to _____.

Refutation *(X is not true because of Y)*
If you need to refute an opposing statement that is untrue, you should point out any errors or omissions in facts or logic in an opposing argument.

It's not possible for _____ to be true, because the facts, which

include _____ and _____ , prove that it cannot be true.

The opposing side's argument has left out some key facts, such as _____,

_____ , and _____.

If _____ is true, as they claim, then it would not be logically

possible for _____ to be true also.

Concession and Absorption *(X is true, but Y is still the better way)*
In some situations, the opposing side has produced factual evidence that you must concede to be true. In these cases, a good strategy is to absorb their argument.

Due to the current circumstances, we need to admit _____ is true, but

we still believe that in the long run _____ is the better way forward.

The other side makes some good points, and we grant that they are right

about _____ and _____; however, being right about a few

minor issues does not address the larger issue that involves _____.

Commonplaces are not recipes or templates to follow in a fixed or mechanical way. Instead, they are flexible patterns and phrasings you should adapt to suit your argument. They are especially helpful at the sentence and paragraph levels because they allow you to skillfully assert your ideas and respond effectively to the ideas of others. You can use a combination of these moves to help you prove your thesis.

Strategy 5: Avoid Fallacies

Logical fallacies indicate errors in reasoning or weak spots in an argument. You should avoid using logical fallacies in your arguments because they are vulnerable places that can be exploited by your opponents. Plus, they can lead you or others to draw inaccurate or unsupported conclusions.

Meanwhile, if you find a logical fallacy in the opposing side's argument, that doesn't necessarily mean they are automatically wrong or being unethical. It simply means there is a weak spot or faulty assumption in their argument that you might challenge.

The table in Figure 10 lists some of the most common logical fallacies and offers examples. Fallacies tend to occur for the following three reasons:

False or Weak Premises

Fallacious conclusions happen when the original assumptions are false or unproven. In these situations, the speaker or writer is usually stretching the truth or overreaching in some way. He or she might be supporting the argument on a shaky premise (bandwagon, *post hoc* reasoning, slippery slope, or hasty generalization). Or the speaker or writer may be making flimsy comparisons or relying on "facts" from sources that aren't credible (weak analogy, false authority).

Irrelevance

When people realize that their argument is weak or difficult to prove, they may try to distract the audience or change the topic. They will use name calling (*ad hominem*) or bring up unrelated issues (red herring, *tu quoque, non sequitur*) to put the other side on the defensive or distract them.

Ambiguity

Some people will also try to confuse the audience by clouding the issue with circular reasoning (begging the question) or arguing against a position that no one is defending (straw man). They might also try to present two choices (either/or) to the audience with one unreasonable choice that almost no one would accept. That way, given what seems to be a choice between a bad and a worse option, the audience feels impelled to choose the bad option rather than the worse one.

You should closely study the logical fallacies shown in Figure 10 so you recognize them when they happen. Again, finding a logical fallacy in an argument doesn't mean you will expose someone else's ideas as wrong or false. However, a fallacy does signal a potential weak spot or faulty logic. In some cases, the speaker or writer may be consciously trying to deceive or distract the audience. In most cases, though, logical fallacies happen accidentally when a speaker or writer has not fully thought through his or her argument.

You should try to memorize these fallacies and also play around with them so you can strengthen your own arguments. Being able to recognize logical fallacies in your own arguments will help you eliminate weaknesses and identify places at which your opposition could undermine your case. Even more importantly, though, by testing your own arguments against these logical fallacies, you will develop a deeper and richer understanding of your own beliefs.

Logical Fallacy	Definition	Example
Bandwagon (*Ad populum*)	Suggesting that a person should agree to something because it is popular.	"Over one thousand people have decided to sign up, so you should, too."
Post hoc reasoning	Arguing that one event caused another when they are unrelated.	"Each time my roommate is out of town, it causes my car to break down and I can't get to work."
Slippery slope	Suggesting that one event will automatically lead to a chain of other events.	"If we allow them to ban assault weapons, soon handguns, rifles, and all other guns will be banned, too."
Hasty generalization	Using a part to make an inaccurate claim about a whole.	"The snowboarder who cut me off proved that all snowboarders are rude."
Begging the question	Using circular reasoning to prove a conclusion.	"Conservatives believe in hard work and strong values. That's why most Americans are conservatives."
Weak analogy	Making an improper comparison between two things that share a common feature.	"Paying taxes to the government is the same as handing your wallet over to a mugger in the park."
False authority	Defending a claim with a biased or untrustworthy source.	"My mother read my paper, and she thinks it deserves an A."
Ad hominem	Attacking the character of the arguer rather than the argument.	"Mary has no credibility on the smoking ban issue because she was once a smoker herself."
Red herring	Saying something that distracts from the issue being argued about.	"So, because books can now be found on the Internet, you're suggesting we burn our libraries?"
Tu quoque	Improperly turning an accusation back on the accuser.	"If you cared about global warming, as you claim, you wouldn't have driven a car to this meeting."
Non sequitur	Stating a conclusion that does not follow from the premises.	"Watching *30 Rock* each week will make you smarter and more popular."
Straw man	Arguing against a position that no one is defending.	"Letting children play soccer on a busy highway is wrong, and I won't stand for it."
Either/or	Presenting someone with a limited choice when other choices are possible.	"We either buy this car now, or we spend the rest of the year walking to school."

FIGURE 10 Common Logical Fallacies

Logical fallacies signal weak points in an argument. Look for them in opposing arguments and avoid using them in your own.

The Toulmin System of Argument

3 How to use the Toulmin method for analyzing and inventing arguments

In the late 1950s, British philosopher Steven Toulmin grew concerned that argument was becoming too impractical and too dependent on rigid forms of logic. He pointed out that formal logic could be successfully used to prove or disprove the claims of philosophers, but many of these "arguments" were not persuasive because they didn't reflect how ordinary people debated issues in their everyday lives. Rigid logical arguments were not flexible enough to handle common concerns and issues.

Elements of Toulmin's System

To develop a more practical form of argument, Toulmin devised a system that relied on six interconnected elements:

Claim—An assertion or conclusion that the argument will try to prove: "China will continue to grow as an important economic power in the twenty-first century."

Grounds—The empirical evidence or data that can be used to support or provide a foundation for the claim: "China's economy has been expanding about ten percent each year for three decades, and analysts believe it will continue expanding at this rate. Meanwhile, China's gross domestic product (GDP) makes it the second-largest economy in the world."

Warrant—The assumption that forms a bridge between the claim and the ground. The warrant is often not stated in an argument, but the audience needs to be able to connect the claim to the ground for the argument to be persuasive: "A quickly expanding economy that has a large and growing GDP will be influential in worldwide economics."

Backing—The facts that are needed to support, or "back," the warrant, especially if the warrant's core assumption is not immediately obvious to the audience: "Money means power in world economics, so an expanding economy and increasing GDP mean an increase in economic influence."

Rebuttal—A statement that points out any limitations or qualifications that temper the claim: "However, China's economic growth may be slowed by the growth of organized labor, increasing competition with other nations that also have cheap labor, and its dependence on foreign energy sources."

Qualifiers—The use of words or phrases that speakers or writers use to signal the strength of their cases and show readers you're not overreaching. Some of these words include *perhaps, unless, in all probability, maybe*, and the like. Qualifiers allow speakers or authors to signal the gray areas in the argument and identify places at which movement or compromise is possible. Qualifiers also remind audiences that all arguments are based on what is probably true, not what is absolutely true.

The Warrant

The *warrant* is an especially important component of Toulmin's system of argument. It is the bridge that connects the evidence with the claim that the arguer wants to make.

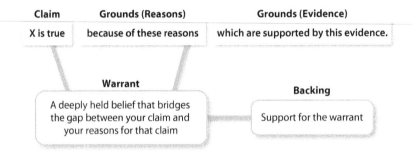

In most arguments, the warrant is typically not stated directly, while other features of the argument like the claim, reasons, and evidence are stated directly. Instead, the warrant is something that the writer or speaker assumes is true without explanation or additional proof. For example,

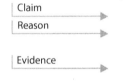

Claim

Reason

Evidence

Domestic terrorists should not be tortured or tried in secretive military courts because terrorism is a crime against civilians; therefore, putting the accused on trial through our civilian courts demonstrates to the world our democracy's respect for judicial transparency and basic human rights.

Unstated Warrant: *An accused person, no matter how heinous the crime, deserves a fair trial and is innocent until proven guilty.*

Toulmin believed that warrants should be revealed, acknowledged, and occasionally challenged, because their unspoken nature can allow speakers or writers to support claims or draw conclusions that may or may not be true. Toulmin used a diagram like the one in Figure 11 to explain what he had in mind.

FIGURE 11
Toulmin's System of Argument In Toulmin's system, a key assumption (a warrant) holds together the grounds and the claim.

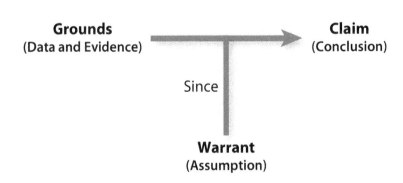

Using Toulmin's System to Form Solid Arguments

When using Toulmin's system, you might find it helpful to break down your argument into the six elements, answering the following kinds of questions:

1. **Claim:** What claim am I trying to prove? What is my thesis?

2. **Grounds:** What reasoning and evidence (empirical facts or data) support my claim?

3. **Warrant:** What is the unstated assumption that connects the grounds to my claim?

4. **Backing:** What facts are available to support my warrant?

5. **Rebuttal:** What are the possible exceptions or limitations of my claim?

6. **Qualifiers:** How strong is my argument and what words would appropriately signal my confidence in the claim?

Answering these questions will help you put together your argument while revealing any of its weaknesses. The following student example demonstrates an argument using Toulmin's system of argument. This example argument demonstrates how the Toulmin system stresses the importance of paying attention to unstated assumptions while relying on solid evidence.

Sally Reynolds

English 105

April 24, 2013

Boston Marathon Bombing: Can Democracy Pass the Test?

Last week's bombings of the Boston Marathon brought out the best and worst of America. On our screens, we saw ordinary people doing extraordinary things, including risking their own lives to help victims who had lost legs or were severely burned. Certainly, these brave heroes must have known that other bombs might be waiting to go off. And yet, they ran to help, rather than run away. We saw Boston police and firefighters quickly restoring order and helping people to safety. Within a few days, investigators released photos of the suspects, who were then killed or captured the following day in a dramatic manhunt.

Our worst was also on display. The alleged bombers turned out to be two brothers. The older and now dead brother was a violent hothead who was called a "loser" by his own uncle. The younger and still alive brother was a pothead who apparently could not say 'no' to his crazy brother but could say 'yes' to killing and maiming innocent people (Martinez, 2013). Our other worsts included a demand by Greg Ball, a New York state senator, to "use torture on this punk" and calls by Senator Lindsey Graham to consider trying the surviving bomber, who is a U.S. citizen, in a military tribunal as an "enemy combatant." Talk radio buzzed with similar calls for revenge on Muslims and fear-driven doubts whether civilian courts can successfully try terrorism cases.

Qualifier →

There is no doubt that this crime is a heinous incident of terrorism, and if proven guilty the surviving brother deserves life in prison or even the death penalty. However, these kinds of incidents are also a test of our democracy. They help us measure whether we are still a nation of laws and human rights, or whether we are devolving into a society where laws and human rights are casually set aside when people get scared.

Reason →

Domestic terrorists should not be tortured or tried in secretive military courts because terrorism is a crime against civilians.

Claim →

Putting the accused on trial in our civilian courts demonstrates to the world our democracy's respect for judicial transparency and basic human rights.

Review of the Evidence

Let's review the facts. The older brother, Tamerlan Tsarnaev, was an amateur boxer who took classes at a community college, beat up his girlfriend, and became radicalized through a friend and an anti-American al-Qaida affiliated website. The younger brother, Dzhokar, was a student at UMass-Dartmouth, who friends say was passive, friendly, and liked to smoke pot.

Evidence →

Both brothers, especially Tamerlan, were struggling to assimilate to American life, even though they had lived in the United States since they were young boys. Detectives believe the two brothers were not connected to any terrorist networks, instead acting on their own in a "lone-wolf" attack.

Grounds →

The day of the Boston Marathon, they ignited two homemade bombs that killed three people, including a 10-year-old boy, and maimed over a hundred more. Then, while trying to escape, they assassinated an MIT campus police officer. These crimes are, by any measure, horrific forms of terrorism.

Torture Would be Wrong

Given these facts, torturing the younger brother would be wrong. Torture would serve no purpose other than sating some blood-thirsty need for revenge. For one thing, the effectiveness of torture as an interrogation tactic is questionable and perhaps even counterproductive. Research has shown that people being tortured will say anything they believe their torturers want to hear ("Tortured," par. 2). As a result, the "intelligence" gathered may indeed confirm what the torturers wanted to hear, but there is a good chance the information is not accurate or true. Even more problematic, neuropsychologists have shown that a traumatized person, including someone under torture, has impaired cognitive function and confused working memory (Morgan, Doran, Steffian, Hazlett, & Southwick, 2006). In other words, even if a terrorist had something to reveal, the trauma of torture itself may cause him or her to forget or mix up the facts.

Torturing the younger brother would show that American society is fear-ridden, reactionary, and hypocritical, abandoning our core values because a "loser" and his submissive brother detonated a couple crude bombs. What kind of message would torturing the younger brother send to other parts of the world? To the developed world, it would signal that the United States is no longer the primary defender of human rights. All our high-mindedness about human dignity and inalienable rights would be proven hollow. Meanwhile, petty tyrants and ruthless oligarchs would see that torture is something condoned, even in advanced nations like the United States.

Military Tribunals Would be Inappropriate

Likewise, trying the surviving bomber in a secretive military tribunal would show that we do not believe in our own courts or legal system. A military tribunal is a process for trying enemy soldiers and agents during a declared war (Napolitano, 2009, par. 6). In these tribunals, military officers serve as inquisitors, judges, and jury. Using this kind of military court may be appropriate for war criminals or spies, but trying a domestic terrorist

Grounds

Backing

Backing

Rebuttal

53

Backing →

in a military tribunal would demonstrate a fundamental distrust of an American jury to determine the truth and dispense justice. Meanwhile, to the rest of the world, a panel of uniformed military officers sitting in judgment of an American citizen would look like some kind of showtrial with a predetermined outcome.

Conclusion: Passing the Test

Claim →

Instead of reacting to this heinous crime in a knee-jerk way, let's show the world we are a nation of laws that respects human rights. We can use this tragedy as a way to honor those citizens in Boston who bravely ran to help the injured, even though they knew the risks. We can honor the victims by demonstrating that terrorism does not work and did not fracture our democracy. Let's demonstrate that a democracy is stronger than a couple homemade bombs made by losers. In other words, let's show the world that our nation and our Constitution are strong enough to give even accused terrorists their day in court, being judged by their peers. Let's pass this test.

References

Martinez, M. (2013). Uncle calls Boston Marathon bombers 'losers.' *CNN.com*. Retrieved from http://www.cnn.com/2013/04/19/us/marathon-suspects-uncle

Morgan, C., Doran, A., Steffian, G., Hazlett, G., & Southwick, S. (2006). Stress-induced deficits in working memory and visuo-constructive abilities in special operations soldiers. *Biological Psychiatry 60*, 722–729. doi: 10.1016/j.biopsych.2006.04.021

Napolitano, A. (2009). The case against military tribunals. *Los Angeles Times*. Retrieved from http://articles.latimes.com/2009/nov/29/opinion/la-oe-napolitano29-2009nov29

The tortured brain. (2009). *Newsweek*. Retrieved from http://www.thedailybeast.com/newsweek/2009/09/21/the-tortured-brain.html

Writing persuasive arguments can be challenging and fun.
Here is what you need to know from this chapter:

1 Persuasive arguments are often called "power-over" arguments because they aim to influence the beliefs and actions of others.

2 To persuade effectively, you need to understand the beliefs your audience already holds as true and treat the issues fairly.

3 Persuasive arguments have three basic elements: a claim, reasons that support the claim, and evidence that backs up those reasons.

4 There are five strategies for successful persuasive arguments: (1) State a reasonable and specific claim (your thesis); (2) use appeals to reasoning, authority, and emotion; (3) find evidence, facts, and data for support; (4) use commonplaces to structure your case; and (5) discuss objections and exceptions. Also, avoid fallacies.

5 A persuasive argument's thesis needs to be reasonable, meaning it is a claim that a reasonable person might agree or disagree with.

6 A persuasive argument's thesis can be sharpened by asking questions about definition, causation, evaluation, or recommendation.

7 Three kinds of basic appeals can be used to support claims: reasoning (*logos*), authority (*ethos*), and emotion (*pathos*).

8 Evidence can be evaluated using the STAR model: sufficient, typical, accurate, and relevant.

9 The Toulmin model of argument is helpful for inventing your arguments and finding out if there are unstated assumptions that you need to clarify.

10 Every persuasive argument should take the views of others into account and deal with them fairly.

1. With a small group in class, analyze an argument that clearly aims to persuade its audience. Find one that appears in your local or school newspaper, in an online magazine or newspaper, in this book, or in an online video (e.g., on YouTube). Analyze it using the five persuasive strategies described in this chapter. Finally, determine if you find it a sound argument overall.

2. Visit The Living Room Candidate, which is an online museum of more than 300 presidential campaign television commercials since 1952 (www.livingroom candidate.org). Take some time to explore the website and watch several commercials from past elections, or choose "Type of Commercial" and choose "Children" or "Fear." Every one of these commercials clearly aims to persuade, but how many of them state a specific claim and how many instead make an implied claim ("You should vote for X")?

3. In a small group, choose a topic you all care about. First, compose one or two thesis *questions* (which your group note taker will record). Now compose thesis *statements* that are reasonable and specific, offering at least one major reason for each statement that supports the claim. Share your questions and theses with the class for further discussion.

1. Choose a highly polarized argument that is happening right now. (It could be a national argument or something very local.) In polarized arguments, each side does not want to budge, and perhaps they don't even want to really listen to the other sides' arguments. Now try to identify the very basic questions (issues) that each side considers most important. Write a brief report on this polarized argument in which you discuss whether the issue is a matter of *definition, causation, evaluation,* or *recommendation.*

2. Images can be persuasive, but they rarely make *explicit* claims that are supported by explicit reasons. Instead, those claims and reasons tend to be *implied* by the image itself. Find an image on the Internet that makes an argument. You might use Google to search for images with the words "pregnant smoking," "teen drug addiction," or "natural gas fracking in the United States." Now take that image's argument and write a brief analysis (200 to 300 words) that uses two or three of the strategies discussed in this chapter to describe the image's argument in explicit terms.

3. Analyze a television show that brings advocates on two sides of issues to debate head to head. You can find these highly combative debates on FOX News, MSNBC, CNN, and other national stations. Although each side argues passionately and clearly aims to persuade, are they really persuasive arguments as they are defined in this chapter? Write a brief report in which you discuss whether you think these kinds of shows really engage in persuasive argument or whether they are doing something else.

Credits

Credits are listed in order of appearance.

Photo Credits

(br), M4OS Photos/Alamy; (tl), Fuse/Getty Images; (tr), Craig F. Walker/The Denver Post/Getty Images; Jason Tanner/UNHCR/Getty Images; ASPCA; Library of Congress [8b29516u]

Text Credits

2010 Iowa Gross Greenhouse Gas Emissions.

Generative
Arguments

Most arguments happen within conversations, so your ability to argue effectively in groups, teams, organizations, and networks will be critical in college and your career. We live in a media-centered world in which ongoing conversations are happening all around us. You probably already join these conversations through Facebook, Twitter, Reddit, Tumblr, websites, listservs, blogs, and e-mail. Likewise, in college and your career, you will participate in face-to-face conversations, such as class discussions, staff meetings, brainstorming sessions, strategic planning summits, and video conferences.

These conversations are called *generative arguments* because you and others are collaboratively using spoken and written discourse to come up with new ideas, share your opinions, compare experiences, build understanding, sort out differences, and figure out what each other believes (Figure 1). In generative arguments, you need to think creatively, sort out your beliefs, and make decisions about the best way forward.

Ordinarily, most generative arguments don't *feel* like arguments. In most conversations, people usually aren't openly disagreeing with each other or trying to win others over to their side. Instead, they are working together to develop a common

From Chapter 2 of *Argument Today with Readings*, First Edition. Richard Johnson-Sheehan and Charles Paine. Copyright © 2015 by Pearson Education, Inc. All rights reserved.

FIGURE 1
Generative
Arguments
Generative
arguments happen
when people get
together to discuss
issues in person or
through electronic
media.

understanding or consensus. Generative arguments are also called "power-with" arguments because participants are working together to clarify what they believe, resolve differences, and manage how others view them and their ideas. The arguments might be subtle, but they're still there.

In this chapter, you will learn how to speak and write effectively in these generative situations. Your ability to use generative strategies to argue in groups, teams, organizations, and networks will be vital to your success in college, the workplace, and the public sphere.

1 How generative arguments can be used to communicate successfully with others

Four Strategies for Generative Arguments

Generative arguments rely on your ability to develop a common understanding with others while striving toward consensus. Here are four basic strategies that you can use to communicate effectively in face-to-face and electronic conversations:

Strategy 1: Build a sense of identification.

Strategy 2: Frame the issue to your advantage.

Strategy 3: Tell interesting stories.

Strategy 4: Negotiate disagreements with Rogerian methods.

These strategies will also help you generate new ideas and plan effectively with others. Once you learn how to use these strategies, you will find that you can speak and write with more influence in group or team situations.

2 How to encourage others to identify with you

Strategy 1: Build a Sense of Identification

Kenneth Burke, an influential American rhetorician, pointed out that people rarely change their minds based on good reasoning and facts alone. Instead, most people are influenced by their *identification* with others. They tend to trust and believe people who are similar to them in backgrounds, beliefs, attitudes, and experiences.

So, if you can demonstrate that you share a common identity with others (e.g., common values or interests, same economic class, similar culture, common upbringing, membership in the same groups, and so on), they are more likely to trust you and agree with your ideas.

Of course, at some level we all identify with each other as human beings. You can, however, look for opportunities to build a stronger sense of identification with others by paying attention to the specific qualities you hold in common with them.

This isn't as complicated as it sounds. As a member of a culture, society, or peer group, you share something in common with just about anyone. So, to build a sense of common identity with someone else, you should be clear about your shared values, interests, or background.

Identify Yourself with the Audience

Burke used the word *consubstantial* to explain why people identify with each other. He defined consubstantial as uniting people through "common sensations, concepts, images, ideas and attitudes."[1] People identify with each other by "acting-together."

In a generative argument, using identification means first showing others that you share or at least respect their values, upbringing, experiences, or status. If people accept you as one of their own (i.e., identify with you), they are more likely to believe what you have to say. Even if you are very different from them in some ways, demonstrating that you respect and understand their values will help them better respect and understand your values.

Let's consider an example. Evangelical Christians tend to be highly skeptical about the existence of human-caused climate change, even though the Bible and religious dogma have almost nothing to say about environmental issues, especially climate change. So why do many evangelicals believe climate change is a hoax?

Here's one possible answer. A majority of evangelicals are *social conservatives*, so they tend to identify with *economic conservatives*, who are usually probusiness and anti-regulation. Economic conservatives generally argue against government regulations, including most environmental policies aimed at regulating greenhouse gasses. So due

---

[1] Kenneth Burke, *Rhetoric of Motives* (Berkeley: U of California, 1969) 21.

to identification, evangelical Christians are more likely to side with other conservatives who are skeptical about climate change. They identify with economic conservatives more than environmentalists, because they trust conservatives who they believe share their values (Figure 2).

FIGURE 2
Identifying with Others
In some cases, people will identify with groups that hold similar but not the same values.

Of course, this example doesn't tell the whole story. Increasingly, many evangelical Christians are coming to believe that climate change exists, especially evangelicals in the Creation Care movement. Meanwhile, there are a few environmentalists who don't believe in climate change. In other words, people usually agree with people they identify with—but not always. Individuals have good reasons for identifying themselves with specific groups on some issues and identifying themselves with other groups on other issues.

Identify with the Audience Against a Shared Problem

Burke also suggested that *division* is an effective way to build identification with others. He pointed out that when people feel physically or economically threatened, highlighting issues you and they are commonly *against* is an effective way to unify groups of people who might otherwise not identify with each other.

A good example would be collective efforts against drunk drivers. People who drive while intoxicated are a commonly acknowledged menace on the roadways. Efforts to stop people from driving while intoxicated often bring together groups with widely different backgrounds and values, such as Mothers Against Drunk Driving, state police, college students, brewing companies, lawyers, teachers, and politicians. Drunk drivers are a common problem that all these groups can identify themselves against.

Natural and human-made disasters also offer opportunities for people to identify with each other and unify to achieve common ends (Figure 3). When hurricane Sandy ravaged downtown New York and much of New Jersey in 2012, politicians like Chris Christie, a Republican New Jersey governor, and Barack Obama, a president from the Democratic Party, set aside their differences to work together on storm recovery. Just weeks earlier, Governor Christie had been campaigning vigorously against the reelection of Obama, but the two leaders could set aside their differences to address the common problem of a devastating hurricane.

FIGURE 3 Building Identification by Unifying Against a Problem Natural and human-made disasters often bring people together against a common threat.

Don't Scapegoat or Pander

Identification can be a powerful tool, but when misused it can also be exploited to scapegoat victims or pander to audiences. Burke pointed out that war and violence can be used to unify people while highlighting differences with others. For example, think about the unity and division that were felt after terrorists brought down the World Trade Center and attacked the Pentagon on September 11, 2001. After the attacks, a large majority of Americans felt unified because they identified with each other against a common threat—terrorism. In a good way, they temporarily overlooked their differences out of compassion for the victims and their common fear of terrorism.

However, this identification also had a dark side. After September 11, there were shocking racist incidents in which mosques in the United States were vandalized and people who appeared to be of Middle Eastern descent were scapegoated, targeted, profiled, and harassed. To suppress dissent, people were told, "You are either with us or you are against us." Division can be a powerful tool for unifying people who feel threatened, but it can also be exploited by public figures who are fearmongering and scapegoating.

Another risk of identification is pandering. If you are trying too hard to identify with others, you risk losing a sense of your own identity. You tell them what they want to hear rather than express your own views. Or worse, you come off as a phony who is trying too hard to appeal to them. When using identification as an argument strategy, it's important to draw attention to shared values, interests, or backgrounds, but you should not fabricate or exaggerate these shared characteristics. Most people can spot phonies or fakes.

3 How to frame issues positively and avoid negative frames

Strategy 2: Frame the Issue to Your Advantage

When discussing an issue with others, you should be aware of how the issue is being "framed." A frame is a mental structure that shapes how people interpret and talk about an issue. How an issue is framed often determines what people believe and how they express their ideas. Frames also help us understand why people sometimes draw very different conclusions from the same body of facts (Figure 4).

FIGURE 4 Different Attempts to Frame an Issue
The Occupy Wall Street movement tried to show that the growing wealth gap between the rich and poor was not in line with American beliefs in equality and fairness. The Tea Party movement, similarly, argued effectively that taxation was curbing American freedoms.

For example, "economic inequality" has become an important social issue in American culture. While America has more billionaires than ever, we also have a swelling number of employed people who have fallen below the poverty line. Advocates for the poor would frame this issue as one of "economic inequality." They would argue that it is morally wrong and socially harmful for economic power to be concentrated exclusively in the hands of a few wealthy people. Defenders of free enterprise, meanwhile, would frame this issue in terms of "economic freedom." The freedom to pursue wealth, they would argue, is a creative force that leads to more prosperity for everyone.

When you are aware of how an issue is being framed, you can better use that frame to express your ideas. Or, in some cases, you can reframe the issue in a way that better suits your own beliefs and values. Here are some strategies for framing issues to your advantage.

Listen for Frames

When discussing an issue with other people, listen carefully to how the issue is being framed. For example, in American culture, "freedom" is a common frame. We hear arguments about the freedom of speech, freedom to bear arms, freedom to choose, freedom to marry, and even the freedom to fail. Being free to make our own choices is something almost all Americans value.

As a result, you will hear many arguments being framed in terms of *freedom*. "Increased taxes restrict our economic freedom." "People who love each other should have the freedom to marry." "We should have the freedom to smoke pot." "Speed limits take away our freedom to drive as fast as we want."

Another common frame, *fun*, is widely used with college-age audiences. As a student, you are regularly promised, "This class will be fun." Advertisements imply that you will have more fun if you buy a specific phone (or car, or clothing, or food). Your friends encourage you to "loosen up and have some fun." Having fun is something that college-aged people tend to value, so many arguments are framed in terms of fun.

Other common frames include the following:

security	competitive	creative
success	responsible	reform
self-reliance	low-cost	rights
fairness	realistic	investment
a balanced approach	practical	choice
faith-based	innovative	healthy
middle-class	"green"	high-quality
environmental	honesty	self-sacrifice
being active	independent	achievement

If you listen carefully while you are talking to others, you can identify the frames at work beneath the conversations.

Frame the Conversation

To frame a conversation, you first need to figure out what you value and what others in the conversation value. With these values in mind, choose a frame that will help you *positively* shape that conversation in your favor. Then, as you discuss the issue, you should associate yourself with the positive aspects of the frame.

For example, let's say you and your friends are discussing whether the wealthy (the so-called 1 percent) have too much political and economic power in American society (Figure 4). If you think the wealthy have too much power already, you could frame the discussion around issues of fairness and social responsibility, pointing out that American political and economic systems should be fair to everyone and the wealthy should be asked to pay their fair share.

If you take the other side by defending free enterprise, you might frame the conversation in terms of freedom by suggesting that restraining the wealthy would ultimately harm economic independence and creativity. You could talk about how taxes take away people's freedom to compete, their freedom to be successful, or their freedom to create new businesses.

As you discuss this issue, you should frame the conversation in ways that make your views seem more positive and reasonable to your audience. Meanwhile, avoid using frames that put your views in a negative light. If you can get the others in the group to accept your frame for the issue, then there is a good chance they will accept your views.

George Lakoff, a linguist and political consultant, suggests that the keys to effective framing are to a) know your values and b) frame the debate in positive, constructive terms.[2] In other words, good framing begins by first understanding what you and others value. Then you need to choose a frame that allows you to express those values in positive terms.

A simple way to evoke a frame is to use positive words that fit the frame. To find those words, put a key idea that signals the frame in the middle of your screen or a piece of paper. Use concept mapping to discover other words and phrases that are evoked by that frame (Figure 5). Then train yourself to use these words as much as you can when you are talking about this particular issue.

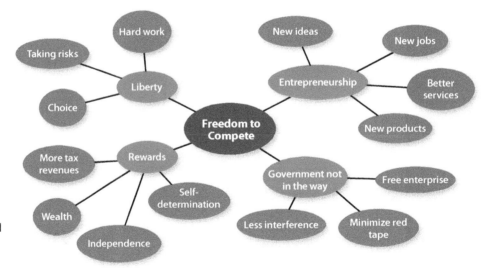

FIGURE 5 Using Concept Mapping to Frame an Issue Concept mapping is a helpful tool for developing words and themes that will help you frame an issue.

When used together, these framed clusters of ideas become *themes*. If you keep using specific words over and over, your audience will connect them into larger themes that frame the issue you are discussing.

---

[2] George Lakoff, *Don't Think of an Elephant: Know Your Values and Frame the Debate* (White River Junction, VT: Chelsea Green, 2004) 4.

Reframe the Conversation

As much as possible, you also want to avoid adopting negative frames that cast your views in an unfavorable light. For example, if you want to argue that wealthy people have too much power in American society, you would not be effective if you argued, "Maybe we need to take away people's freedom to pursue wealth." This negative frame would structure the conversation in a way that makes you sound unreasonable. After all, most Americans would react negatively to taking away the freedom of others.

Likewise, defenders of free enterprise would be ineffective if they stated, "It's all right to treat some people unfairly because they are poor." This negative frame would be resisted by most Americans because treating others unfairly goes against their cultural values.

A common mistake in generative arguments is to let others frame the debate in a way that puts you on the defensive or in a negative light. Others say something like, "We need to protect people's freedom to accumulate as much wealth as they can." If you respond, "No, we need to take that freedom away, because the wealthy already have all the advantages in our society," you are arguing ineffectively from a negative frame.

Instead, you should reframe the conversation by responding from a positive frame of your own choosing: "What we really need is economic fairness and political equality that supports a healthy economy and a sustainable democracy. It's unfair for a small number of wealthy people to control our economy and government simply because they have more money."

Use a Metaphor to Frame or Reframe the Conversation

A metaphor is a special kind of framing device that urges people to visualize an issue from a specific or new perspective. For example, the metaphor "Taxes are chains that hold down America's job creators" establishes a visual frame. With this metaphor, the audience can actually imagine people (those job creators) being weighed down by heavy chains. Of course, the wealthy aren't being put in chains (nor are they always job creators), but the metaphor encourages the audience to visualize them that way. It creates a frame by creating a particular perspective.

Some metaphorical frames become so common that we don't view them as metaphors anymore. For instance, the "war on drugs" is a metaphor that has long shaped the United States' policies toward drug abusers and suppliers (Figure 6). Instead of seeing drug abuse as a health issue, the war on drugs frames the argument in militaristic terms, implying

FIGURE 6 Using a Metaphor to Frame an Argument
The *"War on Drugs"* metaphor has shaped how Americans view the drug abuse problem. Americans tend to view drug abuse in militaristic terms rather than as a health issue.

that high-power weaponry, security sweeps, and armed intervention are needed to stop drug use and trafficking. Metaphors can be used to frame arguments in powerful ways.

Some other commonly used metaphors include, "Our team/company is a family," "Children are wild animals," "Morality is strength," "An election is a campaign," "Love is a game," and "Addiction is a disease." Each of these metaphorical frames encourages you and others to think and talk about issues in specific ways.

4 How to tell good, engaging stories

Strategy 3: Tell Interesting Stories

The third generative argument strategy involves using stories to illustrate and reinforce your beliefs and values. People enjoy listening to stories, so narrative is a particularly effective way to explain your beliefs and describe important events to others. When you're dealing with someone who is especially hostile to your perspectives, a good story can open them up a little so they'll at least give your ideas a fair hearing.

Tell a Funny, Tragic, or Instructive Story

Many of your beliefs and values came about because you or someone you know experienced something funny, tragic, or enlightening. Describing your experience with a story is a good way to explain why you hold some beliefs or opinions to be true.

Most stories have five parts:

Set the scene—Identify the people (the characters) involved and the time and place in which the story happened.

Introduce a conflict or problem to be solved—Stories typically focus on a conflict or problem that alters the characters' lives in some way.

Describe how you and others reacted to the conflict—The people involved evaluate the conflict, event, or problem, trying to figure out what happened.

Describe how you and others resolved the conflict—Your characters come up with a way of resolving or responding to the conflict.

Explain what you or others learned—Not all stories end with a "Here's what we learned" ending. However, explaining how the experience shaped your beliefs or values can be a good way to clarify the meaning of your story.

For example, here is a brief story that makes a simple point:

Sets scene →

One summer, my friends and I were backpacking in the mountains of northern New Mexico. We were exhausted because we had hiked nearly fifteen miles through rough terrain. So, when we arrived at our campsite, we dumped our packs, stripped off our sweaty shirts and shoes, and collapsed under some trees for a rest.

Before long, a large mother black bear and her two cubs ambled out of the forest to check out their new neighbors. It didn't take them long to catch the scent of our food. Before we could head them off, they were tearing into our packs and dining on the food for the rest of our trip. Our yelling and screaming couldn't drive them off. The mother bear would snarl and make feint charges at us. So we had to sit patiently and watch them eat, hoping our unwelcome guests would leave us something for the rest of the trip.

Eventually, the bears had their fill and sauntered back into the woods. We went over to see how much of our food was left. They had eaten about half of the food and damaged much of the rest. As a result, we needed to end our trip a couple days early because we ran out of supplies.

That day, we learned that no matter how tired we were after a day of backpacking, we should always secure our food before doing anything else.

Try the narrative pattern out. Next time you want to make a specific point, look for a story from your or someone else's life that illustrates your point in a meaningful way.

Use Anecdotes to Describe or Clarify

Anecdotes are small stories that can be used in an argument to illustrate specific points. You can draw anecdotes from your own experiences, someone else's experiences, or a historical event. Here is an anecdote about anorexia nervosa from "Kathy Carey" by Teresa Joerger:

Kathy Carey used to rise each morning before her husband and children, even before the sun, to go on a ten-mile run. Many of her friends admired her for her athleticism and physical appearance. She often heard people comment, "I'd love to have legs like yours." Her husband frequently told her how proud he was of how she looked. Even her doctor said that she was impressed with her ability to drop the weight so quickly after giving birth to her third child. What these people did not realize was that they were reinforcing Kathy's beliefs that she had to be athletic and thin to be accepted. They did not realize that Kathy, at 5'4", had gradually dropped from 115 to 85 pounds.

An anecdote like this one could be used within a larger argument about the importance of eating disorder awareness.

Illustrate with Hypothetical Examples

In some situations, you can also use a hypothetical story to connect with your audience. A hypothetical story is designed to put the readers into a story, so it needs to be realistic, and it needs to be something people might actually experience:

Imagine you and your friends have been drinking at a party. You're all under 21, and you all had a few more drinks than you intended. The host of the party, who you don't know, is kicking everyone out, and it's a twelve-mile drive home. There isn't public transportation in the area, and taxis aren't available. Now what?

Hypothetical stories often use the "you" style to put the readers into the story. That way, your readers can identify with the main characters and their problem. Hypothetical examples are a good way to illustrate the dilemmas that people face.

Use Fables or Parables

Though not common in arguments today, fables and parables are still good ways to make a point in an argument. Most people know fables like "The Tortoise and the Hare," "Goldilocks and the Three Bears," or the "The Ant and the Grasshopper." These familiar fables can be referenced or modernized to fit a current problem or issue (Figure 7).

FIGURE 7 Using a Fable to Make a Familiar Point
Fables are a good way to make a simple point with widely known tales.

In religious and some secular arguments, parables are also useful. Parables can be drawn from scriptural texts, such as the Bible, Quran, Bhagavad Gita, Tripitaka, Tao Te Ching, or Book of Mormon. A parable, like a fable, illustrates a point though a fictionalized story. Unlike a fable, though, a parable almost always uses humans as the characters.

Modern-day fables and parables can also be found in popular television shows or movies. People will often use scenes from *The Office, Glee,* or *Modern Family* to explain a point in a funny way. Popular movies, such as *Star Wars, Monty Python and the Holy Grail,* and *The Big Lebowski* are also common places from which to draw fictional stories that make a point. In many ways, these shows are the myths and parables of our time.

5 How to negotiate with others

Strategy 4: Negotiate Differences with Rogerian Methods

You can negotiate differences by focusing on *issues* rather than personalities or feelings. An effective negotiation strategy is to use a form of argument called Rogerian rhetoric, which is based on the theories of psychologist Carl Rogers.

According to Rogers, the problem with most overt attempts to persuade is that persuasive appeals force people to decide whether they agree or disagree with someone else's views.[3] This kind of persuasion is threatening because people feel they are

---

[3] Carl Rogers, "Communication: Its Blocking and its Facilitation." *On Becoming a Person.* (Boston: Houghton Mifflin, 1961) 329-337. Also, see the discussion of Rogerian Rhetoric in Richard Young, Alton Becker and Kenneth Pike, *Rhetoric: Discovery and Change* (New York: Harcourt, 1970).

being asked to change their self-image or worldview. That's why people tend to reject new or different ideas without fully considering them. Given a choice to agree or disagree, most will stay with what they already believe, even if agreeing with something new would be advantageous to them.

Rogers believed that an effective argument needs to first remove this threat to a person's self-image before he or she will consider new ideas or alternate perspectives. Therefore, all sides should strive to listen carefully and understand what others believe. By striving for *understanding* rather than agreement, negotiation allows people to feel less threatened and more open to new ideas and points of view. All sides have the freedom to consider a variety of worldviews and then choose the ideas that fit their own needs and experiences.

According to Rogerian rhetoric, you should follow four steps when negotiating with others:

1. Introduce the problem and demonstrate that you understand and value the others' positions.

2. Identify situations in which the others' positions are valid.

3. Identify situations in which your position is valid.

4. Explain how both you and the others would benefit if you adopted elements from all positions. Stress the places in which the different viewpoints complement and strengthen each other.

When negotiating, your goal is not to *persuade* the others to agree with you in an overt way. Instead, you want to show them that you understand their views and recognize that there are situations in which their views make sense (Figure 8). Likewise, you should help them understand your views and imagine situations in which your views make sense. Then, when all sides understand the others' views, everyone involved can work toward consensus rather than trying to win the others over.

In this way, all sides cooperate to come up with an understanding or plan that is acceptable and beneficial to all. More than likely, everyone won't agree on all points, but each person understands the others' points of view. All sides can then agree to move forward together.

FIGURE 8 Negotiation as a Form of Generative Argument
The best negotiators are people who can focus on issues and negotiate differences. The best outcomes happen when both sides feel like they received something while not giving up too much.

Consensus and Dissensus

In generative arguments, people are usually striving to reach some kind of consensus. Consensus doesn't mean you and the others will agree completely about an issue. It simply means you are identifying places you agree while openly discussing places you disagree. A disagreement doesn't mean one side or the other is right or wrong. Disagreement only means that full consensus hasn't been reached on the issue.

Striving for Consensus

Consensus happens when people figure out where they agree on a particular issue. For example, you and your friends might be talking about a hot-button issue, such as whether abortion should be legal (Figure 9). This issue tends to bring out strong differences in opinion, even among people who agree on most other issues.

Nevertheless, you and the others should be able to reach consensus on some important points. For example, almost all people can agree on the following points:

- Unintended pregnancies should be prevented as much as possible.

- The number of abortions should be as few as possible, ideally zero.

- Adoption should be offered as an alternative to abortion, but no one should be forced or pressured to give a baby away for adoption.

- Abortion is acceptable in very rare cases in which the pregnancy is likely to cause the death of the pregnant woman.

FIGURE 9 Lack of Consensus About a Divisive Issue Even on the most divisive issues, a measure of consensus is possible.

This is what we mean by striving *toward* consensus. There is a good chance you and the others won't reach full agreement about an issue like abortion, especially if you hold opposite opinions. However, discussing this issue in a reasonable way is still important. In fact, you will usually find that people who strongly disagree with you about highly contentious issues can reach consensus on some major points.

When you and the others reach consensus on some major points, you can then figure out how you as a group might achieve common goals. For instance, even though people disagree strongly about abortion, they can agree about preventing unintended pregnancies, reducing the number of abortions, making adoption more available, and defining when a woman's life is threatened by a pregnancy.

Most issues are not as contentious as abortion. You will find that consensus is much easier to reach about issues that are less contentious or polarizing.

Valuing Dissensus

The ability to disagree, or dissent, is important, too. In generative arguments, people should be able to express a disagreement in a reasonable way. Unfortunately, in our polarized and partisan society, many people feel uncomfortable disagreeing with others. So they change the topic, stop listening, walk away, or change the channel instead of actually engaging with the beliefs of others. That's too bad, because even on the most controversial issues, people tend to agree more than they disagree.

Dissensus is important because it urges people to be creative and develop better awareness of issues. All citizens should have the freedom to offer their own viewpoints, even if they know others will disagree with them. Meanwhile, you should encourage people to speak up if they disagree with you or others. That way, you can better understand all points of view.

It takes courage to dissent. When you speak up, people might disagree with you, and they may even get angry. In the end, though, silence and being silenced are the real enemies of civil

FIGURE 10 Silence Is Worse Than Disagreement
Putting duct tape over the mouth has become a common symbol for protesters who feel they are being silenced.

discourse, not the people who have the courage to speak up. A generative argument fails when people cannot say what they believe or, even worse, are being silenced by others (Figure 10). We are all better off when people are allowed to express alternative views, because these disagreements often lead to innovative solutions, stronger plans, and better understanding.

Writing generative arguments can help you argue better in groups and teams. Here is what you need to know from this chapter.

1 Conversations are generative arguments in which people share ideas, compare experiences, build understanding, and figure out the best way forward.

2 Generative arguments are often called "power-with" arguments because people are working together to figure out what to believe or what to do.

3 There are four basic strategies for making a successful generative argument: (1) build a sense of identification, (2) frame the issue, (3) tell an interesting story, and (4) negotiate disagreements.

4 Identification involves demonstrating to others that you share their ideas, values, and experiences.

5 To frame an issue, choose an organizing idea or theme that fits your worldview and use it to promote a specific way of looking at an issue.

6 Telling an interesting story allows you to exhibit and reinforce your or your culture's values.

7 Some common types of stories include (a) funny, tragic, or instructive stories, (b) anecdotes, and (c) fables and parables.

8 Negotiation involves understanding the views of others while sharing your views.

9 Generative arguments strive toward consensus rather than winning people over to one side.

10 Dissensus should be valued rather than avoided because expressing differences often opens the door for creativity and better awareness of issues.

1. With a small group in class, have a conversation about a current topic or issue that is important right now. You could talk about sports, music, movies, commercials, or anything that the entire group knows something about. Ask one member of the group to silently record the kinds of arguments that happen. Talk for about five minutes. Then ask the person who recorded the arguments to list all the moments when he or she felt people were working out differences and shifting their views.

2. If you have an account on a social networking site, such as Facebook, Google+, or Tumblr, look at the postings over the previous month. What kinds of arguments are happening among your friends and family? Are people openly disagreeing with each other? How are they reaching understanding or resolving differences? What happens when people aren't willing to talk about issues that they disagree about?

3. Think about a situation in which you actually changed your mind about an important issue. Then figure out what brought you to a moment when you could change your mind. Did you feel like you were persuaded by facts or logic? Or did you change your mind because you identified with someone else or reached an understanding by sharing ideas with other people? Share your experience with a group of people from your class. How were your experiences similar to the experiences of others in your group? How were your experiences different?

1. List five issues that people find difficult to talk about with a group of others. Pick one of these topics and have a conversation about it with a group of others in your class. Where do people agree? Where do they disagree? At what points did you notice people becoming uptight about this issue? What triggers their negative responses? Using this conversation for support, write an e-mail to your professor in which you describe how people struggle to hold conversations about difficult issues.

2. Pick an issue that interests you. Write a brief argument (200 words) in which you use one of the four generative argument strategies described in this chapter. Then rewrite the argument using a different generative argument strategy (another 200 words). Finally, write an analysis in which you compare these two strategies, discussing their strengths and weaknesses as ways to argue about an issue.

3. List three issues about which you believe people are unable to speak freely. In other words, what are three issues that others will resist talking about? Choose one of these issues. Looking at the four generative argument strategies discussed in this chapter, what strategy would be most effective for talking about this issue with someone who disagrees with you? Write a single-page, single-spaced memo to your instructor in which you describe how you might use this strategy to open a dialogue about this issue with someone who would be uncomfortable talking about it.

Credits

Credits are listed in order of appearance.

Photo Credits

CandyBox Images/Fotolia; Saul Loeb/AFP/Getty Images/Newscom; (l), Shannon Stapleton/Reuters; (r), Seth Perlman/AP Images; Kristopher Skinner/ZUMA Press/Newscom; Barry Chin/The Boston Globe/Getty Images; Official White House Photo by Pete Souza; Shawn Thew/EPA /Landov; Stella/Getty Images

Text Credits

From "Eating Disorder Stories: Kathy Carey" by Teresa Joerger, www.caringonline.com. Used by permission of The Center, Inc.

Graphic from "Understand What the Bible Really Says About The Future..." by Andrew Corbett, www.andrewcorbett.net. Courtesy of Andrew Corbett.

Critical Reading and Rhetorical Analysis

IN THIS CHAPTER, YOU WILL LEARN—

1 Why critical reading is an important skill that you will use in college and your career

2 How to "look through" and "look at" an argument

3 A simple six-step method for reading and responding to an argument critically

4 How to write a rhetorical analysis

Y ou have probably met people who *claim* they like to argue but don't seem to fully understand the issues they want to argue about. Soon, you realize they don't have much support for their opinions, and they don't seem to have good reasons for believing what they believe. In other words, they haven't thought critically about their own beliefs and they don't know how to critically analyze the opinions of others.

In this chapter, you will learn how to read arguments critically and how to analyze them fairly. These critical reading skills will help you better understanding both generative and persuasive arguments, because critical reading and rhetorical analysis help you figure out why people believe what they believe and why they say what they say.

Critical reading goes beyond simply deciding whether you agree with an argument. Instead, it helps you pull arguments apart to better understand how they work and the motivations behind them.

Later in this chapter, you will learn how use a *rhetorical analysis* to investigate the effectiveness of an argument. This kind of analysis uses rhetorical concepts to closely examine how an argument works and whether it is effective. In college, your professors will ask you to write analyses that investigate why specific historical, technologi-

1 Why critical reading is an important skill that you will use in college and your career

cal, theoretical, or political arguments were successful. And, in your career, you and your colleagues will use rhetorical concepts to analyze the behavior of customers, clients, competitors, and markets (Figure 1). This kind of analysis will help you better understand why some kinds of messages work and why some don't.

The purpose of this chapter is to help you interpret and understand arguments at a deeper level. That way, you can better understand what motivates people and how to effectively present your own ideas and beliefs.

FIGURE 1
Presenting an Analysis in the Workplace
In the workplace, rhetorical analyses are called a variety of names, like "marketing research," "impact studies," or "message testing."

2 How to "look through" and "look at" an argument

Looking at and Looking through Arguments

In the past, you have been told to read critically or think critically, but you probably weren't given much advice about how to do it. So let's start out with a few basics.

Richard Lanham, a leading American rhetorician, suggests that critical reading means analyzing an argument on two levels, which he calls "looking through" and "looking at."[1]

> **Looking through an argument**—Most of the time, people *look through* an argument to acquire the information it contains. They look through the words at *what* the author is saying, paying attention to the author's facts, reasoning, statistics, examples, evidence, quotations, descriptions, and other information.

[1]Richard Lanham, *The Electronic Word* (Chicago: U of Chicago P, 1993) 5–14.

***Looking at* an argument**—When people *look at* an argument, they are trying to figure out *how* the argument works, what the argument *does* to readers. They pay attention to its organization, style, and design, as well as its generative and persuasive strategies. They look for the author's motives and values while highlighting any uses of framing, identification, narrative, and negotiation. They look at how the author uses reasoning, authority, and emotion to support his or her claims.

To read critically, you should toggle back and forth between these two kinds of reading. You need to *look through* the argument to figure out what the author is arguing and then *look at* the argument to understand the author's underlying values and argumentative strategies (Figure 2).

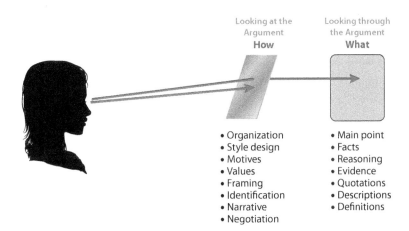

FIGURE 2
Toggling between *Looking through* and *Looking at* an Argument
Reading critically involves both looking through and looking at an argument.

A Simple Method for Reading Critically

3 A simple six-step method for reading and responding to an argument critically

Let's keep this simple. Here are six steps that will help you *look through* and *look at* an argument in a critical way.

Step 1: Read the Argument, Asking Basic Questions

Read through the argument once, primarily paying attention to the information provided by the author and the point the author is trying to make. Then ask some of the following questions:

What Is the Argument's Rhetorical Situation?

An argument's rhetorical situation has five elements: *topic, angle, purpose, audience,* and *context.*

- **Topic**—What specifically is the argument about and what are the topic's boundaries or scope?

- **Angle**—What new perspective, if any, is the author bringing to this topic? What has happened recently that makes this topic interesting to the author and to the intended audience?

- **Purpose**—What exactly is the author trying to achieve in this argument? What is the main point or thesis of the argument and where is it stated?

- **Audience**—Who is the primary audience for this argument? What are their needs, values, and attitudes about what the author is saying? How did the author adjust the argument to meet their needs, values, and attitudes?

- **Context**—How have physical, economic, and political influences shaped the author's decisions about the content, organization, style, design, and medium of the argument? How has the author adjusted or designed the argument to fit these contextual influences?

What is the Argument's Genre?

Once you have identified the elements of the rhetorical situation, you can then explore which genre the argument is using. Figure 3 lists the argument genres that are covered in this text. If you think you have identified the argument's genre, you can flip to that chapter to find a helpful overview of the genre.

When you identify which genre the argument is using, ask the following questions:

- **Content**—Is the content appropriate for this particular genre? What additional information would be helpful to the audience? What unnecessary information did the author include that isn't helpful or need to know?

- **Organization**—What is the structure of the argument? What are the argument's major sections? Is this argument's organization common for the genre it is using? Where is the author stretching or bending the typical organizational pattern for this genre?

- **Style**—How would you characterize the author's writing style or voice? Is the style quarrelsome or friendly? Is it fast paced or plodding? In one word, how would you describe the tone or voice of the argument? Is this tone or voice appropriate for this argument and its genre?

- **Design**—In what ways does the author use design and images effectively or ineffectively? What tone does the argument's design evoke? How does the author use graphics, such as photos, illustrations, charts, or graphs, to support the written text? Are these design features appropriate for this argument's genre?

- **Medium**—How does the medium of the argument (e.g., newspaper, magazine, blog, podcast, poster presentation, website, social networking, etc.) shape how the argument is presented and how the audience receives it? How might the argument be different if it appeared in a different medium?

		FIGURE 3
Description	Evaluation	**Common Argument Genres**
Comparison	Commentary	Once you identify the genre of the argument you are analyzing, you can go to the chapter in this text that discusses that genre.
Causal Analysis	Refutation	
Visual Essay	Proposal	
Narrative	Research Paper or Research Report	
Review		

Analyzing the content, organization, style, and design of the argument will help you decide whether the author has used the genre effectively.

Why is figuring out the genre important? Knowing the genre of an argument helps you better understand what the author is trying to achieve. Each genre reflects how a community gets something done. So, if you can figure out which genre is being used, you can better understand how the argument works and why the author has chosen to argue a particular way.

Step 2: Play the Believing and Doubting Games with the Argument

Peter Elbow, another American scholar of rhetoric, offers a critical reading strategy called the Believing and Doubting Game that will help you to gain some distance from the argument.[2] These "games" will help you see the text from other perspectives, so you will understand it more fully.

> **The Believing Game**—As you read the argument, imagine you are someone who accepts without question what the author is trying to prove. Highlight the argument's strong points and note the places where it seems well reasoned and well supported. Identify and mark places where someone who is inclined to accept this argument would be most enthusiastic about it.

> **The Doubting Game**—Read the argument again, but this time imagine you are someone who is deeply skeptical and even negative about it. Search out and highlight the argument's factual shortcomings and logical flaws. Find any places where the author is overgeneralizing, drawing biased conclusions, or using fallacious reasoning. Repeatedly ask "So what?" as you read the argument to challenge whether the author is saying something important.

Elbow's term, *game*, is a good choice for this kind of critical reading. You are role playing with the argument, first analyzing it in a sympathetic way and then analyzing it in a skeptical way (Figure 4).

---

[2]Peter Elbow, *Writing Without Teachers* (Oxford: Oxford UP, 1973) 147–190.

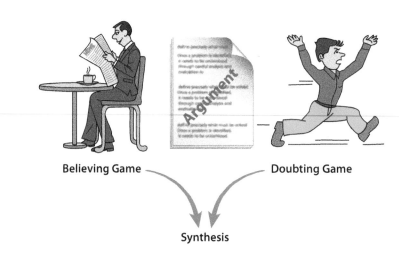

FIGURE 4 Playing the Believing Game and Doubting Game
The Believing Game and Doubting Game can help you analyze an argument from different sides. Then you can synthesize both positions to help you decide what you believe.

After you study the argument from both the believing and doubting perspectives, you can create a *synthesis* that helps you build your own response to the argument. This synthesis of the two perspectives will help you see the argument from different sides so you can figure out how your own opinions compare to the author's views.

Step 3: Look for Features of Generative Arguments

You learned about the features of *generative arguments.* These "power with" arguments tend to be conversation based, and the people involved are typically striving to reach a common understanding or consensus. Usually, generative arguments are open-ended conversations, so look for places in which the author is inviting people to participate in the argument.

Using identification—In what ways is the author trying to build trust by identifying with the audience? Is the author highlighting any common beliefs or values that are shared with the audience? Is the author trying to build identification by drawing attention to a common problem or shared adversary? Do you think the author is inappropriately scapegoating or pandering to get the audience's attention or trust?

Using framing—How is the author framing the argument for the audience? What are the positive frames he or she is using to shape the argument? Is the author using any negative frames that put her or him on the defensive? Can you think of any other ways that this issue might be better framed or reframed?

Using stories—How is the author using narratives (stories, anecdotes, or made-up scenarios) to support or illustrate important points? Are these stories appropriate to the topic, or are they being used to gloss over significant issues or problems?

Using negotiation—In what ways is the author trying to negotiate with the audience? According to the author, what are the major issues that need to be resolved? Has the author identified any situations in which alternative approaches would be valid? Does the argument highlight points on which all sides can agree?

All arguments, even the most obvious attempts to persuade, will have some features of generative arguments. You should identify these features because they will help you better understand how the author is attempting to build understanding and consensus with the audience.

Step 4: Look for Features of Persuasive Arguments

You learned about features of *persuasive arguments*. These "power over" arguments tend to be more one sided because the author is trying to persuade the audience to believe something or take a specific kind of action. Persuasive arguments tend to be constructed with three forms of proof: reasoning (*logos*), authority (*ethos*), and emotion (*pathos*).

Reasoning (*logos*)—In what ways is the author using logic and examples to support the argument's major claims? Highlight the places in which the author is using the following kinds of logical moves:

If . . . then: "If you believe X, then you should believe Y also."

Either . . . or: "Either you believe X or you believe Y."

Cause and effect: "X is why Y happens."

Costs and benefits: "The benefits of doing X are worth/not worth the cost of Y."

Better and worse: "X is better/worse than Y because . . . "

Examples: "For example, X and Y demonstrate that Z happens."

Facts and data: "These facts/data support my argument that X is true (or Y is not true)."

Anecdotes: "X happened to these people, thus demonstrating Y."

Authority (*ethos*)—How is the author trying to establish or draw upon his or her own authority to persuade the audience? How is the author using the authority of experts to support the argument? Highlight the places in which the author is making the following kinds of authority-based moves:

Personal experience: "I have experienced X, so I know it's true and Y is not."

Personal credentials: "I have a degree in Z" or "I am the director of Y." "So I know a lot about the subject of X."

Good moral character: "I have always done the right thing for the right reasons, so you should believe me when I say that X is the best path to follow."

Appeal to experts: "According to Z, who is an expert on this topic, X is true and Y is not true."

Identification with the readers: "You and I come from similar backgrounds and we have similar values; therefore, you would likely agree with me that X is true and Y is not."

Admission of limitations: "I may not know much about Z, but I do know that X is true and Y is not."

Expression of goodwill: "I want what is best for you, so I am recommending X as the best path to follow."

Use of "insider" language: Using jargon or referring to information that primarily insiders would understand.

Emotion (*pathos*)—How is the author trying to inject emotions into the argument? What emotions does the author want the audience to feel as they consider the argument? In what ways is the author using words or images to try to evoke those emotions? Highlight the places in which the author is making some of the following emotional moves:

Promise of gain: "By agreeing with us, you will gain trust, time, money, love, advancement, reputation, comfort, popularity, health, beauty, or convenience."

Promise of enjoyment: "If you do things our way, you will experience joy, anticipation, fun, surprises, enjoyment, pleasure, leisure, or freedom."

Fear of loss: "If you don't do things this way, you risk losing time, money, love, security, freedom, reputation, popularity, health, or beauty."

Fear of pain: "If you don't do things this way, you may feel pain, sadness, grief, frustration, humiliation, embarrassment, loneliness, regret, shame, vulnerability, or worry."

Expressions of anger or disgust: "You should be angry or disgusted because X is unfair to you, me, or others."

Any argument will use a combination of *logos*, *ethos*, and *pathos*. Advertising, of course, relies heavily on *pathos*, but ads also use *logos* and *ethos* to persuade. Scientific texts, meanwhile, are dominated by *logos*, but scientists can draw upon their reputation (*ethos*) and they will occasionally even show emotion (*pathos*) about their topic (Figure 5).

FIGURE 5 Using Emotion in a Scientific Argument
Emotional proofs can be a significant part of any argument even when the topic is scientific. In this picture, scientist Jane Goodall is using emotion to make an important point.

Step 5: Reflect on Your Own Reactions to the Argument

Here's the really tough part. Reflect critically on your own responses and reactions to the argument. No matter how unbiased or impartial you tried to be, as you were reading you still relied on your own existing values and knowledge to help you decide whether the argument was effective. Here are a few questions you can ask yourself:

* What was my first reaction when I started reading the argument?

* How did my first reaction influence how I interpreted the remainder of the argument?

* Where does the argument seem to be agreeing with my views?

* Where is it disagreeing with my views?

* When was I agreeing most with the argument?

* When did I want to argue against it?

* Now that I have spent time analyzing the argument, have my views on this issue changed at all?

Ultimately, critical reading isn't really about the argument you're analyzing. It's about you. Without you, an argument is just ink on a page or pixels on a screen. The argument relies completely on you to interpret and make sense of what the author or presenter is trying to say.

The key to effective critical reading is to continually rethink and reevaluate your own knowledge, values, and beliefs. If an argument challenges you, that's a good thing. If you agree or disagree with it, perhaps the argument will strengthen your convictions. Or maybe you will shift your views or change your mind. Either way, you come away from the experience stronger and better able to understand and articulate the things you believe in.

Step 6: Respond to the Argument

When responding to an argument, you should do more than conclude whether you agree or disagree. In any argument, both sides will have some merit—otherwise, the topic is not really worth arguing about. So you need to explain your response and where your views align with or diverge from the author's views. Here are some questions that will help you form your own response:

Why Does the Argument Matter?

Explain why you think people should care about the argument and why.

_____ is an important issue because _____.

While _____ might not seem important on first glance, it has several important consequences, such as _____, _____, and _____.

Example response: Although childhood obesity might seem like it's just a matter of childhood health that will resolve itself over time, public health studies show that obese children are far more likely to become obese adults, which leads to lifelong health issues for the individuals and skyrocketing healthcare costs for society.

Where and Why Do You Disagree with the Argument?

Describe exactly where the various sides disagree. You learned about four categories of issues on which people tend to agree: definition, causation, evaluation, or recommendation.

At the heart of this debate is a disagreement about that nature of _____, whether it was _____ or _____. **(Definition)**

While most people agree that _____ is caused by _____, they disagree whether we should _____ or _____. **(Causation)**

_____ is something we should pay attention to, but it's not important enough for us to do _____. **(Evaluation)**

I agree that _____ is an issue that needs to be addressed, and I believe the best way forward is to do _____. **(Recommendation)**

Example response: Although childhood obesity is an important issue that is caused primarily by Americans' junk-food and fast-food habits, I disagree that the problem can be solved by imposing taxes on these foods. Instead, the better solution is to educate Americans and provide positive incentives for adopting healthy dietary habits.

Where and Why Do You Personally Agree with the Argument?

Finally, describe exactly where and why you and others agree with the argument you are analyzing. It's unlikely you agree completely with the author, but you can find places at which your values and beliefs align with the author's values and beliefs. Joseph Harris offers a useful four-point system for demonstrating why you agree with an argument. In *Rewriting: How to Do Things with Texts*, he identifies four key activities:

Illustrating—Use points, descriptions, or stories provided by the argument to support your own views. An author may make a point, provide facts, and provide other evidence that strengthen your argument.

Authorizing—Use the authority, expertise, or experience of the author to strengthen your own position and give it more validity. You can cite the author as support for your own argument.

Borrowing—Use a term, definition, or idea developed in the argument. If your own opinion hinges on a technical concept, key term, definition, or idea, you can borrow and cite what the author says.

Extending—Use the author's argument as starting place for launching your own argument. Your argument might extend the author's argument in a new direction or apply it to topics that the author did not consider.

Reacting and responding to an argument is more than a matter of agreeing or disagreeing. Whether the argument is generative or persuasive, you should feel free to add something to the conversation or explain why you agree or disagree with the author.

Writing a Rhetorical Analysis

4 How to write a rhetorical analysis

A rhetorical analysis takes critical reading a step further. The purpose of a rhetorical analysis is to use rhetorical concepts to closely examine how an argument works and determine whether it is *effective* or *ineffective*. You're not figuring out whether the argument is true or false. Instead, you are investigating its effectiveness.

There are a variety of analytical methods available for writing a rhetorical analysis of an argument, but here are a few of the most common:

Analysis of *logos, ethos*, and/or *pathos*—examines how reasoning, credibility, and emotional proofs are used to support an argument, especially a persuasive argument. All three kinds of proofs can be discussed together in the rhetorical analysis, or you can focus on just one of them.

Audience analysis—researches how the argument was written to reflect the needs, values, and attitudes of the targeted audience. An audience analysis also pays attention to how the argument's context (physical, economic, political, and medium) influences how the message was received by the audience.

Genre analysis—studies how an argument uses or deviates from a common genre. You can use the genre to discuss how a specific argument works and whether it is effective.

Narrative analysis—uses elements of narrative to investigate how a story or stories were used to deliver the argument's message.

Metaphor analysis—pays special attention to the author's or presenter's attempts to frame or reframe an argument through the use of metaphors.

Stylistic analysis—looks closely at an argument's use of stylistic devices, such as metaphors, similes, analogies, personification, onomatopoeia, rhythm, voice, and tone.

Visual analysis—uses principles of visual design and visual rhetoric to study how the appearance of an argument shapes its message and its impact on the audience.

You can organize a rhetorical analysis in a variety of ways. One of the most common patterns is shown in Figure 6. In this pattern, after a brief introduction, the

FIGURE 6

Organizing a Rhetorical Analysis Rhetorical analyses tend to follow a pattern similar to this one. After one or more rhetorical concepts are defined and explained, they are used to analyze the argument.

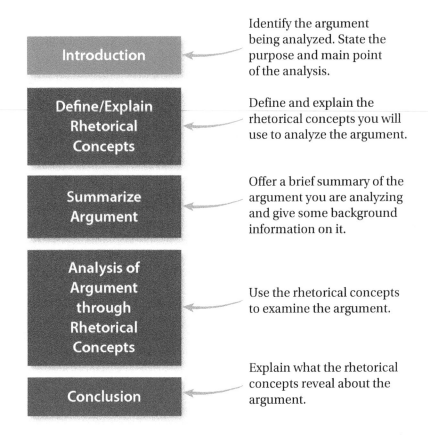

Identify the argument being analyzed. State the purpose and main point of the analysis.

Define and explain the rhetorical concepts you will use to analyze the argument.

Offer a brief summary of the argument you are analyzing and give some background information on it.

Use the rhetorical concepts to examine the argument.

Explain what the rhetorical concepts reveal about the argument.

rhetorical concepts are explained and the argument is summarized. Then the selected rhetorical concepts are used to analyze the argument. Typically a rhetorical analysis ends by explaining what the rhetorical concepts reveal about the argument.

The aim of a rhetorical analysis is to extend your critical reading beyond response into a thorough analysis that can be shared with others. A rhetorical analysis lets you use one or more rhetorical concepts to explore and examine how an argument works. It also helps you explain why an argument was effective or ineffective.

Even more importantly, though, a rhetorical analysis helps you and others understand how certain rhetorical techniques, such as identification, framing, narrative, or the use of *logos*, *ethos*, and *pathos*, can make an argument more effective.

Just want the basics? Here's what you need to know about critical reading and rhetorical analysis.

1 Critical reading gives you the ability to examine arguments to figure out how they work and whether they are reasonable.

2 A rhetorical analysis uses rhetorical concepts to closely examine how an argument works and whether it is effective.

3 When you *look through* an argument, you are paying attention to *what* someone else is saying, and when you *look at* an argument, you are paying attention to *how* that person is arguing.

4 Step 1: Read the argument and ask basic questions about its rhetorical situation and genre.

5 Step 2: Play the Believing and Doubting Games to interpret the argument from two opposite perspectives.

6 Step 3: Look for features of generative arguments.

7 Step 4: Look for features of persuasive arguments.

8 Step 5: Reflect on your own reactions to the argument to help you manage your own bias for or against the argument.

9 Step 6: Develop your own response to the argument, explaining where you agree, where you disagree, and the reasons that you disagree.

10 A rhetorical analysis allows you to discuss why an argument is effective or ineffective.

1. In your group, discuss what you have been taught previously about critical thinking or critical reading. Have you been given strategies for critical reading before? If so, share them with the group and discuss how they differ from the strategies discussed in this chapter. Then discuss the difference between uncritical reading/thinking and critical reading/thinking. Do you know anyone who does not think or read critically? Describe how that person behaves during an argument. Describe how people who don't read or think critically tend to argue.

2. Ask each member of your group to bring an argument from the Internet to class. Using the six critical reading strategies discussed in this chapter, analyze two of the arguments. What do the strategies in this chapter reveal about both arguments? In what ways do they allow you to *look through* and *look at* the argument?

3. List five ways that the ability to read critically will be important to your future career. Think about the kinds of analysis you will need to do at your job. How will the ability to analyze arguments critically help you better understand the arguments at your workplace? Then list three workplace activities that are similar to doing a rhetorical analysis. Share and discuss your two lists with your group.

1. Find a written argument on the Internet or in a print source. Fold a piece of paper in half lengthwise and play the Believing Game and the Doubting Game with the argument. First, imagine that you are completely sold on the argument. On one half of the paper, write down all the positive things you can think of. Second, imagine you are completely skeptical of the argument. Write down all your doubts, questions, and concerns about the argument. Then open the sheet of paper and look at both lists. In an e-mail to your instructor, summarize both your positive and skeptical views of the argument. Then discuss where your own views fit between these two positions.

2. With two other people in your class, use the six critical reading strategies discussed in this chapter to analyze one of the arguments that appears at the end of the genre chapters in this text. You and your teammates should divide up the six strategies, with each of you handling two of them. Then, when you are finished analyzing the argument, get together and share your analyses. Take special note of places your analyses seemed to complement each other and places the analyses seemed to contradict. Combine your notes and present your findings to the class.

3. Find an argument that you disagree with on the Internet or in a print source. Write a rhetorical analysis in which you try to be as objective as possible. You don't need to be completely neutral, but you need to fairly consider the author's ideas and analyze his or her text. Use rhetorical concepts to show why you felt the argument was ineffective or not persuasive. If you haven't written a rhetorical analysis before, you might consider following the pattern shown in Figure 6 to guide your writing.

ONE STUDENT'S WORK

Effective Diplomacy: Examining the Rhetorical Elements of Obama's 2009 Cairo Speech

Jeremy Dellarosa, English 102

Identifies the background and rhetorical situation

Over the course of his first term (and now well into a second), President Barack Obama has proven himself to be an effective and inspiring orator, the likes of which has not been seen perhaps since the presidencies of John F. Kennedy and Ronald Reagan. Time and again, through the power of the spoken word, he has walked a delicate line to reach across the diverse viewpoints that make up this country (and the world). In his most memorable speeches, Obama manages to strike a balance between two rhetorical goals: rousing the emotions of his supporters while simultaneously calming his opponents.

identifies the purpose and states main point of the rhetorical analysis

Of all of the speeches that Obama has delivered, he faced perhaps the most difficult challenge in his 2009 address from Cairo University in Egypt, where he needed to acknowledge the validity of Muslims' displeased feelings toward the United States while simultaneously portraying his nation and his presidency as strong and just. In just shy of an hour, the president managed to address the strained feelings at the heart of U.S.–Muslim relations, acknowledging tensions, conceding mistakes, and painting a hopeful landscape of a potential future for the Muslim world.

The Speech: Acknowledging the Strain Between Cultures

Elaborates on the rhetorical situation and summarizes the rhetorical strategies used in the speech

Throughout his speech, President Obama systematically addresses the myriad issues that will affect the future of the Islamic world. Furthermore, he manages to confront the uneasy (in some cases, contemptuous) relationship that has existed between the Islamic world and America, particularly since 9/11, "nursing the grievances of decades sharpened by the blows of the past eight years that preceded Obama's presidency—the invasion and occupation of Iraq, the collapse of the Arab-Israeli peace process" (Schleifer, 2009, para. 13). He even acknowledges problems going back to the Eisenhower era (Herman, 2009, para. 4–5). Needless to say, acknowledgement of these issues would be an audacious move for any contemporary U.S. politician. Yet Obama does not approach these topics in the same haughty, arrogant, disconnected manner that Americans had grown accustomed to during the previous administration. Instead, the tone of the speech is humble, perhaps even entreating at times, yet it is still full of resolve. Furthermore, the potency of the speech is bolstered by its structure, utilizing simultaneous and overlapping appeals to *ethos, logos,* and *pathos* in order to make a meaningful and effective case for improved American relations with this turbulent region.

Using *Ethos* to Establish Credibility and Goodwill

Almost immediately, President Obama begins his speech with an appeal to *ethos,* establishing his own credibility and his goodwill toward the Islamic world. He shows he understands Islamic culture, recounting his own experience with Islam, from his father's Muslim heritage and his childhood years in Indonesia to his time spent working in and among Muslim communities in Chicago. He develops this display of *ethos* to the Muslim world while simultaneously using *logos,* through reasoning and examples, to remind the West about the significant historical contributions of Islam to the rest of the world. He speaks of "civilization's debt to Islam," saying, "It was Islam ... that carried the light of learning through so many centuries, paving the way for Europe's renaissance and enlightenment" (Obama, 2009, para. 13.) He describes the invaluable progress made by Muslims in the areas of mathematics and science, medicine, literature, art, and architecture. He also supports his point by stating, "throughout history, Islam has demonstrated through words and deeds the possibilities of religious tolerance and racial equality" (para. 12–14). Lastly, Obama shows his knowledge of the Quran, not merely displaying how much he knows, but more importantly employing its authority to back up the points he wants to make:

Describes how *ethos* is used to establish authority and credibility

Quotes Obama to illustrate his use of *ethos,* showing goodwill to both sides

The Holy Quran teaches that whoever kills an innocent... it is as if   5
he has killed all mankind. And the Holy Quran also says whoever
saves a person, it is as if he has saved all mankind. (para. 42)

Using *Logos* to Set Common Goals

At this point, Obama turns more directly to using *logos* to urge Americans
and Muslims to work together toward a common goal. First he offers
several historical examples of Muslims succeeding in and contributing to
America:

> They have fought in our wars. They have served in our government.
> They have stood for civil rights. They have started businesses. They have
> taught at our universities. They've excelled in our sports arenas. They've
> won Nobel Prizes, built our tallest building and lit the Olympic torch.
> And when the first Muslim American was recently elected to Congress,
> he took the oath to defend our Constitution using the same holy Quran
> that one of our founding fathers, Thomas Jefferson, kept in his personal
> library. (para. 17)

In terms of *logos*, Obama is using reason to argue: If these
collaborations are possible, then so are others. By beginning seven
consecutive brief sentences with the word *they*, these examples seem
to come in rapid-fire succession, suggesting that there are many other
examples he could cite.

Then, President Obama continues to deploy *logos*-based appeals alongside
pathos and *ethos* in order to entreat his audience to follow his suggested
course of action. He encourages a mutual understanding between Muslims and
the U.S., saying that a "partnership between America and Islam must be based
on what Islam is, and not what it isn't" (para. 18). He follows up on this point
by stating that he considers it to be part of his "responsibility as president of
the United States to fight against negative stereotypes of Islam wherever they
appear" (para. 18). Nevertheless, he points out that this level of respect must go
both ways, saying,

Analyzes how logical statements and examples (logos) are used to good effect

Describes how style can drive home the logos of an argument

10   Just as Muslims do not fit a crude stereotype, America is not the crude stereotype of a self-interested empire. The United States has been one of the greatest sources of progress that the world has ever known. We were born out of revolution against an empire. (para. 18–20)

Explains how reasoning, emotion, and authority *(logos, pathos, and ethos)* are combined

This particular statement serves a similar purpose as the aforementioned reminder to the West, giving an emotional *pathos*-laden nod to Americans while using *logos* to remind the Islamic world of America's mutually humble beginnings and meaningful contributions.

The president then furthers his appeal by calling on both Islam and the West to act in favor of the common good and against common ills. He points out that people throughout the world are inextricably bound by consequences, mutually hurt by things like economic crises, new diseases, and the threat posed to the global community by nuclear proliferations. He mentions the "stain on our collective conscience" caused by historical acts of violence, and clearly states, "Our problems must be dealt with through partnership, our progress must be shared" (para. 28–32). Having virtually prompted a shaking of hands between Islam and America, Obama set the stage for addressing the larger issues of common importance.

Later in the speech, President Obama also appeals to *logos* by making use of simple reasoning and strong conviction to confront matters pertaining to current affairs in the Middle East, as well as those that stand to affect American relations with the Muslim world. He dives directly into the deep end of the foreign affairs pool with the discussion of Islamic extremism, voicing his continued commitment to the pursuit of terrorists waving the Islamic flag. Nevertheless, he reassures his audience that this is not out of any feeling of spite toward Islam, but rather "because we reject the same thing that people of all faiths reject, the killing of innocent men, women, and children" (para. 35). He follows this by reiterating that his primary responsibility as president is to the continued safety of the American people, but that the harm caused by violent extremism reaches far beyond American borders, saying the following of Al Qaida:

They have killed people of different faiths but, more than any other, they have killed Muslims. Their actions are irreconcilable with the rights of human beings, the progress of nations, and with Islam. (para. 33–40)

With this direct use of common logic, Obama is able to display how   15
the issue of violent religious extremism is widespread, even affecting those of a faith that it claims to stem from. Thus, continued commitment to the problem in places like Afghanistan and Pakistan is necessary, not simply for the safety of America, but for the safety of the world. Obama employs logic in order to instill a sense of community between nations affected by a single problem. Despite his soothing and sympathetic rhetoric earlier in the speech, President Obama makes clear that he has an unwavering resolve to do what is necessary to address the problems at hand while still taking into account the common interest of nations everywhere.

Conclusion: The Speech Was Effective

Obama's purpose is to urge both Muslim nations and America to work together diplomatically. Likewise, his main rhetorical strategies—reason, goodwill, and level-headed *pathos*—are themselves highly diplomatic. One might liken Obama's America to the grammar-school bully who, now in college, has had ample opportunity to reflect on the error of his past ways and who wishes to reconcile his actions with those whom they affected. But how to go about such reconciliation? Clearly, the same old displays of force and aggression would not be effective in this situation. Thus, humility and kindness are far more viable options. In the same way, America can no longer rely on the forceful approach that it has adopted in the past. Good rapport with the international community is not something to be established and enforced. It is something to be nurtured. Such rapport can only come through respect, and although our reputation may not permit such a humble response, we have reached a significant and hopeful turning

> Summarizes and explains what the rhetorical concepts reveal about the argument, concluding with an overall assessment of the speech's effectiveness

point in our life-course as a country. Perhaps we may be able to move forward with a sense of progress, a progress that can only occur through cooperation. In closing, President Obama summarizes in cooperative and conciliatory fashion, quoting the Quran to directly state his main point for his audience in Cairo and his American audience:

> We have the power to make the world we seek, but only if we have the courage to make a new beginning. The Holy Quran tells us, "Mankind, we have created you male and female. And we have made you into nations and tribes so that you may know one another."… The people of the world can live together in peace. We know that is God's vision. Now that must be our work here on Earth. (para. 134–137)

Regardless of differences in faith or ideology, neither side should shoulder the burden of change alone themselves. After all, as the Quran points out, with so many people sharing so small a world, no one is ever acting alone.

References

Herman, C. (2009, November 21). US overthrew Iran's democracy 1953–1979, helped Iraq invade 1980–1988, now US lies for more war. *Examiner.com*. Retrieved from http://www.examiner.com/article/us-overthrew-iran-s-democracy-1953-1979-helped-iraq-invade-1980-1988-now-us-lies-for-more-war

Obama, B. (Speaker). (2009, June 4). Full text of Obama's speech in Cairo. *NBC News*. Retrieved from http://www.nbcnews.com/id/31102929/ns/politics-white_house/#.URnuyTl0vrM

Schleifer, A. S. (2009, June 5). Tears and hard truths in Cairo. *Al Jazeera*. Retrieved from http://www.aljazeera.com/news/middleeast/2009/06/20096503523590820.html

Credits

Credits are listed in order of appearance.

Photo Credits

BananaStock/Thinkstock; Brian Cahn/ZUMAPRESS/
Newscom

Text Credits

"Effective Diplomacy: Examining the Rhetorical
Elements of Obama's 2009 Cairo Speech" by Jeremy
Dellarosa.

Crediting, Quoting, Paraphrasing, and Summarizing

IN THIS CHAPTER YOU WILL LEARN HOW TO—

1 Give credit to a source when you use information exclusive to that source.

2 Quote, paraphrase, and summarize your sources.

3 Frame quotes, paraphrases, and summaries in your texts.

4 Avoid plagiarizing the works and ideas of others.

Previously, you learned how to collect and triangulate a variety of print, electronic, and empirical sources. Now you will learn how to weave those sources seamlessly into your argument. There are four primary ways you can incorporate sources into your argument:

Crediting—You can credit a source for a specific fact or idea with a *parenthetical citation*. The citation names the source and usually identifies the page number where you found the fact or idea.

Quoting—You can quote keywords, phrases, sentences, and longer passages taken directly from a source to explain or support your argument.

Paraphrasing—You can restate or interpret the ideas of someone else in your own words. A paraphrase makes the ideas easier to understand, and it usually mirrors the source's organization or line of reasoning.

From Chapter 17 of *Argument Today with Readings*, First Edition. Richard Johnson-Sheehan and Charles Paine.

Summarizing—You can use your own words to explain the ideas of someone else while also rearranging those ideas to highlight the issues most important to your argument. A summary, unlike a paraphrase, does *not* mirror the source's organization and line of reasoning.

Crediting, quoting, paraphrasing, and summarizing your sources will help you build your argument on solid evidence. Meanwhile, using sources allows you to join the broader conversation about the issue you are arguing about. When you incorporate your sources properly, your argument will have more authority and will be better supported with facts and reasoning.

This chapter will show you how to incorporate the ideas and words of others into your argument while giving credit to your sources.

1 Give credit to a source when you use information exclusive to that source.

Crediting a Source

If you use facts, data, or ideas that are found exclusively in one source, then you should give that source credit with a parenthetical citation. Here are two examples:

Parenthetical Citation →

When Hurricane Katrina hit New Orleans, many things went wrong because of the city's incompetent politicians, corrupt government, poverty, and culture of violence (Flannery 310).

Parenthetical Citation →

As Flannery (2005) points out, many things went wrong when Hurricane Katrina hit New Orleans because of the city's incompetent politicians, corrupt government, poverty, and culture of violence (p. 310).

The first example above uses MLA in-text citation style. In this style, the name and page number are usually placed in parentheses at the end of the sentence. The second example uses APA in-text citation style, placing the year after the name of the source and a page number at the end of the sentence. The correct way to use a parenthetical citation depends on how the source is being used. Turn to "Using MLA Style" or "Using APA Style" to learn how to use these two different in-text citation styles.

There are two benefits to crediting a source with an in-text citation. First, your argument will be stronger because your audience will see where you found your information. Second, you won't be accused of taking or plagiarizing someone else's ideas.

But do you need to cite *everything*? No. You don't need to cite information that is considered common knowledge. Common knowledge includes any facts or ideas that are generally known to most people or can be found in numerous independent sources. For instance, the following items would all be considered common knowledge:

- Ellen DeGeneres is the host of the *Ellen DeGeneres Show*.

- Madison is the capital of Wisconsin.

- The *Declaration of Independence* was signed in 1776.

- The cerebrum is the largest part of the human brain, and it is responsible for most higher functions, such as perception, thought, judgment, and action.

Common knowledge is information that is so widely known that it no longer belongs to anyone. Here's a simple guideline: If you are unsure whether a fact is common knowledge, use a citation.

Using a Quote or Quotation

A quotation is the exact use of a word, phrase, sentence, or passage taken directly from the work of another author or speaker. When using someone else's words, you need to copy their words exactly as they appear in the original. Then put quotation marks around those words or set them off as *block quotes*. Here are some guidelines for quoting brief and long passages from a source.

2 Quote, paraphrase, and summarize your sources.

Brief Quotations

A brief quotation takes a word, phrase, or sentence directly from an original source.

Words

If an author uses a word or term in a unique or special way, you can put quotes around the word or term in your own text. After the first time you quote a word or term, you don't need to continue putting it inside quotation marks.

Acceptable quotation—According to Archer and Rahmstorf, two types of climate-related changes could occur, "abrupt transitions" and "smooth transitions" (6).

Unacceptable quotation—According to Archer and Rahmstorf, two types of climate-related changes could occur, abrupt transitions and smooth transitions (6).

Phrases

If you want to use an entire phrase from a source, you need to put quotation marks around it. Then you should weave the quote into one of your sentences, making sure it flows with the rest of your writing.

Acceptable quotation—Robert Henson explains the global warming mechanism in simple terms when he writes, "the more greenhouse gas we add, the more our planet warms" (26).

Unacceptable quotation—Robert Henson explains the global warming mechanism in simple terms by pointing out that the more greenhouse gas we add, the more our planet warms (26).

Sentences

When using an entire sentence from a source, you should use a *signal phrase* (e.g., "As Hoggan argues,") or a colon to indicate the quotation.

Acceptable quotation—James Hoggan highlights an interesting paradox when he points out, "while scientists were growing more convinced about the proof and more concerned about the risks of climate change, members of the general public were drifting into confusion" (22).

Acceptable quotation—"While scientists were growing more convinced about the proof and more concerned about the risks of climate change," James Hoggan points out, "members of the general public were drifting into confusion" (22).

Unacceptable quotation—While scientists were growing more convinced about the proof and more concerned about the risks of climate change, members of the general public were drifting into confusion, according to Hoggan (22).

Acceptable quotation using a colon—James Hoggan points out the following inconsistency: "While scientists were growing more convinced about the proof and more concerned about the risks of climate change, members of the general public were drifting into confusion" (22).

Unacceptable quotation using a colon—James Hoggan points out the following inconsistency: While scientists were growing more convinced about the proof and more concerned about the risks of climate change, members of the general public were drifting into confusion (22).

Long Quotations (Block Quotes)

Occasionally, you may need to quote a passage at length from a source. A quote that is longer than three lines of text in your argument should be formatted as a *block quote*. To create a block quote, you should indent the entire quotation to separate it visually from your regular text. With block quotes, quotation marks should not be used. Meanwhile, the parenthetical citation appears at the end of the quote, *outside* the final punctuation mark.

> Despite these misinformation campaigns, the general public is gradually beginning to accept that climate change is happening. In response, as Hoggan argues, the fossil-fuel industry is changing tactics:
>
> > As the evidence of climate change has become more compelling—as the science has grown more certain and as people have come to recognize the changes occurring before their eyes—a new and more dangerous form of junk scientist has begun to emerge: the nondenier deniers. These are people who put themselves forth as reasonable interpreters of the science, even as allies in the fight to bring climate change to the public's attention. But then they throw in a variety of arguments that undermine the public appetite for action. (*Climate* 118)
>
> These so-called "scientists," who are often merely public relations agents with titles that sound scientific (e.g., "Director of Ecological Analysis"), will usually agree that human-caused climate change is happening. However, they will then attempt to spin the argument by suggesting that climate change may actually have beneficial or minimal effects.

Note: Block quotes should not be used as an easy way to beef up your word count. When writing an argument, you need to do more than string together a series of block quotes with some of your own words holding them together. You should use block quotes occasionally and only when the original source makes a point in a unique way that cannot be paraphrased or summarized.

Paraphrasing and Summarizing

3 Frame quotes, paraphrases, and summaries in your texts.

When paraphrasing or summarizing, you are using someone else's ideas but putting them into your own words. Paraphrases and summaries are similar and different in some important ways:

Paraphrase—A paraphrase follows the organization and line of thought of the original source. Often, a paraphrase addresses only a portion of a text, and it is about the same length or a little shorter than the portion in the original text.

Summary—a summary strips out many of the details and examples from the original source and reorganizes the author's main points from most important to least important. A summary usually covers the entire content of the source in a condensed and shorter way.

Figure 1 includes a source text that we will be using to discuss paraphrasing and summarizing in this part of the chapter.

It's disgraceful that the media allows such routine distortions in complex system debates like climate change, as if a fact is somehow an "opinion" and all opinions should be aired. If the opinion were that the writer doesn't think the net melting is important enough to build policies to hedge against it—fine, that is an opinion and belongs in the op-ed space. But to allow known falsehoods or misframings of science is not an opinion, just an error or worse. That should in my view be distinguished from real opinions—value judgments on what we should do about it, for example—and a newspaper has a right to demand that such demonstrable factual errors be removed. If a political writer claimed that blacks were better off in the Jim Crow South than now, would that be an "opinion" they would publish in their newspaper? Or that smoking doesn't cause cancer? You get the point.

The question isn't whether reporters, politicians, lawyers, and others or their methods are wrong or that "impartial" scientists are morally superior—but rather the techniques of advocacy-as-usual are suited for a subject like climate change in the public arena. In the advocacy arena, everybody knows the game—spin for the client. But in science, the playing field for public discussions is not level. Any spin on the facts would cause damage to a scientist's reputation—especially young scientists. That is decidedly not true for a status quo defender advocating for client interest. They are rewarded for winning, not for fairly reporting evidence.

Scientists think that advocacy based on a "win for the client" mentality that deliberately selects facts out of context is highly unethical. Unaware of how the advocacy game is played outside the culture of scientific peer review, scientists can stumble into the pitfall of being labeled advocates lobbying for a special interest, even if they had no such intention.

FIGURE 1
Source Text
This excerpt from Stephen Schneider's *Science as a Contact Sport* will be used in this chapter to demonstrate paraphrasing and summarizing.

Paraphrasing

The purpose of paraphrasing is to explain and describe a portion of a source's text in your own words. A paraphrase is usually about the same length as or a little shorter than the source material being paraphrased. For example, the writers of the following acceptable and unacceptable paraphrases of the text in Figure 1 are trying to explain Schneider's claim that scientific facts are not the same as opinion and that scientists should not be treated as special-interest advocates.

Acceptable Paraphrase

Schneider argues in rather strong terms that journalists need to be more mindful of the differences between "opinion" and "factual evidence" when reporting on climate change (207). Factual evidence includes the data and measurements that prove climate change is happening and that burning fossil fuels is the main cause. Opinion is the debate about what people or governments should do to respond to climate change. He points out that journalists often allow distortions and dishonesties to go uncorrected or unchallenged because they want to appear balanced or fair to both sides of an issue. This "balanced" approach, Schneider suggests, puts climate scientists at a distinct disadvantage. After all, the media is well suited to professional advocates, such as politicians, lawyers, advertisers, and corporate spokespeople, who are paid to "win" for their clients (208). Ethical scientists, quite differently, cannot spin or cherry pick the evidence to advocate for one side or another. As a result, Schneider points out, many scientists mistakenly find themselves being challenged as lobbyists for a special interest, even when they are simply trying to explain their findings and the proven facts of climate change (208).

In this acceptable paraphrase, the writer put the ideas from the source into her own words. When she used exact words from Schneider's book, she placed them inside quotation marks.

Now let's look at a paraphrase that is too close to the original source:

Unacceptable Paraphrase

Schneider writes that it's disgraceful that journalists are not more attentive to the differences between opinion and factual evidence when reporting on climate change (207). Scientific facts are not somehow "opinions" that should be aired like all opinions. Opinions are value judgments on what we should do about climate change. Schneider points out that journalists often allow known falsehoods or misframings of science to go unchallenged because they want to seem balanced or fair to the opinions of both sides. This "balanced" approach, Schneider suggests, puts scientists at a distinct disadvantage because the playing field is not level. After all, the media spotlight is well suited to professional advocates, such as politicians, lawyers, advertisers, and corporate spokespeople, who are rewarded for winning, not reporting the evidence fairly (208). Scientists, quite differently, cannot be viewed as deliberately selecting facts out of context to support one position or another. As a result, Schneider points out, many climate scientists stumble into the pitfall of being labeled as advocates lobbying for a special interest, even when they are simply trying to explain their findings and the proven facts of climate change (208).

The highlighted words and phrases are taken directly from Schneider's argument. Even though the writer explicitly cites the source of these ideas, too many words are lifted directly from the source without quotation or attribution. If the writer felt it was important to use these exact words and phrases, she should have placed them inside quotation marks.

Summarizing

When summarizing someone's work, your goal is to capture the source's main ideas while leaving out most of its details and examples. A summary often goes beyond the source's major points to explain the source's structure—its tone, angle, or purpose, its style, its underlying values, or the persuasive strategies it uses to drive home its points.

Acceptable Paragraph-Length Summary

With a passionate appeal, Schneider brings forward his main argument in Chapter 7, titled "The Media Wars: The Stories Behind Persistent Distortion." He argues that the crucial distinction between scientific evidence and opinion is often distorted in the media, making climate scientists appear to be lobbyists for their own special interests and therefore not objective (207). Journalists, Schneider points out, want to appear balanced and fair, so they will routinely pit climate scientists against professional advocates, like politicians, lawyers, and corporate spokespeople. The problem with these so-called balanced debates is that the climate scientist is trying to explain the facts and data objectively, while the professional advocate is doing everything possible to undermine and spin that evidence to "win for the client" (208). As a result, journalists allow many distortions and misrepresentations to go unchallenged, because they assume fairness means allowing both sides to express their opinions. The flaw with this approach is that the existence of climate change is not an opinion—it's based on scientifically proven evidence (207). The media's "balanced" approach inaccurately implies that climate change is just another opinion.

Notice how this summary prioritizes Schneider's key point by putting it up front. Then the summary reorganizes his ideas by order of importance.

An unacceptable summary like the one below usually relies too much on the wording of the original text, and it often does not prioritize the most important points in the source text.

Unacceptable Summary

Schneider brings forward his main argument in Chapter 7, titled "The Media Wars: The Stories Behind Persistent Distortion." He argues that the line between scientific evidence and opinion is often distorted in the media, allowing environmental scientists to be labeled advocates lobbying for a special interest, even if they had no such intention (207). Journalists want to appear balanced and fair, so they will routinely pit climate change scientists against reporters, politicians, lawyers, and others. The problem with these public discussions is that the playing field is not level because the scientist is trying to explain the facts and data, while the professional advocate is using advocacy-as-usual techniques to undermine and spin that evidence to "win for the client," which scientists believe is highly unethical (208). As a result, journalists allow routine distortions in debates about climate change, because they assume a fact is somehow an "opinion" and that all opinions should be aired (207). The flaw with this approach is that the existence of climate change is not an opinion—it's based on scientifically proven evidence. The media's "balanced" approach inaccurately implies that climate change is just another opinion.

The highlighted phrases in this unacceptable summary show places where the author used almost the same wording as the original text.

Framing Quotes, Paraphrases, and Summaries

Your readers should easily see the boundaries between your ideas and the ideas you are taking from your sources. To help them identify these boundaries, you should use signal phrases and parenthetical citations to *frame* the quotation or ideas you took from an outside source. Then you should connect your source's words and ideas to your overall argument (Figure 2). Here is how to do it:

Signal Phrase

A signal phrase indicates where the source material came from. The words "as" and "in" are often at the heart of a signal phrase (e.g., As Hoggan suggests. In Chapter 2 of his *Rough Guide to Climate Change*, Henson argues).

Source Material

Material taken from your source should be separated from your own words with commas, quotation marks, and other punctuation to indicate which words and ideas came directly from the source and which are your own.

Parenthetical Citation

A citation allows readers to find the exact page or website of the source. In MLA or APA documentation style, an in-text citation is used to cite the source. In other documentation styles, you might use a footnote or endnote.

Connection

When you connect the source's ideas to your ideas, you will make it clear how the source material fits in with your own statements and claims.

Figure 2 offers a diagram that color codes these features. The following three examples use these colors to highlight signal phrases, source material, citations, and connections.

> **As Charles Schmidt points out,** a gulf is widening between two types of climate change skeptics. The arguments by conservative bloggers, politicians, and pundits, who deny climate change is happening, are increasingly out of line with the arguments of skeptical scientists, who now generally believe that climate change is happening but are unconvinced about its causes and effects ("Closer," 2010, p. A53). As a result, the footing beneath climate change deniers is crumbling away, leaving their arguments sounding increasingly baseless.

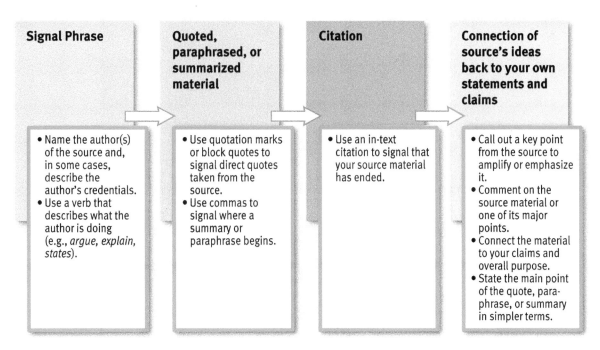

FIGURE 2 Framing Material from a Source
Material taken from a source should be clearly framed with a signal phrase, a citation, and a connection to your own statements and claims.

107

For now, though, as Hoffman demonstrates, the quarrel between the climate change "convinced" and climate change "skeptics" still means both sides are talking past each other (p. 3). Consequently, we are currently in a stalemate position, or what Hoffman calls a "logic schism," waiting for the tipping point when the ever-increasing amount of evidence of human-caused climate change finally overcomes the fossil-fuel industry's marketing and political campaigns.

Studies show, however, that getting others to change their minds about climate change is more than a matter of presenting facts and using good reasoning (Moser & Dilling, 2011; Nisbet & Scheufele, 2009). Even when presented with rock-solid evidence, climate skeptics are reluctant to change their minds, because their beliefs have become part of their identity. They fear that changing their minds on an issue like climate change threatens who they are and how they will live their lives.

As shown in this example, each frame begins with a signal phrase. Signal phrases typically rely on an action verb that signals what the author of the source is trying to achieve in the material that is being quoted, paraphrased, or summarized. Figure 3 provides a helpful list of verbs you can use to signal quotes, paraphrases, and summaries.

The frame usually ends with a *connection* that shows how the source material fits into your overall discussion or argument. Your connection should do one of the following things for your readers:

- call out a key point from the source to amplify or emphasize it

- expand on the source material or one of its major points

- connect the source material to your claims and overall purpose

- rephrase the main point of the source material in simpler terms

When handled properly, framing allows you to clearly signal the boundaries between your source's ideas and your ideas.

Developing an Annotated Bibliography

For a research project, your instructor may ask you to create an *annotated bibliography*. An annotated bibliography is an alphabetical list of your sources that briefly summarizes and offers commentary on each source. Figure 4 shows part of an annotated bibliography that includes an electronic and print source.

Each entry in your annotated bibliography should offer an unbiased summary of the source and a commentary that explains how the source might be useful to your research project. In each commentary, you might also explain how a source complements or contradicts other sources you have collected.

accepts	accuses	acknowledges
adds	admits	advises
agrees	alleges	allows
analyzes	announces	answers
argues	asks	asserts
believes	charges	claims
comments	compares	complains
concedes	concludes	confirms
considers	contends	countercharges
criticizes	declares	demonstrates
denies	describes	disagrees
discusses	disputes	emphasizes
explains	expresses	finds
grants	holds	illustrates
implies	insists	interprets
maintains	notes	objects
observes	offers	point outs
proclaims	proposes	provides
quarrels	reacts	reasons
refutes	rejects	remarks
replies	reports	responds
reveals	shows	states
suggests	supports	thinks
urges	writes	

FIGURE 3

Verbs for Signal Phrases
Use verbs like these to introduce quotations, paraphrases, and summaries. You can also use them in signal phrases.

When developing your annotated bibliography, you should follow the bibliographic format you will use in your argument. For example, you could use either MLA or APA documentation styles. That way, when you list your sources in a Works Cited or References list, they will already be in the proper format.

An annotated bibliography is helpful in a few important ways. First, it will help you remember and keep track of your sources. As your research project grows larger and the sources add up, you won't be able to remember the details of each one. The summaries in your annotated bibliography will give you easy-to-access synopses for review. Second, your annotated bibliography will help you think about your sources in depth and figure out how they work together. The act of summarizing each source will allow you to gain a thorough understanding of the public conversation about your topic. Third, your instructor might use your annotated bibliography to help you identify gaps in your research or places where you could expand on interesting issues.

While putting together your annotated bibliography, you should be mindful about the risk of plagiarism. When you take a quote or an idea from a source, make sure you label it properly in your summary. Clearly identify any direct quotes with quotation marks, and write down the pages where specific quotes or ideas were found. If you are copying a large quotation, you should use a block quote in your entry. Being careful about plagiarism is important while making your annotated bibliography, because otherwise you will eventually forget which words and ideas came from your sources and which didn't. You might innocently use them in your work, thinking they were your own.

"2012 Was One of the 10 Warmest Years on Record." NOAAnews.com. National Oceanic and Atmospheric Administration (NOAA), 6 Aug. 2013. Web. 3 Sep. 2013.

On this webpage, the NOAA summarizes the major findings of its *State of the Climate in 2012* report. Some of the highlights of the report include a) the Arctic continues to warm with sea ice reaching a record low, while the Antarctic sea ice reached a record high, b) sea surface temperatures across the globe are increasing, c) ocean heat content continues to be near record levels, d) the occurrences of cyclones have not seen an increase, and e) the amounts of greenhouse gases continue to climb. The authors write, "Conditions in the Arctic were a major story of 2012, with the region experiencing unprecedented change and breaking several records" (par. 3).

Commentary: This webpage summarizes the eye-opening findings in the full report. Basically, their findings show that climate change is continuing to have a significant effect on the Earth's surface, especially in the Northern Hemisphere. The report confirms the concerns of many of the other sources I have found. However, there are some interesting countertrends such as the increase in Antarctic ice levels. I need to look into that issue further to see what that means.

Weber, Elke and Paul Stern. "Public Understanding of Climate Change in the United States." *American Psychologist* 66.4 (2011): 315-28. Print.

In this article, the authors argue that climate change is an especially difficult issue for the public to understand because there is a "mismatch between people's usual modes of understanding and the task" (317). They point out that much of the problem isn't the public's inability to understand climate change science. Instead, it is "a deficit in trust in the conveyors of climate models and data" (323). They argue that the problem is often an issue of "framing" rather than facts or logic (333).

Commentary: This article explains why there is such a gap between the views of climate scientists and much of the American public. As the authors point out, the resistance to climate change science is often due to a political pre-disposition to not believe the messengers (i.e. climate scientists and environmentalists). Like other articles (Hampton and Smith; Jenkins), these authors seem to be suggesting that re-framing the issue may be the best way forward, not trying to convince people with more facts.

FIGURE 4
Excerpt from an Annotated Bibliography
In this excerpt from an annotated bibliography, the writer has used MLA documentation style to list her sources. Then, for each source, she offers a summary and a paragraph that comments on how the source relates to her research project.

Avoiding Plagiarism

The Council of Writing Program Administrators defines plagiarism this way:

> In an instructional setting, plagiarism occurs when a writer deliberately uses someone else's language, ideas, or other original (not common-knowledge) material without acknowledging its source (par. 4).

In college, plagiarism is a form of academic dishonesty—the same as cheating on an exam—and it can lead to a failing grade on an assignment or even failure of the class. In the workplace, plagiarism is a form of copyright infringement in which one person illegally takes the ideas or words of someone else without their permission. Copyright infringement can lead to costly lawsuits and the firing of any employee who commits it.

Plagiarism is not always intentional. Sometimes writers forget to copy down their sources in their notes. Sometimes they forget where specific ideas came from. But even if you plagiarize accidentally, you may find yourself in serious trouble with your professors, your university, or your employer. So it is crucial that you understand the kinds of plagiarism and learn how to avoid them.

Academic Dishonesty

The most obvious form of plagiarism occurs when someone hands in work that is not his or her own. Everyone, including your professors, knows about "cheater" websites that sell college papers. Everyone also knows about "borrowing" a friend's or roommate's paper. And everyone knows it's easy to cut and paste a sample paper from the Internet. (If you found it, chances are good your professor will find it, too).

And yet, some students still foolishly try to get away with this kind of academic dishonesty. Your professors aren't that stupid. If you hand in a paper that's not your own, you're being dishonest. When students get caught, they often fail the class, which looks bad on their transcripts and is very difficult to explain to future employers or graduate school admissions committees. Students who intentionally plagiarize might even be expelled. Academic dishonesty is clearly deliberate, and few people will have sympathy for someone who is so obviously cheating.

Ironically, people who buy, download, or copy papers often spend more time and energy finding the paper and worrying about the consequences of getting caught than they would if they just wrote the paper in the first place. Plus, they missed the opportunity to improve their writing and research skills.

Patchwriting

Usually, patchwriting happens when someone cuts and pastes one or more paragraphs from a website or other source and then alters words and sentences to make them look like his or her own. Writing scholar Rebecca Moore Howard defines patchwriting as "copying from a source text and then deleting some words, altering grammatical structures, or plugging in one synonym for another" (xvii).

When done intentionally, patchwriting is clearly a form of academic dishonesty, because the writer is presenting someone else's ideas as his or her own without attribution. Some students have even tried to patchwrite an entire paper. They cut and paste several paragraphs from a variety of sources. Then they add some transitions and a few of their own sentences while altering the words and sentences from the original. As a result, little of the paper is based on their own ideas. This kind of dishonesty, when caught, usually leads to a failing grade on the paper and for the class.

Patchwriting can also happen unintentionally, especially when a writer copies sentences or paragraphs from a source and then forgets the material was taken from somewhere else. The writer might even cite the source, not realizing that the included text is too close to the original. Unfortunately, your professor cannot tell whether you were intentionally being dishonest or just made an honest mistake.

To avoid patchwriting, make sure you carefully identify your sources in your notes. Clearly mark any direct quotes taken from your sources with quotation marks, brackets, or some other kind of distinguishing mark. Then, when you use these materials in your document, make sure you quote, paraphrase, and summarize them using proper citations.

Ideas and Words Taken without Attribution

In college and in the workplace, you will often need to use the ideas, words, phrases, or sentences from a source. When you do this, *you must correctly quote and cite that source*. That is, you must place those words inside quotation marks (or use a block quote) and provide a citation that tells your reader precisely where you got those words. If you use ideas, words, phrases, or sentences without attribution, you could be charged with academic dishonesty or copyright infringement.

Sometimes it is difficult to determine whether someone else "owns" the ideas that you are using in your document. If you aren't sure, cite the source. Citing a source will add support to your work, and it will help you avoid being accused of plagiarism.

The Real Problem with Plagiarism

No doubt, plagiarism is easier than ever with the Internet. It's also easier than ever to catch someone who is plagiarizing. Your professors use Google, Yahoo, and Bing, too, and they have access to plagiarism-checking websites like Turnitin. They also often have access to collections of prior papers that were handed in.

If you plagiarize, there is a good chance you will get caught, and the price will be steep. But the real problem with plagiarism is that you are cheating yourself. You are probably paying many thousands of dollars for your education. Cheating robs you of the chance to strengthen your communication skills and prepare for advanced courses and your career.

Of course, there is pressure to do well in your classes, and you don't always have enough time to do everything as well as you could. In the end, though, doing your own work will help you improve and strengthen your mind and abilities. Don't miss that opportunity.

Using sources properly is critical to making a reasonable
and credible argument. Here are the basics.

1 There are four primary ways to use sources to support an argument: crediting, quoting, paraphrasing, and summarizing.

2 Crediting is the use of parenthetical citations to signal places where information was taken from an exclusive source.

3 Quoting is the use of keywords, phrases, sentences, and longer passages to explain or support your argument or someone else's argument.

4 Paraphrasing is the use of your own words to restate or interpret the ideas of someone else, usually to make those ideas easier to understand.

5 Summarizing is the use of your own words to explain the ideas of someone else while also rearranging those ideas to highlight the ones most important to your argument.

6 Common knowledge includes any information that is generally known to most people or can be found in numerous independent sources.

7 Framing quotes, paraphrases, and summaries involves using signal phrases, citations, and connections to develop a context for a source's words or ideas.

8 An annotated bibliography is a useful tool for keep track of your sources and gaining a deeper understanding of the issues related to your topic.

9 Patchwriting is a form of plagiarism in which a writer loosely rewrites the ideas and words of others and presents them as his or her own.

10 Plagiarism, whether intentional or unintentional, robs writers of the opportunity to strengthen their own writing skills and express their own ideas.

1. Find an argument on the Internet that you want to discuss with your group. Go through the argument and highlight any words, phrases, or sentences that you might quote in an argument of your own. Then, in a different color, highlight information that you might paraphrase, summarize, or just cite. With your group, discuss the differences between the information that you would quote directly and the information that you would paraphrase or summarize. With your group, come up with a list of five reasons you might quote something instead of summarizing or paraphrasing it.

2. On the Internet, find a document that quotes sources. Look at how the author of the document frames quotations and other material taken from sources. Did the author do a good job of framing the material from sources? Are there any awkward places where the framing does not work? Write an e-mail to your instructor in which you critique the document's framing of source material. Explain what the author did well and what could be improved.

3. Find an argument that is 1,000 words or more on a topic that interests you. Write a summary that boils the argument down to 500 words. Then write a summary that boils the argument down to 200 words. Then summarize the argument in 50 words. Finally, summarize the argument in 10 words or less. With your group, talk about what kinds of information was left out of each successive summary as you were forced to use fewer and fewer words.

1. Sometimes it seems like our concerns about plagiarism are overblown, especially in the age of remixing, reposting, sampling, and cutting and pasting. Write an argument in which you explore both sides of the plagiarism issue. Start with the definition of plagiarism from the Council of Writing Program Administrators that is printed in this chapter. Then explore the pros and cons of holding to this kind of definition. At the end of your argument, discuss whether you believe the concept of plagiarism needs to change as communication technologies evolve.

2. As more texts are read on screen, citing sources can be handled effectively through links. In other words, a citation could simply be a direct link to the source itself, not a reference to the bibliography in the Works Cited list. Write an argument in which you come up with an electronic alternative to MLA and APA bibliographic styles for citing sources. What are the advantages of using links, and what are some of the potential disadvantages?

3. On the Internet, find an argument you disagree with that uses sources. In a rebuttal to the argument, directly challenge its use of sources. You might point out that its sources are weak or unsubstantiated, which allows the argument to make some unsubstantiated claims. Or you could point out that the author does not use sources from the other side of the issue, which is why the argument is biased or one sided. In your rebuttal, your goal is not to argue against the argument itself. Instead, challenge the argument by undermining its sources.

Credits

Credits are listed in order of appearance.

Text Credits

Reprinted with permission from *Science as a Contact Sport : Inside the Battle to Save Earth's Climate*. By Stephen Schneider. Copyright © 2009 Stephen H. Schneider.

From Council of Writing Program Administrators, www.wpacouncil.org. Licensed under a Creative commons Attribution - No Derivative Works 3.0 United States License, http://creativecommons.org/licenses/by-nd/3.0/us/

Research Papers and Reports—
Arguing with Research

Research papers and reports are often used as capstone projects for college courses. When professors ask you to do a "research project," they want you to study a topic in depth and use your research to make a thorough argument. They also want you to write in an organized and engaging way, using multiple sources to back up your argument.

The terms "research paper" and "research report" are often used interchangeably, which can cause some confusion. Though similar, these two related genres are distinct in some significant ways:

Research papers—Research papers are common in the humanities, business, law, and the arts. They are often assigned in courses like management, political science, prelaw, history, philosophy, literature, languages, film studies, music, religion, and art history. Research papers are typically used to argue about current issues, business ethics, politics, legal issues, historical events, literary criticism, cultures, and social trends.

FIGURE 1 Doing Research in College and Your Career
Research will be important to your success in college and your career.

Research reports—Research reports are common in the sciences, marketing, engineering, economics, and technology. A research report typically includes a section called the "Methodology" or "Methods" in which the researcher explains how the report's evidence was collected, especially any empirical facts, data, and observations. A research report presents research results and discusses those results.

The QuickView illustrates some of the key differences between research papers and research reports. They are similar genres, but the differences are important and worth keeping in mind.

Today, employers often rank the ability to do research at the top of desired skills for job applicants. Research allows you and others to make informed decisions and contribute knowledge to your field (Figure 1). Your ability to do high-quality research will be critical to your success in college and your career.

2 How to use research to generate the content of a research paper or report

Inventing the Content of Your Research Paper or Report

Let's begin by stating the obvious. To write a research paper or report, you need to do a substantial amount of research. The results of your research will then be used to develop a thorough and informed argument.

Let's summarize a six-step research process, focusing specifically on the needs of a research paper or report.

QUICK View

Generative

Persuasive

Generative Argument—Research papers and reports tend to be more generative than persuasive. Essentially, the purpose of a research project is to synthesize and explain existing evidence so your audience can better understand an important issue.

Persuasive Argument—In some cases, research papers and reports are persuasive arguments, especially when you are using research-based evidence to argue a controversial point or support a specific course of action. Persuasive research papers and reports often conclude with specific recommendations or calls to action.

Genre Patterns

These patterns for research papers and reports are suggestions. You should adjust the organization of your research paper or report to suit your argument's specific topic, purpose, audience, and context.

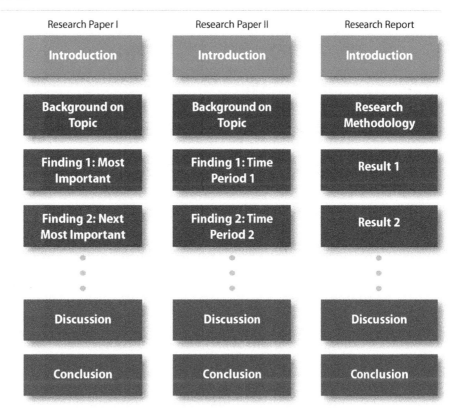

Research Paper I

- Introduction
- Background on Topic
- Finding 1: Most Important
- Finding 2: Next Most Important
- Discussion
- Conclusion

Research Paper II

- Introduction
- Background on Topic
- Finding 1: Time Period 1
- Finding 2: Time Period 2
- Discussion
- Conclusion

Research Report

- Introduction
- Research Methodology
- Result 1
- Result 2
- Discussion
- Conclusion

Step 1: Define Your Research Question

When starting a research project, you first need to formulate your *research question*. Your research question identifies the basic unknown that you want your research to solve. Here are some example research questions:

Research Question: Will concussion-related lawsuits pose a threat to the existence of college football programs?

Research Question: How was the War of 1812 a critical turning point in the unification of the United States?

Research Question: Why have vampires become such powerful sex symbols in popular novels and movies?

Research Question: Why do guys in college like to cross-dress as women for Halloween?

Step 2: Develop Your Working Thesis (Hypothesis)

When you have figured out your research question, you can then formulate your *working thesis,* or *hypothesis.* Your working thesis states your best answer, at this point, to your research question.

Working Thesis: If current concussion-related lawsuits against professional football are successful, it is only a matter of time before college football programs find themselves threatened by similar lawsuits from former players.

Working Thesis: The War of 1812 was the first time the United States as one nation felt threatened, forcing it to behave like a unified republic and not a federation of states.

Working Thesis: Because vampires are portrayed as seductive, physically strong, and impulsive, they represent the "forbidden mate" that many people secretly fantasize about.

Working Thesis: There are two reasons college males cross-dress on Halloween: (1) for straight males, it is a safe opportunity to step outside traditional gender roles, and (2) for some gay males, it's an opportunity to outwardly express a felt identity in a non-threatening way.

Your working thesis (or hypothesis) is your best guess about where you believe the research question will lead you. However, as you do your research, your working thesis will evolve as you make new discoveries and draw more informed conclusions. Eventually, your working thesis will become the main point (thesis statement) of your research paper or report.

Step 3: Develop Your Research Methodology

Now, you need to figure out how you are going to collect the evidence needed to answer your research question. Your research methodology describes the series of steps you will follow to collect evidence from electronic, print, and empirical sources.

Electronic sources—If your topic involves current events, electronic sources may be your best forms of evidence. You should search for evidence on websites, blogs, and listservs, because these sources often contain the most up-to-date information. Other electronic media can also be useful, such as television and radio broadcasts, podcasts, documentaries, and videos.

Note: Online encyclopedias like Wikipedia can be helpful starting places for your research; however, your instructors probably won't let you use them as citable sources because the authors are unknown and the information can be easily altered.

Print sources—Print sources are typically your most reliable sources. They include books, journal articles, magazine articles, newspaper articles, government publications, and other items that were originally written to appear on paper. You can collect a variety of print sources from libraries, especially your university's library (Figure 2). Many print sources, such as newspaper and magazine articles, are also available for viewing and downloading through the Internet.

FIGURE 2 Go to the Library! Your university library is still one of the best sources of evidence for your research project. Don't let a short walk across campus keep you from rounding out your research.

Empirical sources—You can collect your own evidence with empirical methods, such as field observations, surveys, interviews, experiments, and personal experiences.

Your research project should draw evidence from all three of these kinds of sources. If you are too reliant on one kind of source, such as electronic sources, you probably won't gain a full understanding of your subject.

Step 4: Triangulate Your Sources

In you will learn about using the "Research Triangle" to *triangulate* your print, electronic, and empirical sources. Triangulation involves using all three types of sources to compare and corroborate the evidence you collect. Here is triangulation in brief:

- **Three-sided information (reliable):** Reliable evidence is being found in all three types of sources (electronic, print, and empirical).

- **Two-sided information (open to doubt):** Reliable evidence can only be found in two of the three types of sources (e.g., electronic and print only).

- **One-sided information (unreliable):** Key evidence is only being found in one of the three types of sources (e.g., electronic only).

If your research project does not have evidence from all three sides of the Research Triangle, you should find a way to collect evidence from the missing sides.

Step 5: Identify Your Major Findings and Draw Your Conclusions

Your major findings and conclusions are the discoveries and big ideas that your argument will present to your audience.

Major Findings

Use your sources to identify two to five *major findings* about your topic. List them out on your screen. If you have more than five major findings, you should determine whether you can consolidate findings or cross out less important ones. Of course, your research paper can present more than five major findings, but if you have too many "major" findings, your research paper or report will begin to sound tedious to your audience.

Conclusions

Use your major findings to draw two to five *major conclusions* about your research topic. Your conclusions present the big ideas you want your audience to take away from your research. You can have more than five major conclusions, but again you risk making your research paper or report sound tedious to your audience if you discuss too many.

Step 6: Turn Your Working Thesis into a Final Thesis

As you complete your research, you should revise your thesis one last time. Your final thesis will be the main claim or main point that your research paper or research report will prove. This thesis statement will probably appear in both the introduction and conclusion of your argument.

MOVES for Arguing

Research papers and reports can be both generative and persuasive. Here are some common moves they will make.

This issue is important because _____, _____, and _____.

People generally believe _____, but my research shows that _____ is more likely.

My research question was _____, and my hypothesis was _____.

My research methods included _____ major steps.

The results of my research show _____, _____, and _____.

My findings demonstrate that _____, _____, and _____ are likely true.

I recommend that the following actions be taken: _____, _____, and _____.

Organizing and Drafting Your Research Paper or Research Report

3 Methods for organizing and drafting large arguments

The research paper and research report genres are similar in many ways, but they can also differ in content and organization. The QuickView illustrates those differences. Let's look at their similarities and differences.

Introduction: Tell Them What You Are Going to Tell Them

The introduction should establish the framework for the rest of the argument. In other words, you are going to "tell the audience what you are going to tell them." Typically, an introduction will make most or all of the following opening moves:

Identify your topic—Clearly identify and define the topic of your research project. Clarify the scope and boundaries of the project by telling the audience what you are writing about and perhaps what you are not writing about.

State your purpose—Using one sentence, tell your audience the purpose of your research project. Your purpose statement should be straightforward so your audience knows what you are trying to achieve.

> In this research paper, I will argue that concussion-related lawsuits pose a significant threat to the existence of many college football programs.

> My aim is to demonstrate that the War of 1812 was an important turning point in the history of the United States because it was the first time Americans felt unified as part of a greater nation, not as citizens of separate states.

> The purpose of my research paper is to show that today's vampire novels and movies appeal to young women because they combine two age-old storylines: the princess narrative with the forbidden mate narrative.

> In this report, I will demonstrate that straight and gay males cross-dress on Halloween for different reasons, even though their behaviors are often the same.

Your purpose statement should be direct because you want your audience to understand exactly what you are trying to achieve.

State your main point (thesis)—Most readers, including your professors, will expect you to state your argument's main point in the introduction. That way, they can evaluate your evidence as they read the body of the text. You should sharpen your thesis down to a clear point.

> **Weak:** Concussions threaten the viability of college football.

> **Better:** Concussion-related lawsuits against professional football will almost certainly be used as a legal basis for filing lawsuits against college football programs.

Weak: The War of 1812 was an important event in American history.

Better: Though mostly forgotten today, the War of 1812 was a turning point in the history of the United States because this war allowed citizens to unite around a common cause and develop a strong sense of national identity.

Weak: Vampire novels are a guilty pleasure for many women.

Better: Vampire novels tap into deep-seated princess and forbidden mate narratives, making them pleasurable reads even in an age when women no longer fantasize about a prince whisking them away.

Weak: College males cross-dress on Halloween for a variety of reasons.

Stronger: Interestingly, my research shows that straight college males cross-dress on Halloween to experience being feminine, while some gay men see the holiday as a safe way to outwardly express a felt identity.

Your main point (thesis) is your big idea (your main conclusion) for the research paper or report.

Provide background information—Briefly, give your audience enough background information about your topic to familiarize them with it. Usually historical information or references to recent events are good ways to give your audience some background on your topic.

Stress the importance of the topic—Explain to your audience why they should pay attention to this particular issue and why it is important.

These introductory moves can be made in just about any order. Most research papers and reports will include all five moves. At a minimum, your introduction should tell your readers your topic, purpose, and main point (thesis).

Background Section (Research Papers Only)

In your Background section, your goal is to give your audience a brief overall understanding of your subject's history. Specifically, you want to explain the *who, what, where, when, why,* and *how* issues that define it.

As you describe the historical background of your subject, you should use quotes from experts and cite your sources. These authoritative sources will strengthen your argument's credibility. They will also help your audience understand where your information came from and who has already written something about your subject.

The Background section is typically organized one of two ways:

Chronological Review

The section walks the audience chronologically through the topic, explaining how it began, what has happened, how people have responded, and where the situation stands at the moment.

Review of the Two or More Sides of the Issue

Usually, one side is explained first and then the other side is explained. Then, the positions are compared and contrasted to show where they agree and disagree.

Research Methodology or Methods Section (Research Reports Only)

In a research report, a Methodology section or Methods section typically follows the introduction. The purpose of a Methodology section is to describe step by step how you completed your research.

Opening

Your Methodology section should start with an opening paragraph (one or two sentences) that offers an overall description of your research methods.

> To test our hypothesis, we used a 10-question survey to confirm or challenge the facts and figures we found in print and electronic sources. Our research methods followed three major steps: (1) develop the survey, (2) circulate the survey on campus, and (3) analyze its results.

Body of the Methodology Section

In a college research report, each major step will usually receive one or two paragraphs of explanation in the body of your Methodology section (Figure 3). Explain *how* each major step was completed and *why* you thought each step was needed.

Limitations (Closing)

In the closing of your Methodology section, include a paragraph that identifies any major limitations of your research methods. No research methodology is perfect, so identify places where your findings might be limited due to time, access to information, or financial resources.

The Methodology section for a college-level paper will usually run about four to six paragraphs. You should describe your methods with enough detail to allow someone else to replicate your research methodology.

Findings or Results Section

In your Findings section (also called a Results section), you should describe and explain your three to five major findings separately and in depth. Typically, each major finding will receive one or two paragraphs of coverage. Your major findings can be organized two ways:

- **By importance.** They are arranged from most important to least important.

- **By the order in which they occurred.** They are arranged in the order in which they occured or were discovered.

Support each of your findings by citing the evidence you found while doing your research. Where possible, you should use properly labeled graphs, photographs, or other visuals to illustrate your results.

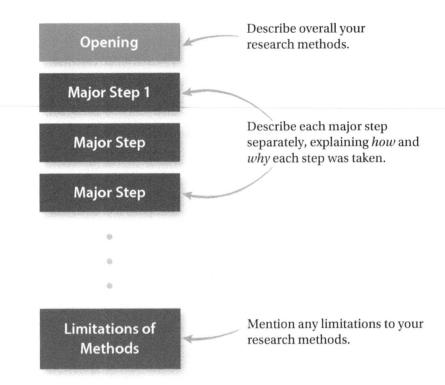

FIGURE 3
A Methodology
Section
A typical
Methodology section
explains the how
and why of your
research methods
while identifying any
limitations.

Discussion Section

The Discussion section interprets your findings for the audience and states your major conclusions. Revisit your thesis, as well as your purpose and main point. Explain how the findings of your research support the thesis of your argument. You might also account for or explain any findings that don't support your thesis.

The purpose of the Discussion section is to present your two to five major conclusions about your topic. In a college-level research paper or report, this section will usually comprise about two to three paragraphs.

Conclusion/Recommendations

The conclusion should summarize your major ideas, restate your main point with more emphasis, and, if appropriate, make some recommendations. You should not include any new evidence or information at this point.

In your conclusion, make some or all of the following four moves:

Signal clearly that you are concluding—You should use a heading or transitional phrase to signal to the audience that you are concluding the argument. This signal is important, because it will indicate that you are about to restate your main point and offer any recommendations.

Restate your main point (with emphasis)—Use similar but new phrasing to the restate your thesis. Your goal is to show your audience that you have proven what you set out to prove.

Offer two to five recommendations (optional)—Most argumentative research reports and some argumentative research papers offer recommendations. You might place your recommendations in a bulleted list to make them easy to locate.

Look to the future—Research papers and reports often end with a brief look into the future. In a few sentences, explain where you think the issue will go from here. You might also mention future possibilities for research on this topic.

Your conclusion should be relatively brief. A one- or two-paragraph conclusion is usually enough for most college research papers or reports.

References or Works Cited

Beginning on a separate page, you should include a list of your sources in a standard bibliographic style, such as the MLA or APA bibliographic style. For MLA style, you should use the heading "Works Cited." For APA style, your sources should appear under the heading "References." list your sources.

Developing Your Style and Design: Sounding and Looking Professional

4 Strategies for achieving an academic or professional tone in research papers or reports

Research papers and reports are formal assignments, so your instructors and supervisors will expect you to use a style and design that is academic and professional.

Style: Make It Plain and Straightforward

Your style should be straightforward and plain, establishing an academic or professional voice. Here are some strategies for writing with an academic or professional style:

Use Plain Sentences

Your sentences should be simple, straightforward, and breathing length. Move the subject of each sentence (i.e., what the sentence is about) to an early position in the sentence. Use active verbs where possible. Try to minimize the number of prepositional phrases, especially chains of prepositional phrases. Also, keep your sentences breathing length to avoid overly complex and convoluted sentences.

Avoid Bureaucratic or Pompous Phrasings

Phrasings like "in lieu of," "regarding," "indeed," "in accordance with," or "pursuant to" sometimes find their way into research papers and reports. These kinds of bureaucratic phrasings make the author sound uncomfortable with the material. A good guideline is to only use words or phrases that you would use in everyday speech.

Define Technical Terms, Jargon, and Acronyms

When you use technical terms or acronyms, offer a sentence definition or parenthetical definition to explain what they mean:

Sentence definition—A concussion is a traumatic brain injury that can lead to temporary problems with balance, attention, decision making, and agility.

Parenthetical definition—Childhood obesity has been linked to type II diabetes, <u>a chronic disease in which the body cannot produce the proper amount of insulin to maintain healthy blood sugar levels.</u>

Technical terms, jargon, and acronyms are useful and appropriate in research papers and reports, but they need to be defined for the audience.

Limit the Use of Passive Voice

The passive voice is fine if used in moderation. However, writers often overuse passive voice in research papers and reports because the ideas are often complex.

Passive—The survey's results <u>were confirmed</u> by our student interviews.

Active—Our student interviews <u>confirmed</u> the survey's results.

Passive—In 1814, the U.S. Capitol Building and White House in Washington, D.C., <u>were captured and burned</u> by British soldiers.

Active—In 1814, British soldiers <u>captured and burned</u> the U.S. Capitol Building and White House in Washington, D.C.

Using passive voice isn't wrong. Passive voice just makes your writing less active and harder to read because it conceals *who* or *what* is doing the action.

Minimize the Use of Nominalizations

A nominalization occurs when the action of the sentence appears as a noun rather than a verb.

Nominalization—This research paper offers a <u>presentation</u> of our findings into football-related concussions and their potential effects on college sports programs.

Revised—This research paper <u>presents</u> our findings into football-related concussions and their potential effects on college sports programs.

Nominalizations are often called "shun" words because they typically end with the suffixes "-tion" or "-sion." In your draft, look for places where you use these shun words. Then, where appropriate, change them into active verbs or adjectives.

Designing Your Research Paper or Report

The design of your research paper or report should highlight the important information that the audience needs, while making the text attractive.

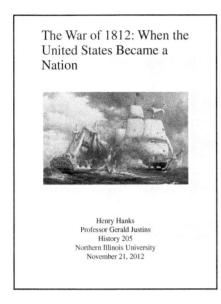

The War of 1812: When the United States Became a Nation

Henry Hanks
Professor Gerald Justins
History 205
Northern Illinois University
November 21, 2012

The Imminent Collision: How Football-Related Concussions Threaten the Existence of College Sports

Jamie Hendrickson
English 102
Ms. Gina Carlton
May 12, 2012

FIGURE 4 Cover Pages
A cover page can be used to set a tone for the entire document.

Follow Your Instructor's Formatting Guidelines

Your instructor will likely give you some specific guidelines about how the document or presentation should look (e.g., margins, line spacing, font, headings, header/footer, page numbers, etc.). You should follow those instructions exactly.

Include a Cover Page

The cover page should include the title of the document, your name, your professor's name, the course, and the date (Figure 4). You might also include an image to set a specific tone for the document.

Use Headings

Headings give the audience an overall sense of how the information is organized, while helping them locate the information they need. Headings also help you bridge the transitions between larger sections.

Add Visuals to Illustrate Key Points

You can use photographs, tables, graphs, and charts to support or amplify what is in the written text. If you find an idea difficult to describe in writing, perhaps you can find a photograph that illustrates what you mean. If you have data and facts that could be turned into a graph or chart, you can use these kinds of visuals to illustrate trends.

Add a Table of Contents

If your research paper or report is ten pages or longer, you might consider adding a table of contents. Most word processors can quickly generate a table of contents for your document. Use tabs, especially "leader" tabs, to line up the page numbers vertically on the right side of the sheet.

The design of your research paper or report is important. If your document is accessible and visually attractive, your audience will likely spend more time considering your argument.

Ready to write that research paper or report? Here's what you need to know.

1 Research papers and research reports are similar in many ways, but there are also important differences in content and organization.

2 The Background section in a research paper gives an overview of the issue being discussed, answering the Five W and How questions.

3 The Methodology section in a research report describes step by step how the research was completed.

4 The Findings or Results section describes and explains the major findings from the research.

5 The Discussion section interprets the major findings and states your major conclusions about your topic.

6 The style and design of your research paper or report should be academic and professional.

7 Your argument's style should use plain, straightforward sentences while minimizing the use of bureaucratic phrasings, passive voice, and nominalizations.

8 When designing the document, make sure the instructor's formatting guidelines are followed closely.

9 Additional design features like a cover page and headings, even if not required, can set a positive, professional tone for the audience.

10 Visuals, such as graphs, charts, and photographs, can be used to reinforce and illustrate important points in the argument.

1. On the Internet, find a research paper or report that you believe is poorly researched. Highlight the places in the text where the author makes claims that are unsupported or seem to be based purely on opinion. As the reader of the document, how do you feel about this kind of unsupported argument? If you were to disagree with this author's views, where would you challenge his or her points? How might you use research to support an opposing view? Show this article to your group and discuss how its weaknesses undermine its argument.

2. Find one example of a research paper and of a research report, preferably on a similar topic. Compare and contrast the two documents. What are some of the similarities? What are some of the differences? In what fields are research papers, like the one you found, most common? In what fields are research reports most common? With your group, discuss why the authors of these documents chose to write research papers instead of research reports and vice versa.

3. A simple search on the Internet will turn up a variety of websites from which you can buy a research paper. Find a few of these websites and look them over. If you were an instructor, how easy would it be to detect a purchased research paper? What would be some of the telltale signs that a student did not write the paper that was handed in? What would be an appropriate sanction for someone who handed in a research paper that is not their own? Discuss these issues with your group and come up with a policy that you would like your instructor to follow if someone were to buy or copy a research paper.

1. Choose a current topic on which you would like to do some research and contribute your viewpoint. Develop a research question about this topic and come up with a working thesis or hypothesis. Try to narrow your topic to something that could be handled in a research paper or research report. Send your topic, research question, and your working thesis to your instructor via e-mail.

2. What kind of evidence (print, electronic, or empirical) do you think is most trustworthy when writing a research project? Does the most appropriate evidence depend on the topic that is being researched, or is one kind of evidence more compelling than the others? In a group of three people, choose three different topics for the group and ask each person to work out the pros and cons of the three kinds of evidence for each topic. Then share the strengths and weaknesses of the three kinds of evidence. As a group, write a briefing (one page) in which you discuss whether you feel some kinds of evidence are more trustworthy than others.

3. Choose a topic, develop a research question, and state a working thesis. Write an outline of a research paper or research report based on the diagrams in the QuickView Guide at the beginning of this chapter. Then list the moves you would need to make in the introduction and conclusion of the document. Share your outline with your group. Ask each group member to critique the others' research questions, working theses, and outlines. In a written comment to each of your group members, explain their research projects' strengths and what you find most interesting about them. Then offer ideas for improvement. Offer suggestions about the kinds of sources that would be most helpful for supporting each research paper or report.

ONE STUDENT'S WORK

In this research paper, student Khizer Amin explores the available research on concussions in ice hockey. Though the paper is specifically about hockey, his evidence and his conclusions can be applied to all contact sports, including football and soccer. As you read his argument, notice how he uses research-based evidence to logically build his argument that concussions are a significant problem in hockey and other contact sports.

Concussions in Ice Hockey: Is it Time to Worry?

Khizer Amin

After receiving two hits to the head in the span of two games, Sidney Crosby, the All-Star center for the Pittsburgh Penguins, was sidelined from hockey in February (Joyce, par. 6). The long and arduous recovery process that ensued garnered continuous questions about when Crosby would return, and upon his return, whether he would be able to regain his high calibre of play. A concussion with consequences of this magnitude is by no means a rare occurrence in sport; in fact, head injuries are the most common cause of death amongst athletes (Cantu, 289). However, Sidney Crosby's reputation as one of the best in the game has pointed the public spotlight on the severity and consequences of concussions and head injury. Since the incident, researchers have seized the opportunity eager to engage the general public in dialogue regarding the issues of aggression and unnecessary physicality in sport.

Definition of Concussion

A concussion is defined by the American Association of Neurological Surgeons (AANS) as, "a clinical syndrome characterized by immediate and transient alteration in brain function, including alteration of mental status and level of consciousness, resulting from mechanical force or trauma" (AANS, par. 2). Immediate symptoms vary from case to case, ranging from a temporary loss of consciousness to amnesia, dizziness, and prolonged confusion (Ropper and Gorson, par. 5).

The generally accepted guidelines for what constitutes a concussion have evolved greatly over recent years as the scientific community has furthered its understanding and knowledge of traumatic brain injuries. In the past, researchers and clinicians characterized loss of consciousness as a necessary and defining symptom of concussions. Furthermore, concussions were not believed to result in long-term debilitations. In contrast to these old beliefs, recent research has found that concussions are a serious risk factor for neurological disorders that may only become apparent years after the original incident (Webbe, 46; Tator, 715).

The development of modern diagnostic techniques has decreased the number of concussions that go undetected and thus untreated. Neurological testing and on-field evaluations for potentially concussed athletes are now more robust and comprehensive. In particular, 'day-after-concussion' examinations are valuable diagnostic tools, since the onset of symptoms may only present themselves at a later time (Casson, Pellman, and Vianno, 236). The injured individual is able to report any changes in mood, appetite, tiredness and sleep patterns. Computerized neuropsychological testing is a recent development that allows athletes, trainers, and parents to monitor cognitive functioning (Lovell, 96). After a concussion, results from this test can be compared to baseline scores (from a test done prior to any injury) to monitor an individual's recovery process.

The Mechanism of Concussion

5 Concussions are generally a functional injury and can often occur without any externally visible impression or contusion to the body (McCrory, et al., 437). They occur when the brain is accelerated into the skull due to some sort of impact or external force. Concussions are caused by a combination of two major types of forces: translational and

rotational (Webbe, 47). Translational forces cause linear accelerations, resulting in stretching and compression of the brain (Meaney and Smith, 21). The collision of the brain against the inner walls of the cranium causes brain tissue damage and elevated intracranial pressure. Conversely, rotational forces cause the brain to accelerate angularly along its mid-vertical axis. This force often results in the shearing of brain tissue and temporary loss of consciousness due to the impact from rotation at the midbrain (Ropper and Gorson, 167). Current evidence suggests that rotational accelerations imparted on the brain are the more severe and important force implicated in the onset of concussions (Webbe, 169).

Concussions in Sport

Concussions are most commonly a result of falling or striking an object or another person (Colantonio, et al. 784). Athletes are prone to such injuries due to the physicality and aggressive behaviour often associated with sport. Amongst individuals 16—34 years of age, a Canadian National Population Health Survey found that 85% of concussions are sport-related (Gordon, Dooley, and Wood, 377). A study in Alberta monitoring the number of emergency department visits due to sport and recreational head injuries reported that ice hockey players accounted for the largest proportion of head injuries, at about 21% (Kelly et al. 79). This may be due to the excessively physical nature of the game, or simply because of the sheer number of participants in the sport, which is after all 'Canada's game'. Other major causes of head injuries were – in order from least to most frequent—cycling, playground activities, soccer, football, and rugby (Kelly et al. 79). It is clear, therefore, that concussions and head injuries are of concern across a variety of sports and activities, and an exploration of both general and activity-specific intervention methods is warranted.

Recent studies have associated concussions in sports with a decline in long-term brain function (de Beaumont et al. 697). Athletes incurring a concussion in early adulthood were found to score lower on neuropsychological testing and suffer from bradykinesia (slowed movement) decades after diagnosis (de Beaumont et al. 705). A link between concussions and the onset of clinical depression in later life has also been made; athletes who have incurred one or two concussions are 1.5 times more likely to suffer from depression in later years (Guskiewicz et al. 906).

Youth athletes are prone to the most negative sequelae of concussions. Concussions can inhibit proper development of the brain resulting in developmental disabilities, severe motor dysfunctions and psychiatric conditions that will burden the child for the entirety of their life (Marchie and Cusimano 124). This is of great concern when considering that 10-12% of Canadian minor league hockey players aged 9-17 report being victims of head injuries each season (126).

Second-impact syndrome is a condition that has gained scientific and media recognition in recent years. Essentially, this refers to incurring a second concussion while an individual is still suffering from the adverse effects of an earlier one (Saunders and Harbaugh 538). It is possible that the two concussions have a compounding effect in terms of the damage caused to the brain. Even a very minor blow to the head after an initial concussion has been associated with sharp increases in intracranial pressure, haemorrhaging, and subsequent death (539). Due to the severity of concussions and the danger of second-impact syndrome, it is important for players, coaches, trainers, and team doctors to follow appropriate return-to-play guidelines.

Increased awareness of the consequences of concussions in sport has 10 prompted many athletes to donate their brains towards concussion research ("Athlete" par. 4). These donations have fuelled much research towards discerning important details about the mechanisms and long-term impacts of concussions. For example, researchers at Boston University recently studied the brain of Rick Martin, a former NHL star. Analysis of Martin's brain revealed that he had chronic traumatic encephalopathy, a disease which leads to cognitive decline and ultimately dementia (Christie par. 1).

Implications on The Culture of Ice Hockey

Concussions in hockey are most often caused by body checking (Warsh et al. 134), a form of physical contact between players, which is legal in the NHL and many minor leagues. However, the newfound dangers of concussions in recent findings has called into question the current culture that exists around aggression and fighting in hockey and other sports (Marchie and Cusimano 125).

Athletes, officials, fans, and the general public often become desensitized to aggression in sport and begin to accept it as part of the game (Fields, Collins, and Comstock 35). In fact, many individuals display elevated levels of aggression while engaged in sports (Boardley and Kavussanu 177), which begs the question of why physical aggression is accepted and legal in athletics but not in other facets of everyday life.

In the past, proponents of physical contact in sports have argued that safety equipment such as helmets and mouth-guards provide ample protection from injuries. While there is evidence of a reduced number of general injuries, there is little scientific evidence demonstrating that current equipment is capable of preventing concussions (McCrory et al. 155; Daneshvar et al. 160). Furthermore, while helmets do indeed reduce the force of impact to the head, there is no evidence that wearing helmets corresponds to a reduced rate of concussions in athletes. As such, there has been a gradual paradigm shift in the scientific community regarding the best means of reducing concussions. Rather than advocating for increased use of safety equipment, there is now an increased focus on changing rules, regulations, and the culture of sport to reduce the number of falls and hits to the head in the first place (McCrory et al. 156; Warsh et al. 140).

The minimum age at which hockey associations should allow participants to body check has become a highly controversial and debated topic in the hockey community. Proponents for lowering the minimum age argue that it allows youth to properly learn and adjust to the techniques behind giving and taking a hit. However, a systematic review exploring the relationship between body checking and injuries found that leagues which permit checking in younger players are associated with higher rates of injuries and fractures (Warsch et al. 140). Based on their findings, the authors recommended that body checking be removed from leagues for younger athletes, with the minimum age for introduction of physical contact being at least 13 years. In line with this, the Ontario Hockey Federation recently introduced new regulations that effectively banned body checking in all house leagues and some select leagues (Lee par. 1).

Conclusion

Concussions are serious injuries with potential serious long-term   15
neurological and psychiatric consequences. Based on current scientific evidence, it is apparent that modifications to the rules surrounding hockey are warranted and could potentially reduce rates of concussion. Imposing greater sanctions on actions such as head hits and checks from behind may help to make Canada's game safer for all participants. Only 1 in every 4000 minor hockey league players will ever fulfill the ultimate dream of playing in the NHL (Marchie and Cusimano, 124). In this light, is it reasonable for our youth to have to–or be allowed to–put their future livelihoods on the line every time they step onto the ice?

Works Cited

"Athlete Brain Donations for Concussion Study Reach 300." *ESPN. com*. 12 Oct. 2010. Web. 16 Oct. 2011.

American Association of Neurological Surgeons [AANS]. "Concussion." *Patient Information*. 2005. Web. 10 Oct. 2011.

Boardley, Ian, and Maria Kavussanu. "Effects of Goal Orientation and Perceived Value of Toughness on Antisocial Behavior in Soccer: The Mediating Role of Moral Disengagement." *Journal of Sport & Exercise Psychology* 32.2 (2010): 176–92. Print.

Cantu, Robert. "Head Injuries in Sport." *British Journal of Sports Medicine* 30.4 (1996): 289–96. Print.

Casson, Ira, Elliot Pellman, and David Viano. "Concussion in Athletes: Information for Team Physicians on the Neurologic Evaluation." *Seminars in Spine Surgery* 22.4 (2010): 234–44. Print.

Christie, James. "Former Sabres Rick Martin Had Brain Disease." *The Globe and Mail*. 5 Oct. 2011. Web. 16 Oct. 2011.

Colantonio, Angela, Christine Saverino, Brandon Zagorski, B. Swaine, John Lewko, Susan Jaglal, and Lee Vernich. "Hospitalizations and Emergency Department Visits for TBI in Ontario." *The Canadian Journal of Neurological Sciences* 37.6 (2010): 783–90. Print.

Daneshvar, Daniel, Christie Baugh, Christopher Nowinski, Ann McKee, Robert Stern, and Robert Cantu. "Helmets and Mouth Guards: The Role of Personal Equipment in Preventing Sport-Related Concussions." *Clinics in Sports Medicine* 30.1 (2011): 145–63. Print.

de Beaumont, Louis, Hugo Théoret, David Mongeon, Julie Messier, Suzanne Leclerc, Sebastian Tremblay, Dave Ellemberg, and Maryse Lassonde. "Brain Function Decline in Healthy Retired Athletes Who Sustained Their Last Sports Concussion in Early Adulthood."*Brain: A Journal of Neurology* 132.3 (2009): 695–708. Print.

Fields, Sarah, Christy Collins, and R. Dawn Comstock. "Violence in Youth Sports: Hazing, Brawling, and Foul Play." *British Journal of Sports Medicine* 44 (2010): 32–7. Print.

Gordon, Kevin, Joseph Dooley, and Ellen Wood. "Descriptive Epidemiology of Concussion." *Pediatric Neurology* 34.5 (2006): 376–78. Print.

Guskiewicz, Kevin, Steven Marshall, Julian Bailes, Michael McCrea, Hernden Harding, Amy Matthews, Johna Mihalik, and Robert Cantu. "Recurrent Concussion and Risk of Depression in Retired Professional Football Players." *Medicine and Science in Sports and Exercise* 39.6 (2007): 903–09. Print.

Joyce, Gare. "Will Sid Ever be the Same?" *Sportsnet Magazine*. 29 Sep. 2011. Web. 11 Oct. 2011.

Kelly, Kaven, H. Lissel, Brian Rowe, JoAnnVincenten, and Don Voaklander. "Sport and Recreation-Related Head Injuries Treated in the Emergency Department." *Clinical Journal of Sport Medicine* 11.2 (2001): 77–81. Print.

Lee, Eddie. "Ontario Hockey Federation Bans Bodychecking in
House Leagues." *TheStar.com.* 6 May 2011. Web. 11 Oct. 2011.

Lovell, Mark. "The Management of Sports-Related Concussion:
Current Status and Future Trends." *Clinics in Sports Medicine*
28.1 (2009): 95–111. Print.

Marchie, Anthony, and Michael Cusimano. "Bodychecking
and Concussions in Ice Hockey: Should Our Youth Pay the
Price?" *Canadian Medical Association Journal* 169.2 (2003):
124–28. Print

McCrory, Paul, Willem Meeuwisse, Karen Johnston, Jiri Dvorak, Mark
Aubry, Mick Molloy, and Robert Cantu. "Consensus Statement
on Concussion in Sport." *The Physician and Sportsmedicine*
37.2 (2009): 141–59. Print.

Meaney, Douglas, and Douglass H. Smith. "Biomechanics of
Concussion." *Clinics in Sports Medicine* 30.1 (2011): 19–31. Print.

Ropper Allen, and Kenneth Gorson. "Concussion." *The New England
Journal of Medicine* 356.2 (2007): 166–72. Print.

Saunders, Richard, and Robert Harbaugh. "The Second Impact
in Catastrophic Contact-Sports Head Trauma." *Journal of
the American Medical Association* 252.4 (1984): 538–39.
Print.

Tator, Charles. "Brain Injury is a Major Problem in Canada and
Annual Incidence is Not Declining." *The Canadian Journal of
Neurological Sciences* 37.6 (2010): 714–15. Print.

Warsh, Joel, SAerban Constantin, Andrew Howard, and Alison
Macpherson. "A Systematic Review of the Association Between
Body Checking and Injury in Youth Ice Hockey." *Clinical
Journal of Sport Medicine* 19.2 (2009): 134–44. Print.

Webbe, Frank. "Definition, Physiology, and Severity of
Cerebral Concussion." *Sports Neuropsychology: Assessment
and Management of Traumatic Brain Injury.* Ed. R. J.
Echemendia. New York: Guilford Press, 2006. 45–70. Print.

A CLOSER LOOK AT
A CLOSER LOOK AT
Concussions in Hockey

1. Consulting the QuickView at the beginning of this chapter, decide which of the four organizational structures most closely resembles the structure of "Concussions in Hockey." Find three ways in which it doesn't follow the patterns in the QuickView.

2. Does Amin present the research of both sides of the controversy, or does he focus more on one side? How could he make his coverage more balanced?

3. Where exactly does Amin reveal his main point in the introduction and conclusion? Highlight the sentences where the main point appears. Compare these two statements. How are they similar? How are they different?

IDEAS FOR
Arguing

1. Write a refutation of Amin's research paper. You could choose to disagree entirely by pointing out lapses in his logic or challenging his research. Or you could extend his argument into another direction and advance a more compelling main point (thesis) or offer further recommendations.

2. Conduct your own local research project into sports-related concussions. Describe what has been happening recently with this issue and the specific controversies and debates. Conclude with your interpretation of the findings and offer two to five recommendations.

Does TV Help Make Americans Passive and Accepting of Authority?

BRUCE E. LEVINE

In this research-based argument, clinical psychology and social critic Bruce E. Levine argues that while television watching is enjoyable and in some ways benefits society, overall it causes Americans to passively accept the status quo. As you read, notice how he offers a new and interesting angle on this issue by combining research with his own personal observations.

Historically, television viewing has been used by various authorities to quiet potentially disruptive people—from kids to psychiatric inpatients to prison inmates. In 1992, *Newsweek* reported, "Faced with severe overcrowding and limited budgets for rehabilitation and counseling, more and more prison officials are using TV to keep inmates quiet" (Springen & Kantrowitz, par. 1). Joe Corpier, a convicted murderer, was quoted, "If there's a good movie, it's usually pretty quiet through the whole institution." Both public and private-enterprise prisons have recognized that providing inmates with cable television can be a more economical method to keep them quiet and subdued than it would be to hire more guards.

Just as I have not emptied my refrigerator of beer, I have not gotten rid of my television, but I recognize the effects of beer and TV. During some dismal periods of my life, TV has been my "drug of choice," and I've watched thousands of hours of TV sports and escapist crap. When I don't need to take the edge off, I have watched Bill Moyers, *Frontline* and other "good television." But I don't kid myself—the research shows that the more TV of any kind we watch, the more passive most of us become.

American TV Viewing

Sociologist Robert Putnam in Bowling Alone (2000) reported that in 1950, about 10 percent of American homes had television sets, but this had grown to more than 99 percent. Putnam also reported that the number of TVs in the average U.S. household had grown to 2.24 sets, with 66 percent of households having three or more sets; the TV set is turned on in the average U.S. home for seven hours a day; two-thirds of Americans regularly watch TV during dinner; and about 40 percent of Americans' leisure time is spent on television. And Putnam also reported that spouses spend three to four times more time watching television together than they do talking to each other.

In 2009, the Nielsen Company reported that U.S. TV viewing was at an all-time high, the average American viewing television 151 hours per month if one includes the following "three screens": a television set, a laptop/personal computer and a cell phone (Gandossey). This increase, according to Nielson, is part of a long-term trend attributable to not only greater availability of screens, increased variety of different viewing methods, more digital recorders, DVR, and TiVo devices but also a tanking economy creating the need for low-cost diversions. And in 2011, the *New York Times* reported, "Americans watched more television than ever in 2010, according to the Nielsen Company. Total viewing of broadcast networks and basic cable channels rose about

1 percent for the year, to an average of 34 hours per person per week" (Stelter, 2011, par. 3)

In February 2012, the *New York Times* reported that young people were watching slightly less television in 2011 than the record highs in 2010 (Stelter, 2012). In 2011, as compared to 2010, those 25-34 and 12-17 years of age were watching nine minutes less a day, and 18-24 year olds were watching television six fewer minutes a day. Those 35 and older are spending slightly more time watching TV. However, there is some controversy about trends here, as the New York Times also reported: "According to data for the first nine months of 2011, children spent as much time in front of the television set as they did in 2010, and in some cases spent more. But the proportion of live viewing is shrinking while time-shifted viewing is expanding" (par. 13).

Online television viewing is increasingly significant, especially so for young people. In one marketing survey of 1,000 Americans reported in 2010 , 64% of said they watched at least some TV online (O'Dell). Among those younger than 25 in this survey, 83% watched at least some of their TV online, with 23% of this younger group watching "most" of their TV online, and 6% watching "all" of their TV online.

How does the United States compare to the rest of the world in TV viewing? There aren't many cross-national studies, and precise comparisons are difficult because of different measurements and different time periods. NOP World, a market research organization, interviewed more than 30,000 people in 30 countries in a study released in 2005, and reported that the United States was one of the highest TV-viewing nations. NationMaster.com, more than a decade ago, reporting on only the United States, Australia, and 11 European countries, found the following: the United States and the United Kingdom were the highest-viewing nations at 28 hours per week, with the lowest-viewing nations being Finland, Norway, and Sweden at 18 hours per week ("Television," 2012).

The majority of what Americans view on television—whether on the TV, laptop, or smartphone screen—is through channels owned by six corporations: General Electric (NBC, MSNBC,

CNBC, Bravo, and SyFi); Walt Disney (ABC, the Disney Channel, A&E, and Lifetime); Rupert Murdoch's News Corporation (Fox, Fox Business Channel, National Geographic, and FX); Time Warner (CNN, CW, HBO, Cinemax, Cartoon Network, TBS, TNT); Viacom (MTV, Nickelodeon/Nick@Nite, VH1, BET, Comedy Central); and CBS (CBS Television Network, CBS Television Distribution Group, Showtime, and CW, a joint venture with Time Warner). In addition to their television holdings, these media giants have vast holdings in radio, movie studios and publishing.

However, while progressives lament the concentrated corporate control of the media, there is evidence that the mere act of watching TV—regardless of the content—may well have a primary pacifying effect.

How TV Viewing Can Make Us Passive

10 Who among us hasn't spent time watching a show we didn't actually like, or found ourselves flipping through the channels long after we've concluded there isn't anything worth watching?

Jerry Mander is a "reformed sinner" of sorts who left his job in advertising to publish *Four Arguments for the Elimination of Television* in 1978. He explains how viewers are mesmerized by what TV insiders call "technical events"— quick cuts, zoom-ins, zoom-outs, rolls, pans, animation, music, graphics, and voice-overs, all of which lure viewers to continue watching even though they have no interest in the content. TV insiders know that it's these technical events—in which viewers see and hear things that real life does not present—that spellbind people to continue watching.

The "hold on us" of TV technical events, according to Robert Kubey and Mihaly Csikszentmihalyi's 2002 *Scientific American* article "Television Addiction Is No Mere Metaphor," is due to our "orienting response"— our instinctive reaction to any sudden or novel stimulus (p. 51). They report that:

In 1986 Byron Reeves of Stanford University, Esther Thorson of the University of Missouri and their colleagues began to study whether the simple formal features of television—cuts,

edits, zooms, pans, sudden noises— activate the orienting response, thereby keeping attention on the screen. By watching how brain waves were affected by formal features, the researchers concluded that these stylistic tricks can indeed trigger involuntary responses and "derive their attentional value through the evolutionary significance of detecting movement. . . . It is the form, not the content, of television that is unique." (p. 51)

Kubey and Csikszentmihalyi claim that TV addiction is, at least psychologically, similar to drug addiction. Using their Experience Sampling Method (in which participants carried a beeper and were signaled six to eight times a day at random to report their activity), Kubey and Csikszentmihalyi found that almost immediately after turning on the TV, subjects reported feeling more relaxed, and because this occurs so quickly and the tension returns so rapidly after the TV is turned off, people are conditioned to associate TV viewing with a lack of tension. They concluded:

Habit-forming drugs work in similar ways. A tranquilizer that leaves the body rapidly is much more likely to cause dependence than one that leaves the body slowly, precisely because the user is more aware that the drug's effects are wearing off. Similarly, viewers' vague learned sense that they will feel less relaxed if they stop viewing may be a significant factor in not turning the set off. (p. 51)

15 Mander (1978) documents research showing that regardless of the programming, viewers' brainwaves slow down, transforming them to a more passive, nonresistant state. In one study that Mander reports comparing brainwave activity in reading versus television watching, it was found the brain's response to reading is more active, unlike the passive response to television— this no matter what the TV content. Comparing the brain effects of TV viewing to reading, Kubey and Csikszentmihalyi report similar EEG results as measured by alpha brain-wave production. Maybe that's why when I view a fantastic Bill

Moyers interview on TV, I can recall almost nothing except that I enjoyed it; this in contrast to how many content specifics I can remember when I read a transcript of a Moyers interview. Kubey and Csikszentmihalyi's survey also revealed that:

> The sense of relaxation ends when the set is turned off, but the feelings of passivity and lowered alertness continue. Survey participants commonly reflect that television has somehow absorbed or sucked out their energy, leaving them depleted. They say they have more difficulty concentrating after viewing than before. In contrast, they rarely indicate such difficulty after reading. (p. 51)

Mander strongly disagrees with the idea that TV is merely a window through which any perception, any argument, or reality may pass. Instead, he claims TV is inherently biased by its technology. For a variety of technical reasons, including TV's need for sharp contrast to maintain interest, Mander explains that authoritarian-based programming is more technically interesting to viewers than democracy-based programming. War and violence may be unpleasant in real life; however, peace and cooperation make for "boring television." And charismatic authority figures are more "interesting" on TV than are ordinary citizens debating issues.

In a truly democratic society, one is gaining knowledge directly through one's own experience with the world, not through the filter of an authority or what Mander calls a mediated experience (p. 55). TV-dominated people ultimately accept others' mediated version of the world rather than discovering their own version based on their own experiences. Robert Keeshan, who played Captain Kangaroo in the long-running children's program, was critical of television—including so-called "good television"—in a manner rarely heard from those who work in it:

20

> When you are spending time in front of the television, you are not doing other things. The young child of three or four years is in the stage of the greatest emotional development that human beings undergo. And we only develop when we experience things, real-life things: a conversation with Mother, touching Father, going places, doing things, relating to others. This kind of experience is critical to a young child, and when the child spends thirty-five hours per week in front of the TV set, it is impossible to have the full range of real-life experience that a young child must have. Even if we had an overabundance of good television programs, it wouldn't solve the problem. (quoted in Mander, p. 265)

Whatever the content of the program, television watching is an isolating experience. Most people are watching alone, but even when watching it with others, they are routinely glued to the TV rather than interacting with one another. TV keeps us indoors, and it keeps us from mixing it up in real life. People who are watching TV are isolated from other people, from the natural world, even from their own thoughts and senses. TV creates isolation, and because it also reduces our awareness of our own feelings, when we start to feel lonely we are tempted to watch more so as to dull the ache of isolation.

Television is a "dream come true" for an authoritarian society. Those with the most money own most of what people see. Fear-based TV programming makes people more afraid and distrustful of one another, which is good for an authoritarian society depending on a "divide and conquer" strategy. Television isolates people so they are not joining together to govern themselves. Viewing television puts one in a brain state that makes it difficult to think critically, and it quiets and subdues a population. And spending one's free time isolated and watching TV interferes with the connection to one's own humanity, and thus makes it easier to accept an authority's version of society and life.

Whether it is in American penitentiaries or homes, TV is a staple of American pacification. When there's no beer in our refrigerators, when our pot hookup has been busted, and when we can't score a psychotropic drug prescription, there is always TV to take off the edge and chill us out.

REFERENCES

Gandossey, T. (2009, February 24). TV viewing at 'all time high,' Nielson says. *CNN.com.* Retrieved from http://edition.cnn.com/2009/SHOWBIZ/TV/02/24/us.video.nielsen/

Kubey, R, Csikszentmihalyi, M. (2002, February 23). Television addition is no mere metaphor. *Scientific American, 286,* 48–55.

Mander, J. (1978). *Four arguments for the elimination of television.* New York: Quill.

O'Dell, J. (2010, April 12). TV viewing's shift to the web [stats]. *Mashable.com.* Retrieved from http://mashable.com/2010/04/12/tv-online/

Springen, K, Kantrowitz, B. (1992, May 31). Hooking up at the big house. *Newsweek Magazine.* Retrieved from http://www.thedailybeast.com/newsweek/1992/05/31/hooking-up-at-the-big-house.html.

Stelter, B. (2011, January 2). TV viewing continues to edge up. *New York Times.* Retrieved from http://www.nytimes.com/2011/01/03/business/media/03ratings.html?_r=4&amp&

Stelter, B. (2012, February 8). Youths are watching, but less often on TV. *New York Times.* Retrieved from http://www.nytimes.com/2012/02/09/business/media/young-people-are-watching-but-less-often-on-tv.html?

Television viewing (most recent) by country. (2012). *Nationmaster.com.* Retrieved from http://www.nationmaster.com/red/graph/med_tel_vie-media-television-viewing&amp

A CLOSER LOOK AT
Does TV Help Make Americans Passive and Accepting of Authority?

1. Find the places where Levine discusses his own personal interactions with television. How do these brief anecdotes help his readers identify with his position? Do you think these passages strengthen his argument, or do they merely distract readers?

2. According to Levine, why does television viewing make us passive? List the reasons he cites. In what other ways does television make us passive? On the other hand, in what ways can television empower us and spur us to action?

3. Some people would argue that while Levine shows why television is a significant problem, he fails to offer solutions. What recommendations could he have proposed for reducing the problems associated with television viewing, or for improving television itself? List three to five possible solutions for dealing with this problem.

IDEAS FOR
Arguing

1. Write a factual personal narrative argument that supports, extends, or challenges Levine's argument. Explore your own television viewing experiences or explore instead other forms of entertainment, such as Internet social sites, online gaming, movies, or gambling.

2. Choose a television show or other multimedia event (movie, video, podcast, etc.) and write a rhetorical analysis that explains how it causes people to become passive or spurs them toward social action.

Credits

Credits are listed in order of appearance.

Photo Credits

(l), Slavomir Kubes/MAFRA/isifa/Getty Images; (r), Tetra images/Thinkstock; David H. Lewis/Getty Images; (l), U.S. Naval Historical Center Photograph; (r), Kiichiro Sato/AP Images

Text Credits

"Does TV Help Make Americans Passive and Accepting of Authority?" by Bruce E. Levine, *AlterNet*, October 26, 2012. Used with permission of AlterNet, www.alternet.org.

"Concussions in Ice Hockey" Is It Time to Worry?" by Khizer Amin, *The Meducator*. Vol. 1: Issue 20. Used by permission of *The Meducator, McMaster Undergraduate Health Sciences Journal*. Reproduction or retransmission of the materials, in whole or in any part, requires prior written consent of the copyright holder, *The Meducator*.

Developing
Your Research
Process

From Chapter 16 of *Argument Today with Readings*, First Edition. Richard Johnson-Sheehan and Charles Paine.

Developing
Your Research
Process

Students often cringe when a professor asks them to do research for a project. That's too bad, because doing research can be both fun and rewarding. Researching a topic is like solving a mystery or discovering new places. Once you know how to do research quickly and efficiently, you will see that exploring new issues is both challenging and fun. Meanwhile, doing research is easier than ever with computers and mobile devices (Figure 1).

Research is the systematic investigation of a topic or issue. The ability to do research will be vital to your success in college and your career. In college, many of your courses will require you to study topics methodically and write arguments that are supported with research-based sources. In the workplace, research is an every-day task that will help you and your colleagues gather information, make informed decisions, and take action. Many employers prominently mention the ability to do research as a critical skill they look for in new employees.

FIGURE 1 Doing Research Is Like Solving a Mystery Doing research is challenging and fun. Usually, once you get started, you will find yourself immersed in the project.

Developing Your Research Process

1 How to develop your own research process

The best way to do research is to follow a *research process* that fits your personal work habits. Everyone does research a little differently, but here is a model that you can use to develop a research process that works for you:

Step 1: Define your research question.

Step 2: Develop a working thesis or hypothesis.

Step 3: Collect print, electronic, and empirical sources.

Step 4: Triangulate your sources.

Step 5: Identify your major findings.

Step 6: Modify or accept your working thesis/hypothesis.

This six-step research process is loosely based on the scientific method. It is designed to help you pose good questions and test a *working thesis* or *hypothesis* (Figure 2). You can modify this process to fit your own work habits and style.

Step 1: Define Your Research Question

To start, you first need to figure out the *research question* you are trying to answer. Defining a research question will help you accomplish two things. First, it will help you sharpen your understanding of your research topic. Second, it will help you develop a new angle on that topic.

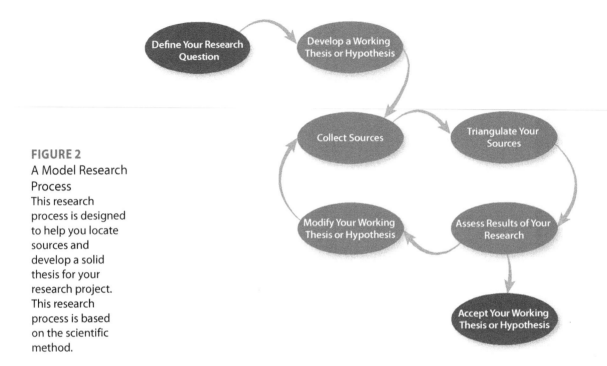

FIGURE 2
A Model Research Process
This research process is designed to help you locate sources and develop a solid thesis for your research project. This research process is based on the scientific method.

Here are some example research topics and research questions:

Research Topic: Fashion on a College Campus

Research Question: How can college students dress well on a limited budget?

Research Topic: Slave Narratives in the Pre–Civil War Era

Research Question: How did slave narratives influence and energize the abolition movement before the American Civil War?

Research Topic: Nutrition in high school lunches

Research Question: If offered healthy options along with standard cafeteria food, will high school students make good choices about what to eat?

Each of these research questions sets a direction or angle for the topic. Your research question identifies the topic, angle, and the purpose of your project.

Step 2: Develop a Working Thesis or Hypothesis

Your *working thesis* or *hypothesis* is your best prediction, right now, about how you will answer your research question. Of course, you can't answer the question with certainty at this point—you haven't done any research. However, you can probably take an educated guess about how the research project will likely turn out. By forming a working thesis right now, you can figure out what kinds of evidence will be needed to answer your question.

In one sentence, write down your working thesis. Here are some working theses based on the research questions above:

Working Thesis: Being fashionable at college often means staying with basics that can be used interchangeably (jeans, cotton dresses, high-heeled loafers) while accessorizing with unique items that set the "look" apart (scarves, fedoras, blazers).

Working Thesis: The publication of slave narratives before the American Civil War kept the embers of Northern dissatisfaction with the South glowing, which helped abolitionists spur Northerners to arms when the Confederate states seceded.

Hypothesis: Given healthy options, some high school students will make better dietary choices at school lunch; however, the majority of students will simply continue to choose the high-calorie foods that taste good and are promoted by mass-media advertising.

Your working thesis should be limited to one sentence so you can focus your research project. If you need more than one sentence to state your working thesis, your topic may be too complex or broad to be handled in a college paper.

Step 3. Collect Print, Electronic, and Empirical Sources

Now it's time to collect sources to determine whether your working thesis holds up. You should search for information from three types of sources:

Electronic sources—websites, blogs, listservs, television and radio broadcasts, podcasts, documentaries, and videos. Many of these sources can be located with Internet search engines like Google, Bing, or Yahoo. Some electronic sources not available through the Internet but may be available through your campus library.

Print sources—books, journals, magazines, newspapers, government publications, reference materials, and microform/microfiche. Your campus library's online catalog should help you locate these materials. Otherwise, Google Scholar is a useful tool for finding print sources.

Empirical sources—field observations, surveys, interviews, case studies, experiments, and personal experiences. Empirical sources require you to experience your subject directly by observing it, measuring it, or discussing it with experts.

As you search for information on your topic, you should try to collect material from all three types of sources. A mixture of sources will help you understand your topic from a variety of perspectives.

Step 4: Triangulate Your Sources

Triangulation involves using the Research Triangle to compare and corroborate the evidence you find in online, print, and empirical sources (Figure 3). That way, you can determine whether the evidence is reliable. Here is how triangulation works.

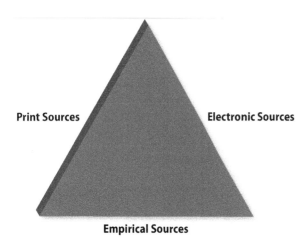

Print Sources

Electronic Sources

Empirical Sources

FIGURE 3 The Research Triangle
When collecting information, you should look for sources on all three sides of the research triangle.

Three-sided information—If you find comparable information from all three sides of the Research Triangle, there is a good chance that the information is reliable.

Two-sided information—If you can gather similar facts from only two sides of the Research Triangle, the information is probably still reliable but open to doubt.

One-sided information—If you can only find evidence from one side of the Research Triangle, then you should question whether the information can be trusted.

Of course, triangulating your sources with the Research Triangle will not guarantee that your sources are reliable or trustworthy. The "truth" and even the "facts" are usually a bit more slippery than that. Instead, triangulation helps you challenge your sources and look for corroborating evidence in diverse places.

You need to be especially skeptical of sources that seem to be drawing their information from just one common source. A blog, for example, could be drawing its evidence from a magazine article, which took the evidence from an interview. In this kind of situation, triangulation really isn't possible, because you're simply finding the same evidence even though it appears in three different media.

You should also be skeptical of sources that are biased toward one perspective on an issue, especially sources that agree with your own personal opinion. When doing research, your aim is to gain a full understanding of the argument, not just back up what you already believe. So, look for a variety of sources that allow you to see all sides of the issue.

Step 5: Identify Your Major Findings

With your sources collected and triangulated, you are ready to identify the *major findings* of your research.

Ask yourself: What are the two to five most important discoveries I made while doing research? These two to five items are your *major findings*. List them and rank them from most important to least important.

Pushing yourself to choose only two to five major findings might seem a bit artificial, but it has two benefits. First, when you limit yourself to a handful of major findings, you can examine and explain them in depth for your audience. Second, if you identify too many major findings, your audience won't be able to figure out which ones are most important. By focusing on a few major findings, you will highlight them for your audience.

Step 6: Modify or Accept Your Working Thesis

You should now revisit your working thesis. More than likely, your sources revealed some interesting new points of view and evidence that you didn't expect. If so, it's likely you will need to modify your working thesis to fit this new evidence. At this point you have a few options:

- **Revise your working thesis**—You can revise your working thesis and do some additional research to see if it holds up.

- **Accept your revised working thesis**—If you're comfortable with your revised working thesis, you're ready to start organizing and drafting your argument.

- **Abandon your working thesis**—If your working thesis now seems incorrect, you can abandon it and formulate a new working thesis.

The decision to abandon a working thesis is always a difficult choice in research projects, but sometimes your research will reveal that your original working thesis missed the mark. That's fine, and it happens regularly in the sciences. If you are really open to finding the truth (and not just confirming what you previously believed), you should be willing to change your beliefs to fit what your research reveals.

Eventually, you will settle on a working thesis you can back up with research. At this point, your working thesis becomes the main point or final thesis that will be the cornerstone of your argument.

Finding Primary and Secondary Sources

2 The differences between primary sources and secondary sources

Researchers often make a distinction between *primary sources* and *secondary sources*.

Primary sources—Primary sources include the artifacts, records, statements, or other items that were created or used by the people directly involved with the subject of the research (Figure 4). Primary sources might include personal papers, letters, e-mails, objects, clothing, tools, creative works, music, or quotes from interviews. Primary sources also include any data or statistics that you or others collected from experiments, observations, or other empirical research.

Secondary sources—Secondary sources include the published works of scholars, journalists, experts, and other knowledgeable people who have analyzed, studied, or commented on the subject. For example, secondary sources can include books, journal articles, magazine articles, newspapers, and blogs.

FIGURE 4
Primary Sources
Primary sources
are typically items
that were directly
connected in
some way with the
events and people
involved with the
topic.

For college papers, most of your research will rely on secondary sources because you will tend to use articles and books to explain and support your views. For many topics, though, you should able to locate primary sources by visiting archives, historic sites, museums, or galleries. Any empirical research you do, such as experiments, surveys, interviews, observations, will also be considered primary sources. You should always look for ways to incorporate at least one primary source in your research.

3 How to collect
evidence from print,
electronic, and
empirical sources

Finding Print Sources

Today, the distinctions between print sources and electronic sources are becoming blurred, especially as print sources are increasingly available through the Internet. For the purpose of research, print sources are texts that originally appeared or were designed to appear in a print format, usually on paper.

With today's easy access to the Internet, you might be tempted to bypass print sources altogether. That would be a mistake. After all, the most reliable evidence is often found in books and articles. Moreover, printed information cannot be easily changed from one day to the next, which typically makes it more reliable than electronic sources.

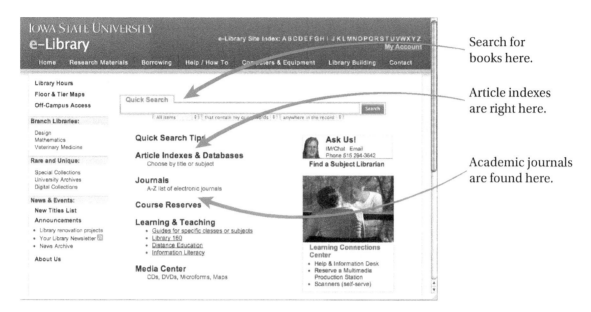

Search for books here.

Article indexes are right here.

Academic journals are found here.

FIGURE 5 A Library Portal

Your library's website gives you access to a variety of print and electronic information.

To find print sources, your best approach is to use your campus library's website, which is also sometimes called a "library portal" or "catalog" (Figure 5). Your library's website will give you access to online catalogs, search engines, and databases that can help you locate the print sources shelved in the library or available through *interlibrary loan.* Here are the kinds of sources that you should look for:

Books—Books are often considered the most reliable print sources. The time and expense of producing a book usually ensures a level of fact-checking, review, and editing that exceeds other sources. Books, however, are not neutral or unbiased sources of information. Their authors have their own opinions, biases, and agendas, so you still need to read books critically and corroborate the facts you find.

Academic journals—Academic journal articles are written and reviewed by scholars, consultants, and subject-matter experts (SMEs), so they tend to be reliable sources of evidence. On your library's website, look for a link, button, or tab that will allow you to search for articles through *periodical indexes.* Some of the more popular periodical indexes include ArticleFirst, EBSCOhost, LexisNexis, PsychINFO, and IEEE Explore.

Magazines—Magazines offer a variety of articles, which you can find through the *Readers' Guide to Periodical Literature.* The *Readers' Guide* is an online index that is probably available through your library's website.

Your library will also keep recent copies of many magazines in its periodical room or reference room. If you are looking for an article from a past issue, you might go directly to the magazine's website. Some other useful indexes for finding magazine articles include Find Articles, MagPortal, and InfoTrac.

Newspapers—Local newspapers are often your best sources of information on current or local issues. Newspaper articles are not as rigorously fact-checked as books, journals, or even magazines, but they are often the most up-to-date sources of information on breaking stories and popular culture. You can find articles through newspaper indexes, such as ProQuest Newspapers, Chronicling America, LexisNexis, New York Times Index, and EBSCOhost. Then you can go to the newspaper's website to access the article itself.

Government documents—You might be surprised at how many useful documents are available from the federal and state governments. These documents tend to be thoroughly researched and are written in an accessible style. You can find them through government websites, such as The Catalog of U.S. Government Publications. At the state level, you can explore state government websites or you can check the online catalogs at the libraries of larger public universities.

Much of your "library research" can be handled from your computer, phone, tablet, or laptop. Copies of many print items can often be downloaded directly to your computer. Otherwise, a trip to the library will usually take less than an hour.

Two increasingly helpful online sources for print texts are Google Books and Google Scholar. Google Books is an online library that has full or partial copies of many books that might not be available in your library. Plus, Google Books is searchable, allowing you to target specific information in a wide variety of books. Google Scholar is a good way to search for a variety of academic articles that are available on the Internet.

Finding Electronic Sources

Electronic sources are texts that were designed to be viewed on a screen or listened to through an electronic medium. They include sources like websites, blogs, wikis, podcasts, television and radio broadcasts, movies, and documentaries.

Using Internet Search Engines

Your professors will often say something like, "I don't want you to just use the first five results you find through Google, Bing, or Yahoo." Internet search engines are extremely sophisticated and helpful, but they can't do your research for you. You need to be selective about the kinds of electronic sources you use.

Knowing a few search engine tricks can help you better target the information you need. For example, let's say you are doing research on the abuse of energy drinks among college students. You might start by entering a phrase into a search engine:

energy drinks

The search engine, as you would expect, will bring up millions of web pages that refer to this topic. Obviously, you don't have time to look through even a fraction of these sites. Also, most of them don't have useful information that pertains to your project.

What should you do? You need to narrow your search to find the handful of useful web pages among these millions (Figure 6). Here are some tricks that will focus your search when using a search engine:

Use exact words—Use exact words that will target the kinds of information you are looking for. Choose words that exactly describe your topic and your angle on that topic.

effects of energy drinks on college students taking final exams

Use quotation marks—When terms are put in quotation marks, the search engine will only look for pages on which those words appear.

effects of "energy drinks" on college students taking "final exams"

Use the minus (–) sign—If you are receiving results you don't want, you can use the minus sign (–) to remove topics that you don't need.

effects of energy drinks on college student final exams –driving –alcohol –obesity

FIGURE 6
Narrowing Your Search on a Search Engine
You can use specific keywords and symbols to help you sharpen your search for sources with a search engine. Dogpile, the search engine shown here, is a good alternative to some of the better-known search engines.

Use the plus (+) sign—Using the plus (+) sign will ensure that some topics will be specifically searched for. The plus sign will stress some words over others when web pages are ranked by the search engine.

> effects of +energy drinks on college student final +exams

Use wildcard symbols—Most search engines will allow the use of wildcard symbols (*, %, or ?) that help you fill in words of a phrase, title, or lyric you can't remember.

> "Red Bull * you wings" energy drinks college students

Using specific words, quotation marks, and symbols will help you quickly narrow your search to websites that will be most useful.

Evaluating Information from the Internet

Just about anyone can put up a website that provides so-called "facts." So you need to be critical and even skeptical about the information you find on the Internet.

Research the background of each source—A quick Internet search on each source will usually help you determine whether an author or organization is credible and basing their information on solid facts and reasoning.

Confirm each source's facts—Any source's facts should generally match up with facts in other credible sources. If one source is saying something that seems out of line with other sources, you should be skeptical.

Look out for deceptive websites—Some websites are specifically created to mislead the public about important issues, usually for political reasons. A website might look professional and sophisticated, but it could be peddling junk information.

Follow the money—If the person, organization, or corporation behind the website stands to gain financially, then you should be even more cautious about the information provided. The possibility of financial gain can bias even credible sources.

All sources have some bias, so do some backchecking on each one to determine whether its information is trustworthy.

Using Wikis and Blogs

Your Internet search will turn up potentially useful information stored on wikis and blogs. A helpful guideline for using wikis and blogs is to not rely on them as your main sources of evidence. Instead, they are helpful for figuring out the scope of the issue and understanding the major points of disagreement.

Wikis—Just about any Internet search will turn up information housed on Wikipedia. Some other popular wikis include WikiHow, WikiAnswers, and Wikibooks. The information on these major wikis can give you a good overview of your topic and the issues involved. The main problem with Wikipedia and other wikis is that users are allowed to change the content. So inaccurate or even misleading facts might be placed on a page. Another problem is that the authors of the information are not known; therefore, you have no one to cite as an authority. Wikis are a fine as a starting place for research, but most professors will not allow you to use them as citable sources.

Blogs—Likewise, blogs are rarely acceptable as citable sources of information. They are sometimes authored by experts, but many blogs are just the opinions of people who may or may not know what they are talking about. Treat blogs as you would a wiki. They are good places to figure out what others are saying about your topic, and they can help you identify the issues about which people disagree.

Using Documentaries, Broadcasts, and Podcasts

Some other electronic sources include documentaries, television and radio broadcasts, and podcasts. Many of these sources are available through the Internet or at your local library. A number of helpful documentaries and broadcasts can also be found on Netflix, Hulu, and YouTube. Your university's library may have access to documentaries on DVD or as downloads.

Documentaries—Documentaries are nonfiction films, television programs, or radio broadcasts that document some aspect of reality. They use facts and stories to help people understand places, historical events, and the lives of others through video, images, sounds, and artifacts. Keep in mind that documentaries are opinionated arguments and they should be treated as such. You can draw facts and quotes from them, but you should always remember that the people behind the documentary have a particular point of view that they would like you to accept.

Broadcasts—You can also draw information from television and radio broadcasts. Often, the news media will create special programs or news segments that discuss the topic you are researching. If you missed the program when it was first aired, you can usually find it archived on the source's website. Keep in mind, though, that even the news media, which usually claim to be objective, will have some bias. You should be aware of any bias and look for evidence that corroborates and challenges what you find in a broadcast.

Podcasts—A podcast is an audio or video program that is available for download through the Internet. You can listen to or view podcasts through your mobile phone, portable media player, or computer. Popular places to find podcasts include iTunes, PodcastAlley.com, Podcast.net, Podcast-bunker, and the NPR Podcast Directory. Podcasts tend to be less formal than news broadcasts. Because they are low-budget media, they can be produced quickly and easily. Podcasts can be good sources of information, but before trusting a podcast as a source, you need to check into the background of the people or organization that made it.

Electronic sources have become a regular part of doing research, so using them is fine. However, you should triangulate the information you find in electronic sources with print and empirical sources.

Finding Empirical Sources

Empirical sources of information give you the opportunity to generate your own evidence. You can interview people, do a survey, run an experiment, or conduct field observations. These hands-on experiences help you confirm or challenge the information you are finding in print and electronic sources.

Gathering empirical evidence might seem like a lot of work, but it's not—and it can be fun. You will find it interesting to check whether the factual claims made by others hold up in the real world.

Interviewing People

Interviews are a great way to go behind the facts to explore the views of experts and regular people (Figure 7). Plus, interviewing others is a good way to collect quotes that support your argument. Here are some strategies for interviewing people:

FIGURE 7
Conducting an Interview
Interviewing an expert is a good way to confirm or challenge what you are finding in secondary sources. Also, interviews are a good way to collect quotes for your argument.

Prepare for the Interview

1. **Do your research.** You need to know as much as possible about your topic before you interview someone about it.

2. **Create a list of three to five fact-based questions.** Your research will probably turn up some facts that you want your interviewee to confirm or challenge.

3. **Create a list of five to ten open-ended questions.** Write down five to ten questions that cannot be answered with a simple "yes" or "no." Your questions should urge the interviewee to offer a detailed explanation or opinion.

4. **Decide how you will record the interview.** Decide whether you want to record the interview as a video or make an audio recording. Or do you want to take written notes? Each of these methods has its pros and cons. For example, audio recording captures the whole conversation, but interviewees are often more guarded about their answers when they are being recorded.

5. **Set up the interview.** The best place to do an interview is at a neutral site, like a classroom, a room in the library, or perhaps a café. The second best place is at the interviewee's office. If necessary, you can do interviews over the phone.

Conduct the Interview

1. **Explain the purpose of your project and how long the interview will take.** Start out by explaining to the interviewee the purpose of your project and how the information from the interview will be used. Also, tell the interviewee how long you expect the interview will take.

2. **Ask permission to record.** If you are recording the interview in any way, ask permission to make the recording. First, ask if recording is all right before you turn on your recorder. Then, once the recorder is on, ask again so you record the interviewee's verbal permission.

3. **Ask your fact-based questions first.** Warm up the interviewee by asking questions that allow him or her to confirm or deny the facts you have already collected.

4. **Ask your open-ended questions next.** Ask the interviewee about his or her opinions, feelings, experiences, and views about the topic.

5. **Ask if he or she would like to provide any other information.** Often people want to tell you things you did not expect or know about. You can wrap up the interview by asking, "Is there anything else you would like to add about this topic?"

6. **Thank the interviewee.** Don't forget to thank the interviewee for his or her time and thoughts.

Follow Up the Interview

1. **Write down everything you remember.** As soon as possible after the interview, describe the interviewee in your notes and fill out any details you couldn't write down during the interview. Do this even if you recorded the interview.

2. **Get your quotes right.** Clarify any direct quotations you collected from your interviewee. If appropriate, you might e-mail your quotes to the interviewee for confirmation.

3. **Back-check the facts.** If the interviewee said something that was new to you or that conflicted with your previous findings, you should use electronic or print sources to back-check the facts. If there is a conflict you cannot resolve, you can send an e-mail to the interviewee to ask for clarification.

4. **Send a thank you note.** Usually an e-mail that thanks your interviewee is sufficient, but some people prefer a card or brief letter of thanks.

Using an Informal Survey

Unless you are majoring in a field that has taught you how to conduct scientific surveys, the surveys you will devise for your arguments will be informal and unscientific. These kinds of "unscientific" surveys are helpful for gaining an overall sense of people's opinions, but they won't give you solid data on which to base conclusions.

Conducting an informal survey is easier than ever. Many free online services, such as SurveyMonkey and Zoomerang, allow you to create and distribute your own surveys. These websites will also collect and tabulate the results for you. Here is how to create a useful, though unscientific, survey:

1. **Identify the population you want to survey.** Some surveys target specific kinds of people (e.g., college students, women from ages 18–22, medical doctors). Others are designed to be filled out by anyone.

2. **Develop your questions.** Create a list of five to ten questions that can be answered quickly. Surveys typically use four basic types of questions: rating scales, multiple choice, numeric open-ended, and open-ended. Figure 8 shows examples of all four types.

3. **Check your questions for neutrality.** Make sure your questions are as neutral as possible. Don't influence the people you are surveying by asking biased or slanted questions that fit your own beliefs or an outcome you are seeking.

4. **Distribute the survey.** Ask a number of people to complete your survey, and note the kinds of people who agree to do it. Not everyone will be interested in completing your survey, so remember that your results might reflect the views of specific kinds of people.

5. **Tabulate your results.** When your surveys are returned, convert any quantitative responses into data. If you collected written answers, pull out phrases and quotes that seem to reflect how the people you surveyed felt about your topic.

A critic might point out that your informal survey is not objective and that your results are not statistically valid. That's fine, as long as you are not using your survey to make important decisions or claim you have discovered some kind of truth. Your informal survey will still give you some helpful information about the opinions of others.

Rating Scale

Birth control should be free and easily available to high school students.

Strongly Agree	Agree	Disagree	Strongly Disagree	No Opinion
☐	☐	☐	☐	☐

Multiple Choice

Who gave you the most information about birth control when you were in high school?

☐ Parents   ☐ Sex ed in school

☐ Friends   ☐ Magazines

☐ Brother or sister   ☐ Internet

☐ Television programs   ☐ School nurse or health center

☐ Doctor or nonschool health center   ☐ Other

Numeric Open-Ended

At what age do you think adolescents should be taught about birth control options?

_____

Text Open-Ended

In a brief answer, describe what role you believe schools should have in educating adolescents about birth control options. _____

_____

_____

_____

_____

_____

Doing Field Observations

Field observations are a good way to confirm or challenge whether people, nature, or animals behave in expected ways (Figure 8). Your observations will likely be informal and unscientific. After all, doing a formal scientific observation (ethnography or case study) typically requires more time than you will have available to write a college argument. Nevertheless, you can still make useful observations as long as you are aware of the limitations of your methods. Here are some techniques for doing field observations.

FIGURE 8
Doing Field Observations
Your field observations can help you figure out how people, nature, or animals behave.

1. **Choose an appropriate location (field site).** You want to choose a field site that allows you to see as much as possible while not making it obvious that you are watching and taking notes. People will typically change their behavior if they think someone is watching them.

2. **Take notes in a two-column format.** A good field note technique is to use two columns to record what you see. On the left side, list the people, things, and events you observed. On the right side, write down how you interpret what you observed.

3. **Use the Five W and How questions.** Keep notes about the *who, what, where, when, why,* and *how* elements that you observe. Try to include as much detail as possible.

4. **Use your senses.** Take notes about the things you see, hear, smell, touch, and taste while you are observing.

5. **Pay attention to things that are moving or changing.** Take special note of the things that moved or changed while you were observing and what caused them to do so.

When you are finished taking notes, spend some time interpreting what you observed. Look for patterns in your observations to help you make sense of your field site.

4 Strategies for triangulating and evaluating sources

Evaluating Your Sources

All sources are not created equal. Depending on your research project, some of the sources you find will be better and more reliable than others. So you should spend time asking the following five questions of each source:

Question 1: Is This Source Credible?

The credibility of a source depends on who wrote it, who sponsored or published it, and where the facts or data came from. You should conduct some background research on the authors or sponsors of the source. A quick Internet search should turn up biographical information on the people who wrote or produced the information you want to use. Check their credentials and determine whether they have the background to offer reliable evidence.

Then figure out who is sponsoring the research behind the source. Obviously, a person, company, or organization that stands to gain financially will have some bias. So follow the money to determine whether the author or sponsor will gain financially if people accept the evidence provided. There is nothing wrong with a source having a financial incentive, but you should always keep in mind that these incentives will usually create more bias.

Also, look at each source's sources. Where did the author get his or her information? Make sure you can track down where the author collected his or her facts and data. If the sources behind the facts and data aren't cited in some way, then you should be skeptical about whether the information is accurate. Meanwhile, if a source is using empirical methods (surveys, interviews, experiments) to generate data, you should analyze whether those methods were reasonably impartial. Look for any indication that the author used methods that were slanted toward a preferred outcome.

Question 2: Is This Source Accurate?

The accuracy of a source can be hard to determine. Earlier in this chapter, you learned how to triangulate sources. Triangulation helps you figure out whether a source's information is accurate. If a source is presenting facts and data that are significantly out of line with your other sources, you should treat that evidence with added skepticism.

Accuracy might also depend on the tools and methods used to collect the evidence. A more exact experiment or closer observation might yield results that make some sources more accurate or reliable than others.

Question 3: Is This Source Current?

Depending on your topic, the currency of your source might help you determine whether its evidence is still reliable. In quickly evolving fields, such as medicine, technology, or popular culture, even the best sources can be outdated within a couple years. In fields that don't change quickly, such as history, geology, or anthropology, a decades-old source might still be current.

To help you determine whether the source is current, look at the date when it was published. Some sources will have been updated or revised, so pay attention to how often the information has been changed or brought up to date. Electronic sources can be especially problematic for determining currency. A reliable electronic source should give you a clear sense of when the information was originally published and last updated. If you can't find a publication or revision date, then you will need to be extra careful about triangulating the source's evidence with other sources.

Question 4: Does the Source Engage Two or More Sides of the Issue?

A reliable source will usually explain and engage at least two sides of an issue. You should have a clear sense that the author understands and has considered the other sides of the issue. Meanwhile, you should be skeptical of an author who is only telling one side of the story or seems to be unaware that other views may exist.

If a source only offers one side of the issue, the information might still be useful but chances are good the author isn't telling you everything. You should do extra research to determine how others might view the issue differently than the author.

Question 5: Are You Biased for or against the Information in This Source?

Finally, be honest about how your own personal beliefs will influence or bias your understanding of each source. We all believe some things are true and some aren't. You cannot set those biases completely aside. So, as you evaluate each source, ask yourself whether you trust the source because it happens to agree with your own personal views. And if you disagree with a source, ask yourself whether your own biases taint whether you believe the source is reliable or credible.

Collecting evidence for your argument is not difficult and it's fun. This is what you need to know.

1 Developing your own research process is a good way to do better research in a more efficient way.

2 A model research process includes these steps: (1) define a research question, (2) develop a working thesis, (3) collect sources, (4) triangulate sources, (5) identify major findings, and (6) modify or accept your working thesis.

3 Primary sources include artifacts, records, statements, or other items that were created or used by the people directly involved with the issue.

4 Secondary sources include the published works of experts, scholars, journalists, and other knowledgeable people who have analyzed, studied, or commented on the issue.

5 Print sources offer some of the most reliable information available on just about any topic.

6 Electronic sources are items that were designed to be viewed on a screen or listened to through an electronic medium.

7 Empirical sources give you hands-on ways to confirm or challenge the information you find in print and electronic sources.

8 Some common empirical methods for a college argument include interviews, surveys, and field observations.

9 You need to evaluate your sources to determine if they are credible, accurate, current, and balanced.

10 When evaluating a source, you should both "follow the money" to see if financial issues might bias it and figure out whether you are personally biased for or against the source.

1. Think about a recent argument you had with a friend or family member. The argument could have been contentious, or it could have just been a discussion about a current issue. During the argument, what kinds of evidence were offered to support the sides of the issue? Were there moments at which you wished you had better evidence to offer? If so, what kinds of evidence might have been helpful? Were there moments when you thought your friend's or family member's argument was weakened by a lack of solid evidence? Describe this argument to your group.

2. Using the Internet, find an argument that is well supported with evidence. Then trace that evidence by finding the sources the author uses. Keep tracing the evidence until you find a primary source. Now that you have reached this basic level, do you still think the argument is well supported? If someone were to challenge this argument, how could a close look at the primary sources be used to raise doubts?

3. With your group, choose a contentious issue that is often argued about in our society (gun control, reproductive rights, freedom of speech, etc.). Then ask each member of your group to gather five secondary sources on that topic, including at least two print sources. Compare the sources you found. Whether you agree with the sources or not, did you find their use of evidence effective? According to your group, which side of the argument best used evidence to support its views? Why? What made that use of evidence stronger?

LET'S **ARGUE**
ABOUT THIS

1. Write a brief commentary in which you argue for (or against) the claim that "all the information necessary for a research project can be found through the Internet." In your argument, explain some of the advantages and shortcomings of doing exclusively electronic research. If you are challenging the claim, explain why you think print and empirical sources are still needed, even though it seems that just about everything is on the Internet.

2. A research plan is a step-by-step description of your research methods. For the research project you are working on right now, write up a step-by-step research plan that describes how you will gather print, electronic, and empirical sources that will help you better understand your topic and support your argument. Then put those steps on a calendar and assign completion dates to each one. In an e-mail to your instructor, describe your research plan and explain why you think it offers the most effective way to explore your topic.

3. You are probably working on a paper right now that involves research. Using your campus library's website, locate five possible print sources (two books and three articles) that might offer evidence for your argument. Then, using the Internet, find five possible electronic sources that would also offer useful evidence. Finally, list two ways in which you could generate empirical evidence for your argument. In an e-mail to your instructor, list your ten print and electronic sources using MLA or APA bibliographic style. Then, list your two possible empirical sources.

Credits

Credits are listed in order of appearance.

Photo Credits

l i g h t p o e t/Shutterstock; Martin Shields/Alamy; Geri Engberg/The Image Works; 360: David R. Frazier Photolibrary, Inc./Alamy; (bl), Lordprice Collection/Alamy; (br), Alexander Raths/Fotolia; (tl), Gianni Dagli Orti/Corbis; (tr), Library of Congress Prints and Photographs Division [LC-USZ62-107110]

Text Credits

Screen Capture from http://www.lib.iastate.edu. Courtesy Iowa State University Library.
Screen Capture, www.dogpile.com. Courtesy Blucora, Inc.

How to Mark a Book

Mortimer Adler

Mortimer Adler (1902–2001) received his Ph.D. from Columbia University in 1928. A conservative thinker, Adler advocated education based on the "truths" found in the classical works of Western civilization. Many academic intellectuals have scorned his simple formulas for progress, but the larger culture has often embraced his ideas, as his post as chairman of the editorial board of the Encyclopedia Britannica *indicated. His Great Books project, for which he is widely known, resulted in the publication and wide circulation of handsome bound sets of important works of world literature. As you read his essay on how to mark a book, you will see a man who thought that the world is, or ought to be, clear and simple.*

1   You know you have to read "between the lines" to get the most out of anything. I want to persuade you to do something equally important in the course of your reading. I want to persuade you to "write between the lines." Unless you do, you are not likely to do the most efficient kind of reading.

I contend, quite bluntly, that marking up a book is not an act of mutilation but of love.

You shouldn't mark up a book which isn't yours. Librarians (or your friends) who lend you books expect you to keep them clean, and you should. If you decide that I am right about the usefulness of marking books, you will have to buy them. Most of the world's great books are available today, in reprint editions, at less than a dollar.

There are two ways in which you can own a book. The first is the property right you establish by paying for it, just as you pay for clothes and furniture. But this act of purchase is only the prelude to possession. Full ownership comes only when you have made it a part of yourself, and the best way to make yourself a part of it is by writing in it. An illustration may make the point clear. You buy a beefsteak and transfer it from the butcher's ice-box to your own. But you do not own the beefsteak in the most important sense until you consume it and get it into your bloodstream. I am arguing that books, too, must be absorbed in your bloodstream to do you any good.

5 Confusion about what it means to *own* a book leads people to a false reverence for paper, binding, and type—a respect for the physical thing—the craft of the printer rather than the genius of the author. They forget that it is possible for a man to acquire the idea, to possess the beauty, which a great book contains, without staking his claim by pasting his bookplate inside the cover. Having a fine library doesn't prove that its owner has a mind enriched by books; it proves nothing more than that he, his father, or his wife, was rich enough to buy them.

There are three kinds of book owners. The first has all the standard sets and best-sellers—unread, untouched. (This deluded individual owns woodpulp and ink, not books.) The second has a great many books—a few of them read through, most of them dipped into, but all of them as clean and shiny as the day they were bought. (This person would probably like to make books his own, but is restrained by a false respect for their physical appearance.) The third has a few books or many—everyone of them dog-eared and dilapidated, shaken and loosened by continual use, marked and scribbled in from front to back. (This man owns books.)

Is it false respect, you may ask, to preserve intact and unblemished a beautifully printed book, an elegantly bound edition? Of course not. I'd no more scribble all over a first edition of *Paradise Lost* than I'd give my baby a set of crayons and an original Rembrandt! I wouldn't mark up a painting or a statue. Its soul, so to speak, is inseparable from its body. And the beauty of a rare edition or of a richly manufactured volume is like that of a painting or a statue.

But the soul of a book *can* be separated from its body. A book is more like the score of a piece of music than it is like a painting. No great musician confuses a symphony with the printed sheets of music. Arturo Toscanini reveres Brahms, but Toscanini's score of the C-minor Symphony is so thoroughly marked up that no one but the maestro himself can read it. The reason why a great conductor makes notations on his musical scores—marks them up again and again each time he returns to study them—is the reason why you should mark your books.

If your respect for magnificent binding or typography gets in the way, buy yourself a cheap edition and pay your respects to the author.

Why is marking up a book indispensable to reading? First, it keeps you awake. (And I don't mean merely conscious; I mean wide awake.) In the second place, reading, if it is active, is thinking, and thinking tends to express itself in words, spoken or written. The marked book is usually the thought-through book. Finally, writing helps you remember the thoughts you had, or the thoughts the author expressed. Let me develop these three points.

10

If reading is to accomplish anything more than passing time, it must be active. You can't let your eyes glide across the lines of a book and come up with an understanding of what you have read. Now an ordinary piece of light fiction, like say, *Gone With the Wind,* doesn't require the most active kind of reading. The books you read for pleasure can be read in a state of relaxation, and nothing is lost. But a great book, rich in ideas and beauty, a book that raises and tries to answer great fundamental questions, demands the most active reading of which you are capable. You don't absorb the ideas of John Dewey the way you absorb the crooning of Mr. Vallee. You have to reach for them. That you cannot do while you're asleep.

If, when you've finished reading a book, the pages are filled with your notes, you know that you read actively. The most famous *active* reader of great books I know is President Hutchins, of the University of Chicago. He also has the hardest schedule of business activities of any man I know. He invariably reads with a pencil, and sometimes, when he picks up a book and pencil in the evening, he finds himself, instead of making intelligent notes, drawing what he calls "caviar factories" on the margins. When that happens, he puts the book down. He knows he's too tired to read, and he's just wasting time.

But, you may ask, why is writing necessary? Well, the physical act of writing, with your own hand, brings words and sentences more sharply before your mind and preserves them better in your memory. To set down your reaction to important words and sentences you have read, and the questions they have raised in your mind, is to preserve those reactions and sharpen those questions.

Even if you wrote on a scratch pad, and threw the paper away when you had finished writing, your grasp of the book would be surer. But you don't have to throw the paper away. The margins (top and bottom, as well as side), the end-papers, the very space between the lines, are all available. They aren't sacred. And, best of all, your marks and notes become an integral part of the book and stay there forever. You can pick up the book the following week or year, and there are all your points of agreement, disagreement, doubt, and inquiry. It's like resuming an interrupted conversation with the advantage of being able to pick up where you left off.

And that is exactly what reading a book should be: a conversation between you and the author. Presumably he knows more about the subject than you do; naturally, you'll have the proper humility as you approach him. But don't let anybody tell you that a reader is supposed to be solely on the receiving end. Understanding is a two-way operation; learning doesn't consist in being an empty receptacle. The learner has to question himself and question the teacher. He even has to argue with the teacher, once he understands what the teacher is saying. And marking a book is literally an expression of your differences, or agreements of opinion, with the author.

15   There are all kinds of devices for marking a book intelligently and   15
fruitfully. Here's the way I do it:

1. *Underlining:* Of major points, of important or forceful statements.
2. *Vertical lines at the margin:* To emphasize a statement already underlined.
3. *Star, asterisk, or other doo-dad at the margin:* To be used sparingly, to emphasize the ten or twenty most important statements in the book. (You may want to fold the bottom corner of each page on which you use such marks. It won't hurt the sturdy paper on which most modern books are printed, and you will be able to take the book off the shelf at any time and, by opening it at the folded corner page, refresh your recollection of the book.)
4. *Numbers in the margin:* To indicate the sequence of points the author makes in developing a single argument.
20   5. *Numbers of other pages in the margin:* To indicate where else in the   20
book the author made points relevant to the point marked; to tie up the ideas in a book, which, though they may be separated by many pages, belong together.
6. *Circling of key words or phrases.*
7. *Writing in the margin, or at the top or bottom of the page, for the sake of:* Recording questions (and perhaps answers) which a passage raised in your mind; reducing a complicated discussion to a simple statement; recording the sequence of major points right through the books. I use the end-papers at the back of the book

to make a personal index of the author's points in the order of their appearance.

The front end-papers are, to me, the most important. Some people reserve them for a fancy bookplate. I reserve them for fancy thinking. After I have finished reading the book and making my personal index on the back end-papers, I turn to the front and try to outline the book, not page by page, or point by point (I've already done that at the back), but as an integrated structure, with a basic unity and an order of parts. This outline is, to me, the measure of my understanding of the work.

If you're a die-hard anti-book-marker, you may object that the margins, the space between the lines, and the end-papers don't give you room enough. All right. How about using a scratch pad slightly smaller than the page-size of the book—so that the edges of the sheets won't protrude? Make your index, outlines, and even your notes on the pad, and then insert these sheets permanently inside the front and back covers of the book.

25 Or, you may say that this business of marking books is going to 25 slow up your reading. It probably will. That's one of the reasons for doing it. Most of us have been taken in by the notion that speed of reading is a measure of our intelligence. There is no such thing as the right speed for intelligent reading. Some things should be read quickly and effortlessly, and some should be read slowly and even laboriously. The sign of intelligence in reading is the ability to read different things differently according to their worth. In the case of good books, the point is not to see how many of them you can get through, but rather how many can get through you—how many you can make your own. A few friends are better than a thousand acquaintances. If this be your aim, as it should be, you will not be impatient if it takes more time and effort to read a great book than it does a newspaper.

You may have one final objection to marking books. You can't lend them to your friends because nobody else can read them without being distracted by your notes. Furthermore, you won't want to lend them because a marked copy is a kind of intellectual diary, and lending it is almost like giving your mind away.

If your friend wishes to read your *Plutarch's Lives,* "Shakespeare," or *The Federalist Papers,* tell him gently but firmly to buy a copy. You will lend him your car or your coat—but your books are as much a part of you as your head or your heart.

Questions on Meaning

1. Paraphrase the point Adler is making in comparing buying a book to buying a beefsteak.
2. Critique Adler's comparison of a book's meaning to the concept of a soul. Look up the word *soul* in a dictionary and organize your critique by the points of the dictionary definitions.
3. Explain Adler's assertion that "There is no such thing as the right speed for intelligent reading."

Questions on Rhetorical Strategy and Style

1. Where is Adler's description of how to mark a book least clear? Explain why.
2. Adler's style is based on very short sentences. Try combining the sentences in a single paragraph (e.g., the one beginning, "There are two ways in which you can own a book . . ."). Compare your revision with the original and describe the alteration in tone you note from the longer sentences.

Writing Assignments

1. Write an essay that describes a few of the most influential books you've ever read. Did you read them actively, as Adler recommends? How did they affect your thinking or behavior?
2. Compile a list of five books you think you should read but haven't yet. Write an essay that tells the story of how you found out about these books.

Shitty First Drafts

Anne Lamott

Anne Lamott (1954–), a writer who writes on writing, among many other subjects, is both a creator of fiction and nonfiction and a commentator on religious subjects. She acquired her interest in writing from her father, Kenneth Lamott, the model and inspiration for her first novel, Hard Laughter *(1987).* Bird by Bird: Some Instructions on Writing and Life, *from which the following excerpt has been taken, is a much read and taught book that looks at the experiences of a writer at work. She is also known for her works on family life, including* Operating Instructions: A Journal of My Son's First Year *(1994) and* Crooked Little Heart *(1997) about the stuff that keeps a family together. Her religious works include* Traveling Mercies: Some Thoughts on Faith *(2000),* Plan B: Further Thoughts on Faith *(2005), and* Grace (Eventually): Thoughts on Faith *(2007). Lamott writes the books she would like to have discovered to read, and helps other aspiring writers to do the same.*

Most writers write terrible stuff in their first drafts, and sometimes the fear of those drafts keeps writers from writing at all. In this humorous book chapter, Lamott tells how to go right ahead and write no matter how bad the first try.

Reprinted from *Bird By Bird: Some Instructions on Writing and Life* (1995), by permission of Pantheon Books, a division of Random House, Inc.

Now, practically even better news than that of short assignments is the idea of shitty first drafts. All good writers write them. This is how they end up with good second drafts and terrific third drafts. People tend to look at successful writers, writers who are getting their books published and maybe even doing well financially, and think that they sit down at their desks every morning feeling like a million dollars, feeling great about who they are and how much talent they have and what a great story they have to tell; that they take in a few deep breaths, push back their sleeves, roll their necks a few times to get all the cricks out, and dive in, typing fully formed passages as fast as a court reporter. But this is just the fantasy of the uninitiated. I know some very great writers, writers you love who write beautifully and have made a great deal of money, and not *one* of them sits down routinely feeling wildly enthusiastic and confident. Not one of them writes elegant first drafts. All right, one of them does, but we do not like her very much. We do not think that she has a rich inner life or that God likes her or can even stand her. (Although when I mentioned this to my priest friend Tom, he said you can safely assume you've created God in your own image when it turns out that God hates all the same people you do.)

Very few writers really know what they are doing until they've done it. Nor do they go about their business feeling dewy and thrilled. They do not type a few stiff warm-up sentences and then find themselves bounding along like huskies across the snow. One writer I know tells me that he sits down every morning and says to himself nicely, "It's not like you don't have a choice, because you do— you can either type or kill yourself." We all often feel like we are pulling teeth, even those writers whose prose ends up being the most natural and fluid. The right words and sentences just do not come pouring out like ticker tape most of the time. Now, Muriel Spark is said to have felt that she was taking dictation from God every morning—sitting there, one supposes, plugged into a Dictaphone, typing away, humming. But this is a very hostile and aggressive position. One might hope for bad things to rain down on a person like this.

For me and most of the other writers I know, writing is not rapturous. In fact, the only way I can get anything written at all is to write really, really shitty first drafts.

The first draft is the child's draft, where you let it all pour out and then let it romp all over the place, knowing that no one is going to see it and that you can shape it later. You just let this childlike part of you channel whatever voices and visions come through and onto the page. If one of the characters wants to say, "Well, so what, Mr. Poopy Pants?," you let her. No one is going to see it. If the kid wants to get into really sentimental, weepy, emotional territory, you let him. Just get it all down on paper, because there may be something great in those six crazy pages that you would never have gotten to by more rational, grown-up means. There may be something in the very last line of the very last paragraph on page six that you just love, that is so beautiful or wild that you now know what you're supposed to be writing about, more or less, or in what direction you might go—but there was no way to get to this without first getting through the first five and a half pages.

5   I used to write food reviews for *California* Magazine before it folded. (My writing food reviews had nothing to do with the magazine folding, although every single review did cause a couple of canceled subscriptions. Some readers took umbrage at my comparing mounds of vegetable puree with various ex-presidents' brains.) These reviews always took two days to write. First I'd go to a restaurant several times with a few opinionated, articulate friends in tow. I'd sit there writing down everything anyone said that was at all interesting or funny. Then on the following Monday I'd sit down at my desk with my notes, and try to write the review. Even after I'd been doing this for years, panic would set in. I'd try to write a lead, but instead I'd write a couple of dreadful sentences, XX them out, try again, XX everything out, and then feel despair and worry settle on my chest like an x-ray apron. It's over, I'd think, calmly. I'm not going to be able to get the magic to work this time. I'm ruined. I'm through. I'm toast. Maybe, I'd think, I can get my old job back as a clerk-typist. But probably not. I'd get up and study my teeth in the mirror for a while. Then I'd stop, remember to breathe, make a few phone calls, hit the kitchen and chow down. Eventually I'd go back and sit down at my desk, and sigh for the next ten minutes. Finally I would pick up my one-inch picture frame, stare into it as if for the answer, and every time the answer would come: all I had to do was to write a really shitty first draft of, say, the opening paragraph. And no one was going to see it.

So I'd start writing without reining myself in. It was almost just typing, just making my fingers move. And the writing would be *terrible*. I'd write a lead paragraph that was a whole page, even though the entire review could only be three pages long, and then I'd start writing up descriptions of the food, one dish at a time, bird by bird, and the critics would be sitting on my shoulders, commenting like cartoon characters. They'd be pretending to snore, or rolling their eyes at my overwrought descriptions, no matter how hard I tried to tone those descriptions down, no matter how conscious I was of what a friend said to me gently in my early days of restaurant reviewing. "Annie," she said, "it is just a piece of *chicken*. It is just a bit of *cake*."

But because by then I had been writing for so long, I would eventually let myself trust the process—sort of, more or less. I'd write a first draft that was maybe twice as long as it should be, with a self-indulgent and boring beginning, stupefying descriptions of the meal, lots of quotes from my black-humored friends that made them sound more like the Manson girls than food lovers, and no ending to speak of. The whole thing would be so long and incoherent and hideous that for the rest of the day I'd obsess about getting creamed by a car before I could write a decent second draft. I'd worry that people would read what I'd written and believe that the accident had really been a suicide, that I had panicked because my talent was waning and my mind was shot.

The next day, though, I'd sit down, go through it all with a colored pen, take out everything I possibly could, find a new lead somewhere on the second page, figure out a kicky place to end it, and then write a second draft. It always turned out fine, sometimes even funny and weird and helpful. I'd go over it one more time and mail it in.

Then, a month later, when it was time for another review, the whole process would start again, complete with the fears that people would find my first draft before I could rewrite it.

10   Almost all good writing begins with terrible first efforts. You need   10
to start somewhere. Start by getting something—anything down on paper. A friend of mine says that the first draft is the down draft—you just get it down. The second draft is the up draft—you fix it up. You try to say what you have to say more accurately. And the third draft is the dental draft, where you check every tooth, to see if it's loose or cramped or decayed, or even, God help us, healthy.

What I've learned to do when I sit down to work on a shitty first draft is to quiet the voices in my head. First there's the vinegar-lipped Reader Lady, who says primly, "Well, *that's* not very interesting, is it?" And there's the emaciated German male who writes these Orwellian memos detailing your thought crimes. And there are your parents, agonizing over your lack of loyalty and discretion; and there's William Burroughs, dozing off or shooting up because he finds you as bold and articulate as a houseplant; and so on. And there are also the dogs: let's not forget the dogs, the dogs in their pen who will surely hurtle and snarl their way out if you ever *stop* writing, because writing is, for some of us, the latch that keeps the door of the pen closed, keeps those crazy ravenous dogs contained.

Quieting these voices is at least half the battle I fight daily. But this is better than it used to be. It used to be 87 percent. Left to its own devices, my mind spends much of its time having conversations with people who aren't there. I walk along defending myself to people, or exchanging repartee with them, or rationalizing my behavior, or seducing them with gossip, or pretending I'm on their TV talk show or whatever. I speed or run an aging yellow light or don't come to a full stop, and one nanosecond later am explaining to imaginary cops exactly why I had to do what I did, or insisting that I did not in fact do it.

I happened to mention this to a hypnotist I saw many years ago, and he looked at me very nicely. At first I thought he was feeling around on the floor for the silent alarm button, but then he gave me the following exercise, which I still use to this day.

Close your eyes and get quiet for a minute, until the chatter starts up. Then isolate one of the voices and imagine the person speaking as a mouse. Pick it up by the tail and drop it into a mason jar. Then isolate another voice, pick it up by the tail, drop it in the jar. And so on. Drop in any high-maintenance parental units, drop in any contractors, lawyers, colleagues, children, anyone who is whining in your head. Then put the lid on, and watch all these mouse people clawing at the glass, jabbering away, trying to make you feel like shit because you won't do what they want—won't give them more money, won't be more successful, won't see them more often. Then imagine that there is a volume-control button on the bottle. Turn it all the way up for a minute, and listen to the stream of angry, neglected, guilt-mongering voices. Then turn it all the way down and watch the frantic mice lunge at the glass, trying to get to you. Leave it down, and get back to your shitty first draft.

15   A writer friend of mine suggests opening the jar and shooting 15 them all in the head. But I think he's a little angry, and I'm sure nothing like this would ever occur to you.

Questions on Meaning

1. How do most writers write a first draft? What do they put into the draft, and how do they feel about beginning to write?
2. What did Lamott learn from her experience as a food columnist for a magazine that no longer exists?
3. Lamott suggests that a writer should plunge past the voices that say the work will never be any good. What does she say to do with those voices?

Questions on Rhetorical Strategy and Style

1. Lamott is funny. What does she say about the one writer she knows who writes good first drafts? How does she feel about this person, and how does her humor explain her perspective?
2. This chapter is a small narration of Lamott's processes for getting past the first draft and on to the later work of revision. How does she tell the story of her writing progress?
3. The chapter ends with an example of putting mice into a jar. What does she say about the writer friend who would just shoot the mice? Why does she end the chapter this way?

Writing Assignments

1. Write a first draft. Then write about the first draft. What did you include that you might cut later? What might you add in the next draft? Write about yourself as a first draft writer.
2. Talk to five of your friends about how they approach writing a paper. Take notes on what they do. Then write a paper comparing and contrasting their processes.
3. Choose some aspect of your life or personality that annoys or troubles you. Then devise a way of getting rid of this aspect as Lamott does the voices that tell her she cannot write. Write about the way that you would quiet the annoying aspect of your life.

The Maker's Eye: Revising Your Own Manuscripts

Donald M. Murray

Donald M. Murray (1924–2006), born in Boston, spent most of his life writing, editing, and teaching writing. He published fiction, poetry, and a variety of nonfiction. He was an editor for Time *magazine and in 1954 won a Pulitzer Prize for editorial writing. His textbooks on writing include* Writing for Your Readers, A Writer Teaches Writing, Write to Learn, Read to Write, *and* The Craft of Revision. *The following essay was published in the journal* The Writer *in 1973. As you read about how Murray approached revision, think about your own writing and revising habits.*

1   When students complete a first draft, they consider the job of writing done—and their teachers too often agree. When professional writers complete a first draft, they usually feel that they are at the start of the writing process. When a draft is completed, the job of writing can begin.

That difference in attitude is the difference between amateur and professional, inexperience and experience, journeyman and craftsman. Peter F. Drucker, the prolific business writer, calls his first draft "the zero draft"—after that he can start counting. Most writers share the feeling that the first draft, and all of those which follow, are opportunities to discover what they have to say and how best they can say it.

To produce a progression of drafts, each of which says more and says it more clearly, the writer has to develop a special kind of reading skill. In school we are taught to decode what appears on the page as finished writing. Writers, however, face a different category of possibility and responsibility when they read their own drafts. To them the words on the page are never finished. Each can be changed and rearranged, can set off a chain reaction of confusion or clarified meaning. This is a different kind of reading, which is possibly more difficult and certainly more exciting.

Writers must learn to be their own best enemy. They must accept the criticism of others and be suspicious of it; they must accept the praise of others and be even more suspicious of it. Writers cannot depend on others. They must detach themselves from their own pages so that they can apply both their caring and their craft to their own work.

5   Such detachment is not easy. Science fiction writer Ray Bradbury supposedly puts each manuscript away for a year to the day and then rereads it as a stranger. Not many writers have the discipline or the time to do this. We must read when our judgment may be at its worst, when we are close to the euphoric moment of creation.

Then the writer, counsels novelist Nancy Hale, "should be critical of everything that seems to him most delightful in his style. He should excise what he most admires, because he wouldn't thus admire it if he weren't . . . in a sense protecting it from criticism." John Ciardi, the poet, adds, "The last act of the writing must be to become one's own reader. It is, I suppose, a schizophrenic process, to begin passionately and to end critically, to begin hot and to end cold; and, more important, to be passion-hot and critic-cold at the same time."

Most people think that the principal problem is that writers are too proud of what they have written. Actually, a greater problem for most professional writers is one shared by the majority of students. They are overly critical, think everything is dreadful, tear up page after page, never complete a draft, see the task as hopeless.

The writer must learn to read critically but constructively, to cut what is bad, to reveal what is good. Eleanor Estes, the children's book author, explains: "The writer must survey his work critically, coolly, as though he were a stranger to it. He must be willing to prune, expertly and hard-heartedly. At the end of each revision, a manuscript may look . . . worked over, torn apart, pinned together, added to, deleted from, words changed and words changed back. Yet the book must maintain its original freshness and spontaneity."

Most readers underestimate the amount of rewriting it usually takes to produce spontaneous reading. This is a great disadvantage to the student writer, who sees only a finished product and never watches the craftsman who takes the necessary step back, studies the work carefully, returns to the task, steps back, returns, steps back, again and again. Anthony Burgess, one of the most prolific writers in the English-speaking world, admits, "I might revise a page twenty times." Roald Dahl, the popular children's writer, states, "By the time I'm nearing the end of a story, the first part will have been reread and altered and corrected at least 150 times. . . . Good writing is essentially rewriting. I am positive of this."

10   Rewriting isn't virtuous. It isn't something that ought to be done. 10 It is simply something that most writers find they have to do to discover what they have to say and how to say it. It is a condition of the writer's life.

There are, however, a few writers who do little formal rewriting, primarily because they have the capacity and experience to create and review a large number of invisible drafts in their minds before they approach the page. And some writers slowly produce finished pages, performing all the tasks of revision simultaneously, page by page, rather than draft by draft. But it is still possible to see the sequence followed by most writers most of the time in rereading their own work.

Most writers scan their drafts first, reading as quickly as possible to catch the larger problems of subject and form, then move in closer and closer as they read and write, reread and rewrite.

The first thing writers look for in their drafts is information. They know that a good piece of writing is built from specific, accurate, and interesting information. The writer must have an abundance of information from which to construct a readable piece of writing.

Next writers look for *meaning* in the information. The specifics must build a pattern of significance. Each piece of specific information must carry the reader toward meaning.

15   Writers reading their own drafts are aware of *audience*. They put 15 themselves in the reader's situation and make sure that they deliver information which a reader wants to know or needs to know in a manner which is easily digested. Writers try to be sure that they anticipate and answer the questions a critical reader will ask when reading the piece of writing.

Writers make sure that the *form* is appropriate to the subject and the audience. Form, or genre, is the vehicle which carries meaning to the reader, but form cannot be selected until the writer has adequate information to discover its significance and an audience which needs or wants that meaning.

Once writers are sure the form is appropriate, they must then look at the *structure,* the order of what they have written. Good writing is built on a solid framework of logic, argument, narrative, or motivation which runs through the entire piece of writing and holds it together. This is the time when many writers find it most effective to outline as a way of visualizing the hidden spine by which the piece of writing is supported.

The element on which writers may spend a majority of their time is *development.* Each section of a piece of writing must be adequately developed. It must give readers enough information so that they are satisfied. How much information is enough? That's as difficult as asking how much garlic belongs in a salad. It must be done to taste, but most beginning writers underdevelop, underestimating the reader's hunger for information.

As writers solve development problems, they often have to consider questions of *dimension.* There must be a pleasing and effective proportion among all the parts of the piece of writing. There is a continual process of subtracting and adding to keep the piece of writing in balance.

20 Finally, writers have to listen to their own voices. *Voice* is the force 20 which drives a piece of writing forward. It is an expression of the writer's authority and concern. It is what is between the words on the page, what glues the piece of writing together. A good piece of writing is always marked by a consistent, individual voice.

As writers read and reread, write and rewrite, they move closer and closer to the page until they are doing line-by-line editing. Writers read their own pages with infinite care. Each sentence, each line, each clause, each phrase, each word, each mark of punctuation, each section of white space between the type has to contribute to the clarification of meaning.

Slowly the writer moves from word to word, looking through language to see the subject. As a word is changed, cut, or added, as a construction is rearranged, all the words used before that moment and all those that follow that moment must be considered and reconsidered.

Writers often read aloud at this stage of the editing process, muttering or whispering to themselves, calling on the ear's experience with language. Does this sound right—or that? Writers edit, shifting back and forth from eye to page to ear to page. I find I must do this careful editing in short runs, no more than fifteen or twenty minutes at a stretch, or I become too kind with myself. I begin to see what I hope is on the page, not what actually is on the page.

This sounds tedious if you haven't done it, but actually it is fun. Making something right is immensely satisfying, for writers begin to learn what they are writing about by writing. Language leads them to meaning, and there is the joy of discovery, of understanding, of making meaning clear as the writer employs the technical skills of language.

25   Words have double meanings, even triple and quadruple meanings. Each word has its own potential for connotation and denotation. And when writers rub one word against the other, they are often rewarded with a sudden insight, an unexpected clarification.   25

The maker's eye moves back and forth from word to phrase to sentence to paragraph to sentence to phrase to word. The maker's eye sees the need for variety and balance, for a firmer structure, for a more appropriate form. It peers into the interior of the paragraph, looking for coherence, unity, and emphasis, which make meaning clear.

I learned something about this process when my first bifocals were prescribed. I had ordered a larger section of the reading portion of the glass because of my work, but even so, I could not contain my eyes within this new limit of vision. And I still find myself taking off my glasses and bending my nose towards the page, for my eyes unconsciously flick back and forth across the page, back to another page, forward to still another, as I try to see each evolving line in relation to every other line.

When does this process end? Most writers agree with the great Russian writer Tolstoy, who said, "I scarcely ever reread my published writings, if by chance I come across a page, it always strikes me: all this must be rewritten; this is how I should have written it."

The maker's eye is never satisfied, for each word has the potential to ignite new meaning. This article has been twice written all the way through the writing process, and it was published four years ago. Now it is to be republished in a book. The editors make a few small suggestions, and then I read it with my maker's eye. Now it has been re-edited, re-revised, re-read, re-re-edited, for each piece of writing to the writer is full of potential and alternatives.

30   A piece of writing is never finished. It is delivered to a deadline, torn   30 out of the typewriter on demand, sent off with a sense of accomplishment and shame and pride and frustration. If only there were a couple more days, time for just another run at it, perhaps then . . .

186

Questions on Meaning

1. Why should writers be suspicious of the criticism of others and even more suspicious of the praise of others?
2. Explain why and how rewriting is an opportunity for writers "to discover what they have to say." Why don't, or can't, writers know in advance what they want to say?

Questions on Rhetorical Strategy and Style

1. Describe the essay's thesis in your own words. Does Murray express it in one statement anywhere in the essay?
2. How does Murray analyze the process of rewriting? Is there one set process all writers go through, with steps in the same order, or does it vary? Describe this process fully.
3. Murray defines eight specific elements of writing that the writer examines and works on in the rewriting process. List these and define each in our own words.
4. Murray quotes a number of different writers on how they go about rewriting. The use of these quotations involves which of the eight elements?

Writing Assignments

1. Search your belongings for any piece of writing you did long ago—a letter, a school paper, anything. Read it and critique it objectively. What are its strengths? What would you want to rewrite now? How do you see it differently now from when you wrote it?
2. Write an essay in which you describe your own rewriting process—the method you use when you don't "have to" rewrite as part of an assignment. Be honest with yourself about how you actually work, and discuss what constraints of time and other factors affect your process. Analyze the strengths and weaknesses of your approach to rewriting.

Learning to Read and Write

Frederick Douglass

Frederick Douglass (1817–1895)—abolitionist, author, and the first black American to become a prominent public figure—was born into slavery near Tuckahoe, Maryland. As a youth, Douglass worked as a household servant, a field hand, and a shipyard apprentice. In 1838, after several failed attempts to escape (for which he received beatings), he successfully reached New York. He took the surname "Douglass" and eventually settled in New Bedford, Massachusetts. In 1841, the Massachusetts Anti-Slavery League, impressed by his great oratory skills, hired Douglass to help promote the abolition of slavery. Douglass bought his freedom in 1847, using money contributed both by Americans and by sympathizers in England, where he had fled to preserve his freedom. For the next 13 years, Douglass edited the abolitionist periodical North Star *(changed to* Frederick Douglass's Paper *in 1851). During the Civil War, Douglass urged President Lincoln to emancipate the slaves and helped recruit black troops. After the war, he held a series of government posts, including Assistant Secretary to the Santo Domingo Commission, Marshall of the District of Columbia, District Recorder of Deeds, and Ambassador to Haiti. This essay, which comes from Douglass's autobiography,* Narrative of the Life of Frederick Douglass, an American Slave *(1845), reveals the guile and determination that Douglass employed to teach himself to read. As you read the words of a former slave, written more than a century ago, think of how closed the world was to Douglass, yet how he recognized that literacy could help open the door.*

¹

I lived in Master Hugh's family about seven years. During this time, I succeeded in learning to read and write. In accomplishing this, I was compelled to resort to various stratagems. I had no regular teacher. My mistress, who had kindly commenced to instruct me, had, in compliance with the advice and direction of her husband, not only ceased to instruct, but had set her face against my being instructed by any one else. It is due, however, to my mistress to say of her, that she did not adopt this course of treatment immediately. She at first lacked the depravity indispensable to shutting me up in mental darkness. It was at least necessary for her to have some training in the exercise of irresponsible power, to make her equal to the task of treating me as though I were a brute.

My mistress was, as I have said, a kind and tender-hearted woman; and in the simplicity of her soul she commenced, when I first went to live with her, to treat me as she supposed one human being ought to treat another. In entering upon the duties of a slaveholder, she did not seem to perceive that I sustained to her the relation of a mere chattel, and that for her to treat me as a human being was not only wrong, but dangerously so. Slavery proved as injurious to her as it did to me. When I went there, she was a pious, warm, and tender-hearted woman. There was no sorrow or suffering for which she had not a tear. She had bread for the hungry, clothes for the naked, and comfort for every mourner that came within her reach. Slavery soon proved its ability to divest her of these heavenly qualities. Under its influence, the tender heart became stone, and the lamb-like disposition gave way to one of tiger-like fierceness. The first step in her downward course was in her ceasing to instruct me. She now commenced to practise her husband's precepts. She finally became even more violent in her opposition than her husband himself. She was not satisfied with simply doing as well as he had commanded; she seemed anxious to do better. Nothing seemed to make her more angry than to see me with a newspaper. She seemed to think that here lay the danger. I have had her rush at me with a face made all up of fury, and snatch from me a newspaper, in a manner that fully revealed her apprehension. She was an apt woman; and a little experience soon demonstrated, to her satisfaction, that education and slavery were incompatible with each other.

From this time I was most narrowly watched. If I was in a separate room any considerable length of time, I was sure to be suspected

¹

of having a book, and was at once called to give an account of myself. All this, however, was too late. The first step had been taken. Mistress, in teaching me the alphabet, had given me the *inch,* and no precaution could prevent me from taking the *ell.*

The plan which I adopted, and the one by which I was most successful, was that of making friends of all the little white boys whom I met in the street. As many of these as I could, I converted into teachers. With their kindly aid, obtained at different times and in different places, I finally succeeded in learning to read. When I was sent on errands, I always took my book with me, and by going one part of my errand quickly, I found time to get a lesson before my return. I used also to carry bread with me, enough of which was always in the house, and to which I was always welcome; for I was much better off in this regard than many of the poor white children in our neighborhood. This bread I used to bestow upon the hungry little urchins, who, in return, would give me that more valuable bread of knowledge. I am strongly tempted to give the names of two or three of those little boys, as a testimonial of the gratitude and affection I bear them; but prudence forbids;—not that it would injure me, but it might embarrass them; for it is almost an unpardonable offense to teach slaves to read in this Christian country. It is enough to say of the dear little fellows, that they lived on Philpot Street, very near Durgin and Bailey's shipyard. I used to talk this matter of slavery over with them. I would sometimes say to them, I wished I could be as free as they would be when they got to be men. "You will be free as soon as you are twenty-one, *but I am a slave for life!* Have not I as good a right to be free as you have?" These words used to trouble them; they would express for me the liveliest sympathy, and console me with the hope that something would occur by which I might be free.

5 I was now about twelve years old, and the thought of being *a slave for life* began to bear heavily upon my heart. Just about this time, I got hold of a book entitled "The Columbian Orator." Every opportunity I got, I used to read this book. Among much of other interesting matter, I found in it a dialogue between a master and his slave. The slave was represented as having run away from his master three times. The dialogue represented the conversation which took place between them, when the slave was retaken the third time. In this dialogue, the whole argument in behalf of slavery was brought forward by the master, all of which was disposed of by the slave. The slave was made to

say some very smart as well as impressive things in reply to his master—things which had the desired though unexpected effect; for the conversation resulted in the voluntary emancipation of the slave on the part of the master.

In the same book, I met with one of Sheridan's mighty speeches on and in behalf of Catholic emancipation. These were choice documents to me. I read them over and over again with unabated interest. They gave tongue to interesting thoughts of my own soul, which had frequently flashed through my mind, and died away for want of utterance. The moral which I gained from the dialogue was the power of truth over the conscience of even a slaveholder. What I got from Sheridan was a bold denunciation of slavery, and a powerful vindication of human rights. The reading of these documents enabled me to utter my thoughts, and to meet the arguments brought forward to sustain slavery; but while they relieved me of one difficulty, they brought on another even more painful than the one of which I was relieved. The more I read, the more I was led to abhor and detest my enslavers. I could regard them in no other light than a band of successful robbers, who had left their homes, and gone to Africa, and stolen us from our homes, and in a strange land reduced us to slavery. I loathed them as being the meanest as well as the most wicked of men. As I read and contemplated the subject, behold! that very discontentment which Master Hugh had predicted would follow my learning to read had already come, to torment and sting my soul to unutterable anguish. As I writhed under it, I would at times feel that learning to read had been a curse rather than a blessing. It had given me a view of my wretched condition, without the remedy. It opened my eyes to the horrible pit, but to no ladder upon which to get out. In moments of agony, I envied my fellow-slaves for their stupidity. I have often wished myself a beast. I preferred the condition of the meanest reptile to my own. Any thing, no matter what, to get rid of thinking! It was this everlasting thinking of my condition that tormented me. There was no getting rid of it. It was pressed upon me by every object within sight or hearing, animate or inanimate. The silver trump of freedom had roused my soul to eternal wakefulness. Freedom now appeared, to disappear no more forever. It was heard in every sound, and seen in every thing. It was ever present to torment me with a sense of my wretched condition. I saw nothing without seeing it, I heard nothing without hearing it, and felt nothing without feeling it. It looked from every star, it smiled in every calm, breathed in every wind, and moved in every storm.

I often found myself regretting my own existence, and wishing myself dead; and but for the hope of being free, I have no doubt but that I should have killed myself, or done something for which I should have been killed. While in this state of mind, I was eager to hear any one speak of slavery. I was a ready listener. Every little while, I could hear something about the abolitionists. It was some time before I found what the word meant. It was always used in such connections as to make it an interesting word to me. If a slave ran away and succeeded in getting clear, or if a slave killed his master, set fire to a barn, or did any thing very wrong in the mind of a slaveholder, it was spoken of as the fruit of *abolition.* Hearing the word in this connection very often, I set about learning what it meant. The dictionary afforded me little or no help. I found it was "the act of abolishing," but then I did not know what was to be abolished. Here I was perplexed. I did not dare to ask any one about its meaning, for I was satisfied that it was something they wanted me to know very little about. After a patient waiting, I got one of our city papers, containing an account of the number of petitions from the north, praying for the abolition of slavery in the District of Columbia, and of the slave trade between the States. From this time I understood the words *abolition* and *abolitionist,* and always drew near when that word was spoken, expecting to hear something of importance to myself and fellow-slaves. The light broke in upon me by degrees. I went one day down on the wharf of Mr. Waters; and seeing two Irishmen unloading a scow of stone, I went, unasked, and helped them. When we had finished, one of them came to me and asked me if I were a slave. I told him I was. He asked, "Are ye a slave for life?" I told him that I was. The good Irishman seemed to be deeply affected by the statement. He said to the other that it was a pity so fine a little fellow as myself should be a slave for life. He said it was a shame to hold me. They both advised me to run away to the north; that I should find friends there, and that I should be free. I pretended not to be interested in what they said, and treated them as if I did not understand them; for I feared they might be treacherous. White men have been known to encourage slaves to escape, and then, to get the reward, catch them and return them to their masters. I was afraid that these seemingly good men might use me so; but I nevertheless remembered their advice, and from that time I resolved to run away. I looked forward to a time at which it would be safe for me to escape. I was too young to think of doing so immediately; besides, I wished to learn how to write, as I might have occasion to write my own pass. I consoled myself with the hope that I should one day find a good chance. Meanwhile, I would learn to write.

The idea as to how I might learn to write was suggested to me by being in Durgin and Bailey's ship-yard, and frequently seeing the ship carpenters, after hewing, and getting a piece of timber ready for use, write on the timber the name of that part of the ship for which it was intended. When a piece of timber was intended for the larboard side, it would be marked thus—"L." When a piece was for the starboard side, it would be marked thus—"S." A piece for the larboard side forward, would be marked thus—"L. F." When a piece was for starboard side forward, it would be marked thus—"S. F." For larboard aft, it would be marked thus—"L. A." For starboard aft, it would be marked thus—"S. A." I soon learned the names of these letters, and for what they were intended when placed upon a piece of timber in the shipyard. I immediately commenced copying them, and in a short time was able to make the four letters named. After that, when I met with any boy who I knew could write, I would tell him I could write as well as he. The next word would be, "I don't believe you. Let me see you try it." I would then make the letters which I had been so fortunate as to learn, and ask him to beat that. In this way I got a good many lessons in writing, which it is quite possible I should never have gotten in any other way. During this time, my copy-book was the board fence, brick wall, and pavement; my pen and ink was a lump of chalk. With these, I learned mainly how to write. I then commenced and continued copying the Italics in Webster's Spelling Book, until I could make them all without looking on the book. By this time, my little Master Thomas had gone to school, and learned how to write, and had written over a number of copy-books. These had been brought home, and shown to some of our near neighbors, and then laid aside. My mistress used to go to class meeting at the Wilk Street meetinghouse every Monday afternoon, and leave me to take care of the house. When left thus, I used to spend the time in writing in the spaces left in Master Thomas's copy-book, copying what he had written. I continued to do this until I could write a hand very similar to that of Master Thomas. Thus, after a long, tedious effort for years, I finally succeeded in learning how to write.

Questions on Meaning

1. Douglass stated that by teaching him the alphabet, his mistress had "given me the *inch,* and no precaution could prevent me from taking the *ell.* " What did he mean by that statement? If you are not certain, look up the English/European definition of the word "ell." What expression would a writer most often use today to convey that meaning?

2. From reading *The Columbian Orator,* Douglass learned some invaluable lessons about the power of education and the ability to express oneself intelligently. What is the *moral* lesson that he attributes to this book?

3. What is the single word that gave Douglass hope, that made him believe that there was a way out of his slavery? What is the irony about learning this word that delayed his revelation?

Questions on Rhetorical Strategy and Style

1. What is the primary rhetorical strategy used in this essay? Give examples of two other rhetorical strategies also used.

2. Although Douglass is sparing with dates, this essay is vaguely chronological. Read through the essay again and see if you can determine how old he was when he began working as a servant, when he apprenticed at the boatyard, and when he "finally succeeded in learning how to write." Does Douglass's inattention to dates affect the impact of the essay?

Writing Assignments

1. As Douglass learned more about slavery, he came to despise slaveholders and what they were doing to his people. In time, he would come to realize that the discontent his knowledge gave him was why his master did not want him to become educated. This is a common theme in oppression: Keep the oppressed from gaining a foothold, be it through wisdom or material possessions. Research how white South Africa oppressed black South Africans during Apartheid. What parallels can you draw between oppression in South Africa and the oppression experienced by Douglass?

2. As Douglass became more literate and more aware of his plight as a slave, he sometimes felt that "learning to read had been a curse

rather than a blessing." Write an essay about something you have learned that you later wished you did not know. Did your enlightenment eventually enrich your life, or has it continued to torment you? Has it made you a less curious person? What lesson did you learn from this experience?

3. In the second paragraph, Douglass explains how his mistress "did not perceive" how to act as a slaveowner and thus acted contrary to her position by treating Douglass with kindness. Later, in the fourth paragraph, he describes how other boys who had befriended him might be embarrassed if identified. Think of a time when you have crossed an invisible barrier of class, race, education, or wealth to treat someone with equality. Perhaps you had a friend in high school who your parents did not feel was "your kind," or maybe you have become friends with someone in college whom other college acquaintances look down upon. Write an essay describing the reactions of others to your relationship with this person and how his or her reactions, in turn, have affected this relationship. Did the barrier damage your relationship with this person or strengthen your resolve?

The Act of Writing: One Man's Method

William Zinsser

William Zinsser (1922–) was born in New York City. A graduate of Princeton University (1944), Zinsser has worked as a feature and editorial writer, drama editor, and film critic for the New York Herald Tribune; *a columnist for* Life, Look, *and the* New York Times; *an editor for the Book-of-the-Month Club; and an English instructor at Yale University. Zinsser's books include* Pop Goes America *(1963),* On Writing Well: An Informal Guide to Writing Nonfiction *(1976),* Writing With a Word Processor *(1983),* Writing to Learn *(1988),* Willie and Dwike *(1984), and* Spring Training *(1989). In the following excerpt from* Writing With a Word Processor, *Zinsser explains why a word processor helps him do what he already does well even better: write clearly.*

1   Writing is a deeply personal process, full of mystery and surprise. No two people go about it in exactly the same way. We all have little devices to get us started, or to keep us going, or to remind us of what we think we want to say, and what works for one person may not work for anyone else. The main thing is to get something written—to get the words out of our heads. There is no "right" method. Any method that will do the job is the right method for you.

It helps to remember that writing is hard. Most nonwriters don't know this; they think that writing is a natural function, like breathing, that ought to come easy, and they're puzzled when it doesn't. If you find that writing is hard, it's because it is hard. It's one of the hardest things that people do. Among other reasons, it's hard because it requires thinking. You won't write clearly unless you keep forcing yourself to think clearly. There's no escaping the question that has to be constantly asked: What do I want to say next?

So painful is this task that writers go to remarkable lengths to postpone their daily labor. They sharpen their pencils and change their typewriter ribbon and go out to the store to buy more paper. Now these sacred rituals, as [the computer manuals] would say, have been obsoleted.

When I began writing this book on my word processor I didn't have any idea what would happen. Would I be able to write anything at all? Would it be any good? I was bringing to the machine what I assumed were wholly different ways of thinking about writing. The units massed in front of me looked cold and sterile. Their steady hum reminded me that they were waiting. They seemed to be waiting for information, not for writing. Maybe what I wrote would also be cold and sterile.

5   I was particularly worried about the absence of paper. I knew that I would only be able to see as many lines as the screen would hold—twenty lines. How could I review what I had already written? How could I get a sense of continuity and flow? With paper it was always possible to flick through the preceding pages to see where I was coming from—and where I ought to be going. Without paper I would have no such periodic fix. Would this be a major hardship?

The only way to find out was to find out. I took a last look at my unsharpened pencils and went to work.

My particular hang-up as a writer is that I have to get every paragraph as nearly right as possible before I go on to the next paragraph. I'm somewhat like a bricklayer: I build very slowly, not adding a new row until I feel that the foundation is solid enough to hold up the house. I'm the exact opposite of the writer who dashes off his entire first draft, not caring how sloppy it looks or how badly it's written. His only objective at this early stage is to let his creative motor run the full course at full speed; repairs can always be made later. I envy this writer and would like to have his metabolism. But I'm stuck with the one I've got.

I also care how my writing looks while I'm writing it. The visual arrangement is important to me: the shape of the words, of the sentences, of the paragraphs, of the page. I don't like sentences that are dense with long words, or paragraphs that never end. As I write I want to see the design that my piece will have when the reader sees it in type, and I want that design to have a rhythm and a pace that will invite the reader to keep reading. O.K., so I'm a nut. But I'm not alone; the visual component is important to a large number of people who write.

One hang-up we visual people share is that our copy must be neat. My lifelong writing method, for instance, has gone like this. I put a piece of paper in the typewriter and write the first paragraph. Then I take the paper out and edit what I've written. I mark it up horribly, crossing words out and scribbling new ones in the space between the lines. By this time the paragraph has lost its nature and shape for me as a piece of writing. It's a mishmash of typing and handwriting and arrows and balloons and other directional symbols. So I type a clean copy, incorporating the changes, and then I take that piece of paper out of the typewriter and edit it. It's better, but not much better. I go over it with my pencil again, making more changes, which again make it too messy for me to read critically, so I go back to the typewriter for round three. And round four. Not until I'm reasonably satisfied do I proceed to the next paragraph.

10   This can get pretty tedious, and I have often thought that there   10
must be a better way. Now there is. The word processor is God's gift, or at least science's gift, to the tinkerers and the refiners and the neatness freaks. For me it was obviously the perfect new toy. I began playing on page 1—editing, cutting and revising—and have been on a rewriting high ever since. The burden of the years has been lifted.

Mostly I've been cutting. I would guess that I've cut at least as many words out of this book as the number that remain. Probably half of those words were eliminated because I saw that they were unnecessary— the sentence worked fine without them. This is where the word processor can improve your writing to an extent that you will hardly believe. Learn to recognize what is clutter and to use the DELETE key to prune it out.

How will you know clutter when you see it? Here's a device I used when I was teaching writing at Yale that my students found helpful; it may be a help here. I would put brackets around every component in a student's paper that I didn't think was doing some kind of work. Often it was only one word—for example, the useless preposition that gets appended to so many verbs (order up, free up), or the adverb whose meaning is already in the verb (blare loudly, clench tightly), or the adjective that tells us what we already know (smooth marble, green grass). The brackets might surround the little qualifiers that dilute a writer's authority (a bit, sort of, in a sense), or the countless phrases in which the writer explains what he is about to explain (it might be pointed out, I'm tempted to say). Often my brackets would surround an entire sentence—the sentence that essentially repeats what the previous sentence has said, or tells the reader something that is implicit, or adds a detail that is irrelevant. Most people's writing is littered with phrases that do no new work whatever. Most first drafts, in fact, can be cut by fifty percent without losing anything organic. (Try it; it's a good exercise.)

By bracketing these extra words, instead of crossing them out, I was saying to the student: "I may be wrong, but I think this can go and the meaning of the sentence won't be affected in any way. But *you* decide: read the sentence without the bracketed material and see if it works." In the first half of the term, the students' papers were festooned with my brackets. Whole paragraphs got bracketed. But gradually the students learned to put mental brackets around their many different kinds of clutter, and by the end of the term I was returning papers to them that had hardly any brackets, or none. It was always a satisfying moment. Today many of those students are professional writers. "I still see your brackets," they tell me. "They're following me through life."

You can develop the same eye. Writing is clear and strong to the extent that it has no superfluous parts. (So is art and music and dance and typography and design.) You will really enjoy writing on a word processor when you see your sentences growing in strength, literally before your eyes, as you get rid of the fat. Be thankful for everything that you can throw away.

15   I was struck by how many phrases and sentences I wrote in this 15
book that I later found I didn't need. Many of them hammered home a point that didn't need hammering because it had already been made. This kind of overwriting happens in almost everybody's first draft, and it's perfectly natural—the act of putting down our thoughts makes us garrulous. Luckily, the act of editing follows the act of writing, and this is where the word processor will bail you out. It intercedes at the point where the game can be won or lost. With its help I cut hundreds of unnecessary words and didn't replace them.

Hundreds of others were discarded because I later thought of a better word—one that caught more precisely or more vividly what I was trying to express. Here, again, a word processor encourages you to play. The English language is rich in words that convey an exact shade of meaning. Don't get stuck with a word that's merely good if you can find one that takes the reader by surprise with its color or aptness or quirkiness. Root around in your dictionary of synonyms and find words that are fresh. Throw them up on the screen and see how they look.

Also learn to play with whole sentences. If a sentence strikes you as awkward or ponderous, move your cursor to the space after the period and write a new sentence that you think is better. Maybe you can make it shorter. Or clearer. Maybe you can make it livelier by turning it into a question or otherwise altering its rhythm. Change the passive verbs into active verbs. (Passive verbs are the death of clarity and vigor.) Try writing two or three new versions of the awkward sentence and then compare them, or write a fourth version that combines the best elements of all three. Sentences come in an infinite variety of shapes and sizes. Find one that pleases you. If it's clear, and if it pleases you and expresses who you are, trust it to please other people. Then delete all the versions that aren't as good. Your shiny new sentence will jump into position and the rest of the paragraph will rearrange itself as quickly and neatly as if you had never pulled it apart.

Another goal that the word processor will help you to achieve is unity. No matter how carefully you write each sentence as you assemble a piece of writing, the final product is bound to have some ragged edges. Is the tone consistent throughout? And the point of view? And the pronoun? And the tense? How about the transitions? Do they pull the reader along, or is the piece jerky and disjointed? A good piece of writing should be harmonious from beginning to end in the voice of the writer and the flow of its logic. But the harmony usually requires some last-minute patching.

I've been writing this book by the bricklayer method, slowly and carefully. That's all very well as far as it goes—at the end of every chapter the individual bricks may look fine. But what about the wall? The only way to check your piece for unity is to go over it one more time from start to finish, preferably reading it aloud. See if you have executed all the decisions that you made before you started writing. . . .

[20] I mention this [in part] because word processors are going to be [20] widely used by people who need to impart technical information: matters of operating procedure in business and banking, science and

technology, medicine and health, education and government and dozens of other specialized fields. The information will only be helpful if readers can grasp it quickly and easily. If it's muddy they will get discouraged or angry, or both, and will stop reading.

You can avoid this dreaded fate for your message, whatever it is, by making sure that every sentence is a logical sequel to the one that preceded it. One way to approach this goal is to keep your sentences short. A major reason why technical prose becomes so tangled is that the writer tries to make one sentence do too many jobs. It's a natural hazard of the first draft. But the solution is simple: see that every sentence contains only one thought. The reader can accommodate only one idea at a time. Help him by giving him only one idea at a time. Let him understand A before you proceed to B.

In writing this book I was eager to explain the procedures that I had learned about how word processors work, and I would frequently lump several points together in one sentence. Later, editing what I had written, I asked myself if the procedure would be clear to someone who was puzzling through it for the first time—someone who hadn't struggled to figure the procedure out. Often I felt that it wouldn't be clear. I was giving the reader too much. He was being asked to picture himself taking various steps that were single and sequential, and that's how he deserved to get them.

I therefore divided all troublesome long sentences into two short sentences, or even three. It always gave me great pleasure. Not only is it the fastest way for a writer to get out of a quagmire that there seems to be no getting out of; I also like short sentences for their own sake. There's almost no more beautiful sight than a simple declarative sentence. This book is full of simple declarative sentences that have no punctuation and that carry one simple thought. Without a word processor I wouldn't have chopped as many of them down to their proper size, or done it with so little effort. This is one of the main clarifying jobs that your machine can help you to perform, especially if your writing requires you to guide the reader into territory that is new and bewildering.

Not all my experiences, of course, were rosy. The machine had disadvantages as well as blessings. Often, for instance, I missed not being able to see more than twenty lines at a time—to review what I had written earlier. If I wanted to see more lines I had to "scroll" them back into view.

25   But even this wasn't as painful as I had thought it would be. I   25
found that I could hold in my head the gist of what I had written and
didn't need to keep looking at it. Was this need, in fact, still another
writer's hang-up that I could shed? To some extent it was. I discovered,
as I had at so many other points in this journey, that various crutches
I had always assumed I needed were really not necessary. I made a decision to just throw them away and found that I could still function.
The only real hardship occurred when a paragraph broke at the bottom of the screen. This meant that the first lines of the paragraph were
on one page and the rest were on the next page, and I had to keep
flicking the two pages back and forth to read what I was writing. But
again, it wasn't fatal. I learned to live with it and soon took it for
granted as an occupational hazard.

The story that I've told in this chapter is personal and idiosyn-
cratic: how the word processor helped one writer to write one book.
In many of its details it's everybody's story. All writers have different
methods and psychological needs. . . .

Questions on Meaning

1. "The main thing," Zinsser writes, "is to get something written." What does Zinsser believe is the "right" method to accomplish this?
2. Why does Zinsser (in 1983) consider the "word processor" to be "God's gift"? How relevant are his comments to students today? Find some of Zinsser's descriptions of computers that reveal that he is writing about "word processors" during their early years on the market.
3. Why does Zinsser advise writers about deleting words from drafts? Why does he feel the computer facilitates this exercise?

Questions on Rhetorical Strategy and Style

1. Analyze Zinsser's writing process. What are the steps he takes as he composes? What is the rigidity of his writing process that he wishes he were not constrained by? How does the visual aspect of what he is writing affect the way he writes?
2. Find where Zinsser uses examples to illustrate the use of brackets while editing, a writing tip he taught his students at Yale. Reread something you have written and bracket superfluous words. How would the use of brackets help you tighten your writing?
3. Zinsser uses a cause-and-effect writing strategy to tout the impact of the "word processor" on refining word choice, fine-tuning sentences, and unifying writing. What are some other advantages of a computer over longhand and/or using a typewriter?

Writing Assignments

1. Describe your writing process. How do you write your first draft? When do you format your material? Do you use desktop publishing to improve the look of your documents? *Do you backup your work?*
2. Most people have pet distractions they employ to keep from facing a blank screen (or blank sheet of paper)—straightening their desk, making coffee, checking their e-mail, or cleaning their fingernails with a paper clip, for example. Describe the little habits or rituals that you use to delay the inevitable. How do you finally force yourself to get to work? Explain why you agree or disagree with Zinsser that writing is hard.

3. Zinsser, who grew up writing longhand and with a typewriter, was older than 60 before he began using a "word processor." Write an essay *longhand,* comparing and contrasting what it is like to write by hand versus writing with a personal computer. Do your first and second drafts by hand, then input your third draft. Explain what you missed most about using a computer. Describe anything you discovered you *liked* about composing longhand. Would you voluntarily write a first draft longhand for your next writing assignment?

How to Say Nothing in 500 Words

Paul Roberts

Paul Roberts (1917–1967) wrote clear and helpful writing textbooks, among them English Syntax *(1954),* Patterns of English *(1956),* Understanding English *(1958) and* English Sentences *(1962). He approached writing with the scientific discipline of a linguist. In the following excerpt from* Understanding English, *note his tendency to categorize and classify, to write descriptions and rules. In this way, the "art" of writing is transformed to the science (Latin for knowledge) of composition.*

Nothing About Something

1   It's Friday afternoon, and you have almost survived another week of classes. You are just looking forward dreamily to the weekend when the English instructor says: "For Monday you will turn in a five-hundred-word composition on college football."

Well, that puts a good big hole in the weekend. You don't have any strong views on college football one way or the other. You get rather excited during the season and go to all the home games and find it rather more fun than not. On the other hand, the class has been reading Robert Hutchins in the anthology and perhaps Shaw's "Eighty-Yard Run," and from the class discussion you have got the idea that the instructor thinks college football is for the birds. You are no fool, you. You can figure out what side to take.

After dinner you get out the portable typewriter that you got for high school graduation. You might as well get it over with and enjoy Saturday and Sunday. Five hundred words is about two double-spaced pages with normal margins. You put in a sheet of paper, think up a title, and you're off:

Why College Football Should Be Abolished

College football should be abolished because it's bad for the school and also bad for the players. The players are so busy practicing that they don't have any time for their studies.

5   This, you feel, is a mighty good start. The only trouble is that it's only thirty-two words. You still have four hundred and sixty-eight to go, and you've pretty well exhausted the subject. It comes to you that you do your best thinking in the morning, so you put away the typewriter and go to the movies. But the next morning you have to do your washing and some math problems, and in the afternoon you go to the game. The English instructor turns up too, and you wonder if you've taken the right side after all. Saturday night you have a date, and Sunday morning you have to go to church. (You shouldn't let English assignments interfere with your religion.) What with one thing and another, it's ten o'clock Sunday night before you get out the typewriter again. You make a pot of coffee and start to fill out your views on college football. Put a little meat on the bones.

Why College Football Should Be Abolished

In my opinion, it seems to me that college football should be abolished. The reason why I think this to be true is because I feel that football is bad for the colleges in nearly every respect. As Robert Hutchins says in his article in our anthology in which he discusses college football, it would be better if the colleges had race horses and had races with one another, because then the horses would not have to attend classes. I firmly agree with Mr. Hutchins on this point, and I am sure that many other students would agree too.

One reason why it seems to me that college football is bad is that it has become too commercial. In the olden times when people played football just for the fun of it, maybe college football was all right, but they do not play football just for the fun of it now as they used to in the old days. Nowadays college football is what you might call a big business. Maybe this is not true at all schools, and I don't think it is especially true here at State, but certainly this is the case at most colleges and universities in America nowadays, as Mr. Hutchins points out in his very interesting article. Actually the coaches and alumni go around to the high schools and offer the high school stars large salaries to come to their colleges and play football for them. There was one case where a high school star was offered a convertible if he would play football for a certain college.

Another reason for abolishing college football is that it is bad for the players. They do not have time to get a college education, because they are so busy playing football. A football player has to practice every afternoon from three to six, and then he is so tired that he can't concentrate on his studies. He just feels like dropping off to sleep after dinner, and then the next day he goes to his classes without having studied and maybe he fails the test.

(Good ripe stuff so far, but you're still a hundred and fifty-one words from home. One more push.)

Also I think college football is bad for the colleges and the universities because not very many students get to participate in it. Out of a college of ten thousand students only seventy-five or a hundred play football, if that many. Football is what you might call a spectator sport. That means that most people go to watch it but do not play it themselves.

(Four hundred and fifteen. Well, you still have the conclusion, and when you retype it, you can make the margins a little wider.)

These are the reasons why I agree with Mr. Hutchins that college football should be abolished in American colleges and universities.

On Monday you turn it in, moderately hopeful, and on Friday it comes back marked "weak in content" and sporting a big "D."

This essay is exaggerated a little, not much. The English instructor will recognize it as reasonably typical of what an assignment on college football will bring in. He knows that nearly half of the class will contrive in five hundred words to say that college football is too commercial and bad for the players. Most of the other half will inform him that college football builds character and prepares one for life and brings prestige to the school. As he reads paper after paper all saying the same thing in almost the same words, all bloodless, five hundred words dripping out of nothing, he wonders how he allowed himself to get trapped into teaching English when he might have had a happy and interesting life as an electrician or a confidence man.

Well, you may ask, what can you do about it? The subject is one on which you have few convictions and little information. Can you be expected to make a dull subject interesting? As a matter of fact, this is precisely what you are expected to do. This is the writer's essential task. All subjects, except sex, are dull until somebody makes them interesting. The writer's job is to find the argument, the approach, the angle, the wording that will take the reader with him. This is seldom easy, and it is particularly hard in subjects that have been much discussed: College Football, Fraternities, Popular Music, Is Chivalry Dead?, and the like. You will feel that there is nothing you can do with such subjects except repeat the old bromides. But there are some things you can do which will make your papers, if not throbbingly alive, at least less insufferably tedious than they might otherwise be.

Avoid the Obvious Content

Say the assignment is college football. Say that you've decided to be against it. Begin by putting down the arguments that come to your mind: it is too commercial, it takes the students' minds off their studies, it is hard on the players, it makes the university a kind of circus instead of an intellectual center, for most schools it is financially ruinous. Can you think of any more arguments just off hand! All right.

Now when you write your paper, *make sure that you don't use any of the material on this list.* If these are the points that leap to your mind, they will leap to everyone else's too, and whether you get a "C" or a "D" may depend on whether the instructor reads your paper early when he is fresh and tolerant or late, when the sentence "In my opinion, college football has become too commercial," inexorably repeated, has brought him to the brink of lunacy.

15   Be against college football for some reason or reasons of your own.   15
If they are keen and perceptive ones, that's splendid. But even if they are trivial or foolish or indefensible, you are still ahead so long as they are not everybody else's reasons too. Be against it because the colleges don't spend enough money on it to make it worth while, because it is bad for the characters of the spectators, because the players are forced to attend classes, because the football stars hog all the beautiful women, because it competes with baseball and is therefore un-American and possibly Communist inspired. There are lots of more or less unused reasons for being against college football.

Sometimes it is a good idea to sum up and dispose of the trite and conventional points before going on to your own. This has the advantage of indicating to the reader that you are going to be neither trite nor conventional. Something like this:

> We are often told that college football should be abolished because it has become too commercial or because it is bad for the players. These arguments are no doubt very cogent, but they don't really go to the heart of the matter. Then you go to the heart of the matter.

Take the Less Usual Side

One rather simple way of getting interest into your paper is to take the side of the argument that most of the citizens will want to avoid. If the assignment is an essay on dogs, you can, if you choose, explain that dogs are faithful and lovable companions, intelligent, useful as guardians of the house and protectors of children, indispensable in police work—in short, when all is said and done, man's best friends. Or you can suggest that those big brown eyes conceal, more often than not, a vacuity of mind and an inconstancy of purpose; that the dogs you have known most intimately have been mangy, ill-tempered brutes, incapable of instruction; and that only your nobility of mind and fear of arrest prevent you from kicking the flea-ridden animals when you pass them on the street.

Naturally, personal convictions will sometimes dictate your approach. If the assigned subject is "Is Methodism Rewarding to the individual?" and you are a pious Methodist, you have really no choice. But few assigned subjects, if any, will fall in this category. Most of them will lie in broad areas of discussion with much to be said on both sides. They are intellectual exercises and it is legitimate to argue now one way and now another, as debaters do in similar circumstances. Always take the side that looks to you hardest, least defensible. It will almost always turn out to be easier to write interestingly on that side.

20 This general advice applies where you have a choice of subjects. If 20 you are to choose among "The Value of Fraternities" and "My Favorite High School Teacher" and "What I Think About Beetles," by all means plump for the beetles. By the time the instructor gets to your paper, he will be up to his ears in tedious tales about the French teacher at Bloombury High and assertions about how fraternities build character and prepare one for life. Your views on beetles, whatever they are, are bound to be a refreshing change.

Don't worry too much about figuring out what the instructor thinks about the subject so that you can cuddle up with him. Chances are his views are no stronger than yours. If he does have convictions and you oppose them, his problem is to keep from grading you higher than you deserve in order to show he is not biased. This doesn't mean that you should always cantankerously dissent from what the instructor says; that gets tiresome too. And if the subject assigned is "My Pet Peeve," do not begin, "My pet peeve is the English instructor who assigns papers on 'my pet peeve.'" This was still funny during the War of 1812, but it has sort of lost its edge since then. It is in general good manners to avoid personalities.

Slip out of Abstraction

If you will study the essay on college football . . . you will perceive that one reason for its appalling dullness is that it never gets down to particulars. It is just a series of not very glittering generalities: "football is bad for the colleges," "it has become too commercial," "football is a big business," "it is bad for the players," and so on. Such round phrases thudding against the reader's brain are unlikely to convince him, though they may well render him unconscious.

If you want the reader to believe that college football is bad for the players, you have to do more than say so. You have to display the evil. Take your roommate, Alfred Simkins, the second-string center. Picture poor old Alfy coming home from football practice every evening, bruised and aching, agonizingly tired, scarcely able to shovel the mashed potatoes into his mouth. Let us see him staggering up to the room, getting out his econ textbook, peering desperately at it with his good eye, falling asleep and failing the test in the morning. Let us share his unbearable tension as Saturday draws near. Will he fail, be demoted, lose his monthly allowance, be forced to return to the coal mines? And if he succeeds, what will be his reward? Perhaps a slight ripple of applause when the third-string center replaces him, a moment of elation in the locker room if the team wins, of despair if it loses. What will he look back on when he graduates from college? Toil and torn ligaments. And what will be his future? He is not good enough for pro football, and he is too obscure and weak in econ to succeed in stocks and bonds. College football is tearing the heart from Alfred Simkins and, when it finishes with him, will callously toss aside the shattered hulk.

This is no doubt a weak enough argument for the abolition of college football, but it is a sight better than saying, in three or four variations, that college football (in your opinion) is bad for the players.

25 Look at the work of any professional writer and notice how consistently he is moving from the generality, the abstract statement, to the concrete example, the facts and figures, the illustration. If he is writing on juvenile delinquency, he does not just tell you that juveniles are (it seems to him) delinquent and that (in his opinion) something should be done about it. He shows you juveniles being delinquent, tearing up movie theatres in Buffalo, stabbing high school principals in Dallas, smoking marijuana in Palo Alto. And more than likely he is moving toward some specific remedy, not just a general wringing of the hands.

It is no doubt possible to be *too* concrete, too illustrative or anecdotal, but few inexperienced writers err this way. For most the soundest advice is to be seeking always for the picture, to be always turning general remarks into seeable examples. Don't say, "Sororities teach girls the social graces." Say "Sorority life teaches a girl how to carry on a conversation while pouring tea, without sloshing the tea into the saucer." Don't say, "I like certain kinds of popular music very much."

Say, "Whenever I hear Gerber Spinklittle play 'Mississippi Man' on the trombone, my socks creep up my ankles."

Get Rid of Obvious Padding

The student toiling away at his weekly English theme is too often tormented by a figure: five hundred words. How, he asks himself, is he to achieve this staggering total? Obviously by never using one word when he can somehow work in ten.

He is therefore seldom content with a plain statement like "Fast driving is dangerous." This has only four words in it. He takes thought, and the sentence becomes:

> In my opinion, fast driving is dangerous.

30 Better, but he can do better still: 30

> In my opinion, fast driving would seem to be rather dangerous.

If he is really adept, it may come out:
> In my humble opinion, though I do not claim to be an expert on this complicated subject, fast driving, in most circumstances, would seem to be rather dangerous in many respects, or at least so it would seem to me.

Thus four words have been turned into forty, and not an iota of content has been added.

35 Now this is a way to go about reaching five hundred words, and 35 if you are content with a "D" grade, it is as good a way as any. But if you aim higher, you must work differently. Instead of stuffing your sentences with straw, you must try steadily to get rid of the padding, to make your sentences lean and tough. If you are really working at it, your first draft will greatly exceed the required total, and then you will work it down, thus:

> It is thought in some quarters that fraternities do not contribute as much as might be expected to campus life.

Some people think that fraternities contribute little to campus life.

The average doctor who practices in small towns or in the country must toil night and day to heal the sick.
Most country doctors work long hours.

40   When I was a little girl, I suffered from shyness and embarrassment in the presence of others.
I was a shy little girl.

It is absolutely necessary for the person employed as a marine fireman to give the matter of steam pressure his undivided attention at all times.
The fireman has to keep his eye on the steam gauge.

You may ask how you can arrive at five hundred words at this rate. Simply. You dig up more real content. Instead of taking a couple of obvious points off the surface of the topic and then circling warily around them for six paragraphs, you work in and explore, figure out the details. You illustrate. You say that fast driving is dangerous, and then you prove it. How long does it take to stop a car at forty and at eighty? How far can you see at night? What happens when a tire blows?! What happens in a head-on collision at fifty miles an hour! Pretty soon your paper will be full of broken glass and blood and headless torsos, and reaching five hundred words will not really be a problem.

Call a Fool a Fool

45   Some of the padding in freshman themes is to be blamed not on anxiety about the word minimum but on excessive timidity. The student writes, "In my opinion, the principal of my high school acted in ways that I believe every unbiased person would have to call foolish." This isn't exactly what he means. What he means is, "My high school principal was a fool." If he was a fool, call him a fool. Hedging the thing about with "in-my-opinion's" and "it-seems-to-me's" and "as-I-see-it's" and "at-least-from-my-point-of-view's" gains you nothing. Delete these phrases whenever they creep into your paper.

The student's tendency to hedge stems from a modesty that in other circumstances would be commendable. He is, he realizes, young and inexperienced, and he half suspects that he is dopey and fuzzy-minded beyond the average. Probably only too true. But it doesn't help to announce your incompetence six times in every paragraph. Decide what you want to say and say it as vigorously as possible, without apology and in plain words.

Linguistic diffidence can take various forms. One is what we call *euphemism*. This is the tendency to call a spade "a certain garden implement" or women's underwear "unmentionables." It is stronger in some eras than others and in some people than others but it always operates more or less in subjects that are touchy or taboo: death, sex, madness, and so on. Thus we shrink from saying "He died last night" but say instead "passed away," "left us," "joined his Maker," "went to his reward." Or we try to take off the tension with a lighter cliché: "kicked the bucket," "cashed in his chips," "handed in his dinner pail." We have found all sorts of ways to avoid saying *mad*: "mentally ill," "touched," "not quite right upstairs," "feeble-minded," "innocent," "simple," "off his trolley," "not in his right mind. "Even such a now plain word as *insane* began as a euphemism with the meaning "not healthy."

Modern science, particularly psychology, contributes many polysyllables in which we can wrap our thoughts and blunt their force. To many writers there is no such thing as a bad schoolboy. Schoolboys are maladjusted or unoriented or misunderstood or in need of guidance or lacking in continued success toward satisfactory integration of the personality as a social unit, but they are never bad. Psychology no doubt makes us better men or women, more sympathetic and tolerant, but it doesn't make writing any easier. Had Shakespeare been confronted with psychology, "To be or not to be" might have come out, "To continue as a social unit or not to do so. That is the personality problem. Whether 'tis a better sign of integration at the conscious level to display a psychic tolerance toward the maladjustments and repressions induced by one's lack of orientation in one's environment or—" But Hamlet would never have finished the soliloquy.

Writing in the modern world, you cannot altogether avoid modern jargon. Nor, in an effort to get away from euphemism, should you salt your paper with four-letter words. But you can do much if you will mount guard against those roundabout phrases, those echoing polysyllables that tend to slip into your writing to rob it of its crispness and force.

Beware of the Pat Expression

50   Other things being equal, avoid phrases like "other things being 50 equal." Those sentences that come to you whole, or in two or three doughy lumps, are sure to be bad sentences. They are no creation of yours but pieces of common thought floating in the community soup.

Pat expressions are hard, often impossible, to avoid, because they come too easily to be noticed and seem too necessary to be dispensed with. No writer avoids them altogether, but good writers avoid them more often than poor writers.

By "pat expressions" we mean such tags as "to all practical intents and purposes," "the pure and simple truth," "from where I sit," "the time of his life," "to the ends of the earth," "in the twinkling of an eye," "as sure as you're born," "over my dead body," "under cover of darkness," "took the easy way out," "when all is said and done," "told him time and time again," "parted the best of friends," "stand up and be counted," "gave him the best years of her life," "worked her fingers to the bone." Like other clichés, these expressions were once forceful. Now we should use them only when we cant possibly think of anything else.

Some pat expressions stand like a wall between the writer and thought. Such a one is "the American way of life." Many student writers feel that when they have said that something accords with the American way of life or does not they have exhausted the subject. Actually, they have stopped at the highest level of abstraction. The American way of life is the complicated set of bonds between a hundred and eighty million ways. All of us know this when we think about it, but the tag phrase too often keeps us from thinking about it.

So with many another phrase dear to the politician: "this great land of ours," "the man in the street," "our national heritage." These may prove our patriotism or give a clue to our political beliefs, but otherwise they add nothing to the paper except words.

Colorful Words

The writer builds with words, and no builder uses a raw material more slippery and elusive and treacherous. A writer's work is a constant struggle to get the right word in the right place, to find that particular word that will convey his meaning exactly, that will persuade the reader or soothe him or startle or amuse him. He never succeeds altogether—sometimes he feels that he scarcely succeeds at all—but such successes as he has are what make the thing worth doing.

There is no book of rules for this game. One progresses through everlasting experiment on the basis of ever-widening experience. There are few useful generalizations that one can make about words as words, but there are perhaps a few.

Some words are what we call "colorful." By this we mean that they are calculated to produce a picture or induce an emotion. They are dressy instead of plain, specific instead of general, loud instead of soft. Thus, in place of "Her heart beat," we may write "Her heart *pounded, throbbed, fluttered, danced.*" Instead of "He sat in his chair," we may say, "He *lounged, sprawled, coiled.*" Instead of "It was hot," we may say, "It was *blistering, sultry, muggy, suffocating, steamy, wilting.*"

However, it should not be supposed that the fancy word is always better. Often it is as well to write "Her heart beat" or "It was hot" if that is all it did or all it was. Ages differ in how they like their prose. The nineteenth century liked it rich and smoky. The twentieth has usually preferred it lean and cool. The twentieth-century writer, like all writers, is forever seeking the exact word, but he is wary of sounding feverish. He tends to pitch it low, to understate it, to throw it away. He knows that if he gets too colorful, the audience is likely to giggle.

See how this strikes you: "As the rich, golden glow of the sunset died away along the eternal western hills, Angela's limpid blue eyes looked softly and trustingly into Montague's flashing brown ones, and her heart pounded like a drum in time with the joyous song surging in her soul." Some people like that sort of thing, but most modern readers would say, "Good grief," and turn on the television.

Colored Words

Some words we would call not so much colorful as colored—that is, loaded with associations, good or bad. All words—except perhaps structure words—have associations of some sort. We have said that the meaning of a word is the sum of the contexts in which it occurs. When we hear a word, we hear with it an echo of all the situations in which we have heard it before.

In some words, these echoes are obvious and discussable. The word *mother,* for example, has, for most people, agreeable associations. When you hear *mother* you probably think of home, safety, love, food, and various other pleasant things. If one writes, "She was like a *mother* to me," he gets an effect which he would not get in "She was like an aunt to me." The advertiser makes use of the associations of *mother* by working it in when he talks about his product. The politician works it in when he talks about himself.

So also with such words as *home, liberty, fireside, contentment, patriot, tenderness, sacrifice, childlike, manly, bluff, limpid.* All of these words are loaded with favorable associations that would be rather hard to indicate in a straightforward definition. There is more than a literal difference between "They sat around the fireside" and "They sat around the stove." They might have been equally warm and happy around the stove, but *fireside* suggests leisure, grace, quiet tradition, congenial company, and *stove* does not.

Conversely, some words have bad associations. *Mother* suggests pleasant things, but *mother-in-law* does not. Many mothers-in-law are heroically lovable and some mothers drink gin all day and beat their children insensible, but these facts of life are beside the point. The thing is that *mother* sounds good and *mother-in-law* does not.

Or consider the word *intellectual.* This would seem to be a complimentary term, but in point of fact it is not, for it has picked up associations of impracticality and ineffectuality and general dopiness. So also with such words as *liberal, reactionary, Communist, socialist, capitalist, radical, schoolteacher, truck driver, undertaker, operator, salesman, huckster, speculator.* These convey meanings on the literal level, but beyond that—sometimes, in some places—they convey contempt on the part of the speaker.

65 The question of whether to use loaded words or not depends on what is being written. The scientist, the scholar, try to avoid them; for the poet, the advertising writer, the public speaker, they are standard equipment. But every writer should take care that they do not substitute for thought. If you write, "Anyone who thinks that is nothing but a Socialist (or Communist or capitalist)," you have said nothing ex-

cept that you don't like people who think that, and such remarks are effective only with the most naive readers. It is always a bad mistake to think your readers more naive than they really are.

Colorless Words

But probably most student writers come to grief not with words that are colorful or those that are colored but with those that have no color at all. A pet example is *nice*, a word we would find it hard to dispense with in casual conversation but which is no longer capable of adding much to a description. Colorless words are those of such general meaning that in a particular sentence they mean nothing. Slang adjectives, like *cool* ("That's real cool") tend to explode all over the language. They are applied to everything, lose their original force, and quickly die.

Beware also of nouns of very general meaning, like *circumstances, cases, instances, aspects, factors, relationships, attitudes, eventualities,* etc. In most circumstances you will find that those cases of writing which contain too many instances of words like these will in this and other aspects have factors leading to unsatisfactory relationships with the reader resulting in unfavorable attitudes on his part and perhaps other eventualities, like a grade of "D." Notice also what "etc." means. It means "I'd like to make this list longer, but I can't think of any more examples."

Questions on Meaning

1. Did the description of the student struggling with an English assignment remind you of yourself? In what ways? If it did not, describe the ways your writing process works with assignments like "College Football."
2. List the "rules" Roberts offers for successful college writing. Which of them do you already follow? Which have you been taught but so far not used much? Which are new to you? Which do you feel you may want to adopt?

Questions on Rhetorical Strategy and Style

1. Roberts's essay is a process analysis, like a set of directions for assembling something, complete with a troubleshooting section. The best test of a process analysis is to try to follow the directions. So try writing and revising a paragraph using the process that Roberts describes. Once you have finished, report any problems you encountered.
2. Sets of directions usually require the writer to use the second person pronoun "you." Try revising one of Roberts's paragraphs to put it in first person, "I," or third person, "one," or "he or she." Note that when Roberts uses third person, he allows the masculine pronoun, "he," to stand for both genders. That is now considered sexist usage.

Writing Assignments

1. List and explain any additional steps in writing that you find necessary to your comfort or personal creativity or focus.
2. Most writing processes are not as linear—that is not so tidy and orderly—as process analysis leads us to infer. Recall the process by which you wrote the essay you completed most recently, or the one you remember most clearly. In an essay intended to clarify your writing processes for yourself, your peers, and your teacher, describe the process of writing that essay.
3. Roberts uses a form of wry humor often associated with English teachers (e.g., "Many mothers-in-law are heroically loveable and some mothers drink gin all day and beat their children insensible, but these facts of life are beside the point. The thing is that mother sounds good and mother-in-law does not.") Find other examples of his humor to get the idea, and write a process analysis essay that uses this tone.

The Death of Reading

Mitchell Stephens

Mitchell Stephens teaches at New York University where he directed the university's selection of the "Top 100" works of journalism of the twentieth century. He has traveled widely and written about globalization for LonelyPlanet.com and frequently records commentaries for NPR. His articles have appeared in the New York Times, Washington Post, *and* Los Angeles Times. *He co-edited* Covering Catastrophe *(2002), which describes firsthand accounts by TV and radio journalists who were on the scene during the September 11 terrorist attacks. He authored* A History of News *(1996) and* Writing and Reporting News *(1993), the latter of which received the New York Times Notable Book of the Year award.*

1 What's missing from these pictures?

- Three people sit in a doctor's waiting room. One stares at the television that rests on an end table; the second fiddles with a hand-held video game; the head of the third is wrapped in earphones.
- A couple of kids, waiting for bedtime, lie on the floor of a brightly painted room, busy manipulating the controls of a video game.
- Two hundred people sit in an airplane. Some have brought their own tapes, some doze, most stare up at a small movie screen.

What is missing from these pictures, and increasingly from our lives, is the activity through which most of us learned much of what we know of the wider world. What's missing is the force that, according to a growing consensus of historians, established our patterns of thought and, in an important sense, made our civilization. What's missing is the venerable, increasingly dated activity that you—what's the matter? bored with all your CDs and videotapes?—are engaged in right now.

Ironically, but not coincidentally, reading has begun fading from our culture at the very moment that its importance to that culture is finally being established. Its decline, many theorists believe, is as profound as, say, the fall of communism, and some have taken to prophesying that the downturn in reading could result in the modern world's cultural and political decline.

"A mode of thinking is being lost," laments Neil Postman, whose book, *Amusing Ourselves to Death,* is a warning about the consequences of a falloff in reading. "We are losing a sort of psychic habit, a logic, a sense of complexity, an ability to spot contradictions and even falsity." Postman, a professor of communication arts at New York University, believes this loss is now being felt in our cultural activities and in our politics, as well as in our children's SAT scores, and that it could get worse. But of course such prophecies are delivered in print, so no one pays much heed.

5   The anecdotal evidence that reading is in decline is copious and compelling. "When I go out socially in Washington," confides Daniel Boorstin, a historian and former librarian of Congress, "I'm careful not to embarrass my dinner companions by asking what they have read lately. Instead I say, 'I suppose you don't have much time to read books nowadays.'"

That is a courtesy, alas, for which most of us would be grateful. The fact is that few of us, and few of our friends and few of our children, have the time to read as much as we would like. We're too busy working or working out or playing or—OK, let's admit it—watching TV.

Our homes barely make room for reading. Those old islands of quiet—libraries, studies, and dens—long ago were invaded by flat screens and Nintendos. Now they are called "family rooms" or, more accurately, "television rooms." And our architects seem to have given up providing us with bookshelves; instead they busy themselves designing "entertainment centers."

So we haven't quite gotten around to Stephen M. Hawking's *A Brief History of Time* yet. We're saving Amy Tan's latest novel for vacation, maybe. And that pile of unread *New Yorkers* or *Rolling Stones* or *Los Angeles Times Magazines* keeps growing, each unread issue an additional piece of anecdotal evidence.

Those whose livelihoods depend on our reading suggest, optimistically, that the widespread notion that it is in decline is an oversimplification. "I believe that people who used to read a lot of books read less now," concedes Alberto Vitale, chairman of Random House, the nation's largest publisher of trade (nontext) books. "But in my opinion, there are many *more* people reading books."

10 The optimists do have some statistics on their side. Books, the oldest form of print, seem to be doing reasonably well. Publishers, in fact, are churning out more and more of them: 133,196 new titles listed in *Books in Print* in the past year. That is about 16 times the number of titles printed 40 years ago (one of the reasons "keeping up" may seem so much harder for us than it did for our parents and grandparents). And publishers are selling more, too: about 2 billion books in 1990, an 11% increase over 1985. Reports of the death of the book seem greatly exaggerated.

Ah, but are these books actually being read? Not, in many cases, from cover-to-cover. A recent Gallup Poll found many more people in 1990 than in 1957 who say they are currently reading a book or novel, but many fewer now than in 1975 who say they have completed a book in the past week. In a society where professional success now requires acquaintance with masses of esoteric information, books are often purchased to be consulted, not read. About 15% of the new titles in *Books in Print* are scientific or technical books.

Fiction and general-interest nonfiction works would seem to be designed to be read, but lately these books also serve other functions. Their authors often employ them as routes to movie contracts or to tenure or to the intellectual renown that apparently comes with having catalogued definitively, in two or three dense volumes, how George Bernard Shaw, say, spent each of his evenings. Their publishers increasingly see these books not as collections of sentences and paragraphs that might be clarified and sharpened but as product that must be publicized and marketed so the balance sheets of the large conglomerates they now work for might tilt in the right direction.

Given the pace of modern life, the readers of these books, too, may have other purposes in mind—a quick, conversation-enhancing skim perhaps. "People tend to read too rapidly," moans Russell Jacoby, author of *The Last Intellectual.* "They tend to read while commuting, watching a game on TV, or playing Nintendo." Jacoby, who recently taught history at UC Riverside, keeps threatening to open "slow-reading centers."

And books increasingly have another function for those who purchase them. They have begun replacing the bottle of Scotch or the tie as gifts—giving them about the same chance of being opened as those tied had of being worn. The number of bookstores in the United States has been growing in recent decades, at a rate second only to that of fast-food restaurants, but according to statistics supplied by the American Booksellers Assn., more than one quarter of all their sales are in November and December—for the holidays.

15   In 1985, Michael Kinsley of the *New Republic* conducted an experiment. Notes offering a $5 reward to anyone who saw them and called the magazine were hidden about three-quarters of the way through 70 copies of the hottest nonfiction books in Washington, D.C., bookstores. These were the books that all of Washington seemed to be talking about. "Washington" was apparently basing its comments on the reviews and maybe a quick skim. No one called.

"Fortunately for booksellers," Kinsley wrote, "their prosperity depends on people buying books, not on people actually reading the bulky things." (Kinsley's advice to authors who would like their words actually to be read: "Cut out the middleman, and just write the review.")

Those of us with less disposable income, or less inclination to dispose of it in bookstores, can still get our books from libraries. "You can't say people take books out of the library just to put them on the coffee table," says Simon Michael Bessie, chairman of the Center for the Book at the Library of Congress.

And library use is up. Public-library circulation in the United States has grown from 4.7 "units" per capita per year in 1980 to 6.1 in 1989, according to a study by the Library Research Center at the University of Illinois. However, the "units" we are checking out of the library now include not only lots of school and business readings but also cassettes, CDs and videotapes.

Here is perhaps the most frightening of the statistics on books: According to the Gallup Poll, the number of Americans who admitted to having read *no* books during the past year—and this is not an easy thing to admit to a pollster—doubled from 1978 to 1990, from

8% to 16%. "I cannot live without books," Thomas Jefferson, whose collection helped start the Library of Congress, told John Adams. More and more of us apparently can.

20   Magazines would appear to be better suited to our hectic lives, if for no other reason than that they require much less of a time commitment than do books. Gathering evidence to confirm or deny this surmise, however, is not easy. There are too many different kinds of magazines and too many individual variations in their popularity. We do know that the magazine business has been in dire straits lately, but this has been caused by a falloff in advertising, not necessarily in circulation.

The best indicator of whether we are spending more or less time with magazines may be "time-use" studies such as those compiled at the University of Maryland. These show that the proportion of the population that reads a magazine on a typical day proportion of the population that reads a magazine on a typical day dropped from 38% in 1946 to 28% in 1985. Magazine publishers, however, can take some encouragement from the fact that most of that drop had occurred by the 1950s.

The statistics on newspaper readership are much less ambiguous and much grimmer. According to the University of Maryland time-use studies, the share of the adult population that "read a newspaper yesterday" has declined from 85% in 1946 to 73% in 1965 to 55% in 1985. The numbers on per capita newspaper circulation and the percentage of American homes that receive a daily newspaper form similar graphs—graphs you could ski down.

"What has changed is the strength of the habit of reading a newspaper," notes Al Gollin of the Newspaper Advertising Bureau. "it used to be one of those things that almost everybody did." No more. Americans on average now read newspapers much less frequently than they did 30 years ago, 20 years ago, even 10 years ago.

And young people have been losing the newspaper habit even faster than their parents. "We are developing a generation that has no interest in reading except insofar as it is assigned in school," concludes Daniel Kevles, professor of humanities at Caltech. "They don't read newspapers or magazines. I sense a general lack of interest in public affairs among my students." A recent *Times Mirror* survey found that only 30% of Americans under the age of 35 said they had read a newspaper the previous day, compared to 67% in 1965.

25   The Gulf War provided further evidence of how far the news-   25
paper has fallen. According to a survey by Birch/Scarborough, a grand
total of 8.9% of us said we kept up with war news primarily through
newspapers. The days when we found most of our news set in type on
a page are long gone.

Those time-use studies actually discovered a slight increase from
1965 to 1985 in the amount of time people said they spend reading
books and magazines: from 1.7 to 1.9 hours a week. But if you throw
in newspapers, the total time people spent with reading as their primary activity has dropped more than 30% in those years, from 4.2
hours a week to 2.8.

And this drop has occurred at the same time that the amount of
education Americans obtain has been rising dramatically. The percentage of Americans who have completed four years of high school
has more than tripled since 1940, according to the Bureau of the
Census Current Population Survey, and the percentage of Americans
completing four years of college has more than quadrupled.

If education still stimulated the desire to read, all the statistics on
reading would be shooting up. That they are not may say something
about the quality of our educational system and about the interests of
the students it now attracts. It certainly says something about reading
and its future. If dramatically increased exposure to an educational
system based on the printed word cannot get us to read, what will?

Reading's troubles are not difficult to explain. A hundred years
ago, on days when no circus was in town, people looking for entertainment had three alternatives: fulfilling biological needs, talking, or
reading. Those looking for information were restricted to the latter
two. Many of our ancestors, to be sure, were unable to read, but those
who could relied upon it, as Thomas Jefferson did, with a desperation
that is difficult for us to imagine.

30   Books, in those days, had a unique power to transport. "There is   30
no Frigate like a Book," wrote 19th-Century poet Emily Dickinson,
"To take us lands away." Now, of course, there are many easier ways
of getting there.

"Our society is particularly ingenious at thinking up alternatives
to the book," notes Boorstin. Indeed, we have thought up an entire
communications revolution, and there have not been many of those
in human history. The first such revolution was the development of
language hundreds of thousands of years ago; the second, the devel-

opment of reading and writing in the Middle East about 5,000 years ago; the third, the invention of the printing press 500 years ago.

The fourth communications revolution—ours—began, perhaps, with the experiments of Samuel Morse, Guglielmo Marconi, and Thomas Edison in the 19th Century, and it has been picking up steam ever since. Movies, recordings, radio, telephones, computers, photocopiers, and fax machines are all part of it. But, of course, the most powerful product of this revolution, so far, and the one that has posed the largest threat to reading, has been television.

Some print lovers have taken heart from the recent troubles of the TV networks or from the fact that the amount of time the average American family keeps the TV on each day, as measured by Nielsen, finally leveled off in the mid 1980s—at about seven hours a day. But, of course, we have since supplemented broadcast and even cable TV with other equally diverting forms of programming.

The first television wave washed over us in the 1950s and '60s. But then, while we were still getting used to having this perky new friend in our bedrooms, a second wave hit. In 1982, only 5.5% of American homes had videocassette recorders. Now 72.5% of them do, and, according to Nielsen, videotapes keep the set on an average of an extra half-hour each day in those homes. Add still more minutes for video games. So much for that leveling-off.

35   Russell Jacoby and his wife have found a sure way to protect 35 themselves and their two children from the siren songs of the tube: When their set was stolen a number of years ago, they simply didn't replace it. But most of the rest of us now share our homes with one or more TV sets, which we turn on more than we would like to admit. "Everyone lies about how much time they and their families spend watching TV," Jacoby asserts. It is a wonder that we manage to find the time to read even as much as we do.

"There are only so many hours in the days," says Alberto Vitale of Random house, wistfully.

As a youth, Abraham Lincoln is reported to have spent so many hours buried in his books that the neighbors labeled him lazy. When Lincoln arrived in Congress, his fellow congressmen, by one account, dismissed him as a "bookworm.' That insult is not heard much nowadays, nor are readers disparaged as lazy.

Instead, the more dedicated parents among us feel guilty if we don't manage to read to our children each evening, hoping the kids will pick up the habit we parents are rapidly losing. The First Lady campaigns for literacy. We end TV shows with pleas to read books. And, according to the Gallup Poll, 61% of us proclaim reading "more rewarding" than watching television; 73% lament that we read too few books; 92% attest that reading is a "good use" of our time. And 45% of the poll's respondents believe, against all the evidence, that they will be "reading more in the months and years ahead."

Reading certainly is well loved now that it is in decline. Yet it is no longer something that we ache to do. How many kids today surreptitiously finish books by flashlight under the covers? Instead, reading, like eating broccoli, has now become something that we feel we *should* do (always a bad sign).

40   Some teenagers and—says Michael Silverblatt, host of KCRW's   40
"Bookworm" show—some Southern Californians actually find it hip to pretend to read less than they really do, but the vast majority of us sincerely, vigorously, and guiltily genuflect in front of the printed page. Never in human history has reading been more respected.

This is not surprising. One of the characteristics of any technological revolution is nostalgia for the old order. Socrates, who lived a few hundred years after the invention of the Greek alphabet, when writing was transforming Greek culture, strenuously argued the superiority of the oral culture it was replacing. According to Plato's (written) account, Socrates predicted that the use of writing would weaken memories and deprive "learners" of the chance to question what they were being taught.

Such nostalgia for the methods of oral tradition—memorization, rhetoric, recital—kept them alive in the schools well into this century. Now similar calls are going out to defend the schools against the incursions of the new information technologies so that our educational institutions can serve as repositories of another fading tradition—reading.

We did not realize that we were living in the age of print until it began to end. Only then did we gain the perspective to see the effects of reading on our thoughts. Those effects are profound, as anthropological studies of societies without reading have begun to show.

For example, the following statements were presented to members of a mostly preliterate tribe in a remote area of the Soviet Union: "In the far north, where there is snow, all bears are white. Novaya Zembla is in the far north, and there is always snow there." Then these people were asked what color the bears are in Novaya Zembla. A typical response, as reported by Father Walter Ong in his book *Orality and Literacy:* "I don't know. I've seen a black bear. I've never seen any others. Each locality has its own animals." These people could not solve this simplest of logical puzzles.

45 It is not that such preliterate people are less intelligent than we are. They simply think differently—"situationally." When words are written down, not just enunciated, they are freed from the subjective situations and experiences ("I've seen a black bear") in which they were imbedded. Written words can be played with, analyzed, rearranged, and organized into categories (black bears, white bears, places where there is always snow). The correspondences, connections, or contradictions among various statements can be carefully examined. As investigators such as Ong and anthropologist Jack Goody have explained, our system of logic—our ability to find principles that apply independently of situations—is a product of literacy. This logic, which goes back to the Egyptians, Hebrews, and Greeks, led to mathematics and philosophy and history. Among its accomplishments is our culture.

And when written words are set in print, they gain additional powers. Our sentences grow even less connected to our persons as they are spelled out in the interchangeable letters of movable type. Our thoughts grow more abstract, more removed from the situations in which we happen to find ourselves. Superstitions, biases, and legendary characters like dragons and kings have difficulty fitting into these straight precise lines of type. Charts, maps, and columns of figures can be duplicated exactly for the first time. According to seminal media theorist Marshall McLuhan and historian Elizabeth Eisenstein, the scientific revolution and the Enlightenment were both products of the printing press.

"Reading is central to our culture," states Ong, a professor of humanities at Saint Louis University. "It is connected to virtually all the forces that shaped our culture." Among those who ponder such matters, there is no longer much controversy about that. The question, as we leave the age of print for the uncharted waters of this new electronic age, is whether we risk losing much of what reading enabled us to gain.

Neil Postman, for one, fears that the answer is yes. "New communications technologies giveth," he proclaims, "and they taketh away."

On the debit side Postman would place recent developments in art, education, religion, journalism, and politics—all of which, in his view, are losing the seriousness and intellectual content print gave them as they are transformed into "show business" to meet the needs of electronic media.

Reading demands that we sit still, be quiet, and concentrate hard enough to decode a system of symbols and follow extended arguments. This is an injunction that increasingly is falling on earphoned-plugged ears. Television and its electronic brethren are much less strict. We can be cleaning, daydreaming or half dozing; they don't seem to care. All television demands is our gaze. Dazzling collages of imagery and rhythm are assembled just to get us to open our eyelids a bit wider.

50   Kings used to turn thumbs down on spectacles that bored them;   50
we simply press thumb to remote control, zapping any scene, exposition, or argument that takes much more than a fraction of a minute to unfold. "Thinking," Postman writes, "does not play well on TV."

Our entertainers, pundits, professors, ministers, and leaders, therefore, are judged not so much on their ability to reason but on their ability to project a diverting image. Amuse us or we'll change the channel. Whether or not the points being made are valid is of less importance. Somehow this does not seem what Jefferson and the other founders had in mind when they entrusted us with governing a country.

Pessimists like Postman do not have much difficulty convincing us that life on a late-20th-Century couch can be frivolous and vegetable-like. We already feel guilty that we are watching "the boob tube" rather than reading. However, making the case that life in that supposed golden age of reading was really much more noble than life today is more difficult.

As his example of political discourse before TV, Postman chooses those astoundingly literate, three-hour-long debates between Lincoln and Stephen A. Douglas in 1858. But 18th- and 19th-Century American politics was not all conducted on this level. The slogans with which William Henry Harrison made his case for the presidency in 1840, for example—"Log Cabin and Hard Cider," "Tippecanoe and Tyler, too"—are as vacuous as anything concocted by Ronald Reagan's media wizards.

The arguments against TV are based on a certain amount of such false nostalgia. People then did not read quite so much, and their reading material was not quite so exemplary as those pining for a lost golden age suggest. "We have no figures on how much or how well books were read in the past," Ong notes. "All we have are the comments of bibliophiles. There is no evidence, for example, that all the copies of the books printed in the 16th and 17th centuries were read. There is plenty of evidence that a lot of them were not read." Nevertheless, the doomsayers do have some harder evidence on their side.

55   There is, to begin with, the decline in writing skills, much fretted   55
over by educators in recent years. Written language demands stricter rules of syntax and grammar than spoken language, and these are the rules, first codified in printed dictionaries and grammar books, that we learn (or now fail to learn) in school. The sentences of the electronic age, because they are supplemented by images, can get away with playing by looser rules. Try, sometimes, to diagram the sentences of a TV-football "analyst."

It is not surprising, therefore, that students who watch and listen more and read less are losing command of their writing. As anyone who has seen that rare thing, a letter written by a student, knows, young people today often have considerable difficulty filling a page with clear, exact sentences. Their performance on recent SATs raises the question of whether they also have difficulty producing clear, exact thought.

The average score on the SAT verbal test, taken by a large number of college-bound high school students, was 466 (on a scale of 200 to 800) in 1968. Then, as the first TV generation began taking the test, scores began tumbling. The average score leveled off from 1978 to 1987, but now, with the arrival of the MTV kids, it has begun skidding again—down to 422 this year.

The College Boards do not test a representative sample of American teenagers. More—and perhaps less qualified—students are now going to college and therefore taking the test, which may be driving scores down. Still, the correspondence between verbal scores and the two waves of TV's assault upon reading is hard to overlook.

"The decline in SAT scores has a lot to do with not reading," asserts College Board President Donald M. Stewart. Why? "The ability to read is linked to the ability to process, analyze, and comprehend information," Stewart explains. "I guess that's called thinking."

60   Michael Silverblatt of "Bookworm" uses an analogy that young   60
people might find more persuasive: "Just as people who don't work
out can't do certain things with their bodies, people who don't read
can't do certain things with their minds."

Boorstin puts the problem even more bluntly. He calls people
who do not read "self-handicapped" and says, "A person who doesn't
read books is only half-alive." And if the members of a society stop
reading? "Then you have a half-alive society."

From the perspective of enthusiasts of the new culture of videos,
videotapes, video games, and CDs, all this must sound like the whining of a ragged, nearly defeated old order. Not everyone is convinced
that all that is deep and serious in our society is in fact under siege. "I
know a number of extremely intelligent adults who don't read more
than a book or two a year but still remain healthy, active contributors
to society," says Wendy Lesser, editor of *Three Penny Review,* a respected
Berkeley literary publication. "I think if you can get people to learn to
discriminate between good and bad TV programs, you've done more
for them than you would by simply forcing them to read a book,
however trashy."

And even those who believe that the decline in reading does herald some profound cultural changes are not convinced those changes
will necessarily be for the worse. Perhaps, they might argue, the logic
inculcated by writing and print is not the only way of processing
information about the world. Perhaps in immersion in electronic
forms of communication might lead to different but equally valid
ways of being smart—forms of intelligence that go unrecognized by
SAT tests. "I'm listening to that argument with more and more sympathy," concedes Stewart of the College Boards.

It is possible, moreover, that electronic forms of communication
have more potential than is currently being expressed in either the
vapid fantasies of Madonna videos or the static talk shows and cos-
tume dramas of public television. These media might be capable,
given time, of creating a culture as profound and deep as that of reading. These technologies might, in other words, have more to "giveth"
than we can yet imagine.

65   It took 2,000 years of writing before an alphabet was developed.   65
It took a century and a half of printing before someone thought to
print a novel or a newspaper. New communications technologies do

not arrive upon the scene fully grown; they need time to develop the methods and forms that best exploit their potential.

Our communications revolution, from this perspective, is still quite young. TV has been around for only half a century. Most of its programming is still recycled theater—mini-dramas and comedies; its more stylistically adventurous forms—commercials and music videos— are little more than demonstrations of the visual capabilities of the medium.

Television's technicians have mastered the art of mating laugh track to quip; they can make everything from cats to toothbrushes dance. But TV still may not have stumbled upon the grammar and syntax of video—the patterns and relations of images and sounds that will enable us to communicate complex ideas with clarity and exactness. Television may not yet have discovered the forms that will do for that medium what the novel and the newspaper did for print.

TV today grapples with difficult subjects only by getting slow and boring. It is possible to imagine a television program that would be difficult for the opposite reason: because it is too fast, too busy, too full of information. Perhaps such super-dense television would be able to plumb depths quickly enough to fit the video generation's short attention spans, or perhaps this TV would be stimulating enough to stretch those attention spans.

Does television really have such potential? Does a whole culture's worth of new perspectives, new ideas, new creations in fact lie slumbering in our television sets, just waiting for programming capable of awakening them? "Possibly," Daniel Kevles comments with some skepticism, "but I think any more intelligent programming will still have to coexist with MTV and action dramas."

70 Still, if the electronic media can, even intermittently, transform 70 themselves into vehicles for ideas with the reach and capacity of print it would be good news for our society. The Postmans of the world could rest easy; we would not go giggling off into decadence and dictatorship. But such a development would represent still more bad news for reading.

Is reading likely to survive the electronic age? Of course, Daniel Boorstin says. He scoffs at the notion that books, magazines, or newspapers are going to disappear any time soon. Boorstin calls this the "displacement fallacy" and points out that radio survived and prospered after the introduction of TV, despite many gloomy predictions to the contrary. "New technologies tend to discover unique opportunities for the old," Boorstin maintains.

Not every outdated communication technology succeeds in finding such an opportunity. Consider smoke signals, for example, or town criers or the telegram. Nevertheless, Boorstin has a point.

Books already have found some new functions for themselves—as reference manuals for example. Magazines have survived in part by discovering audiences too small and specialized for TV to reach. And newspapers? Well, maybe *USA Today,* with its brief, snappy stories, is responding to a new opportunity presented by the TV generation's shortened attention spans. Or maybe newspapers are still searching for their niche in the electronic age.

Print and electronics also collaborate more than is generally recognized. According to the preliminary results of a study by Robert Kubey, communications professor at Rutgers University, words appear in about 20% of the images in a sample of 30 channels available on cable. And the alphabet has recently found a new life for itself on the keyboards of computers.

75 "I'm using about 20 times as much paper since I started using a 75 computer," Ong adds. "A new technology does not wipe out what went before; it transforms and enhances it. When people started writing, they didn't quit talking." Indeed, they probably spoke more logically.

However, the introduction of writing undoubtedly did cause people to spend less time talking—because of the old not-enough-hours-in-the-day problem. And it probably did cause them to rely less on speech for communicating important information. So, whatever new forms print may assume in response to electronics, it is unlikely that print will regain its position as our major source of information or entertainment.

Reading still plays and, for the foreseeable future, will continue to play, a crucial role in our society. Nevertheless, there is no getting around the fact that reading's role has diminished and likely will continue to shrink.

This does not mean we should begin turning first-grade classes over to video lessons. Until the new technologies grow up a bit, it would not hurt any of us to read more to our children or take a book with us the next time we must sit and wait. And perhaps it was not a bad idea that you chose, instead of watching the Rams game or renting *Dances With Wolves,* to make it through this article.

Questions on Meaning

1. This essay is full of data on the decline of reading of all kinds. Review some of the statistics on this decline. What would happen if the decline continued?

2. Stephens notes that as reading declines, writing scores decline as well. He notes SAT essay scores and their decline. Why does reading contribute to better writing?

3. What causes reading to decline? What do people do rather than read? What do people check out of the library these days? If you have the chance to choose between a book and a CD, which do you choose?

Questions on Rhetorical Strategy and Style

1. This essay is built around numbers. Why are these numbers so rhetorically effective? Why do we tend to believe statistics rather than mere argument? Why is it better to believe an argument that is based on numbers?

2. The center of the essay attacks TV by showing that the rise of TV exactly parallels the decline in reading. Why does this framing of the argument work well? Is the reader already likely to think that TV is the culprit?

3. The essay ends by congratulating you for reading the essay instead of watching a video or a football game. What kind of reader would have been likely to read the *L.A. Times Magazine*, where this essay originally appeared? Would this reader feel complimented by the ending of the essay? Why?

Writing Assignments

1. List the last ten things you read. Now write an essay about what you read; why you read; and how you read.

2. How much time do you spend watching television? How much time do your parents spend watching TV? How about your grandparents? What can you assume about television in our culture from your own family? Write about these assumptions.

3. The essay argues that newspaper reading is declining in America. How do you get your news? Write about the typical ways that young people learn about the world today. Include comments on what young people want to know about and why.

Education and Learning

Suppose a friend has suggested that the two of you start a business. Your business will offer clients a variety of professional services, so your friend wants to hire a group of people with bachelor's and master's degrees and maybe even a few doctorates. Your employees will screen your clients by ability levels, train them to interact socially with one another, teach them values and ethics, foster their sense of pride in the community, counsel those with special needs and provide them the support they need, involve them in programs to lower the crime rate, and help them to furnish entertainment to the community in the form of sports and artistic activities. With no extra time or resources, your employees will cover the basics of reading, writing, math, science, and a number of other subjects for a clientele of various ages, interests, and intentions.

Hearing such a proposition, you take a deep breath and inquire just how your friend will finance such a staggeringly complex undertaking. "Well," your friend says, "we'll ask each family for a contribution, and we'll have to live within whatever money they give us." That sounds a little shaky to you, so you ask how much you will make. "Ummm," your friend stammers, "I can promise you it will be more than minimum wage." Of course, the "business" in question is education, in particular, American public education, and you wisely tell your friend you will have to think it over. Teachers are expected to supply a democracy with functioning citizens, at the lowest possible price, and despite violence, racism, drugs, divorce, child abuse, and a host of other social ills that may make it virtually impossible even to maintain order.

As difficult as education appears from the outside, it becomes even more difficult looking at it from the inside. If you decide to go into the education business, you will soon find that many teachers and researchers question the very existence of the quantity known as "intelligence," the thing that education is supposed to cultivate. Most IQ tests favor verbal and mathematical ability, which is assumed to represent intelligence. But other measurements of ability do not correlate well with IQ test intelligence. Performance skills such as dance, athletics, music, and even writing seem to operate independently of IQ. And IQ tests also seem to favor upper-middle-class white males and discriminate systematically against certain minorities. Thus teachers may differ sharply over how to measure educational potential and achievement, and those differences may lead to disagreements over how and what to teach. Among many other problems within education, ideas themselves have caused conflicts within the schools. Some teachers and parents have never become comfortable with the disparities between the Bible's account of creation and the theory of evolution's account. Many schools and communities have quarreled over whether to allow Spanish or some other language to supplement instruction in English, or over whether "standard English" should be the only dialect, or whether black English should be taught as well. Colleges and universities plagued with race, gender, and sexual orientation conflicts have struggled with whether, and/or how, to limit free speech on campus in order to control verbal harassment.

Given all these problems of education, it may seem surprising that learning occurs at all. But we must not confuse the institution of education—the curriculum, books, buildings, teachers, researchers, parents, legislators, and the rest of the community—with the process of learning, which is a basic human drive. Before the age of three, every normal child learns most of the enormously complex grammar of his or her native language. At the age of five or six, a child enters the classroom able only to recite the alphabet, yet by the beginning of the new year—miraculously—the child can read and write. The energy fueling this powerful process comes from within the child, and though the energy may wane as the child grows older, learning continues. The accomplishments of the early years are refined into the skills that prepare the adult to earn a living, and the drive to learn is supplemented by the need to survive and to prevail. The problematic institution of education and the fascinating processes of learning have drawn the attention of many bright minds: writers such as Russell Baker, Carl Rowan, James Thurber, and Virginia Woolf; scientists such as Francis Bacon, Stephen Jay Gould, Robin Lakoff, and Stanley Milgram; theorists such as Bruno Bettelheim, Aaron Copland, Jonathan Kozol, and Mary Wollstonecraft; and a host of teachers.

Are Too Many People Going to College?

Charles Murray

Charles Murray is a political scientist and holds a Ph.D. in Political Science from MIT. Currently he works at the American Enterprise Institute in Washington, D.C. Early in his career he was a Peace Corps volunteer in Thailand and later served as a researcher at the American Institutes for Research, a private research organization. From 1981-1990 Murray was a Senior Fellow at the Manhattan Institute for Policy Research where he wrote Losing Ground: American Social Policy, 1950–1980 *(1984). It was in this book that he concluded that social welfare programs should be eliminated. In 1988 he published* In Pursuit: Of Happiness and Good Government. *This book was followed by* What It Means to Be a Libertarian: A Personal Interpretation *(1996);* Human Accomplishment: The Pursuit of Excellence in the Arts and Sciences, 800 B.C. to 1950 *(2003); and* In Our Hands: A Plan to Replace the Welfare State *(2006). His most controversial work was* The Bell Curve: Intelligence and Class Structure in American Life *(1994). Co-authored with Richard Herrnstein, the book argues that IQ plays a greater role than socio-economic status in predicting success in life. Murray's most recent book is* Real Education: Four Simple Truths for Bringing America's Schools Back to Reality *(2008). In the following article published in* The American Magazine *in 2008 Murray asserts that the real reason for going to college is to gain a liberal education, not to get a job.*

Reprinted from the *American Magazine*, September 8, 2008, by permission of the American Enterprise Institute Press.

1 To ask whether too many people are going to college requires us to think about the importance and nature of a liberal education. "Universities are not intended to teach the knowledge required to fit men for some special mode of gaining their livelihood," John Stuart Mill told students at the University of St. Andrews in 1867. "Their object is not to make skillful lawyers, or physicians, or engineers, but capable and cultivated human beings." If this is true (and I agree that it is), why say that too many people are going to college? Surely a mass democracy should encourage as many people as possible to become "capable and cultivated human beings" in Mill's sense. We should not restrict the availability of a liberal education to a rarefied intellectual elite. More people should be going to college, not fewer.

Yes and no. More people should be getting the basics of a liberal education. But for most students, the places to provide those basics are elementary and middle school. E. D. Hirsch Jr. is the indispensable thinker on this topic, beginning with his 1987 book *Cultural Literacy: What Every American Needs to Know*. Part of his argument involves the importance of a body of core knowledge in fostering reading speed and comprehension. With regard to a liberal education, Hirsch makes three points that are germane here:

Full participation in any culture requires familiarity with a body of core knowledge. To live in the United States and not recognize Teddy Roosevelt, Prohibition, the Minutemen, Wall Street, smoke-filled rooms, or Gettysburg is like trying to read without knowing some of the ten thousand most commonly used words in the language. It signifies a degree of cultural illiteracy about America. But the core knowledge transcends one's own country. Not to recognize Falstaff, Apollo, the Sistine Chapel, the Inquisition, the twenty-third Psalm, or Mozart signifies cultural illiteracy about the West. Not to recognize the solar system, the Big Bang, natural selection, relativity, or the periodic table is to be scientifically illiterate. Not to recognize the Mediterranean, Vienna, the Yangtze River, Mount Everest, or Mecca is to be geographically illiterate.

This core knowledge is an important part of the glue that holds the culture together. All American children, of whatever ethnic heritage, and whether their families came here 300 years ago or three months ago, need to learn about the Pilgrims, Valley Forge, Duke Ellington, Apollo 11, Susan B. Anthony, George C. Marshall, and the Freedom Riders. All students need to learn the iconic stories. For a society of immigrants such as ours, the core knowledge is our shared identity that makes us Americans together rather than hyphenated Americans.

5   *K–8 are the right years to teach the core knowledge, and the effort should get off to a running start in elementary school.* Starting early is partly a matter of necessity: There's a lot to learn, and it takes time. But another reason is that small children enjoy learning myths and fables, showing off names and dates they have memorized, and hearing about great historical figures and exciting deeds. The educational establishment sees this kind of curriculum as one that forces children to memorize boring facts. That conventional wisdom is wrong on every count. The facts can be fascinating (if taught right); a lot more than memorization is entailed; yet memorizing things is an indispensable part of education, too; and memorizing is something that children do much, much better than adults. The core knowledge is suited to ways that young children naturally learn and enjoy learning. Not all children will be able to do the reading with the same level of comprehension, but the fact-based nature of the core knowledge actually works to the benefit of low ability students—remembering facts is much easier than making inferences and deductions. The core knowledge curriculum lends itself to adaptation for students across a wide range of academic ability.

In the 20 years since *Cultural Literacy* was published, Hirsch and his colleagues have developed and refined his original formulation into an inventory of more than 6,000 items that approximate the core knowledge broadly shared by literate Americans. Hirsch's Core Knowledge Foundation has also developed a detailed, grade by-grade curriculum for K–8, complete with lists of books and other teaching materials.

The Core Knowledge approach need not stop with eighth grade. High school is a good place for survey courses in the humanities, social sciences, and sciences taught at a level below the demands of a college course and accessible to most students in the upper two-thirds of the distribution of academic ability. Some students will not want to take these courses, and it can be counterproductive to require them to do so, but high school can put considerable flesh on the liberal education skeleton for students who are still interested.

Liberal Education in College

Saying "too many people are going to college" is not the same as saying that the average student does not need to know about history, science, and great works of art, music, and literature. They do need to know—and to know more than they are currently learning. So let's teach it to them, but let's not wait for college to do it.

Liberal education in college means taking on the tough stuff. A high-school graduate who has acquired Hirsch's core knowledge will know, for example, that John Stuart Mill was an important 19th-century English philosopher who was associated with something called Utilitarianism and wrote a famous book called *On Liberty*. But learning philosophy in college, which is an essential component of a liberal education, means that the student has to be able to read and understand the actual text of *On Liberty*. That brings us to the limits set by the nature of college-level material. Here is the first sentence of *On Liberty*: "The subject of this essay is not the so-called liberty of the will, so unfortunately opposed to the misnamed doctrine of philosophical necessity; but civil, or social liberty: the nature and limits of the power which can be legitimately exercised by society over the individual." I will not burden you with *On Liberty*'s last sentence. It is 126 words long. And Mill is one of the more accessible philosophers, and *On Liberty* is one of Mill's more accessible works. It would be nice if everyone could acquire a fully formed liberal education, but they cannot.

10   Specifically: When College Board researchers defined "college readiness" as the SAT score that is associated with a 65 percent chance of getting at least a 2.7 grade point average in college during the freshman year, and then applied those criteria (hardly demanding in an era of soft courses and grade inflation) to the freshmen in a sample of 41 major colleges and universities, the threshold "college readiness" score was found to be 1180 on the combined SAT math and verbal tests. It is a score that only about 10 percent of American 18-year-olds would achieve if they all took the SAT, in an age when more than 30 percent of 18-year-olds go to college.

Should all of those who do have the academic ability to absorb a college-level liberal education get one? It depends. Suppose we have before us a young woman who is in the 98th percentile of academic ability and wants to become a lawyer and eventually run for political office. To me, it seems essential that she spend her undergraduate years getting a rigorous liberal education. Apart from a liberal education's value to her, the nation will benefit. Everything she does as an attorney or as an elected official should be informed by the kind of wisdom that a rigorous liberal education can encourage. It is appropriate to push her into that kind of undergraduate program.

But the only reason we can get away with pushing her is that the odds are high that she will enjoy it. The odds are high because she is good at this sort of thing—it's no problem for her to read *On Liberty* or *Paradise Lost*. It's no problem for her to come up with an interesting perspective on what she's read and weave it into a term paper. And because she's good at it, she is also likely to enjoy it. It is one of Aristotle's central themes in his discussion of human happiness, a theme that John Rawls later distilled into what he called the Aristotelian Principle: "Other things equal, human beings enjoy the exercise of the irrealized capacities (their innate or trained abilities), and this enjoyment increases the more the capacity is realized, or the greater its complexity." And so it comes to pass that those who take the hardest majors and who enroll in courses that look most like an old fashioned liberal education are concentrated among the students in the top percentiles of academic ability. Getting a liberal education consists of dealing with complex intellectual material day after day, and dealing with complex intellectual material is what students in the top few percentiles are really good at, in the same way that other people are really good at cooking or making pottery. For these students, doing it well is fun.

Every percentile down the ability ladder—and this applies to all abilities, not just academic—the probability that a person will enjoy the hardest aspects of an activity goes down as well. Students at the 80th percentile of academic ability are still smart kids, but the odds that they will respond to a course that assigns Mill or Milton are considerably lower than the odds that a student in the top few percentiles will respond. Virtue has nothing to do it. Maturity has nothing to do with it. Appreciation of the value of a liberal education has nothing to do with it. The probability that a student will enjoy *Paradise Lost* goes down as his linguistic ability goes down, but so does the probability that he works on double acrostic puzzles in his spare time or regularly plays online Scrabble, and for the identical reason. The lower down the linguistic ladder he is, the less fun such activities are.

And so we return to the question: Should all of those who have the academic ability to absorb a college-level liberal education get one? If our young woman is at the 80th percentile of linguistic ability, should she be pushed to do so? She has enough intellectual capacity, if she puts her mind to it and works exceptionally hard.

15   The answer is no. If she wants to, fine. But she probably won't, and there's no way to force her. Try to force her (for example, by setting up a demanding core curriculum), and she will transfer to another school, because she is in college for vocational training. She wants to write computer code. Start a business. Get a job in television. She uses college to take vocational courses that pertain to her career interests. A large proportion of people who are theoretically able to absorb a liberal education have no interest in doing so.

And reasonably so. Seen dispassionately, getting a traditional liberal education over four years is an odd way to enjoy spending one's time. Not many people enjoy reading for hour after hour, day after day, no matter what the material may be. To enjoy reading *On Liberty* and its ilk—and if you're going to absorb such material, you must in some sense enjoy the process—is downright peculiar. To be willing to spend many more hours writing papers and answers to exam questions about that material approaches masochism.

We should look at the kind of work that goes into acquiring a liberal education at the college level in the same way that we look at the grueling apprenticeship that goes into becoming a master chef: something that understandably attracts only a few people. Most students at today's colleges choose not to take the courses that go into a liberal education because the capabilities they want to develop lie elsewhere. These students are not lazy, any more than students who don't want to spend hours learning how to chop carrots into a perfect eighth-inch dice are lazy. A liberal education just doesn't make sense for them.

For Learning How to Make a Living, the Four-Year Brick-and-Mortar Residential College is Increasingly Obsolete

We now go from one extreme to the other, from the ideal of liberal education to the utilitarian process of acquiring the knowledge that most students go to college to acquire—practical and vocational. The question here is not whether the traditional four-year residential college is fun or valuable as a place to grow up, but when it makes sense as a place to learn how to make a living. The answer is: in a sensible world, hardly ever.

Start with the time it takes—four years. Assuming a semester system with four courses per semester, four years of class work means 32 semester-long courses. The occupations for which "knowing enough" requires 32 courses are exceedingly rare. For some professions—medicine and law are the obvious examples—a rationale for four years of course work can be concocted (combining pre-med and pre-law undergraduate courses with three years of medical school and law school), but for every other occupation, the body of knowledge taught in classrooms can be learned more quickly. Even Ph.D.s don't require four years of course work. The Ph.D. is supposed to signify expertise, but that expertise comes from burrowing deep in to a specialty, not from dozens of courses.

20   Those are the jobs with the most stringent academic requirements. For the student who wants to become a good hotel manager, software designer, accountant, hospital administrator, farmer, high-school teacher, social worker, journalist, optometrist, interior designer, or football coach, four years of class work is ridiculous. Actually becoming good in those occupations will take longer than four years, but most of the competence is acquired on the job. The two year community college and online courses offer more flexible options for tailoring course work to the real needs of the job.

A brick-and-mortar campus is increasingly obsolete. The physical infrastructure of the college used to make sense for three reasons. First, a good library was essential to higher learning, and only a college faculty and student body provided the economies of scale that made good libraries affordable. Second, scholarship flourishes through colleagueships, and the college campus made it possible to put scholars in physical proximity to each other. Third, the best teaching requires interaction between teachers and students, and physical proximity was the only way to get it. All three rationales for the brick-and-mortar campus are fading fast.

The rationale for a physical library is within a few years of extinction. Even now, the Internet provides access, for a price, to all the world's significant technical journals. The books are about to follow. Google is scanning the entire text of every book in the libraries of Harvard, Princeton, Stanford, Oxford, the New York Public Library, the Bavarian State

Library, Ghent University Library, Keio Library (Tokyo), the National Library of Catalonia, University of Lausanne, and an expanding list of others. Collectively, this project will encompass close to the sum total of human knowledge. It will be completely searchable. Everything out of copyright will be free. Everything still under copyright will be accessible for a fee. Libraries will still be a selling point for colleges, but as a place for students to study in pleasant surroundings—an amenity in the same way that an attractive student union is an amenity. Colleges and universities will not need to exist because they provide libraries.

The rationale for colleges based on colleagueships has eroded. Until a few decades ago, physical proximity was important because correspondence and phone calls just weren't as good. As email began to spread during the 1980s, physical proximity became less important. As the capacity of the Internet expanded in the 1990s, other mechanisms made those interactions richer. Now, regular emails from professional groups inform scholars of the latest publications in their field of interest. Specialized chat groups enable scholars to bounce new ideas off other people working on the same problems. Drafts are exchanged effortlessly and comments attached electronically. Whether physical proximity still has any advantages depends mostly on the personality of the scholar. Some people like being around other people during the workday and prefer face-to-face conversations to emails. For those who don't, the value of being on a college campus instead of on a mountaintop in Montana is nil. Their electronic access to other scholars is incomparably greater than any scholar enjoyed even within the world's premier universities before the advent of the Internet. Like the library, face-to-face colleagueships will be an amenity that colleges continue to provide. But colleges and universities will not need to exist because they provide a community of scholars.

The third rationale for the brick-and-mortar college is that it brings teachers together with students. Working against that rationale is the explosion in the breadth and realism of what is known as distance learning. The idea of distance learning is surprisingly old—Isaac Pitman was teaching his shorthand system to British students through the postal service in the 1840s, and the University of London began offering degrees for correspondence students in 1858—but the technology of distance learning changed little for the next century. The advent of inexpensive videocassettes in the 1980s opened up a way for students to hear and see lectures without being in the classroom. By the early 1990s, it was possible to buy college-level courses on audio- or videotape, taught by first-rate teaching professors, on a wide range of topics, for a few hundred dollars. But without easy interaction between teacher and student, distance learning remained a poor second-best to a good college seminar.

25   Once again, the Internet is revolutionizing everything. As personal computers acquired the processing power to show high-definition video and the storage capacity to handle big video files, the possibilities for distance learning expanded by orders of magnitude. We are now watching the early expression of those possibilities: podcasts and streaming videos in real time of professors' lectures, online discussions among students scattered around the country, online interaction between students and professors, online exams, and tutorials augmented by computer-aided instruction software.   25

Even today, the quality of student-teacher interactions in a virtual classroom competes with the interactions in a brick-and-mortar classroom. But the technology is still in its early stages of development and the rate of improvement is breathtaking. Compare video games such as Myst and SimCity in the 1990s to their descendants today; the Walkman you used in the 1990s to the iPod you use today; the cell phone you used in the 1990s to the BlackBerry or iPhone you use today. Whatever technical limitations might lead you to say, "Yes, but it's still not the same as being there in the classroom," are probably within a few years of being outdated.

College Isn't All It's Cracked Up to Be

College looms so large in the thinking of both parents and students because it is seen as the open sesame to a good job. Reaping the economic payoff for college that shows up in econometric analyses is a long shot for large numbers of young people.

When high-school graduates think that obtaining a B.A. will help them get a higher-paying job, they are only narrowly correct. Economists have established beyond doubt that people with B.A.s earn more on average than people without them. But why does the B.A. produce that result? For whom does the B.A. produce that result? For some jobs, the economic premium for a degree is produced by the actual education that has gone into getting the degree.

Lawyers, physicians, and engineers can earn their high incomes only by deploying knowledge and skills that take years to acquire, and degrees in law, medicine, and engineering still signify competence in those knowledges and skills. But for many other jobs, the economic premium for the B.A. is created by a brutal fact of life about the American job market: Employers do not even interview applicants who do not hold a B.A. Even more brutal, the advantage conferred by the B.A. often has nothing to do with the content of the education. Employers do not value what the student learned, just that the student has a degree.

Employers value the B.A. because it is a no-cost (for them) screening device for academic ability and perseverance. The more people who go to college, the more sense it makes for employers to require a B.A. When only a small percentage of people got college degrees, employers who required a B.A. would have been shutting themselves off from access to most of the talent. With more than a third of 23-year-olds now getting a B.A., many employers can reasonably limit their hiring pool to college graduates because bright and ambitious high-school graduates who can go to college usually do go to college. An employer can believe that exceptions exist but rationally choose not to expend time and money to identify them. Knowing this, large numbers of students are in college to buy their admission ticket—the B.A.

30   But while it is true that the average person with a B.A. makes more than the average person without a B.A., getting a B.A. is still going to be the wrong economic decision for many high-school graduates. Wages within occupations form a distribution. Young people with okay-but-not-great academic ability who are thinking about whether to go after a B.A. need to consider the competition they will face after they graduate. Let me put these calculations in terms of a specific example, a young man who has just graduated from high school and is trying to decide whether to become an electrician or go to college and major in business, hoping to become a white-collar manager. He is at the 70th percentile in linguistic ability and logical mathematical ability—someone who shouldn't go to college by my standards, but who can, in today's world, easily find a college that will give him a degree. He is exactly average in interpersonal and intrapersonal ability. He is at the 95th percentile in the small-motor skills and spatial abilities that are helpful in being a good electrician.

He begins by looking up the average income of electricians and managers on the Bureau of Labor Statistics website, and finds that the mean annual income for electricians in 2005 was $45,630, only about half of the $88,450 mean for management occupations. It looks as if getting a B.A. will buy him a huge wage premium. Should he try to get the B.A. on economic grounds?

To make his decision correctly, our young man must start by throwing out the averages. He has the ability to become an excellent electrician and can reasonably expect to be near the top of the electricians' income distribution. He does not have it in him to be an excellent manager, because he is only average in interpersonal and intrapersonal ability and only modestly above average in academic ability, all of which are important for becoming a good manager, while his competitors for those slots will include many who are high in all of those abilities. Realistically, he should be looking at the incomes toward the bottom of the distribution of managers. With that in mind, he goes back to the Bureau of Labor Statistics website and discovers that an electrician at the 90th percentile of electricians' incomes made $70,480 in 2005, almost twice the income of a manager at the 10th percentile of managers' incomes ($37,800). Even if our young man successfully completes college and gets a B.A. (which is far from certain), he is likely to make less money than if he becomes an electrician.

Then there is job security to consider. A good way to make sure you always can find work is to be among the best at what you do. It also helps to have a job that does not require you to compete with people around the globe. When corporations downsize, they lay off mediocre managers before they lay off top electricians. When the economy gets soft, top electricians can find work when mediocre managers cannot. Low-level management jobs can often be outsourced to India, whereas electricians' jobs cannot.

What I have said of electricians is true throughout the American job market. The income for the top people in a wide variety of occupations that do not require a college degree is higher than the average income for many occupations that require a B.A. Furthermore, the range and number of such jobs are expanding rapidly. The need for assembly-line workers in factories (one of the most boring jobs ever invented) is falling, but the demand for skilled technicians of every kind—in healthcare, information technology, transportation networks, and every other industry that relies on high-tech equipment—is expanding. The service sector includes many low-skill, low-paying jobs, but it also includes growing numbers of specialized jobs that pay well (for example, in healthcare and the entertainment and leisure industries). Construction offers an array of high-paying jobs for people who are good at what they do. It's not just skilled labor in the standard construction trades that is in high demand. The increase in wealth in American society has increased the demand for all sorts of craftsmanship. Today's high-end homes and office buildings may entail the work of specialized skills in stonework, masonry, glazing, painting, cabinetmaking, machining, landscaping, and a dozen other crafts. The increase in wealth is also driving an increased demand for the custom-made and the exquisitely wrought, meaning demand for artisans in everything from pottery to jewelry to metalworking. There has never been a time in history when people with skills not taught in college have been in so much demand at such high pay as today, nor a time when the range of such jobs has been so wide. In today's America, finding a first-rate lawyer or physician is easy. Finding first-rate skilled labor is hard.

Intrinsic Rewards

35   The topic is no longer money but job satisfaction—intrinsic rewards.   35
We return to our high-school graduate trying to decide between going to college and becoming an electrician. He knows that he enjoys working with his hands and likes the idea of not being stuck in the same place all day, but he also likes the idea of being a manager sitting behind a desk in a big office, telling people what to do and getting the status that goes with it.

However, he should face facts that he is unlikely to know on his own, but that a guidance counselor could help him face. His chances of getting the big office and the status are slim. He is more likely to remain in a cubicle, under the thumb of the boss in the big office. He is unlikely to have a job in which he produces something tangible during the course of the day.

If he becomes a top electrician instead, he will have an expertise that he exercises at a high level. At the end of a workday, he will often be able to see that his work made a difference in the lives of people whose problems he has solved. He will not be confined to a cubicle and, after his apprenticeship, will be his own supervisor in the field. Top electricians often become independent contractors who have no boss at all.

The intrinsic rewards of being a top manager can be just as great as those of a top electrician (though I would not claim they are greater), but the intrinsic rewards of being a mediocre manager are not. Even as people in white-collar jobs lament the soullessness of their work, the intrinsic rewards of exercising technical skills remain undiminished.

Finally, there is an overarching consideration so important it is hard to express adequately: the satisfaction of being good at what one does for a living (and knowing it), compared to the melancholy of being mediocre at what one does for a living (and knowing it). This is another truth about living a human life that a 17-year-old might not yet understand on his own, but that a guidance counselor can bring to his attention. Guidance counselors and parents who automatically encourage young people to go to college straight out of high school regardless of their skills and interests are being thoughtless about the best interests of young people in their charge.

The Dark Side of the B.A. as Norm

40 It is possible to accept all that I have presented as fact and still disagree with the proposition that too many people are going to college. The argument goes something like this:

The meaning of a college education has evolved since the 19th century. The traditional liberal education is still available for students who want it, but the curriculum is appropriately broader now, and includes many courses for vocational preparation that today's students want. Furthermore, intellectual requirements vary across majors. It may be true that few students can complete a major in economics or biology, but larger proportions can handle the easier majors. A narrow focus on curriculum also misses the important nonacademic functions of college. The lifestyle on today's campuses may leave something to be desired, but four years of college still give youngsters in late adolescence a chance to encounter different kinds of people, to discover new interests, and to decide what they want to make of their lives. And if it is true that some students spend too much of their college years partying, that was also true of many Oxford students in the 18th century. Lighten up.

If the only people we had to worry about were those who are on college campuses and doing reasonably well, this position would have something to be said for it. It does not address the issues of whether four years makes sense or whether a residential facility makes sense; nevertheless, college as it exists is not an intrinsically evil place for the students who are there and are coping academically. But there is the broader American society to worry about as well. However unintentionally, we have made something that is still inaccessible to a majority of the population—the B.A.—into a symbol of first-class citizenship. We have done so at the same time that other class divisions are becoming more powerful. Today's college system is implicated in the emergence of class-riven America.

The problem begins with the message sent to young people that they should aspire to college no matter what. Some politicians are among the most visible offenders, treating every failure to go to college as an injustice that can be remedied by increasing government help. American educational administrators reinforce the message by instructing guidance counselors to steer as many students as possible toward a college-prep track (more than 90 percent of high-school students report that their guidance counselors encouraged them to go to college). But politicians and educators are only following the lead of the larger culture. As long as it remains taboo to acknowledge that college is intellectually too demanding for most young people, we will continue to create crazily unrealistic expectations among the next generation. If "crazily unrealistic" sounds too strong, consider that more than 90 percent of high school seniors expect to go to college, and more than 70 percent of them expect to work in professional jobs.

One aspect of this phenomenon has been labeled misaligned ambitions, meaning that adolescents have career ambitions that are inconsistent with their educational plans. Data from the Sloan Study of Youth and Social Development conducted during the 1990s indicate that misaligned ambitions characterized more than half of all adolescents. Almost always, the misalignment is in the optimistic direction, as adolescents aspire to be attorneys or physicians without understanding the educational hurdles they must surmount to achieve their goals. They end up at a four-year institution not because that is where they can take the courses they need to meet their career goals, but because college is the place where B.A.s are handed out, and everyone knows that these days you've got to have a B.A. Many of them drop out. Of those who entered a four-year college in 1995, only 58 percent had gotten their B.A. five academic years later. Another 14 percent were still enrolled. If we assume that half of that 14 percent eventually get their B.A.s, about a third of all those who entered college hoping for a B.A. leave without one.

45   If these numbers had been produced in a culture where the B.A. was a nice thing to have but not a big deal, they could be interpreted as the result of young adults deciding that they didn't really want a B.A. after all. Instead, these numbers were produced by a system in which having a B.A. is a very big deal indeed, and that brings us to the increasingly worrisome role of the B.A. as a source of class division. The United States has always had symbols of class, and the college degree has always been one of them. But through the first half of the 20th century, there were all sorts of respectable reasons a person might not go to college—not enough money to pay for college; needing to work right out of high school to support a wife, parents, or younger siblings; or the commonly held belief that going straight to work was better preparation for a business career than going to college. As long as the percentage of college graduates remained small, it also remained true, and everybody knew it, that the majority of America's intellectually most able people did not have B.A.s.

Over the course of the 20th century, three trends gathered strength. The first was the increasing proportion of jobs screened for high academic ability due to the advanced level of education they require—engineers, physicians, attorneys, college teachers, scientists, and the like. The second was the increasing market value of those jobs. The third was the opening up of college to more of those who had the academic ability to go to college, partly because the increase in American wealth meant that more parents could afford college for their children, and partly because the proliferation of scholarships and loans made it possible for most students with enough academic ability to go.

The combined effect of these trends has been to overturn the state of affairs that prevailed through World War II. Now the great majority of America's intellectually most able people do have a B.A. Along with that transformation has come a downside that few anticipated. The acceptable excuses for not going to college have dried up. The more people who go to college, the more stigmatizing the failure to complete college becomes. Today, if you do not get a B.A., many people assume it is because you are too dumb or too lazy. And all this because of a degree that seldom has an interpretable substantive meaning.

Let's approach the situation from a different angle. Imagine that America had no system of postsecondary education and you were made a member of a task force assigned to create one from scratch. Ask yourself what you would think if one of your colleagues submitted this proposal:

First, we will set up a common goal for every young person that represents educational success. We will call it a B.A. We will then make it difficult or impossible for most people to achieve this goal. For those who can, achieving the goal will take four years no matter what is being taught. We will attach an economic reward for reaching the goal that often has little to do with the content of what has been learned. We will lure large numbers of people who do not possess adequate ability or motivation to try to achieve the goal and then fail. We will then stigmatize everyone who fails to achieve it.

50   What I have just described is the system that we have in place.   50
There must be a better way.

Questions on Meaning

1. Murray begins his essay with what is essentially a definition of a liberal education. How does he characterize it? What kind of person is a liberal education designed to create? What should be the role of such a person within society?

2. What does the author mean by "core knowledge"? Why is it important, in the author's view, for people to have it? State the reasons why the author believes this kind of knowledge should be taught in the K-8 years of schooling.

3. Summarize the main points in Murray's argument. How would you describe his approach? What kinds of evidence does he provide? In your opinion, what parts of the argument do you find most persuasive? At what points in the essay are you less convinced?

4. Early in the essay the author asserts the premise that "full participation in any culture requires familiarity with a body of core knowledge." Do you agree or disagree? Explain your reasons.

Questions on Rhetorical Strategy and Style

1. Expand your answer to question #3 above. Identify the kinds of evidence Murray uses to support his perspective. Look specifically at the kinds of sources he references. What kinds of sources are they? What makes them credible? How does he establish his own credibility on the subject at hand?

2. How does the author display his awareness that the topic is controversial? Knowing this, how does he anticipate and deal with those who will disagree with his perspective?

3. Review the hypothetical example of "a young man who has just graduated from high school and is trying to decide whether to become an electrician or go to college and major in business hoping to become a white-collar manager." Why has the author included this example? Did it accomplish its purpose for us? Why or why not?

Writing Assignments

1. Higher education has become a critical issue of late for several reasons. The cost of tuition has outpaced inflation as states have cut their higher education appropriations. Student debt is a virtual national crisis. Competition has come from the for-profit sector. The government is concerned about our ability to compete on a global scale fostering an intense focus on job and career training, particularly in the STEM areas. Write a literature review gathering together various sources of the debate. In your review, annotate each source in a brief paragraph that captures the standpoint of the author on the issue. Include in your review a brief introduction to the issue and brief remarks at the conclusion.

2. Write a personal essay in which you discuss why you decided to attend college. Discuss how your background prepared your for college. But also you may discuss the reasons why you were not prepared for college. In thinking about your essay, consider how you fit one of the profiles of people Murray writes about in this selection.

College Pressures

William Zinsser

William Zinsser (1922–) was born in New York City. A graduate of Princeton University (1944), Zinsser has worked as a feature and editorial writer, drama editor, and film critic for The New York Herald Tribune; *a columnist for* Life, Look, *and* The New York Times; *an editor for the Book-of-the-Month Club; and an English instructor at Yale University. Zinsser's books include* Pop Goes America *(1963),* On Writing Well: An Informal Guide to Writing Nonfiction *(1976),* Writing With a Word Processor *(1983),* Writing to Learn *(1988),* Willie and Dwike *(1984), and* Spring Training *(1989). In the essay that follows, published in* Blair and Ketchum's Country Journal *magazine in 1979, Zinsser describes the pressures experienced by college students in the late 1970s that make them rigidly goal-driven and unable to explore.*

Dear Carlos: I desperately need a dean's excuse for my chem midterm which will begin in about 1 hour. All I can say is that I totally blew it this week. I've fallen incredibly, inconceivably behind.

Carlos: Help! I'm anxious to hear from you. I'll be in my room and won't leave it until I hear from you. Tomorrow is the last day for . . .

Carlos: I left town because I started bugging out again. I stayed up all night to finish a take-home make-up exam & am typing it to hand in on the 10th. It was due on the 5th. P.S. I'm going to the dentist. Pain is pretty bad.

Carlos: Probably by Friday I'll be able to get back to my studies. Right now I'm going to take a long walk. This whole thing has taken a lot out of me.

Carlos: I'm really up the proverbial creek. The problem is I really bombed the history final. Since I need that course for my major I . . .

Carlos: Here follows a tale of woe. I went home this weekend, had to help my Mom, & caught a fever so didn't have much time to study. My professor . . .

Carlos: Aargh! Trouble. Nothing original but everything's piling up at once. To be brief, my job interview . . .

Hey Carlos, good news! I've got mononucleosis.

1   Who are these wretched supplicants, scribbling notes so laden with anxiety, seeking such miracles of postponement and balm? They are men and women who belong to Branford College, one of the twelve residential colleges at Yale University, and the messages are just a few of the hundreds that they left for their dean, Carlos Hortas—often slipped under his door at 4 A.M.—last year.

But students like the ones who wrote those notes can also be found on campuses from coast to coast—especially in New England and at many other private colleges across the country that have high academic standards and highly motivated students. Nobody could doubt that the notes are real. In their urgency and their gallows humor they are authentic voices of a generation that is panicky to succeed.

My own connection with the message writers is that I am master of Branford College. I live in its Gothic quadrangle and know the students well. (We have 485 of them.) I am privy to their hopes and fears—and also to their stereo music and their piercing cries in the dead of night ("Does anybody *ca-a-are?*"). If they went to Carlos to ask how to get through tomorrow, they come to me to ask how to get through the rest of their lives.

Mainly I try to remind them that the road ahead is a long one and that it will have more unexpected turns than they think. There will be plenty of time to change jobs, change careers, change whole attitudes and approaches. They don't want to hear such liberating news. They want a map—right now—that they can follow unswervingly to career security, financial security, Social Security and, presumably, a prepaid grave.

5   What I wish for all students is some release from the clammy grip of the future. I wish them a chance to savor each segment of their

education as an experience in itself and not as a grim preparation for the next step. I wish them the right to experiment, to trip and fall, to learn that defeat is as instructive as victory and is not the end of the world.

My wish, of course, is naïve. One of the few rights that America does not proclaim is the right to fail. Achievement is the national god, venerated in our media—the million-dollar athlete, the wealthy executive—and glorified in our praise of possessions. In the presence of such a potent state religion, the young are growing up old.

I see four kinds of pressure working on college students today: economic pressure, parental pressure, peer pressure, and self-induced pressure. It is easy to look around for villains—to blame the colleges for charging too much money, the professors for assigning too much work, the parents for pushing their children too far, the students for driving themselves too hard. But there are no villains; only victims.

"In the late 1960s," one dean told me, "the typical question that I got from students was 'Why is there so much suffering in the world?' or 'How can I make a contribution?' Today it's 'Do you think it would look better for getting into law school if I did a double major in history and political science, or just majored in one of them?' " Many other deans confirmed this pattern. One said: "They're trying to find an edge—the intangible something that will look better on paper if two students are about equal."

Note the emphasis on looking better. The transcript has become a sacred document, the passport to security. How one appears on paper is more important than how one appears in person. *A* is for Admirable and *B* is for Borderline, even though, in Yale's official system of grading, *A* means "excellent" and *B* means "very good." Today, looking very good is no longer good enough, especially for students who hope to go on to law school or medical school. They know that entrance into the better schools will be an entrance into the better law firms and better medical practices where they will make a lot of money. They also know that the odds are harsh. Yale Law School, for instance, matriculates 170 students from an applicant pool of 3,700; Harvard enrolls 550 from a pool of 7,000.

10   It's all very well for those of us who write letters of recommenda-   10
tion for our students to stress the qualities of humanity that will make them good lawyers or doctors. And it's nice to think that admission officers are really reading our letters and looking for the extra dimension of commitment or concern. Still, it would be hard for a student not to

visualize these officers shuffling so many transcripts studded with *As* that they regard a *B* as positively shameful.

The pressure is almost as heavy on students who just want to graduate and get a job. Long gone are the days of the "gentleman's C," when students journeyed through college with a certain relaxation, sampling a wide variety of courses—music, art, philosophy, classics, anthropology, poetry, religion—that would send them out as liberally educated men and women. If I were an employer I would rather employ graduates who have this range and curiosity than those who narrowly pursued safe subjects and high grades. I know countless students whose inquiring minds exhilarate me. I like to hear the play of their ideas. I don't know if they are getting *As* or *Cs*, and I don't care. I also like them as people. The country needs them, and they will find satisfying jobs. I tell them to relax. They can't.

Nor can I blame them. They live in a brutal economy. Tuition, room, and board at most private colleges now comes to at least $7,000, not counting books and fees. This might seem to suggest that the colleges are getting rich. But they are equally battered by inflation. Tuition covers only 60 percent of what it costs to educate a student, and ordinarily the remainder comes from what colleges receive in endowments, grants, and gifts. Now the remainder keeps being swallowed by the cruel costs—higher every year—of just opening the doors. Heating oil is up. Insurance is up. Postage is up. Health-premium costs are up. Everything is up. Deficits are up. We are witnessing in America the creation of a brotherhood of paupers—colleges, parents, and students, joined by the common bond of debt.

Today it is not unusual for a student, even if he works part time at college and full time during the summer, to accrue $5,000 in loans after four years—loans that he must start to repay within one year after graduation. Exhorted at commencement to go forth into the world, he is already behind as he goes forth. How could he not feel under pressure throughout college to prepare for this day of reckoning? I have used "he," incidentally, only for brevity. Women at Yale are under no less pressure to justify their expensive education to themselves, their parents, and society. In fact, they are probably under more pressure. For although they leave college superbly equipped to bring fresh leadership to traditionally male jobs, society hasn't yet caught up with this fact.

Along with economic pressure goes parental pressure. Inevitably, the two are deeply intertwined.

15   I see many students taking pre-medical courses with joyless tenacity. They go off to their labs as if they were going to the dentist. It saddens me because I know them in other corners of their life as cheerful people.

"Do you want to go to medical school?" I ask them.

"I guess so," they say, without conviction, or "Not really."

"Then why are you going?"

"Well, my parents want me to be a doctor. They're paying all this money and . . . "

20   Poor students, poor parents. They are caught in one of the oldest webs of love and duty and guilt. The parents mean well; they are trying to steer their sons and daughters toward a secure future. But the sons and daughters want to major in history or classics or philosophy—subjects with no "practical" value. Where's the payoff on the humanities? It's not easy to persuade such loving parents that the humanities do indeed pay off. The intellectual faculties developed by studying subjects like history and classics—an ability to synthesize and relate, to weigh cause and effect, to see events in perspective—are just the faculties that make creative leaders in business or almost any general field. Still, many fathers would rather put their money on courses that point toward a specific profession—courses that are pre-law, pre-medical, pre-business, or, as I sometimes heard it put, "pre-rich."

But the pressure on students is severe. They are truly torn. One part of them feels obligated to fulfill their parents' expectations; after all, their parents are older and presumably wiser. Another part tells them that the expectations that are right for their parents are not right for them.

I know a student who wants to be an artist. She is very obviously an artist and will be a good one—she has already had several modest local exhibits. Meanwhile she is growing as a well-rounded person and taking humanistic subjects that will enrich the inner resources out of which her art will grow. But her father is strongly opposed. He thinks that an artist is a "dumb" thing to be. The student vacillates and tries to please everybody. She keeps up with her art somewhat furtively and takes some of the "dumb" courses her father wants her to take—at least they are dumb courses for her. She is a free spirit on a campus of tense students—no small achievement in itself—and she deserves to follow her muse.

Peer pressure and self-induced pressure are also intertwined, and they begin almost at the beginning of freshman year.

"I had a freshman student I'll call Linda," one dean told me, "who came in and said she was under terrible pressure because her roommate, Barbara, was much brighter and studied all the time. I couldn't tell her that Barbara had come in two hours earlier to say the same thing about Linda."

25   The story is almost funny except that it's not. It's symptomatic of all the pressures put together. When every student thinks every other student is working harder and doing better, the only solution is to study harder still. I see students going off to the library every night after dinner and coming back when it closes at midnight. I wish they would sometimes forget about their peers and go to a movie. I hear the clacking of typewriters in the hours before dawn. I see the tension in their eyes when exams are approaching and papers are due: *"Will I get everything done?"*

Probably they won't. They will get sick. They will get "blocked." They will sleep. They will oversleep. They will bug out. *Hey Carlos, help!*

Part of the problem is that they do more than they are expected to do. A professor will assign five-page papers. Several students will start writing ten-page papers to impress him. Then more students will write ten-page papers, and a few will raise the ante to fifteen. Pity the poor student who is still just doing the assignment.

"Once you have 20 or 30 percent of the student population deliberately overexerting," one dean points out, "it's bad for everybody. When a teacher gets more and more effort from his class, the student who is doing normal work can be perceived as not doing well. The tactic works, psychologically."

Why can't the professor just cut back and not accept longer papers? He can, and he probably will. But by then the term will be half over and the damage done. Grade fever is highly contagious and not easily reversed. Besides, the professor's main concern is with his course. He knows his students only in relation to the course and doesn't know that they are also overexerting in their other courses. Nor is it really his business. He didn't sign up for dealing with the student as a whole person and with all the emotional baggage the student brought along from home. That's what deans, masters, chaplains, and psychiatrists are for.

30   To some extent this is nothing new: a certain number of professors have always been self-contained islands of scholarship and shyness, more comfortable with books than with people. But the new pauperism has widened the gap still further, for professors who actually like to spend time with students don't have as much time to spend. They also are overexerting. If they are young, they are busy trying to publish in order not to perish, hanging by their finger nails onto a shrinking profession. If they are old and tenured, they are buried under the duties of administering departments—as departmental chairmen or members of committees—that have been thinned out by the budgetary axe.

Ultimately it will be the students' own business to break the circles in which they are trapped. They are too young to be prisoners of their parents' dreams and their classmates' fears. They must be jolted into believing in themselves as unique men and women who have the power to shape their own future.

"Violence is being done to the undergraduate experience," says Carlos Hortas. "College should be open-ended: at the end it should open many, many roads. Instead, students are choosing their goal in advance, and their choices narrow as they go along. It's almost as if they think that the country has been codified in the type of jobs that exist—that they've got to fit into certain slots. Therefore, fit into the best-paying slot.

"They ought to take chances. Not taking chances will lead to a life of colorless mediocrity. They'll be comfortable. But something in the spirit will be missing."

I have painted too drab a portrait of today's students, making them seem a solemn lot. That is only half of their story; if they were so dreary I wouldn't so thoroughly enjoy their company. The other half is that they are easy to like. They are quick to laugh and to offer friendship. They are not introverts. They are unusually kind and are more considerate of one another than any student generation I have known.

35   Nor are they so obsessed with their studies that they avoid sports and extracurricular activities. On the contrary, they juggle their crowded hours to play on a variety of teams, perform with musical and dramatic groups, and write for campus publications. But this in turn is one more cause of anxiety. There are too many choices. Academically,

they have 1,300 courses to select from; outside class they have to decide how much spare time they can spare and how to spend it.

This means that they engage in fewer extracurricular pursuits than their predecessors did. If they want to row on the crew and play in the symphony they will eliminate one; in the '60s they would have done both. They also tend to choose activities that are self-limiting. Drama, for instance, is flourishing in all twelve of Yale's residential colleges as it never has before. Students hurl themselves into these productions— as actors, directors, carpenters, and technicians—with a dedication to create the best possible play, knowing that the day will come when the run will end and they can get back to their studies.

They also can't afford to be the willing slave of organizations like the *Yale Daily News.* Last spring at the one-hundredth anniversary banquet of that paper—whose past chairmen include such once and future kings as Potter Stewart, Kingman Brewster, and William F. Buckley, Jr.—much was made of the fact that the editorial staff used to be small and totally committed and that "Newsies" routinely worked fifty hours a week. In effect they belonged to a club; Newsies is how they defined themselves at Yale. Today's student will write one or two articles a week, when he can, and he defines himself as a student. I've never heard the word Newsie except at the banquet.

If I have described the modern undergraduate primarily as a driven creature who is largely ignoring the blithe spirit inside who keeps trying to come out and play, it's because that's where the crunch is, not only at Yale but throughout American education. It's why I think we should all be worried about the values that are nurturing a generation so fearful of risk and so goal-obsessed at such an early age.

I tell students that there is no one "right" way to get ahead—that each of them is a different person, starting from a different point and bound for a different destination. I tell them that change is a tonic and that all the slots are not codified nor the frontiers closed. One of my ways of telling them is to invite men and women who have achieved success outside the academic world to come and talk informally with my students during the year. They are heads of companies or ad agencies, editors of magazines, politicians, public officials, television magnates, labor leaders, business executives, Broadway producers, artists, writers, economists, photographers, scientists, historians—a mixed bag of achievers.

40 I ask them to say a few words about how they got started. The students assume that they started in their present profession and knew all along that it was what they wanted to do. Luckily for me, most of them got into their field by a circuitous route, to their surprise, after many detours. The students are startled. They can hardly conceive of a career that was not pre-planned. They can hardly imagine allowing the hand of God or chance to nudge them down some unforseen trail. 40

Questions on Meaning

1. Why does Zinsser identify "achievement" as the "national god"? What is his wish for students? Who does he say is responsible for getting students out of their achievement trap?
2. In this 1979 essay, Zinsser expresses the opinion that female students are under more pressure than male students. Do you believe that is the case today?

Questions on Rhetorical Strategy and Style

1. In the second paragraph after the notes to Carlos, Zinsser identifies students who are "panicky to succeed" as often being students at "New England and other private colleges that have high academic standards and highly motivated students." How do you react to this comment? Do you feel that Zinsser becomes more inclusive as he continues the essay, or does he maintain this somewhat elitist perspective?
2. How does Zinsser use the writing strategy of classification and division to describe the various pressures students face? How do these pressures compare to the pressures students feel today? Using his divisions, how would you classify the pressures you feel at school?
3. How does Zinsser compare and contrast the outlook of students in the 1960s to students in the late 1970s? How would you compare and contrast the outlook of students today to those he describes?

Writing Assignments

1. Find where Zinsser uses an example of an artistic student to illustrate parental pressure. How well do you relate to the trials and tribulations of an artistic student at Yale in the late 1970s? What are the characteristics of a student who would best reflect the pressures *you* feel?
2. Reread paragraph 11 ("The pressure is almost as heavy . . .") and paragraph 20 ("Poor students, poor parents.") and compare and contrast how you are approaching your college years to the approach Zinsser would like to see students take. Explain why you feel you are headed in the right direction or not.

3. It is not difficult for students to get caught up in competing with their peers in terms of time spent studying, pages of reports, and, of course, grades. Describe the peer pressures you have felt at college. How have they affected the way you study and your feelings of accomplishment?

4. In the 1960s, students used to joke that they would like to collect Social Security upon graduation and work a few years extra when they reached retirement age so they could enjoy life while they were young. Write an essay about what you would do if you were given a living allowance and told to take a few years off after college *without penalty on your resume.* Would you take courses you couldn't because of requirements in your major, perform volunteer work, travel, live alone in a cabin and read, help your family at home, wait tables at a resort? How do you think this spontaneous, experimental time would affect your outlook on life? What "unforeseen trails" do you think you might be "nudged down"?

The Human Cost of an Illiterate Society

Jonathan Kozol

*Jonathan Kozol (1936–) was born in Boston and gradu-
ated from Harvard University. He has taught at Yale University, Trinity College, and the University of Massachusetts
at Amherst as well as several public schools. He is well
known for his writing on social and educational issues,
often calling for educational reform and more realistic examination of societal problems. His books include* Death
at an Early Age *(1967),* Free Schools *(1972),* On Being
a Teacher *(1981),* Illiterate America *(1985),* Rachel and
Her Children: Homeless Families in America *(1986),
and* Savage Inequalities: Children in America's Schools
(1991). The following selection is an excerpt from Illiterate America. *Kozol does not explore the causes of illiteracy
in this selection, as he does elsewhere in this book, but instead looks at a wide range of effects, or costs, of illiteracy,
both for society and the individual. Before beginning to
read, think for a moment about what it might mean to be
illiterate. Try to imagine how many ways your life would
be different if you couldn't read. Regardless of how imagi-
native you are, you are likely to be shocked by all the ways
illiteracy affects an illiterate person and society as a whole.*

PRECAUTIONS. READ BEFORE USING.
Poison: Contains sodium hydroxide (caustic soda-lye).
Corrosive: Causes severe eye and skin damage, may cause blindness.
Harmful or fatal if swallowed.
If swallowed, give large quantities of milk or water.

Do not induce vomiting.
Important: Keep water out of can at all times to prevent contents from violently erupting . . .

—warning on a can of Drano

1   Questions of literacy, in Socrates' belief, must at length be judged as matters of morality. Socrates could not have had in mind the moral compromise peculiar to a nation like our own. Some of our Founding Fathers did, however, have this question in their minds. One of the wisest of those Founding Fathers (one who may not have been most compassionate but surely was more prescient than some of his peers) recognized the special dangers that illiteracy would pose to basic equity in the political construction that he helped to shape.

"A people who mean to be their own governors," James Madison wrote, "must arm themselves with the power knowledge gives. A popular government without popular information or the means of acquiring it, is but a prologue to a farce or a tragedy, or perhaps both."

Tragedy looms larger than farce in the United States today. Illiterate citizens seldom vote. Those who do are forced to cast a vote of questionable worth. They cannot make informed decisions based on serious print information. Sometimes they can be alerted to their interests by aggressive voter education. More frequently, they vote for a face, a smile, or a style, not for a mind or character or body of beliefs.

The number of illiterate adults exceeds by 16 million the entire vote cast for the winner in the 1980 presidential contest. If even one third of all illiterates could vote, and read enough and do sufficient math to vote in their self-interest, Ronald Reagan would not likely have been chosen president. There is, of course, no way to know for sure. We do know this: Democracy is a mendacious term when used by those who are prepared to countenance the forced exclusion of one third of our electorate. So long as 60 million people are denied significant participation, the government is neither of, nor for, nor by, the people. It is a government, at best, of those two thirds whose wealth, skin color, or parental privilege allows them opportunity to profit from the provocation and instruction of the written word.

5   The undermining of democracy in the United States is one "expense" that sensitive Americans can easily deplore because it represents a contradiction that endangers citizens of all political positions. The human price is not so obvious at first.

Since I first immersed myself within this work I have often had the following dream: I find that I am in a railroad station or a large department store within a city that is utterly unknown to me and where I cannot understand the printed words. None of the signs or symbols is familiar. Everything looks strange: like mirror writing of some kind. Gradually I understand that I am in the Soviet Union. All the letters on the walls around me are Cyrillic. I look for my pocket dictionary but I find that it has been mislaid. Where have I left it? Then I recall that I forgot to bring it with me when I packed my bags in Boston. I struggle to remember the name of my hotel. I try to ask somebody for directions. One person stops and looks at me in a peculiar way. I lose the nerve to ask. At last I reach into my wallet for an ID card. The card is missing. Have I lost it? Then I remember that my card was confiscated for some reason, many years before. Around this point, I wake up in a panic.

This panic is not so different from the misery that millions of adult illiterates experience each day within the course of their routine existence in the U.S.A.

Illiterates cannot read the menu in a restaurant.

They cannot read the cost of items on the menu in the *window* of the restaurant before they enter.

10 Illiterates cannot read the letters that their children bring home 10 from their teachers. They cannot study school department circulars that tell them of the courses that their children must be taking if they hope to pass the SAT exams. They cannot help with homework. They cannot write a letter to the teacher. They are afraid to visit in the classroom. They do not want to humiliate their child or themselves.

Illiterates cannot read instructions on a bottle of prescription medicine. They cannot find out when a medicine is past the year of safe consumption; nor can they read of allergenic risks, warnings to diabetics, or the potential sedative effect of certain kinds of nonprescription pills. They cannot observe preventive health care admonitions. They cannot read about "the seven warning signs of cancer" or the indications of blood-sugar fluctuations or the risks of eating certain foods that aggravate the likelihood of cardiac arrest.

Illiterates live, in more than literal ways, an uninsured existence. They cannot understand the written details on a health insurance form. They cannot read the waivers that they sign preceding surgical procedures. Several women I have known in Boston have entered a slum hospital with the intention of obtaining a tubal ligation and have emerged a few days later after having been subjected to a hysterectomy. Unaware of their rights, incognizant of jargon, intimidated by the unfamiliar air of fear and atmosphere of ether that so many of us find oppressive in the confines even of the most attractive and expensive medical facilities, they have signed their names to documents they could not read and which nobody, in the hectic situation that prevails so often in those overcrowded hospitals that serve the urban poor, had even bothered to explain.

Childbirth might seem to be the last inalienable right of any female citizen within a civilized society. Illiterate mothers, as we shall see, already have been cheated of the power to protect their progeny against the likelihood of demolition in deficient public schools and, as a result, against the verbal servitude within which they themselves exist. Surgical denial of the right to bear that child in the first place represents an ultimate denial, an unspeakable metaphor, a final darkness that denies even the twilight gleamings of our own humanity. What greater violation of our biological, our biblical, our spiritual humanity could possibly exist than that which takes place nightly, perhaps hourly these days, within such over-burdened and benighted institutions as the Boston City Hospital? Illiteracy has many costs; few are so irreversible as this.

Even the roof above one's head, the gas or other fuel for heating that protects the residents of northern city slums against the threat of illness in the winter months become uncertain guarantees. Illiterates cannot read the lease that they must sign to live in an apartment which, too often, they cannot afford. They cannot manage check accounts and therefore seldom pay for anything by mail. Hours and entire days of difficult travel (and the cost of bus or other public transit) must be added to the real cost of whatever they consume. Loss of interest on the check accounts they do not have, and could not manage if they did, must be regarded as another of the excess costs paid by the citizen who is excluded from the common instruments of commerce in a numerate society.

15   "I couldn't understand the bills," a woman in Washington, D.C.,   15
reports, "and then I couldn't write the checks to pay them. We signed things we didn't know what they were."

Illiterates cannot read the notices that they receive from welfare offices or from the IRS. They must depend on word-of-mouth instruction from the welfare worker—or from other persons whom they have good reason to mistrust. They do not know what rights they have, what deadlines and requirements they face, what options they might choose to exercise. They are half-citizens. Their rights exist in print but not in fact.

Illiterates cannot look up numbers in a telephone directory. Even if they can find the names of friends, few possess the sorting skills to make use of the yellow pages; categories are bewildering and trade names are beyond decoding capabilities for millions of nonreaders. Even the emergency numbers listed on the first page of the phone book—"Ambulance," "Police," and "Fire"—are too frequently beyond the recognition of nonreaders.

Many illiterates cannot read the admonition on a pack of cigarettes. Neither the Surgeon General's warning nor its reproduction on the package can alert them to the risks. Although most people learn by word of mouth that smoking is related to a number of grave physical disorders, they do not get the chance to read the detailed stories which can document this danger with the vividness that turns concern into determination to resist. They can see the handsome cowboy or the slim Virginia lady lighting up a filter cigarette; they cannot heed the words that tell them that this product is (not "may be") dangerous to their health. Sixty million men and women are condemned to be the unalerted, high-risk candidates for cancer.

Illiterates do not buy "no-name" products in the supermarkets. They must depend on photographs or the familiar logos that are printed on the packages of brand-name groceries. The poorest people, therefore, are denied the benefits of the least costly products.

20   Illiterates depend almost entirely upon label recognition. Many 20 labels, however, are not easy to distinguish. Dozens of different kinds of Campbell's soup appear identical to the nonreaders The purchaser who cannot read and does not dare to ask for help, out of the fear of being stigmatized (a fear which is unfortunately realistic), frequently comes home with something which she never wanted and her family never tasted.

Illiterates cannot read instructions on a pack of frozen food. Packages sometimes provide an illustration to explain the cooking preparations; but illustrations are of little help to someone who must "boil water, drop the food—*within* its plastic wrapper—in the boiling water, wait for it to simmer, instantly remove."

Even when labels are seemingly clear, they may be easily mistaken. A woman in Detroit brought home a gallon of Crisco for her children's dinner. She thought that she had bought the chicken that was pictured on the label. She had enough Crisco now to last a year—but no more money to go back and buy the food for dinner.

Recipes provided on the packages of certain staples sometimes tempt a semiliterate person to prepare a meal her children have not tasted. The longing to vary the uniform and often starchy content of low-budget meals provided to the family that relies on food stamps commonly leads to ruinous results. Scarce funds have been wasted and the food must be thrown out. The same applies to distribution of food-surplus produce in emergency conditions. Government inducements to poor people to "explore the ways" by which to make a tasty meal from tasteless noodles, surplus cheese, and powdered milk are useless to nonreaders. Intended as benevolent advice, such recommendations mock reality and foster deeper feelings of resentment and of inability to cope. (Those, on the other hand, who cautiously refrain from "innovative" recipes in preparation of their children's meals must suffer the opprobrium of "laziness," "lack of imagination. . . .")

Illiterates cannot travel freely. When they attempt to do so, they encounter risks that few of us can dream of. They cannot read traffic signs and, while they often learn to recognize and to decipher symbols, they cannot manage street names which they haven't seen before. The same is true for bus and subway stops. While ingenuity can sometimes help a man or woman to discern directions from familiar landmarks, buildings, cemeteries, churches, and the like, most illiterates are virtually immobilized. They seldom wander past the streets and neighborhoods they know. Geographical paralysis becomes a bitter metaphor for their entire existence. They are immobilized in almost every sense we can imagine. They can't move up. They can't move out. They cannot see beyond. Illiterates may take an oral test for drivers' permits in most sections of America. It is a questionable concession. Where will they go? How will they get there? How will they get home? Could it be that some of us might like it better if they stayed where they belong?

25   Travel is only one of many instances of circumscribed existence.   25
Choice, in almost all its facets, is diminished in the life of an illiterate adult. Even the printed TV schedule, which provides most people with the luxury of preselection, does not belong within the arsenal of options in illiterate existence. One consequence is that the viewer watches only what appears at moments when he happens to have time to turn the switch. Another consequence, a lot more common, is that the TV set remains in operation night and day. Whatever the program offered at the hour when he walks into the room will be the nutriment

that he accepts and swallows. Thus, to passivity, is added frequency—indeed, almost uninterrupted continuity. Freedom to select is no more possible here than in the choice of home or surgery or food.

"You don't choose," said one illiterate woman. "You take your wishes from somebody else." Whether in perusal of a menu, selection of highways, purchase of groceries, or determination of affordable enjoyment, illiterate Americans must trust somebody else: a friend, a relative, a stranger on the street, a grocery clerk, a TV copywriter.

"All of our mail we get, it's hard for her to read. Settin' down and writing a letter, she can't do it. Like if we get a bill . . . we take it over to my sister-in-law . . . My sister-in-law reads it."

Billing agencies harass poor people for the payment of the bills for purchases that might have taken place six months before. Utility companies offer an agreement for a staggered payment schedule on a bill past due. "You have to trust them," one man said. Precisely for this reason, you end up by trusting no one and suspecting everyone of possible deceit. A submerged sense of distrust becomes the corollary to a constant need to trust. "They are cheating me . . . I have been tricked . . . I do not know . . ."

Not knowing: This is a familiar theme. Not knowing the right word for the right thing at the right time is one form of subjugation. Not knowing the world that lies concealed behind those words is a more terrifying feeling. The longitude and latitude of one's existence are beyond all easy apprehension. Even the hard, cold stars within the firmament above one's head begin to mock the possibilities for self-location. Where am I? Where did I come from? Where will I go?

30   "I've lost a lot of jobs," one man explains. "Today, even if you're 30 a janitor, there's still reading and writing . . . They leave a note saying, 'Go to room so-and-so . . .' You can't do it. You can't read it. You don't know."

"The hardest thing about it is that I've been places where I didn't know where I was. You don't know where you are . . . You're lost."

"Like I said: I have two kids. What do I do if one of my kids starts choking? I go running to the phone . . . I can't look up the hospital phone number. That's if we're at home. Out on the street, I can't read the sign. I get to a pay phone. 'Okay, tell us where you are. We'll send an ambulance.' I look at the street sign. Right there, I can't tell you what it says. I'd have to spell it out, letter for letter. By that time, one of my kids would be dead . . . These are the kinds of fears you go with, every single day . . ."

"Reading directions, I suffer with. I work with chemicals . . . That's scary to begin with . . . "

"You sit down. They throw the menu in front of you. Where do you go from there? Nine times out of ten you say, 'Go ahead. Pick out something for the both of us.' I've eaten some weird things, let me tell you!"

35 Menus. Chemicals. A child choking while his mother searches for a word she does not know to find assistance that will come too late. Another mother speaks about the inability to help her kids to read: "I can't read to them. Of course that's leaving them out of something they should have. Oh, it matters. You believe it matters! I ordered all these books. The kids belong to a book club. Donny wanted me to read a book to him. I told Donny: 'I can't read,' He said: 'Mommy, you sit down. I'll read it to you.' I tried it one day, reading from the pictures. Donny looked at me. He said, 'Mommy, that's not right.' He's only five. He knew I couldn't read . . .'"

A landlord tells a woman that her lease allows him to evict her if her baby cries and causes inconvenience to her neighbors. The consequence of challenging his words conveys a danger which appears, unlikely as it seems, even more alarming than the danger of eviction. Once she admits that she can't read, in the desire to maneuver for the time in which to call a friend, she will have defined herself in terms of an explicit impotence that she cannot endure. Capitulation in this case is preferable to self-humiliation. Resisting the definition of oneself in terms of what one cannot do, what others take for granted, represents a need so great that other imperatives (even one so urgent as the need to keep one's home in winter's cold) evaporate and fall away in face of fear. Even the loss of home and shelter, in this case, is not so terrifying as the loss of self.

"I come out of school. I was sixteen. They had their meetings. The directors meet. They said that I was wasting their school paper. I was wasting pencils . . ."

Another illiterate, looking back, believes she was not worthy of her teacher's time. She believes that it was wrong of her to take up space within her school. She believes that it was right to leave in order that somebody more deserving could receive her place.

Children choke. Their mother chokes another way: on more than chicken bones.

40 People eat what others order, know what others tell them, struggle not to see themselves as they believe the world perceives them. A

man in California speaks about his own loss of identity, of self-location, definition:

"I stood at the bottom of the ramp. My car had broke down on the freeway. There was a phone. I asked for the police. They was nice. They said to tell them where I was. I looked up at the signs. There was one that I had seen before. I read it to them: ONE WAY STREET. They thought it was a joke. I told them I couldn't read. There was other signs above the ramp. They told me to try. I looked around for somebody to help. All the cars was going by real fast. I couldn't make them understand that I was lost. The cop was nice. He told me: 'Try once more,' I did my best. I couldn't read. I only knew the sign above my head. The cop was trying to be nice. He knew that I was trapped. 'I can't send out a car to you if you can't tell me where you are.' I felt afraid. I nearly cried. I'm forty-eight years old. I only said: 'I'm on a one-way street . . .'"

The legal problems and the courtroom complications that confront illiterate adults have been discussed above. The anguish that may underlie such matters was brought home to me this year while I was working on this book. I have spoken, in the introduction, of a sudden phone call from one of my former students, now in prison for a criminal offense. Stephen is not a boy today. He is twenty-eight years old. He called to ask me to assist him in his trial, which comes up next fall. He will be on trial for murder. He has just knifed and killed a man who first enticed him to his home, then cheated him, and then insulted him—as "an illiterate subhuman."

Stephen now faces twenty years to life. Stephen's mother was illiterate. His grandparents were illiterate as well. What parental curse did not destroy was killed off finally by the schools. Silent violence is repaid with interest. It will cost us $25,000 yearly to maintain this broken soul in prison. But what is the price that has been paid by Stephen's victim? What is the price that will be paid by Stephen?

Perhaps we might slow down a moment here and look at the realities described above. This is the nation that we live in. This is a society that most of us did not create but which our President and other leaders have been willing to sustain by virtue of malign neglect. Do we possess the character and courage to address a problem which so many nations, poorer than our own, have found it natural to correct?

45   The answers to these questions represent a reasonable test of our   45
belief in the democracy to which we have been asked in public school to swear allegiance.

Questions on Meaning

1. Define what Kozol means by "human cost." You might start your thinking by considering how this cost is different from the literal monetary costs that are also described at different points in the essay.
2. Kozol relates illiteracy to the concept of subjugation. Brainstorm what your think he means by this. Who are the subjugators? What is their motivation for subjugating illiterate people?
3. In a sentence or two, express the primary theme of this essay.

Questions on Rhetorical Strategy and Style

1. One characteristic of Kozol's style is passages that link concrete examples with larger abstractions or generalizations. For example, in paragraph 24, in the context of the difficulties of an illiterate person traveling, Kozol writes, "Geographical paralysis becomes a bitter metaphor for their entire existence. They are immobilized in almost every sense we can imagine." Another example occurs in paragraphs 12 and 13, where Kozol speaks of women given a hysterectomy without being informed of the meaning of this surgery as "a final darkness that denies even the twilight gleamings of our own humanity." Analyze this passage and explain why Kozol calls this the "ultimate denial."
2. Kozol frequently uses description as a rhetorical device for developing the essay. Read back through the essay and identify at least three examples of illiterate people whose problem Kozol describes in detail. How does each of these examples contribute to the effectiveness of the essay overall?
3. How successful is Kozol in building his argument about the costs of illiteracy? What specific characteristics of the essay contribute to your evaluation?

Writing Assignments

1. To better understand the difficulty illiterates face in many types of communication, use your imagination to solve the following problem. You are the director of a new program at your college or university for teaching reading at no cost to adult illiterates in the community. You have funding to hire teachers and pay for classrooms and materials, but very little money left over to publicize the

program. How do you inform illiterates in the community about your reading classes? How do you give them basic information such as where to come and what times and how to get there? Brainstorm with others to reach the most effective solution that overcomes the problems of communication.

2. Kozol says our political leaders sustain the problem of illiteracy through "malign neglect." What does he mean by this phrase? Why is this neglect "malign"? Consider other social problems, such as homelessness or lack of good health care for people in poverty. Do you see "malign neglect" with these problems too? Write an essay in which you explore the reasons why leaders might be neglectful in these ways.

3. In paragraph 3 Kozol states that illiterate persons can only "cast a vote of questionable worth" because their decision is not based on "serious print information" but on "a face, a smile, or a style." Some social critics would say the same is true of many people who can read: that they vote based on television images and sound bytes rather than careful reading of the issues. If true, this only heightens the resulting national tragedy to which Kozol refers. What do you think about this idea? Do most people take the time to study the issues in depth before voting? Ask a few other people about how much they read before the last election. Think about what you learn from their comments, and formulate your own thesis about what really happens in an election and what you think *should* happen. Write a persuasive essay that develops your thesis.

Civic Engagement: The University as a Public Good

Nancy E. Cantor

Nancy Cantor (1952–) graduated from Sarah Lawrence College (1974) and Stanford University (Ph.D. 1978). She taught at Princeton where she chaired the Department of Psychology. She moved on to be dean of the graduate schools at the University of Michigan, where she led the university's defense of affirmative action in the cases Grutter v. Bollinger *and* Gratz v. Bollinger—*which were decided by the Supreme Court in 2003. She wrote several papers on the issues involved in those decisions. She then became chancellor at the University of Illinois-Urbana-Champaign (2001). She is now chancellor at Syracuse University. She is a fellow of the American Academy of Arts and Sciences and has served as chair of the board of directors of the American Association of Higher Education. Her awards include Distinguished Scientific Award for an Early Career Contribution to Psychology, awarded by the American Psychological Association (1985), and Woman of Achievement Award, given by the Anti-Defamation League (2001). She co-authored* Personality and Social Intelligence, *Century Psychology Series, (Prentice Hall, 1987) and* Personality Psychology: Recent Trends and Emerging Directions *(Springer, 1989); and she edited* Personality, Cognition, and Social Interaction *(1981).*

Civic engagement at a great public university requires many kinds of involvement, including work across colleges and departments and work across student boundaries. In this speech, Cantor explains her views of civic engagement and academic diversity.

1   As a public good, universities have a rare and critical role to play. While we educate leaders for the future, we also address important societal issues of the day. Our discoveries can and do change the world. We lay the groundwork for the future as we work to preserve the culture of the past. At the same time, we try out new ways to build community.

The university's role is "rare" because it is positioned to the side of everyday life, unconstrained by requirements for rigid adherence to social norms or intellectual paradigms. The university can foster an experimental attitude—playful, if you will—that can give rise to both intellectual discovery and social innovation.

The university takes on a "critical" role when it opens its gates far enough to listen to the different voices in the debate over the issues of greatest concern to society and to learn about them firsthand. The university must face outward toward work that changes the culture of the day.

We are at our best when we build a community of scholars and learners who feel empowered to be both playful in examining their world and responsible for affecting societal progress. Just as we want to open our gates and look outward, we also want to build model communities on campus to invite the world in as partners.

Liberal learning and civic engagement

5   As AAC&U eloquently states in its Statement on Liberal Learning: "Liberal learning is society's best investment in our shared future." Likewise I would argue that the best way for society to fulfill its dreams of a shared, productive, and harmonious future is to maintain universities as public goods. We can do this by intertwining the playfulness of liberal learning as a mode of thought and action with the responsibility of civic engagement with diverse stakeholders whose voices need to matter more in our shared future. In so doing, we will be able to educate socially responsible citizens who will not be complacent in the face of entrenched societal norms, but will take the initiative in shaping our diverse democracy and its global interconnections.[1]

This can happen because, at their best, liberal education and civic engagement have much in common. Each requires vibrant and sustained exchanges of both people and ideas. Universities can offer safe havens for people from different backgrounds, races, ethnic groups, and generations to talk, argue, and reflect as equals in exchanges that can and should bridge the boundaries between the university and the wider world.

Now, just one generation away from a time when white children will be the minority in our public schools, children of different races still grow up in different neighborhoods without attending each other's birthday parties, proms, weddings, and funerals. Because they and we do not know each other, the stereotypes that result have led to great inequality and injustice in such vital areas as employment, health care, and the criminal justice system.

Mirroring our divisions at home is ethnic, religious, and intergroup conflict in virtually every corner of the globe. The result is untold human and cultural carnage. To make matters worse, we have reacted to the very real pain and losses we have suffered on our own shores by turning inward, "battening the hatches" if you will, presenting real problems for the free and vital exchanges of people and ideas that are the foundation of our democracy.

The task of universities is urgent: to build on themes of diversity, not only in admissions and in recruiting, but also in creating living and learning communities that will produce a citizenry that is both engaged and informed. It is not enough to affirmatively provide access to educational opportunity. We must also create opportunities and settings in which to pursue true integration. Universities can take a leadership role in shaping a dialogue that goes beyond differences by supporting environments in which students learn from and about each other—environments in which differences are neither privileged nor ignored. (See Patricia Gurin's discussion of Benjamin Barber's distinction between ignoring and privileging differences in *Defending Diversity*, 2004.)

Building sustained exchanges: The arts as a prototype

10 Universities can fulfill this mission by offering contexts for the exchanges of people and ideas that are sustained, rather than one-shot efforts over a day, a week, or even a semester. These exchanges must 10

appeal to people of different expertise and backgrounds. They should allow for open-mindedness, permit the suspension of everyday norms and judgments, and give standing to everyone, across generations.

In trying to envision how such exchanges might actually work, we might look to the arts—which I would define broadly as "expressive culture" in all forms—for a natural prototype. The arts stand to the side of daily life, and they allow the expression of self and of social tensions in a safe way. They can also forge sustained connections between peoples and ideas and cultures that otherwise either simply remain invisible, unexpressed, or worse yet, clash in destructive ways.

As an example, I invite you to consider the blues, a creation of African-Americans that made its way from rural slavery to our nation's cities, to people and places all over the world with different musical traditions, to young and old, and to other art forms. It is shown in a brilliant traveling exhibition entitled "Visualizing the Blues," photographs of the Mississippi Delta collected by the Dixon Gallery and Gardens in Memphis.

In the catalog for this exhibition, which was shown at the Krannert Art Museum at the University of Illinois, Deborah Willis Kennedy (2000) writes, "The blues is a life-and-death struggle. The blues permits the living to defend life/living." To visualize the blues, one must contend with prejudice and racism, blood and spit, malice and murder.

Ernest Withers took a photograph that illustrates this point. Its title is "Boarding House Bathroom From Which James Earl Ray Shot Dr. King, 422 South Main Street, Memphis, April 1968." The photograph shows a filthy toilet, an old tub, a pockmarked wall, the open window from which a killer silenced our nation's greatest voice for peace in the twentieth century. The room is repellent. Normally, we would turn away, but as soon as we realize where we are, we stay to stare. We are at the vantage point of the assassin. The image draws us into dialogue, across history and between groups.

15 The arts often serve this way, as the medium, not just the reflection, of intergroup dialogue. They offer an escape from the silencing that tends to come in "normal" society, making it possible to face highly charged and even taboo subjects. And everyone has some "standing" in the "conversation" that ensues. In the arts, for example, it is not only diplomats who can discuss and negotiate peace. Without money, limousines, or hotel reservations, children are taking it up, 15

one-to-one, through a "Peace through Poetry" exchange on the Internet, sponsored by iEARN, an international educational and resource network. The sixteen schools participating in this project are located in Chicago, Lithuania, Japan, Bulgaria, Moscow, and in Urbana, a few blocks from our campus at Illinois.

"Before the war commences the end is clear," writes Rositsa Kuneva, a student from Bulgaria. "All taking part are losers, nobody wins/Never wins the one who fights against his fear/Sluicing down the earth with bloody rinse."[2]

Dialogues such as these strip away the armor that we think we need to protect our place in the world, and there is nothing quite like the voices of students when they are given standing through artistic expression. The arts demonstrate that the kinds of exchanges we need in the nation's colleges and universities are possible, but we must construct ways for these exchanges to occur.

Exchanges across the boundaries of race and ethnicity

In our increasingly multiracial democracy it is vital that universities create exchanges across the rigid boundaries of race and ethnicity, religion and culture. But the exchanges that come so naturally in the arts need something more in higher education: structures that let these exchanges happen.

Our students, faculty, and community partners need settings in which we can let down our guard, acknowledge each other's standing in the conversation, and feel able to express both discomfort and ignorance. We need to be able to do this formally and informally, on and off campus, and across the groups in which we have been socialized. Then and only then will our nation come close to realizing the educational benefits of diversity. Then and only then will we begin to more fully embrace the fifty-year-old promise of *Brown v. Board of Education.*

20 So, why are we in higher education still talking about race? 20 Because our failure to discard the legacy of Jim Crow has left our nation so segregated that our students, for the most part, do not meet as equals until they arrive at our doors. I will never forget a Latina student who told me, "I've never lived with so many white people before." It is up to us to shift that perspective to: "They've never had

the chance to live with ME before," with all the opportunities and optimism that implies. We must create learning and living communities that will make true integration possible, and we must create ways to assess how well we're doing.

We must understand that the idea of "civic engagement" goes beyond service or volunteer work. We must immerse ourselves in environments of genuine exchange, and these can start at home, on our own campuses. Vibrant multiracial/multicultural exchanges that bring the issues of society to our doorstep are as much about civic engagement as are our programs in neighboring communities. We should also take the extra step of inviting our community neighbors onto our campuses as we build new models of community.

Experiments in exchange at Illinois

What would such communities look like? And how can we use what we know about the arts as a model? At Illinois, as on many campuses, we have been asking these questions for several years and I thought it might be useful to describe a few of our efforts, keeping in mind the analogies with the artistic exchanges I have already described.

Exchanges that eschew boundaries. One of the most powerful aspects of artistic exchanges is that they eschew the "normal" boundaries and distinctions of social life—anyone and everyone can be engaged in artistic expression, and frequently these exchanges draw diverse peoples and generations together. In a similar vein, when we created our new Center for Democracy in a Multiracial Society in 2002, we resolved that it would bring together scholars, students, and community activists to engage in conversation about the many racialized positions of different groups and individuals in our society.

The Center drew its advisory board from the leadership of all of our ethnic studies programs on campus. It invited community activists to come to campus for sabbaticals at the Center. It engaged students from different campus communities in intergroup conversations and analyses that go beyond "black and white." And it funded projects to examine the experience of democracy in daily life from these different positions.

Many of the Center's initiatives intentionally engage multiple generations of both novices and experts. They circumvent the "silencing" that comes with power and status, and they give "standing" to those who often are the most affected but the least heard. For example, the Center faculty have mobilized with Latino/a community activists in Illinois to address two issues of critical importance to their community—narrowing the K-12 achievement gap and lobbying for the rights of children of undocumented families. As they define what it means to "mobilize with the community," the goal is to position the families and the students to be heard.

It is the families themselves who are helping to design interventions in the schools. It is our students, many of whom have firsthand experience with being excluded by virtue of their parents' status, who are speaking to the legislators in Springfield, dialoguing at the Center with statewide leaders of the newest Freedom Rides, and learning in action as they take part in opening up educational opportunity to our fastest-growing student population in Illinois. Their voices have authenticity and power when they are finally given the stage. Listen to the words of Yesenia Sanchez, who came to our campus on a Freedom Ride:

> I am fighting for my dignity. I am an undocumented student and, just like many others, feel helpless because my dreams and goals are being snatched away. I wake up every morning and feel that my life is in limbo, nothing is certain . . . I am also here for my mother. When she was a young girl, she was only able to go up to the sixth grade because she was a woman and was supposed to be at home. She tells me how every night she dreamed about going to school. Her dreams are also mine, and I am determined to be someone.

Exchanges that take a lesson from history. We also take a lesson from the arts in trying to encourage cross-talk about race and opportunity, contrasting historical dreams and contemporary realities. At the moment, for example, we are in the middle of a year-long commemoration of the fiftieth anniversary of *Brown v. Board,* honoring those who put their lives on the line for the cause of justice, reexamining their struggle, and rededicating ourselves to their still unfulfilled dream.

At our entering student convocation last August, we began with a speech from the director of our women's studies program, Professor Kal Alston, about what *Brown v. Board* had meant to her African-American family and to her own education in predominantly white schools. We'll end the year with a commencement address by legal scholar and activist, Professor Lani Guinier. In between we have sponsored symposia, performances, book clubs, community research projects and partnerships, and dialogues. We are seeing both synergy and exchange.

30 As part of the commemoration, we invited back to campus 30 alumni from Project 500, which in 1968 recruited African-American students from all over the nation to enroll at Illinois. As graduates, many continued the struggle for civil rights their entire lives and our current students took note of their lessons. Numbers of current students told us later they were so moved by hearing the stories of this older generation that afterwards they met as a group on their own to do some soul-searching about themselves.

In fact, that kind of storytelling and social introspection is a key component in creating new contexts for exchange on campus. The *Brown v. Board* commemoration itself, for example, is now the object of study by undergraduates participating in a new initiative we are calling The Ethnography of the University. This initiative is giving students the opportunity to examine deliberately their own and their peers' experiences of race at the university and then to report their work, their interviews, their data, and their conclusions on a Web archive for future use by other students as well as faculty, staff, and members of our larger community. As the Web archive develops, we too will be able to better assess the impact of our efforts to foster multiracial exchange.

So far, the students' research on the *Brown v. Board* commemoration indicates that a big event, such as the convocation that all first year students are expected to attend, can make a big difference. Their interviews showed that, while only some of our 38,000 students knew about *Brown,* and many did not, every single first-year student interviewed knew something about it and had something to say. A massive one-time effort can create interest that then carries over to the book clubs, symposia, performances, and other venues that offer smaller, ongoing contexts for exchange.

Understanding difference in the service of building common cause happens one person at a time, and it requires that we be able to reflect on our experience and see it in relation to the experiences of others. This, of course, is what happens frequently between artist and audience, as each critiques the other's expressions. It is also what is happening to the students who are doing the research in the Ethnography of the University initiative and we hope it is happening with other students as they gather together to reflect on *Brown*.

Living and learning together in safe havens. Of course, nothing can quite match the awakening that occurs when students come together informally as peers, and in those rare but critical moments, let down their guard, shed their protective armor, and enter into what can then become sustained dialogues about diversity.

35   In this light, I'd like to share a comment from a University of   35 Michigan undergraduate who answered an e-mail request to all students from the president of the Michigan Student Assembly, to describe the impact, positive or negative, of diversity on their lives. This is what she said, in her words, in 1997:

> My roommate and I roomed blind. I had no idea whom I would end up with. In mid-August I found out all about her. She was from Detroit and black. This didn't bother me one bit. So far we have gotten along great. . . . Here is one thing that I found funny. . . . My roommate has a flat iron that she uses to straighten AND curl her hair with. She had been bugging me for a while to let her try it on my hair. This one Friday night I decided to let her give it a try. . . . So she reached for my hair with her hand so that she could grab a chunk to brush. "EEEE," she shrieked. "What is that? . . . No, nothing is wrong. I just can't believe what your hair feels like! . . . I've never felt any white girl's hair before," she said. "I had no idea it was so different." We spent the next hour discussing how we take care of our hair, how much it costs to get it done, and we also argued about what a perm is. This isn't a great educational story, but now I feel a little more "worldly" and not as sheltered as I had before. It's the little things like this that make impacts on my life. Small, but nonetheless important. Diversity helps to make the world a little smaller.

In one brief moment, two students who were already friends and even shared the same room really *saw* each other in new ways, as women with hair that was different and bad hair days that were the same. One more blind spot disappeared in the slow way things happen when real integration finally occurs, when differences can be affirmed, talked about, and shared.

So how do we foster this sense of safety to express the self and social tensions in nonjudgmental and authentic ways in both living and learning environments—and preferably at the place that living and learning intersect? Again using the insight we can get from the arts, compare the difference in the courage of expression we typically see in campus theater to the muted "politeness" of many classroom discussions.

Classroom conversations can be just as courageous, but first we must structure the context to provide just enough safety for students to try to get to know each other and experience alternative perspectives on the world. At Illinois, we are building on the work of a model developed at Michigan in our Program in Intergroup Relations, which facilitates structured dialogues across small groups to create environments in which discomfort, ignorance, and even conflict are tolerated in the service of building trust and a sense of common fate.

40 Next fall, we will take another step by opening a new living and 40 learning residence for first and second year students. It will be dedicated to Intergroup Relations and Multiracial Integration, with cultural programming, structured dialogues, and classes taught by faculty fellows from our Center for Democracy. The idea here is a simple one: Since most students have had very little, if any, experience in crossing the boundaries of race and ethnicity in their daily lives, we need to structure safe environments for integration, for learning how to do the hard work of reaching out and living and learning in a multiracial community.

We know that most students, majority and minority, will say that there are substantial racial tensions on campus. At the same time, they will also say that at college they have made, often for the first time in their lives, some very good, close relationships with persons of other races and ethnicities. It is our responsibility to foster these kinds of intergroup experiences, preparing the ground of daily life in our campus community. We want to encourage the actual reaching out, on the ground, from one person to another. And we recognize that if we want students to become engaged citizens of the world, people who can question that world and prod it to be a better place—somewhere they want to live—we must invite them to change higher education, to share it, and to make it stretch to fit them. We want our students to change our university and to make it better.

Knowing the other, shaping the self

We have a hope in this nation that we can draw on the talent, skill, insight, and imagination of all of our citizens, and higher education must help to lead the way. With a nod to Walt Whitman, the poet Langston Hughes expressed this hope—this conviction—in an equally powerful way, in a poem entitled "I, Too."[3]

I, too, sing America.

I am the darker brother.
They send me to eat in the kitchen
When company comes,
But I laugh,
And eat well,
And grow strong.

Tomorrow,
I'll be at the table
When company comes.
Nobody'll dare
Say to me,
"Eat in the kitchen,"
Then.

Besides,
They'll see how beautiful I am
And be ashamed—

I, too, am America.

To lead the way toward fulfilling this hope, we in higher education must figure out how to sit together around our table and engage with difference. It is through this social introspection, done in the company of others and informed by the clash of perspectives, that liberal learning occurs, sustained by difference and strengthened by the solidarity that follows.

End Notes

1. See the Guiding Principles for the Center for Liberal Education and Civic Engagement, a cooperative effort of AAC&U and Campus Compact.

2. www.vceducation.org/peace/schools/ukraine208.html.
3. From *The Collected Poems of Langston Hughes,* by Langston Hughes, copyright © 1994 by The Estate of Langston Hughes. Used by permission of Alfred A. Knof, a division of Random House, Inc.

Works Cited

Grutter v. Bollinger, U.S. Supreme Court, No. 02–214, June 23, 2003.

Gurin, Patricia, ed., Earl Lewis, Eric Dey, Sylvia Hurtado, Jeffrey S. Lehman. 2004. *Defending diversity: Affirmative Action at the University of Michigan.* Ann Arbor: University of Michigan Press.

Kennedy, Deborah Willis. 2000. Coda: Imagine the blues. In Wendy McDoris, *Visualizing the blues: Images of the American South.* Memphis: The Dixon Gallery and Garden.

National Advisory Commission on Civil Disorders. 1968. *Report of the National Advisory Commission on Civil Disorders.* Washington, DC: Government Printing Office, March 1.

Questions on Meaning

1. What does it mean to be engaged civically? What does a university have to do to help its students and faculty understand the demands of diversity?
2. The arts is an area where everyone has a chance to cross boundaries, especially the boundaries between people of different races and backgrounds. How can the arts help us cross these boundaries?
3. What did the university do for its freshman orientation to help students see something of the history of multicultural experiences at the school? What did the returning alumni tell the freshmen about the lessons that a liberal education had taught them?

Questions on Rhetorical Strategy and Style

1. Cantor begins by letting the audience know that the situation calls for critical change. What major change in demographics does she note? What is happening to the white majority in American culture?
2. In the body of the work, Cantor discusses the many values that come from the arts. Why is this area her main focus? What does she show by talking about different artists and different programs?
3. The speech ends by quoting the great black poet of the Harlem Renaissance, Langston Hughes. Who is he reflecting in his poem? Why does a reference to both Langston Hughes and Walt Whitman make a fitting end for the speech?

Writing Assignments

1. Choose a picture, sculpture, or poem that reflects your idea of diversity and multiculturalism. Write about the work and how it expresses your views.
2. Cantor says that the liberal arts help us to understand diverse points of view. What different perspectives does a student get by studying science, history, and the arts? How can these perspectives help to expand horizons? Give examples.
3. Cantor talks of expressing oneself in safety. Describe what you see as a safe environment. Use experiences that you have had in situations that you consider to be both safe and not safe. Compare and contrast the experiences.

School vs. Education

Russell Baker

Russell Baker (1925–) was born in a rural town in Virginia and grew up in New Jersey and Maryland. He received his B. A. in English from Johns Hopkins University in 1947 and worked as a reporter for the Baltimore Sun *and then the* New York Times. *In 1962 he began writing his "Observer" column for the* Times, *which was syndicated in over 400 newspapers for more than two decades. His topics range from the mundane everyday annoyances to serious social problems, and his style is generally casual but thoughtful. In 1979 he received the Pulitzer Prize for distinguished commentary; he received the Prize again for his autobiography* Growing Up *(1982). His collections of columns and essays include* All Things Considered *(1965),* Poor Russell's Almanac *(1972),* So This is Depravity *(1980)* The Rescue of Miss Yaskell and Other Pipe Dreams *(1983), and* There's a Country in My Cellar *(1990). The following piece, first published in his* New York Times *column in 1975, intertwines serious commentary on American education and values with a spoof on what our schools teach. As you read it, think about the serious message Baker wants to communicate to us.*

By the age of six the average child will have completed the basic American education and be ready to enter school. If the child has been attentive in these preschool years, he or she will already have mastered many skills.

From television, the child will have learned how to pick a lock, commit a fairly elaborate bank holdup, prevent wetness all day long, get the laundry twice as white, and kill people with a variety of sophisticated armaments.

From watching his parents, the child, in many cases, will already know how to smoke, how much soda to mix with whiskey, what kind of language to use when angry, and how to violate the speed laws without being caught.

At this point, the child is ready for the second stage of education, which occurs in school. There, a variety of lessons may be learned in the very first days.

5 The teacher may illustrate the economic importance of belonging to a strong union by closing down the school before the child arrives. Fathers and mothers may demonstrate to the child the social cohesion that can be built on shared hatred by demonstrating their dislike for children whose pigmentation displeases them. In the latter event, the child may receive visual instruction in techniques of stoning buses, cracking skulls with a nightstick, and subduing mobs with tear gas. Formal education has begun.

During formal education, the child learns that life is for testing. This stage lasts twelve years, a period during which the child learns that success comes from telling testers what they want to hear.

Early in this stage, the child learns that he is either dumb or smart. If the teacher puts intelligent demands upon the child, the child learns he is smart. If the teacher expects little of the child, the child learns he is dumb and soon quits bothering to tell the testers what they want to hear.

At this point, education becomes more subtle. The child taught by school that he is dumb observes that neither he, she, nor any of the many children who are even dumber, ever fails to be promoted to the next grade. From this, the child learns that while everybody talks a lot about the virtue of being smart, there is very little incentive to stop being dumb.

What is the point of school, besides attendance? the child wonders. As the end of the first formal stage of education approaches, school answers this question. The point is to equip the child to enter college.

10 Children who have been taught they are smart have no difficulty. They have been happily telling testers what they want to hear for twelve years. Being artists at telling testers what they want to hear, they

are admitted to college joyously, where they promptly learn that they are the hope of America.

Children whose education has been limited to adjusting themselves to their schools' low estimates of them are admitted to less joyous colleges which, in some cases, may teach them to read.

At this stage of education, a fresh question arises for everyone. If the point of lower education was to get into college, what is the point of college? The answer is soon learned. The point of college is to prepare the student—no longer a child now—to get into graduate school. In college the student learns that it is no longer enough simply to tell the testers what they want to hear. Many are tested for graduate school; few are admitted.

Those excluded may be denied valuable certificates to prosper in medicine, at the bar, in the corporate boardroom. The student learns that the race is to the cunning and often, alas, to the unprincipled.

Thus, the student learns the importance of destroying competitors and emerges richly prepared to play his role in the great simmering melodrama of American life.

15   Afterward, the former student's destiny fulfilled, his life rich with   15
Oriental carpets, rare porcelain, and full bank accounts, he may one day find himself with the leisure and the inclination to open a book with a curious mind, and start to become educated.

Questions on Meaning

1. What kinds of things does Baker say children learn before going to school?
2. Does Baker use any positive examples of what children learn either in or out of school? Why do you think Baker is so critical of both American society and our system of education?
3. Reread the essay's closing paragraph. Why does he say "*start* to become educated" (emphasis added)? What is different about the learning described at that moment from the schooling and lessons learned previously?

Questions on Rhetorical Strategy and Style

1. Analyze Baker's newspaper column style in this essay. What are the effects of short paragraphs, simple sentences, sweeping generalizations, and so on? How would you describe his tone?
2. Baker does not explicitly define schooling or education in a definitive way, but his meanings emerge clearly by the end of the essay. Summarize in your own words Baker's definitions of school learning and education.
3. Although Baker does not use all the rhetorical devices of persuasion in this essay, he does argue different points along the way. How does he develop his arguments that schools primarily teach one how to take tests, and that college teaches one how to succeed in a rapacious world?

Writing Assignments

1. How would you evaluate the American educational system as you have experienced it? To what extent is Baker correct in his judgment? What other statements about school and education do you think are necessary to add in order to complete a fair description of American education?
2. What does it mean to be truly educated—apart from having a college degree? Write an essay in which you define your own ideas about what education—at its best—really means.

Idiot Nation

Michael Moore

Born in Davison, Michigan to an automobile assembly line worker and a secretary, Michael Moore (1954–) attended the University of Michigan-Flint. In 1976, after dropping out of college, he founded an alternative newspaper, the Flint Voice, *the success of which led to a stint on National Public Radio's* All Things Considered *and a position on the editorial board of* Mother Jones *magazine. Moore began making independent documentary films in 1986 after founding his own Dog Eat Dog production company. His first film,* Roger & Me, *was released to critical and popular acclaim in 1989. It chronicles Moore's futile attempts to corner General Motors CEO Roger Smith after GM closed the plant in Flint and moved its operations to Mexico. Moore's next full-length film was the 1994 comedy* Canadian Bacon, *featuring a U.S. president played by Alan Alda declaring war on Canada. A parody of weekly newsmagazines, "TV Nation," followed the same year. Moore's first book,* Downsize This!, *was published in 1996, and another documentary—*The Big One, *focusing on labor practices at Nike—appeared in 1997. Moore's 2002 documentary* Bowling for Columbine, *exploring the American propensity for gun violence, became one of the most controversial and successful films of the year. In summer 2004 Moore released his most provocative film to date:* Fahrenheit 9/11, *a searing indictment of the Bush administration's response to the September 11 events (particularly the invasion of Iraq), won the Best Picture Award at the prestigious Cannes Film Festival.*

This chapter from his 2002 book Stupid White Men . . . and other sorry excuses for the state of the

Reprinted from *Stupid White Men . . . And Other Sorry Excuses for the State of the Nation!*, by permission of HarperCollins Publishers. Copyright © 2002 by Michael Moore.

nation! features the same level of scathing commentary found in his films. In it Moore shines a light on what he considers the abysmal state of American education, alternating raucous humor with bitter social commentary.

1   Do you feel like you live in a nation of idiots?

I used to console myself about the state of stupidity in this country by repeating this to myself: *Even if there are two hundred million stone-cold idiots in this country, that leaves at least eighty million who'll get what I'm saying—and that's still more than the populations of the United Kingdom and Iceland combined!*

Then came the day I found myself sharing an office with the ESPN game show *Two-Minute Drill*. This is the show that tests your knowledge of not only who plays what position for which team, but who hit what where in a 1925 game between Boston and New York, who was rookie of the year in 1965 in the old American Basketball Association, and what Jake Wood had for breakfast the morning of May 12, 1967.

I don't know the answer to any of those questions—but for some reason I do remember Jake Wood's uniform number: 2. Why on earth am I retaining that useless fact?

5   I don't know, but after watching scores of guys waiting to audition for that ESPN show, I think I do know something about intelligence and the American mind. Hordes of these jocks and lunkheads hang out in our hallway awaiting their big moment, going over hundreds of facts and statistics in their heads and challenging each other with questions I can't see why anyone would be able to answer other than God Almighty Himself. To look at these testosterone-loaded bruisers you would guess that they were a bunch of illiterates who would be lucky if they could read the label on a Bud.

In fact, they are geniuses. They can answer all thirty obscure trivia questions in less than 120 seconds. That's four seconds a question—including the time used by the slow-reading celebrity athletes who ask the questions.

I once heard the linguist and political writer Noam Chomsky say that if you want proof the American people aren't stupid, just turn on any sports talk radio show and listen to the incredible retention of facts. It is amazing—and it's proof that the American mind is alive and well. It just isn't challenged with anything interesting or exciting. *Our* challenge, Chomsky said, was to find a way to make politics as gripping and engaging as sports. When we do that, watch how Americans will do nothing but talk about who did what to whom at the WTO.

But first, they have to be able to read the letters *WTO*.

There are forty-four million Americans who cannot read and write above a fourth-grade level—in other words, who are functional illiterates.

How did I learn this statistic? Well, I *read* it. And now you've read it. So we've already eaten into the mere 99 hours a *year* an average American adult spends reading a book—compared with 1,460 hours watching television.

I've also read that only 11 percent of the American public bothers to *read* a daily newspaper, beyond the funny pages or the used car ads.

So if you live in a country where forty-four million can't read— and perhaps close to another two hundred million can read but usually don't—well, friends, you and I are living in one very scary place. A nation that not only churns out illiterate students BUT GOES OUT OF ITS WAY TO REMAIN IGNORANT AND STUPID is a nation that should not be running the world—at least not until a majority of its citizens can locate Kosovo (or any other country it has bombed) on the map.

It comes as no surprise to foreigners that Americans, who love to revel in their stupidity, would "elect" a president who rarely reads *anything*—including his own briefing papers—and thinks Africa is a nation, not a continent. An idiot leader of an idiot nation. In our glorious land of plenty, less is always more when it comes to taxing any lobe of the brain with the intake of facts and numbers, critical thinking, or the comprehension of anything that isn't . . . well, sports.

Our Idiot-in-Chief does nothing to hide his ignorance—he even brags about it. During his commencement address to the Yale Class of 2001, George W. Bush spoke proudly of having been a mediocre student at Yale. "And to the C students, I say you, too, can be President of the United States!" The part where you also need an ex-President father, a brother as governor of a state with missing ballots, and a Supreme Court full of your dad's buddies must have been too complicated to bother with in a short speech.

15   As Americans, we have quite a proud tradition of being repre-   15
sented by ignorant high-ranking officials. In 1956 President Dwight
D. Eisenhower's nominee as ambassador to Ceylon (now Sri Lanka)
was unable to identify either the country's prime minister or its capital during his Senate confirmation hearing. Not a problem—Maxwell
Gluck was confirmed anyway. In 1981 President Ronald Reagan's
nominee for deputy secretary of state, William Clark, admitted to a
wide-ranging lack of knowledge about foreign affairs at his confirmation hearing. Clark had no idea how our allies in Western Europe felt
about having American nuclear missiles based there, and didn't know
the names of the prime ministers of South Africa or Zimbabwe. Not
to worry—he was confirmed, too. All this just paved the way for Baby
Bush, who hadn't quite absorbed the names of the leaders of India or
Pakistan, two of the seven nations that possess the atomic bomb.

And Bush went to Yale *and* Harvard.

Recently a group of 556 seniors at fifty-five prestigious American
universities (e.g., Harvard, Yale, Stanford) were given a multiple-choice
test consisting of questions that were described as "high school level."
Thirty-four questions were asked. These top students could only answer
53 percent of them correctly. And only one student got them all right.

A whopping 40 percent of these students did not know when
the Civil War took place—even when given a wide range of choices:
A. 1750–1800; B. 1800–1850; C. 1850–1900; D. 1900–1950; or
E. after 1950. *(The answer is C, guys.)* The two questions the college
seniors scored highest on were (1) Who is Snoop Doggy Dog? (98 percent got that one right), and (2) Who are Beavis and Butt-head?
(99 percent knew). For my money, Beavis and Butt-head represented
some of the best American satire of the nineties, and Snoop and his
fellow rappers have much to say about America's social ills, so I'm not
going down the road of blaming MTV.

What I *am* concerned with is why politicians like Senators Joe
Lieberman of Connecticut and Herbert Kohl of Wisconsin want to
go after MTV when *they* are the ones responsible for the massive failure of American education. Walk into any public school, and the
odds are good that you'll find overflowing classrooms, leaking ceil-
ings, and demoralized teachers. In 1 out of 4 schools, you'll find students "learning" from textbooks published in the 1980s—or earlier.

20 Why is this? Because the political leaders—and the people who 20 vote for them—have decided it's a bigger priority to build another bomber than to educate our children. They would rather hold hearings about the depravity of a television show called *Jackass* than about their own depravity in neglecting our schools and children and maintaining our title as Dumbest Country on Earth.

I hate writing these words. I *love* this big lug of a country and the crazy people in it. But when I can travel to some backwater village in Central America, as I did back in the eighties, and listen to a bunch of twelve-year-olds tell me their concerns about the World Bank, I get the feeling that *something* is lacking in the United States of America.

Our problem isn't just that our kids don't know nothin' but that the adults who pay their tuition are no better. I wonder what would happen if we tested the U.S. Congress to see just how much our representatives know. What if we were to give a pop quiz to the commentators who cram our TVs and radios with all their nonstop nonsense? How many would *they* get right?

A while back, I decided to find out. It was one of those Sunday mornings when the choice on TV was the *Parade of Homes* real estate show or *The McLaughlin Group.* If you like the sound of hyenas on Dexedrine, of course, you go with *McLaughlin.* On this particular Sunday morning, perhaps as my punishment for not being at Mass, I was forced to listen to magazine columnist Fred Barnes (now an editor at the right-wing *Weekly Standard* and co-host of the Fox News show *The Beltway Boys)* whine on and on about the sorry state of American education, blaming the teachers and their evil union for why students are doing so poorly.

"These kids don't even know what *The Iliad* and *The Odyssey* are!" he bellowed, as the other panelists nodded in admiration at Fred's noble lament.

25 The next morning I called Fred Barnes at his Washington office. 25 "Fred," I said, "tell me what *The Iliad* and *The Odyssey* are."

He started hemming and hawing. "Well, they're . . . uh . . . you know . . . uh . . . okay, fine, you got me—I don't know what they're about. Happy now?"

No, not really. You're one of the top TV pundits in America, seen every week on your own show and plenty of others. You gladly hawk your "wisdom" to hundreds of thousands of unsuspecting citizens, gleefully scorning others for their ignorance. Yet you and your guests know little or nothing yourselves. Grow up, get some books, and go to your room.

Yale and Harvard. Princeton and Dartmouth. Stanford and Berkeley. Get a degree from one of those universities, and you're set for life. So what if, on that test of the college seniors I previously mentioned, 70 percent of the students at those fine schools had never heard of the Voting Rights Act or President Lyndon Johnson's Great Society initiatives? Who needs to know stuff like that as you sit in your Tuscan villa watching the sunset and checking how well your portfolio did today?

So what if *not one* of these top universities that the ignorant students attend requires that they take even one course in American history to graduate? Who needs history when you are going to be tomorrow's master of the universe?

Who cares if 70 percent of those who graduate from America's colleges are not required to learn a foreign language? Isn't the rest of the world speaking English now? And if they aren't, hadn't all those damn foreigners better GET WITH THE PROGRAM?

And who gives a rat's ass if, out of the seventy English Literature programs at seventy major American universities, only twenty-three now require English majors to take a course in Shakespeare? Can somebody please explain to me what Shakespeare and English have to do with each other? What good are some moldy old plays going to be in the business world, anyway?

Maybe I'm just jealous because I don't have a college degree. Yes, I, Michael Moore, am a college dropout.

Well, I never *officially* dropped out. One day in my sophomore year, I drove around and around the various parking lots of our commuter campus in Flint, searching desperately for a parking space. There simply was no place to park—every spot was full, and no one was leaving. After a frustrating hour spent circling around in my '69 Chevy Impala, I shouted out the window, "That's it, I'm dropping out!" I drove home and told my parents I was no longer in college.

"Why?" they asked.

"Couldn't find a parking spot," I replied, grabbing a Redpop and moving on with the rest of my life. I haven't sat at a school desk since.

My dislike of school started somewhere around the second month of first grade. My parents—and God Bless Them Forever for doing this—had taught me to read and write by the time I was four. So when

I entered St. John's Elementary School, I had to sit and feign interest while the other kids, like robots, sang, "A-B-C-D-E-F-G . . . Now I know my ABCs, tell me what you think of me!" Every time I heard that line, I wanted to scream out, "Here's what I think of you—quit singing that damn song! Somebody get me a Twinkie!"

I was bored beyond belief. The nuns, to their credit, recognized this, and one day Sister John Catherine took me aside and said that they had decided to skip me up to second grade, effective immediately. I was thrilled. When I got home I excitedly announced to my parents that I had already advanced a grade in my first month of school. They seemed underwhelmed by this new evidence of my genius. Instead they let out a "WHAT THE—," then went into the kitchen and closed the door. I could hear my mother on the phone explaining to the Mother Superior that there was *no way* her little Michael was going to be attending class with kids bigger and older than him, so please, Sister, put him back in first grade.

I was crushed. My mother explained to me that if I skipped first grade I'd always be the youngest and littlest kid in class all through my school years (well, inertia and fast food eventually proved her wrong on that count). There would be no appeals to my father, who left most education decisions to my mother, the valedictorian of her high school class. I tried to explain that if I was sent back to first grade it would appear that I'd *flunked* second grade on my first day— putting myself at risk of having the crap beaten out of me by the first graders I'd left behind with a rousing "See ya, suckers!" But Mom wasn't falling for it; it was then I learned that the only person with higher authority than Mother Superior was Mother Moore.

The next day I decided to ignore all instructions from my parents to go back to first grade. In the morning, before the opening bell, all the students had to line up outside the school with their classmates and then march into the building in single file. Quietly, but defiantly, I went and stood in the second graders' line, praying that God would strike the nuns blind so they wouldn't see which line I was in. The bell rang—and no one had spotted me! The second grade line started to move, and I went with it. *Yes!* I thought. *If I can pull this off, if I can just get into that second grade classroom and take my seat, then nobody will be able to get me out of there.* Just as I was about to enter the door of the school, I felt a hand grab me by the collar of my coat. It was Sister John Catherine.

40 "I think you're in the wrong line, Michael," she said firmly. "You 40
are now in first grade again." I began to protest: my parents had it "all
wrong," or "those weren't *really* my parents," or . . .

For the next twelve years I sat in class, did my work, and remained
constantly preoccupied, looking for ways to bust out. I started an
underground school paper in fourth grade. It was shut down. I started
it again in sixth. It was shut down. In eighth grade I not only started
the paper again, I convinced the good sisters to let me write a play for
our class to perform at the Christmas pageant. The play had something to do with how many rats occupied the parish hall and how all
the rats in the country had descended on St. John's Parish Hall to have
their annual "rat convention." The priest put a stop to that one—and
shut down the paper again. Instead, my friends and I were told to go
up on stage and sing three Christmas carols and then leave the stage
without uttering a word. I organized half the class to go up there and
utter nothing. So we stood there and refused to sing the carols, our
silent protest against censorship. By the second song, intimidated by
the stern looks from their parents in the audience, most of the protesters joined in on the singing—and by the third song, I too, had capitu-
lated, joining in on "O Holy Night," and promising myself to live to
fight another day.

High school, as we all know, is some sort of sick, sadistic punishment of kids by adults seeking vengeance because they can no longer
lead the responsibility-free, screwing-around-24/7 lives young people
enjoy. What other explanation could there be for those four brutal
years of degrading comments, physical abuse, and the belief that
you're the only one not having sex?

As soon as I entered high school—and the public school system—
all the grousing I'd done about the repression of the Sisters of St. Joseph
was forgotten; suddenly they all looked like scholars and saints. I was
now walking the halls of a two-thousand-plus-inmate holding pen.
Where the nuns had devoted their lives to teaching for no earthly
reward, those running the public high school had one simple mission:
"Hunt these little pricks down like dogs, then cage them until we can
either break their will or ship them off to the glue factory!" Do this,
don't do that, tuck your shirt in, wipe that smile off your face, where's
your hall pass, THAT'S THE WRONG PASS! *YOU—DETENTION!!*

One day I came home from school and picked up the paper. The
headline read: "26th Amendment Passes—Voting Age Lowered to 18."

Below that was another headline: "School Board President to Retire, Seat Up for Election."

45   Hmm. I called the county clerk.

"Uh, I'm gonna be eighteen in a few weeks. If I can vote, does that I mean I can also run for office?"

"Let me see," the lady replied. "That's a new question!"

She ruffled through some papers and came back on the phone. "Yes," she said, "you can run. All you need to do is gather twenty signatures to place your name on the ballot."

Twenty signatures? That's it? I had no idea running for elective office required so little work. I got the twenty signatures, submitted my petition, and started campaigning. My platform? "Fire the high school principal and the assistant principal!"

50   Alarmed at the idea that a high school student might actually find a legal means to remove the very administrators he was being paddled by, five local "adults" took out petitions and got themselves added to the ballot, too.

Of course, they ended up splitting the older adult vote five ways—and I won, getting the vote of every single stoner between the ages of eighteen and twenty-five (who, though many would probably never vote again, relished the thought of sending their high school wardens to the gallows).

The day after I won, I was walking down the hall at school (I had one more week to serve out as a student), and I passed the assistant principal, my shirt tail proudly untucked.

"Good morning, Mr. Moore," he said tersely. The day before, my name had been "Hey-You!" Now I was his boss.

Within nine months after I took my seat on the school board, the principal and assistant principal had submitted their "letters of resignation," a face-saving device employed when one is "asked" to step down. A couple of years later the principal suffered a heart attack and died.

55   I had known this man, the principal, for many years. When I was eight years old, he used to let me and my friends skate and play hockey on this little pond beside his house. He was kind and generous, and always left the door to his house open in case any of us needed to change into our skates or if we got cold and just wanted to get warm. Years later, I was asked to play bass in a band that was forming, but I didn't own a bass. He let me borrow his son's.

I offer this to remind myself that all people are actually good at their core, and to remember that someone with whom I grew to have serious disputes was also someone with a free cup of hot chocolate for us shivering little brats from the neighborhood.

Teachers are now the politicians' favorite punching bag. To listen to the likes of Chester Finn, a former assistant secretary of education in Bush the Elder's administration, you'd think all that has crumbled in our society can be traced back to lax, lazy, and incompetent teachers. "If you put out a Ten-Most-Wanted list of who's killing American education, I'm not sure who you would have higher on the list: the teachers' union or the education school faculties," Finn said.

Sure, there are a lot of teachers who suck, and they'd be better suited to making telemarketing calls for Amway. But the vast majority are dedicated educators who have chosen a profession that pays them less than what some of their students earn selling Ecstasy, and for that sacrifice we seek to punish them. I don't know about you, but I want the people who have the direct attention of my child more hours a day than I do treated with tender loving care. Those are my kids they're "preparing" for this world, so why on earth would I want to piss them off?

You would think society's attitude would be something like this:

Teachers, thank you so much for devoting your life to my child. Is there ANYTHING I can do to help you? Is there ANYTHING you need? I am here for you. Why? Because you are helping my child—MY BABY—learn and grow. Not only will you be largely responsible for her ability to make a living, but your influence will greatly affect how she views the world, what she knows about other people in this world, and how she will feel about herself. I want her to believe she can attempt anything—that no doors are closed and that no dreams are too distant. I am entrusting the most valuable person in my life to you for seven hours each day. You are thus one of the most important people in my life! Thank you.

60 No, instead, this is what teachers hear: 60

- "You've got to wonder about teachers who claim to put the interests of children first—and then look to milk the system dry through wage hikes." (*New York Post*, 12/26/00)
- "Estimates of the number of bad teachers range from 5 percent to 18 percent of the 2.6 million total." (Michael Chapman, *Investor's Business Daily*, 9/21/98)
- "Most education professionals belong to a closed community

of devotees . . . who follow popular philosophies rather than research on what works." (Douglas Carminen, quoted in the *Montreal Gazette,* 1/6/01)

- "Teachers unions have gone to bat for felons and teachers who have had sex with students, as well as those who simply couldn't teach." (Peter Schweizen, *National Review,* 8/17/98)

What kind of priority do we place on education in America? Oh, it's on the funding list—somewhere down between OSHA and meat inspectors. The person who cares for our child every day receives an average of $41,351 annually. A Congressman who cares only about which tobacco lobbyist is taking him to dinner tonight receives $145,100.

Considering the face-slapping society gives our teachers on a daily basis, is it any wonder so few choose the profession? The national teacher shortage is so big that some school systems are recruiting teachers outside the United States. Chicago recently recruited and hired teachers from twenty-eight foreign countries, including China, France, and Hungary. By the time the new term begins in New York City, seven thousand veteran teachers will have retired—and 60 percent of the new teachers hired to replace them are uncertified.

But here's the kicker for me: 163 New York City schools opened the 2000–2001 school year *without a principal!* You heard right—school, with *no one in charge.* Apparently the mayor and the school board are experimenting with chaos theory—throw five hundred poor kids into a crumbling building, and watch nature take its course! In the city from which most of the wealth in the world is controlled, where there are more millionaires per square foot than there is gum on the sidewalk, we somehow can't find the money to pay a starting teacher more than $31,900 a year. And we act surprised when we can't get results.

And it's not just teachers who have been neglected—American schools are *literally* falling apart. In 1999 one-quarter of U.S. public schools reported that the condition of at least one of their buildings was inadequate. In 1997 the entire Washington, D.C., school system had to delay the start of school for three weeks because nearly *one-third* of the schools were found to be unsafe.

65   Almost 10 percent of U.S. public schools have enrollments that are   65

306

more than 25 percent greater than the capacity of their permanent buildings. Classes have to be held in the hallways, outdoors, in the gym, in the cafeteria; one school I visited even held classes in a janitor's closet. It's not as if the janitor's closets are being used for anything related to cleaning, anyway—in New York almost 15 percent of the eleven hundred public schools are without full-time custodians, forcing teachers to mop their own floors and students to do without toilet paper. We already send our kids out into the street to hawk candy bars so their schools can buy band instruments—what's next? Car washes to raise money for toilet paper?

Further proof of just how special our little offspring are is the number of public and even school libraries that have been shut down or had their hours cut back. The last thing we need is a bunch of kids hanging out around a bunch of books!

Apparently "President" Bush agrees: in his first budget he proposed cutting federal spending on libraries by $39 million, down to $168 million—a nearly 19 percent reduction. Just the week before, his wife, former school librarian Laura Bush, kicked off a national campaign for America's libraries, calling them "community treasure chests, loaded with a wealth of information available to everyone, equally." The President's mother, Barbara Bush, heads the Foundation for Family Literacy. Well, there's nothing like having firsthand experience with illiteracy in the family to motivate one into acts of charity.

For kids who are exposed to books at home, the loss of a library is sad. But for kids who come from environments where people don't read, the loss of a library is a tragedy that might keep them from ever discovering the joys of reading—or from gathering the kind of information that will decide their lot in life. Jonathan Kozol, for decades an advocate for disadvantaged children, has observed that school libraries "remain the clearest window to a world of noncommercial satisfactions and enticements that most children in poor neighborhoods will ever know."

Kids deprived of access to good libraries are also being kept from developing the information skills they need to keep up in workplaces that are increasingly dependent on rapidly changing information. The ability to conduct research is "probably the most essential skill [today's students] can have," says Julie Walker, executive director of the American Association of School Librarians. "The knowledge [students] acquire in school is not going to serve them throughout their lifetimes. Many of them will have four to five careers in a lifetime. It will be their ability to navigate information that will matter."

70   Who's to blame for the decline in libraries? Well, when it comes   70
to school libraries, you can start by pointing the finger (yes, *that*
finger) at Richard Nixon. From the 1960s until 1974, school libraries
received specific funding from the government. But in 1974 the
Nixon administration changed the rules, stipulating that federal education money be doled out in "block grants" to be spent by states
however they chose. Few states chose to spend the money on libraries,
and the downslide began. This is one reason that materials in many
school libraries today date from the 1960s and early 1970s, before
funding was diverted. ("No, Sally, the Soviet Union isn't our enemy.
The Soviet Union has been kaput for ten years. . . .")

This 1999 account by an *Education Week* reporter about the
"library" at a Philadelphia elementary school could apply to any number of similarly neglected schools:

> Even the best books in the library at T. M. Pierce Elementary School
> are dated, tattered, and discolored. The worst—many in a latter
> state of disintegration—are dirty and fetid and leave a moldy
> residue on hands and clothing. Chairs and tables are old, mis-
> matched, or broken. There isn't a computer in sight. . . . Outdated
> facts and theories and offensive stereotypes leap from the authorita-
> tive pages of encyclopedias and biographies, fiction and nonfiction
> tomes. Among the volumes on these shelves a student would find it
> all but impossible to locate accurate information on AIDS or other
> contemporary diseases, explorations of the moon and Mars, or the
> past five U.S. presidents.

The ultimate irony in all of this is that the very politicians who
refuse to fund education in America adequately are the same ones
who go ballistic over how our kids have fallen behind the Germans,
the Japanese, and just about every other country with running water
and an economy not based on the sale of Chiclets. Suddenly they
want "accountability." They want the teachers held responsible and
to be tested. And they want the kids to be tested—over and over
and over.

There's nothing terribly wrong with the concept of using stan-
dardized testing to determine whether kids are learning to read and
write and do math. But too many politicians and education bureau-
crats have created a national obsession with testing, as if everything
that's wrong with the educational system in this country would be
magically fixed if we could just raise those scores.

The people who really should be tested (besides the yammering pundits) are the so-called political leaders. Next time you see your state representative or congressman, give him this pop quiz—and remind him that any future pay raises will be based on how well he scores:

1. What is the annual pay of your average constituent?
2. What percent of welfare recipients are children?
3. How many known species of plants and animals are on the brink of extinction?
4. How big is the hole in the ozone layer?
5. Which African countries have a lower infant mortality rate than Detroit?
6. How many American cities still have two competing newspapers?
7. How many ounces in a gallon?
8. Which do I stand a greater chance of being killed by: a gun shot in school or a bolt of lightning?
9. What's the only state capital without a McDonald's?
10. Describe the story of either *The Iliad* or *The Odyssey.*

Answers

1. $28,548
2. 67 percent
3. 11,046
4. 10.5 million square miles
5. Libya, Mauritius, Seychelles
6. 34
7. 128 ounces
8. You're twice as likely to be killed by lightning as by a gunshot in school.
9. Montpelier, Vermont
10. *The Iliad* is an ancient Greek epic poem by Homer about the Trojan War. *The Odyssey* is another epic poem by Homer recounting the ten-year journey home from the Trojan War made by Odysseus, the king of Ithaca.

75 Chances are, the genius representing you in the legislature won't 75 score 50 percent on the above test. The good news is that you get to flunk him within a year or two.

There is one group in the country that isn't just sitting around carping about all them lamebrain teachers—a group that cares deeply about what kinds of students will enter the adult world. You could say they have a vested interest in this captive audience of millions of young people . . . or in the billions of dollars they spend each year. (Teenagers alone spent more than $150 billion last year.) Yes, it's Corporate America, whose generosity to our nation's schools is just one more example of their continuing patriotic service.

Just how committed are these companies to our children's schools?

According to numbers collected by the Center for the Analysis of Commercialism in Education (CACE), their selfless charity has seen a tremendous boom since 1990. Over the past ten years, school programs and activities have seen corporate sponsorship increase by 248 percent. In exchange for this sponsorship, schools allow the corporation to associate its name with the events.

For example, Eddie Bauer sponsors the final round of the National Geography Bee. Book covers featuring Calvin Klein and Nike ads are distributed to students. Nike and other shoemakers, looking for early access to tomorrow's stars, sponsor inner-city high school basketball teams.

Pizza Hut set up its "Book-It!" program to encourage children to read. When students meet the monthly reading goal, they are rewarded with a certificate for a Pizza Hut personal pan pizza. At the restaurant, the store manager personally congratulates the children and gives them each a sticker and a certificate. Pizza Hut suggests school principals place a "Pizza Hut Book-It!" honor roll list in the school for everyone to see.

General Mills and Campbell's Soup thought up a better plan. Instead of giving free rewards, they both have programs rewarding schools for getting parents to buy their products. Under General Mills's "Box Tops for Education" program, schools get ten cents for each box top logo they send in, and can earn up to $10,000 a year. That's 100,000 General Mills products sold. Campbell's Soup's "Labels for Education" program is no better. It touts itself as "Providing America's children with FREE school equipment!" Schools can earn one "free" Apple iMac computer for only 94,950 soup labels. Campbell's suggests setting a goal of a label a day from each student. With Campbell's conservative estimate of five labels per week per child, all you need is a school of 528 kids to get that free computer.

80

It's not just this kind of sponsorship that brings these schools and corporations together. The 1990s saw a phenomenal 1,384 percent increase in exclusive agreements between schools and soft-drink bottlers. Two hundred and forty school districts in thirty-one states have sold exclusive rights to one of the big three soda companies (Coca-Cola, Pepsi, Dr. Pepper) to push their products in schools. Anybody wonder why there are more overweight kids than ever before? Or more young women with calcium deficiencies because they're drinking less milk? And even though federal law prohibits the sale of soft drinks in schools until lunch periods begin, in some overcrowded schools "lunch" begins in midmorning. Artificially flavored carbonated sugar water—the breakfast of champions! (In March 2001 Coke responded to public pressure, announcing that it would add water, juice, and other sugar-free, caffeine-free, and calcium-rich alternatives to soda to its school vending machines.)

I guess they can afford such concessions when you consider their deal with the Colorado Springs school district. Colorado has been a trailblazer when it comes to tie-ins between the schools and soft drink companies. In Colorado Springs, the district will receive $8.4 million over ten years from its deal with Coca-Cola—and more if it exceeds its "requirement" of selling seventy thousand cases of Coke products a year. To ensure the levels are met, school district officials urged principals to allow students unlimited access to Coke machines and allow students to drink Coke in the classroom.

But Coke isn't alone. In the Jefferson County, Colorado, school district (home of Columbine High School), Pepsi contributed $1.5 million to help build a new sports stadium. Some county schools tested a science course, developed in part by Pepsi, called "The Carbonated Beverage Company." Students taste-tested colas, analyzed cola samples, watched a video tour of a Pepsi bottling plant, and visited a local plant.

85 The school district in Wylie, Texas, signed a deal in 1996 that 85 shared the rights to sell soft drinks in the schools between Coke and Dr. Pepper. Each company paid $31,000 a year. Then, in 1998, the county changed its mind and signed a deal with Coke worth $1.2 million over fifteen years. Dr. Pepper sued the county for breach of contract. The school district bought out Dr. Pepper's contract, costing them $160,000—plus another $20,000 in legal fees.

It's not just the companies that sometimes get sent packing. Students who lack the proper corporate school spirit do so at considerable risk. When Mike Cameron wore a Pepsi shirt on "Coke Day" at Greenbrier High School in Evans, Georgia, he was suspended for a day. "Coke Day" was part of the school's entry in a national "Team Up With Coca-Cola" contest, which awards $10,000 to the high school that comes up with the best plan for distributing Coke discount cards. Greenbrier school officials said Cameron was suspended for "being disruptive and trying to destroy the school picture" when he removed an outer shirt and revealed the Pepsi shirt as a photograph was being taken of students posed to spell out the word *Coke.* Cameron said the shirt was visible all day, but he didn't get in trouble until posing for the picture. No slouch in the marketing department, Pepsi quickly sent the high school senior a box of Pepsi shirts and hats.

If turning the students into billboards isn't enough, schools and corporations sometimes turn the school itself into one giant neon sign for corporate America. Appropriation of school space, including scoreboards, rooftops, walls, and textbooks, for corporate logos and advertising is up 539 percent.

Colorado Springs, not satisfied to sell its soul only to Coca-Cola, has plastered its school buses with advertisements for Burger King, Wendy's, and other big companies. Free book covers and school planners with ads for Kellogg's Pop-Tarts and pictures of FOX TV personalities were also handed out to the students.

After members of the Grapevine-Colleyville Independent School District in Texas decided they didn't want advertisements in the classrooms, they allowed Dr. Pepper and 7-Up logos to be painted on the rooftops of two high schools. The two high schools, not coincidentally, lie under the Dallas airport flight path.

90 The schools aren't just looking for ways to advertise; they're also concerned with the students' perceptions of various products. That's why, in some schools, companies conduct market research in classrooms during school hours. Education Market Resources of Kansas reports that "children respond openly and easily to questions and stimuli" in the classroom setting. (Of course, that's what they're *supposed* to be doing in a classroom—but for their own benefit, not that of some corporate pollsters.) Filling out marketing surveys instead of learning, however, is probably *not* what they should be doing.

Companies have also learned they can reach this confined audience by "sponsoring" educational materials. This practice, like the others, has exploded as well, increasing 1,875 percent since 1990.

Teachers have shown a Shell Oil video that teaches students that the way to experience nature is by driving there—after filling your Jeep's gas tank at a Shell station. ExxonMobil prepared lesson plans about the flourishing wildlife in Prince William Sound, site of the ecological disaster caused by the oil spill from the Exxon *Valdez*. A third-grade math book features exercises involving counting Tootsie Rolls. A Hershey's-sponsored curriculum used in many schools features "The Chocolate Dream Machine," including lessons in math, science, geography—and nutrition.

In a number of high schools, the economics course is supplied by General Motors. GM writes and provides the textbooks and the course outline. Students learn from GM's example the benefits of capitalism and how to operate a company—like GM.

And what better way to imprint a corporate logo on the country's children than through television and the Internet beamed directly into the classroom. Electronic marketing, where a company provides programming or equipment to schools for the right to advertise to their students, is up 139 percent.

95   One example is the ZapMe! Corporation, which provides schools   95 with a free computer lab and access to pre-selected Web sites. In return, schools must promise that the lab will be in use at least four hours a day. The catch? The ZapMe! Web browser has constantly scrolling advertisements—and the company gets to collect information on students' browsing habits, information they can then sell to other companies.

Perhaps the worst of the electronic marketers is Channel One Television. Eight million students in 12,000 classrooms watch Channel One, an in-school news *and advertising* program, every day. (That's right: EVERY day.) Kids are spending the equivalent of six full school days a year watching Channel One in almost 40 percent of U.S. middle and high schools. Instructional time lost to the ads alone? One entire day per year. That translates into an annual cost to taxpayers of more than $1.8 billion.

Sure, doctors and educators agree that our kids can never watch enough TV. And there's probably a place in school for some television programs—I have fond memories of watching astronauts blasting off on the television rolled into my grade school auditorium. But out of the daily twelve-minute Channel One broadcasts, only 20 percent of the airtime is devoted to stories about politics, the economy, and cultural and social issues. That leaves a whopping 80 percent for advertising, sports, weather, features, and Channel One promotions.

Channel One is disproportionately shown in schools in low income communities with large minority populations, where the least money is available for education, and where the least amount is spent on textbooks and other academic materials. Once these districts receive corporate handouts, government's failure to provide adequate school funding tends to remain unaddressed.

For most of us, the only time we enter an American high school is to vote at our local precinct. (There's an irony if there ever was one—going to participate in democracy's sacred ritual while two thousand students in the same building live under some sort of totalitarian dictatorship.) The halls are packed with burned-out teenagers shuffling from class to class, dazed and confused, wondering what the hell they're doing there. They learn how to regurgitate answers the state wants them to give, and any attempt to be an individual is now grounds for being suspected to be a member of the trench coat mafia. I visited a school recently, and some students asked me if I noticed that they and the other students in the school were all wearing white or some neutral color. Nobody dares wear black, or anything else wild and distinct. That's a sure ticket to the principal's office—where the school psychologist will be waiting to ascertain whether that Limp Bizkit shirt you have on means that you intend to shoot up Miss Nelson's fourth hour geometry class.

100   So the kids learn to submerge any personal expression. They learn that it's better to go along so that you get along. They learn that to rock the boat could get them rocked right out of the school. Don't question authority. Do as you're told. Don't think, just do as I say.

Oh, and have a good and productive life as an active, well-adjusted participant in our thriving democracy!

Questions on Meaning

1. How does Moore characterize politicians and pundits with regard to the state of American education? Why does he consider them more responsible than educators for the poor performance of students?
2. According to Moore, why is the lack of funding for libraries such a crucial problem? Why are libraries so significant not only to education in general, but to the education of disadvantaged children?
3. What problems, according to Moore, are associated with corporate funding for schools? Based on your experience, do you agree or disagree with his assessment? Explain your response.

Questions on Rhetorical Strategy and Style

1. Effective persuasion depends on evidence. List the evidence Moore offers in support of his position, and explain its significance to his argument.
2. Moore cites a number of causes for what he calls America's idiocy (e.g., poor funding for education and libraries, autocratic school systems, corporate sponsorship). Choose three or four of these causes and evaluate their persuasive value. How effective is Moore in establishing these cause-and-effect relationships?
3. *Satire,* the use of humor to ridicule a subject, often involves saying one thing while meaning another. For example, Moore refers to corporations' "continuing patriotic service" to schools. Identify several examples of satire in this piece, and explain how they help to establish Moore's tone.

Writing Assignments

1. Think back to your own experience in school, and write an essay describing that experience. Use specific examples to illustrate your essay. To what extent does your experience support or refute Moore's characterization of American education? (If you did not attend American schools, consider how your experience is similar to or different from what Moore describes.)
2. Moore criticizes colleges and universities as well as schools. Examine your institution's catalog, focusing on the mission statement and the description of general education requirements. Based on

this information and your experience so far, write a report on the value placed on education at your institution.

3. Read Moore's other work, watch his films, and read accounts of his career by credible sources. Then write a profile of Moore, focusing on his political beliefs, his social concerns, his style, and his place in American culture.

Why Don't We Complain?

William F. Buckley, Jr.

William F. Buckley, Jr. (1925–) was born in New York. One of ten children of a lawyer who had earned great wealth from Texas oil, Buckley was educated as a youth at St. Thomas More School in London and Millbrook School in New York. After a stint in the Navy during World War II, he attended Yale University, where he wrote for The Yale Daily News *and was a member of the debating team. Shortly after his graduation from Yale, he published* God and Man at Yale *(1951), a memoir in which he discusses his conservative political philosophy and basic Christian principles. An erudite and articulate spokesman for American conservatives, Buckley has published a number of books on politics and government, including* Happy Days Were Here Again: Reflections of a Libertarian Journalist *(1993); written a syndicated newspaper column; founded and edited a magazine expounding conservative viewpoints,* The National Review; *and hosted a weekly television program,* Firing Line. *He has also written novels and books on sailing, another passion. Buckley received the Presidential Medal of Freedom in 1991 from President Bush. Although liberals disagree vociferously with some of his viewpoints, they just as strongly respect his intelligence and forthrightness. The following essay, written in 1961, reflects not only Buckley's verbal precision, but also his trademark wry sense of humor.*

1   It was the very last coach and the only empty seat on the entire train, so there was no turning back. The problem was to breathe. Outside, the temperature was below freezing. Inside the railroad car the temperature must have been about 85 degrees. I took off my overcoat,

and a few minutes later my jacket, and noticed that the car was flecked with the white shirts of the passengers. I soon found my hand moving to loosen my tie. From one end of the car to the other, as we rattled through Westchester County, we sweated; but we did not moan.

I watched the train conductor appear at the head of the car. "Tickets, all tickets, please!" In a more virile age, I thought, the passengers would seize the conductor and strap him down on a seat over the radiator to share the fate of his patrons. He shuffled down the aisle, picking up tickets, punching commutation cards. *No one addressed a word to him.* He approached my seat, and I drew a deep breath of resolution. "Conductor," I began with a considerable edge to my voice. . . . Instantly the doleful eyes of my seatmate turned tiredly from his newspaper to fix me with a resentful stare: what question could be so important as to justify my sibilant intrusion into his stupor? I was shaken by those eyes. I am incapable of making a discreet fuss, so I mumbled a question about what time were we due in Stamford (I didn't even ask whether it would be before or after dehydration could be expected to set in), got my reply, and went back to my newspaper and to wiping my brow.

The conductor had nonchalantly walked down the gauntlet of eighty sweating American freemen, and not one of them had asked him to explain why the passengers in that car had been consigned to suffer. There is nothing to be done when the temperature *outdoors* is 85 degrees, and indoors the air conditioner has broken down; obviously when that happens there is nothing to do, except perhaps curse the day that one was born. But when the temperature outdoors is below freezing, it takes a positive act of will on somebody's part to set the temperature *indoors* at 85. Somewhere a valve was turned too far, a furnace overstocked, a thermostat maladjusted: something that could easily be remedied by turning off the heat and allowing the great outdoors to come indoors. All this is so obvious. What is not obvious is what has happened to the American people.

It isn't just the commuters, whom we have come to visualize as a supine breed who have got on to the trick of suspending their sensory faculties twice a day while they submit to the creeping dissolution of the railroad industry. It isn't just they who have given up trying to rectify irrational vexations. It is the American people everywhere.

5   A few weeks ago at a large movie theatre I turned to my wife and said, "The picture is out of focus." "Be quiet," she answered. I obeyed.   5

But a few minutes later I raised the point again, with mounting impatience. "It will be all right in a minute," she said apprehensively. (She would rather lose her eyesight than be around when I make one of my infrequent scenes.) I waited, it was *just* out of focus—not glaringly out, but out. My vision is 20–20, and I assume that is the vision, adjusted, of most people in the movie house. So, after hectoring my wife throughout the first reel, I finally prevailed upon her to admit that it *was* off, and very annoying. We then settled down, coming to rest on the presumption that: a) someone connected with the management of the theatre must soon notice the blur and make the correction; or b) that someone seated near the rear of the house would make the complaint in behalf of those of us up front; or c) that—any minute now—the entire house would explode into catcalls and foot stamping, calling dramatic attention to the irksome distortion.

What happened was nothing. The movie ended, as it had begun, *just* out of focus, and as we trooped out, we stretched our faces in a variety of contortions to accustom the eye to the shock of normal focus.

I think it is safe to say that everybody suffered on that occasion. And I think it is safe to assume that everyone was expecting someone else to take the initiative in going back to speak to the manager. And it is probably true even that if we had supposed the movie would run right through the blurred image, someone surely would have summoned up the purposive indignation to get up out of his seat and file his complaint.

But notice that no one did. And the reason no one did is because we are all increasingly anxious in America to be unobtrusive, we are reluctant to make our voices heard, hesitant about claiming our rights; we are afraid that our cause is unjust, or that if it is not unjust, that it is ambiguous; or if not even that, that it is too trivial to justify the horrors of a confrontation with Authority; we will sit in an oven or endure a racking headache before undertaking a head-on, I'm-here-to-tell-you complaint. That tendency to passive compliance, to a heedless endurance, is something to keep one's eyes on—in sharp focus.

I myself can occasionally summon the courage to complain, but I cannot, as I have intimated, complain softly. My own instinct is so strong to let the thing ride, to forget about it—to expect that someone will take the matter up, when the grievance is collective, in my behalf—that it is only when the provocation is at a very special key, whose vibrations touch simultaneously a complexus of nerves, allergies, and passions, that I catch fire and find the reserves of courage and assertiveness to speak up. When that happens, I get quite carried away. My blood gets hot, my brow wet, I become unbearably and unconscionably sarcastic and bellicose; I am girded for a total showdown.

10   Why should that be? Why could not I (or anyone else) on that   10
railroad coach have said simply to the conductor, "Sir"—I take that back: that sounds sarcastic—"Conductor, would you be good enough to turn down the heat? I am extremely hot. In fact I tend to get hot every time the temperature reaches 85 degr—" Strike that last sentence. Just end it with the simple statement that you are extremely hot, and let the conductor infer the cause.

Every New Year's Eve I resolve to do something about the Milquetoast in me and vow to speak up, calmly, for my rights, and for the betterment of our society, on every appropriate occasion. Entering last New Year's Eve I was fortified in my resolve because that morning at breakfast I had had to ask the waitress three times for a glass of milk. She finally brought it—after I had finished my eggs, which is when I don't want it any more. I did not have the manliness to order her to take the milk back, but settled instead for a cowardly sulk, and ostentatiously refused to drink the milk—though I later paid for it—rather than state plainly to the hostess, as I should have, why I had not drunk it, and would not pay for it.

So by the time the New Year ushered out the Old, riding in on my morning's indignation and stimulated by the gastric juices of resolution that flow so faithfully on New Year's Eve, I rendered my vow. Henceforward I would conquer my shyness, my despicable disposition to supineness. I would speak out like a man against the unnecessary annoyances of our time.

Forty-eight hours later, I was standing in line at the ski repair store in Pico Peak, Vermont. All I needed, to get on with my skiing, was the loan, for one minute, of a small screwdriver, to tighten a loose binding. Behind the counter in the workshop were two men. One was industriously engaged in serving the complicated requirements of a young lady at the head of the line, and obviously he would be tied up for quite a while. The other—"Jiggs," his workmate called him—was a middle-aged man, who sat in a chair puffing a pipe, exchanging small talk with his working partner. My pulse began its telltale acceleration. The minutes ticked on. I stared at the idle shopkeeper, hoping to shame him into action, but he was impervious to my telepathic reproof and continued his small talk with his friend, brazenly insensitive to the nervous demands of six good men who were raring to ski.

Suddenly my New Year's Eve resolution struck me. It was now or never. I broke from my place in line and marched to the counter. I was going to control myself. I dug my nails into my palms. My effort was only partially successful:

15 "If you are not too busy," I said icily, "would you mind handing me a screwdriver?" 15

Work stopped and everyone turned his eyes on me, and I experienced the mortification I always feel when I am the center of centripetal shafts of curiosity, resentment, perplexity.

But the worst was yet to come. "I am sorry, sir," said Jiggs defensively, moving the pipe from his mouth. "I am not supposed to move. I have just had a heart attack." That was the signal for a great whirring noise that descended from heaven. We looked, stricken, out the window, and it appeared as though a cyclone had suddenly focused on the snowy courtyard between the shop and the ski lift. Suddenly a gigantic army helicopter materialized, and hovered down to a landing. Two men jumped out of the plane carrying a stretcher, tore into the ski shop, and lifted the shopkeeper onto the stretcher. Jiggs bade his companion good-by, was whisked out the door, into the plane, up to the heavens, down—we learned—to a near-by army hospital. I looked up manfully—into a score of man-eating eyes. I put the experience down as a reversal.

As I write this, on an airplane, I have run out of paper and need to reach into my briefcase under my legs for more. I cannot do this until my empty lunch tray is removed from my lap. I arrested the stewardess as she passed empty-handed down the aisle on the way to the kitchen to fetch the lunch trays for the passengers up forward who haven't been served yet. "Would you please take my tray?" "Just a *moment, sir!*" she said, and marched on sternly. Shall I tell her that since she is headed for the kitchen *anyway,* it could not delay the feeding of the other passengers by more than two seconds necessary to stash away my empty tray? Or remind her that not fifteen minutes ago she spoke unctuously into the loudspeaker the words undoubtedly devised by the airline's highly paid public relations counselor: "If there is anything I or Miss French can do for you to make your trip more enjoyable, *please* let us—" I have run out of paper.

I think the observable reluctance of the majority of Americans to assert themselves in minor matters is related to our increased sense of helplessness in an age of technology and centralized political and economic power. For generations, Americans who were too hot, or too cold, got up and did something about it. Now we call the plumber, or the electrician, or the furnace man. The habit of looking after our own needs obviously had something to do with the assertiveness that characterized the American family familiar to readers of American literature. With the technification of life goes our direct responsibility for our material environment, and we are conditioned to adopt a position of helplessness not only as regards the broken air conditioner, but as regards the overheated train. It takes an expert to fix the former, but not the latter; yet these distinctions, as we withdraw into helplessness, tend to fade away.

20   Our notorious political apathy is a related phenomenon. Every   20
year, whether the Republican or the Democratic Party is in office, more and more power drains away from the individual to feed vast reservoirs in far-off places; and we have less and less say about the shape of events which shape our future. From this alienation of personal power comes the sense of resignation with which we accept the political dispensations of a powerful government whose hold upon us continues to increase.

An editor of a national weekly news magazine told me a few years ago that as few as a dozen letters of protest against an editorial stance of his magazine was enough to convene a plenipotentiary meeting of the board of editors to review policy. "So few people complain, or make their voices heard," he explained to me, "that we assume a dozen letters represent the inarticulated views of thousands of readers." In the past ten years, he said, the volume of mail has noticeably decreased, even though the circulation of his magazine has risen.

When our voices are finally mute, when we have finally suppressed the natural instinct to complain, whether the vexation is trivial or grave, we shall have become automatons, incapable of feeling. When Premier Khrushchev first came to this country late in 1959 he was primed, we are informed, to experience the bitter resentment of the American people against his tyranny, against his persecutions, against the movement which is responsible for the great number of American deaths in Korea, for billions in taxes every year, and for life everlasting on the brink of disaster; but Khrushchev was pleasantly surprised, and reported back to the Russian people that he had been met with overwhelming cordiality (read: apathy), except, to be sure, for "a few fascists who followed me around with their wretched posters, and should be horsewhipped."

I may be crazy, but I say there would have been lots more posters in a society where train temperatures in the dead of winter are not allowed to climb to 85 degrees without complaint.

Questions on Meaning

1. Buckley feels that the "reluctance" of Americans to complain is partly related to a "sense of helplessness" related to the "age of technology"—this written nearly 20 years before the first personal computer. Explain how you feel computer technology and Internet communications have either retarded or enhanced our ability to complain.

2. Given that this essay was written when the cold war with the Soviet Union was quite hot, what is Buckley's serious message in his next-to-the-last paragraph? What danger is symbolized by sweating, compliant commuters?

Questions on Rhetorical Strategy and Style

1. Buckley describes himself as a shy man, a Milquetoast. How does this compare or contrast with your image of Buckley? Do you think it possible that a man with Buckley's stature and public life could truly be shy?

2. Buckley lets on that he is loud when he does complain—"I am incapable of making a discreet fuss" and "I cannot complain softly," he says. Reread his description of what happens when he *does* complain. What is your image of him—both externally and internally?

3. What is the impact of the dialogue that Buckley uses in a number of places in the essay? Rewrite one of the passages without dialogue. Describe the effect of your revision on his argument.

Writing Assignments

1. Describe an incident when you complained publicly. What motivated you to complain? What were the reactions of other people? Did you lose your temper? How did the person you complained to respond? What would you do differently in the same circumstances?

2. Buckley wrote this essay in the early 1960s, during the civil rights movement (when Americans most definitely were speaking out), but before the so-called sexual revolution, the women's movement, and protest against the war in Vietnam were sweeping the country. Is it still relevant today? Describe what you think would occur *now* on a commuter train seriously overheated in the

middle of winter, in a theater with an out-of-focus picture, or in a line at a ski shop?

3. Buckley complains in this essay about political apathy—one of his complaints that is certainly justified today. Write an essay about voter apathy in America. Compare and contrast voter turnout in national and local elections when Buckley wrote this essay to that in recent elections. Discuss the causes and effects of this apathy. What suggestions would you make to reverse the apathetic trend?

Letter from Birmingham Jail

Martin Luther King, Jr.

Martin Luther King, Jr. (1929–1968), was born in Atlanta, Georgia. The son and grandson of Baptist ministers, he attended Morehouse College, Crozer Theological Seminary, and Boston University where he received a Ph.D. (1955) and met his future wife, Coretta Scott. King's active involvement in the civil rights movement began in 1955, when he led a boycott of segregated buses in Montgomery, Alabama. From the mid 1950s until he was shot and killed in Memphis, Tennessee, while supporting striking city workers, King organized boycotts, sit-ins, mass demonstrations, and other protest activities. As a black civil rights leader, King was arrested, jailed, stoned, stabbed, and beaten; his house was bombed; he was placed under secret surveillance by Federal Bureau of Investigation (FBI) director J. Edgar Hoover; and in 1966 he was awarded the Nobel Peace Prize. Through his leadership— always underscored by his nonviolent beliefs—King's name has become synonymous with the watersheds of the civil rights movement in the United States: Rosa Parks; the Southern Christian Leadership Conference (which King founded); Selma, Alabama; the Civil Rights Act; the Voting Rights Act; and the 1963 civil rights march on Washington, D. C. His published works include Strength to Love *(1963) and* Conscience for Change *(1967). This essay—published in a revised form in* Why We Can't Wait *(1964)—is King's stern response to eight clergymen from Alabama who were asking civil rights activists to give up public demonstrations in Birmingham, Alabama, and turn to the courts. Read the clergymen's public statement first, then King's detailed rebuttal (printed here as it appeared originally). Keep in mind that King wrote these words four months before he delivered his famous "I Have a Dream" speech during the August 1963 civil rights march on Washington; after long years of activism, he was clearly impatient with the slow progress of the civil rights movement.*

Public Statement by Eight Alabama Clergymen

(April 12, 1963)

1   We the undersigned clergymen are among those who, in January, issued "An Appeal for Law and Order and Common Sense," in dealing with racial problems in Alabama. We expressed understanding that honest convictions in racial matters could properly be pursued in the courts, but urged that decisions of those courts should in the meantime be peacefully obeyed.

Since that time there had been some evidence of increased forbearance and a willingness to face facts. Responsible citizens have undertaken to work on various problems which cause racial friction and unrest. In Birmingham, recent public events have given indication that we all have opportunity for a new constructive and realistic approach to racial problems.

However, we are now confronted by a series of demonstrations by some of our Negro citizens, directed and led in part by outsiders. We recognize the natural impatience of people who feel that their hopes are slow in being realized. But we are convinced that these demonstrations are unwise and untimely.

We agree rather with certain local Negro leadership which has called for honest and open negotiation of racial issues in our area. And we believe this kind of facing of issues can best be accomplished by citizens of our own metropolitan area, white and Negro, meeting with their knowledge and experience of the local situation. All of us need to face that responsibility and find proper channels for its accomplishment.

5   Just as we formerly pointed out that "hatred and violence have no   5
sanction in our religious and political traditions," we also point out
that such actions as incite to hatred and violence, however technically
peaceful those actions may be, have not contributed to the resolution
of our local problems. We do not believe that these days of new hope
are days when extreme measures are justified in Birmingham.

We commend the community as a whole, and the local news
media and law enforcement officials in particular, on the calm manner in which these demonstrations have been handled. We urge the
public to continue to show restraint should the demonstrations continue, and the law enforcement officials to remain calm and continue
to protect our city from violence.

We further strongly urge our own Negro community to withdraw
support from these demonstrations, and to unite locally in working
peacefully for a better Birmingham. When rights are consistently denied, a cause should be pressed in the courts and in negotiations
among local leaders, and not in the streets. We appeal to both our
white and Negro citizenry to observe the principles of law and order
and common sense.

Signed by:

C.C. J. CARPENTER, D.D., LL.D., *Bishop of Alabama*
JOSEPH A. DURICK, D.D., *Auxiliary Bishop, Diocese of
      Mobile, Birmingham*
RABBI MILTON L. GRAFMAN, *Temple Emanu-El,
      Birmingham, Alabama*
BISHOP PAUL HARDIN, *Bishop of the Alabama-West Florida
      Conference of the Methodist Church*
BISHOP NOLAN B. HARMON, *Bishop of the North Alabama
      Conference of the Methodist Church*
GEORGE M. MURRAY, D.D., LL.D., *Bishop Coadjutor,
      Episcopal Diocese of Alabama*
EDWARD V. RAMAGE, *Moderator, Synod of the Alabama
      Presbyterian Church in the United States*
EARL STALLINGS, *Pastor, First Baptist Church, Birmingham,
      Alabama*

Letter from Birmingham Jail

MARTIN LUTHER KING, JR.
Birmingham City Jail
April 16, 1963

Bishop C. C. J. Carpenter
Bishop Joseph A. Durick
Rabbi Milton L. Grafman
Bishop Paul Hardin
Bishop Nolan B. Harmon
The Rev. George M. Murray
The Rev. Edward V. Ramage
The Rev. Earl Stallings

My dear Fellow Clergymen,

While confined here in the Birmingham City Jail, I came across your recent statement calling our present activities "unwise and untimely." Seldom, if ever, do I pause to answer criticism of my work and ideas. If I sought to answer all of the criticisms that cross my desk, my secretaries would be engaged in little else in the course of the day and I would have no time for constructive work. But since I feel that you are men of genuine good will and your criticisms are sincerely set forth, I would like to answer your statement in what I hope will be patient and reasonable terms.

I think I should give the reason for my being in Birmingham, since you have been influenced by the argument of "outsiders coming in." I have the honor of serving as president of the Southern Christian Leadership Conference, an organization operating in every Southern state with headquarters in Atlanta, Georgia. We have some eighty-five affiliate organizations all across the South—one being the Alabama Christian Movement for Human Rights. Whenever necessary and possible we share staff, educational, and financial resources with our affiliates. Several months ago our local affiliate here in Birmingham invited us to be on call to engage in a nonviolent direct action program if such were deemed necessary. We readily consented, and when the hour came we lived up to our promises. So I, along with several members of my staff, am here, because I was invited here. I am here because I have basic organizational ties here.

10   But more basically, I am in Birmingham because injustice is here.   10 Just as the eighth century prophets left their little villages and carried their "thus saith the Lord" far beyond the boundaries of their home town, and just as the Apostle Paul left his little village of Tarsus and carried the gospel of Jesus Christ to practically every hamlet and city of the Greco-Roman world, I too am compelled to carry the gospel of freedom beyond my particular home town. Like Paul, I must constantly respond to the Macedonian call for aid.

Moreover, I am cognizant of the interrelatedness of all communities and states. I cannot sit idly by in Atlanta and not be concerned about what happens in Birmingham. Injustice anywhere is a threat to justice everywhere. We are caught in an inescapable network of mutuality, tied in a single garment of destiny. Whatever affects one directly affects all indirectly. Never again can we afford to live with the narrow, provincial "outside agitator" idea. Anyone who lives inside the United States can never be considered an outsider anywhere in this country.

You deplore the demonstrations that are presently taking place in Birmingham. But I am sorry that your statement did not express a similar concern for the conditions that brought the demonstrations into being. I am sure that each of you would want to go beyond the superficial social analyst who looks merely at effects, and does not grapple with underlying causes. I would not hesitate to say that it is unfortunate that so-called demonstrations are taking place in Birmingham at this time, but I would say in more emphatic terms that it is even more unfortunate that the white power structure of this city left the Negro community with no other alternative.

In any nonviolent campaign there are four basic steps: (1) collection of the facts to determine whether injustices are alive; (2) negotiation; (3) self-purification; and (4) direct action. We have gone through all of these steps in Birmingham. There can be no gainsaying of the fact that racial injustice engulfs this community. Birmingham is probably the most thoroughly segregated city in the United States. Its ugly record of police brutality is known in every section of this country. Its unjust treatment of Negroes in the courts is a notorious reality. There have been more unsolved bombings of Negro homes and churches in Birmingham than any city in this nation. These are the hard, brutal, and unbelievable facts. On the basis of these conditions, Negro leaders sought to negotiate with the city fathers. But the political leaders consistently refused to engage in good faith negotiation.

Then came the opportunity last September to talk with some of the leaders of the economic community. In these negotiating sessions certain promises were made by the merchants—such as the promise to remove the humiliating racial signs from the stores. On the basis of these promises Rev. Shuttlesworth and the leaders of the Alabama Christian Movement for Human Rights agreed to call a moratorium on any type of demonstrations. As the weeks and months unfolded we realized that we were the victims of a broken promise. The signs remained. As in so many experiences of the past we were confronted with blasted hopes, and the dark shadow of a deep disappointment settled upon us. So we had no alternative except that of preparing for direct action, whereby we would present our very bodies as a means of laying our case before the conscience of the local and national community. We were not unmindful of the difficulties involved. So we decided to go through a process of self-purification. We started having workshops on nonviolence and repeatedly asked ourselves the questions, "Are you able to accept blows without retaliating?" "Are you able to endure the ordeals of jail?"

15 We decided to set our direct action program around the Easter season, realizing that with the exception of Christmas, this was the largest shopping period of the year. Knowing that a strong economic withdrawal program would be the by-product of direct action, we felt that this was the best time to bring pressure on the merchants for the needed changes. Then it occurred to us that the March election was ahead, and so we speedily decided to postpone action until after election day. When we discovered that Mr. Connor was in the run-off, we decided again to postpone so that the demonstrations could not be used to cloud the issues. At this time we agreed to begin our nonviolent witness the day after the run-off.

This reveals that we did not move irresponsibly into direct action. We too wanted to see Mr. Connor defeated; so we went through postponement after postponement to aid in this community need. After this we felt that direct action could be delayed no longer.

You may well ask, "Why direct action? Why sit-ins, marches, etc.? Isn't negotiation a better path?" You are exactly right in your call for negotiation. Indeed, this is the purpose of direct action. Nonviolent direct action seeks to create such a crisis and establish such creative tension that a community that has constantly refused to negotiate is forced to confront the issue. It seeks so to dramatize the issue that it can no longer be ignored. I just referred to the creation of tension as a part of the work of the nonviolent resister. This may sound rather shocking. But I must confess that I am not afraid of the word tension. I have earnestly worked and preached against violent tension, but there is a type of constructive nonviolent tension that is necessary for growth. Just as Socrates felt that it was necessary to create a tension in the mind so that individuals could rise from the bondage of myths and half-truths to the unfettered realm of creative analysis and objective appraisal, we must see the need of having nonviolent gadflies to create the kind of tension in society that will help men rise from the dark depths of prejudice and racism to the majestic heights of understanding and brotherhood. So the purpose of the direct action is to create a situation so crisis-packed that it will inevitably open the door to negotiation. We, therefore, concur with you in your call for negotiation. Too long has our beloved Southland been bogged down in the tragic attempt to live in monologue rather than dialogue.

One of the basic points in your statement is that our acts are untimely. Some have asked, "Why didn't you give the new administration time to act?" The only answer that I can give to this inquiry is that the new administration must be prodded about as much as the outgoing one before it acts. We will be sadly mistaken if we feel that the election of Mr. Boutwell will bring the millennium to Birmingham. While Mr. Boutwell is much more articulate and gentle than Mr. Connor, they are both segregationists dedicated to the task of maintaining the status quo. The hope I see in Mr. Boutwell is that he will be reasonable enough to see the futility of massive resistance to desegregation. But he will not see this without pressure from the devotees of civil rights. My friends, I must say to you that we have not made a single gain in civil rights without determined legal and nonviolent pressure. History is the long and tragic story of the fact that privileged groups seldom give up their privileges voluntarily. Individuals may see the moral light and voluntarily give up their unjust posture; but as Reinhold Niebuhr has reminded us, groups are more immoral than individuals.

We know through painful experience that freedom is never voluntarily given by the oppressor; it must be demanded by the oppressed. Frankly I have never yet engaged in a direct action movement that was "well timed," according to the timetable of those who have not suffered unduly from the disease of segregation. For years now I have heard the word "Wait!" It rings in the ear of every Negro with a piercing familiarity. This "wait" has almost always meant "never." It has been a tranquilizing thalidomide, relieving the emotional stress for a moment, only to give birth to an ill-formed infant of frustration. We must come to see with the distinguished jurist of yesterday that "justice too long delayed is justice denied." We have waited for more than three hundred and forty years for our constitutional and God-given rights. The nations of Asia and Africa are moving with jet-like speed toward the goal of political independence, and we still creep at horse and buggy pace toward the gaining of a cup of coffee at a lunch counter.

20   I guess it is easy for those who have never felt the stinging darts of segregation to say wait. But when you have seen vicious mobs lynch your mothers and fathers at will and drown your sisters and brothers at whim; when you have seen hate filled policemen curse, kick, brutalize, and even kill your black brothers and sisters with impunity; when you see the vast majority of your twenty million Negro brothers smothering in an air-tight cage of poverty in the midst of an affluent society; when you suddenly find your tongue twisted and your speech stammering as you seek to explain to your six-year-old daughter why she can't go to the public amusement park that has just been advertised on television, and see tears welling up in her little eyes when she is told that Funtown is closed to colored children, and see the depressing clouds of inferiority begin to form in her little mental sky, and see her begin to distort her little personality by unconsciously developing a bitterness toward white people; when you have to concoct an answer for a five-year-old son asking in agonizing pathos: "Daddy, why do white people treat colored people so mean?"; when you take a cross country drive and find it necessary to sleep night after night in the uncomfortable corners of your automobile because no motel will accept you; when you are humiliated day in and day out by nagging signs reading "white" and "colored"; when your first name becomes "nigger" and your middle name becomes "boy" (however old you are) and your last name becomes "John," and when your wife and mother are never given the respected title "Mrs."; when you are harried by day and haunted by night by the fact that you are a Negro, living constantly at tip-toe stance never quite knowing what to expect next, and plagued with inner fears and outer resentments; when you are forever

fighting a degenerating sense of "nobodiness";——then you will understand why we find it difficult to wait. There comes a time when the cup of endurance runs over, and men are no longer willing to be plunged into an abyss of injustice where they experience the bleakness of corroding despair. I hope, sirs, you can understand our legitimate and unavoidable impatience.

You express a great deal of anxiety over our willingness to break laws. This is certainly a legitimate concern. Since we so diligently urge people to obey the Supreme Court's decision of 1954 outlawing segregation in the public schools, it is rather strange and paradoxical to find us consciously breaking laws. One may well ask, "How can you advocate breaking some laws and obeying others?" The answer is found in the fact that there are two types of laws. There are *just* laws and there are *unjust* laws. I would be the first to advocate obeying just laws. One has not only a legal but moral responsibility to obey just laws. Conversely, one has a moral responsibility to disobey unjust laws. I would agree with Saint Augustine that "An unjust law is no law at all."

Now what is the difference between the two? How does one determine when a law is just or unjust? A just law is a man-made code that squares with the moral law or the law of God. An unjust law is a code that is out of harmony with the moral law. To put it in the terms of Saint Thomas Aquinas, an unjust law is a human law that is not rooted in eternal and natural law. Any law that uplifts human personality is just. Any law that degrades human personality is unjust. All segregation statutes are unjust because segregation distorts the soul and damages the personality. It gives the segregator a false sense of superiority and the segregated a false sense of inferiority. To use the words of Martin Buber, the great Jewish philosopher, segregation substitutes an "I-it" relationship for the "I-thou" relationship, and ends up relegating persons to the status of things. So segregation is not only politically, economically, and sociologically unsound, but it is morally wrong and sinful. Paul Tillich has said that sin is separation. Isn't segregation an existential expression of man's tragic separation, an expression of his awful estrangement, his terrible sinfulness? So I can urge men to obey the 1954 decision of the Supreme Court because it is morally right, and I can urge them to disobey segregation ordinances because they are morally wrong.

Let us turn to a more concrete example of just and unjust laws. An unjust law is a code that a majority inflicts on a minority that is not binding on itself. This is *difference* made legal. On the other hand a just law is a code that a majority compels a minority to follow that it is willing to follow itself. This is *sameness* made legal.

Let me give another explanation. An unjust law is a code inflicted upon a minority which that minority had no part in enacting or creating because they did not have the unhampered right to vote. Who can say the legislature of Alabama which set up the segregation laws was democratically elected? Throughout the state of Alabama all types of conniving methods are used to prevent Negroes from becoming registered voters and there are some counties without a single Negro registered to vote despite the fact that the Negro constitutes a majority of the population. Can any law set up in such a state be considered democratically structured?

25   These are just a few examples of unjust and just laws. There are 25 some instances when a law is just on its face but unjust in its application. For instance, I was arrested Friday on a charge of parading without a permit. Now there is nothing wrong with an ordinance which requires a permit for a parade, but when the ordinance is used to preserve segregation and to deny citizens the First Amendment privilege of peaceful assembly and peaceful protest, then it becomes unjust.

I hope you can see the distinction I am trying to point out. In no sense do I advocate evading or defying the law as the rabid segregationist would do. This would lead to anarchy. One who breaks an unjust law must do it *openly, lovingly* (not hatefully as the white mothers did in New Orleans when they were seen on television screaming "nigger, nigger, nigger") and with a willingness to accept the penalty. I submit that an individual who breaks a law that conscience tells him is unjust, and willingly accepts the penalty by staying in jail to arouse the conscience of the community over its injustice, is in reality expressing the very highest respect for law.

Of course there is nothing new about this kind of civil disobedience. It was seen sublimely in the refusal of Shadrach, Meshach, and Abednego to obey the laws of Nebuchadnezzar because a higher moral law was involved. It was practiced superbly by the early Christians who were willing to face hungry lions and the excruciating pain of chopping blocks, before submitting to certain unjust laws of the Roman Empire. To a degree academic freedom is a reality today because Socrates practiced civil disobedience.

We can never forget that everything Hitler did in Germany was "legal" and everything the Hungarian freedom fighters did in Hungary was "illegal." It was "illegal" to aid and comfort a Jew in Hitler's Germany. But I am sure that, if I had lived in Germany during that time, I would have aided and comforted my Jewish brothers even though it was illegal. If I lived in a communist country today where certain principles dear to the Christian faith are suppressed, I believe I would openly advocate disobeying those antireligious laws.

I must make two honest confessions to you, my Christian and Jewish brothers. First I must confess that over the last few years I have been gravely disappointed with the white moderate. I have almost reached the regrettable conclusion that the Negroes' great stumbling block in the stride toward freedom is not the White Citizens' "Counciler" or the Ku Klux Klanner, but the white moderate who is more devoted to "order" than to justice; who prefers a negative peace which is the absence of tension to a positive peace which is the presence of justice; who constantly says "I agree with you in the goal you seek, but I can't agree with your methods of direct action;" who paternalistically feels that he can set the timetable for another man's freedom; who lives by the myth of time and who constantly advises the Negro to wait until a "more convenient season." Shallow understanding from people of good will is more frustrating than absolute misunderstanding from people of ill will. Lukewarm acceptance is much more bewildering than outright rejection.

30   I had hoped that the white moderate would understand that law and order exist for the purpose of establishing justice, and that when they fail to do this they become the dangerously structured dams that block the flow of social progress. I had hoped that the white moderate would understand that the present tension in the South is merely a necessary phase of the transition from an obnoxious negative peace, where the Negro passively accepted his unjust plight, to a substance-filled positive peace, where all men will respect the dignity and worth of human personality. Actually, we who engage in nonviolent direct action are not the creators of tension. We merely bring to the surface the hidden tension that is already alive. We bring it out in the open where it can be seen and dealt with. Like a boil that can never be cured as long as it is covered up but must be opened with all its pus-flowing ugliness to the natural medicines of air and light, injustice must likewise be exposed, with all of the tension its exposing creates, to the light

of human conscience and the air of national opinion before it can be cured.

In your statement you asserted that our actions, even though peaceful, must be condemned because they precipitate violence. But can this assertion be logically made? Isn't this like condemning the robbed man because his possession of money precipitated the evil act of robbery? Isn't this like condemning Socrates because his unswerving commitment to truth and his philosophical delvings precipitated the misguided popular mind to make him drink the hemlock? Isn't this like condemning Jesus because His unique God consciousness and never-ceasing devotion to His will precipitated the evil act of crucifixion? We must come to see, as federal courts have consistently affirmed, that it is immoral to urge an individual to withdraw his efforts to gain his basic constitutional rights because the quest precipitates violence. Society must protect the robbed and punish the robber.

I had also hoped that the white moderate would reject the myth of time. I received a letter this morning from a white brother in Texas which said: "All Christians know that the colored people will receive equal rights eventually, but is it possible that you are in too great of a religious hurry? It has taken Christianity almost 2,000 years to accomplish what it has. The teachings of Christ take time to come to earth." All that is said here grows out of a tragic misconception of time. It is the strangely irrational notion that there is something in the very flow of time that will inevitably cure all ills. Actually time is neutral. It can be used either destructively or constructively. I am coming to feel that the people of ill will have used time much more effectively than the people of good will. We will have to repent in this generation not merely for the vitriolic words and actions of the bad people, but for the appalling silence of the good people. We must come to see that human progress never rolls in on wheels of inevitability. It comes through the tireless efforts and persistent work of men willing to be co-workers with God, and without this hard work time itself becomes an ally of the forces of social stagnation.

We must use time creatively, and forever realize that the time is always ripe to do right. Now is the time to make real the promise of democracy, and transform our pending national elegy into a creative psalm of brotherhood. Now is the time to lift our national policy from the quicksand of racial injustice to the solid rock of human dignity.

You spoke of our activity in Birmingham as extreme. At first I was rather disappointed that fellow clergymen would see my nonviolent efforts as those of the extremist. I started thinking about the fact that I stand in the middle of two opposing forces in the Negro community. One is a force of complacency made up of Negroes who, as a result of long years of oppression, have been so completely drained of self-respect and a sense of "somebodiness" that they have adjusted to segregation, and of a few Negroes in the middle class who, because of a degree of academic and economic security, and because at points they profit by segregation, have unconsciously become insensitive to the problems of the masses. The other force is one of bitterness and hatred and comes perilously close to advocating violence. It is expressed in the various black nationalist groups that are springing up over the nation, the largest and best known being Elijah Muhammad's Muslim movement. This movement is nourished by the contemporary frustration over the continued existence of racial discrimination. It is made up of people who have lost faith in America, who have absolutely repudiated Christianity, and who have concluded that the white man is an incurable "devil." I have tried to stand between these two forces saying that we need not follow the "do-nothingism" of the complacent or the hatred and despair of the black nationalist. There is the more excellent way of love and nonviolent protest. I'm grateful to God that, through the Negro church, the dimension of nonviolence entered our struggle. If this philosophy had not emerged I am convinced that by now many streets of the South would be flowing with floods of blood. And I am further convinced that if our white brothers dismiss us as "rabble rousers" and "outside agitators"—those of us who are working through the channels of nonviolent direct action—and refuse to support our nonviolent efforts, millions of Negroes, out of frustration and despair, will seek solace and security in black nationalist ideologies, a development that will lead inevitably to a frightening racial nightmare.

35   Oppressed people cannot remain oppressed forever. The urge for freedom will eventually come. This is what has happened to the American Negro. Something within has reminded him of his birthright of freedom; something without has reminded him that he can gain it. Consciously and unconsciously, he has been swept in by what the Germans call the *Zeitgeist*, and with his black brothers of Africa, and his brown and yellow brothers of Asia, South America, and the

Caribbean, he is moving with a sense of cosmic urgency toward the promised land of racial justice. Recognizing this vital urge that has engulfed the Negro community, one should readily understand public demonstrations. The Negro has many pent-up resentments and latent frustrations. He has to get them out. So let him march sometime; let him have his prayer pilgrimages to the city hall; understand why he must have sit-ins and freedom rides. If his repressed emotions do not come out in these nonviolent ways, they will come out in ominous expressions of violence. This is not a threat; it is a fact of history. So I have not said to my people, "Get rid of your discontent." But I have tried to say that this normal and healthy discontent can be channeled through the creative outlet of nonviolent direct action. Now this approach is being dismissed as extremist. I must admit that I was initially disappointed in being so categorized.

But as I continued to think about the matter I gradually gained a bit of satisfaction from being considered an extremist. Was not Jesus an extremist in love? "Love your enemies, bless them that curse you, pray for them that despitefully use you." Was not Amos an extremist for justice— "Let justice roll down like waters and righteousness like a mighty stream." Was not Paul an extremist for the gospel of Jesus Christ— "I bear in my body the marks of the Lord Jesus." Was not Martin Luther an extremist— "Here I stand; I can do none other so help me God." Was not John Bunyan an extremist— "I will stay in jail to the end of my days before I make a butchery of my conscience." Was not Abraham Lincoln an extremist— "This nation cannot survive half slave and half free." Was not Thomas Jefferson an extremist— "We hold these truths to be self evident that all men are created equal." So the question is not whether we will be extremist but what kind of extremist will we be. Will we be extremists for hate or will we be extremists for love? Will we be extremists for the preservation of injustice or will we be extremists for the cause of justice? In that dramatic scene on Calvary's hill three men were crucified. We must never forget that all three were crucified for the same crime—the crime of extremism. Two were extremists for immorality, and thus fell below their environment. The other, Jesus Christ, was an extremist for love, truth, and goodness, and thereby rose above His environment. So, after all, maybe the South, the nation, and the world are in dire need of creative extremists.

I had hoped that the white moderate would see this. Maybe I was too optimistic. Maybe I expected too much. I guess I should have realized that few members of a race that has oppressed another race can understand or appreciate the deep groans and passionate yearnings of those that have been oppressed, and still fewer have the vision to see that injustice must be rooted out by strong, persistent, and determined action. I am thankful, however, that some of our white brothers have grasped the meaning of this social revolution and committed themselves to it. They are still all too small in quantity, but they are big in quality. Some like Ralph McGill, Lillian Smith, Harry Golden, and James Dabbs have written about our struggle in eloquent, prophetic, and understanding terms. Others have marched with us down nameless streets of the South. They have languished in filthy, roach-infested jails, suffering the abuse and brutality of angry policemen who see them as "dirty nigger lovers." They, unlike so many of their moderate brothers and sisters, have recognized the urgency of the moment and sensed the need for powerful "action" antidotes to combat the disease of segregation.

Let me rush on to mention my other disappointment. I have been so greatly disappointed with the white Church and its leadership. Of course there are some notable exceptions. I am not unmindful of the fact that each of you has taken some significant stands on this issue. I commend you, Rev. Stallings, for your Christian stand on this past Sunday, in welcoming Negroes to your worship service on a nonsegregated basis. I commend the Catholic leaders of this state for integrating Springhill College several years ago.

But despite these notable exceptions I must honestly reiterate that I have been disappointed with the Church. I do not say that as one of those negative critics who can always find something wrong with the Church. I say it as a minister of the gospel, who loves the Church; who was nurtured in its bosom; who has been sustained by its spiritual blessings and who will remain true to it as long as the cord of life shall lengthen.

40 I had the strange feeling when I was suddenly catapulted into the 40 leadership of the bus protest in Montgomery several years ago that we would have the support of the white Church. I felt that the white ministers, priests, and rabbis of the South would be some of our strongest allies. Instead, some have been outright opponents, refusing to understand the

freedom movement and misrepresenting its leaders; all too many others have been more cautious than courageous and have remained silent behind the anesthetizing security of stained glass windows.

In spite of my shattered dreams of the past, I came to Birmingham with the hope that the white religious leadership of the community would see the justice of our cause and, with deep moral concern, serve as the channel through which our just grievances could get to the power structure. I had hoped that each of you would understand. But again I have been disappointed.

I have heard numerous religious leaders of the South call upon their worshippers to comply with a desegregation decision because it is the law, but I have longed to hear white ministers say follow this decree because integration is morally right and the Negro is your brother. In the midst of blatant injustices inflicted upon the Negro, I have watched white churches stand on the sideline and merely mouth pious irrelevancies and sanctimonious trivialities. In the midst of a mighty struggle to rid our nation of racial and economic injustice, I have heard so many ministers say, "Those are social issues with which the Gospel has no real concern," and I have watched so many churches commit themselves to a completely otherworldly religion which made a strange distinction between body and soul, the sacred and the secular.

So here we are moving toward the exit of the twentieth century with a religious community largely adjusted to the status quo, standing as a tail light behind other community agencies rather than a headlight leading men to higher levels of justice.

I have travelled the length and breadth of Alabama, Mississippi, and all the other Southern states. On sweltering summer days and crisp autumn mornings I have looked at her beautiful churches with their spires pointing heavenward. I have beheld the impressive outlay of her massive religious education buildings. Over and over again I have found myself asking: "Who worships here? Who is their God? Where were their voices when the lips of Governor Barnett dripped with words of interposition and nullification? Where were they when Governor Wallace gave the clarion call for defiance and hatred? Where were their voices of support when tired, bruised, and weary Negro men and women decided to rise from the dark dungeons of complacency to the bright hills of creative protest?"

45 Yes, these questions are still in my mind. In deep disappointment, 45 I have wept over the laxity of the Church. But be assured that my tears

have been tears of love. There can be no deep disappointment where there is not deep love. Yes, I love the Church; I love her sacred walls. How could I do otherwise? I am in the rather unique position of being the son, the grandson, and the great grandson of preachers. Yes, I see the Church as the body of Christ. But, oh! How we have blemished and scarred that body through social neglect and fear of being nonconformists.

There was a time when the Church was very powerful. It was during that period when the early Christians rejoiced when they were deemed worthy to suffer for what they believed. In those days the Church was not merely a thermometer that recorded the ideas and principles of popular opinion; it was a thermostat that transformed the mores of society. Wherever the early Christians entered a town the power structure got disturbed and immediately sought to convict them for being "disturbers of the peace" and "outside agitators." But they went on with the conviction that they were a "colony of heaven" and had to obey God rather than man. They were small in number but big in commitment. They were too God-intoxicated to be "astronomically intimidated." They brought an end to such ancient evils as infanticide and gladiatorial contest.

Things are different now. The contemporary Church is so often a weak, ineffectual voice with an uncertain sound. It is so often the archsupporter of the status quo. Far from being disturbed by the presence of the Church, the power structure of the average community is consoled by the Church's silent and often vocal sanction of things as they are.

But the judgment of God is upon the Church as never before. If the Church of today does not recapture the sacrificial spirit of the early Church, it will lose its authentic ring, forfeit the loyalty of millions, and be dismissed as an irrelevant social club with no meaning for the twentieth century. I am meeting young people every day whose disappointment with the Church has risen to outright disgust.

Maybe again I have been too optimistic. Is organized religion too inextricably bound to the status quo to save our nation and the world? Maybe I must turn my faith to the inner spiritual Church, the church within the Church, as the true *ecclesia* and the hope of the world. But again I am thankful to God that some noble souls from the ranks of organized religion have broken loose from the paralyzing chains of conformity and joined us as active partners in the struggle for freedom. They have left their secure congregations and walked the streets of Albany, Georgia, with us. They have gone through the highways of the South on torturous rides for freedom. Yes, they have gone to jail with us. Some have been kicked out of their churches and lost the support of their bishops and fellow ministers. But they have gone with the faith that right defeated is stronger than evil triumphant. These men have been the leaven in the lump of the race. Their witness has been the spiritual salt that has preserved the true meaning of the Gospel in these troubled times. They have carved a tunnel of hope through the dark mountain of disappointment.

50   I hope the Church as a whole will meet the challenge of this decisive hour. But even if the Church does not come to the aid of justice, I have no despair about the future. I have no fear about the outcome of our struggle in Birmingham, even if our motives are presently misunderstood. We will reach the goal of freedom in Birmingham and all over the nation, because the goal of America is freedom. Abused and scorned though we may be, our destiny is tied up with the destiny of America. Before the pilgrims landed at Plymouth, we were here. Before the pen of Jefferson etched across the pages of history the majestic words of the Declaration of Independence, we were here. For more than two centuries our foreparents labored in this country without wages; they made cotton "king"; and they built the homes of their masters in the midst of brutal injustice and shameful humiliation—and yet out of a bottomless vitality they continued to thrive and develop. If the inexpressible cruelties of slavery could not stop us, the opposition we now face will surely fail. We will win our freedom because the sacred heritage of our nation and the eternal will of God are embodied in our echoing demands.

I must close now. But before closing I am impelled to mention one other point in your statement that troubled me profoundly. You warmly commended the Birmingham police force for keeping "order" and "preventing violence." I don't believe you would have so warmly commended the police force if you had seen its angry violent dogs literally biting six unarmed, nonviolent Negroes. I don't believe you would so quickly commend the policemen if you would observe their ugly and inhuman treatment of Negroes here in the city jail; if you would watch them push and curse old Negro women and young Negro girls; if you would see them slap and kick old Negro men and young Negro boys; if you will observe them, as they did on two occasions, refuse to give us food because we wanted to sing our grace together. I'm sorry that I can't join you in your praise for the police department.

It is true that they have been rather disciplined in their public handling of the demonstrators. In this sense they have been rather publicly "nonviolent." But for what purpose? To preserve the evil system of segregation. Over the last few years I have consistently preached that nonviolence demands that the means we use must be as pure as the ends we seek. So I have tried to make it clear that it is wrong to use immoral means to attain moral ends. But now I must affirm that it is just as wrong, or even more so, to use moral means to preserve immoral ends. Maybe Mr. Connor and his policemen have been rather publicly nonviolent, as Chief Pritchett was in Albany, Georgia, but they have used the moral means of nonviolence to maintain the immoral end of flagrant racial injustice. T. S. Eliot has said that there is no greater treason than to do the right deed for the wrong reason.

I wish you had commended the Negro sit-inners and demonstrators of Birmingham for their sublime courage, their willingness to suffer, and their amazing discipline in the midst of the most inhuman provocation. One day the South will recognize its real heroes. They will be the James Merediths, courageously and with a majestic sense of purpose, facing jeering and hostile mobs and the agonizing loneliness that characterizes the life of the pioneer. They will be old, oppressed, battered Negro women, symbolized in a seventy-two year old woman of Montgomery, Alabama, who rose up with a sense of dignity and with her people decided not to ride the segregated buses, and responded to one who inquired about her tiredness with ungrammatical profundity: "My feets is tired, but my soul is rested." They will be young high school and college students, young ministers of the gospel and a host of the elders, courageously and nonviolently sitting in at lunch counters and willingly going to jail for conscience sake. One day the South will know that when these disinherited children of God sat down at lunch counters they were in reality standing up for the best in the American dream and the most sacred values in our Judeo-Christian heritage, and thus carrying our whole nation back to great wells of democracy which were dug deep by the founding fathers in the formulation of the Constitution and the Declaration of Independence.

Never before have I written a letter this long (or should I say a book?). I'm afraid that it is much too long to take your precious time.

I can assure you that it would have been much shorter if I had been writing from a comfortable desk, but what else is there to do when you are alone for days in the dull monotony of a narrow jail cell other than write long letters, think strange thoughts, and pray long prayers!

55   If I have said anything in this letter that is an overstatement of the truth and is indicative of an unreasonable impatience, I beg you to forgive me. If I have said anything in this letter that is an understatement of the truth and is indicative of my having a patience that makes me patient with anything less than brotherhood, I beg God to forgive me.

I hope this letter finds you strong in the faith. I also hope that circumstances will soon make it possible for me to meet each of you, not as an integrationist or a civil rights leader, but as a fellow clergyman and a Christian brother. Let us all hope that the dark clouds of racial prejudice will soon pass away and the deep fog of misunderstanding will be lifted from our fear-drenched communities and in some not too distant tomorrow the radiant stars of love and brotherhood will shine over our great nation with all of their scintillating beauty.

Yours for the cause of
Peace and Brotherhood
MARTIN LUTHER KING, JR.

Questions on Meaning

1. At the time that this essay was written, King had been active in the civil rights movement for nearly 10 years. How had he usually handled criticisms of his work and ideas? Why?

2. The public statement by the eight clergymen exhibits a distrust for *outsiders.* How does King address that common fear and skepticism? If you had been one of the *local* clergymen, how do you think you would have reacted to King's explanation? Would you have respected his convictions? Embraced his beliefs?

3. Often in this essay, King addresses the issue of the timeliness of nonviolent demonstrations and other political activities. This urgency of action is a common theme of King's. "For years I have heard the word 'Wait!' " he writes. "It rings in the ear of every Negro with a piercing familiarity." What does the word *wait* mean to King?

Questions on Rhetorical Strategy and Style

1. King's dominant rhetorical strategy is clear: persuasion. He is not telling a story; he is not using flowery language or a preacher's oratory. This essay is logos and ethos: a sound argument supported by credibility, integrity, and experience. Analyze how he builds the argument one step at a time through the essay.

2. Repetition helps to drive home an argument. Show two places in this essay where King effectively uses repetition. Rewrite one of the passages without the repeated phrase and compare its effectiveness with the original.

3. Find King's discussion of just and unjust laws and locate the two paragraphs in which he gives examples of these laws ("Let us turn to a more concrete example . . . " and "Let me give another explanation . . . "). What is your reaction to his use of examples here?

Writing Assignments

1. A student of Gandhi, King based his political activities on nonviolent confrontation. In this essay, King outlines four steps of nonviolent activism: collect facts, negotiate, self-purify, and take direct action. Identify an injustice in your lifetime that people are trying or have tried to change through nonviolent activism.

Examples may include a physical barrier to people with physical handicaps, an employment restriction that discriminates against elderly people, or a city ordinance that unfairly restricts the activities of teenagers. Describe the political activity that has occurred, then relate it to King's four steps. Were these steps applied? If not, discuss how the outcome might have been different if these steps had been applied.

2. In this essay, King responds to the charge of being an extremist by admitting that he initially was put off by the label, but then realized that he wore it proudly. What is your reaction to the term? Does "extremist" hold negative or positive connotations for you? Is it used to credit or discredit? Identify some current political figures who are called extremists. Write an essay defining the term and describing how it is commonly applied, using current extremist political figures as examples.

3. King writes that one "has a moral responsibility to disobey unjust laws." Do you agree? Reread his defense of that statement. Does King's stance help overturn unjust laws or create anarchy? Choose a "law" that affects your life that you feel is unjust—perhaps a dormitory rule or campus restriction or a local law. Would you, or do you, intentionally break it? Write an essay describing the "law" and your action, arguing your viewpoint on obeying or disobeying it.

Address to the Prisoners in the Cook County Jail

Clarence Darrow

Clarence Darrow (1857–1938) was born in Kinsman, Ohio. Admitted to the bar in 1878, Darrow began his legal career as a small-town Ohio lawyer. In 1887, he moved to Chicago and began a successful practice in civil suits and labor law. Darrow rose to national prominence defending Eugene V. Debs and other union leaders in the 1894 Pullman strike. His notoriety grew with the Leob-Leopold kidnap, murder, and ransom case (1924) and with the case he is most often associated with today, the Scopes anti-evolution trial (1925), in which he argued against the politician and esteemed orator William Jennings Bryan. Darrow, who opposed capital punishment, often gave speeches on social and political issues. His books include Crime: Its Cause and Treatment *(1922). In this speech given to a group of prisoners, Darrow explains that they are in jail because they lack opportunity.*

1   If I looked at jails and crimes and prisoners in the way the ordinary person does, I should not speak on this subject to you. The reason I talk to you on the question of crime, its cause and cure, is that I really do not in the least believe in crime. There is no such thing as a crime as the word is generally understood. I do not believe there is any sort of distinction between the real moral conditions of the people in and out of jail. One is just as good as the other. The people here can no more help being here than the people outside can avoid being outside. I do not believe that people are in jail because they deserve to be. They are in jail simply because they cannot avoid it on account of circumstances which are entirely beyond their control and for which they are in no way responsible.

I suppose a great many people on the outside would say I was doing you harm if they should hear what I say to you this afternoon, but you cannot be hurt a great deal anyway, so it will not matter. Good people outside would say that I was really teaching you things that were calculated to injure society, but it's worth while now and then to hear something different from what you ordinarily get from preachers and the like. These will tell you that you should be good and then you will get rich and be happy. Of course we know that people do not get rich by being good, and that is the reason why so many of you people try to get rich some other way, only you do not understand how to do it quite as well as the fellow outside.

There are people who think that everything in this world is an accident. But really there is no such thing as an accident. A great many folks admit that many of the people in jail ought to be there, and many who are outside ought to be in. I think none of them ought to be here. There ought to be no jails; and if it were not for the fact that people on the outside are so grasping and heartless in their dealings with the people on the inside, there would be no such institution as jails.

I do not want you to believe that I think all you people here are angels. I do not think that. You are people of all kinds, all of you doing the best you can—and that is evidently not very well. You are people of all kinds and conditions and under all circumstances. In one sense everybody is equally good and equally bad. We all do the best we can under the circumstances. But as to the exact things for which you are sent here, some of you are guilty and did the particular act because you needed the money. Some of you did it because you are in the habit of doing it, and some of you because you are born to it, and it comes to be as natural as it does, for instance, for me to be good.

5 Most of you probably have nothing against me, and most of you 5
would treat me the same way as any other person would, probably better than some of the people on the outside would treat me, because you think I believe in you and they know I do not believe in them. While you would not have the least thing against me in the world, you might pick my pockets. I do not think all of you would, but I think some of you would. You would not have anything against me, but that's your profession, a few of you. Some of the rest of you, if my doors were unlocked, might come in if you saw anything you wanted—not out of any malice to me, but because that is your trade. There is no doubt there are quite a number of people in this jail who

would pick my pockets. And still I know this—that when I get outside pretty nearly everybody picks my pocket. There may be some of you who would hold up a man on the street, if you did not happen to have something else to do, and needed the money; but when I want to light my house or my office the gas company holds me up. They charge me one dollar for something that is worth twenty-five cents. Still all these people are good people; they are pillars of society and support the churches, and they are respectable.

When I ride on the streetcars I am held up—I pay five cents for a ride that is worth two and a half cents, simply because a body of men have bribed the city council and the legislature, so that all the rest of us have to pay tribute to them.

If I do not want to fall into the clutches of the gas trust and choose to burn oil instead of gas, then good Mr. Rockefeller holds me up, and he uses a certain portion of his money to build universities and support churches which are engaged in telling us how to be good.

Some of you are here for obtaining property under false pretenses—yet I pick up a great Sunday paper and read the advertisements of a merchant prince—"Shirtwaists for 39 cents, marked down from $3.00."

When I read the advertisements in the paper I see they are all lies. When I want to get out and find a place to stand anywhere on the face of the earth, I find that it has all been taken up long ago before I came here, and before you came here, and somebody says, "Get off, swim into the lake, fly into the air; go anywhere, but get off." That is because these people have the police and they have the jails and the judges and the lawyers and the soldiers and all the rest of them to take care of the earth and drive everybody off that comes in their way.

10   A great many people will tell you that all this is true, but that it   10 does not excuse you. These facts do not excuse some fellow who reaches into my pocket and takes out a five-dollar bill. The fact that the gas company bribes the members of the legislature from year to year, and fixes the law, so that all you people are compelled to be "fleeced" whenever you deal with them; the fact that the streetcar companies and the gas companies have control of the streets; and the fact that the landlords own all the earth—this, they say, has nothing to do with you.

Let us see whether there is any connection between the crimes of the respectable classes and your presence in the jail. Many of you people are in jail because you have really committed burglary; many of you, because you have stolen something. In the meaning of the law, you have taken some other person's property. Some of you have entered a store and carried off a pair of shoes because you did not have the price. Possibly some of you have committed murder. I cannot tell what all of you did. There are a great many people here who have done some of these things who really do not know themselves why they did them. I think I know why you did them—every one of you; you did these things because you were bound to do them. It looked to you at the time as if you had a chance to do them or not, as you saw fit; but still, after all, you had no choice. There may be people here who had some money in their pockets and who still went out and got some more money in a way society forbids. Now, you may not yourselves see exactly why it was you did this thing, but if you look at the question deeply enough and carefully enough you will see that there were circumstances that drove you to do exactly the thing which you did. You could not help it any more than we outside can help taking the positions that we take. The reformers who tell you to be good and you will be happy, and the people on the outside who have property to protect—they think that the only way to do it is by building jails and locking you up in cells on weekdays and praying for you Sundays.

I think that all of this has nothing whatever to do with right conduct. I think it is very easily seen what has to do with right conduct. Some so-called criminals—and I will use this word because it is handy, it means nothing to me—I speak of the criminals who get caught as distinguished from the criminals who catch them—some of these so-called criminals are in jail for their first offenses, but nine tenths of you are in jail because you did not have a good lawyer and, of course, you did not have a good lawyer because you did not have enough money to pay a good lawyer. There is no very great danger of a rich man going to jail.

Some of you may be here for the first time. If we would open the doors and let you out, and leave the laws as they are today, some of you would be back tomorrow. This is about as good a place as you can get anyway. There are many people here who are so in the habit of coming that they would not know where else to go. There are people who are born with the tendency to break into jail every chance they get, and they cannot avoid it. You cannot figure out your life and see why it was, but still there is a reason for it; and if we were all wise and knew all the facts, we could figure it out.

In the first place, there are a good many more people who go to jail in the wintertime than in the summer. Why is this? Is it because people are more wicked in winter? No, it is because the coal trust begins to get in its grip in the winter. A few gentlemen take possession of the coal, and unless the people will pay seven or eight dollars a ton for something that is worth three dollars, they will have to freeze. Then there is nothing to do but to break into jail, and so there are many more in jail in the winter than in summer. It costs more for gas in the winter because the nights are longer, and people go to jail to save gas bills. The jails are electric-lighted. You may not know it, but these economic laws are working all the time, whether we know it or do not know it.

15   There are more people who go to jail in hard times than in good   15
times—few people, comparatively, go to jail except when they are hard up. They go to jail because they have no other place to go. They may not know why, but it is true all the same. People are not more wicked in hard times. That is not the reason. The fact is true all over the world that in hard times more people go to jail than in good times, and in winter more people go to jail than in summer. Of course it is pretty hard times for people who go to jail at any time. The people who go to jail are almost always poor people—people who have no other place to live, first and last. When times are hard, then you find large numbers of people who go to jail who would not otherwise be in jail.

Long ago, Mr. Buckle, who was a great philosopher and historian, collected facts, and he showed that the number of people who are arrested increased just as the price of food increased. When they put up the price of gas ten cents a thousand, I do not know who will go to jail, but I do know that a certain number of people will go. When the meat combine raises the price of beef, I do not know who is going to jail, but I know that a large number of people are bound to go. Whenever the Standard Oil Company raises the price of oil, I know that a certain number of girls who are seamstresses, and who work night after night long hours for somebody else, will be compelled to go out on the streets and ply another trade, and I know that Mr. Rockefeller and his associates are responsible and not the poor girls in the jails.

First and last, people are sent to jail because they are poor. Sometimes, as I say, you may not need money at the particular time, but you wish to have thrifty forehanded habits, and do not always wait until you are in absolute want. Some of you people are perhaps plying the trade, the profession, which is called burglary. No man in his right senses will go into a strange house in the dead of night and prowl around with a dark lantern through unfamiliar rooms and take chances of his life, if he has plenty of the good things of the world in his own home. You would not take any such chances as that. If a man had clothes in his clothespress and beefsteak in his pantry and money in the bank, he would not navigate around nights in houses where he knows nothing about the premises whatever. It always requires experience and education for this profession, and people who fit themselves for it are no more to blame than I am for being a lawyer. A man would not hold up another man on the street if he had plenty of money in his own pocket. He might do it if he had one dollar or two dollars, but he wouldn't if he had as much money as Mr. Rockefeller has. Mr. Rockefeller has a great deal better hold-up game than that.

The more that is taken from the poor by the rich, who have the chance to take it, the more poor people there are who are compelled to resort to these means for a livelihood. They may not understand it, they may not think so at once, but after all they are driven into that line of employment.

There is a bill before the legislature of this state to punish kidnaping children with death. We have wise members of the legislature. They know the gas trust when they see it and they always see it—they can furnish light enough to be seen; and this legislature thinks it is going to stop kidnaping children by making a law punishing kidnapers of children with death. I don't believe in kidnaping children, but the legislature is all wrong. Kidnaping children is not a crime, it is a profession. It has been developed with the times. It has been developed with our modern industrial conditions. There are many ways of making money—many new ways that our ancestors knew nothing about. Our ancestors knew nothing about a billion-dollar trust; and here comes some poor fellow who has no other trade and he discovers the profession of kidnaping children.

20   This crime is born, not because people are bad; people don't kidnap other people's children because they want the children or because they are devilish, but because they see a chance to get some money out of it. You cannot cure this crime by passing a law punishing by death kidnapers of children. There is one way to cure it. There is one way to cure all these offenses, and that is to give the people a chance to live. There is no other way, and there never was any other way since the

world began; and the world is so blind and stupid that it will not see. If every man and woman and child in the world had a chance to make a decent, fair, honest living, there would be no jails and no lawyers and no courts. There might be some persons here or there with some peculiar formation of their brain, like Rockefeller, who would do these things simply to be doing them; but they would be very, very few, and those should be sent to a hospital and treated, and not sent to jail; and they would entirely disappear in the second generation, or at least in the third generation.

I am not talking pure theory. I will just give you two or three illustrations.

The English people once punished criminals by sending them away. They would load them on a ship and export them to Australia. England was owned by lords and nobles and rich people. They owned the whole earth over there, and the other people had to stay in the streets. They could not get a decent living. They used to take their criminals and send them to Australia—I mean the class of criminals who got caught. When these criminals got over there, and nobody else had come, they had the whole continent to run over, and so they could raise sheep and furnish their own meat, which is easier than stealing it. These criminals then became decent, respectable people because they had a chance to live. They did not commit any crimes. They were just like the English people who sent them there, only better. And in the second generation the descendants of those criminals were as good and respectable a class of people as there were on the face of the earth, and then they began building churches and jails themselves.

A portion of this country was settled in the same way, landing prisoners down on the southern coast; but when they got here and had a whole continent to run over and plenty of chances to make a living, they became respectable citizens, making their own living just like any other citizen in the world. But finally the descendants of the English aristocracy who sent the people over to Australia found out they were getting rich, and so they went over to get possession of the earth as they always do, and they organized land syndicates and got control of the land and ores, and then they had just as many criminals in Australia as they did in England. It was not because the world had grown bad; it was because the earth had been taken away from the people.

Some of you people have lived in the country. It's prettier than it is here. And if you have ever lived on a farm you understand that if you put a lot of cattle in a field, when the pasture is short they will jump over the fence; but put them in a good field where there is plenty of pasture, and they will be law-abiding cattle to the end of time. The human animal is just like the rest of the animals, only a little more so. The same thing that governs in the one governs in the other.

25   Everybody makes his living along the lines of least resistance. A 25 wise man who comes into a country early sees a great undeveloped land. For instance, our rich men twenty-five years ago saw that Chicago was small and knew a lot of people would come here and settle, and they readily saw that if they had all the land around here it would be worth a good deal, so they grabbed the land. You cannot be a landlord because somebody has got it all. You must find some other calling. In England and Ireland and Scotland less than five per cent own all the land there is, and the people are bound to stay there on any kind of terms the landlords give. They must live the best they can, so they develop all these various professions—burglary, picking pockets, and the like.

Again, people find all sorts of ways of getting rich. These are diseases like everything else. You look at people getting rich, organizing trusts and making a million dollars, and somebody gets the disease and he starts out. He catches it just as a man catches the mumps or the measles; he is not to blame, it is in the air. You will find men speculating beyond their means, because the mania of money-getting is taking possession of them. It is simply a disease—nothing more, nothing less. You cannot avoid catching it; but the fellows who have control of the earth have the advantage of you. See what the law is: when these men get control of things, they make the laws. They do not make the laws to protect anybody; courts are not instruments of justice. When your case gets into court it will make little difference whether you are guilty or innocent, but it's better if you have a smart lawyer. And you cannot have a smart lawyer unless you have money. First and last it's a question of money. Those men who own the earth make the laws to protect what they have. They fix up a sort of fence or pen around what they have, and they fix the law so the fellow on the outside cannot get in. The laws are really organized for the protection of the men who rule the world. They were never organized or enforced to do justice. We have no system for doing justice, not the slightest in the world.

Let me illustrate: Take the poorest person in this room. If the community had provided a system of doing justice, the poorest person in this room would have as good a lawyer as the richest, would he not? When you went into court you would have just as long a trial and just as fair a trial as the richest person in Chicago. Your case would not be tried in fifteen or twenty minutes, whereas it would take fifteen days to get through with a rich man's case.

Then if you were rich and were beaten, your case would be taken to the Appellate Court. A poor man cannot take his case to the Appellate Court; he has not the price. And then to the Supreme Court. And if he were beaten there he might perhaps go to the United States Supreme Court. And he might die of old age before he got into jail. If you are poor, it's a quick job. You are almost known to be guilty, else you would not be there. Why should anyone be in the criminal court if he were not guilty? He would not be there if he could be anywhere else. The officials have no time to look after all these cases. The people who are on the outside, who are running banks and building churches and making jails, they have no time to examine 600 or 700 prisoners each year to see whether they are guilty or innocent. If the courts were organized to promote justice the people would elect somebody to defend all these criminals, somebody as smart as the prosecutor—and give him as many detectives and as many assistants to help, and pay as much money to defend you as to prosecute you. We have a very able man for state's attorney, and he has many assistants, detectives, and policemen without end, and judges to hear the cases—everything handy.

Most all of our criminal code consists in offenses against property. People are sent to jail because they have committed a crime against property. It is of very little consequence whether one hundred people more or less go to jail who ought not to go—you must protect property, because in this world property is of more importance than anything else.

30 How is it done? These people who have property fix it so they can 30 protect what they have. When somebody commits a crime it does not follow that he has done something that is morally wrong. The man on the outside who has committed no crime may have done something. For instance: to take all the coal in the United States and raise the price two dollars or three dollars when there is no need of it, and thus kill thousands of babies and send thousands of people to the poorhouse and tens of thousands to jail, as is done every year in the United States—this is a greater crime than all the people in our jails ever committed; but the law does not punish it. Why? Because the fellows

who control the earth make the laws. If you and I had the making of the laws, the first thing we would do would be to punish the fellow who gets control of the earth. Nature put this coal in the ground for me as well as for them and nature made the prairies up here to raise wheat for me as well as for them, and then the great railroad companies came along and fenced it up.

Most all of the crimes for which we are punished are property crimes. There are a few personal crimes, like murder—but they are very few. The crimes committed are mostly those against property. If this punishment is right the criminals must have a lot of property. How much money is there in this crowd? And yet you are all here for crimes against property. The people up and down the Lake Shore have not committed crime; still they have so much property they don't know what to do with it. It is perfectly plain why these people have not committed crimes against property; they make the laws and therefore do not need to break them. And in order for you to get some property you are obliged to break the rules of the game. I don't know but what some of you may have had a very nice chance to get rich by carrying a hod for one dollar a day, twelve hours. Instead of taking that nice, easy profession, you are a burglar. If you had been given a chance to be a banker you would rather follow that. Some of you may have had a chance to work as a switchman on a railroad where you know, according to statistics, that you cannot live and keep all your limbs more than seven years, and you can get fifty dollars or seventy-five dollars a month for taking your lives in your hands; and instead of taking that lucrative position you chose to be a sneak thief, or something like that. Some of you made that sort of choice. I don't know which I would take if I was reduced to this choice. I have an easier choice.

I will guarantee to take from this jail, or any jail in the world, five hundred men who have been the worst criminals and law-breakers who ever got into jail, and I will go down to our lowest streets and take five hundred of the most abandoned prostitutes, and go out somewhere where there is plenty of land, and will give them a chance to make a living, and they will be as good people as the average in the community.

There is one remedy for the sort of condition we see here. The world never finds it out, or when it does find it out it does not enforce it. You may pass a law punishing every person with death for burglary, and it will make no difference. Men will commit it just the same. In

England there was a time when one hundred different offenses were punishable with death, and it made no difference. The English people strangely found out that so fast as they repealed the severe penalties and so fast as they did away with punishing men by death, crime decreased instead of increased; that the smaller the penalty the fewer the crimes.

Hanging men in our county jails does not prevent murder. It makes murderers.

35

And this has been the history of the world. It's easy to see how to do away with what we call crime. It is not so easy to do it. I will tell you how to do it. It can be done by giving the people a chance to live—by destroying special privileges. So long as big criminals can get the coal fields, so long as the big criminals have control of the city council and get the public streets for streetcars and gas rights—this is bound to send thousands of poor people to jail. So long as men are allowed to monopolize all the earth, and compel others to live on such terms as these men see fit to make, then you are bound to get into jail.

The only way in the world to abolish crime and criminals is to abolish the big ones and the little ones together. Make fair conditions of life. Give men a chance to live. Abolish the right of private ownership of land, abolish monopoly, make the world partners in production, partners in the good things of life. Nobody would steal if he could get something of his own some easier way. Nobody will commit burglary when he has a house full. No girl will go out on the streets when she has a comfortable place at home. The man who owns a sweatshop or a department store may not be to blame himself for the condition of his girls, but when he pays them five dollars, three dollars, and two dollars a week, I wonder where he thinks they will get the rest of their money to live. The only way to cure these conditions is by equality. There should be no jails. They do not accomplish what they pretend to accomplish. If you would wipe them out there would be no more criminals than now. They terrorize nobody. They are a blot upon any civilization, and a jail is an evidence of the lack of charity of the people on the outside who make the jails and fill them with the victims of their greed.

Questions on Meaning

1. Darrow repeatedly states that jails should be done away with. What happens to "criminals" if there are no jails? What does he contend will happen to the crime rate if there are no jails? What evidence does he provide to support these beliefs?
2. Explain what Darrow means when he states that there are people born with the tendency to break *into* jail. Why does he say there are more people in jail in the winter than summer? When else do jails tend to fill up?
3. State Darrow's thesis in this speech in your own words. Explain why you do or do not agree with it.

Questions on Rhetorical Strategy and Style

1. How does Darrow compare and contrast the crimes of "criminals" with the crimes of people outside jails in terms of pickpocketing and holdups? How does he propose to "abolish crime and criminals"? Explain why you think his solution to crime would or would not work.
2. How does Darrow use a rhetorical strategy of cause and effect to explain why being poor and needy and without a bright future results in more people being in jail? Find other examples of cause and effect, such as the impact of strict punishment on the crime rate.
3. Throughout this essay, Darrow makes sardonic comments, such as "be good and then you will get rich and be happy" and "building jails and locking you up in cells on weekdays and praying for you Sundays" and "then they began building churches and jails themselves." What does this rhetorical strategy tell you about his feeling for the people "outside," the "good people"? Who are the wealthy and controlling people outside he castigates the most?

Writing Assignments

1. Explain why you agree or disagree with Darrow that almost all the people in jail are there because they cannot help it. What do you think would happen if 500 "men who have been the worst criminals" and 500 "abandoned prostitutes" were given land and a chance to make a living? Describe what you think this hypothetical community would be like 1, 5, and 10 years after it was set up.

2. Darrow repeatedly takes verbal swipes at "Rockefeller." Research the Rockefeller family and fortunes at the turn of the century. Whom was he referring to? Why did he hold this Rockefeller in such disdain? What controversies surrounded Rockefeller?

3. Write an essay in support of or opposition to capital punishment. In the essay, compare the rates of various crimes in states that have capital punishment with states that do not. What do you feel are deterrents to crime if not capital punishment?

Civil Disobedience

Henry David Thoreau

Henry David Thoreau (1817–1862), American philosopher, essayist, and poet, was born in Concord, Massachusetts. Following his graduation from Harvard University (1837), he worked for a short time as a teacher, but quit over his disagreement with the practice of punishing students by whipping them. A follower of transcendentalism, the literary and philosophical movement led by Ralph Waldo Emerson, Bronson Alcott, and Orestes Brownson, Thoreau with his brother John opened a private school based on transcendentalism in 1838, but it closed soon after when his brother became fatally ill. For a while, Thoreau lived in Emerson's house as a handyman, while he continued to write in his journal—a practice he had begun at Harvard. A few years later he erected a small cabin on Emerson's land on Walden Pond in Concord and lived on and off at the cabin from 1845–1847, writing journal entries that later would form his most well-known book, Walden, or Life in the Woods *(1854). During the years of* Walden, *he was jailed one night for his refusal to pay a poll tax to support the United States' war on Mexico, an experience that led to the essay, "Resistance to Civil Government" (1849) (later titled "On the Duty of Civil Disobedience"). Thoreau's advocacy of using passive resistance to protest unjust laws inspired many other individuals to use civil disobedience, including Mohandas Gandhi and Martin Luther King. As you will learn in this famous 1849 essay, Thoreau believed that it is not only your right but your duty to break laws that perpetuate an injustice.*

1   I heartily accept the motto, "That government is best which governs least;" and I should like to see it acted up to more rapidly and systematically. Carried out, it finally amounts to this, which

also I believe,—"That government is best which governs not at all;" and when men are prepared for it, that will be the kind of government which they will have. Government is at best but an expedient; but most governments are usually, and all governments are sometimes, inexpedient. The objections which have been brought against a standing army, and they are many and weighty, and deserve to prevail, may also at last be brought against a standing government. The standing army is only an arm of the standing government. The government itself, which is only the mode which the people have chosen to execute their will, is equally liable to be abused and perverted before the people can act through it. Witness the present Mexican war, the work of comparatively a few individuals using the standing government as their tool; for, in the outset, the people would not have consented to this measure.

This American government,—what is it but a tradition, though a recent one, endeavoring to transmit itself unimpaired to posterity, but each instant losing some of its integrity? It has not the vitality and force of a single living man; for a single man can bend it to his will. It is a sort of wooden gun to the people themselves. But it is not the less necessary for this; for the people must have some complicated machinery or other, and hear its din, to satisfy that idea of government which they have. Governments show thus how successfully men can be imposed on, even impose on themselves, for their own advantage. It is excellent, we must all allow. Yet this government never of itself furthered any enterprise, but by the alacrity with which it got out of its way. *It* does not keep the country free. *It* does not settle the West. *It* does not educate. The character inherent in the American people has done all that has been accomplished; and it would have done somewhat more, if the government had not sometimes got in its way. For government is an expedient by which men would fain succeed in letting one another alone; and, as has been said, when it is most expedient, the governed are most let alone by it. Trade and commerce, if they were not made of india-rubber, would never manage to bounce over the obstacles which legislators are continually putting in their way; and, if one were to judge these men wholly by the effects of their actions and not partly by their intentions, they would deserve to be classed and punished with those mischievous persons who put obstructions on the railroads.

But, to speak practically and as a citizen, unlike those who call themselves no-government men, I ask for, not at once no government, but *at once* a better government. Let every man make known what kind of government would command his respect, and that will be one step toward obtaining it.

After all, the practical reason why, when the power is once in the hands of the people, a majority are permitted, and for a long period continue, to rule is not because they are most likely to be in the right, nor because this seems fairest to the minority, but because they are physically the strongest. But a government in which the majority rule in all cases cannot be based on justice, even as far as men understand it. Can there not be a government in which majorities do not virtually decide right and wrong, but conscience?—in which majorities decide only those questions to which the rule of expediency is applicable? Must the citizen ever for a moment, or in the least degree, resign his conscience to the legislator? Why has every man a conscience, then? I think that we should be men first, and subjects afterward. It is not desirable to cultivate a respect for the law, so much as for the right. The only obligation which I have a right to assume is to do at any time what I think right. It is truly enough said that a corporation has no conscience; but a corporation of conscientious men is a corporation *with* a conscience. Law never made men a whit more just; and, by means of their respect for it, even the well-disposed are daily made the agents of injustice. A common and natural result of an undue respect for law is, that you may see a file of soldiers, colonel, captain, corporal, privates, powder-monkeys, and all, marching in admirable order over hill and dale to the wars, against their wills, ay, against their common sense and consciences, which makes it very steep marching indeed, and produces a palpitation of the heart. They have no doubt that it is a damnable business in which they are concerned; they are all peaceably inclined. Now, what are they? Men at all? or small movable forts and magazines, at the service of some unscrupulous man in power? Visit the Navy-Yard, and behold a marine, such a man as an American government can make, or such as it can make a man with its black arts, —a mere shadow and reminiscence of humanity, a man laid out alive and standing, and already, as one may say, buried under arms with funeral accompaniments, though it may be,—

> "Not a drum was heard, not a funeral note, 5
> As his corse to the rampart we hurried;

Not a soldier discharged his farewell shot
O'er the grave where our hero we buried."

The mass of men serve the state thus, not as men mainly, but as machines, with their bodies. They are the standing army, and the militia, jailers, constables, *posse comitatus,* etc. In most cases there is no free exercise whatever of the judgment or of the moral sense; but they put themselves on a level with wood and earth and stones; and wooden men can perhaps be manufactured that will serve the purpose as well. Such command no more respect than men of straw or a lump of dirt. They have the same sort of worth only as horses and dogs. Yet such as these even are commonly esteemed good citizens. Others—as most legislators, politicians, lawyers, ministers, and office-holders—serve the state chiefly with their heads; and, as they rarely make any moral distinctions, they are as likely to serve the devil, without *intending* it, as God. A very few—as heroes, patriots, martyrs, reformers in the great sense, and *men*—serve the state with their consciences also, and so necessarily resist it for the most part; and they are commonly treated as enemies by it. A wise man will only be useful as a man, and will not submit to be "clay," and "stop a hole to keep the wind away," but leave that office to his dust at least:—

"I am too high-born to be propertied,
To be a secondary at control,
Or useful serving-man and instrument
To any sovereign state throughout the world."

He who gives himself entirely to his fellow-men appears to them useless and selfish; but he who gives himself partially to them is pronounced a benefactor and philanthropist.

How does it become a man to behave toward this American government today? I answer, that he cannot without disgrace be associated with it. I cannot for an instant recognize that political organization as *my* government which is the *slave's* government also.

All men recognize the right of revolution; that is, the right to refuse allegiance to, and to resist, the government, when its tyranny or its inefficiency are great and unendurable. But almost all say that such is not the case now. But such was the case, they think, in the Revolution of '75. If one were to tell me that this was a bad government be-

10

cause it taxed certain foreign commodities brought to its ports, it is most probable that I should not make an ado about it, for I can do without them. All machines have their friction; and possibly this does enough good to counterbalance the evil. At any rate, it is a great evil to make a stir about it. But when the friction comes to have its machine, and oppression and robbery are organized, I say, let us not have such a machine any longer. In other words, when a sixth of the population of a nation which has undertaken to be the refuge of liberty are slaves, and a whole country is unjustly overrun and conquered by a foreign army, and subjected to military law, I think that it is not too soon for honest men to rebel and revolutionize. What makes this duty the more urgent is the fact that the country so overrun is not our own, but ours is the invading army.

Paley, a common authority with many on moral questions, in his chapter on the "Duty of Submission to Civil Government," resolves all civil obligation into expediency; and he proceeds to say that "so long as the interest of the whole society requires it, that is, so long as the established government cannot be resisted or changed without public inconveniency, it is the will of God . . . that the established government be obeyed,—and no longer. This principle being admitted, the justice of every particular case of resistance is reduced to a computation of the quantity of the danger and grievance on the one side, and of the probability and expense of redressing it on the other." Of this, he says, every man shall judge for himself. But Paley appears never to have contemplated those cases to which the rule of expediency does not apply, in which a people, as well as an individual, must do justice, cost what it may. If I have unjustly wrested a plank from a drowning man, I must restore it to him though I drown myself. This, according to Paley, would be inconvenient. But he that would save his life, in such a case, shall lose it. This people must cease to hold slaves, and to make war on Mexico, though it cost them their existence as a people.

In their practice, nations agree with Paley; but does any one think that Massachusetts does exactly what is right at the present crisis?

"A drab of state, a cloth-o'-silver slut,
To have her train borne up, and her soul trail in the dirt."

Practically speaking, the opponents to a reform in Massachusetts are not a hundred thousand politicians at the South, but a hundred thousand merchants and farmers here, who are more interested in commerce and agriculture than they are in humanity, and are not prepared to do justice to the slave and to Mexico, *cost what it may.* I quarrel not with far-off foes, but with those who, near at home, coöperate with, and do the bidding of, those far away, and without whom the latter would be harmless. We are accustomed to say, that the mass of men are unprepared; but improvement is slow, because the few are not materially wiser or better than the many. It is not so important that many should be as good as you, as that there be some absolute goodness somewhere; for that will leaven the whole lump. There are thousands who are *in opinion* opposed to slavery and to the war, who yet in effect do nothing to put an end to them; who, esteeming themselves children of Washington and Franklin, sit down with their hands in their pockets, and say that they know not what to do, and do nothing; who even postpone the question of freedom to the question of free trade, and quietly read the prices-current along with the latest advices from Mexico, after dinner, and, it may be, fall asleep over them both. What is the price-current of an honest man and patriot to-day? They hesitate, and they regret, and sometimes they petition; but they do nothing in earnest and with effect. They will wait, well disposed, for others to remedy the evil, that they may no longer have it to regret. At most, they give only a cheap vote, and a feeble countenance and God-speed, to the right, as it goes by them. There are nine hundred and ninety-nine patrons of virtue to one virtuous man. But it is easier to deal with the real possessor of a thing than with the temporary guardian of it.

All voting is a sort of gaming, like checkers or backgammon, with a slight moral tinge to it, a playing with right and wrong, with moral questions; and betting naturally accompanies it. The character of the voters is not staked. I cast my vote, perchance, as I think right; but I am not vitally concerned that that right should prevail. I am willing to leave it to the majority. Its obligation, therefore, never exceeds that of expediency. Even voting *for the right* is *doing* nothing for it. It is only expressing to men feebly your desire that it should prevail. A wise man will not leave the right to the mercy of chance, nor wish it to prevail through the power of the majority. There is but little virtue in the action of masses of men. When the majority shall at length vote for the abolition of slavery, it will be because they are indifferent to slavery, or because there is but little slavery left to be abolished by their

15

vote. *They* will then be the only slaves. Only *his* vote can hasten the abolition of slavery who asserts his own freedom by his vote.

I hear of a convention to be held at Baltimore, or elsewhere, for the selection of a candidate for the Presidency, made up chiefly of editors, and men who are politicians by profession; but I think, what is it to any independent, intelligent, and respectable man what decision they may come to? Shall we not have the advantage of his wisdom and honesty, nevertheless? Can we not count upon some independent votes? Are there not many individuals in the country who do not attend conventions? But no: I find that the respectable man, so called, has immediately drifted from his position, and despairs of his country, when his country has more reason to despair of him. He forthwith adopts one of the candidates thus selected as the only *available* one, thus proving that he is himself *available* for any purposes of the demagogue. His vote is of no more worth than that of any unprincipled foreigner or hireling native, who may have been bought. O for a man who is a *man*, and, as my neighbor says, has a bone in his back which you cannot pass your hand through! Our statistics are at fault: the population has been returned too large. How many *men* are there to a square thousand miles in this country? Hardly one. Does not America offer any inducement for men to settle here? The American has dwindled into an Odd Fellow,—one who may be known by the development of his organ of gregariousness, and a manifest lack of intellect and cheerful self-reliance; whose first and chief concern, on coming into the world, is to see that the almshouses are in good repair; and, before yet he has lawfully donned the virile garb, to collect a fund for the support of the widows and orphans that may be; who, in short, ventures to live only by the aid of the Mutual Insurance company, which has promised to bury him decently.

It is not a man's duty, as a matter of course, to devote himself to the eradication of any, even the most enormous, wrong; he may still properly have other concerns to engage him; but it is his duty, at least, to wash his hands of it, and, if he gives it no thought longer, not to give it practically his support. If I devote myself to other pursuits and contemplations, I must first see, at least, that I do not pursue them sitting upon another man's shoulders. I must get off him first, that he may pursue his contemplations too. See what gross inconsistency is tolerated. I have heard some of my townsmen say, "I should like to have them order me out to help put down an insurrection of the slaves, or to march to Mexico;—see if I would go;" and yet these very men have each, directly by their allegiance, and so indirectly, at least, by their money, furnished a substitute. The soldier is applauded who refuses to serve in an unjust war by those who do not refuse to sustain the unjust government which makes the war; is applauded by those whose own act and authority he disregards and sets at naught; as if the state were penitent to that degree that it hired one to scourge it while it sinned, but not to that degree that it left off sinning for a moment. Thus, under the name of Order and Civil Government, we are all made at last to pay homage to and support our own meanness. After the first blush of sin comes its indifference; and from immoral it becomes, as it were, *un*moral, and not quite unnecessary to that life which we have made.

The broadest and most prevalent error requires the most disinterested virtue to sustain it. The slight reproach to which the virtue of patriotism is commonly liable, the noble are most likely to incur. Those who, while they disapprove of the character and measures of a government, yield to it their allegiance and support are undoubtedly its most conscientious supporters, and so frequently the most serious obstacles to reform. Some are petitioning the State to dissolve the Union, to disregard the requisitions of the President. Why do they not dissolve it themselves,—the union between themselves and the State,—and refuse to pay their quota into its treasury? Do not they stand in the same relation to the State that the State does to the Union? And have not the same reasons prevented the State from resisting the Union which have prevented them from resisting the State?

How can a man be satisfied to entertain an opinion merely, and enjoy *it*? Is there any enjoyment in it, if his opinion is that he is aggrieved? If you are cheated out of a single dollar by your neighbor, you do not rest satisfied with knowing that you are cheated, or with saying that you are cheated, or even with petitioning him to pay you your due; but you take effectual steps at once to obtain the full amount, and see that you are never cheated again. Action from principle, the perception and the performance of right, changes things and relations; it is essentially revolutionary, and does not consist wholly with anything which was. It not only divides States and churches, it divides families; ay, it divides the *individual,* separating the diabolical in him from the divine.

Unjust laws exist: shall we be content to obey them, or shall we
endeavor to amend them, and obey them until we have succeeded, or
shall we transgress them at once? Men generally, under such a government as this, think that they ought to wait until they have persuaded the majority to alter them. They think that, if they should
resist, the remedy would be worse than the evil. But it is the fault of
the government itself that the remedy *is* worse than the evil. *It* makes
it worse. Why is it not more apt to anticipate and provide for reform?
Why does it not cherish its wise minority? Why does it cry and resist
before it is hurt? Why does it not encourage its citizens to be on the
alert to point out its faults, and *do* better than it would have them?
Why does it always crucify Christ, and excommunicate Copernicus
and Luther, and pronounce Washington and Franklin rebels?

One would think, that a deliberate and practical denial of its authority was the only offence never contemplated by government; else,
why has it not assigned its definite, its suitable and proportionate,
penalty? If a man who has no property refuses but once to earn nine
shillings for the State, he is put in prison for a period unlimited by any
law that I know, and determined only by the discretion of those who
placed him there; but if he should steal ninety times nine shillings
from the State, he is soon permitted to go at large again.

If the injustice is part of the necessary friction of the machine of
government, let it go, let it go: perchance it will wear smooth,—certainly the machine will wear out. If the injustice has a spring, or a pul-
ley, or a rope, or a crank, exclusively for itself, then perhaps you may
consider whether the remedy will not be worse than the evil; but if it
is of such a nature that it requires you to be the agent of injustice to
another, then, I say, break the law. Let your life be a counter-friction
to stop the machine. What I have to do is to see, at any rate, that I do
not lend myself to the wrong which I condemn.

As for adopting the ways which the State has provided for remedying the evil, I know not of such ways. They take too much time,
and a man's life will be gone. I have other affairs to attend to. I came
into this world, not chiefly to make this a good place to live in, but to
live in it, be it good or bad. A man has not everything to do, but something; and because he cannot do *everything,* it is not necessary that he
should do *something* wrong. It is not my business to be petitioning the
Governor or the Legislature any more than it is theirs to petition me;
and if they should not hear my petition, what should I do then? But

20

in this case the State has provided no way: its very Constitution is the evil. This may seem to be harsh and stubborn and unconciliatory; but it is to treat with the utmost kindness and consideration the only spirit that can appreciate or deserves it. So is all change for the better, like birth and death, which convulse the body.

I do not hesitate to say, that those who call themselves Abolitionists should at once effectually withdraw their support, both in person and property, from the government of Massachusetts, and not wait till they constitute a majority of one, before they suffer the right to prevail through them. I think that it is enough if they have God on their side, without waiting for that other one. Moreover, any man more right than his neighbors constitutes a majority of one already.

I meet this American government, or its representative, the State government, directly, and face to face, once a year—no more—in the person of its tax-gatherer; this is the only mode in which a man situated as I am necessarily meets it; and it then says distinctly, Recognize me; and the simplest, the most effectual, and, in the present posture of affairs, the indispensablest mode of treating with it on this head, of expressing your little satisfaction with and love for it, is to deny it then. My civil neighbor, the tax-gatherer, is the very man I have to deal with,—for it is, after all, with men and not with parchment that I quarrel,—and he has voluntarily chosen to be an agent of the government. How shall he ever know well what he is and does as an officer of the government, or as a man, until he is obliged to consider whether he shall treat me, his neighbor, for whom he has respect, as a neighbor and well-disposed man, or as a maniac and disturber of the peace, and see if he can get over this obstruction to his neighborliness without a ruder and more impetuous thought or speech corresponding with his action. I know this well, that if one thousand, if one hundred, if ten men whom I could name,—if ten *honest* men only,—ay, if *one* HONEST man, in this State of Massachusetts, *ceasing to hold slaves,* were actually to withdraw from this copartnership, and be locked up in the county jail therefor, it would be the abolition of slavery in America. For it matters not how small the beginning may seem to be: what is once well done is done forever. But we love better to talk about it: that we say is our mission. Reform keeps many scores of newspapers in its service, but not one man. If my esteemed neighbor, the State's ambassador, who will devote his days to the settlement of the question of human rights in the Council Chamber, instead of being threatened

25

with the prisons of Carolina, were to sit down the prisoner of Massachusetts, that State which is so anxious to foist the sin of slavery upon her sister,—though at present she can discover only an act of inhospitality to be the ground of a quarrel with her,—the Legislature would not wholly waive the subject the following winter.

Under a government which imprisons any unjustly, the true place for a just man is also a prison. The proper place to-day, the only place which Massachusetts has provided for her freer and less desponding spirits, is in her prisons, to be put out and locked out of the State by her own act, as they have already put themselves out by their principles. It is there that the fugitive slave, and the Mexican prisoner on parole, and the Indian come to plead the wrongs of his race should find them; on that separate, but more free and honorable ground, where the State places those who are not *with* her, but *against* her,—the only house in a slave State in which a free man can abide with honor. If any think that their influence would be lost there, and their voices no longer afflict the ear of the State, that they would not be as an enemy within its walls, they do not know by how much truth is stronger than error, nor how much more eloquently and effectively he can combat injustice who has experienced a little in his own person. Cast your whole vote, not a strip of paper merely, but your whole influence. A minority is powerless while it conforms to the majority; it is not even a minority then; but it is irresistible when it clogs by its whole weight. If the alternative is to keep all just men in prison, or give up war and slavery, the State will not hesitate which to choose. If a thousand men were not to pay their tax-bills this year, that would not be a violent and bloody measure, as it would be to pay them, and enable the State to commit violence and shed innocent blood. This is, in fact, the definition of a peaceable revolution, if any such is possible. If the tax-gatherer, or any other public officer, asks me, as one has done, "But what shall I do?" my answer is, "If you really wish to do anything, resign your office." When the subject has refused allegiance, and the officer has resigned his office, then the revolution is accomplished. But even suppose blood should flow. Is there not a sort of blood shed when the conscience is wounded? Through this wound a man's real manhood and immortality flow out, and he bleeds to an everlasting death. I see this blood flowing now.

I have contemplated the imprisonment of the offender, rather than the seizure of his goods,—though both will serve the same purpose,—because they who assert the purest right, and consequently are most dangerous to a corrupt State, commonly have not spent much time in accumulating property. To such the State renders comparatively small service, and a slight tax is wont to appear exorbitant, particularly if they are obliged to earn it by special labor with their hands. If there were one who lived wholly without the use of money, the State itself would hesitate to demand it of him. But the rich man—not to make any invidious comparison—is always sold to the institution which makes him rich. Absolutely speaking, the more money, the less virtue; for money comes between a man and his objects, and obtains them for him; and it was certainly no great virtue to obtain it. It puts to rest many questions which he would otherwise be taxed to answer; while the only new question which it puts is the hard but superfluous one, how to spend it. Thus his moral ground is taken from under his feet. The opportunities of living are diminished in proportion as what are called the "means" are increased. The best thing a man can do for his culture when he is rich is to endeavour to carry out those schemes which he entertained when he was poor. Christ answered the Herodians according to their condition. "Show me the tribute-money," said he;—and one took a penny out of his pocket;—if you use money which has the image of Cæsar on it, and which he has made current and valuable, that is, *if you are men of the State,* and gladly enjoy the advantages of Cæsar's government, then pay him back some of his own when he demands it. "Render therefore to Cæsar that which is Cæsar's, and to God those things which are God's," —leaving them no wiser than before as to which was which; for they did not wish to know.

When I converse with the freest of my neighbors, I perceive that, whatever they may say about the magnitude and seriousness of the question, and their regard for the public tranquillity, the long and the short of the matter is, that they cannot spare the protection of the existing government, and they dread the consequences to their property and families of disobedience to it. For my own part, I should not like to think that I ever rely on the protection of the State. But, if I deny the authority of the State when it presents its tax-bill, it will soon take and waste all my property, and so harass me and my children without end. This is hard. This makes it impossible for a man to live honestly, and at the same time comfortably, in outward respects. It will not be worth the while to accumulate property; that would be sure to go again. You must hire or squat somewhere, and raise but a small crop, and eat that soon. You must live within yourself, and depend upon yourself always tucked up and ready for a start, and not have many affairs. A man may grow rich in Turkey even, if he will be in all respects a good subject of the Turkish government. Confucius said: "If a state is governed by the principles of reason, poverty and misery are subjects of shame; if a state is not governed by the principles of reason, riches and honors are the subjects of shame." No: until I want the protection of Massachusetts to be extended to me in some distant Southern port, where my liberty is endangered, or until I am bent solely on building up an estate at home by peaceful enterprise, I can afford to refuse allegiance to Massachusetts, and her right to my property and life. It costs me less in every sense to incur the penalty of disobedience to the State than it would to obey. I should feel as if I were worth less in that case.

Some years ago, the State met me in behalf of the Church, and commanded me to pay a certain sum toward the support of a clergyman whose preaching my father attended, but never I myself. "Pay" it said, "or be locked up in the jail." I declined to pay. But, unfortunately, another man saw fit to pay it. I did not see why the schoolmaster should be taxed to support the priest, and not the priest the schoolmaster; for I was not the State's schoolmaster, but I supported myself by voluntary subscription. I did not see why the lyceum should not present its tax-bill, and have the State to back its demand, as well as the Church. However, at the request of the selectmen, I condescended to make some such statement as this in writing:—"Know all men by these presents, that I, Henry Thoreau, do not wish to be regarded as a member of any incorporated society which I have not joined." This I gave to the town clerk; and he has it. The State, having thus learned that I did not wish to be regarded as a member of that church, has never made a like demand on me since; though it said that it must adhere to its original presumption that time. If I had known how to name them, I should then have signed off in detail from all the societies which I never signed on to; but I did not know where to find a complete list.

I have paid no poll-tax for six years. I was put into a jail once on this account, for one night; and, as I stood considering the walls of solid stone, two or three feet thick, the door of wood and iron, a foot thick, and the iron grating which strained the light, I could not help

30

being struck with the foolishness of that institution which treated me as if I were mere flesh and blood and bones, to be locked up. I wondered that it should have concluded at length that this was the best use it could put me to, and had never thought to avail itself of my services in some way. I saw that, if there was a wall of stone between me and my townsmen, there was a still more difficult one to climb or break through before they could get to be as free as I was. I did not for a moment feel confined, and the walls seemed a great waste of stone and mortar. I felt as if I alone of all my townsmen had paid my tax. They plainly did not know how to treat me, but behaved like persons who are underbred. In every threat and in every compliment there was a blunder; for they thought that my chief desire was to stand the other side of that stone wall. I could not but smile to see how industriously they locked the door on my meditations, which followed them out again without let or hindrance, and *they* were really all that was dangerous. As they could not reach me, they had resolved to punish my body; just as boys, if they cannot come at some person against whom they have a spite, will abuse his dog. I saw that the State was half-witted, that it was timid as a lone woman with her silver spoons, and that it did not know its friends from its foes, and I lost all my remaining respect for it, and pitied it.

Thus the State never intentionally confronts a man's sense, intellectual or moral, but only his body, his senses. It is not armed with superior wit or honesty, but with superior physical strength. I was not born to be forced. I will breathe after my own fashion. Let us see who is the strongest. What force has a multitude? They only can force me who obey a higher law than I. They force me to become like themselves. I do not hear of *men* being *forced* to live this way or that by masses of men. What sort of life were that to live? When I meet a government which says to me, "Your money or your life," why should I be in haste to give it my money? It may be in a great strait, and not know what to do: I cannot help that. It must help itself; do as I do. It is not worth the while to snivel about it. I am not responsible for the successful working of the machinery of society. I am not the son of the engineer. I perceive that, when an acorn and a chestnut fall side by side, the one does not remain inert to make way for the other, but both obey their own laws, and spring and grow and flourish as best they can, till one, perchance, overshadows and destroys the other. If a plant cannot live according to its nature, it dies; and so a man.

The night in prison was novel and interesting enough. The prisoners in their shirt-sleeves were enjoying a chat and the evening air in the doorway, when I entered. But the jailer said, "Come, boys, it is time to lock up;" and so they dispersed, and I heard the sound of their steps returning into the hollow apartments. My roommate was introduced to me by the jailer, as "a first-rate fellow and a clever man." When the door was locked, he showed me where to hang my hat, and how he managed matters there. The rooms were whitewashed once a month; and this one, at least, was the whitest, most simply furnished, and probably the neatest apartment in the town. He naturally wanted to know where I came from, and what brought me there; and, when I had told him, I asked him in turn how he came there, presuming him to be an honest man of course; and, as the world goes, I believe he was. "Why," said he, "they accused me of burning a barn; but I never did it." As near as I could discover, he had probably gone to bed in a barn when drunk, and smoked his pipe there; and so a barn was burnt. He had the reputation of being a clever man, had been there some three months waiting for his trial to come on, and would have to wait as much longer; but he was quite domesticated and contented, since he got his board for nothing, and thought that he was well treated.

He occupied one window, and I the other; and I saw that if one stayed there long, his principal business would be to look out the window. I had soon read all the tracts that were left there, and examined where former prisoners had broken out, and where a grate had been sawed off, and heard the history of the various occupants of that room; for I found that even here there was a history and a gossip which never circulated beyond the walls of the jail. Probably this is the only house in the town where verses are composed, which are afterward printed in a circular form, but not published. I was shown quite a long list of verses which were composed by some young men who had been detected in an attempt to escape, who avenged themselves by singing them.

I pumped my fellow-prisoner as dry as I could, for fear I should never see him again; but at length he showed me which was my bed, and left me to blow out the lamp.

It was like traveling into a far country, such as I had never expected to behold, to lie there for one night. It seemed to me that I never had heard the town clock strike before, nor the evening sounds of the village; for we slept with the windows open, which were inside

35

the grating. It was to see my native village in the light of the Middle Ages, and our Concord was turned into a Rhine stream, and visions of knights and castles passed before me. They were the voices of old burghers that I heard in the streets. I was an involuntary spectator and auditor of whatever was done and said in the kitchen of the adjacent village inn,—a wholly new and rare experience to me. It was a closer view of my native town. I was fairly inside of it. I never had seen its institutions before. This is one of its peculiar institutions; for it is a shire town. I began to comprehend what its inhabitants were about.

In the morning, our breakfasts were put through the hole in the door, in small oblong-square tin pans, made to fit, and holding a pint of chocolate, with brown bread, and an iron spoon. When they called for the vessels again, I was green enough to return what bread I had left; but my comrade seized it, and said that I should lay that up for lunch or dinner. Soon after he was let out to work at haying in a neighboring field, whither he went every day, and would not be back till noon; so he bade me good-day, saying that he doubted if he should see me again.

When I came out of prison,—for some one interfered, and paid that tax,—I did not perceive that great changes had taken place on the common, such as he observed who went in a youth and emerged a tottering and gray-headed man; and yet a change had to my eyes come over the scene,—the town, and State, and country,—greater than any that mere time could effect. I saw yet more distinctly the State in which I lived. I saw to what extent the people among whom I lived could be trusted as good neighbors and friends; that their friendship was for summer weather only; that they did not greatly purpose to do right; that they were a distinct race from me by their prejudices and superstitions, as the Chinamen and Malays are; that in their sacrifices to humanity they ran no risks, not even to their property; that after all they were not so noble but they treated the thief as he had treated them, and hoped, by a certain outward observance and a few prayers, and by walking in a particular straight though useless path from time to time, to save their souls. This may be to judge my neighbors harshly; for I believe that many of them are not aware that they have such an institution as the jail in their village.

It was formerly the custom in our village, when a poor debtor came out of jail, for his acquaintances to salute him, looking through their fingers, which were crossed to represent the grating of a jail window, "How do ye do?" My neighbors did not thus salute me, but first looked at me, and then at one another, as if I had returned from a long journey. I was put into jail as I was going to the shoemaker's to get a shoe which was mended. When I was let out the next morning, I proceeded to finish my errand, and, having put on my mended shoe, joined a huckleberry party, who were impatient to put themselves under my conduct; and in half an hour,—for the horse was soon tackled,—was in the midst of a huckleberry field, on one of our highest hills, two miles off, and then the State was nowhere to be seen.

This is the whole history of "My Prisons."

I have never declined paying the highway tax, because I am as desirous of being a good neighbor as I am of being a bad subject; and as for supporting schools, I am doing my part to educate my fellow-countrymen now. It is for no particular item in the tax-bill that I refuse to pay it. I simply wish to refuse allegiance to the State, to withdraw and stand aloof from it effectually. I do not care to trace the course of my dollar, if I could, till it buys a man or a musket to shoot one with,—the dollar is innocent,—but I am concerned to trace the effects of my allegiance. In fact, I quietly declare war with the State, after my fashion, though I will still make what use and get what advantage of her I can, as is usual in such cases. 40

If others pay the tax which is demanded of me, from a sympathy with the State, they do but what they have already done in their own case, or rather they abet injustice to a greater extent than the State requires. If they pay the tax from a mistaken interest in the individual taxed, to save his property, or prevent his going to jail, it is because they have not considered wisely how far they let their private feelings interfere with the public good.

This, then, is my position at present. But one cannot be too much on his guard in such a case, lest his action be biased by obstinacy or an undue regard for the opinions of men. Let him see that he does only what belongs to himself and to the hour.

I think sometimes, Why, this people mean well, they are only ignorant; they would do better if they knew how: why give your neighbors this pain to treat you as they are not inclined to? But I think, again, This is no reason why I should do as they do, or permit others to suffer much greater pain of a different kind. Again, I sometimes say to myself, When many millions of men, without heat, without ill will, without personal feeling of any kind, demand of you a few shillings only, without the possibility, such is their constitution, of retracting or altering their present demand, and without the possibility, on your side, of appeal to any other millions, why expose yourself to this overwhelming brute force? You do not resist cold and hunger, the winds and the waves, thus obstinately; you quietly submit to a thousand similar necessities. You do not put your head into the fire. But just in proportion as I regard this as not wholly a brute force, but partly a human force, and consider that I have relations to those millions as to so many millions of men, and not of mere brute or inanimate things, I see that appeal is possible, first and instantaneously, from them to the Maker of them, and, secondly, from them to themselves. But if I put my head deliberately into the fire, there is no appeal to fire or to the Maker of fire, and I have only myself to blame. If I could convince myself that I have any right to be satisfied with men as they are, and to treat them accordingly, and not according, in some respects, to my requisitions and expectations of what they and I ought to be, then, like a good Mussulman and fatalist, I should endeavor to be satisfied with things as they are, and say it is the will of God. And, above all, there is this difference between resisting this and a purely brute or natural force, that I can resist this with some effect; but I cannot expect, like Orpheus, to change the nature of the rocks and trees and beasts.

I do not wish to quarrel with any man or nation. I do not wish to split hairs, to make fine distinctions, or set myself up as better than my neighbors. I seek rather, I may say, even an excuse for conforming to the laws of the land. I am but too ready to conform to them. Indeed I have reason to suspect myself on this head; and each year, as the tax-gatherer comes round, I find myself disposed to review the acts and position of the general and State governments, and the spirit of the people, to discover a pretext for conformity.

> "We must affect our country as our parents,
> And if at any time we alienate
> Our love or industry from doing it honor,
> We must respect effects and teach the soul
> Matter of conscience and religion,
> And not desire of rule or benefit."

45

I believe that the State will soon be able to take all my work of this sort out of my hands, and then I shall be no better a patriot than my fellow-countrymen. Seen from a lower point of view, the Constitution, with all its faults, is very good; the law and the courts are very respectable; even this State and this American government are, in many respects, very admirable and rare things, to be thankful for, such as a great many have described them; but seen from a point of view a little higher, they are what I have described them; seen from a higher still, and the highest, who shall say what they are, or that they are worth looking at or thinking of at all?

However, the government does not concern me much, and I shall bestow the fewest possible thoughts on it. It is not many moments that I live under a government, even in this world. If a man is thought-free, fancy-free, imagination-free, that which *is not* never for a long time appearing *to be* to him, unwise rulers or reformers cannot fatally interrupt him.

I know that most men think differently from myself; but those whose lives are by profession devoted to the study of these or kindred subjects content me as little as any. Statesmen and legislators, standing so completely within the institution, never distinctly and nakedly behold it. They speak of moving society, but have no resting-place without it. They may be men of a certain experience and discrimination, and have no doubt invented ingenious and even useful systems, for which we sincerely thank them; but all their wit and usefulness lie within certain not very wide limits. They are wont to forget that the world is not governed by policy and expediency. Webster never goes behind government, and so cannot speak with authority about it. His words are wisdom to those legislators who contemplate no essential reform in the existing government; but for thinkers, and those who legislate for all time, he never once glances at the subject. I know of those whose serene and wise speculations on this theme would soon reveal the limits of his mind's range and hospitality. Yet, compared with the cheap professions of most reformers, and the still cheaper wisdom and eloquence of politicians in general, his are almost the only sensible and valuable words, and we thank Heaven for him. Comparatively, he is always strong, original, and, above all, practical. Still, his quality is not wisdom, but prudence. The lawyer's truth is not Truth, but consistency or a consistent expediency. Truth is always in harmony with herself, and is not concerned chiefly to reveal the justice that may consist with wrong-doing. He well deserves to be called, as he has been called, the Defender of the Constitution. There are really no blows to be given by him but defensive ones. He is not a leader, but a follower. His leaders are the men of '87. "I have never made an effort," he says, "and never propose to make an effort; I have never countenanced an effort, and never mean to countenance an effort, to disturb the arrangement as originally made, by which the various States came into the Union." Still thinking of the sanction which the Constitution gives to slavery, he says, "Because it was a part of the original compact,—let it stand." Notwithstanding his special acuteness and ability, he is unable to take a fact out of its merely political relations, and behold it as it lies absolutely to be disposed of by the intellect,—what, for instance, it behooves a man to do here in America to-day with regard to slavery,—but ventures, or is driven, to make some such desperate answer as the following, while professing to speak absolutely, and as a private man,—from which what new and singular code of social duties might be inferred? "The manner," says he, "in which the governments of those States where slavery exists are to regulate it is for their own consideration, under their responsibility to their constituents, to the general laws of propriety, humanity, and justice, and to God. Associations formed elsewhere, springing from a feeling of humanity, or any other cause, have nothing whatever to do with it. They have never received any encouragement from me, and they never will."

They who know of no purer sources of truth, who have traced up its stream no higher, stand, and wisely stand, by the Bible and the Constitution, and drink at it there with reverence and humility; but they who behold where it comes trickling into this lake or that pool, gird up their loins once more, and continue their pilgrimage toward its fountain-head.

No man with a genius for legislation has appeared in America. 50 They are rare in the history of the world. There are orators, politicians, and eloquent men, by the thousand; but the speaker has not yet opened his mouth to speak who is capable of settling the much-vexed questions of the day. We love eloquence for its own sake, and not for any truth which it may utter, or any heroism it may inspire. Our legislators have not yet learned the comparative value of free trade and of freedom, of union, and of rectitude, to a nation. They have no genius or talent for comparatively humble questions of taxation and finance, commerce and manufactures and agriculture. If we were left solely to the wordy wit of legislators in Congress for our guidance, uncorrected by the seasonable experience and the effectual complaints of the people, America would not long retain her rank among the nations. For eighteen hundred years, though perchance I have no right to say it, the New Testament has been written; yet where is the legislator who has wisdom and practical talent enough to avail himself of the light which it sheds on the science of legislation?

The authority of government, even such as I am willing to submit to,—for I will cheerfully obey those who know and can do better than I, and in many things even those who neither know nor can do so well,—is still an impure one: to be strictly just, it must have the sanction and consent of the governed. It can have no pure right over my person and property but what I concede to it. The progress from an absolute to a limited monarchy, from a limited monarchy to a democracy, is a progress toward a true respect for the individual. Is a democracy, such as we know it, the last improvement possible in government? Is it not possible to take a step further towards recognizing and organizing the rights of man? There will never be a really free and enlightened State until the State comes to recognize the individual as a higher and independent power, from which all its own power and authority are derived, and treats him accordingly. I please myself with imagining a State at last which can afford to be just to all men, and to treat the individual with respect as a neighbor; which even would not think it inconsistent with its own repose if a few were to live aloof from it, not meddling with it, nor embraced by it, who fulfilled all the duties of neighbors and fellow-men. A State which bore this kind of fruit, and suffered it to drop off as fast as it ripened, would prepare the way for a still more perfect and glorious State, which also I have imagined, but not yet anywhere seen.

[1849]

Questions on Meaning

1. Explain Thoreau's comment at the beginning of the essay, "that government is best which governs least." Do you agree? How would Thoreau be described politically if he made that comment in America today?

2. What does Thoreau believe would be the beginning of the end of slavery? Why does he say that the acts that would initiate the end of slavery will not occur?

3. What is the broad ramification of Thoreau's statement, "I did not see why the schoolmaster should be taxed to support the priest, and not the priest the schoolmaster"? What did Thoreau do when he was confronted with a tax for the priest? What do you think the governing body of Concord—the selectmen—thought of Thoreau?

Questions on Rhetorical Strategy and Style

1. Thoreau exhibits impressive command of the language as well as broad knowledge of philosophy and the politics of his day. Identify examples of how he uses logos (logic), pathos (appeals to the audience's beliefs or emotions), and ethos (claims based on his authority or character) in making his argument. Which of these factors of argumentation does Thoreau use most persuasively?

2. Reread Thoreau's description of the night he spent in jail for refusing to pay his poll tax. How does he compare and contrast the confining structure of the jail with his "meditations," which "followed them out." Who did he believe was more dangerous, the jailer or the jailed?

3. What is the effect of the repetition Thoreau employs in three sentences in the middle of the second paragraph? What does Thoreau mean by the italicized word "it"? Do you agree with his castigation of the role or purpose of government? How does his argument make a shift in the following paragraph when he speaks of a "better" government? Describe the characteristics of this improved government as he presents them in his closing paragraph.

Writing Assignments

1. Civil disobedience has been used effectively on many occasions to protest unjust laws. Explain why you would or would not feel

comfortable initiating an act of civil disobedience to protest a law or regulation or rule that you feel is unjust. Would you join in if a group were protesting together? How much risk would you expose yourself to: arrest? teargassing? water cannons? Overall, would you advocate or discourage civil disobedience?

2. Research acts of civil disobedience in the United States—such as sit-ins during the civil rights movement, protests over the United States' involvement in the Vietnam War, or demonstrations against nuclear power. What happened to the individuals who disobeyed the law? In the end, how effective were their actions? Compare the effect of a large number of individuals disobeying the law versus a small number.

3. "Call your congressman" or "let them know at the ballot box" are common arguments against civil disobedience. Write an essay expressing your agreement or disagreement with using conventional means for (as Thoreau stated) "remedying the evil" rather than civil disobedience. Are conventional means of rescinding unjust (or just plain stupid) laws effective? Are they too slow? Review incidents of civil disobedience and review the alternatives.

The Ethic of Compassion

The Dalai Lama

His Holiness the Dalai Lama (1935–) was born a peasant in Taktser, Tibet under the birth name of Lhamo Dhondrub. He is the fourteenth Dalai Lama (spiritual leader of Tibet, reincarnation of the thirteenth Dalai Lama, and an incarnation of the Buddha of Compassion). He lives in Dharamsala, India. He was recognized at age two as the Dalai Lama and was enthroned on February 22, 1940. He completed the Geshe Lharampa Degree (equivalent to a Doctorate of Buddhist Philosophy) in 1959 and became head of Tibet—but was driven out by a Chinese invasion. He has worked on behalf of Tibet from India, asking the United Nations for help and working to bring Buddhist beliefs back to the country. He received the Albert Schweitzer Humanitarian Award (1987); Raoul Wallenberg Congressional Human Rights Award (1989); the Nobel Peace Prize (1989); Franklin D. Roosevelt Freedom Medal (1994); and the Hessian Peace Prize (2005). His books include Kindness, Clarity and Insight *(Snow Lion, 1984);* Compassion and the Individual *(Wisdom Publications, 1991); and* The Power of Compassion *(Harper Collins, 1995).*

Compassion is good when first considered, for it is easy to feel compassion for one who suffers. Compassion is harder to muster for wealthy and powerful people and even harder to feel when true compassion leads to a career change or an even greater life upheaval.

1 We noted earlier that all the world's major religions stress the importance of cultivating love and compassion. In the Buddhist philosophical tradition, different levels of attainment

are described. At a basic level, compassion (*nying je*) is understood mainly in terms of empathy—our ability to enter into and, to some extent, share others' suffering. But Buddhist—and perhaps others—believe that this can be developed to such a degree that not only does our compassion arise without any effort, but it is unconditional, undifferentiated, and universal in scope. A feeling of intimacy toward all other sentient beings, including of course those who would harm us, is generated, which is likened in the literature to the love a mother has for her only child.

But this sense of equanimity toward all others is not seen as an end in itself. Rather, it is seen as the springboard to a love still greater. Because our capacity for empathy is innate, and because the ability to reason is also an innate faculty, compassion shares the characteristics of consciousness itself. The potential we have to develop it is therefore stable and continuous. It is not a resource which can be used up—as water is used up when we boil it. And though it can be described in terms of activity, it is not like a physical activity which we train for, like jumping, where once we reach a certain height we can go no further. On the contrary, when we enhance our sensitivity toward others' suffering through deliberately opening ourselves up to it, it is believed that we can gradually extend out compassion to the point where the individual feels so moved by even the subtlest suffering of others that they come to have an over-whelming sense of responsibility toward those others. This causes the one who is compassionate to dedicate themselves entirely to helping others overcome both their suffering and the causes of their suffering. In Tibetan, this ultimate level of attainment is called *nying je chenmo*, literally "great compassion."

Now I am not suggesting that each individual must attain these advanced states of spiritual development in order to lead an ethically wholesome life. I have described *nying je chenmo* not because it is a precondition of ethical conduct but rather because I believe that pushing the logic of compassion to the highest level can act as a powerful inspiration. If we can just keep the aspiration to develop *nying je chenmo,* or great compassion, as an ideal, it will naturally have a significant impact on our outlook. Based on the simple recognition that, just as I do, so do all others desire to be happy and not to suffer, it will serve as a constant reminder against selfishness and partiality. It will remind us that there is little to be gained from being kind and generous because we hope to win something in return. It will remind us that actions motivated by the desire to create a good name for ourselves are still selfish, however much they may appear to be acts of kindness. It will also remind us that there is nothing exceptional about acts of charity toward those we already feel close to. And it will help us to recognize that the bias we naturally feel toward our families and friends is actually a highly unreliable thing on which to base ethical conduct. If we reserve ethical conduct for those whom we feel close to, the danger is that we will neglect our responsibilities toward those outside this circle.

Why is this? So long as the individuals in question continue to meet our expectations, all is well. But should they fail to do so, someone we consider a dear friend one day can become our sworn enemy the next. As we saw earlier, we have a tendency to react badly to all who threaten fulfillment of our cherished desires, though they may be our closest relations. For this reason, compassion and mutual respect offer a much more solid basis for our relations with others. This is also true of partnerships. If our love for someone is based largely on attraction, whether it be their looks or some other superficial characteristic, our feelings for that person are liable, over time, to evaporate. When they lose the quality we found alluring, or when we find ourselves no longer satisfied by it, the situation can change completely, this despite their being the same person. This is why relationships based purely on attraction are almost always unstable. On the other hand, when we begin to perfect our compassion, neither the other's appearance nor their behavior affects our underlying attitude.

Consider, too, that habitually our feelings toward others depend very much on their circumstances. Most people, when they see someone who is handicapped, feel sympathetic toward that person. But then when they see others who are wealthier, or better educated, or better placed socially, they immediately feel envious and competitive toward them. Our negative feelings prevent us from seeing the sameness of ourselves and all others. We forget that just like us, whether fortunate or unfortunate, distant or near, they desire to be happy and not to suffer.

The struggle is thus to overcome these feelings of partiality. Certainly, developing genuine compassion for our loved ones is the obvious and appropriate place to start. The impact our actions have on our close ones will generally be much greater than on others, and therefore our responsibilities toward them are greater. Yet we need to recognize that, ultimately, there are no grounds for discriminating in their favor. In this sense, we are all in the same position as a doctor confronted by ten patients suffering the same serious illness. They are each equally deserving of treatment. The reader should not suppose that what is being advocated here is a state of detached indifference, however. The further essential challenge, as we begin to extend our compassion toward all others, is to maintain the same level of intimacy as we feel toward those closest to us. In other words, what is being suggested is that we need to strive for even-handedness in our approach toward all others, a level ground into which we can plant the seed of *nying je chenmo,* of great love and compassion.

If we can begin to relate to others on the basis of such equanimity, our compassion will not depend on the fact that so and so is my husband, my wife, my relative, my friend. Rather, a feeling of closeness toward all others can be developed based on the simple recognition that, just like myself, all wish to be happy and to avoid suffering. In other words, we will start to relate to others on the basis of their sentient nature. Again, we can think of this in terms of an ideal, one which it is immensely difficult to attain. But, for myself, I find it one which is profoundly inspiring and helpful.

Let us now consider the role of compassionate love and kind-heartedness in our daily lives. Does the ideal of developing it to the point where it is unconditional mean that we must abandon our own interests entirely? Not at all. In fact, it is the best way of serving them—indeed, it could even be said to constitute the wisest course for fulfilling self-interest. For if it is correct that those qualities such as love, patience, tolerance, and forgiveness are what happiness consists in, and if it is also correct that *nying je,* or compassion, as I have defined it, is both the source and the fruit of these qualities, then the more we are compassionate, the more we provide for our own happiness. Thus, any idea that concern for others, though a noble quality, is a matter for our private lives only, is simply short-sighted. Compassion belongs to every sphere of activity, including, of course, the workplace.

Here, though, I must acknowledge the existence of a perception—shared by many, it seems—that compassion is, if not actually an impediment, at least irrelevant to professional life. Personally, I would argue that not only is it relevant, but that when compassion is lacking, our activities are in danger of becoming destructive. This is because when we ignore the question of the impact our actions have on others' well-being, inevitably we end up hurting them. The ethic of compassion helps provide the necessary foundation and motivation for both restraint and the cultivation of virtue. When we begin to develop a genuine appreciation of the value of compassion, our outlook on others begins automatically to change. This alone can serve as a powerful influence on the conduct of our lives. When, for example, the temptation to deceive others arises, our compassion for them will prevent us from entertaining the idea. And when we realize that our work itself is in danger of being exploited to the detriment of others, compassion will cause us to disengage from it. So to take an imaginary case of a scientist whose research seems likely to be a source of suffering, they will recognize this and act accordingly, even if this means abandoning the project.

10   I do not deny that genuine problems can arise when we dedicate ourselves to the ideal of compassion. In the case of a scientist who felt unable to continue in the direction their work was taking them, this could have profound consequences both for themselves and for their families. Likewise, those engaged in the caring professions—in medicine, counseling, social work, and so on—or even those looking after someone at home may sometimes become so exhausted by their duties that they feel overwhelmed. Constant exposure to suffering, coupled occasionally with a feeling of being taken for granted, can induce feelings of helplessness and even despair. Or it can happen that individuals may find themselves performing outwardly generous actions merely for the sake of it—simply going through the motions, as it were. Of course this is better than nothing. But when left unchecked, this can lead to insensitivity toward others' suffering. If this starts to happen, it is best to disengage for a short while and make a deliberate effort to reawaken that sensitivity. In this it can be helpful to remember that despair is never a solution. It is, rather, the ultimate failure. Therefore, as the Tibetan expression has it, even if the rope breaks nine times, we must splice it back together a tenth time. In this way, even if ultimately we do fail, at least there will be no feelings of regret. And when we combine this insight with a clear appreciation of our potential to benefit others, we find that we can begin to restore our hope and confidence.

Some people may object to this ideal on the grounds that by entering into others' suffering, we bring suffering on ourselves. To an extent, this is true. But I suggest that there is an important qualitative distinction to be made between experiencing one's own suffering and experiencing suffering in the course of sharing in others'. In the case of one's own suffering, given that it is involuntary, there is a sense of oppression: it seems to come from outside us. By contrast, sharing in someone else's suffering must at some level involve a degree of voluntariness, which itself is indicative of a certain inner strength. For this reason, the disturbance it may cause is considerably less likely to paralyze us than our own suffering.

Of course, even as an ideal, the notion of developing unconditional compassion is daunting. Most people, including myself, must struggle even to reach the point where putting others' interests on a par with our own becomes easy. We should not allow this to put us off, however. And while undoubtedly there will be obstacles on the way to developing a genuinely warm heart, there is the deep consolation of knowing that in doing so we are creating the conditions for our own happiness. As I mentioned earlier, the more we truly desire to benefit others, the greater the strength and confidence we develop and the greater the peace and happiness we experience. If this still seems unlikely, it is worth asking ourselves how else we are to do so. With violence and aggression? Of course not. With money? Perhaps up to a point, but no further. But with love, by sharing in others' suffering, by recognizing ourselves clearly in all others—especially those who are disadvantaged and those whose rights are not respected—by helping them to, be happy: yes. Through love, through kindness, through compassion we establish understanding between ourselves and others. This is how we forge unity and harmony.

Compassion and love are not mere luxuries. As the source both of inner and external peace, they are fundamental to the continued survival of our species. On the one hand, they constitute non-violence in action. On the other, they are the source of all spiritual qualities: of forgiveness, tolerance, and all the virtues. Moreover, they are the very thing that gives meaning to our activities and makes them constructive. There is nothing amazing about being highly educated; there is nothing amazing about being rich. Only when the individual has a warm heart do these attributes become worthwhile.

So to those who say that the Dalai Lama is being unrealistic in advocating this ideal of unconditional love, I urge them to experiment with it nonetheless. They will discover that when we reach beyond the confines of narrow self-interest, our hearts become filled with strength. Peace and joy become our constant companion. It breaks down barriers of every kind and in the end destroys the notion of my interest as independent from others' interest. But most important, so far as ethics is concerned, where love of one's neighbor, affection, kindness, and compassion live, we find that ethical conduct is automatic. Ethically wholesome actions arise naturally in the context of compassion.

Questions on Meaning

1. Compassion means to empathize with another, to feel that person's joy, pain, and hope. Why does the author say that feeling compassion for the disabled or the poor is easy? Why is it hard to feel sympathy for those we envy?

2. What would happen to our ordinary, selfish lives if we were to start feeling real compassion? Would we be able to use the environment and the rest of the world as we do now? What would we have to change?

3. What does the individual gain by feeling compassion? Is the kind of peace and love that are described in this essay really what people want? Why do most of us live lives that are aimed at making money and winning, rather than loving?

Questions on Rhetorical Strategy and Style

1. The tone of this essay is very gentle and kind, but the message is quite tough. How does the author warn the reader in the introduction that the essay is going to be demanding and maybe a bit disturbing?

2. The essay moves to a cause and effect structure: If one feels true compassion, the feeling may cause one to have to change one's life. The feeling, though a good one, may lead to uncomfortable results. How does this causality affect the reader of the essay? Is a reader likely to change behavior in light of this cause and effect explanation?

3. The end of the essay promises that great good can come from feeling compassion. How does the writer hope to persuade the reader that these benefits are worthwhile? Does this ending promise better things for the world if many readers are persuaded? Is it even possible?

Writing Assignments

1. A wise person once said that we should feel compassion rather than guilt, for we will act from compassion, but we will merely suffer from guilt. Think of someone you know whom you consider compassionate. Write about what that person does with life. What kind of work does the person do? What kind of entertainment and leisure activities does that person pursue?

2. Write about a world leader whom you consider compassionate. Show how this feeling is displayed in the person's actions. What would happen to world politics if everyone acted with compassion?
3. Consider a world conflict, either one occurring now or one in history. Write about how the events could be or would have been different had the parties shown more compassion and less aggression.

What to the Slave is the Fourth of July?

Frederick Douglass

Frederick Douglass (1817–1895)—abolitionist, author, and the first black American to become a prominent public figure—was born into slavery near Tuckahoe, Maryland. As a youth, Douglass worked as a household servant, a field hand, and a shipyard apprentice. In 1838, after several failed attempts to escape (for which he received beatings), he successfully reached New York. He took the surname "Douglass" and eventually settled in New Bedford, Massachusetts. In 1841, the Massachusetts Anti-Slavery League, impressed by his great oratory skills, hired Douglass to help promote the abolition of slavery. Douglass bought his freedom in 1847, using money contributed both by Americans and by sympathizers in England, where he had fled to preserve his freedom. For the next 13 years, Douglass edited the abolitionist periodical North Star *(changed to* Frederick Douglass's Paper *in 1851). During the Civil War, Douglass urged President Lincoln to emancipate the slaves and helped recruit black troops. After the war, he held a series of government posts, including Assistant Secretary to the Santo Domingo Commission, Marshal of the District of Columbia, District Recorder of Deeds, and Ambassador to Haiti. In this 1852 speech delivered in Rochester, New York, Douglass rails against the hypocrisy of celebrating independence in a country in which slavery is the law of the land.*

Reprinted from *The Frederick Douglass Papers* (1991), by permission of Yale University Press.

1   Fellow citizens, pardon me, and allow me to ask, why am I called   1
upon to speak here today? What have I or those I represent to
do with your national independence? Are the great principles of
political freedom and of natural justice, embodied in that Declaration
of Independence, extended to us? And am I, therefore, called upon to
bring our humble offering to the national altar, and to confess the
benefits, and express devout gratitude for the blessings resulting from
your independence to us?

Would to God, both for your sakes and ours, that an affirmative
answer could be truthfully returned to these questions. Then would
my task be light, and my burden easy and delightful. For who is there
so cold that a nation's sympathy could not warm him? Who so obdu-
rate and dead to the claims of gratitude, that would not thankfully
acknowledge such priceless benefits? Who so stolid and selfish that
would not give his voice to swell the hallelujahs of a nation's jubilee,
when the chains of servitude had been torn from his limbs? I am not
that man. In a case like that, the dumb might eloquently speak, and
the "lame man leap as an hart."

But such is not the state of the case. I say it with a sad sense of dis-
parity between us. I am not included within the pale of this glorious
anniversary! Your high independence only reveals the immeasurable
distance between us. The blessings in which you this day rejoice are
not enjoyed in common. The rich inheritance of justice, liberty, prosperity, and independence bequeathed by your fathers is shared by you,
not by me. The sunlight that brought life and healing to you has
brought stripes and death to me. This Fourth of July is yours, not
mine. You may rejoice, I must mourn. To drag a man in fetters into
the grand illuminated temple of liberty, and call upon him to join you
in joyous anthems, were inhuman mockery and sacrilegious irony. Do
you mean, citizens, to mock me, by asking me to speak today? If so,
there is a parallel to your conduct. And let me warn you, that it is dangerous to copy the example of a nation (Babylon) whose crimes, tow-
ering up to heaven, were thrown down by the breath of the Almighty,
burying that nation in irrecoverable ruin.

Fellow citizens, above your national, tumultuous joy, I hear the
mournful wail of millions, whose chains, heavy and grievous yesterday, are today rendered more intolerable by the jubilant shouts that
reach them. If I do forget, if I do not remember those bleeding children of sorrow this day, "may my right hand forget her cunning, and
may my tongue cleave to the roof of my mouth!"

5   To forget them, to pass lightly over their wrongs and to chime in
with the popular theme would be treason most scandalous and shocking, and would make me a reproach before God and the world.

My subject, then, fellow citizens, is "American Slavery." I shall see
this day and its popular characteristics from the slave's point of view.
Standing here, identified with the American bondman, making his
wrongs mine, I do not hesitate to declare, with all my soul, that the
character and conduct of this nation never looked blacker to me than
on this Fourth of July.

Whether we turn to the declarations of the past, or to the professions of the present, the conduct of the nation seems equally hideous
and revolting. America is false to the past, false to the present, and
solemnly binds herself to be false to the future. Standing with God
and the crushed and bleeding slave on this occasion, I will, in the
name of humanity, which is outraged, in the name of liberty, which is
fettered, in the name of the Constitution and the Bible, which are
disregarded and trampled upon, dare to call in question and to
denounce, with all the emphasis I can command, everything that
serves to perpetuate slavery—the great sin and shame of America! "I
will not equivocate—I will not excuse." I will use the severest language I can command, and yet not one word shall escape me that any
man, whose judgment is not blinded by prejudice, or who is not at
heart a slave-holder, shall not confess to be right and just.

But I fancy I hear some of my audience say it is just in this circumstance that you and your brother Abolitionists fail to make a
favorable impression on the public mind. Would you argue more and
denounce less, would you persuade more and rebuke less, your cause
would be much more likely to succeed. But, I submit, where all is
plain there is nothing to be argued. What point in the anti-slavery
creed would you have me argue? On what branch of the subject do the
people of this country need light? Must I undertake to prove that the
slave is a man? That point is conceded already. Nobody doubts it. The
slave-holders themselves acknowledge it in the enactment of laws for
their government. They acknowledge it when they punish disobedience
on the part of the slave. There are seventy-two crimes in the State of
Virginia, which, if committed by a black man (no matter how ignorant he be), subject him to the punishment of death; while only two of
these same crimes will subject a white man to like punishment.

What is this but the acknowledgment that the slave is a moral,
intellectual, and responsible being? The manhood of the slave is

conceded. It is admitted in the fact that Southern statute books are covered with enactments, forbidding, under severe fines and penalties, the teaching of the slave to read and write. When you can point to any such laws in reference to the beasts of the field, then I may consent to argue the manhood of the slave. When the dogs in your streets, when the fowls of the air, when the cattle on your hills, when the fish of the sea, and the reptiles that crawl, shall be unable to distinguish the slave from a brute, then I will argue with you that the slave is a man!

10   For the present it is enough to affirm the equal manhood of the Negro race. Is it not astonishing that, while we are plowing, planting, and reaping, using all kinds of mechanical tools, erecting houses, constructing bridges, building ships, working in metals of brass, iron, copper, silver, and gold; that while we are reading, writing, and ciphering, acting as clerks, merchants, and secretaries, having among us lawyers, doctors, ministers, poets, authors, editors, orators, and teachers; that we are engaged in all the enterprises common to other men—digging gold in California, capturing the whale in the Pacific, feeding sheep and cattle on the hillside, living, moving, acting, thinking, planning, living in families as husbands, wives, and children, and above all, confessing and worshipping the Christian God, and looking hopefully for life and immortality beyond the grave—we are called upon to prove that we are men?

Would you have me argue that man is entitled to liberty? That he is the rightful owner of his own body? You have already declared it. Must I argue the wrongfulness of slavery? Is that a question for republicans? Is it to be settled by the rules of logic and argumentation, as a matter beset with great difficulty, involving a doubtful application of the principle of justice, hard to understand? How should I look today in the presence of Americans, dividing and subdividing a discourse, to show that men have a natural right to freedom, speaking of it relatively and positively, negatively and affirmatively? To do so would be to make myself ridiculous, and to offer an insult to your understanding. There is not a man beneath the canopy of heaven who does not know that slavery is wrong for him.

What! Am I to argue that it is wrong to make men brutes, to rob them of their liberty, to work them without wages, to keep them ignorant of their relations to their fellow men, to beat them with sticks, to flay their flesh with the lash, to load their limbs with irons, to hunt them with dogs, to sell them at auction, to sunder their families, to knock out their teeth, to burn their flesh, to starve them into obedience and submission to their masters? Must I argue that a system thus marked with blood and stained with pollution is wrong? No—I will not. I have better employment for my time and strength than such arguments would imply.

What, then, remains to be argued? Is it that slavery is not divine; that God did not establish it; that our doctors of divinity are mistaken? There is blasphemy in the thought. That which is inhuman cannot be divine. Who can reason on such a proposition? They that can, may—I cannot. The time for such argument is past.

At a time like this, scorching irony, not convincing argument, is needed. Oh! had I the ability, and could I reach the nation's ear, I would today pour out a fiery stream of biting ridicule, blasting reproach, withering sarcasm, and stern rebuke. For it is not light that is needed, but fire; it is not the gentle shower, but thunder. We need the storm, the whirlwind, and the earthquake. The feeling of the nation must be quickened; the conscience of the nation must be roused; the propriety of the nation must be startled; the hypocrisy of the nation must be exposed; and its crimes against God and man must be denounced.

15 What to the American slave is your Fourth of July? I answer, a day that reveals to him more than all other days of the year, the gross injustice and cruelty to which he is the constant victim. To him your celebration is a sham; your boasted liberty an unholy license; your national greatness, swelling vanity; your sounds of rejoicing are empty and heartless; your shouts of liberty and equality, hollow mock; your prayers and hymns, your sermons and thanksgivings, with all your religious parade and solemnity, are to him mere bombast, fraud, deception, impiety, and hypocrisy—a thin veil to cover up crimes which would disgrace a nation of savages. There is not a nation of the earth guilty of practices more shocking and bloody than are the people of these United States at this very hour.

Go search where you will, roam through all the monarchies and despotisms of the Old World, travel through South America, search out every abuse and when you have found the last, lay your facts by the side of the everyday practices of this nation, and you will say with me that, for revolting barbarity and shameless hypocrisy, America reigns without a rival.

Delivered July 4, 1852 Rochester, NY

Questions on Meaning

1. Why does Douglass insist that the plight of the slave is so much more intolerable on the Fourth of July than on any other day? How does he make this point clear to his audience?
2. What does Douglass mean by "where all is plain there is nothing to be argued"? What specific points does he insist are already understood?
3. What is Douglass calling for when he says that in order to abolish slavery, what is needed is fire, thunder, and earthquake?

Questions on Rhetorical Strategy and Style

1. What is the impact of the series of questions with which Douglass opens his speech? Identify several other questions in the speech and comment on their effectiveness as well.
2. Douglass presents a series of contrasts in his speech, most notably that between the slave and the free American. Identify several of these contrasts and explain their significance to the speech.
3. Why do you think Douglass makes so many references to the Bible? Why would this technique be particularly effective to his audience at the time?

Writing Assignments

1. Douglass lists a number of points that should not have to be argued, beginning with the point that a slave is a man. Identify those points and present his reasoning in traditional essay form. Without the oratory, how effective do you find his arguments? Explain your response.
2. Write an essay analyzing the effectiveness of Douglass's rhetoric in this speech. Focus on such features as questions, repetition, contrasts, biblical references, and word choice.
3. During the 2008 presidential primary season, a post 9/11 sermon by the Reverend Jeremiah Wright became the subject of significant controversy. In that sermon Wright condemns America for its oppression and imperialism. After watching a video of the entire sermon, compare it to Douglass's speech. What specific similarities and differences can you identify in the two addresses? Based on the popular response to the Wright sermon, how do you think Douglass's compatriots might have responded to him?

Race Matters

Cornel West

Cornel West (1953–) was born and reared in Tulsa, Oklahoma. He graduated from two Ivy League Universities—Harvard and Princeton—and has taught at three: Harvard, Princeton, and Yale. He currently directs the African-American Studies Department at Princeton. He has written many books. Recent works on race include Breaking Bread: Insurgent Black Intellectual Life *(1991) and* Race Matters *(1993). West takes a global viewpoint toward race issues, preferring to lay out the problem and the basic materials for a solution rather than to propose detailed responses to the issues. In this article he takes the moral high ground, seeking consensus through shared understanding. Note as you read his comments on issues of injustice that he takes the scholar's detached and analytical view where another writer might grow emotionally involved.*

Since the beginning of the nation, white Americans have suffered from a deep inner uncertainty as to who they really are. One of the ways that has been used to simplify the answer has been to seize upon the presence of black Americans and use them as a marker, a symbol of limits, a metaphor for the "outsider." Many whites could look at the social position of blacks and feel that color formed an easy and reliable gauge for determining to what extent one was or was not American. Perhaps that is why one of the first epithets that many European immigrants learned when they got off the boat was the term "nigger"—it made them feel instantly American. But this is tricky magic. Despite his racial difference and social status, something indisputably American about Negroes not only raised doubts about the white man's value system but aroused the troubling suspicion that whatever else the true American is, he is also somehow black.

—RALPH ELLISON, "What America
Would Be Like without Blacks" (1970)

What happened in Los Angeles in April of 1992 was neither a race riot nor a class rebellion. Rather, this monumental upheaval was a multiracial, trans-class, and largely male display of justified social rage. For all its ugly, xenophobic resentment, its air of adolescent carnival, and its downright barbaric behavior, it signified the sense of powerlessness in American society. Glib attempts to reduce its meaning to the pathologies of the black underclass, the criminal actions of hoodlums, or the political revolt of the oppressed urban masses miss the mark. Of those arrested, only 36 percent were black, more than a third had full-time jobs, and most claimed to shun political affiliation. What we witnessed in Los Angeles was the consequence of a lethal linkage of economic decline, cultural decay, and political lethargy in American life. Race was the visible catalyst, not the underlying cause.

The meaning of the earthshaking events in Los Angeles is difficult to grasp because most of us remain trapped in the narrow framework of the dominant liberal and conservative views of race in America, which with its worn-out vocabulary leaves us intellectually debilitated, morally disempowered, and personally depressed. The astonishing disappearance of the event from public dialogue is testimony to just how painful and distressing a serious engagement with race is. Our truncated public discussions of race suppress the best of who and what we are as a people because they fail to confront the complexity of the issue in a candid and critical manner. The predictable pitting of liberals against conservatives, Great Society Democrats against self-help Republicans, reinforces intellectual parochialism and political paralysis.

The liberal notion that more government programs can solve racial problems is simplistic—precisely because it focuses *solely* on the economic dimension. And the conservative idea that what is needed is a change in the moral behavior of poor black urban dwellers (especially poor black men, who, they say, should stay married, support their children, and stop committing so much crime) highlights immoral actions while ignoring public responsibility for the immoral circumstances that haunt our fellow citizens.

The common denominator of these views of race is that each still sees black people as a "problem people," in the words of Dorothy I. Height, president of the National Council of Negro Women, rather than as fellow American citizens with problems. Her words echo the poignant "unasked question" of W. E. B. Du Bois, who, in *The Souls of Black Folk* (1903), wrote:

> *They approach me in a half-hesitant sort of way, eye me curiously or compassionately, and then instead of saying directly, How does it feel to be a problem? they say, I know an excellent colored man in my town. . . . Do not these Southern outrages make your blood boil? At these I smile, or am interested, or reduce the boiling to a simmer, as the occasion may require. To the real question, How does it feel to be a problem? I answer seldom a word.*

Nearly a century later, we confine discussions about race in America to the "problems" black people pose for whites rather than consider what this way of viewing black people reveals about us as a nation.

This paralyzing framework encourages liberals to relieve their guilty consciences by supporting public funds directed at "the problems"; but at the same time, reluctant to exercise principled criticism of black people, liberals deny them the freedom to err. Similarly, conservatives blame the "problems" on black people themselves—and thereby render black social misery invisible or unworthy of public attention.

Hence, for liberals, black people are to be "included" and "integrated" into "our" society and culture, while for conservatives they are to be "well behaved" and "worthy of acceptance" by "our" way of life. Both fail to see that the presence and predicaments of black people are neither additions to nor defections from American life, but rather *constitutive elements of that life.*

To engage in a serious discussion of race in America, we must begin not with the problems of black people but with the flaws of American society—flaws rooted in historic inequalities and longstanding cultural stereotypes. How we set up the terms for discussing racial issues shapes our perception and response to these issues. As long as black people are viewed as a "them," the burden falls on blacks to do all the "cultural" and "moral" work necessary for healthy race relations. The implication is that only certain Americans can define what it means to be American—and the rest must simply "fit in."

The emergence of strong black-nationalist sentiments among blacks, especially among young people, is a revolt against this sense of having to "fit in." The variety of black-nationalist ideologies, from the moderate views of Supreme Court justice Clarence Thomas in his youth to those of Louis Farrakhan today, rest upon a fundamental truth: White America has been historically weak-willed in ensuring racial justice and has continued to resist fully accepting the humanity of blacks. As long as double standards and differential treatment abound—as long as the rap performer Ice-T is harshly condemned while former Los Angeles Police Chief Daryl F. Gates's antiblack comments are received in polite silence, as long as Dr. Leonard Jeffries's anti-Semitic statements are met with vitriolic outrage while presidential candidate Patrick J. Buchanan's anti-Semitism receives a genteel response black nationalisms will thrive.

Afrocentrism, a contemporary species of black nationalism, is a gallant yet misguided attempt to define an African identity in a white society perceived to be hostile. It is gallant because it puts black doings and sufferings, not white anxieties and fears, at the center of discussion. It is misguided because—out of fear of cultural hybridization and through silence on the issue of class, retrograde views on black women, gay men, and lesbians, and a reluctance to link race to the common good—it reinforces the narrow discussions about race.

10   To establish a new framework, we need to begin with a frank acknowledgment of the basic humanness and Americanness of each of us. And we must acknowledge that as a people—*E Pluribus Unum*—we are on a slippery slope toward economic strife, social turmoil, and cultural chaos. If we go down, we go down together. The Los Angeles upheaval forced us to see not only that we are not connected in ways we would like to be but also, in a more profound sense, that this failure to connect binds us even more tightly together. The paradox of race in America is that our common destiny is more pronounced and imperiled precisely when our divisions are deeper. The Civil War and its legacy speak loudly here. And our divisions are growing deeper. Today, eighty-six percent of white suburban Americans live in neighborhoods that are less than one percent black, meaning that the prospects for the country depend largely on how its cities fare in the hands of a suburban electorate. There is no escape from our interracial interdependence, yet enforced racial hierarchy dooms us as a nation to collective paranoia and hysteria—the unmaking of any democratic order.

The verdict in the Rodney King case which sparked the incidents in Los Angeles was perceived to be wrong by the vast majority of

Americans. But whites have often failed to acknowledge the widespread mistreatment of black people, especially black men, by law enforcement agencies, which helped ignite the spark. The verdict was merely the occasion for deep-seated rage to come to the surface. This rage is fed by the "silent" depression ravaging the country—in which real weekly wages of all American workers since 1973 have declined nearly twenty percent, while at the same time wealth has been upwardly distributed.

The exodus of stable industrial jobs from urban centers to cheaper labor markets here and abroad, housing policies that have created "chocolate cities and vanilla suburbs" (to use the popular musical artist George Clinton's memorable phrase), white fear of black crime, and the urban influx of poor Spanish-speaking and Asian immigrants—all have helped erode the tax base of American cities just as the federal government has cut its supports and programs. The result is unemployment, hunger, homelessness, and sickness for millions.

And a pervasive spiritual impoverishment grows. The collapse of meaning in life—the eclipse of hope and absence of love of self and others, the breakdown of family and neighborhood bonds—leads to the social deracination and cultural denudement of urban dwellers, especially children. We have created rootless, dangling people with little link to the supportive networks—family, friends, school—that sustain some sense of purpose in life. We have witnessed the collapse of the spiritual communities that in the past helped Americans face despair, disease, and death and that transmit through the generations dignity and decency, excellence and elegance.

The result is lives of what we might call "random nows," of fortuitous and fleeting moments preoccupied with "getting over" with acquiring pleasure, property, and power by any means necessary. (This is not what Malcolm X meant by this famous phrase.) Post-modern culture is more and more a market culture dominated by gangster mentalities and self-destructive wantonness. This culture engulfs all of us—yet its impact on the disadvantaged is devastating, resulting in extreme violence in everyday life. Sexual violence against women and homicidal assaults by young black men on one another are only the most obvious signs of this empty quest for pleasure, property, and power.

15 Last, this rage is fueled by a political atmosphere in which images, 15 not ideas, dominate, where politicians spend more time raising money

than debating issues. The functions of parties have been displaced by public polls, and politicians behave less as thermostats that determine the climate of opinion than as thermometers registering the public mood. American politics has been rocked by an unleashing of greed among opportunistic public officials—who have followed the lead of their counterparts in the private sphere, where, as of 1989, one percent of the population owned thirty-seven percent of the wealth and ten percent of the population owned eighty-six percent of the wealth—leading to a profound cynicism and pessimism among the citizenry.

And given the way in which the Republican Party since 1968 has appealed to popular xenophobic images—playing the black, female, and homophobic cards to realign the electorate along race, sex, and sexual-orientation lines—it is no surprise that the notion that we are all part of one garment of destiny is discredited. Appeals to special interests rather than to public interests reinforce this polarization. The Los Angeles upheaval was an expression of utter fragmentation by a powerless citizenry that includes not just the poor but all of us.

What is to be done? How do we capture a new spirit and vision to meet the challenges of the post-industrial city, post-modern culture, and post-party politics?

First, we must admit that the most valuable sources for help, hope, and power consist of ourselves and our common history. As in the ages of Lincoln, Roosevelt, and King, we must look to new frameworks and languages to understand our multilayered crisis and overcome our deep malaise.

Second, we must focus our attention on the public square—the common good that undergirds our national and global destinies. The vitality of any public square ultimately depends on how much we care about the quality of our lives together. The neglect of our public infrastructure, for example—our water and sewage systems, bridges, tunnels, highways, subways, and streets—reflects not only our myopic economic policies, which impede productivity, but also the low priority we place on our common life.

20   The tragic plight of our children clearly reveals our deep disregard   20
for public well-being. About one out of every five children in this country lives in poverty, including one out of every two black children and two out of every five Hispanic children. Most of our children—neglected by overburdened parents and bombarded by the market

values of profit-hungry corporations—are ill-equipped to live lives of spiritual and cultural quality. Faced with these facts, how do we expect ever to constitute a vibrant society?

One essential step is some form of large-scale public intervention to ensure access to basic social goods—housing, food, health care, education, child care, and jobs. We must invigorate the common good with a mixture of government, business, and labor that does not follow any existing blueprint. After a period in which the private sphere has been sacralized and the public square gutted, the temptation is to make a fetish of the public square. We need to resist such dogmatic swings.

Last, the major challenge is to meet the need to generate new leadership. The paucity of courageous leaders—so apparent in the response to the events in Los Angeles—requires that we look beyond the same elites and voices that recycle the older frameworks. We need leaders—neither saints nor sparkling television personalities—who can situate themselves within a larger historical narrative of this country and our world, who can grasp the complex dynamics of our peoplehood and imagine a future grounded in the best of our past, yet who are attuned to the frightening obstacles that now perplex us. Our ideals of freedom, democracy, and equality must be invoked to invigorate all of us, especially the landless, propertyless, and luckless. Only a visionary leadership that can motivate "the better angels of our nature," as Lincoln said, and activate possibilities for a freer, more efficient, and stable America—only that leadership deserves cultivation and support.

This new leadership must be grounded in grass-roots organizing that highlights democratic accountability. Whoever our leaders will be as we approach the twenty-first century, their challenge will be to help Americans determine whether a genuine multiracial democracy can be created and sustained in an era of global economy and a moment of xenophobic frenzy.

Let us hope and pray that the vast intelligence, imagination, humor, and courage of Americans will not fail us. Either we learn a new language of empathy and compassion, or the fire this time will consume us all.

Questions on Meaning

1. What, according to West, are the liberal and conservative attitudes about how to solve racial problems? What do the two views have in common? Why do both viewpoints lead to more subtle forms of racism?

2. West says that young black people take up black-nationalist sentiments, that is, that they want to see themselves as a nation of people separate from the predominantly white American mainstream. What other reasons besides racism might provoke people in their late teens and early twenties to try to build an identity separate from their parents' and their culture's assumptions?

3. West suggests that the loss of industrial jobs, spiritual impoverishment, and a cynical political system have caused the racial problems that we are currently experiencing. Explain as well as you can how those forces could lead someone to hostility toward a person of another race.

Questions on Rhetorical Strategy and Style

1. West uses an intellectual's vocabulary. Based on the context, what is your best guess concerning the meanings of xenophobic, lethargy, ideologies, afrocentrism, deracination, post-modern, and sacralized. Check your guesses against a dictionary. Why does West use such a seemingly detached tone?

2. Locate in the text the places where West makes appeals to reason, and the places where the appeals are emotional.

Writing Assignments

1. Use the *Reader's Guide to Periodical Literature* to locate some news accounts of the Los Angeles riots of April, 1992. Read several accounts of the events and write a brief description of what happened including the various contributing causes.

2. This essay does not provide a clear practical plan for resolving the problems of racism. Instead it focuses on general goals and attitudes. List the goals and attitudes West mentions, and add any that you think important.

3. Recall an incident of racist speech or action from your personal experience. Write an essay in which you briefly retell the incident; then at greater length analyze the causes and effects of the

incident, and speculate about what changes in the people or the environment could have prevented the incident.

4. Write a letter to the editor of your local newspaper describing the racial problems in an organization to which you belong.

White Privilege: Unpacking the Invisible Knapsack

Peggy McIntosh

Feminist and anti-racism activist Peggy McIntosh graduated from Radcliffe College in 1956 and earned a Ph.D. from Harvard University in 1967. Currently the Associate Director of the Wellesley Centers for Women at Wellesley College in Massachusetts, McIntosh has also taught at Harvard University, Trinity College (Washington, D.C.), the University of Denver, and the University of Durham, England. She has long been involved with the movement to make education more inclusive, co-founding the Rocky Mountain Women's Institute and founding the SEED (Seeking Educational Equity and Diversity) Project to assist teachers in developing race- and gender-sensitive curricula in public and private schools. McIntosh has worked with institutions in the United States, Europe, and Asia on issues of racial and gender equity, and has lectured and published widely on these issues. McIntosh is perhaps best known for "White Privilege and Male Privilege: A Personal Account of Coming to See Correspondences through Work on Women's Studies," published by the Wellesley College Center for Women in 1988. The concept of white privilege explored by McIntosh in this article has influenced scholarly and political work on racial issues for more than two decades. The following selection, adapted from that article, originally appeared in 1988 in the journal Peace and Freedom. *In it, McIntosh examines the unacknowledged advantages enjoyed by white people in U.S. culture, arguing that these invisible privileges inevitably lead to oppression of people of color.*

1   Through work to bring materials from Women's Studies into the rest of the curriculum, I have often noticed men's unwillingness to grant that they are over-privileged, even though they may grant that women are disadvantaged. They may say they will work to improve women's status, in the society, the university, or the curriculum, but they can't or won't support the idea of lessening men's. Denials which amount to taboos surround the subject of advantages which men gain from women's disadvantages. These denials protect male privilege from being fully acknowledged, lessened or ended.

Thinking through unacknowledged male privilege as a phenomenon, I realized that since hierarchies in our society are interlocking, there was most likely a phenomenon of white privilege which was similarly denied and protected. As a white person, I realized I had been taught about racism as something which puts others at a disadvantage, but had been taught not to see one of its corollary aspects, white privilege, which puts me at an advantage.

I think whites are carefully taught not to recognize white privilege, as males are taught not to recognize male privilege. So I have begun in an untutored way to ask what it is like to have white privilege. I have come to see white privilege as an invisible package of unearned assets which I can count on cashing in each day, but about which I was "meant" to remain oblivious. White privilege is like an invisible weightless knapsack of special provisions, maps, passports, codebooks, visas, clothes, tools and blank checks.

Describing white privilege makes one newly accountable. As we in Women's Studies work to reveal male privilege and ask men to give up some of their power, so one who writes about having white privilege must ask, "Having described it, what will I do to lessen or end it?"

5   After I realized the extent to which men work from a base of unacknowledged privilege, I understood that much of their oppressiveness was unconscious. Then I remembered the frequent charges from women of color that white women whom they encounter are oppressive. I began to understand why we are justly seen as oppressive, even when we don't see ourselves that way. I began to count the ways in which I enjoy unearned skin privilege and have been conditioned into oblivion about its existence.

My schooling gave me no training in seeing myself as an oppressor, as an unfairly advantaged person, or as a participant in a damaged culture. I was taught to see myself as an individual whose moral state depended on her individual moral will. My schooling followed the pattern my colleague Elizabeth Minnich has pointed out: whites are taught to think of their lives as morally neutral, normative, and average, and also ideal, so that when we work to benefit others, this is seen as work which will allow "them" to be more like "us."

I decided to try to work on myself at least by identifying some of the daily effects of white privilege in my life. I have chosen those conditions which I think in my case attach somewhat more to skin-color privilege than to class, religion, ethnic status, or geographical location, though of course all these other factors are intricately intertwined. As far as I can see, my African American co-workers, friends and acquaintances with whom I come into daily or frequent contact in this particular time, place, and line of work cannot count on most of these conditions.

1. I can if I wish arrange to be in the company of people of my race most of the time.
2. If I should need to move, I can be pretty sure of renting or purchasing housing in an area which I can afford and in which I would want to live.
3. I can be pretty sure that my neighbors in such a location will be neutral or pleasant to me.
4. I can go shopping alone most of the time, pretty well assured that I will not be followed or harassed.
5. I can turn on the television or open to the front page of the paper and see people of my race widely represented.
6. When I am told about our national heritage or about "civilization," I am shown that people of my color made it what it is.
7. I can be sure that my children will be given curricular materials that testify to the existence of their race.
8. If I want to, I can be pretty sure of finding a publisher for this piece on white privilege.
9. I can go into a music shop and count on finding the music of my race represented, into a supermarket and find the staple foods which fit with my cultural traditions, into a hairdresser's shop and find someone who can cut my hair.
10. Whether I use checks, credit cards, or cash, I can count on my skin color not to work against the appearance of financial reliability.
11. I can arrange to protect my children most of the time from people who might not like them.

12. I can swear, or dress in secondhand clothes, or not answer letters, without having people attribute these choices to the bad morals, the poverty, or the illiteracy of my race.

13. I can speak in public to a powerful male group without putting my race on trial.

14. I can do well in a challenging situation without being called a credit to my race.

15. I am never asked to speak for all the people of my racial group.

16. I can remain oblivious of the language and customs of persons of color who constitute the world's majority without feeling in my culture any penalty for such oblivion.

17. I can criticize our government and talk about how much I fear its policies and behavior without being seen as a cultural outsider.

18. I can be pretty sure that if I ask to talk to "the person in charge," I will be facing a person of my race.

19. If a traffic cop pulls me over or if the IRS audits my tax return, I can be sure I haven't been singled out because of my race.

20. I can easily buy posters, postcards, picture books, greeting cards, dolls, toys, and children's magazines featuring people of my race.

21. I can go home from most meetings of organizations I belong to feeling somewhat tied in, rather than isolated, out-of-place, out-numbered, unheard, held at a distance, or feared.

22. I can take a job with an affirmative action employer without having co-workers on the job suspect that I got it because of race.

23. I can choose public accommodation without fearing that people of my race cannot get in or will be mistreated in the places I have chosen.

24. I can be sure that if I need legal or medical help, my race will not work against me.

25. If my day, week, or year is going badly, I need not ask of each negative episode or situation whether it has racial overtones.

26. I can choose blemish cover or bandages in "flesh" color and have them more or less match my skin.

I repeatedly forgot each of the realizations on this list until I wrote it down. For me white privilege has turned out to be an elusive and fugitive subject. The pressure to avoid it is great, for in facing it I must give up the myth of meritocracy. If these things are true, this is not such a free country; one's life is not what one makes it; many doors open for certain people through no virtues of their own.

In unpacking this invisible backpack of white privilege, I have listed conditions of daily experience which I once took for granted.

Nor did I think of any of these perquisites as bad for the holder. I now think that we need a more finely differentiated taxonomy of privilege, for some of these varieties are only what one would want for everyone in a just society, and others give licence to be ignorant, oblivious, arrogant and destructive.

10   I see a pattern running through the matrix of white privilege, a   10
pattern of assumptions which were passed on to me as a white person. There was one main piece of cultural turf; it was my own turf, and I was among those who could control the turf. My skin color was an asset for any move I was educated to want to make. I could think of myself as belonging in major ways, and of making social systems work for me. I could freely disparage, fear, neglect, or be oblivious to anything outside of the dominant cultural forms. Being of the main culture, I could also criticize it fairly freely.

In proportion as my racial group was being made confident, comfortable, and oblivious, other groups were likely being made inconfident, uncomfortable, and alienated. Whiteness protected me from many kinds of hostility, distress, and violence, which I was being subtly trained to visit in turn upon people of color.

For this reason, the word "privilege" now seems to me misleading. We usually think of privilege as being a favored state, whether earned or conferred by birth or luck. Yet some of the conditions I have described here work to systematically overempower certain groups. Such privilege simply *confers dominance* because of one's race or sex.

I want, then, to distinguish between earned strength and unearned power conferred systematically. Power from unearned privilege can look like strength when it is in fact permission to escape or to dominate. But not all of the privileges on my list are inevitably damaging. Some, like the expectation that neighbors will be decent to you, or that your race will not count against you in court, should be the norm in a just society. Others, like the privilege to ignore less powerful people, distort the humanity of the holders as well as the ignored groups.

We might at least start by distinguishing between positive advantages which we can work to spread, and negative types of advantages which unless rejected will always reinforce our present hierarchies. For example, the feeling that one belongs within the human circle, as Native Americans say, should not be seen as privilege for a few. Ideally it is an *unearned entitlement.* At present, since only a few have it, it is an *unearned advantage* for them. This paper results from a process of coming to see that some of the power which I originally saw as attendant on being a human being in the U.S. consisted in *unearned advantage* and *conferred dominance*.

15   I have met very few men who are truly distressed about systemic, unearned male advantage and conferred dominance. And so one question for me and others like me is whether we will be like them, or whether we will get truly distressed, even outraged, about unearned race advantage and conferred dominance and if so, what we will do to lessen them. In any case, we need to do more work in identifying how they actually affect our daily lives. Many, perhaps most, of our white students in the U.S. think that racism doesn't affect them because they are not people of color; they do not see "whiteness" as a racial identity. In addition, since race and sex are not the only advantaging systems at work, we need similarly to examine the daily experience of having age advantage, or ethnic advantage, or physical ability, or advantage related to nationality, religion, or sexual orientation.

It seems to me that obliviousness about white advantage, like obliviousness about male advantage, is kept strongly inculturated in the United States so as to maintain the myth of meritocracy, the myth that democratic choice is equally available to all. Keeping most people unaware that freedom of confident action is there for just a small number of people props up those in power, and serves to keep power in the hands of the same groups that have most of it already.

Though systematic change takes many decades, there are pressing questions for me and I imagine for some others like me if we raise our daily consciousness on the perquisites of being light-skinned. What will we do with such knowledge? As we know from watching men, it is an open question whether we will choose to use unearned advantage to weaken hidden systems of advantage, and whether we will use any of our arbitrarily-awarded power to try to reconstruct power systems on a broader base.

Questions on Meaning

1. What is the relationship, according to McIntosh, between unacknowledged privilege and unconscious oppression? How does such privilege lead to oppression, and how does she propose that the issue be addressed?

2. How does McIntosh distinguish between earned strength and unearned power? What is the significance of this distinction to her argument?

3. What does McIntosh mean by "the myth of meritocracy"? How is the notion of meritocracy related to issues of privilege and power?

Questions on Rhetorical Strategy and Style

1. A key to effective persuasion is the establishment of *ethos*, or the credibility of the writer. How does McIntosh establish *ethos* in the opening paragraphs of this essay? Specifically, how does her reference to women's studies work enhance her credibility?

2. How do you respond to the simile of the invisible knapsack? In what ways does the simile contribute to the effectiveness of the essay?

3. What is the effect of McIntosh's list of white privileges? How would the essay's impact have been altered had she placed this material in a paragraph rather than a numbered list?

Writing Assignments

1. Write a brief essay explaining your immediate response to this essay. Examine how your response is informed by your own gender, race, class, or ethnicity.

2. This essay was originally published in 1988. Focusing on several items in McIntosh's list, write an essay describing the extent to which the issue she raises remains relevant today.

3. Identify items on McIntosh's list that resonate with your own experience. Using these items as a focal point, write an essay responding to her question, "What will we do with such knowledge?"

American Ignorance of War

Czeslaw Milosz

*Czeslaw Milosz (1911–) was born in Lithuania, under
Czarist Russia's control, and was living in Poland when
Germany invaded and occupied that country in 1939. In
1946, he became a diplomat for Poland's Communist government, until 1951 when he defected to the West and
eventually settled in the United States. He began writing
poetry when still a university student in Lithuania and became what many critics have called Poland's greatest modern poet, although his works were not published in that
country before 1980. In America, he became a professor at
the University of California at Berkeley and continued
writing poetry, fiction, and nonfiction. His key books include over a dozen books of poetry, two novels and the nonfiction books* The Captive Mind *(1953), from which the
following selection comes;* Native Realm *(1983); and* The
History of Polish Literature *(1983). In 1980 Milosz received the Nobel Prize for Literature. The excerpt following was published soon after Milosz came to the United
States, and in it he explains to Americans a great difference
between our perceptions of the world and what he has experienced under totalitarian regimes.*

1   "Are Americans *really* stupid?" I was asked in Warsaw. In the   1
voice of the man who posed the question, there was despair,
as well as the hope that I would contradict him. This question reveals the attitude of the average person in the people's democra-
cies toward the West: it is despair mixed with a residue of hope.

During the last few years, the West has given these people a number of reasons to despair politically. In the case of the intellectual, other, more complicated reasons come into play. Before the countries of Central and Eastern Europe entered the sphere of the Imperium, they lived through the Second World War. That war was much more devastating there than in the countries of Western Europe. It destroyed not only their economies, but also a great many values which had seemed till then unshakable.

Man tends to regard the order he lives in as *natural*. The houses he passes on his way to work seem more like rocks rising out of the earth than like products of human hands. He considers the work he does in his office or factory as essential to the harmonious functioning of the world. The clothes he wears are exactly what they should be, and he laughs at the idea that he might equally well be wearing a Roman toga or medieval armor. He respects and envies a minister of state or a bank director, and regards the possession of a considerable amount of money as the main guarantee of peace and security. He cannot believe that one day a rider may appear on a street he knows well, where cats sleep and children play, and start catching passersby with his lasso. He is accustomed to satisfying those of his physiological needs which are considered private as discreetly as possible, without realizing that such a pattern of behavior is not common to all human societies. In a word, he behaves a little like Charlie Chaplin in *The Gold Rush,* bustling about in a shack poised precariously on the edge of a cliff.

His first stroll along a street littered with glass from bomb-shattered windows shakes his faith in the "naturalness" of his world. The wind scatters papers from hastily evacuated offices, papers labeled "Confidential" or "Top Secret" that evoke visions of safes, keys, conferences, couriers, and secretaries. Now the wind blows them through the street for anyone to read; yet no one does, for each man is more urgently concerned with finding a loaf of bread. Strangely enough, the world goes on even though the offices and secret files have lost all meaning. Farther down the street, he stops before a house split in half by a bomb, the privacy of people's homes—the family smells, the warmth of the beehive life, the furniture preserving the memory of loves and hatreds—cut open to public view. The house itself, no longer a rock, but a scaffolding of plaster, concrete, and brick; and on the third floor, a solitary white bathtub, rain-rinsed of all recollection of those who once bathed in it. Its formerly influential and respected owners, now destitute, walk the fields in search of stray potatoes. Thus overnight money loses its value and becomes a meaningless mass of printed paper. His walk takes him past a little boy poking a stick into a heap of smoking ruins and whistling a song about the great leader who will preserve the nation against all enemies. The song remains, but the leader of yesterday is already part of an extinct past.

5   He finds he acquires new habits quickly. Once, had he stumbled upon a corpse on the street, he would have called the police. A crowd would have gathered, and much talk and comment would have ensued. Now he knows he must avoid the dark body lying in the gutter, and refrain from asking unnecessary questions. The man who fired the gun must have had his reasons; he might well have been executing an Underground sentence.

Nor is the average European accustomed to thinking of his native city as divided into segregated living areas, but a single decree can force him to this new pattern of life and thought. Quarter A may suddenly be designated for one race; B, for a second; C, for a third. As the resettlement deadline approaches, the streets become filled with long lines of wagons, carts, wheelbarrows, and people carrying bundles, beds, chests, caldrons, and bird cages. When all the moves are effected, 2,000 people may find themselves in a building that once housed 200, but each man is at last in the proper area. Then high walls are erected around quarter C, and daily a given lot of men, women, and children are loaded into wagons that take them off to specially constructed factories where they are scientifically slaughtered and their bodies burned.

And even the rider with the lasso appears, in the form of a military van waiting at the corner of a street. A man passing that corner meets a leveled rifle, raises his hands, is pushed into the van, and from that moment is lost to his family and friends. He may be sent to a concentration camp, or he may face a firing squad, his lips sealed with plaster lest he cry out against the state; but, in any case, he serves as a warning to his fellow men. Perhaps one might escape such a fate by remaining at home. But the father of a family must go out in order to provide bread and soup for his wife and children; and every night they worry about whether or not he will return. Since these conditions last for years, everyone gradually comes to look upon the city as a jungle, and upon the fate of twentieth-century man as identical with that of a caveman living in the midst of powerful monsters.

It was once thought obvious that a man bears the same name and surname throughout his entire life; now it proves wiser for many reasons to change them and to memorize a new and fabricated biography. As a result, the records of the civilian state become completely confused. Everyone ceases to care about formalities, so that marriage, for example, comes to mean little more than living together.

Respectable citizens used to regard banditry as a crime. Today, bank robbers are heroes because the money they steal is destined for the Underground. Usually they are young boys, mothers' boys, but their appearance is deceiving. The killing of a man presents no great moral problem to them.

10 The nearness of death destroys shame. Men and women change as soon as they know that the date of their execution has been fixed by a fat little man with shiny boots and a riding crop. They copulate in public, on the small bit of ground surrounded by barbed wire—their last home on earth. Boys and girls in their teens, about to go off to the barricades to fight against tanks with pistols and bottles of gasoline, want to enjoy their youth and lose their respect for standards of decency.

Which world is "natural"? That which existed before, or the world of war? Both are natural, if both are within the realm of one's experience. All the concepts men live by are a product of the historic formation in which they find themselves. Fluidity and constant change are the characteristics of phenomena. And man is so plastic a being that one can even conceive of the day when a thoroughly self-respecting citizen will crawl on all fours, sporting a tail of brightly colored feathers as a sign of conformity to the order he lives in.

The man of the East cannot take Americans seriously because they have never undergone the experiences that teach men how relative their judgements and thinking habits are. Their resultant lack of imagination is appalling. Because they were born and raised in a given social order and in a given system of values, they believe that any other order must be "unnatural," and that it cannot last because it is incompatible with human nature. But even they may one day know fire, hunger, and the sword. In all probability this is what will occur; for it is hard to believe that when one half of the world is living through terrible disasters, the other half can continue a nineteenth-century mode of life, learning about the distress of its distant fellow men only from movies and newspapers. Recent examples teach us that this cannot be. An inhabitant of Warsaw or Budapest once looked at newsreels of bombed Spain or burning Shanghai, but in the end he learned how these and many other catastrophes appear in actuality. He read a gloomy tale of the NKVD until one day he found he himself had to deal with it. *If something exists in one place, it will exist everywhere.* This is the conclusion he draws from his observations, and so he has no particular faith in the momentary prosperity of America. He suspects that the years 1933–1945 in Europe prefigure what will occur elsewhere. A hard school, where ignorance was punished not by bad marks but by death, has taught him to think sociologically and historically. But it has not freed him from irrational feelings. He is apt to believe in theories that foresee violent changes in the countries of the West, for he finds it unjust that they should escape the hardships he had to undergo.

Questions on Meaning

1. What does Milosz mean by "the natural world"?
2. Why is it that Eastern Europeans "cannot take Americans seriously"? How seriously can Americans take themselves in this respect?
3. Fully explain the meaning of Milosz's statement: "If something exists in one place, it will exist everywhere."

Questions on Rhetorical Strategy and Style

1. The essay uses examples to show us what life is like under a totalitarian government. Reread that section of the essay and identify three specific descriptions that you find vivid, and explain how the language used creates this effect.
2. Milosz describes the Nazi occupation of Poland without referring to Nazis or historical specifics. In this section of the essay, from paragraph 4 through 10, he uses the present tense to describe these changed conditions. What are the effects on the reader of his decisions to write the essay in this way? What would be lost if it had been written as conventional history in past tense with names, places, and dates?

Writing Assignments

1. Milosz's statement that the peaceful democratic world in which Americans live is no more natural than the uncertain, violent world of authoritarian and military rule is somewhat shocking to many readers. How did you react as you read this? What is the difference between *knowing about* a horrible experience such as Milosz describes, or the fact of 6 million Jews put to death in Nazi death camps, and actually *experiencing or observing* it firsthand?
2. The title of this 1953 essay implies Americans are ignorant of war, but the essay actually means Americans are ignorant of the effects of being occupied by an opposing force during wartime. How ignorant are Americans of war itself, particularly after the extensive television coverage of our last two wars: the Vietnam War and the Gulf War? Neither was fought on American soil, of course, but in both the death of American soldiers was well publicized. Write an essay in which you describe how the country as a whole views war.

3. This essay, like almost any reading in world history, is a blunt re-
    minder that human beings are capable of great atrocities and vio-
    lence. What is your view of human nature? Write an essay in
    which you address this question. Try to define your view of
    human nature in a way that includes both your everyday outlook
    and your understanding of the darker realities.

The Singer Solution to World Poverty

Peter Singer

One of the most renowned–and reviled–philosophers in recent times, Peter Singer (1946–) was born in Melbourne, Australia and educated at the University of Melbourne and Oxford University. In addition to writing extensively on a wide range of ethical issues, he has also taught at universities around the world, including his two alma maters, Harvard, Stanford, Yale, Wesleyan, and New York University. Perhaps his most famous (or infamous) appointment, however, came in 1998, when he was named Ira W. DeCamp Professor of Bioethics, University Center for Human Values, Princeton University. Protests against the appointment focused largely on his exploration of sensitive issues such as euthanasia, as well as his critique of traditional Judeo-Christian ethics. Singer himself claims that his "entire philosophy is shaped by an abhorrence of suffering and cruelty." That abhorrence led to one of his most acclaimed books, Animal Liberation: A New Ethics for Our Treatment of Animals, *published in 1975. He has written and edited more than a dozen other books, most of them controversial, including* Practical Ethics *(1979),* Should the Baby Live? The Problem of Handicapped Infants *(1985),* Rethinking Life and Death *(1994), and* The Life You Can Save: Acting Now to End World Poverty *(2009). The impact of Singer's work has been significant; his books have been translated into more than twenty different languages, and he was named one of "The* Time *100," Time Magazine's list of the world's most influential people, in 2005. In the following selection, originally published in 1999, Singer contends that spending money on luxuries when children around the world are starving constitutes a moral choice.*

1 In the Brazilian film *Central Station*, Dora is a retired school-teacher who makes ends meet by sitting at the station writing letters for illiterate people. Suddenly she has an opportunity to pocket a thousand dollars. All she has to do is persuade a homeless nine-year-old boy to follow her to an address she has been given. (She is told he will be adopted by wealthy foreigners.) She delivers the boy, gets the money, spends some of it on a television set, and settles down to enjoy her new acquisition. Her neighbor spoils the fun, however, by telling her that the boy was too old to be adopted— he will be killed and his organs sold for transplantation. Perhaps Dora knew this all along, but after her neighbor's plain speaking, she spends a troubled night. In the morning Dora resolves to take the boy back.

Suppose Dora had told her neighbor that it is a tough world, other people have nice new TVs too, and if selling the kid is the only way she can get one, well, he was only a street kid. She would then have become, in the eyes of the audience, a monster. She redeems herself only by being prepared to bear considerable risks to save the boy.

At the end of the movie, in cinemas in the affluent nations of the world, people who would have been quick to condemn Dora if she had not rescued the boy go home to places far more comfortable than her apartment. In fact, the average family in the United States spends almost one third of its income on things that are no more necessary to them than Dora's new TV was to her. Going out to nice restaurants, buying new clothes because the old ones are no longer stylish, vacationing at beach resorts—so much of our income is spent on things not essential to the preservation of our lives and health. Donated to one of a number of charitable agencies, that money could mean the difference between life and death for children in need.

All of which raises a question: in the end, what is the ethical distinction between a Brazilian who sells a homeless child to organ peddlers and an American who already has a TV and upgrades to a better one, knowing that the money could be donated to an organization that would use it to save the lives of kids in need?

Of course, there are several differences between the two situations that could support different moral judgments about them. For one thing, to be able to consign a child to death when he is standing right in front of you takes a chilling kind of heartlessness; it is much easier to ignore an appeal for money to help children you will never meet. Yet for a utilitarian philosopher like myself—that is, one who judges whether acts are right or wrong by their consequences—if the upshot of the American's failure to donate the money is that one more kid dies on the streets of a Brazilian city, then it is in some sense just as bad as selling the kid to the organ peddlers. But one doesn't need to embrace my utilitarian ethic to see that at the very least, there is a troubling incongruity in being so quick to condemn Dora for taking the child to the organ peddlers while at the same time not regarding the American consumer's behavior as raising a serious moral issue.

In his 1996 book, *Living High and Letting Die*, the New York University philosopher Peter Unger presented an ingenious series of imaginary examples designed to probe our intuitions about whether it is wrong to live well without giving substantial amounts of money to help people who are hungry, malnourished, or dying from easily treatable illness like diarrhea. Here's my paraphrase of one of these examples:

Bob is close to retirement. He has invested most of his savings in a very rare and valuable old car, a Bugatti, which he has not been able to insure. The Bugatti is his pride and joy. In addition to the pleasure he gets from driving and caring for his car, Bob knows that its rising market value means that he will always be able to sell it and live comfortably after retirement. One day when Bob is out for a drive, he parks the Bugatti near the end of a railway siding and goes for a walk up the track. As he does so, he sees that a runaway train, with no one aboard, is running down the railway track. Looking farther down the track, he sees the small figure of a child very likely to be killed by the runaway train. He can't stop the train and the child is too far away to warn of the danger, but he can throw a switch that will divert the train down the siding where his Bugatti is parked. Then nobody will be killed—but the train will destroy his Bugatti. Thinking of his joy in owning the car and the financial security it represents, Bob decides not to throw the switch. The child is killed. For many years to come, Bob enjoys owning his Bugatti and the financial security it represents.

Bob's conduct, most of us will immediately respond, was gravely wrong. Unger agrees. But then he reminds us that we too have opportunities to save the lives of children. We can give to organizations like UNICEF or Oxfam America. How much would we have to give one of these organizations to have a high probability of saving the life of a child threatened by easily preventable diseases? (I do not believe that children are more worth saving than adults, but since no one can argue that children have brought their poverty on themselves, focusing on them simplifies the issues.) Unger called up some experts and used the information they provided to offer some plausible estimates that include the cost of raising money, administrative expenses, and the cost of delivering aid where it is most needed. By his calculation, $200 in donations would help a sickly two-year-old transform into a healthy six-year-old—offering safe passage through childhood's most dangerous years. To show how practical philosophical argument can be, Unger even tells his readers that they can easily donate funds by using their credit card and calling one of these toll-free numbers: (800) 367-5437 for UNICEF; (800) 693-2687 for Oxfam America.

Now you too have the information you need to save a child's life. How should you judge yourself if you don't do it? Think again about Bob and his Bugatti. Unlike Dora, Bob did not have to look into the eyes of the child he was sacrificing for his own material comfort. The child was a complete stranger to him and too far away to relate to in an intimate, personal way. Unlike Dora too, he did not mislead the child or initiate the chain of events imperiling him. In all these respects, Bob's situation resembles that of people able but unwilling to donate to overseas aid and differs from Dora's situation.

10   If you still think that it was very wrong of Bob not to throw the   10 switch that would have diverted the train and saved the child's life, then it is hard to see how you could deny that it is also very wrong not to send money to one of the organizations listed above. Unless, that is, there is some morally important difference between the two situations that I have overlooked.

Is it the practical uncertainties about whether aid will really reach the people who need it? Nobody who knows the world of overseas aid can doubt that such uncertainties exist. But Unger's figure of $200 to save a child's life was reached after he had made conservative assumptions about the proportion of the money donated that will actually reach its target.

One genuine difference between Bob and those who can afford to donate to overseas aid organizations but don't is that only Bob can save the child on the tracks, whereas there are hundreds of millions of people who can give $200 to overseas aid organizations. The problem is that most of them aren't doing it. Does this mean that it is all right for you not to do it?

Suppose that there were more owners of priceless vintage cars—Carol, Dave, Emma, Fred, and so on, down to Ziggy—all in exactly the same situation as Bob, with their own siding and their own switch, all sacrificing the child in order to preserve their own cherished car. Would that make it all right for Bob to do the same? To answer this question affirmatively is to endorse follow-the-crowd ethics—the kind of ethics that led many Germans to look away when the Nazi atrocities were being committed. We do not excuse them because others were behaving no better.

We seem to lack a sound basis for drawing a clear moral line between Bob's situation and that of any reader of this article with $200 to spare who does not donate it to an overseas aid agency. These readers seem to be acting at least as badly as Bob was acting when he chose to let the runaway train hurtle toward the unsuspecting child. In the light of this conclusion, I trust that many readers will reach for the phone and donate that $200. Perhaps you should do it before reading further.

15 Now that you have distinguished yourself morally from people who put their vintage cars ahead of a child's life, how about treating yourself and your partner to dinner at your favorite restaurant? But wait. The money you will spend at the restaurant could also help save the lives of children overseas! True, you weren't planning to blow $200 tonight, but if you were to give up dining out just for one month, you would easily save that amount. And what is one month's dining out compared to a child's life? There's the rub. Since there are a lot of desperately needy children in the world, there will always be another child whose life you could save for another $200. Are you therefore obliged to keep giving until you have nothing left? At what point can you stop?

Hypothetical examples can easily become farcical. Consider Bob. How far past losing the Bugatti should he go? Imagine that Bob had got his foot stuck in the track of the siding, and if he diverted the train, then before it rammed the car it would also amputate his big toe. Should he still throw the switch? What if it would amputate his foot? His entire leg?

As absurd as the Bugatti scenario gets when pushed to extremes, the point it raises is a serious one: only when the sacrifices become very significant indeed would most people be prepared to say that Bob does nothing wrong when he decides not to throw the switch. Of course, most people could be wrong; we can't decide moral issues by taking opinion polls. But consider for yourself the level of sacrifice that you would demand of Bob, and then think about how much money you would have to give away in order to make a sacrifice that is roughly equal to that. It's almost certainly much, much more than $200. For most middle-class Americans, it could easily be more like $200,000.

Isn't it counterproductive to ask people to do so much? Don't we run the risk that many will shrug their shoulders and say that morality, so conceived, is fine for saints but not for them? I accept that we are unlikely to see, in the near or even medium-term future, a world in which it is normal for wealthy Americans to give the bulk of their wealth to strangers. When it comes to praising or blaming people for what they do, we tend to use a standard that is relative to some conception of normal behavior. Comfortably off Americans who give, say, 10 percent of their income to overseas aid organizations are so far ahead of most of their equally comfortable fellow citizens that I wouldn't go out of my way to chastise them for not doing more. Nevertheless, they should be doing much more, and they are in no position to criticize Bob for failing to make the much greater sacrifice of his Bugatti.

At this point various objections may crop up. Someone may say, "If every citizen living in the affluent nations contributed his or her share, I wouldn't have to make such a drastic sacrifice, because long before such levels were reached the resources would have been there to save the lives of all those children dying from lack of food or medical care. So why should I give more than my fair share?" Another, related objection is that the government ought to increase its overseas aid allocations, since that would spread the burden more equitably across all taxpayers.

20   Yet the question of how much we ought to give is a matter to be decided in the real world—and that, sadly, is a world in which we know that most people do not, and in the immediate future will not, give substantial amounts to overseas aid agencies. We know too that at least in the next year, the United States government is not going to meet even the very modest United Nations-recommended target of 0.7 percent of gross national product; at the moment it lags far below that, at 0.09 percent, not even half of Japan's 0.22 percent or a tenth of Denmark's 0.97 percent. Thus, we know that the money we can give beyond that theoretical "fair share" is still going to save lives that would otherwise be lost. While the idea that no one need do more than his or her fair share is a powerful one, should it prevail if we know that others are not doing their fair share and that children will die preventable deaths unless we do more than our fair share? That would be taking fairness too far.

Thus, this ground for limiting how much we ought to give also fails. In the world as it is now, I can see no escape from the conclusion that each one of us with wealth surplus to his or her essential needs should be giving most of it to help people suffering from poverty so dire as to be life-threatening. That's right: I'm saying that you shouldn't buy that new car, take that cruise, redecorate the house, or get that pricy new suit. After all, a thousand-dollar suit could save five children's lives.

So how does my philosophy break down in dollars and cents? An American household with an income of $50,000 spends around $30,000 annually on necessities, according to the Conference Board, a nonprofit economic research organization. Therefore, for a household bringing in $50,000 a year, donations to help the world's poor should be as close as possible to $20,000. The $30,000 required for necessities holds for higher incomes as well. So a household making $100,000 could cut a yearly check for $70,000. Again, the formula is simple: whatever money you're spending on luxuries, not necessities, should be given away.

Now, evolutionary psychologists tell us that human nature just isn't sufficiently altruistic to make it plausible that many people will sacrifice so much for strangers. On the facts of human nature, they might be right, but they would be wrong to draw a moral conclusion from those facts. If it is the case that we ought to do things that, predictably, most of us won't do, then let's face that fact head-on. Then, if we value the life of a child more than going to fancy restaurants, the next time we dine out we will know that we could have done something better with our money. If that makes living a morally decent life extremely arduous, well, then that is the way things are. If we don't do it, then we should at least know that we are failing to live a morally decent life—not because it is good to wallow in guilt but because knowing where we should be going is the first step toward heading in that direction.

When Bob first grasped the dilemma that faced him as he stood by that railway switch, he must have thought how extraordinarily unlucky he was to be placed in a situation in which he must choose between the life of an innocent child and the sacrifice of most of his savings. But he was not unlucky at all. We are all in that situation.

Questions on Meaning

1. Singer explains that a utilitarian philosopher "judges whether acts are right or wrong by their consequences." How do other philosophies or value systems judge right and wrong? How significant do you consider the differences between philosophies?
2. How is the failure to donate substantial amounts to lifesaving charities equivalent to killing children, according to Singer? How compelling do you find this analogy? Explain your response.
3. How do you think Singer would measure the success of his appeal—by how many minds he opens, by how much money people give, or by some other measure?

Questions on Rhetorical Strategy and Style

1. What is the impact of Singer's opening example? How does the story of *Central Station* set the tone for the entire essay?
2. The legitimacy of Singer's argument relies on the validity of the comparisons he makes between his two primary examples and the reality of middle- and upper-class lives. List the points of comparison and evaluate their effectiveness in supporting his argument.
3. Midway through the essay Singer shifts from analysis to directly addressing the reader; in fact, he calls upon the reader to act in the moment. How effective do you find this technique? Explain your response.

Writing Assignments

1. Conduct a general analysis of your family's financial situation, subtracting the cost of necessities from your household income— the resulting figure being what Singer believes you should contribute to fight world poverty. Using this information, write a response to Singer's essay. What arguments can you make for not contributing that figure?
2. Conduct research on the operations of either Oxfam America or UNICEF, consulting not only the organization's own materials but commentaries from other sources. Write a report based on your research, focusing on the effectiveness of the organization in dealing with world poverty.

Small Change: Why the Revolution Will Not be Tweeted

Malcolm Gladwell

Malcolm Gladwell (1963–) was born in England but grew up in Canada. He majored in history at the University of Toronto, graduating in 1984. In 1987 he began work as a reporter for the Washington Post *where he worked first as a science writer and then as New York bureau chief. In 1996 he moved to* The New Yorker *where he works as a staff writer. His published works include* The Tipping Point *(2001), a best-selling book theorizing the impact of building trends on events and ideas;* Blink: The Power of Thinking Without Thinking *(2005), in which he explores the power of the mind to make splitsecond decisions; and* Outliers: The Story of Success *(2008). In this selection, first published in* The New Yorker, *Gladwell asks whether the activism that occurs through social media today carries any risk and produces the level of change effected by the social activism during the height of the civil rights movement in the U.S.*

1   At four-thirty in the afternoon on Monday, February 1, 1960, four college students sat down at the lunch counter at the Woolworth's in downtown Greensboro, North Carolina. They were freshmen at North Carolina A.&T., a black college a mile or so away.

"I'd like a cup of coffee, please," one of the four, Ezell Blair, said to the waitress.

"We don't serve Negroes here," she replied.

The Woolworth's lunch counter was a long L-shaped bar that could seat sixty-six people, with a standup snack bar at one end. The seats were for whites. The snack bar was for blacks. Another employee, a black woman who worked at the steam table, approached the students and tried to warn them away. "You're acting stupid, ignorant!" she said. They didn't move. Around five-thirty, the front doors to the store were locked. The four still didn't move. Finally, they left by a side door. Outside, a small crowd had gathered, including a photographer from the Greensboro *Record*. "I'll be back tomorrow with A.&T. College," one of the students said.

5   By next morning, the protest had grown to twenty-seven men and four women, most from the same dormitory as the original four. The men were dressed in suits and ties. The students had brought their schoolwork, and studied as they sat at the counter. On Wednesday, students from Greensboro's "Negro" secondary school, Dudley High, joined in, and the number of protesters swelled to eighty. By Thursday, the protesters numbered three hundred, including three white women, from the Greensboro campus of the University of North Carolina. By Saturday, the sit-in had reached six hundred. People spilled out onto the street. White teen-agers waved Confederate flags. Someone threw a firecracker. At noon, the A.&T. football team arrived. "Here comes the wrecking crew," one of the white students shouted.

By the following Monday, sit-ins had spread to Winston-Salem, twenty-five miles away, and Durham, fifty miles away. The day after that, students at Fayetteville State Teachers College and at Johnson C. Smith College, in Charlotte, joined in, followed on Wednesday by students at St. Augustine's College and Shaw University, in Raleigh. On Thursday and Friday, the protest crossed state lines, surfacing in Hampton and Portsmouth, Virginia, in Rock Hill, South Carolina, and in Chattanooga, Tennessee. By the end of the month, there were sit-ins throughout the South, as far west as Texas. "I asked every student I met what the first day of the sitdowns had been like on his campus," the political theorist Michael Walzer wrote in *Dissent*. "The answer was always the same: 'It was like a fever. Everyone wanted to go.' " Some seventy thousand students eventually took part. Thousands were arrested and untold thousands more radicalized. These events in the early sixties became a civil-rights war that engulfed the South for the rest of the decade—and it happened without e-mail, texting, Facebook, or Twitter.

The world, we are told, is in the midst of a revolution. The new tools of social media have reinvented social activism. With Facebook and Twitter and the like, the traditional relationship between political authority and popular will has been upended, making it easier for the powerless to collaborate, coördinate, and give voice to their concerns. When ten thousand protesters took to the streets in Moldova in the spring of 2009 to protest against their country's Communist government, the action was dubbed the Twitter Revolution, because of the means by which the demonstrators had been brought together. A few months after that, when student protests rocked Tehran, the State Department took the unusual step of asking Twitter to suspend scheduled maintenance of its Web site, because the Administration didn't want such a critical organizing tool out of service at the height of the demonstrations. "Without Twitter the people of Iran would not have felt empowered and confident to stand up for freedom and democracy," Mark Pfeifle, a former national-security adviser, later wrote, calling for Twitter to be nominated for the Nobel Peace Prize. Where activists were once defined by their causes, they are now defined by their tools. Facebook warriors go online to push for change. "You are the best hope for us all," James K. Glassman, a former senior State Department official, told a crowd of cyber activists at a recent conference sponsored by Facebook, A. T. & T., Howcast, MTV, and Google. Sites like Facebook, Glassman said, "give the U.S. a significant competitive advantage over terrorists. Some time ago, I said that Al Qaeda was 'eating our lunch on the Internet.' That is no longer the case. Al Qaeda is stuck in Web 1.0. The Internet is now about interactivity and conversation."

These are strong, and puzzling, claims. Why does it matter who is eating whose lunch on the Internet? Are people who log on to their Facebook page really the best hope for us all? As for Moldova's so-called Twitter Revolution, Evgeny Morozov, a scholar at Stanford who has been the most persistent of digital evangelism's critics, points out that Twitter had scant internal significance in Moldova, a country where very few Twitter accounts exist. Nor does it seem to have been a revolution, not least because the protests—as Anne Applebaum suggested in the Washington *Post*—may well have been a bit of stagecraft cooked up by the government. (In a country paranoid about Romanian revanchism, the protesters flew a Romanian flag over the Parliament building.) In the Iranian case, meanwhile, the people tweeting about the demonstrations were almost all in the West. "It is time to get Twitter's role in the events in Iran right," Golnaz Esfandiari wrote, this past summer, in *Foreign Policy*. "Simply put: There was no Twitter Revolution inside Iran." The cadre of prominent bloggers, like Andrew Sullivan, who championed the role of social media in Iran, Esfandiari continued, misunderstood the situation. "Western journalists who couldn't reach—or didn't bother reaching?—people on the ground in Iran simply scrolled through the English-language tweets post with tag #iranelection," she wrote. "Through it all, no one seemed to wonder why people trying to coordinate protests in Iran would be writing in any language other than Farsi."

10   Some of this grandiosity is to be expected. Innovators tend to be solipsists. They often want to cram every stray fact and experience into their new model. As the historian Robert Darnton has written, "The marvels of communication technology in the present have produced a false consciousness about the past—even a sense that communication has no history, or had nothing of importance to consider before the days of television and the Internet." But there is something else at work here, in the outsized enthusiasm for social media. Fifty years after one of the most extraordinary episodes of social upheaval in American history, we seem to have forgotten what activism is.

Greensboro in the early nineteen-sixties was the kind of place where racial insubordination was routinely met with violence. The four students who first sat down at the lunch counter were terrified. "I suppose if anyone had come up behind me and yelled 'Boo,' I think I would have fallen off my seat," one of them said later. On the first day, the store manager notified the police chief, who immediately sent two officers to the store. On the third day, a gang of white toughs showed up at the lunch counter and stood ostentatiously behind the protesters, ominously muttering epithets such as "burr-head nigger." A local Ku Klux Klan leader made an appearance. On Saturday, as tensions grew, someone called in a bomb threat, and the entire store had to be evacuated.

The dangers were even clearer in the Mississippi Freedom Summer Project of 1964, another of the sentinel campaigns of the civil-rights movement. The Student Nonviolent Coordinating Committee recruited hundreds of Northern, largely white unpaid volunteers to run Freedom Schools, register black voters, and raise civil-rights awareness in the Deep South. "No one should go *any where* alone, but certainly not in an automobile and certainly not at night," they were instructed. Within days of arriving in Mississippi, three volunteers—Michael Schwerner, James Chaney, and Andrew Goodman—were kidnapped and killed, and, during the rest of the summer, thirty-seven black churches were set on fire and dozens of safe houses were bombed; volunteers were beaten, shot at, arrested, and trailed by pickup trucks full of armed men. A quarter of those in the program dropped out. Activism that challenges the status quo—that attacks deeply rooted problems—is not for the faint of heart.

What makes people capable of this kind of activism? The Stanford sociologist Doug McAdam compared the Freedom Summer dropouts with the participants who stayed, and discovered that the key difference wasn't, as might be expected, ideological fervor. "*All* of the applicants—participants and withdrawals alike—emerge as highly committed, articulate supporters of the goals and values of the summer program," he concluded. What mattered more was an applicant's degree of personal connection to the civil-rights movement. All the volunteers were required to provide a list of personal contacts—the people they wanted kept apprised of their activities—and participants were far more likely than dropouts to have close friends who were also going to Mississippi. High-risk activism, McAdam concluded, is a "strong-tie" phenomenon.

This pattern shows up again and again. One study of the Red Brigades, the Italian terrorist group of the nineteen-seventies, found that seventy per cent of recruits had at least one good friend already in the organization. The same is true of the men who joined the mujahideen in Afghanistan. Even revolutionary actions that look spontaneous, like the demonstrations in East Germany that led to the fall of the Berlin Wall, are, at core, strong-tie phenomena. The opposition movement in East Germany consisted of several hundred groups, each with roughly a dozen members. Each group was in limited contact with the others: at the time, only thirteen per cent of East Germans even had a phone. All they knew was that on Monday nights, outside St. Nicholas Church in downtown Leipzig, people gathered to voice their anger at the state. And the primary determinant of who showed up was "critical friends"—the more friends you had who were critical of the regime the more likely you were to join the protest.

15   So one crucial fact about the four freshmen at the Greensboro   15
lunch counter—David Richmond, Franklin McCain, Ezell Blair, and
Joseph McNeil—was their relationship with one another. McNeil was
a roommate of Blair's in A.&T.'s Scott Hall dormitory. Richmond
roomed with McCain one floor up, and Blair, Richmond, and
McCain had all gone to Dudley High School. The four would smug-
gle beer into the dorm and talk late into the night in Blair and
McNeil's room. They would all have remembered the murder of
Emmett Till in 1955, the Montgomery bus boycott that same year,
and the showdown in Little Rock in 1957. It was McNeil who
brought up the idea of a sit-in at Woolworth's. They'd discussed it for
nearly a month. Then McNeil came into the dorm room and asked
the others if they were ready. There was a pause, and McCain said, in
a way that works only with people who talk late into the night with
one another, "Are you guys chicken or not?" Ezell Blair worked up the
courage the next day to ask for a cup of coffee because he was flanked
by his roommate and two good friends from high school.

The kind of activism associated with social media isn't like this at all.
The platforms of social media are built around weak ties. Twitter is a
way of following (or being followed by) people you may never have
met. Facebook is a tool for efficiently managing your acquaintances,
for keeping up with the people you would not otherwise be able to
stay in touch with. That's why you can have a thousand "friends" on
Facebook, as you never could in real life.

This is in many ways a wonderful thing. There is strength in
weak ties, as the sociologist Mark Granovetter has observed. Our
acquaintances—not our friends—are our greatest source of new ideas
and information. The Internet lets us exploit the power of these kinds
of distant connections with marvellous efficiency. It's terrific at the
diffusion of innovation, interdisciplinary collaboration, seamlessly
matching up buyers and sellers, and the logistical functions of the
dating world. But weak ties seldom lead to high-risk activism.

In a new book called "The Dragonfly Effect: Quick, Effective,
and Powerful Ways to Use Social Media to Drive Social Change," the
business consultant Andy Smith and the Stanford Business School
professor Jennifer Aaker tell the story of Sameer Bhatia, a young Silicon Valley entrepreneur who came down with acute myelogenous
leukemia. It's a perfect illustration of social media's strengths. Bhatia

needed a bone-marrow transplant, but he could not find a match among his relatives and friends. The odds were best with a donor of his ethnicity, and there were few South Asians in the national bone-marrow database. So Bhatia's business partner sent out an e-mail explaining Bhatia's plight to more than four hundred of their acquaintances, who forwarded the e-mail to their personal contacts; Facebook pages and YouTube videos were devoted to the Help Sameer campaign. Eventually, nearly twenty-five thousand new people were registered in the bone-marrow database, and Bhatia found a match.

But how did the campaign get so many people to sign up? By not asking too much of them. That's the only way you can get someone you don't really know to do something on your behalf. You can get thousands of people to sign up for a donor registry, because doing so is pretty easy. You have to send in a cheek swab and—in the highly unlikely event that your bone marrow is a good match for someone in need—spend a few hours at the hospital. Donating bone marrow isn't a trivial matter. But it doesn't involve financial or personal risk; it doesn't mean spending a summer being chased by armed men in pickup trucks. It doesn't require that you confront socially entrenched norms and practices. In fact, it's the kind of commitment that will bring only social acknowledgment and praise.

The evangelists of social media don't understand this distinction; they seem to believe that a Facebook friend is the same as a real friend and that signing up for a donor registry in Silicon Valley today is activism in the same sense as sitting at a segregated lunch counter in Greensboro in 1960. "Social networks are particularly effective at increasing motivation," Aaker and Smith write. But that's not true. Social networks are effective at increasing *participation*—by lessening the level of motivation that participation requires. The Facebook page of the Save Darfur Coalition has 1,282,339 members, who have donated an average of nine cents apiece. The next biggest Darfur charity on Facebook has 22,073 members, who have donated an average of thirty-five cents. Help Save Darfur has 2,797 members, who have given, on average, fifteen cents. A spokesperson for the Save Darfur Coalition told *Newsweek,* "We wouldn't necessarily gauge someone's value to the advocacy movement based on what they've given. This is a powerful mechanism to engage this critical population. They inform their community, attend events, volunteer. It's not something you can measure by looking at a ledger." In other words, Facebook activism succeeds not by motivating people to make a real sacrifice but by motivating them to do the things that people do when they are not motivated enough to make a real sacrifice. We are a long way from the lunch counters of Greensboro.

The students who joined the sit-ins across the South during the winter of 1960 described the movement as a "fever." But the civil-rights movement was more like a military campaign than like a contagion. In the late nineteen-fifties, there had been sixteen sit-ins in various cities throughout the South, fifteen of which were formally organized by civil-rights organizations like the N.A.A.C.P. and CORE. Possible locations for activism were scouted. Plans were drawn up. Movement activists held training sessions and retreats for would-be protesters. The Greensboro Four were a product of this groundwork: all were members of the N.A.A.C.P. Youth Council. They had close ties with the head of the local N.A.A.C.P. chapter. They had been briefed on the earlier wave of sit-ins in Durham, and had been part of a series of movement meetings in activist churches. When the sit-in movement spread from Greensboro throughout the South, it did not spread indiscriminately. It spread to those cities which had preëxisting "movement centers"—a core of dedicated and trained activists ready to turn the "fever" into action.

20 The civil-rights movement was high-risk activism. It was also,20 crucially, strategic activism: a challenge to the establishment mounted with precision and discipline. The N.A.A.C.P. was a centralized organization, run from New York according to highly formalized operating procedures. At the Southern Christian Leadership Conference, Martin Luther King, Jr., was the unquestioned authority. At the center of the movement was the black church, which had, as Aldon D. Morris points out in his superb 1984 study, "The Origins of the Civil Rights Movement," a carefully demarcated division of labor, with various standing committees and disciplined groups. "Each group was task-oriented and coordinated its activities through authority structures," Morris writes. "Individuals were held accountable for their assigned duties, and important conflicts were resolved by the minister, who usually exercised ultimate authority over the congregation."

This is the second crucial distinction between traditional activism and its online variant: social media are not about this kind of hierarchical organization. Facebook and the like are tools for building *networks*, which are the opposite, in structure and character, of hierarchies. Unlike hierarchies, with their rules and procedures, networks aren't controlled by a single central authority. Decisions are made through consensus, and the ties that bind people to the group are loose.

This structure makes networks enormously resilient and adaptable in low-risk situations. Wikipedia is a perfect example. It doesn't have an editor, sitting in New York, who directs and corrects each entry. The effort of putting together each entry is self-organized. If every entry in Wikipedia were to be erased tomorrow, the content would swiftly be restored, because that's what happens when a network of thousands spontaneously devote their time to a task.

25   There are many things, though, that networks don't do well. Car   25
companies sensibly use a network to organize their hundreds of suppliers, but not to design their cars. No one believes that the articulation of a coherent design philosophy is best handled by a sprawling, leaderless organizational system. Because networks don't have a centralized leadership structure and clear lines of authority, they have real difficulty reaching consensus and setting goals. They can't think strategically; they are chronically prone to conflict and error. How do you make difficult choices about tactics or strategy or philosophical direction when everyone has an equal say?

The Palestine Liberation Organization originated as a network, and the international-relations scholars Mette Eilstrup-Sangiovanni and Calvert Jones argue in a recent essay in *International Security* that this is why it ran into such trouble as it grew: "Structural features typical of networks—the absence of central authority, the unchecked autonomy of rival groups, and the inability to arbitrate quarrels through formal mechanisms—made the P.L.O. excessively vulnerable to outside manipulation and internal strife."

In Germany in the nineteen-seventies, they go on, "the far more unified and successful left-wing terrorists tended to organize hierarchically, with professional management and clear divisions of labor. They were concentrated geographically in universities, where they could establish central leadership, trust, and camaraderie through regular, face-to-face meetings." They seldom betrayed their comrades in arms during police interrogations. Their counterparts on the right were organized as decentralized networks, and had no such discipline.

These groups were regularly infiltrated, and members, once arrested, easily gave up their comrades. Similarly, Al Qaeda was most dangerous when it was a unified hierarchy. Now that it has dissipated into a network, it has proved far less effective.

The drawbacks of networks scarcely matter if the network isn't interested in systemic change—if it just wants to frighten or humiliate or make a splash—or if it doesn't need to think strategically. But if you're taking on a powerful and organized establishment you have to be a hierarchy. The Montgomery bus boycott required the participation of tens of thousands of people who depended on public transit to get to and from work each day. It lasted a *year*. In order to persuade those people to stay true to the cause, the boycott's organizers tasked each local black church with maintaining morale, and put together a free alternative private carpool service, with forty-eight dispatchers and forty-two pickup stations. Even the White Citizens Council, King later said, conceded that the carpool system moved with "military precision." By the time King came to Birmingham, for the climactic showdown with Police Commissioner Eugene (Bull) Connor, he had a budget of a million dollars, and a hundred full-time staff members on the ground, divided into operational units. The operation itself was divided into steadily escalating phases, mapped out in advance. Support was maintained through consecutive mass meetings rotating from church to church around the city.

30 Boycotts and sit-ins and nonviolent confrontations—which were 30
the weapons of choice for the civil-rights movement—are high-risk strategies. They leave little room for conflict and error. The moment even one protester deviates from the script and responds to provocation, the moral legitimacy of the entire protest is compromised. Enthusiasts for social media would no doubt have us believe that King's task in Birmingham would have been made infinitely easier had he been able to communicate with his followers through Facebook, and contented himself with tweets from a Birmingham jail. But networks are messy: think of the ceaseless pattern of correction and revision, amendment and debate, that characterizes Wikipedia. If Martin Luther King, Jr., had tried to do a wiki-boycott in Montgomery, he would have been steamrollered by the white power structure. And of what use would a digital communication tool be in a town where ninety-eight per cent of the black community could be reached every Sunday morning at church? The things that King

needed in Birmingham—discipline and strategy—were things that online social media cannot provide.

The bible of the social-media movement is Clay Shirky's "Here Comes Everybody." Shirky, who teaches at New York University, sets out to demonstrate the organizing power of the Internet, and he begins with the story of Evan, who worked on Wall Street, and his friend Ivanna, after she left her smart phone, an expensive Sidekick, on the back seat of a New York City taxicab. The telephone company transferred the data on Ivanna's lost phone to a new phone, where-upon she and Evan discovered that the Sidekick was now in the hands of a teen-ager from Queens, who was using it to take photographs of herself and her friends.

When Evan e-mailed the teen-ager, Sasha, asking for the phone back, she replied that his "white ass" didn't deserve to have it back. Miffed, he set up a Web page with her picture and a description of what had happened. He forwarded the link to his friends, and they forwarded it to their friends. Someone found the MySpace page of Sasha's boyfriend, and a link to it found its way onto the site. Some-one found her address online and took a video of her home while dri-ving by; Evan posted the video on the site. The story was picked up by the news filter Digg. Evan was now up to ten e-mails a minute. He created a bulletin board for his readers to share their stories, but it crashed under the weight of responses. Evan and Ivanna went to the police, but the police filed the report under "lost," rather than "stolen," which essentially closed the case. "By this point millions of readers were watching," Shirky writes, "and dozens of mainstream news outlets had covered the story." Bowing to the pressure, the N.Y.P.D. reclassified the item as "stolen." Sasha was arrested, and Evan got his friend's Sidekick back.

Shirky's argument is that this is the kind of thing that could never have happened in the pre-Internet age—and he's right. Evan could never have tracked down Sasha. The story of the Sidekick would never have been publicized. An army of people could never have been assembled to wage this fight. The police wouldn't have bowed to the pressure of a lone person who had misplaced something as trivial as a cell phone. The story, to Shirky, illustrates "the ease and speed with which a group can be mobilized for the right kind of cause" in the Internet age.

Shirky considers this model of activism an upgrade. But it is simply a form of organizing which favors the weak-tie connections that give us access to information over the strong-tie connections that help us persevere in the face of danger. It shifts our energies from organizations that promote strategic and disciplined activity and toward those which promote resilience and adaptability. It makes it easier for activists to express themselves, and harder for that expression to have any impact. The instruments of social media are well suited to making the existing social order more efficient. They are not a natural enemy of the status quo. If you are of the opinion that all the world needs is a little buffing around the edges, this should not trouble you. But if you think that there are still lunch counters out there that need integrating it ought to give you pause.

35   Shirky ends the story of the lost Sidekick by asking, portentously, 35 "What happens next?"—no doubt imagining future waves of digital protesters. But he has already answered the question. What happens next is more of the same. A networked, weak-tie world is good at things like helping Wall Streeters get phones back from teen-age girls. *Viva la revolución.*

Questions on Meaning

1. What is the popular view of how social media helped to shape events in Moldova, Romania, and Iran? What does Gladwell assert about how social change actually did occur in those countries?
2. What is the author's explanation to his question, "What makes people capable of this kind of activism?" What conditions did the civil rights activists encounter in the South in 1964?
3. How does social media activism differ from the kind of activism associated with the civil rights movement? What are the critical distinctions, according to the author?
4. What is Clay Shirky's perspective on the "organizing power of the Internet"? In what ways does Gladwell disagree with him?"

Questions on Rhetorical Strategy and Style

1. Why does the author begin his essay with the protest staged by the students at Woolworth's in 1960? In what way does it form the foundation for his argument?
2. What kinds of sources does the author reference in order to strengthen his argument? How does he set up and integrate those sources to establish their credibility?
3. How would you characterize Gladwell's style of writing? What makes that style credible for intelligent readers, but accessible and engaging enough to gain a large readership?

Writing Assignments

1. Write an essay about the recent Occupy Wall Street movement. In your essay describe the structure of the movement and where it fits within the author's analysis.
2. What is your opinion of the author's view of digital protest activity? Do you feel he treats social networks fairly? Why or why not? Write an essay stating your position on such questions.
3. Gladwell claims that social media are not effective at creating motivation. Write a position essay in which you agree or disagree with this statement.

The Tipping Point

Malcolm Gladwell

Malcolm Gladwell (1963–   ) was born in England but grew up in Canada. He majored in history at the University of Toronto, graduating in 1984. In 1987 he began as a reporter for the Washington Post *where he worked first as a science writer and then as New York bureau chief. In 1996 he moved to the* New Yorker *where he works as a staff writer.* The Tipping Point *(2001), his best-selling book, is the source of this essay. The book theorizes the impact of building trends on events and ideas, showing that change takes place in sudden events rather than by gradual shifting.*

1 For Hush Puppies—the classic American brushed-suede shoes with the lightweight crepe sole—the Tipping Point came somewhere between late 1994 and early 1995. The brand had been all but dead until that point. Sales were down to 30,000 pairs a year, mostly to backwoods outlets and small-town family stores. Wolverine, the company that makes Hush Puppies, was thinking of phasing out the shoes that made them famous. But then something strange happened. At a fashion shoot, two Hush Puppies executives—Owen Baxter and Geoffrey Lewis—ran into a stylist from New York who told them that the classic Hush Puppies had suddenly become hip in the clubs and bars of downtown Manhattan. "We were being told," Baxter recalls, "that there were resale shops in the Village, in Soho, where the shoes were being sold. People were going to the Ma and Pa stores, the little stores that still carried them, and buying them up." Baxter and Lewis were baffled at first. It made no sense to them that shoes that were so obviously out of fashion could make a comeback. "We were told that Isaac Mizrahi was wearing the shoes himself,"

Lewis says. "I think it's fair to say that at the time we had no idea who Isaac Mizrahi was."

By the fall of 1995, things began to happen in a rush. First the designer John Bartlett called. He wanted to use Hush Puppies in his spring collection. Then another Manhattan designer, Anna Sui, called, wanting shoes for her show as well. In Los Angeles, the designer Joe Fitzgerald put a twenty-five-foot inflatable basset hound—the symbol of the Hush Puppies brand—on the roof of his Hollywood store and gutted an adjoining art gallery to turn it into a Hush Puppies boutique. While he was still painting and putting up shelves, the actor Pee-wee Herman walked in and asked for a couple of pairs. "It was total word of mouth," Fitzgerald remembers.

In 1995, the company sold 430,000 pairs of the classic Hush Puppies, and the next year it sold four times that, and the year after that still more, until Hush Puppies were once again a staple of the wardrobe of the young American male. In 1996, Hush Puppies won the prize for best accessory at the Council of Fashion Designers awards dinner at Lincoln Center, and the president of the firm stood up on the stage with Calvin Klein and Donna Karan and accepted an award for an achievement that—as he would be the first to admit— his company had almost nothing to do with. Hush Puppies had suddenly exploded, and it all started with a handful of kids in the East Village and Soho.

How did that happen? Those first few kids, whoever they were, weren't deliberately trying to promote Hush Puppies. They were wearing them precisely because no one else would wear them. Then the fad spread to two fashion designers who used the shoes to peddle something else—haute couture. The shoes were an incidental touch. No one was trying to make Hush Puppies a trend. Yet, somehow, that's exactly what happened. The shoes passed a certain point in popularity and they tipped. How does a thirty-dollar pair of shoes go from a handful of downtown Manhattan hipsters and designers to every mall in America in the space of two years?

I

5 There was a time, not very long ago, in the desperately poor New York City neighborhoods of Brownsville and East New York, when the streets would turn into ghost towns at dusk. Ordinary working

people wouldn't walk on the sidewalks. Children wouldn't ride their bicycles on the streets. Old folks wouldn't sit on stoops and park benches. The drug trade ran so rampant and gang warfare was so ubiquitous in that part of Brooklyn that most people would take to the safety of their apartment at nightfall. Police officers who served in Brownsville in the 1980s and early 1990s say that, in those years, as soon as the sun went down their radios exploded with chatter between beat officers and their dispatchers over every conceivable kind of violent and dangerous crime. In 1992, there were 2,154 murders in New York City and 626,182 serious crimes, with the weight of those crimes falling hardest in places like Brownsville and East New York. But then something strange happened. At some mysterious and critical point, the crime rate began to turn. It tipped. Within five years, murders had dropped 64.3 percent to 770 and total crimes had fallen by almost half to 355,893. In Brownsville and East New York, the sidewalks filled up again, the bicycles came back, and old folks reappeared on the stoops. "There was a time when it wasn't uncommon to hear rapid fire, like you would hear somewhere in the jungle in Vietnam," says Inspector Edward Messadri, who commands the police precinct in Brownsville. "I don't hear the gunfire anymore."[1]

The New York City police will tell you that what happened in New York was that the city's policing strategies dramatically improved. Criminologists point to the decline of the crack trade and the aging of the population. Economists, meanwhile, say that the gradual improvement in the city's economy over the course of the 1990s had the effect of employing those who might otherwise have become criminals. These are the conventional explanations for the rise and fall of social problems, but in the end none is any more satisfying than the statement that kids in the East Village caused the Hush Puppies revival. The changes in the drug trade, the population, and the economy are all long-term trends, happening all over the country. They don't explain why crime plunged in New York City so much more than in other cities around the country, and they don't explain why it all happened in such an extraordinarily short time. As for the improvements made by the police, they are important too. But there is a puzzling gap between the scale of the changes in policing and the size of the effect on places like Brownsville and East New York. After all, crime didn't just slowly ebb in New York as conditions gradually improved.

It plummeted. How can a change in a handful of economic and social indices cause murder rates to fall by two-thirds in five years?

II

The idea of the Tipping Point is very simple. It is that the best way to understand the emergence of fashion trends, the ebb and flow of crime waves, or, for that matter, the transformation of unknown books into bestsellers, or the rise of teenage smoking, or the phenomena of word of mouth, or any number of other mysterious changes that mark everyday life is to think of them as epidemics. Ideas and products and messages and behaviors spread just like viruses do.

The rise of Hush Puppies and the fall of New York's crime rate are textbook examples of epidemics in action. Although they may sound as if they don't have very much in common, they share a basic, underlying pattern. First of all, they are clear examples of contagious behavior. No one took out an advertisement and told people that the traditional Hush Puppies were cool and they should start wearing them. Those kids simply wore the shoes when they went to clubs or cafes or walked the streets of downtown New York, and in so doing exposed other people to their fashion sense. They infected them with the Hush Puppies "virus."

The crime decline in New York surely happened the same way. It wasn't that some huge percentage of would-be murderers suddenly sat up in 1993 and decided not to commit any more crimes. Nor was it that the police managed magically to intervene in a huge percentage of situations that would otherwise have turned deadly. What happened is that the small number of people in the small number of situations in which the police or the new social forces had some impact started behaving very differently, and that behavior somehow spread to other would-be criminals in similar situations. Somehow a large number of people in New York got "infected" with an anti-crime virus in a short time.

10 The second distinguishing characteristic of these two examples is 10 that in both cases little changes had big effects. All of the possible reasons for why New York's crime rate dropped are changes that happened at the margin; they were incremental changes. The crack trade leveled off. The population got a little older. The police force got a little better. Yet the effect was dramatic. So too with Hush Puppies.

How many kids are we talking about who began wearing the shoes in downtown Manhattan? Twenty? Fifty? One hundred—at the most? Yet their actions seem to have single-handedly started an international fashion trend.

Finally, both changes happened in a hurry. They didn't build steadily and slowly. It is instructive to look at a chart of the crime rate in New York City from, say, the mid-1960s to the late 1990s. It looks like a giant arch. In 1965, there were 200,000 crimes in the city and from that point on the number begins a sharp rise, doubling in two years and continuing almost unbroken until it hits 650,000 crimes a year in the mid-1970s. It stays steady at that level for the next two decades, before plunging downward in 1992 as sharply as it rose thirty years earlier. Crime did not taper off. It didn't gently decelerate. It hit a certain point and jammed on the brakes.

These three characteristics—one, contagiousness; two, the fact that little causes can have big effects; and three, that change happens not gradually but at one dramatic moment—are the same three principles that define how measles moves through a grade-school classroom or the flu attacks every winter. Of the three, the third trait—the idea that epidemics can rise or fall in one dramatic moment—is the most important, because it is the principle that makes sense of the first two and that permits the greatest insight into why modern change happens the way it does. The name given to that one dramatic moment in an epidemic when everything can change all at once is the Tipping Point.

III

A world that follows the rules of epidemics is a very different place from the world we think we live in now. Think, for a moment, about the concept of contagiousness. If I say that word to you, you think of colds and the flu or perhaps something very dangerous like HIV or Ebola. We have, in our minds, a very specific, biological notion of what contagiousness means. But if there can be epidemics of crime or epidemics of fashion, there must be all kinds of things just as contagious as viruses. Have you ever thought about yawning, for instance? Yawning is a surprisingly powerful act. Just because you read the word "yawning" in the previous two sentences—and the two additional "yawns" in this sentence—a good number of you will probably yawn within the next few minutes. Even as I'm writing this, I've yawned twice. If you're reading this in a public place, and you've just yawned, chances are that a good proportion of everyone who saw you yawn is now yawning too, and a good proportion of the people watching the people who watched you yawn are now yawning as well, and on and on, in an ever-widening, yawning circle.[2]

Yawning is incredibly contagious. I made some of you reading this yawn simply by writing the word "yawn." The people who yawned when they saw you yawn, meanwhile, were infected by the sight of you yawning—which is a second kind of contagion. They might even have yawned if they only heard you yawn, because yawning is also aurally contagious: if you play an audiotape of a yawn to blind people, they'll yawn too. And finally, if you yawned as you read this, did the thought cross your mind—however unconsciously and fleetingly—that you might be tired? I suspect that for some of you it did, which means that yawns can also be emotionally contagious. Simply by writing the word, I can plant a feeling in your mind. Can the flu virus do that? Contagiousness, in other words, is an unexpected property of all kinds of things, and we have to remember that, if we are to recognize and diagnose epidemic change.

15   The second of the principles of epidemics—that little changes   15
can somehow have big effects—is also a fairly radical notion. We are, as humans, heavily socialized to make a kind of rough approximation between cause and effect. If we want to communicate a strong emotion, if we want to convince someone that, say, we love them, we realize that we need to speak passionately and forthrightly. If we want to break bad news to someone, we lower our voices and choose our words carefully. We are trained to think that what goes into any transaction or relationship or system must be directly related, in intensity and dimension, to what comes out. Consider, for example, the following puzzle. I give you a large piece of paper, and I ask you to fold it over once, and then take that folded paper and fold it over again, and then again, and again, until you have refolded the original paper 50 times. How tall do you think the final stack is going to be? In answer to that question, most people will fold the sheet in their mind's eye, and guess that the pile would be as thick as a phone book, or, if they're really courageous, they'll say that it would be as tall as a refrigerator. But the real answer is that the height of the stack would approximate the distance to the sun. And if you folded it over one

more time, the stack would be as high as the distance to the sun and back. This is an example of what in mathematics is called a geometric progression. Epidemics are another example of geometric progression: when a virus spreads through a population, it doubles and doubles again, until it has (figuratively) grown from a single sheet of paper all the way to the sun in fifty steps. As human beings we have a hard time with this kind of progression, because the end result—the effect—seems far out of proportion to the cause. To appreciate the power of epidemics, we have to abandon this expectation about proportionality. We need to prepare ourselves for the possibility that sometimes big changes follow from small events, and that sometimes these changes can happen very quickly.

This possibility of sudden change is at the center of the idea of the Tipping Point and might well be the hardest of all to accept. The expression first came into popular use in the 1970s to describe the flight to the suburbs of white living in the older cities of the American Northeast. When the number of incoming African Americans in a particular neighborhood reached a certain point—20 percent, say—sociologists observed that the community would "tip": most of the remaining whites would leave almost immediately. The Tipping Point is the moment of critical mass, the threshold, the boiling point. There was a Tipping Point for violent crime in New York in the early 1990s, and a Tipping Point for the reemergence of Hush Puppies, just as there is a Tipping Point for the introduction of any new technology. Sharp introduced the first low-priced fax machine in 1984, and sold about 80,000 of those machines in the United States in that first year. For the next three years, businesses slowly and steadily bought more and more faxes, until, in 1987, enough people had faxes that it made sense for everyone to get a fax. Nineteen eighty-seven was the fax machine Tipping Point. A million machines were sold that year, and by 1989 two million new machines had gone into operation. Cellular phones have followed the same trajectory. Through the 1990s, they got smaller and cheaper, and service got better until 1998, when the technology hit a Tipping Point and suddenly everyone had a cell phone[3]. . . .

All epidemics have Tipping Points. Jonathan Crane, a sociologist at the University of Illinois, has looked at the effect the number of role models in a community—the professionals, managers, teachers whom the Census Bureau has defined as "high status"—has on the lives of teenagers in the same neighborhood. He found little difference in pregnancy rates or school drop-out rates in neighborhoods of between 40 and 5 percent of high-status workers. But when the number of professionals dropped below 5 percent, the problems exploded. For black schoolchildren, for example, as the percentage of high-status workers falls just 2.2 percentage points—from 5.6 percent to 3.4 percent—drop-out rates more than double. At the same Tipping Point, the rates of childbearing for teenaged girls—which barely move at all up to that point—nearly double. We assume, intuitively, that neighborhoods and social problems decline in some kind of steady progression. But sometimes they may not decline steadily at all; at the Tipping Point, schools can lose control of their students, and family life can disintegrate all at once.

I remember once as a child seeing our family's puppy encounter snow for the first time. He was shocked and delighted and overwhelmed, wagging his tail nervously, sniffing about in this strange, fluffy substance, whimpering with the mystery of it all. It wasn't much colder on the morning of his first snowfall than it had been the evening before. It might have been 34 degrees the previous evening, and now it was 31 degrees. Almost nothing had changed, in other words, yet—and this was the amazing thing—everything had changed. Rain had become something entirely different. Snow! We are all, at heart, gradualists, our expectations set by the steady passage of time. But the world of the Tipping Point is a place where the unexpected becomes expected, where radical change is more than possibility. It is—contrary to all our expectations—a certainty. . . .

Notes

1. For a good summary of New York City crime statistics, see: Michael Massing, "The Blue Revolution," in the *New York Review of Books,* November 19, 1998, pp. 32–34. There is another good discussion of the anomalous nature of the New York crime drop in William Bratton and William Andrews, "What We've Learned About Policing," in *City Journal,* Spring 1999, p. 25.
2. The leader in research on yawning is Robert Provine, a psychologist at the University of Maryland. Among his papers on the subject are:
   Robert Provine, "Yawning as a Stereotyped Action Pattern and Releasing Stimulus," *Ethology* (1983), vol. 72, pp. 109–122.

Robert Provine, "Contagious Yawning and Infant Imitation," *Bulletin of the Psychonomic Society* (1989), vol. 27, no. 2, pp. 125–126.

3. The best way to understand the Tipping Point is to imagine a hypothetical outbreak of the flu. Suppose, for example, that one summer 1,000 tourists come to Manhattan from Canada carrying an untreatable strain of twenty-four-hour virus. This strain of flu has a 2 percent infection rate, which is to say that one out of every 50 people who come into close contact with someone carrying it catches the bug himself. Let's say that 50 is also exactly the number of people the average Manhattanite—in the course of riding the subways and mingling with colleagues at work—comes in contact with every day. What we have, then, is a disease in equilibrium. Those 1,000 Canadian tourists pass on the virus to 1,000 new people on the day they arrive. And the next day those 1,000 newly infected people pass on the virus to another 1,000 people, just as the original 1,000 tourists who started the epidemic are returning to health. With those getting sick and those getting well so perfectly in balance, the flu chugs along at a steady but unspectacular clip through the rest of the summer and the fall.

But then comes the Christmas season. The subways and buses get more crowded with tourists and shoppers, and instead of running into an even 50 people a day, the average Manhattanite now has close contact with, say, 55 people a day. All of a sudden, the equilibrium is disrupted. The 1,000 flu carriers now run into 55,000 people a day, and at a 2 percent infection rate, that translates into 1,100 cases the following day. Those 1,100, in turn, are now passing on their virus to 55,000 people as well, so that by day three there are 1,210 Manhattanites with the flu and by day four 1,331 and by the end of the week there are nearly 2,000, and so on up, in an exponential spiral, until Manhattan has a full-blown flu epidemic on its hands by Christmas Day. That moment when the average flu carrier went from running into 50 people a day to running into 55 people was the Tipping Point. It was the point at which an ordinary and stable phenomenon—a low-level flu outbreak—turned into a public health crisis. If you were to draw a graph of the progress of the Canadian flu epidemic, the Tipping Point would be the point on the graph where the line suddenly turned upward.

Tipping Points are moments of great sensitivity. Changes made right at the Tipping Point can have enormous consequences. Our Canadian flu became an epidemic when the number of New Yorkers running into a flu carrier jumped from 50 to 55 a day. But had that same small change happened in the opposite direction, if the number had dropped from 50 to 45, that change would have pushed the number of flu victims down to 478 within a week, and with a few weeks more at that rate, the Canadian flu would have vanished from Manhattan entirely. Cutting the number exposed from 70 to 65, or 65 to 60 or 60 to 55 would not have been sufficient to end the epidemic. But a change right at the Tipping Point, from 50 to 45, would.

The Tipping Point model has been described in several classic works of sociology. I suggest:

Mark Granovetter, "Threshold Models of Collective Behavior," *American Journal of Sociology* (1978), vol. 83, pp. 1420–1443.

Mark Granovetter and R. Soong, "Threshold Models of Diffusion and Collective Behavior," *Journal of Mathematical Sociology* (1983), vol. 9, pp. 165–179.

Thomas Schelling, "Dynamic Models of Segregation," *Journal of Mathematical Sociology* (1971), vol. I, pp. 143–186.

Thomas Schelling, *Micromotives and Macrobehavior* (New York: W. W. Norton, 1978).

Jonathan Crane, "The Epidemic Theory of Ghettos and Neighborhood Effects on Dropping Out and Teenage Childbearing," *American Journal of Sociology* (1989), vol. 95, no. 5, pp. 1226–1259.

Questions on Meaning

1. Two examples carry the basic message of the essay: the shoes called Hush Puppies, and crime in two New York City neighborhoods. Why does the rapid increase in Hush Puppies and the rapid decline in crime give the essay its title?
2. Gladwell notes the pattern of all epidemics: They are all contagious behavior; they have big effects; and they happen fast. Why does Gladwell propose that epidemics happen in many more areas than disease?
3. Does the example of the yawn work for you? Did you yawn? What other examples prove that the Tipping Point does exist?

Questions on Rhetorical Strategy and Style

1. The essay has a brief introduction and then three parts marked I, II, and III. What information is in each of the three parts? Why is the essay divided in this way?
2. The author has a reputation for making complex ideas understandable and readable. The style of the essay is conversational and detailed. Why does this style contribute to readability?
3. Many of the points in the essay are backed up with statistics. How does the use of data help to make the arguments both more clear and more understandable?

Writing Assignments

1. Trace a fashion trend that you have noticed and participated in during the past three or four years. Where did it begin (or where did you first notice it)? Why did you follow the trend?
2. Read about a current epidemic, such as AIDS. Where did it begin? When did it start to decline? What scientific explanations have been given? Would the Tipping Point argument work as well?
3. The real point of the essay is that, for the most part, people respond to all kinds of contagions. Try the experiment Gladwell uses in the essay. Sit in a public place and yawn. Count the responses. Then write about the phenomenon you observed.

"Serving in Florida" from *Nickel and Dimed*

Barbara Ehrenreich

Barbara Ehrenreich (1941–) was born in Montana and earned a Ph.D. from Rockefeller University. She is known as—and speaks of herself as—an independent and outspoken feminist, liberal, and democratic socialist. Most of her nonfiction can be classified as social criticism, including a number of books: The Hearts of Men *(1983);* Fear of Falling *(1989);* The Worst Years of Our Lives *(1990); and* Bait and Switch: The (Futile) Pursuit of the American Dream *(2005). Her* New York Times *best seller* Nickel and Dimed: On (Not) Getting By in America *(2001) exposed the reality of the working poor. Her novel* Kipper's Game *was published in 1993. She is a regular essayist for* Time *and other magazines. In this excerpt from* Nickel and Dimed: On (Not) Getting By in America, *Ehrenreich embarks on an experiment starting in a low-wage life. In doing so she learns much about the people she encounters and about herself.*

1   I could drift along like this, in some dreamy proletarian idyll, except for two things. One is management. If I have kept this subject to the margins so far it is because I still flinch to think that I spent all those weeks under the surveillance of men (and later women) whose job it was to monitor my behavior for signs of sloth, theft, drug abuse, or worse. Not that managers and especially "assistant managers" in low-wage settings like this are exactly the class enemy. Mostly, in the restaurant business, they are former cooks still capable of pinch-hitting in the kitchen, just as in hotels they are likely

to be former clerks, and paid a salary of only about $400 a week. But everyone knows they have crossed over to the other side, which is, crudely put, corporate as opposed to human. Cooks want to prepare tasty meals, servers want to serve them graciously, but managers are there for only one reason—to make sure that money is made for some theoretical entity, the corporation, which exists far away in Chicago or New York, if a corporation can be said to have a physical existence at all. Reflecting on her career, Gail tells me ruefully that she swore, years ago, never to work for a corporation again. "They don't cut you no slack. You give and you give and they take."

Managers can sit—for hours at a time if they want—but it's their job to see that no one else ever does, even when there's nothing to do, and this is why, for servers, slow times can be as exhausting as rushes. You start dragging out each little chore because if the manager on duty catches you in an idle moment he will give you something far nastier to do. So I wipe, I clean, I consolidate catsup bottles and recheck the cheesecake supply, even tour the tables to make sure the customer evaluation forms are all standing perkily in their places— wondering all the time how many calories I burn in these strictly theatrical exercises. In desperation, I even take the desserts out of their glass display case and freshen them up with whipped cream and bright new maraschino cherries; anything to look busy. When, on a particularly dead afternoon, Stu finds me glancing at a *USA Today* a customer has left behind, he assigns me to vacuum the entire floor with the broken vacuum cleaner, which has a handle only two feet long, and the only way to do that without incurring orthopedic damage is to proceed from spot to spot on your knees.

On my first Friday at Hearthside there is a "mandatory meeting for all restaurant employees," which I attend, eager for insight into our overall marketing strategy and the niche (your basic Ohio cuisine with a tropical twist?) we aim to inhabit. But there is no "we" at this meeting. Phillip, our top manager except for an occasional "consultant" sent out by corporate headquarters, opens it with a sneer: "The break room—it's disgusting. Butts in the ashtrays, newspapers lying around, crumbs." This windowless little room, which also houses the time clock for the entire hotel, is where we stash our bags and civilian clothes and take our half-hour meal breaks. But a break room is not a right, he tells us, it can be taken away. We should also know that the lockers in the break room and whatever is in them can be searched at any time. Then comes gossip; there has been gossip; gossip (which seems to mean employees talking among themselves) must stop. Off-duty employees are henceforth barred from eating at the restaurant, because "other servers gather around them and gossip." When Phillip has exhausted his agenda of rebukes, Joan complains about the conditions of the ladies' room and I throw in my two bits about the vacuum cleaner. But I don't see any backup coming from my fellow servers, each of whom has slipped into her own personal funk; Gail, my role model, stares sorrowfully at a point six inches from her nose. The meeting ends when Andy, one of the cooks, gets up, muttering about breaking up his day off for this almighty bullshit.

Just four days later we are suddenly summoned into the kitchen at 3:30 P.M., even though there are live tables on the floor. We all—about ten of us—stand around Phillip, who announces grimly that there has been a report of some "drug activity" on the night shift and that, as a result, we are now to be a "drug-free" workplace, meaning that all new hires will be tested and possibly also current employees on a random basis. I am glad that this part of the kitchen is so dark because I find myself blushing as hard as if I had been caught toking up in the ladies' room myself: I haven't been treated this way—lined up in the corridor, threatened with locker searches, peppered with carelessly aimed accusations—since at least junior high school. Back on the floor, Joan cracks, "Next they'll be telling us we can't have *sex* on the job." When I ask Stu what happened to inspire the crackdown, he just mutters about "management decisions" and takes the opportunity to upbraid Gail and me for being too generous with the rolls. From now on there's to be only one per customer and it goes out with the dinner, not with the salad. He's also been riding the cooks, prompting Andy to come out of the kitchen and observe—with the serenity of a man whose customary implement is a butcher knife—that "Stu has a death wish today."

5. Later in the evening, the gossip crystallizes around the theory that Stu is himself the drug culprit, that he uses the restaurant phone to order up marijuana and sends one of the late servers out to fetch it for him. The server was caught and she may have ratted out Stu, at least enough to cast some suspicion on him, thus accounting for his pissy behavior. Who knows? Personally, I'm ready to believe anything bad about Stu, who serves no evident function and presumes too much on our common ethnicity, sidling up to me one night to engage in a little

nativism directed at the Haitian immigrants: "I feel like I'm the foreigner here. They're taking over the country." Still later that evening, the drug in question escalates to crack. Lionel, the busboy, entertains us for the rest of the shift by standing just behind Stu's back and sucking deliriously on an imaginary joint or maybe a pipe.

The other problem, in addition to the less-than-nurturing management style, is that this job shows no sign of being financially viable. You might imagine, from a comfortable distance, that people who live, year in and year out, on $6 to $10 an hour have discovered some survival stratagems unknown to the middle class. But no. It's not hard to get my coworkers talking about their living situations, because housing, in almost every case, is the principal source of disruption in their lives, the first thing they fill you in on when they arrive for their shifts. After a week, I have compiled the following survey:

Gail is sharing a room in a well-known downtown flophouse for $250 a week. Her roommate, a male friend, has begun hitting on her, driving her nuts, but the rent would be impossible alone.

Claude, the Haitian cook, is desperate to get out of the two-room apartment he shares with his girlfriend and two other, unrelated people. As far as I can determine, the other Haitian men live in similarly crowded situations.

Annette, a twenty-year-old server who is six months pregnant and abandoned by her boyfriend, lives with her mother, a postal clerk.

10

Marianne, who is a breakfast server, and her boyfriend are paying $170 a week for a one-person trailer.

Billy, who at $10 an hour is the wealthiest of us, lives in the trailer he owns, paying only the $400-a-month lot fee.

The other white cook, Andy, lives on his dry-docked boat, which, as far as I can tell from his loving descriptions, can't be more than twenty feet long. He offers to take me out on it once it's repaired, but the offer comes with inquiries as to my marital status, so I do not follow up on it.

Tina, another server, and her husband are paying $60 a night for a room in the Days Inn. This is because they have no car and the Days Inn is in walking distance of the Hearth-side. When Marianne is tossed out of her trailer for sublet-ting (which is against trailer park rules), she leaves her boyfriend and moves in with Tina and her husband.

Joan, who had fooled me with her numerous and tasteful outfits (hostesses wear their own clothes), lives in a van parked behind a shopping center at night and showers in Tina's motel room. The clothes are from thrift shops.[1]

15   It strikes me, in my middle-class solipsism, that there is gross improvidence in some of these arrangements. When Gail and I are wrapping silverware in napkins—the only task for which we are per-mitted to sit—she tells me she is thinking of escaping from her room-mate by moving into the Days Inn herself. I am astounded: how she can even think of paying $40 to $60 a day? But if I was afraid of sounding like a social worker, I have come out just sounding like a fool. She squints at me in disbelief: "And where am I supposed to get a month's rent and a month's deposit for an apartment?" I'd been feel-ing pretty smug about my $500 efficiency, but of course it was made possible only by the $1,300 I had allotted myself for start-up costs when I began my low-wage life: $1,000 for the first month's rent and deposit, $100 for initial groceries and cash in my pocket, $200 stuffed away for emergencies. In poverty, as in certain propositions in physics, starting conditions are everything.

There are no secret economies that nourish the poor; on the con-trary, there are a host of special costs. If you can't put up the two months' rent you need to secure an apartment, you end up paying through the nose for a room by the week. If you have only a room, with a hot plate at best, you can't save by cooking up huge lentil stews that can be frozen for the week ahead. You eat fast food or the hot dogs and Styrofoam cups of soup that can be microwaved in a convenience store. If you have no money for health insurance—and the Hearth-side's niggardly plan kicks in only after three months—you go without routine care or prescription drugs and end up paying the price. Gail, for example, was doing fine, healthwise anyway, until she ran out of money for estrogen pills. She is supposed to be on the company health plan by now, but they claim to have lost her application form and to be beginning the paperwork all over again. So she spends $9 a pop for pills to control the migraines she wouldn't have, she insists, if her estrogen supplements were covered. Similarly, Marianne's boyfriend lost his job as a roofer because he missed so much time after getting a cut on his foot for which he couldn't afford the prescribed antibiotic.

My own situation, when I sit down to assess it after two weeks of work, would not be much better if this were my actual life. The seductive thing about waitressing is that you don't have to wait for payday to feel a few bills in your pocket, and my tips usually cover meals and gas, plus something left over to stuff into the kitchen drawer I use as a bank. But as the tourist business slows in the summer heat, I sometimes leave work with only $20 in tips (the gross is higher, but servers share about 15 percent of their tips with the busboys and bartenders). With wages included, this amounts to about the minimum wage of $5.15 an hour. The sum in the drawer is piling up but at the present rate of accumulation will be more than $100 short of my rent when the end of the month comes around. Nor can I see any expenses to cut. True, I haven't gone the lentil stew route yet, but that's because I don't have a large cooking pot, potholders, or a ladle to stir with (which would cost a total of about $30 at Kmart, somewhat less at a thrift store), not to mention onions, carrots, and the indispensable bay leaf. I do make my lunch almost every day— usually some slow-burning, high-protein combo like frozen chicken patties with melted cheese on top and canned pinto beans on the side. Dinner is at the Hearthside, which offers its employees a choice of BLT, fish sandwich, or hamburger for only $2. The burger lasts longest, especially if it's heaped with gut-puckering jalapeños, but by midnight my stomach is growling again.

So unless I want to start using my car as a residence, I have to find a second or an alternative job. I call all the hotels I'd filled out housekeeping applications at weeks ago—the Hyatt, Holiday Inn, Econo Lodge, HoJo's, Best Western, plus a half dozen locally run guest houses. Nothing. Then I start making the rounds again, wasting whole mornings waiting for some assistant manager to show up, even dipping into places so creepy that the front-desk clerk greets you from behind bulletproof glass and sells pints of liquor over the counter. But either someone has exposed my real-life housekeeping habits—which are, shall we say, mellow—or I am at the wrong end of some infallible ethnic equation: most, but by no means all, of the working housekeepers I see on my job searches are African Americans, Spanish-speaking, or refugees from the Central European post-Communist world, while servers are almost invariably white and monolingually English-speaking. When I finally get a positive response, I have been identified once again as server material. Jerry's—again, not the real name—which is part of a well-known national chain and physically attached here to another budget hotel, is ready to use me at once. The prospect is both exciting and terrifying because, with about the same number of tables and counter seats, Jerry's attracts three or four times the volume of customers as the gloomy old Hearthside.

Picture a fat person's hell, and I don't mean a place with no food. Instead there is everything you might eat if eating had no bodily consequences—the cheese fries, the chicken-fried steaks, the fudge-laden desserts—only here every bite must be paid for, one way or another, in human discomfort. The kitchen is a cavern, a stomach leading to the lower intestine that is the garbage and dishwashing area, from which issue bizarre smells combining the edible and the offal: creamy carrion, pizza barf, and that unique and enigmatic Jerry's scent, citrus fart. The floor is slick with spills, forcing us to walk through the kitchen with tiny steps, like Susan McDougal in leg irons. Sinks everywhere are clogged with scraps of lettuce, decomposing lemon wedges, water-logged toast crusts. Put your hand down on any counter and you risk being stuck to it by the film of ancient syrup spills, and this is unfortunate because hands are utensils here, used for scooping up lettuce onto the salad plates, lifting out pie slices, and even moving hash browns from one plate to another. The regulation poster in the single unisex rest room admonishes us to wash our hands thoroughly, and even offers instructions for doing so, but there is always some vital substance missing—soap, paper towels, toilet paper—and I never found all three at once. You learn to stuff your pockets with napkins before going in there, and too bad about the customers, who must eat, although they don't realize it, almost literally out of our hands.

20   The break room summarizes the whole situation: there is none, 20 because there are no breaks at Jerry's. For six to eight hours in a row, you never sit except to pee. Actually, there are three folding chairs at a table immediately adjacent to the bathroom, but hardly anyone ever sits in this, the very rectum of the gastroarchitectural system. Rather, the function of the peri-toilet area is to house the ashtrays in which servers and dishwashers leave their cigarettes burning at all times, like votive candles, so they don't have to waste time lighting up again when they dash back here for a

puff. Almost everyone smokes as if their pulmonary well-being depended on it—the multinational mélange of cooks; the dishwashers, who are all Czechs here; the servers, who are American natives—creating an atmosphere in which oxygen is only an occasional pollutant. My first morning at Jerry's, when the hypoglycemic shakes set in, I complain to one of my fellow servers that I don't understand how she can go so long without food. "Well, I don't understand how *you* can go so long without a cigarette," she responds in a tone of reproach. Because work is what you do for others; smoking is what you do for yourself. I don't know why the antismoking crusaders have never grasped the element of defiant self-nurturance that makes the habit so endearing to its victims—as if, in the American workplace, the only thing people have to call their own is the tumors they are nourishing and the spare moments they devote to feeding them.

Now, the Industrial Revolution is not an easy transition, especially, in my experience, when you have to zip through it in just a couple of days. I have gone from craft work straight into the factory, from the air-conditioned morgue of the Hearthside directly into the flames. Customers arrive in human waves, sometimes disgorged fifty at a time from their tour buses, peckish and whiny. Instead of two "girls" on the floor at once, there can be as many as six of us running around in our brilliant pink-and-orange Hawaiian shirts. Conversations, either with customers or with fellow employees, seldom last more than twenty seconds at a time. On my first day, in fact, I am hurt by my sister servers' coldness. My mentor for the day is a supremely competent, emotionally uninflected twenty-three-year-old, and the others, who gossip a little among themselves about the real reason someone is out sick today and the size of the bail bond someone else has had to pay, ignore me completely. On my second day, I find out why. "Well, it's good to see *you* again," one of them says in greeting. "Hardly anyone comes back after the first day." I feel powerfully vindicated—a survivor—but it would take a long time, probably months, before I could hope to be accepted into this sorority.

I start out with the beautiful, heroic idea of handling the two jobs at once, and for two days I almost do it: working the breakfast/lunch shift at Jerry's from 8:00 till 2:00, arriving at the Hearthside a few minutes late, at 2:10, and attempting to hold out until 10:00. In the few minutes I have between jobs, I pick up a spicy chicken sandwich at the Wendy's drive-through window, gobble it down in the car, and change from khaki slacks to black, from Hawaiian to rust-colored polo. There is a problem, though. When, during the 3:00–4:00 o'clock dead time, I finally sit down to wrap silver, my flesh seems to bond to the seat. I try to refuel with a purloined cup of clam chowder, as I've seen Gail and Joan do dozens of time, but Stu catches me and hisses "No *eating!*" although there's not a customer around to be offended by the sight of food making contact with a server's lips. So I tell Gail I'm going to quit, and she hugs me and says she might just follow me to Jerry's herself.

But the chances of this are minuscule. She has left the flophouse and her annoying roommate and is back to living in her truck. But, guess what, she reports to me excitedly later that evening, Phillip has given her permission to park overnight in the hotel parking lot, as long as she keeps out of sight, and the parking lot should be totally safe since it's patrolled by a hotel security guard! With the Hearthside offering benefits like that, how could anyone think of leaving? This must be Phillip's theory, anyway. He accepts my resignation with a shrug, his main concern being that I return my two polo shirts and aprons.

Gail would have triumphed at Jerry's, I'm sure, but for me it's a crash course in exhaustion management. Years ago, the kindly fry cook who trained me to waitress at a Los Angeles truck stop used to say: Never make an unnecessary trip; if you don't have to walk fast, walk slow; if you don't have to walk, stand. But at Jerry's the effort of distinguishing necessary from unnecessary and urgent from whenever would itself be too much of an energy drain. The only thing to do is to treat each shift as a one-time-only emergency: you've got fifty starving people out there, lying scattered on the battlefield, so get out there and feed them! Forget that you will have to do this again tomorrow, forget that you will have to be alert enough to dodge the drunks on the drive home tonight—just burn, burn, burn! Ideally, at some point you enter what servers call a "rhythm" and psychologists term a "flow state," where signals pass from the sense organs directly to the muscles, bypassing the cerebral cortex, and a Zen-like emptiness sets in. I'm on a 2:00–10:00 P.M. shift now, and a male server from the morning shift tells me about the time he "pulled a triple"—three shifts in a row, all the way around the clock—and then got off and had a drink and met this girl, and maybe he shouldn't tell me this, but they had sex right then and there and it was like *beautiful.*

But there's another capacity of the neuromuscular system, which is pain. I start tossing back drugstore-brand ibuprofens as if they were vitamin C, four before each shift, because an old mouse-related repetitive-stress injury in my upper back has come back to full-spasm strength, thanks to the tray carrying. In my ordinary life, this level of disability might justify a day of ice packs and stretching. Here I comfort myself with the Aleve commercial where the cute blue-collar guy asks: If you quit after working four hours, what would your boss say? And the not-so-cute blue-collar guy, who's lugging a metal beam on his back, answers: He'd fire me, that's what. But fortunately, the commercial tells us, we workers can exert the same kind of authority over our painkillers that our bosses exert over us. If Tylenol doesn't want to work for more than four hours, you just fire its ass and switch to Aleve.

25   True, I take occasional breaks from this life, going home now and then to catch up on e-mail and for conjugal visits (though I am careful to "pay" for everything I eat here, at $5 for a dinner, which I put in a jar), seeing *The Truman Show* with friends and letting them buy my ticket. And I still have those what-am-I-doing-here moments at work, when I get so homesick for the printed word that I obsessively reread the six-page menu. But as the days go by, my old life is beginning to look exceedingly strange. The e-mails and phone messages addressed to my former self come from a distant race of people with exotic concerns and far too much time on their hands. The neighborly market I used to cruise for produce now looks forbiddingly like a Manhattan yuppie emporium. And when I sit down one morning in my real home to pay bills from my past life, I am dazzled by the two- and three-figure sums owed to outfits like Club Body Tech and Amazon.com.

    Management at Jerry's is generally calmer and more "professional" than at the Hearthside, with two exceptions. One is Joy, a plump, blowsy woman in her early thirties who once kindly devoted several minutes of her time to instructing me in the correct one-handed method of tray carrying but whose moods change disconcertingly from shift to shift and even within one. The other is B.J., aka B.J. the Bitch, whose contribution is to stand by the kitchen counter and yell, "Nita, your order's up, move it!" or "Barbara, didn't you see you've got another table out there? Come *on,* girl!" Among other things, she is hated for having replaced the whipped cream squirt cans with big plastic whipped-cream-filled baggies that have to be squeezed with both hands—because, reportedly, she saw or thought she saw employees trying to inhale the propellant gas from the squirt cans, in the hope that it might be nitrous oxide. On my third night, she pulls me aside abruptly and brings her face so close that it looks like she's planning to butt me with her forehead. But instead of saying "You're fired," she says, "You're doing fine." The only trouble is I'm spending time chatting with customers: "That's how they're getting you." Furthermore I am letting them "run me," which means harassment by sequential demands: you bring the catsup and they decide they want extra Thousand Island; you bring that and they announce they now need a side of fries, and so on into distraction. Finally she tells me not to take her wrong. She tries to say things in a nice way, but "you get into a mode, you know, because everything has to move so fast."[2]

I mumble thanks for the advice, feeling like I've just been stripped naked by the crazed enforcer of some ancient sumptuary law: No chatting for *you,* girl. No fancy service ethic allowed for the serfs. Chatting with customers is for the good-looking young college-educated servers in the downtown carpaccio and ceviche joints, the kids who can make $70–$100 a night. What had I been thinking? My job is to move orders from tables to kitchen and then trays from kitchen to tables. Customers are in fact the major obstacle to the smooth transformation of information into food and food into money—they are, in short, the enemy. And the painful thing is that I'm beginning to see it this way myself. There are the traditional asshole types—frat boys who down multiple Buds and then make a fuss because the steaks are so emaciated and the fries so sparse—as well as the variously impaired—due to age, diabetes, or literacy issues—who require patient nutritional counseling. The worst, for some reason, are the Visible Christians—like the ten-person table, all jolly and sanctified after Sunday night service, who run me mercilessly and then leave me $1 on a $92 bill. Or the guy with the crucifixion T-shirt (SOMEONE TO LOOK UP TO) who complains that his baked potato is too hard and his iced tea too icy (I cheerfully fix both) and leaves no tip at all. As a general rule, people wearing crosses or WWJD? ("What Would Jesus Do?") buttons look at us disapprovingly no matter what we do, as if they were confusing waitressing with Mary Magdalene's original profession.

I make friends, over time, with the other "girls" who work my shift: Nita, the tattooed twenty-something who taunts us by going around saying brightly, "Have we started making money yet?" Ellen, whose teenage son cooks on the graveyard shift and who once managed a restaurant in Massachusetts but won't try out for management here because she prefers being a "common worker" and not "ordering people around." Easygoing fiftyish Lucy, with the raucous laugh, who limps toward the end of the shift because of something that has gone wrong with her leg, the exact nature of which cannot be determined without health insurance. We talk about the usual girl things—men, children, and the sinister allure of Jerry's chocolate peanut-butter cream pie— though no one, I notice, ever brings up anything potentially expensive, like shopping or movies. As at the Hearthside, the only recreation ever referred to is partying, which requires little more than some beer, a joint, and a few close friends. Still, no one is homeless, or cops to it anyway, thanks usually to a working husband or boyfriend. All in all, we form a reliable mutual-support group: if one of us is feeling sick or overwhelmed, another one will "bev" a table or even carry trays for her. If one of us is off sneaking a cigarette or a pee, the others will do their best to conceal her absence from the enforcers of corporate rationality.[3]

But my saving human connection—my oxytocin receptor, as it were—is George, the nineteen-year-old Czech dishwasher who has been in this country exactly one week. We get talking when he asks me, tortuously, how much cigarettes cost at Jerry's. I do my best to explain that they cost over a dollar more here than at a regular store and suggest that he just take one from the half-filled packs that are always lying around on the break table. But that would be unthink-able. Except for the one tiny earring signaling his allegiance to some vaguely alternative point of view, George is a perfect straight arrow— crew-cut, hardworking, and hungry for eye contact. "Czech Republic," I ask, "or Slovakia?" and he seems delighted that I know the difference. "Vaclav Havel," I try, "Velvet Revolution, Frank Zappa?" "Yes, yes, 1989," he says, and I realize that for him this is already history.

30   My project is to teach George English. "How are you today,   30 George?" I say at the start of each shift. "I am good, and how are you today, Barbara?" I learn that he is not paid by Jerry's but by the "agent" who shipped him over—$5 an hour, with the agent getting the dollar or so difference between that and what Jerry's pays dishwashers. I learn also that he shares an apartment with a crowd of other Czech "dishers," as he calls them, and that he cannot sleep until one of them goes off for his shift, leaving a vacant bed. We are having one of our ESL sessions late one afternoon when B.J. catches us at it and orders "Joseph" to take up the rubber mats on the floor near the dishwashing sinks and mop underneath. "I thought your name was George," I say loud enough for B.J. to hear as she strides off back to the counter. Is she embarrassed? Maybe a little, because she greets me back at the counter with "George,

Joseph—there are so many of them!" I say nothing, neither nodding nor smiling, and for this I am punished later, when I think I am ready to go and she announces that I need to roll fifty more sets of silverware, and isn't it time I mixed up a fresh four-gallon batch of blue-cheese dressing? May you grow old in this place, B.J., is the curse I beam out at her when I am finally permitted to leave. May the syrup spills glue your feet to the floor.

I make the decision to move closer to Key West. First, because of the drive. Second and third, also because of the drive: gas is eating up $4–$5 a day, and although Jerry's is as high-volume as you can get, the tips average only 10 percent, and not just for a newbie like me. Between the base pay of $2.15 an hour and the obligation to share tips with the busboys and dishwashers, we're averaging only about $7.50 an hour. Then there is the $30 I had to spend on the regulation tan slacks worn by Jerry's servers—a setback it could take weeks to absorb. (I had combed the town's two downscale department stores hoping for something cheaper but decided in the end that these marked-down Dockers, originally $49, were more likely to survive a daily washing.) Of my fellow servers, everyone who lacks a working husband or boyfriend seems to have a second job: Nita does something at a computer eight hours a day; another welds. Without the forty-five-minute commute, I can picture myself working two jobs and still having the time to shower between them.

So I take the $500 deposit I have coming from my landlord, the $400 I have earned toward the next month's rent, plus the $200 reserved for emergencies, and use the $1,100 to pay the rent and deposit on trailer number 46 in the Overseas Trailer Park, a mile from the cluster of budget hotels that constitute Key West's version of an industrial park. Number 46 is about eight feet in width and shaped like a barbell inside, with a narrow region—because of the sink and the stove—separating the bedroom from what might optimistically be called the "living" area, with its two-person table and half-sized couch. The bathroom is so small my knees rub against the shower stall when I sit on the toilet, and you can't just leap out of the bed, you have to climb down to the foot of it in order to find a patch of floor space to stand on. Outside, I am within a few yards of a liquor store, a bar that advertises "free beer tomorrow," a convenience store, and a Burger King—but no supermarket or, alas, Laundromat. By reputation, the Overseas park is a nest of crime and crack, and I am hoping at least for some vibrant multicultural street life. But desolation rules night and day, except for a thin stream of pedestrians heading for their jobs at the Sheraton or the 7-Eleven. There are not exactly people here but what amounts to canned labor, being preserved between shifts from the heat.

In line with my reduced living conditions, a new form of ugliness arises at Jerry's. First we are confronted—via an announcement on the computers through which we input orders—with the new rule that the hotel bar, the Driftwood, is henceforth off-limits to restaurant employees. The culprit, I learn through the grapevine, is the ultra-efficient twenty-three-year-old who trained me—another trailer home dweller and a mother of three. Something had set her off one morning, so she slipped out for a nip and returned to the floor impaired. The restriction mostly hurts Ellen, whose habit it is to free her hair from its rubber band and drop by the Driftwood for a couple of Zins before heading home at the end of her shift, but all of us feel the chill. Then the next day, when I go for straws, I find the dry-storage room locked. It's never been locked before; we go in and out of it all day—for napkins, jelly containers, Styrofoam cups for takeout. Vic, the portly assistant manager who opens it for me, explains that he caught one of the dishwashers attempting to steal something and, unfortunately, the miscreant will be with us until a replacement can be found—hence the locked door. I neglect to ask what he had been trying to steal but Vic tells me who he is—the kid with the buzz cut and the earring, you know, he's back there right now.

I wish I could say I rushed back and confronted George to get his side of the story. I wish I could say I stood up to Vic and insisted that George be given a translator and allowed to defend himself or announced that I'd find a lawyer who'd handle the case pro bono. At the very least I should have testified as to the kid's honesty. The mystery to me is that there's not much worth stealing in the dry-storage room, at least not in any fenceable quantity: "Is Gyorgi here, and am having 200—maybe 250—catsup packets. What do you say?" My guess is that he had taken—if he had taken anything at all—some Saltines or a can of cherry pie mix and that the motive for taking it was hunger.

So why didn't I intervene? Certainly not because I was held back by the kind of moral paralysis that can mask as journalistic objectivity. On the contrary, something new—something loathsome and servile— had infected me, along with the kitchen odors that I could still sniff on my bra when I finally undressed at night. In real life I am moderately

35

brave, but plenty of brave people shed their courage in POW camps, and maybe something similar goes on in the infinitely more congenial milieu of the low-wage American workplace. Maybe, in a month or two more at Jerry's, I might have regained my crusading spirit. Then again, in a month or two I might have turned into a different person altogether—say, the kind of person who would have turned George in.

But this is not something I was slated to find out. When my monthlong plunge into poverty was almost over, I finally landed my dream job—housekeeping. I did this by walking into the personnel office of the only place I figured I might have some credibility, the hotel attached to Jerry's, and confiding urgently that I had to have a second job if I was to pay my rent and, no, it couldn't be front-desk clerk. "All *right,*" the personnel lady fairly spits, "so it's *housekeeping,*" and marches me back to meet Millie, the housekeeping manager, a tiny, frenetic Hispanic woman who greets me as "babe" and hands me a pamphlet emphasizing the need for a positive attitude. The pay is $6.10 an hour and the hours are nine in the morning till "whenever," which I am hoping can be defined as a little before two. I don't have to ask about health insurance once I meet Carlotta, the middle-aged African American woman who will be training me. Carlie, as she tells me to call her, is missing all of her top front teeth.

On that first day of housekeeping and last day—although I don't yet know it's the last—of my life as a low-wage worker in Key West, Carlie is in a foul mood. We have been given nineteen rooms to clean, most of them "checkouts," as opposed to "stay-overs," and requiring the whole enchilada of bed stripping, vacuuming, and bathroom scrubbing. When one of the rooms that had been listed as a stay-over turns out to be a checkout, she calls Millie to complain, but of course to no avail. "So make up the motherfucker," she orders me, and I do the beds while she sloshes around the bathroom. For four hours without a break I strip and remake beds, taking about four and a half minutes per queen-sized bed, which I could get down to three if there were any reason to. We try to avoid vacuuming by picking up the larger specks by hand, but often there is nothing to do but drag the monstrous vacuum cleaner—it weighs about thirty pounds—off our cart and try to wrestle it around the floor. Sometimes Carlie hands me the squirt bottle of "Bam" (an acronym for something that begins, ominously, with "butyric"—the rest of it has been worn off the label) and lets me do the bathrooms. No service ethic challenges me here to new heights of performance. I just concentrate on removing the pubic hairs from the bathtubs, or at least the dark ones that I can see.

I had looked forward to the breaking-and-entering aspect of cleaning the stay-overs, the chance to examine the secret physical existence of strangers. But the contents of the rooms are always banal and surprisingly neat—zipped-up shaving kits, shoes lined up against the wall (there are no closets), flyers for snorkeling trips, maybe an empty wine bottle or two. It is the TV that keeps us going, from Jerry to Sally to *Hawaii Five-0* and then on to the soaps. If there's something especially arresting, like "Won't Take No for an Answer" on Jerry, we sit down on the edge of a bed and giggle for a moment, as if this were a pajama party instead of a terminally dead-end job. The soaps are the best, and Carlie turns the volume up full blast so she won't miss anything from the bathroom or while the vacuum is on. In Room 503, Marcia confronts Jeff about Lauren. In 505, Lauren taunts poor cheated-on Marcia. In 511, Helen offers Amanda $10,000 to stop seeing Eric, prompting Carlie to emerge from the bathroom to study Amanda's troubled face. "You take it, girl," she advises. "I would for sure."

The tourists' rooms that we clean and, beyond them, the far more expensively appointed interiors in the soaps begin after a while to merge. We have entered a better world—a world of comfort where every day is a day off, waiting to be filled with sexual intrigue. We are only gate-crashers in this fantasy, however, forced to pay for our presence with backaches and perpetual thirst. The mirrors, and there are far too many of them in hotel rooms, contain the kind of person you would normally find pushing a shopping cart down a city street—bedraggled, dressed in a damp hotel polo shirt two sizes too large, and with sweat dribbling down her chin like drool. I am enormously relieved when Carlie announces a half-hour meal break, but my appetite fades when I see that the bag of hot dog rolls she has been carrying around on our cart is not trash salvaged from a checkout but what she has brought for her lunch.

40   Between the TV and the fact that I'm in no position, as a first dayer, 40 to launch new topics of conversation, I don't learn much about Carlie except that she hurts, and in more than one way. She moves slowly about her work, muttering something about joint pain, and this is probably going to doom her, since the young immigrant housekeepers—

Polish and Salvadoran—like to polish off their rooms by two in the afternoon, while she drags the work out till six. It doesn't make any sense to hurry, she observes, when you're being paid by the hour. Already, management has brought in a woman to do what sounds like time-motion studies and there's talk about switching to paying by the room.[4] She broods, too, about all the little evidences of disrespect that come her way, and not only from management. "They don't care about us," she tells me of the hotel guests; in fact, they don't notice us at all unless something gets stolen from a room—"then they're all over you." We're eating our lunch side by side in the break room when a white guy in a maintenance uniform walks by and Carlie calls out, "Hey you," in a friendly way, "what's your name?"

"Peter Pan," he says, his back already to us.

"That wasn't funny," Carlie says, turning to me. "That was no kind of answer. Why did he have to be funny like that?" I venture that he has an attitude, and she nods as if that were an acute diagnosis. "Yeah, he got a attitude all right."

"Maybe he's a having a bad day," I elaborate, not because I feel any obligation to defend the white race but because her face is so twisted with hurt.

When I request permission to leave at about 3:30, another house-keeper warns me that no one has so far succeeded in combining housekeeping with serving at Jerry's: "Some kid did it once for five days, and you're no kid." With that helpful information in mind, I rush back to number 46, down four Advils (the name brand this time), shower, stooping to fit into the stall, and attempt to compose myself for the oncoming shift. So much for what Marx termed the "reproduction of labor power," meaning the things a worker has to do just so she'll be ready to labor again. The only unforeseen obstacle to the smooth transition from job to job is that my tan Jerry's slacks, which had looked reasonably clean by 40-watt bulb last night when I hand washed my Hawaiian shirt, prove by daylight to be mottled with catsup and ranch-dressing stains. I spend most of my hour-long break between jobs attempting to remove the edible portions of the slacks with a sponge and then drying them over the hood of my car in the sun.

I can do this two-job thing, is my theory, if I can drink enough caffeine and avoid getting distracted by George's ever more obvious suffering.[5] The first few days after the alleged theft, he seemed not to understand the trouble he was in, and our chirpy little conversations had continued. But the last couple of shifts he's been listless and unshaven, and tonight he looks like the ghost we all know him to be, with dark half-moons hanging from his eyes. At one point, when I am briefly immobilized by the task of filling little paper cups with sour cream for baked potatoes, he comes over and looks as if he'd like to explore the limits of our shared vocabulary, but I am called to the floor for a table. I resolve to give him all my tips that night, and to hell with the experiment in low-wage money management. At eight, Ellen and I grab a snack together standing at the mephitic end of the kitchen counter, but I can only manage two or three mozzarella sticks, and lunch had been a mere handful of McNuggets. I am not tired at all, I assure myself, though it may be that there is simply no more "I" left to do the tiredness monitoring. What I would see if I were more alert to the situation is that the forces of destruction are already massing against me. There is only one cook on duty, a young man named Jesus ("Hay-Sue," that is), and he is new to the job. And there is Joy, who shows up to take over in the middle of the shift dressed in high heels and a long, clingy white dress and fuming as if she'd just been stood up in some cocktail bar.

45   Then it comes, the perfect storm. Four of my tables fill up at once. 45
Four tables is nothing for me now, but only so long as they are obligingly staggered. As I bev table 27, tables 25, 28, and 24 are watching enviously. As I bev 25, 24 glowers because their bevs haven't even been ordered. Twenty-eight is four yuppyish types, meaning everything on the side and agonizing instructions as to the chicken Caesars. Twenty-five is a middle-aged black couple who complain, with some justice, that the iced tea isn't fresh and the tabletop is sticky. But table 24 is the meteorological event of the century: ten British tourists who seem to have made the decision to absorb the American experience entirely by mouth. Here everyone has at least two drinks—iced tea *and* milk shake, Michelob *and* water (with lemon slice in the water, please)—and a huge, promiscuous orgy of breakfast specials, mozz sticks, chicken strips, quesadillas, burgers with cheese and without, sides of hash browns with cheddar, with onions, with gravy, seasoned fries, plain fries, banana splits. Poor Jesus! Poor me! Because when I arrive with their first tray of food—after three prior trips just to refill bevs—Princess Di refuses to eat her chicken strips with her pancake and sausage special since, as she now reveals, the strips were meant to be an

appetizer. Maybe the others would have accepted their meals, but Di, who is deep into her third Michelob, insists that everything else go back while they work on their starters. Meanwhile, the yuppies are waving me down for more decaf and the black couple looks ready to summon the NAACP.

Much of what happens next is lost in the fog of war. Jesus starts going under. The little printer in front of him is spewing out orders faster than he can rip them off, much less produce the meals. A menacing restlessness rises from the tables, all of which are full. Even the invincible Ellen is ashen from stress. I take table 24 their reheated main courses, which they immediately reject as either too cold or fossilized by the microwave. When I return to the kitchen with their trays (three trays in three trips) Joy confronts me with arms akimbo: "What *is* this?" She means the food—the plates of rejected pancakes, hash browns in assorted flavors, toasts, burgers, sausages, eggs. "Uh, scrambled with cheddar," I try, "and that's—" "*No,*" she screams in my face, "is it a traditional, a super-scramble, an eye-opener?" I pretend to study my check for a clue, but entropy has been up to its tricks, not only on the plates but in my head, and I have to admit that the original order is beyond reconstruction. "You don't know an eye-opener from a traditional?" she demands in outrage. All I know, in fact, is that my legs have lost interest in the current venture and have announced their intention to fold. I am saved by a yuppie (mercifully not one of mine) who chooses this moment to charge into the kitchen to bellow that his food is twenty-five minutes late. Joy screams at him to get the hell out of her kitchen, *please,* and then turns on Jesus in a fury, hurling an empty tray across the room for emphasis.

I leave. I don't walk out, I just leave. I don't finish my side work or pick up my credit card tips, if any, at the cash register or, of course, ask Joy's permission to go. And the surprising thing is that you *can* walk out without permission, that the door opens, that the thick tropical night air parts to let me pass, that my car is still parked where I left it. There is no vindication in this exit, no fuck-you surge of relief, just an overwhelming dank sense of failure pressing down on me and the entire parking lot. I had gone into this venture in the spirit of science, to test a mathematical proposition, but somewhere along the line, in the tunnel vision imposed by long shifts and relentless concentration, it became a test of myself, and clearly I have failed. Not only had I flamed out as a housekeeper/server, I had forgotten to give George my tips, and, for reasons perhaps best known to hard-working, generous people like Gail and Ellen, this hurts. I don't cry, but I am in a position to realize, for the first time in many years, that the tear ducts are and still capable of doing their job.

When I moved out of the trailer park, I gave the key to number 46 to Gail and arranged for my deposit to be transferred to her. She told me that Joan was still living in her van and that Stu had been fired from the Hearthside. According to the most up-to-date rumors, the drug he ordered from the restaurant was crack and he was caught dipping into the cash register to pay for it. I never found out what happened to George.

End Notes

1. I could find no statistics on the number of employed people living in cars or vans, but according to a 1997 report of the National Coalition for the Homeless, "Myths and Facts about Homelessness," nearly one-fifth of all homeless people (in twenty-nine cities across the nation) are employed in full- or part-time jobs.

2. In *Workers in a Lean World: Unions in the International Economy* (Verso, 1997), Kim Moody cites studies finding an increase in stress-related workplace injuries and illness between the mid-1980s and the early 1990s. He argues that rising stress levels reflect a new system of "management by stress" in which workers in a variety of industries are being squeezed to extract maximum productivity, to the detriment of their health.

3. Until April 1998, there was no federally mandated right to bathroom breaks. According to Marc Linder and Ingrid Nygaard, authors of *Void Where Prohibited: Rest Breaks and the Right to Urinate on Company Time* (Cornell University Press, 1997), "The right to rest and void at work is not high on the list of social or political causes supported by professional or executive employees, who enjoy personal workplace liberties that millions of factory workers can only dream about . . . While we were dismayed to discover that workers lacked an acknowledged right to void at work, [the workers] were amazed by outsiders' naive belief that their employers would permit them to perform this basic bodily function when necessary. . . . A factory worker, not allowed a break for six-hour stretches voided into pads worn inside her uniform; and a kindergarten teacher in a school without aides had to take all twenty children with her to the bathroom and line them up outside the stall door while she voided."

4. A few weeks after I left, I heard ads on the radio for housekeeping jobs at this hotel at the amazing rate of "up to $9 an hour." When I inquired, I found out that the hotel had indeed started paying by the room, and I suspect that Carlie, if she lasted, was still making the equivalent of $6 an hour or quite a bit less.

5. In 1996 the number of persons holding two or more jobs averaged 7.8 million, or 6.2 percent of the workforce. It was about the same rate for men and for women (6.1 versus 6.2). About two-thirds of multiple jobholders work one job full-time and the other part-time. Only a heroic minority—4 percent of men and 2 percent of women—work two full-time jobs simultaneously (John F. Stinson Jr., "New Data on Multiple Jobholding Available from the CPS," *Monthly Labor Review*, March 1997).

Questions on Meaning

1. Why, in your opinion, did the writer feel it necessary to engage in this experiment? What are the advantages and disadvantages of such an approach to learning about the working conditions of those in low-paying jobs?
2. What is the author's observation about managers, their relationship to corporations, and front line workers?
3. The author seems surprised to learn that "people who live, year in and year out, on $6 to $10 an hour in fact have not discovered some survival stratagems unknown to the middle class." Explain the reasons for the author's assumption and why she was surprised by her discovery.
4. What is meant by the statement "the Industrial Revolution is not an easy transition, especially . . . when you have to zip through it in just a couple of days"?

Questions on Rhetorical Strategy and Style

1. The author notes that she takes "occasional breaks from this life, going home now and then to catch up on e-mail and for conjugal visits . . ." Why is she willing to reveal that she did avail herself of such relative comfort?
2. At several points in this selection the author indicates shifts in her attitude toward others and her sense of self. Note them. In particular, what does it indicate that she did not stand up for George when he was accused of stealing? How do passages such as this affect your interpretation of the author's intent?
3. Why did the author include the background information about her coworkers in the form of a survey?

Writing Assignments

1. Anthropology is the study of other cultures. While Ehrenreich is not an anthropologist, her book raises questions about how one's position in relation to the subject is a matter of interpretation. Write an essay explaining how the author's "participant observer" role influences her understanding of the situations she describes.

2. Write an essay about the most demeaning job you've had (or still have). As Ehrenreich does, make elaborate observations and self-reflections. How has the experience changed your understanding of work and the attitudes and conditions that shape people's opportunities?

On Dumpster Diving

Lars Eighner

Lars Eighner (1948–) became homeless in the 1980s after losing a job and being unable to find another immediately. He had been a student at the University of Texas at Austin before this, at which time he had been thrown out of his mother's house for being gay. While homeless he wrote stories and articles for magazines when he was able to find a typewriter to use and stay in one place long enough to write. He remained homeless for about three years, caring for and traveling with his dog, Lizbeth. In 1993 he published Travels with Lizbeth: Three Years on the Road and on the Streets, *an autobiographical account of that period which is in turns humorous, philosophical, and a good narrative. The following essay is an excerpted chapter from that book. Eighner's writing is successful because of the unabashedly honest and self-aware way he takes on his subject and opens his reader to a new world—here, the contents of trash dumpsters.*

This chapter was composed while the author was homeless. The present tense has been preserved.

1   Long before I began Dumpster diving I was impressed with Dumpsters, enough so that I wrote the Merriam-Webster research service to discover what I could about the word *Dumpster.* I learned from them that it is a proprietary word belonging to the Dempsey Dumpster company. Since then I have dutifully capitalized the word, although it was lowercased in almost all the citations Merriam-Webster photocopied for me. Dempsey's word is too apt. I have never heard these things called anything but Dumpsters. I do not

know anyone who knows the generic name for these objects. From time to time I have heard a wino or hobo give some corrupted credit to the original and call them Dipsy Dumpsters.

I began Dumpster diving about a year before I became homeless.

I prefer the word *scavenging* and use the word *scrounging* when I mean to be obscure. I have heard people, evidently meaning to be polite, use the word *foraging,* but I prefer to reserve that word for gathering nuts and berries and such which I do also according to the season and the opportunity. *Dumpster diving* seems to me to be a little too cute and, in my case, inaccurate because I lack the athletic ability to lower myself into the Dumpsters as the true divers do, much as their increased profit.

I like the frankness of the word *scavenging,* which I can hardly think of without picturing a big black snail on an aquarium wall. I live from the refuse of others. I am a scavenger. I think it a sound and honorable niche, although if I could I would naturally prefer to live the comfortable consumer life, perhaps—and only perhaps—as a slightly less wasteful consumer, owing to what I have learned as a scavenger.

5   While Lizbeth and I were still living in the shack on Avenue B as my savings ran out, I put almost all my sporadic income into rent. The necessities of daily life I began to extract from Dumpsters. Yes, we ate from them. Except for jeans, all my clothes came from Dumpsters. Boom boxes, candles, bedding, toilet paper, a virgin male love doll, medicine, books, a typewriter, dishes, furnishings, and change, sometimes amounting to many dollars—I acquired many things from the Dumpsters.

I have learned much as a scavenger. I mean to put some of what I have learned down here, beginning with the practical art of Dumpster diving and proceeding to the abstract.

What is safe to eat?

After all, the finding of objects is becoming something of an urban art. Even respectable employed people will sometimes find something tempting sticking out of a Dumpster or standing beside one. Quite a number of people, not all of them of the bohemian type, are willing to brag that they found this or that piece in the trash. But eating from Dumpsters is what separates the dilettanti from the professionals. Eating safely from the Dumpsters involves three principles: using the senses and common sense to evaluate the conditions of the found materials, knowing the Dumpsters of a given area and checking them regularly, and seeking always to answer the question "Why was this discarded?"

Perhaps everyone who has a kitchen and a regular supply of groceries has, at one time or another, made a sandwich and eaten half of it before discovering mold on the bread or got a mouthful of milk before realizing the milk had turned. Nothing of the sort is likely to happen to a Dumpster diver because he is constantly reminded that most food is discarded for a reason. Yet a lot of perfectly good food can be found in Dumpsters.

10   Canned goods, for example, turn up fairly often in the Dumpsters I frequent. All except the most phobic people would be willing to eat from a can, even if it came from a Dumpster. Canned goods are among the safest of foods to be found in Dumpsters but are not utterly foolproof.

Although very rare with modern canning methods, botulism is a possibility. Most other forms of food poisoning seldom do lasting harm to a healthy person, but botulism is most certainly fatal and often the first symptom is death. Except for carbonated beverages, all canned goods should contain a slight vacuum and suck air when first punctured. Bulging, rusty, and dented cans and cans that spew when punctured should be avoided, especially when the contents are not very acidic or syrupy.

Heat can break down the botulin, but this requires much more cooking than most people do to canned goods. To the extent that botulism occurs at all, of course, it can occur in cans on pantry shelves as well as in cans from Dumpsters. Need I say that home-canned goods are simply too risky to be recommended

From time to time one of my companions, aware of the source of my provisions, will ask, "Do you think these crackers are really safe to eat?" For some reason it is most often the crackers they ask about.

This question has always made me angry. Of course I would not offer my companion anything I had doubts about. But more than that, I wonder why he cannot evaluate the condition of the crackers for himself. I have no special knowledge and I have been wrong before. Since he knows where the food comes from, it seems to me he ought to assume some of the responsibility for deciding what he will put in his mouth. For myself I have few qualms about dry foods such as crackers, cookies, cereal, chips, and pasta if they are free of visible contaminates and still dry and crisp. Most often such things are found in the original packaging, which is not so much a positive sign as it is the absence of a negative one.

15   Raw fruits and vegetables with intact skins seem perfectly safe to me, excluding of course the obviously rotten. Many are discarded for minor imperfections that can be pared away. Leafy vegetables, grapes, cauliflower, broccoli, and similar things may be contaminated by liquids and may be impractical to wash.

Candy, especially hard candy, is usually safe if it has not drawn ants. Chocolate is often discarded only because it has become discolored as the cocoa butter de-emulsified. Candying, after all, is one method of food preservation because pathogens do not like very sugary substances.

All of these foods might be found in any Dumpster and can be evaluated with some confidence largely on the basis of appearance. Beyond these are foods that cannot be correctly evaluated without additional information.

I began scavenging by pulling pizzas out of the Dumpster behind a pizza delivery shop. In general, prepared food requires caution, but in this case I knew when the shop closed and went to the Dumpster as soon as the last of the help left.

Such shops often get prank orders; both the orders and the products made to fill them are called *bogus*. Because help seldom stays long at these places, pizzas are often made with the wrong topping, refused on delivery for being cold, or baked incorrectly. The products to be discarded are boxed up because inventory is kept by counting boxes: A boxed pizza can be written off; an unboxed pizza does not exist.

20   I never placed a bogus order to increase the supply of pizzas and I believe no one else was scavenging in this Dumpster. But the people in the shop became suspicious and began to retain their garbage in the shop overnight. While it lasted I had a steady supply of fresh, sometimes warm pizza. Because I knew the Dumpster I knew the source of the pizza, and because I visited the Dumpster regularly I knew what was fresh and what was yesterday's.

The area I frequent is inhabited by many affluent college students. I am not here by chance; the Dumpsters in this area are very rich. Students throw out many good things, including food. In particular they tend to throw everything out when they move at the end of a semester, before and after breaks, and around midterm, when many of them despair of college. So I find it advantageous to keep an eye on the academic calendar.

Students throw food away around breaks because they do not know whether it has spoiled or will spoil before they return. A typical discard is a half jar of peanut butter. In fact, nonorganic peanut butter does not require refrigeration and is unlikely to spoil in any reasonable time. The student does not know that, and since it is Daddy's money, the student decides not to take a chance. Opened containers require caution and some attention to the question. "Why was this discarded?" But in the case of discards from student apartments, the answer may be that the item was thrown out through carelessness, ignorance, or wastefulness. This can sometimes be deduced when the item is found with many others, including some that are obviously perfectly good.

Some students, and others, approach defrosting a freezer by chucking out the whole lot. Not only do the circumstances of such a find tell the story, but also the mass of frozen goods stays cold for a long time and items may be found still frozen or freshly thawed.

Yogurt, cheese, and sour cream are items that are often thrown out while they are still good. Occasionally I find a cheese with a spot of mold, which of course I just pare off, and because it is obvious why such a cheese was discarded, I treat it with less suspicion than an apparently perfect cheese found in similar circumstances. Yogurt is often discarded, still sealed, only because the expiration date on the carton had passed. This is one of my favorite finds because yogurt will keep for several days, even in warm weather.

25 Students throw out canned goods and staples at the end of semesters and when they give up college at midterm. Drugs, pornography, spirits, and the like are often discarded when parents are expected—Dad's day, for example. And spirits also turn up after big party weekends, presumably discarded by the newly reformed. Wine and spirits, of course, keep perfectly well even once opened, but the same cannot be said of beer.

My test for carbonated soft drinks is whether they still fizz vigorously. Many juices or other beverages are too acidic or too syrupy to cause much concern, provided they are not visibly contaminated. I have discovered nasty molds in vegetable juices, even when the product was found under its original seal; I recommend that such products be decanted slowly into a clear glass. Liquids always require some care. One hot day I found a large jug of Pat O'Brien's Hurricane mix. The jug had been opened, but it was still ice cold. I drank three large glasses before it became apparent to me that someone had added the rum to the mix, and not a little rum. I never tasted the rum, and by the time I began to feel the effects I had already ingested a very large quantity of the beverage. Some divers would have considered this a boon, but being suddenly intoxicated in a public place in the early afternoon is not my idea of a good time.

I have heard of people maliciously contaminating discarded food and even handouts, but mostly I have heard of this from people with vivid imaginations who have had no experience with the Dumpsters themselves. Just before the pizza shop stopped discarding its garbage at night, jalapeños began showing up on most of the discarded pizzas. If indeed this was meant to discourage me it was a wasted effort because I am native Texan.

For myself, I avoid game, poultry, pork, and egg-based foods, whether I find them raw or cooked. I seldom have the means to cook what I find, but when I do I avail myself of plentiful supplies of beef, which is often in very good condition. I suppose fish becomes disagreeable before it becomes dangerous. Lizbeth is happy to have any such thing that is past its prime and, in fact, does not recognize fish as food until it is quite strong.

Home leftovers, as opposed to surpluses from restaurants, are very often bad. Evidently, especially among students, there is a common type of personality that carefully wraps up even the smallest leftover and shoves it into the back of the refrigerator for six months or so before discarding it. Characteristic of this type are the reused jars and margarine tubs to which the remains are committed. I avoid ethnic foods I am unfamiliar with. If I do not know what it is supposed to look like when it is good, I cannot be certain I will be able to tell if it is bad.

30   No matter how careful I am I still get dysentery at least once a   30
month, oftener in warm weather. I do not want to paint too romantic a picture. Dumpster diving has serious drawbacks as a way of life.

I learned to scavenge gradually, on my own. Since then I have initiated several companions into the trade. I have learned that there is a predictable series of stages a person goes through in learning to scavenge.

At first the new scavenger is filled with disgust and self-loathing. He is ashamed of being seen and may lurk around, trying to duck behind things, or he may try to dive at night. (In fact, most people instinctively look away from a scavenger. By skulking around, the novice calls attention to himself and arouses suspicion. Diving at night is ineffective and needlessly messy.)

Every grain of rice seems to be a maggot. Everything seems to stink. He can wipe the egg yolk off the found can, but he cannot erase from his mind the stigma of eating garbage.

That stage passes with experience. The scavenger finds a pair of running shoes that fit and look and smell brand-new. He finds a pocket calculator in perfect working order. He finds pristine ice cream, still frozen, more than he can eat or keep. He begins to understand: People throw away perfectly good stuff, a lot of perfectly good stuff.

At this stage, Dumpster shyness begins to dissipate. The diver, after all, has the last laugh. He is finding all manner of good things that are his for the taking. Those who disparage his profession are the fools, not he.

He may begin to hang on to some perfectly good things for which he has neither a use nor a market. Then he begins to take note of the things that are not perfectly good but are nearly so. He mates a Walkman with broken earphones and one that is missing a battery cover. He picks up things that he can repair.

At this stage he may become lost and never recover. Dumpsters are full of things of some potential value to someone and also of things that never have much intrinsic value but are interesting. All the Dumpster divers I have known come to the point of trying to acquire everything they touch. Why not take it, they reason, since it is all free? This is, of course, hopeless. Most divers come to realize that they must restrict themselves to items of relatively immediate utility. But in some cases the diver simply cannot control himself. I have met several of these pack-rat types. Their ideas of the values of various pieces of junk verge on the psychotic. Every bit of glass may be a diamond, they think, and all that glisters, gold.

I tend to gain weight when I am scavenging. Partly this is because I always find far more pizza and doughnuts than water-packed tuna, nonfat yogurt, and fresh vegetables. Also I have not developed much faith in the reliability of Dumpsters as a food source, although it has been proven to me many times. I tend to eat as if I have no idea where my next meal is coming from. But mostly I just hate to see food go to waste and so I eat much more than I should. Something like this drives the obsession to collect junk.

As for collecting objects, I usually restrict myself to collecting one kind of small object at a time, such as pocket calculators, sunglasses, or campaign buttons. To live on the street I must anticipate my needs to a certain extent: I must pick up and save warm bedding I find in August because it will not be found in Dumpsters in November. As I have no access to health care, I often hoard essential drugs, such as antibiotics and antihistamines. (This course can be recommended only to those with some grounding in pharmacology. Antibiotics, for example, even when indicated are worse than useless if taken in insufficient amounts.) But even if I had a home with extensive storage space, I could not save everything that might be valuable in some contingency.

40   I have proprietary feelings about my Dumpsters. As I have mentioned, it is no accident that I scavenge from ones where good finds are common. But my limited experience with Dumpsters in other areas suggests to me that even in poorer areas, Dumpsters, if attended with sufficient diligence, can be made to yield a livelihood. The rich students discard perfectly good kiwifruit; poorer people discard perfectly good apples. Slacks and Polo shirts are found in the one place; jeans and T-shirts in the other. The population of competitors rather than the affluence of the dumpers most affects the feasibility of survival by scavenging. The large number of competitors is what puts me off the idea of trying to scavenge in places like Los Angeles.   40

Curiously, I do not mind my direct competition, other scavengers, so much as I hate the can scroungers.

People scrounge cans because they have to have a little cash. I have tried scrounging cans with an able-bodied companion. Afoot a can scrounger simply cannot make more than a few dollars a day. One can extract the necessities of life from the Dumpsters directly with far less effort than would be required to accumulate the equivalent value in cans. (These observations may not hold in places with container redemption laws.)

Can scroungers, then, are people who must have small amounts of cash. These are drug addicts and winos, mostly the latter because the amounts of cash are so small. Spirits and drugs do, like all other commodities, turn up in Dumpsters and the scavenger will from time to time have a half bottle of a rather good wine with his dinner. But the wino cannot survive on these occasional finds; he must have his daily dose to stave off the DTs. All the cans he can carry will buy about three bottles of Wild Irish Rose.

I do not begrudge them the cans, but can scroungers tend to tear up the Dumpsters, mixing the contents and littering the area. They become so specialized that they can see only cans. They earn my contempt by passing up change, canned goods, and readily hockable items.

45   There are precious few courtesies among scavengers. But it is common practice to set aside surplus items: pairs of shoes, clothing, canned goods, and such. A true scavenger hates to see good stuff go to waste, and what he cannot use he leaves in good condition in plain sight.

Can scroungers lay waste to everything in their path and will stir one of a pair of good shoes to the bottom of a Dumpster, to be lost or ruined in the muck. Can scroungers will even go through individual garbage cans, something I have never seen a scavenger do.

Individual garbage cans are set out on the public easement only on garbage days. On other days going through them requires trespassing close to a dwelling. Going through individual garbage cans without scattering litter is almost impossible. Litter is likely to reduce the public's tolerance of scavenging. Individual cans are simply not as productive as Dumpsters; people in houses and duplexes do not move so often and for some reason do not tend to discard as much useful material. Moreover, the time required to go through one garbage can that serves one household is not much less than the time required to go through a Dumpster that contains the refuse of twenty apartments.

But my strongest reservation about going through individual garbage cans is that this seems to me a very personal kind of invasion to which I would object if I were a householder. Although many things in Dumpsters are obviously meant never to come to light, a Dumpster is somehow less personal.

I avoid trying to draw conclusions about the people who dump in the Dumpsters I frequent. I think it would be unethical to do so, although I know many people will find the idea of scavenger ethics too funny for words.

50   Dumpsters contain bank statements, correspondence, and other documents, just as anyone might expect. But there are also less

obvious sources of information. Pill bottles, for example. The labels bear the name of the patient, the name of the doctor, and the name of the drug. AIDS drugs and antipsychotic medicines, to name but two groups, are specific and are seldom prescribed for any other disorders. The plastic compacts for birth-control pills usually have complete label information.

Despite all of this sensitive information, I have had only one apartment resident object to my going through the Dumpster. In that case it turned out the resident was a university athlete who was taking bets and who was afraid I would turn up his wager slips.

Occasionally a find tells a story. I once found a small paper bag containing some unused condoms, several partial tubes of flavored sexual lubricants, a partially used compact of birth-control pills, and the torn pieces of a picture of a young man. Clearly she was through with him and planning to give up sex altogether.

Dumpster things are often sad—abandoned teddy bears, shredded wedding books, despaired-of sales kits. I find many pets lying in state in Dumpsters. Although I hope to get off the streets so that Lizbeth can have a long and comfortable old age, I know this hope is not very realistic. So I suppose when her time comes she too will go into a Dumpster. I will have no better place for her. And after all, it is fitting, since for most of her life her livelihood has come from the Dumpster. When she finds something I think is safe that has been spilled from a Dumpster, I let her have it. She already knows the route around the best ones. I like to think that if she survives me she will have a chance of evading the dog catcher and of finding her sustenance on the route.

Silly vanities also come to rest in the Dumpsters. I am a rather accomplished needleworker. I get a lot of material from the Dumpsters. Evidently sorority girls, hoping to impress someone, perhaps themselves, with their mastery of a womanly art, buy a lot of embroider-by-number kits, work a few stitches horribly, and eventually discard the whole mess. I pull out their stitches, turn the canvas over, and work an original design. Do not think I refrain from chuckling as I make gifts from these kits.

55 I find diaries and journals. I have often thought of compiling a 55 book of literary found objects. And perhaps I will one day. But what I find is hopelessly commonplace and bad without being, even unconsciously, camp. College students also discard their papers. I am

horrified to discover the kind of paper that now merits an A in an undergraduate course. I am grateful, however, for the number of good books and magazines the students throw out.

In the area I know best I have never discovered vermin in the Dumpsters, but there are two kinds of kitty surprise. One is alley cats whom I meet as they leap, claws first, out of Dumpsters. This is especially thrilling when I have Lizbeth in tow. The other kind of kitty surprise is a plastic garbage bag filled with some ponderous, amorphous mass. This always proves to be used cat litter.

City bees harvest doughnut glaze and this makes the Dumpster at the doughnut shop more interesting. My faith in the instinctive wisdom of animals is always shaken whenever I see Lizbeth attempt to catch a bee in her mouth, which she does whenever bees are present. Evidently some birds find Dumpsters profitable, for birdie surprise is almost as common as kitty surprise of the first kind. In hunting season all kinds of small game turn up in Dumpsters, some of it, sadly, not entirely dead. Curiously, summer and winter, maggots are uncommon.

The worst of the living and near-living hazards of the Dumpsters are the fire ants. The food they claim is not much of a loss, but they are vicious and aggressive. It is very easy to brush against some surface of the Dumpster and pick up half a dozen or more fire ants, usually in some sensitive area such as the underarm. One advantage of bringing Lizbeth along as I make Dumpster rounds is that, for obvious reasons, she is very alert to ground-based fire ants. When Lizbeth recognizes a fire-ant infestation around our feet, she does the Dance of the Zillion Fire Ants. I have learned not to ignore this warning from Lizbeth, whether I perceive the tiny ants or not, but to remove ourselves at Lizbeth's first pas de bourrée. All the more so because the ants are the worst in the summer months when I wear flip-flops if I have them. (Perhaps someone will misunderstand this. Lizbeth does the Dance of the Zillion Fire Ants when she recognizes more fire ants than she cares to eat, not when she is being bitten. Since I have learned to react promptly, she does not get bitten at all. It is the isolated patrol of fire ants that falls in Lizbeth's range that deserves pity. She finds them quite tasty.)

By far the best way to go through a Dumpster is to lower yourself into it. Most of the good stuff tends to settle at the bottom because it is usually weightier than the rubbish. My more athletic companions have often demonstrated to me that they can extract much good material from a Dumpster I have already been over.

60   To those psychologically or physically unprepared to enter a Dumpster, I recommend a stout stick, preferably with some barb or hook at one end. The hook can be used to grab plastic garbage bags. When I find canned goods or other objects loose at the bottom of a Dumpster, I lower a bag into it, roll the desired object into the bag, and then hoist the bag out—a procedure more easily described than executed. Much Dumpster diving is a matter of experience for which nothing will do except practice.

Dumpster diving is outdoor work, often surprisingly pleasant. It is not entirely predictable; things of interest turn up every day and some days there are finds of great value. I am always very pleased when I can turn up exactly the thing I most wanted to find. Yet in spite of the element of chance, scavenging more than most other pursuits tends to yield returns in some proportion to the effort and intelligence brought to bear. It is very sweet to turn up a few dollars in change from a Dumpster that has just been gone over by a wino.

The land is now covered with cities. The cities are full of Dumpsters. If a member of the canine race is ever able to know what it is doing, then Lizbeth knows that when we go around to the Dumpsters, we are hunting. I think of scavenging as a modern form of self-reliance. In any event, after having survived nearly ten years of government service, where everything is geared to the lowest common denominator, I find it refreshing to have work that rewards initiative and effort. Certainly I would be happy to have a sinecure again, but I am no longer heartbroken that I left one.

I find from the experience of scavenging two rather deep lessons. The first is to take what you can use and let the rest go by. I have come to think that there is no value in the abstract. A thing I cannot use or make useful, perhaps by trading, has no value however rare or fine it may be. I mean useful in a broad sense—some art I would find useful and some otherwise.

I was shocked to realize that some things are not worth acquiring, but now I think it is so. Some material things are white elephants that eat up the possessor's substance. The second lesson is the transience of material being. This has not quite converted me to a dualist, but it has made some headway in that direction. I do not suppose that ideas are immortal, but certainly mental things are longer lived than other material things.

65 Once I was the sort of person who invests objects with sentimental value. Now I no longer have those objects, but I have the sentiments yet.

Many times in our travels I have lost everything but the clothes I was wearing and Lizbeth. The things I find in Dumpsters, the love letters and rag dolls of so many lives, remind me of this lesson. Now I hardly pick up a thing without envisioning the time I will cast it aside. This I think is a healthy state of mind. Almost everything I have now has already been cast out at least once, proving that what I own is valueless to someone.

Anyway, I find my desire to grab for the gaudy bauble has been largely sated. I think this is an attitude I share with the very wealthy—we both know there is plenty more where what we have came from. Between us are the rat-race millions who nightly scavenge the cable channels looking for they know not what.

I am sorry for them.

Questions on Meaning

1. Describe your initial reaction to this essay, and explain what about the essay caused this reaction. For example if you were surprised, what specifically did you find surprising?

2. As Eighner analyzes the contents of the dumpsters, he also analyzes the motives of the people who threw these things away. How do these two levels of analysis shape the essay and contribute to its theme?

3. By the end of this essay Eighner has moved to reflective comments on society at large, including the "rat-race millions." What ultimately is he saying about our society? Discuss how consistent this ending is with the development of the essay overall.

Questions on Rhetorical Strategy and Style

1. Eighner's polished use of language and his vocabulary are sophisticated, giving the impression of an educated and intelligent person. To what extent is this consistent with your previous image of what most homeless people are like? Explain the effects of Eighner's very careful definition and explanation of his subject.

2. In addition to analyzing types of food and types of motives for throwing things away, the essay analyzes many other aspects of the "dumpster diving" experience, such as his analysis and classification of different sorts of scavengers. How many different types does he identify? Describe how they are different and what they have in common.

3. This essay is powerful in part because of Eighner's vivid use of detail. Choose any part of the essay describing in detail the contents of dumpsters, and identify in his description the words that most successfully evoke a physical image of the dumpster.

Writing Assignments

1. How do you react to Eighner's comments about wasteful, affluent students? Ask some other students about what things they throw away, and consider your own habits. Do Eighner's descriptions apply to you and other students you know? Why or why not? If so, how does that make you feel? Organize your findings into an essay about possessions.

2. What are your own favorite possessions? Think about your feelings for them, and reflect on what these feelings reveal about what makes you happy. Write an essay in which you explore the relationship between "things" and happiness, using yourself and others as examples.

The High Price of Materialism

Tim Kasser

Tim Kasser (1966–), associate professor of psychology at Knox College since 1995, graduated from Vanderbilt (1988) and University of Rochester (M.A. 1990 and Ph.D. 1994). He has been designated Distinguished Research Fellow, for "Substantial Research Contributing to a Better Understanding of Quality of Life Issues," by the International Society for Quality of Life Studies, 2003; received the CHOICE Outstanding Academic Book, for The High Price of Materialism, *American Library Association, 2002; and the Philip Green Wright/Lombard College Prize for Distinguished Teaching, 2000. He is associate editor for the* Journal of Personality and Social Psychology: Personality Processes and Individual Differences. *His book,* The High Price of Materialism, *(Cambridge: MIT Press, 2002) is the source for this excerpt. He is also co-editor with Allen D. Kanner of* Psychology and Consumer Culture: The Struggle for a Good Life in a Materialistic World, *(American Psychological Association, 2004). He studies the ways in which wealth and attractiveness either do or do not make people happy.*

People who worry about making money and having the right education and background are not as happy and fulfilled as people who think more about getting along with others and doing good work. Culture, however, encourages the pursuit of money and prestige thus leading many to be unhappy.

> To continue much longer overwhelmed by business cares and with
> most of my thoughts wholly upon the way to make money in the
> shortest time must degrade me beyond hope of permanent recovery.
> —ANDREW CARNEGIE[1]

1   In recent years, scientific investigators working in a variety of fields   1
have begun to tally the costs of a materialistic lifestyle. Although the
body of empirical literature on materialism is not large, especially
compared with what we know about topics such as depression, stereo-
typing, neurons, and memory, its findings are quite consistent. Indeed,
what stands out across the studies is a simple fact: people who strongly
value the pursuit of wealth and possessions report lower psychological
well-being than those who are less concerned with such aims.

Research from Our Lab

Since 1993 my colleagues and I have been publishing a series of papers
in which we have been exploring how people's values and goals relate to
their well-being. Our focus has been on understanding what people
view as important or valuable in life, and on associating those values
statistically with a variety of other aspects of their lives, such as happiness, depression, and anxiety. What people value clearly varies from one
individual to another. For some, spirituality and religion are of para-
mount importance; for others, home life, relationships, and family are
especially valued; other people focus on having fun and excitement; and
others on contributing to the community.[2] In our work, we have been
particularly interested in individuals for whom materialistic values are
relatively important. That is, compared with other things that might be
deemed central to one's life, what happens psychologically when a person feels that making money and having possessions are relatively high
in the pantheon of values?

Our First Study

To obtain an answer to this question, Richard Ryan and I began by
developing a questionnaire to measure people's values, which we called
the Aspiration Index.[3] People who complete this questionnaire are presented with many different types of goals and asked to rate each one in
terms of whether it is not at all important, somewhat important,
extremely important, and so on. The current version of the Aspiration

Index includes a large number of possible goals people might have, such as desires to feel safe and secure, to help the world be a better place, to have a great sex life, and to have good relationships with others. By assessing different types of goals, we can obtain a valid assessment of how important materialistic values are in the context of a person's entire system of values. Most value researchers view this as crucial and insist that we can know how much someone values a particular outcome only when that value is considered in relation to other things that might possibly be valued.[4]

Table 1 shows items used to assess materialistic values in our first study. Of central interest, participants reported how important several *financial success* aspirations were to them. We also asked participants how much they were concerned with *self-acceptance* (desires for psychological growth, autonomy, and self-esteem), *affiliation* (desires for a good family life and friendships), and *community feeling* (desires to make the world a better place through one's own actions). From these ratings, we could determine how important, or central, the value of financial success was for each person relative to the other three values.

Ryan and I administered the Aspiration Index to a group of individuals who, second to white rats, form the backbone of much scientific research in psychology: college students. Three hundred sixteen students at the University of Rochester completed a survey packet that included the index and four questionnaires that assessed positive feelings of well-being and negative feelings of distress.

The first measure of well-being assessed self-actualization, a concept made popular by the father of humanistic psychology, Abraham Maslow. Maslow conceived of self-actualization as the pinnacle of psychological health, the state attained by people motivated by growth, meaning, and aesthetics, rather than by insecurity and the attempt to fit in with what other people expect.[5] People who score high on this

Table 1   Financial success items from Kasser and Ryan's (1993) Aspiration Index

You will buy things just because you want them.
You will be financially successful.
You will be your own boss.
You will have a job with high social status.
You will have a job that pays well.

Participants rate how important these aspirations are, from not at all to very important. Reprinted by permission of the American Psychological Association.

measure of self-actualization generally agree with statements such as, "It is better to be yourself than to be popular," and "I do not feel ashamed of any of my emotions." Our second measure of well-being, vitality, also assesses psychological growth and the energy that goes along with authentically expressing who one really is. Vital people are likely to feel energized, alert, and overflowing with that wonderful feeling of being alive.

The last two measures assessed two of the most common psychological disorders: depression and anxiety. The depression questionnaire asked participants how frequently they had experienced common depressive symptoms such as feeling down, feeling lonely or disconnected from others, having sleep or appetite troubles, and having little energy or difficulty concentrating. The anxiety measure asked how much they generally experienced nervousness or shakiness inside, felt tense or fearful, or were suddenly scared for no reason.[6]

When we used statistical analyses to examine how people's value orientations related to their well-being, the results were intriguing. Compared with students who were more oriented toward self-acceptance, affiliation, or community feeling, those who considered financial success a relatively central value reported significantly lower levels of self-actualization and vitality, as well as significantly higher levels of depression and anxiety. Notably, such a strong focus was associated with decreased psychological well-being regardless of whether participants were men or women.

These results supported the premise that materialistic values are unhealthy, but we wanted to see if they would be replicated with young adults who were not in college, and with other ways of assessing well-being besides questionnaires. We therefore gave a somewhat shorter version of the Aspiration Index to a wide-ranging group of 140 eighteen-year-olds. These adolescents varied greatly in terms of race, socioeconomic status, and their mothers' psychological health. Their current situation in life was also diverse, with some having dropped out of high school and others going on to college, some already having had children, and others in trouble with the law.

10   We evaluated psychological well-being in a somewhat different way   10 in this sample. Instead of completing questionnaires, participants met with an experienced clinical psychologist who interviewed them using a set of standard questions. From these interviews ratings were made of the extent to which the teens were socially productive and of how much

they exhibited symptoms of behavior disorders. A socially productive adolescent was defined as someone who was doing well in school, was holding down a job, and had hobbies and other outside interests. Behavior disorders, one of the most common of all childhood problems, involved a variety of symptoms expressing oppositional, defiant, and antisocial behavior common in unhappy teens, such as fighting, belonging to a gang, stealing, and torturing small animals. We also measured the teens' general functioning in life by rating them on a 100-point scale commonly used to assess people's level of psychiatric impairment and overall adaptation to life.[7]

Even with these differences in samples and the way we assessed well-being, the results with these teenagers revealed a pattern consistent with our earlier findings: individuals who were focused on financial success, compared with nonmaterialistic values, were not adapting to society well and were acting in rather destructive ways. Specifically, they were not functioning well in school, on the job, or in their extracurricular activities, and were likely to exhibit various symptoms of behavior disorders, such as vandalizing, skipping school, and carrying weapons.

Our first studies therefore showed that when young adults report that financial success is relatively central to their aspirations, low well-being, high distress, and difficulty adjusting to life are also evident. Although we cannot be sure from these results whether materialistic values cause unhappiness, or whether other factors are at work, the results do suggest a rather startling conclusion: the American dream has a dark side, and the pursuit of wealth and possessions might actually be undermining our well-being.

More Recent Work from Our Lab

These results raised a number of further questions in our minds. Were financial success values the only ones that were problematic for people's psychological health? What would happen if we looked at older individuals? Would similar results be found for other aspects of psychological health and distress? These were some of the issues Ryan and I tried to grapple with in our next study.[8]

We began by revising the Aspiration Index to include some other prominent goals and values of consumer culture. Although strivings for money and possessions certainly constitute the core message encouraged by consumeristic and capitalistic cultures, two other goals are also typically encouraged: having the "right" image and being well known socially. Image and fame values are entwined with those for money and possessions in at least a couple of ways. First, the media in consumeristic cultures frequently link these values by having good-looking celebrities sell products. The underlying message is that owning these products will enhance our image and ensure our popularity with others. A second way these values are connected is that image, fame, and money all share a focus of looking for a sense of worth outside of oneself, and involve striving for external rewards and the praise of others. When we focus on these values (which Ryan and I called "extrinsic"), we are seeking sources of satisfaction outside of ourselves, whether in money, in the mirror, or in admiration by others. In capitalistic, consumer cultures such as the United States, these extrinsic values are often encouraged as worthy because they seemingly convey a sense of success and power.

15   Table 2 lists the items we used in the revised version of the Aspiration Index to measure these three types of materialistic values. In several studies, we have found that people who value one of these values, such

Table 2 Sample items from Kasser and Ryan's (1996) revised Aspiration Index

Financial success

You will have a job with high social status.
You will have a job that pays well.
You will be financially successful.
You will have a lot of expensive possessions.

Social recognition

Your name will be known by many people.
You will do something that brings you much recognition.
You will be admired by many people.
You will be famous.
Your name will appear frequently in the media.

Appealing appearance

You will successfully hide the signs of aging.
You will have people comment often about how
    attractive you look.
You will keep up with fashions in hair and clothing.
You will achieve the "look" you've been after.
Your image will be one others find appealing.

as fame, also tend to value money and image. Thus they seem to have "bought into" the prominent goals of consumer society. Notably, this cluster of goals also was found in students from both Russia and Germany, suggesting that the coexistence of money, fame, and image values can be found in cultures less consumeristic than the United States.[9]

Having expanded the Aspiration Index to measure a greater number of values relevant to the messages of consumer culture, Ryan and I set out to determine whether our results would be the same in adults as they were in college students and teenagers. We randomly sampled a group of 100 adults living in a diverse neighborhood of Rochester, New York. The participants ranged from eighteen to seventy-nine years of age and came from lower, middle, and upper socioeconomic backgrounds. The survey packet we left at participants' doors contained the revised Aspiration Index and the four measures of well-being we used previously (self-actualization, vitality, anxiety, depression measures). Participants also reported on their physical health by noting how often they had experienced nine physical symptoms in the past week (headache, stomach aches, backaches, etc.).[10]

The findings largely corroborated those reported with young adults. Adults who focused on money, image, and fame reported less self-actualization and vitality, and more depression than those less concerned with these values. What is more, they also reported significantly more experiences of physical symptoms. That is, people who believed it is important to strive for possessions, popularity, and good looks also reported more headaches, backaches, sore muscles, and sore throats than individuals less focused on such goals. This was really one of the first indicators, to us, of the pervasive negative correlates of materialistic values—not only is people's psychological well-being worse when they focus on money, but so is their physical health.

As in our studies of college students, materialistic values were equally unhealthy for men and women. Because of the nature of this sample, we could also examine whether findings depended on age or income. Analyses showed that regardless of their age or wealth, people with highly central materialistic values also reported lower well-being.

Having documented some of the problems associated with materialism in adults of different ages and backgrounds, we returned to college students and teenagers to explore further the many different ways that these values are associated with low well-being. As a start, we wanted a better sense of the daily lives of people with a strong materialistic orientation. The earlier studies asked individuals to look back on some portion of their lives and tell us about their well-being; although this is a quick method to measure how people are feeling, we wanted to change the focus and obtain a snapshot of people's daily lives. Therefore, in addition to completing our standard packet of questionnaires, we asked 192 students at the University of Rochester to keep a diary for two weeks. In the middle of each day, and then again at the end of each day, they answered several questions about their current experience: how much they had the same nine physical symptoms assessed in the adult sample and how much they felt each of nine emotions (e.g., happy, joyful, unhappy, angry).

20   As before, participants highly focused on materialistic values reported less self-actualization and vitality and more depression than those with less interest in those values. They also experienced more physical symptoms and less in the way of positive emotions over the two weeks. Something about a strong desire for materialistic pursuits actually affected the participants' day-to-day lives and decreased the quality of their daily experience.[11]

Another new element of this study was measurement of participants' narcissistic tendencies. In psychological parlance, narcissism describes people who cover an inner feeling of emptiness and questionable self-worth with a grandiose exterior that brags of self-importance. Narcissists are typically vain, expect special treatment and admiration from others, and can be manipulative and hostile toward others. Social critics and psychologists have often suggested that consumer culture breeds a narcissistic personality by focusing individuals on the glorification of consumption (e.g., "Have it your way"; "Want it? Get it!").[12] Furthermore, narcissists' desire for external validation fits well with our conception of materialistic values as extrinsic and focused on others' praise. Thus it was not surprising to find that students with strong materialistic tendencies scored high on a standard measure of narcissism, agreeing with statements such as, "I am more capable than other people," "I like to start new fads and fashions," "I wish somebody would write my biography one day," and "I can make anybody believe anything I want them to."[13]

More recent studies expanded our measurements of psychological functioning by examining the extent to which materialism is associated with the use of substances such as tobacco, alcohol, and drugs. In one such project, Ryan and I asked 261 students at Montana State

University how many cigarettes they smoked on a typical day, and how often in the last year they had "gotten drunk," "smoked marijuana," and "done hard drugs." When we averaged these four indicators, results showed that people with a strong materialistic value orientation were highly likely to use such substances frequently.[14]

These results were replicated by Geoff Williams in two groups of high school students.[15] In one study, 141 high school students were asked whether they had smoked 100 cigarettes in their lifetime, which is the National Cancer Institute's definition of a smoker. Student smokers were more oriented toward materialistic values than toward values such as self-acceptance, affiliation, and community feeling. Williams next asked 271 ninth- through twelfth-graders about an even broader list of behaviors that put teens at risk for later problems, such as use of cigarettes, chewing tobacco, alcohol, and marijuana, as well as whether they ever had sexual intercourse. Materialistic teens were more likely to engage in each of these five risk behaviors than were teens focused on other values.

End Notes

1. Carnegie quotation is from Hendrick (1932), pp. 146–147.
2. There is no real agreement in psychology as to the exact number or content of values that make up the human value system, although Shalom Schwartz (1992, 1994, 1996) has made an excellent case for a "universal" system of values. Nonetheless, a glance through a review of value measures (Braithwaite & Scott, 1991) will probably impress the reader for how much disagreement exists among psychologists about what values are important to measure.
3. This first study is Kasser and Ryan (1993).
4. Milton Rokeach (1973), a prominent thinker in empirical value research, coined the term "relative centrality" to describe how important a value is relative to other values. His insistence on this means of measurement is relatively well accepted among value researchers.
5. Maslow (1954) described this idea well.
6. Well-being measures include self-actualization (Jones & Crandall, 1986), vitality (Ryan & Frederick, 1997), anxiety (Derogatis et al., 1974), and depression (Radloff, 1977).
7. The scales in this study were social productivity (Ikle et al., 1983), conduct disorders (Herjanic & Reich, 1982), and global functioning (American Psychiatric Association, 1987). See Sameroff et al. (1982) for more information about the heterogeneous sample.
8. Further information on results from the next two samples reviewed can be found in Kasser (1994) or Kasser and Ryan (1996).
9. See Ryan et al. (1999) and Schmuck et al. (2000).

10. Items were taken from Emmons (1991).

11. Another important finding from this study related to an issue relevant to socially desirable responding. Psychologists are often concerned that participants' responses to certain questionnaires are clouded by the desire to answer in a way that fits with what they think society feels is "good." As a result, they may be unlikely to admit to feelings and thoughts that might be seen as deviant or less than optimal. Because a scale exists to measure socially desirable responding (Crowne & Marlowe, 1960), we examined whether this might explain why people strongly focused on materialistic values reported low well-being. Our statistical analysis found no support for this idea, as the effects remained significant even after accounting for socially desirable responses. Notably, however, Mick (1996) reached a different conclusion with other measures of materialism.

12. See Cushman (1990) or Kanner and Gomes (1995).

13. This narcissism scale was developed by Raskin and Terry (1988).

14. Kasser and Ryan (2001).

15. Williams et al. (2000).

References

American Psychiatric Association. (1987). *Diagnostic and statistical manual of mental disorders* (3rd ed., rev.). Washington, DC: American Psychiatric Association.

Braithwaite, V. A., & Scott, W. A. (1991). Values. In J. P. Robinson, P. R. Shaver, & L. S. Wrightsman (Eds.), *Measures of personality and social psychological attitudes* (pp. 661–753). San Diego: Academic Press.

Crowne, D. P., & Marlowe, D. (1960). A new scale of social desirability independent of psychopathology. *Journal of Consulting Psychology, 24,* 349–354.

Cushman, P. (1990). Why the self is empty: Toward a historically situated psychology. *American Psychologist, 45,* 599–611.

Derogatis, L. R., Lipman, R. S., Rickels, K., Uhlenhuth, E. H., & Covi, L. (1974). The Hopkins Symptom Checklist (HSCL): A self-report symptom inventory. *Behavioral Science, 19,* 1–15.

Emmons, R. A. (1991). Personal strivings, daily life events, and psychological and physical well-being. *Journal of Personality, 59,* 453–472.

Hendrick, B. J. (1932). *The life of Andrew Carnegie,* Vol. 1. Garden City, NY: Doubleday.

Herjanic, B., & Reich, W. (1982). Development of a structured psychiatric interview for children: Agreement between child and parent on individual symptoms. *Journal of Abnormal Child Psychology, 10,* 307–324.

Ikle, D. N., Lipp, D. O., Butters, E. A., & Ciarlo, J. (1983). *Development and validation of the adolescent community mental health questionnaire.* Denver, CO: Mental Systems Evaluation Project.

Jones, A., & Crandall, R. (1986). Validation of a short index of self-actualization. *Personality and Social Psychology Bulletin, 12,* 63–73.

Kanner, A. D., & Gomes, M. E. (1995). The all-consuming self. In T. Roszak, M. E. Gomes, & A. D. Kanner (Eds.), *Ecopsychology: Restoring the Earth, healing the mind* (pp. 77–91). San Francisco: Sierra Club Books.

Kasser, T. (1994). *Further dismantling the American dream: Differential well-being correlates of intrinsic and extrinsic goals.* Unpublished doctoral dissertation, University of Rochester, Rochester, NY.

Kasser, T., & Ryan, R. M. (1993). A dark side of the American dream: Correlates of financial success as a central life aspiration. *Journal of Personality and Social Psychology, 65,* 410–422.

Kasser, T., & Ryan, R. M. (1996). Further examining the American dream: Differential correlates of intrinsic and extrinsic goals. *Personality and Social Psychology Bulletin, 22,* 280–287.

Kasser, T., & Ryan R. M. (2001). Be careful what you wish for: Optimal functioning and the relative attainment of intrinsic and extrinsic goals. In P. Schmuck & K. M. Sheldon (Eds.), Life goals and well-being: *Towards a positive psychology of human striving* (pp. 116–131). Goettingen, Germany: Hogrefe & Huber.

Maslow, A. H. (1954). *Motivation and personality.* New York: Harper & Row.

Mick, D. G. (1996). Are studies of dark side variables confounded by socially desirable responding? The case of materialism. *Journal of Consumer Research, 23,* 106–119.

Radloff, L. (1977). The CES-D scale: A self-report depression scale for research in the general population. *Applied Psychological Measurement, 1,* 385–401.

Raskin, R., & Terry, H. (1988). A principal components analysis of the Narcissistic Personality Inventory and further evidence of its construct validity. *Journal of Personality and Social Psychology, 54,* 890–902.

Rokeach, M. (1973). *The nature of human values.* New York: Free Press.

Ryan, R. M., Chirkov, V. I., Little, T. D., Sheldon, K. M., Timoshina, E., & Deci, E. L. (1999). The American dream in Russia: Extrinsic aspirations and well-being in two cultures. *Personality and Social Psychology Bulletin, 25,* 1509–1524.

Ryan, R. M., & Frederick, C. (1997). On energy, personality, and health: Subjectivity vitality as a dynamic reflection of well-being. *Journal of Personality, 65,* 529–565.

Sameroff, A. J., Seifer, R., & Zax, M. (1982). Early development of children at risk for emotional disorders. *Monographs of the Society for Research in Child Development, 47* (serial no. 199).

Schmuck, P., Kasser, T., & Ryan, R. M. (2000). Intrinsic and extrinsic goals: Their structure and relationship to well-being in German and U.S. college students. *Social Indicators Research, 50,* 225–241.

Schwartz, S. H. (1992). Universals in the content and structure of values: Theoretical and empirical tests in 20 countries. In M. Zanna (Ed.), *Advances in experimental and social psychology,* Vol. 25 (pp. 1–65). Orlando, FL: Academic Press.

Schwartz, S. H. (1994). Are there universal aspects in the content and structure of values? *Journal of Social Issues, 50,* 19–45.

Schwartz, S. H. (1996). Values, priorities and behavior: Applying of theory of integrated value systems. In C. Seligman, J. M. Olson, & M. P. Zanna (Eds.), *The psychology of values: The Ontario symposium,* Vol. 8 (pp. 1–24). Hillsdale, NJ: Erlbaum.

Williams, G. C., Cox, E. M., Hedberg, V. A., & Deci, E. L. (2000). Extrinsic life goals and health risk behaviors in adolescents. *Journal of Applied Social Psychology, 30,* 1756–1771.

Questions on Meaning

1. Self-actualization means that a person is satisfied with his or her own goals and aspirations and is not upset by outward expectations. What is the relationship between a desire for money and power and this quality in Kasser's research?
2. Two common psychological disorders are anxiety and depression. How are these related to a desire for money and power? What does this tell us about life in a world where everyone wants to win (note reality TV)?
3. The desire to have money and power is also associated with cigarette and substance abuse. What does this say about what the desire to be rich and famous does to the health and well-being of those who abuse substantives?

Questions on Rhetorical Strategy and Style

1. Oddly enough, this essay—that shows the cost of ambition—begins by talking about what the cost of depression and illness is to the country. Why does this apparent contradiction work as a beginning to the essay? Who is the intended audience of the essay?
2. The essay moves systematically through the studies that have been done in the psychology lab of these investigators. Each investigation leads to another that gives even more distressing results. How does the research move from depression to physical illness?
3. The essay ends with the effects of these feelings on teenagers? Teens who value money and success more than community and self-acceptance are more likely to behave in ways that will hurt them in later life. Why does this ending appeal to a need for change?

Writing Assignments

1. Observe students on your campus. Visit a spot where students drink and/or smoke. What do they talk about? What are their values? Then visit a spot where students are working on a community project or tutoring. What do they talk about? What are their values? Write about the differences.
2. The essay begins with a quote from Andrew Carnegie, who was one of the richest men in America and who died with very little

money because he gave it all away to charity. What do you think of people who give large amounts of money to charity? What do you think of people who try to win the lottery? Describe what you see as typical personalities of both.

3. The essay discusses an Aspiration Index. Write about your aspirations. What do you want from life? What will make you happy? Then think about how you fit with the information in the essay. Reflect on your values.

Notes on Class

Paul Fussell

Paul Fussell (1924-) was born in California, the son of a millionaire. After completing a degree at Pomona College, he served as an infantry officer in World War II and returned to take a Ph.D. in literature at Harvard. His book, Poetic Meter and Poetic Form *(1965, revised 1979), is used widely in literature courses; and his* The Great War and Modern Memory *(1975), written about the British experience of World War I, won the National Book Award in 1976. He has taught at Rutgers and currently occupies a chair in English literature at the University of Pennsylvania. In his delightful book,* Class, *he ironically describes the fascination of an allegedly democratic American society with the details of social class. In the essay reprinted here, taken from* The Boy Scout Handbook and Other Observations *(1982), he is particularly merciless with the middle class.*

1   If the dirty little secret used to be sex, now it is the facts about social class. No subject today is more likely to offend. Over thirty years ago Dr. Kinsey generated considerable alarm by disclosing that despite appearances one-quarter of the male population had enjoyed at least one homosexual orgasm. A similar alarm can be occasioned today by asserting that despite the much-discussed mechanism of "social mobility" and the constant redistribution of income in this country, it is virtually impossible to break out of the social class in which one has been nurtured. Bad news for the ambitious as well as the bogus, but there it is.

Defining class is difficult, as sociologists and anthropologists have learned. The more data we feed into the machines, the less likely it is that significant formulations will emerge. What follows here is based not on interviews, questionnaires, or any kind of quantitative technique but on perhaps a more trustworthy method—perception. Theory may inform us that there are three classes in America, high, middle, and low. Perception will tell us that there are at least nine, which I would designate and arrange like this:

> Top Out-of-Sight
> Upper
> Upper Middle
> _____
> Middle
> High-Proletarian
> Mid-Proletarian
> Low-Proletarian
> _____
> Destitute
> Bottom Out-of-Sight

In addition, there is a floating, class with no permanent location in this hierarchy. We can call it Class X. It consists of well-to-do hippies, "artist," "writers" (who write nothing), floating bohemians, politicians out of office, disgraced athletic coaches, resiresabroad, rock stars, "celebrities," and the shrewder sort of spies.

The quasi-official division of the population into three economic classes called high-, middle-, and low-income groups rather misses the point, because as a class indicator the amount of money is not as important as the source. Important distinctions at both the top and bottom of the class scale arise less from degree of affluence than from the people or institutions to whom one is beholden for support. For example, the main thing distinguishing the top three classes from each other is the amount of money inherited in relation to the amount currently earned. The Top Out-of-Sight Class (Rockefellers, du Ponts, Melons, Fords, Whitneys) lives on inherited capital entirely. Its money is like the hats of the Boston ladies who, asked where they got them, answer, "Oh, we *have* our hats." No one whose money, no matter how ample, comes from his own work, like film stars, can be a member of the Top Out-of-Sights, even if the size of his income and the extravagance of his expenditure permit him temporary social access to it.

Since we expect extremes to meet, we are not surprised to find the very lowest class, Bottom Out-of-Sight, similar to the highest in one crucial respect: It is given its money and kept sort of afloat not by its own efforts but by the welfare machinery or the prison system. Members of the Top Out-of-Sight Class sometimes earn some money, as directors or board members of philanthropic or even profitable enterprises, but the amount earned is laughable in relation to the amount already possessed. Membership in the Top Out-of-Sight Class depends on the ability to flourish without working at all, and it is this that suggests a curious brotherhood between those at the top and the bottom of the scale.

5   It is this also that distinguishes the Upper Class from its betters. It lives on both inherited money and a salary from attractive, if usually slight, work, without which, even if it could survive and even flourish, it would feel bored and a little ashamed. The next class down, the Upper Middle, may possess virtually as much as the two above it. The difference is that it has earned most of it, in law, medicine, oil, real-estate, or even the more honorific forms of trade. The Upper Middles are afflicted with a bourgeois sense of shame, a conviction that to live on the earnings of others, even forebears, is not entirely nice.

The Out-of-Sight Classes at top and bottom have something else in common: They are literally all but invisible (hence their name). The façades of Top Out-of-Sight houses are never seen from the street, and such residences (like Rockefeller's upstate New York premises) are often hidden away deep in the hills, safe from envy and its ultimate attendants, confiscatory taxation and finally expropriation. The Bottom Out-of-Sight Class is equally invisible. When not hidden away in institutions or claustrated in monasteries, lamaseries, or communes, it is hiding from creditors, deceived bail-bondsmen, and merchants intent on repossessing cars and furniture. (This class is visible briefly in one place, in the spring on the streets of New York City, but after this ritual yearly show of itself it disappears again.) When you pass a house with a would-be impressive façade addressing the street, you know it is occupied by a mere member of the Upper or Upper Middle Class. The White House is an example. Its residents, even on those occasions when they are Kennedys, can never be classified as Top Out-of-Sight but only Upper Class. The house is simply too conspicuous, and temporary residence there usually constitutes a come-down for most of its occupants. It is a hopelessly Upper- or Upper-Middle-Class place.

Another feature of both Top and Bottom Out-of-Sight Classes is their anxiety to keep their names out of the papers, and this too suggests that socially the President is always rather vulgar. All the classes in between Top and Bottom Out-of-Sight slaver for personal publicity (monograms on shirts, inscribing one's name on lawn-mowers and power tools, etc.), and it is this lust to be known almost as much as income that distinguishes them from their Top and Bottom neighbors. The High- and Mid-Prole Classes can be recognized immediately by their pride in advertising their physical presence, a way of saying, "Look! We pay our bills and have a known place in the community, and you can find us there any time." Thus hypertrophied house numbers on the front, or house numbers written "Two Hundred Five" ("Two Hundred and Five" is worse) instead of 205, or flamboyant house or family names blazoned on façades, like "The Willows" or "The Polnickis."

(If you go behind the façade into the house itself, you will find a fairly trustworthy class indicator in the kind of wood visible there. The top three classes invariably go in for hardwoods for doors and panelling; the Middle and High-Prole Classes, pine, either plain or "knotty." The knotty-pine "den" is an absolute stigma of the Middle Class, one never to be overcome or disguised by temporarily affected higher usages. Below knotty pine there is plywood.)

Façade study is a badly neglected anthropological field. As we work down from the (largely white-painted) bank-like façades of the Upper and Upper Middle Classes, we encounter such Middle and Prole conventions as these, which I rank in order of social status:

Middle	1.	A potted tree on either side of the front door, and the more pointy and symmetrical the better.
	2.	A large rectangular picture-window in a split-level "ranch" house, displaying a table-lamp between two side curtains. The cellophane on the lampshade must be visibly inviolate.
	3.	Two chairs, usually metal with pipe arms, disposed on the front porch as a "conversation group," in stubborn defiance of the traffic thundering past.

High-Prole	4.	Religious shrines in the garden, which if small and understated, are slightly higher class than
Mid-Prole	5.	Plaster gnomes and flamingoes, and blue or lavender shiny spheres supported by fluted cast-concrete pedestals.
Low-Prole	6.	Defunct truck tires painted white and enclosing flower beds. (Auto tires are a grade higher.)
	7.	Flower-bed designs worked in dead light bulbs or the butts of disused beer bottles.

The Destitute have no façades to decorate, and of course the Bottom Out-of-Sights, being invisible, have none either, although both these classes can occasionally help others decorate theirs–painting tires white on an hourly basis, for example, or even watering and fertilizing the potted trees of the Middle Class. Class X also does not decorate its façades, hoping to stay loose and unidentifiable, ready to re-locate and shape-change the moment it sees that its cover has been penetrated.

10   In this list of façade conventions an important principle emerges. Organic materials have higher status than metal or plastic. We should take warning from Sophie Portnoy's aluminum venetian blinds, which are also lower than wood because the slats are curved, as if "improved," instead of classically flat. The same principle applies, as *The Preppy Handbook* has shown so effectively, to clothing fabrics, which must be cotton or wool, never Dacron or anything of that prole kind. In the same way, yachts with wood hulls, because they must be repaired or replaced (at high cost) more often, are classier than yachts with fiberglass hulls, no matter how shrewdly merchandised. Plastic hulls are cheaper and more practical, which is precisely why they lack class.

As we move down the scale, income of course decreases, but income is less important to class than other seldom-invoked measurements: for example, the degree to which one's work is supervised by an omnipresent immediate superior. The more free from supervision, the higher the class, which is why a dentist ranks higher than a mechanic working under a foreman in a large auto shop, even if he makes considerably more money than the dentist. The two trades may be thought equally dirty: It is the dentist's freedom from supervision that helps confer class upon him. Likewise, a high-school teacher obliged to file weekly "lesson plans" with a principal or "curriculum coordinator" thereby occupies a class position lower than a tenured professor, who reports to no one, even though the high-school teacher may be richer, smarter, and nicer. (Supervisors and Inspectors are titles that go with public schools, post offices, and police departments: The student of class will need to know no more.) It is largely because they must report that even the highest members of the naval and military services lack social status: They all have designated supervisors—even the Chairman of the Joint Chiefs of Staff has to report to the President.

Class is thus defined less by bare income than by constraints and insecurities. It is defined also by habits and attitudes. Take television watching. The Top Out-of-Sight Class doesn't watch at all. It owns the companies and pays others to monitor the thing. It is also entirely devoid of intellectual or even emotional curiosity: It has its ideas the way it has its money. The Upper Class does look at television but it prefers Camp offerings, like the films of Jean Harlow or Jon Hall. The Upper Middle Class regards TV as vulgar except for the highminded emissions of National Educational Television, which it watches avidly, especially when, like the Shakespeare series, they are the most incompetently directed and boring. Upper Middles make a point of forbidding children to watch more than an hour a day and worry a lot about violence in society and sugar in cereal. The Middle-Class watches, preferring the more "beautiful" kinds of non-body-contact sports like tennis or gymnastics or figure-skating (the music is a redeeming feature here). With High-, Mid-, and Low-Proles we find heavy viewing of the soaps in the daytime and rugged body-contact sports (football, hockey, boxing) in the evening. The lower one is located in the Prole classes the more likely one is to watch "Bowling for Dollars" and "Wonder Woman" and "The Hulk" and when choosing a game show to prefer "Joker's Wild" to "The Family Feud," whose jokes are sometimes incomprehensible. Destitutes and Bottom Out-of-Sights have in common a problem involving choice. Destitutes usually "own" about three color sets, and the problem is which three programs to run at once. Bottom Out-of-Sights exercise no choice at all, the decisions being made for them by correctional or institutional personnel.

The time when the evening meal is consumed defines class better than, say, the presence or absence on the table of ketchup bottles and ashtrays shaped like little toilets enjoining the diners to "Put Your Butts Here." Destitutes and Bottom Out-of-Sights eat dinner at 5:30, for the Prole staff on which they depend must clean up and be out roller-skating or bowling early in the evening. Thus Proles eat at 6:00 or 6:30. The Middles eat at 7:00, the Upper Middles at 7:30 or, if very ambitious, at 8:00. The Uppers and Top Out-of-Sights dine at 8:30 or 9:00 or even later, after nightly protracted "cocktail" sessions lasting usually around two hours. Sometimes they forget to eat at all.

Similarly, the physical appearance of the various classes defines them fairly accurately. Among the top four classes thin is good, and the bottom two classes appear to ape this usage, although down there thin is seldom a matter of choice. It is the three Prole classes that tend to fat, partly as a result of their use of convenience foods and plenty of beer. These are the classes too where anxiety about slipping down a rung causes nervous overeating, resulting in fat that can be rationalized as advertising the security of steady wages and the ability to "eat out" often. Even "Going Out for Breakfast" is not unthinkable for Proles, if we are to believe that they respond to the McDonald's TV ads as they're supposed to. A recent magazine ad for a diet book aimed at Proles stigmatizes a number of erroneous assumptions about body weight, proclaiming with some inelegance that "They're all a crock." Among such vulgar errors is the proposition that "All Social Classes Are Equally Over-weight." This the ad rejects by noting quite accurately,

> *Your weight is an advertisement of your social standing. A century ago, corpulence was a sign of success. But no more. Today it is the badge of the lower-middle-class, where obesity is four times more prevalent than it is among the upper-middle and middle classes.*

It is not just four times more prevalent. It is at least four times more visible, as any observer can testify who has witnessed Prole women perambulating shopping malls in their bright, very tight jersey trousers. Not just obesity but the flaunting of obesity is the Prole sign, as if the object were to give maximum aesthetic offense to the higher classes and thus achieve a form of revenge.

15   Another physical feature with powerful class meaning is the wearing of plaster casts on legs and ankles by members of the top three classes. These casts, a sort of white badge of honor, betoken stylish mishaps with frivolous but costly toys like horses, skis, snowmobiles, and mopeds. They signify a high level of conspicuous waste in a social   15

world where questions of unpayable medical bills or missed working days do not apply. But in the matter of clothes, the Top Out-of-Sight is different from both Upper and Upper Middle Classes. It prefers to appear in new clothes, whereas the class just below it prefers old clothes. Likewise, all three Prole classes make much of new garments, with the highest possible polyester content. The question does not arise in the same form with Destitutes and Bottom Out-of-Sights. They wear used clothes, the thrift shop and prison supply room serving as their Bonwit's and Korvette's.

This American class system is very hard for foreigners to master, partly because most foreigners imagine that since America was founded by the British it must retain something of British institutions. But our class system is more subtle than the British, more a matter of gradations than of blunt divisions, like the binary distinction between a gentleman and a cad. This seems to lack plausibility here. One seldom encounters in the United States the sort of absolute prohibitions which (half-comically, to be sure) one is asked to believe define the gentleman in England. Like these:

> *A gentleman never wears brown shoes in the city, or*
> *A gentleman never wears a green suit, or*
> *A gentleman never has soup at lunch, or*
> *A gentleman never uses a comb, or*
> *A gentleman never smells of anything but tar, or*
> *"No gentleman can fail to admire Bellini."*

W. H. Auden

In America it seems to matter much less the way you present yourself—green, brown, neat, sloppy, scented—than what your backing is—that is, where your money comes from. What the upper orders display here is no special uniform but the kind of psychological security they derive from knowing that others recognize their freedom from petty anxieties and trivial prohibitions.

Questions on Meaning

1. Draw a matrix (a shape like a chess board) with 10 rows labeled with Fussell's ten classes. Label the columns "Income," "Facade," and so forth to include all the categories that Fussell uses to distinguish the classes. Insert brief descriptions in the "cells." For example, the cell at the intersection of the row "Top-Out-of-Sight" and the column "Income," would read "more inherited than earned."
2. How does Fussell distinguish the top three classes in his list?
3. How are the Top and Bottom Out-of-Sight classes alike, other than being out of sight?

Questions on Rhetorical Strategy and Style

1. Fussell uses lists of qualities and possessions that distinguish the classes. Re-examine one of his lists and explain what distinguishes the items on his lists. Why is the second item not as good as the first, and the third not as good as the second, and so on?
2. What qualities do the members of Fussell's class X have in common?

Writing Assignments

1. What class would you assign to someone who works as a professor at a university, has the evening meal at 6:30, lives in a condo with a small garden devoid of plaster ornaments, runs daily and plays tennis twice a week? Explain. Add class assignments for people you know.
2. Use Fussell's categories to write an essay examining your roots. Visit or recall the houses of your most significant friends and relatives, and assign them social classes.
3. Fussell's descriptions of classes are ironic or satirical, sometimes a little cruel, and very upper-class. What and whom has Fussell left out of his picture of American social classes? Write an essay that provides a more balanced picture of your own class, or of the class you grew up in.

Glass Ceiling

Scott Adams

Scott Adams (1957–), creator of one of the most recognizable characters in cartoon history, was born and raised in the Catskills region of New York state. He moved to California after graduating from college. He then earned an M.B.A. at the University of California at Berkeley, after which he spent almost 20 years in the banking industry. His creation, the Dilbert *comic strip, emerged first as a feature of Adams's presentations at work. In 1988, he syndicated the cartoon, which began appearing in newspapers in 1989.* Dilbert *proved an almost immediate hit. Workers frustrated with cubicle life, managerial bureaucracy, and the insensitivity of corporate America found a champion in the nerdy little character. Soon office and cubicle walls were covered with* Dilbert *cartoons, and collections of Adams's work consistently made the bestseller lists. In 1995, Adams left his cubicle to devote all of his energies to the strip.*

Original Dilbert *books include* The Dilbert Principle *(1996),* Dogbert's Top Secret Management Handbook *(1996),* The Dilbert Future *(1997), and* The Joy of Work *(1998). In addition, 22 collections of the comic strip have been published, with more than 10 million copies currently in print. Despite the success of the strip and the collections, an animated television program featuring Dilbert lasted only one season on UPN. In the following strip, Adams explores gender issues in the workplace, focusing specifically on power relationships.*

Questions on Meaning

1. What is the relationship between Alice and her coworker in this strip? How does power shift during the story?
2. What does the term "glass ceiling" mean? In your experience, is it still a valid concept? Explain your response.
3. How does Alice's response to her coworker demonstrate her feelings about gender issues in the workplace?

Questions on Rhetorical Strategy and Style

1. How does Adams use facial expressions in the strip to tell his story?
2. In what ways does the glass ceiling disrupt the cause/effect relationship between work and reward?
3. Based on this strip, what do you believe is Adams's attitude toward the glass ceiling?

Writing Assignments

1. Write a report on gender roles in the workplace based on your own experience. Have you observed any discrimination against women in terms of work assignments, compensation, or treatment? If so, try to use specific examples to support your claims.
2. Research the concept of the glass ceiling. Write an essay either recounting its history over the past decade or analyzing the relevance of the concept for women in today's workforce.

Modern Witch Hunts Fueled by Irrational Fear, Media

Paul Campos

Paul Campos (1959–   ), the child of Mexican immigrants, was born in Colorado Springs and grew up in Michigan, the oldest of six children. He received his BA, MA, and JD from the University of Michigan. After practicing law in Chicago, he joined the University of Colorado Law School faculty in 1990. He also writes a newspaper column for the Scripps Howard News Agency. His books include Jurismania: The Madness of American Law *(1999) and* The Obesity Myth: Why America's Obsession with Weight Is Hazardous to Your Health *(2004).*

1   H.L. Mencken once remarked that no fact was ever more firmly established in a court of law than the existence of witches. Anyone who thinks witch hunts are a thing of the past ought to read Barry Glassner's book "The Culture of Fear." Glassner, a sociologist at the University of Southern California, has assembled a catalogue of American cultural hysteria that is both amusing and appalling.

Glassner's book describes how and why Americans come to be terrified of all sorts of small or imaginary risks, while paying little attention to far greater threats. From flesh-eating bacteria and plane crashes, to breast implants, road rage and school shootings, complex sets of cultural forces push Americans toward intermittent (or, in the case of issues such as drug use, continual) outbursts of fear-driven irrationality.

In some cases our fears are based on the invention of imaginary diseases. Consider Oppositional Deficit Disorder, which according to the American Psychiatric Association's Diagnostic and Statistical Manual makes children good candidates for imprisonment in psychiatric wards if they do any five of the following: argue with adults, defy adult requests, do things that annoy others, lose their tempers, become easily annoyed, act spiteful, blame others for their mistakes, get angry and resentful or swear.

As Glassner points out, this definition essentially turns being a teenager into a form of mental illness.

5   The most chilling recent example of how irrational fears can cause enormous social damage is provided by the amazing story of "satanic ritual abuse." In her new book "No Crueler Tyrannies: Accusation, False Witness, and Other Terrors of Our Times," Dorothy Rabinowitz describes how hundreds of child-care workers, teachers and others were accused of, charged with, and in many cases imprisoned for, a series of quite literally incredible crimes.

Rabinowitz points out that some of these people are still in prison, after having been tried and convicted "on the basis of some of the most fantastic claims ever presented to an American jury."

Bowing to pressure from legions of hysterical parents demanding that they "protect the children," prosecutors and judges allowed out of control "experts" to coerce small children into testifying that they had been subjected to horrifying sexual abuse, even after the children denied repeatedly that anything of the sort had occurred.

Glassner and Rabinowitz both describe the crucial role the media play in creating and sustaining our modern witch hunts. And, as the media frenzy over the supposed epidemic of sexual abuse by Roman Catholic priests begins to subside, it would be well to remember the cautionary tales presented by these two books.

No one denies, of course, that some priests have committed terrible crimes, and that in some instances these crimes have been ignored or covered up by negligent or corrupt church officials. But no one denies there are such things as road rage, school shootings and drug abuse, either.

10   The point is that, as these books demonstrate, cultural anxieties, symbolic politics, and media overkill can convert relatively rare incidents into "epidemics" that trigger outbursts of legal and social hysteria.

Given the dynamics of the story, one thing seems certain about the current wave of accusations against priests: Many of those accusations will turn out to be false. It's also safe to predict that the media will get around to discovering this, after the hysteria has died down. But not just yet.

Consider a caveat from a review of Rabinowitz's book in the *New York Times:* "After all, there are charges of sex abuse that prove to be true—just look at the scandal that has overtaken the Roman Catholic Church."

Questions on Meaning

1. Campos quotes H.L. Mencken as saying that, "no fact was ever so firmly established in court of law than the existence of witches." What does Campos mean by this reference? Were there witches? If not, why would the law have said there were? What danger does this information indicate for citizens today?
2. What characteristics of teenagers could cause them to be jailed as mental patients? Why does the essay argue that such treatment would be unethical?
3. What modern day "witch hunts" does Campos describe? What characterizes these persecutions? Are they indeed the same as witch hunts?

Questions on Rhetorical Style and Structure

1. The essay begins and ends with powerful citations and quotes from other writers. How does this technique catch and hold the reader's attention?
2. As an article in newspapers, this essay must appeal to many readers. What techniques does the author use to appeal to the readers, and how does knowing that the author is a law professor give him credibility?
3. The essay uses references from two authors, Glassner and Rabinowitz. How are these two compared in order to make the essay's point stronger?

Writing Assignments

1. Campos argues that the media create some of the public's fears. Find an issue in the media that is being used now to fuel fears (terrorism, SUVs, AIDS), and write about how the media present the threat. How is the reporting accurate, and how is it sensational and fear-inducing?
2. Investigate a current "illness" that worries parents—for example, Attention Deficit Disorder or diet drugs. Find information on the disorder, and write about the ways that young people are affected.

3. Find information on the witch hunts in Europe or America. Write about the real reasons for these accusations. You might look into the blacklisting of writers in the United States in the fifties as well. Find out about the House Un-American Activities Committee and Arthur Miller, as one possibility.

Future Shlock

Neil Postman

Neil Postman (1931–2003) was born in Brooklyn, New York. He was educated at the State University of New York and Columbia, and he taught communications arts and sciences at New York University. A well-known spokesman for educational reform, Postman wrote for a number of periodicals, including the Atlantic *and* The Nation. *Publications include* Teaching as a Conserving Activity *(1980),* The Disappearance of Childhood *(1982),* Amusing Ourselves to Death: Public Discourse in the Age of Show Business *(1985), and* Conscientious Objections: Stirring Up Trouble About Language, Technology, and Education *(1988). Also, he coauthored* Linguistics: A Revolution in Teaching *(1966),* Teaching as a Subversive Activity *(1969), and* The Soft Revolution *(1971). Postman edited* Et Cetera, *the journal of general semantics, for a decade. In this essay, Postman attacked the trivialization of American culture and the loss of intelligent discourse by the show business mindset of mass media.*

1   Human intelligence is among the most fragile things in nature. It doesn't take much to distract it, suppress it, or even annihilate it. In this century, we have had some lethal examples of how easily and quickly intelligence can be defeated by any one of its several nemeses: ignorance, superstition, moral fervor, cruelty, cowardice, neglect. In the late 1920s, for example, Germany was, by any measure, the most literate, cultured nation in the world. Its legendary seats of learning attracted scholars from every corner. Its philosophers, social critics, and scientists were of the first rank; its humane traditions an inspiration to less favored nations. But by the mid-1930s—that

is, in less than ten years—this cathedral of human reason had been transformed into a cesspool of barbaric irrationality. Many of the most intelligent products of German culture were forced to flee—for example, Einstein, Freud, Karl Jaspers, Thomas Mann, and Stefan Zweig. Even worse, those who remained were either forced to submit their minds to the sovereignty of primitive superstition, or—worse still— willingly did so: Konrad Lorenz, Werner Heisenberg, Martin Heidegger, Gerhardt Hauptmann. On May 10, 1933, a huge bonfire was kindled in Berlin and the books of Marcel Proust, André Gide, Emile Zola, Jack London, Upton Sinclair, and a hundred others were committed to the flames, amid shouts of idiot delight. By 1936, Joseph Paul Goebbels, Germany's Minister of Propaganda, was issuing a proclamation which began with the following words: "Because this year has not brought an improvement in art criticism, I forbid once and for all the continuance of art criticism in its past form, effective as of today." By 1936, there was no one left in Germany who had the brains or courage to object.

Exactly why the Germans banished intelligence is a vast and largely unanswered question. I have never been persuaded that the desperate economic depression that afflicted Germany in the 1920s adequately explains what happened. To quote Aristotle: Men do not become tyrants in order to keep warm. Neither do they become stupid—at least not *that* stupid. But the matter need not trouble us here. I offer the German case only as the most striking example of the fragility of human intelligence. My focus here is the United States in our own time, and I wish to worry you about the rapid erosion of our own intelligence. If you are confident that such a thing cannot happen, your confidence is misplaced, I believe, but it is understandable.

After all, the United States is one of the few countries in the world founded by intellectuals—men of wide learning, of extraordinary rhetorical powers, of deep faith in reason. And although we have had our moods of anti-intellectualism, few people have been more generous in support of intelligence and learning than Americans. It was the United States that initiated the experiment in mass education that is, even today, the envy of the world. It was America's churches that laid the foundation of our admirable system of higher education; it was the Land-Grant Act of 1862 that made possible our great state universities; and it is to America that scholars and writers have fled when freedom of the intellect became impossible in their own nations. This is why the great historian of American civilization Henry Steele Commager called

America "the Empire of Reason." But Commager was referring to the United States of the eighteenth and nineteenth centuries. What term he would use for America today, I cannot say. Yet he has observed, as others have, a change, a precipitous decline in our valuation of intelligence, in our uses of language, in the disciplines of logic and reason, in our capacity to attend to complexity. Perhaps he would agree with me that the Empire of Reason is, in fact, gone, and that the most apt term for America today is the Empire of Shlock.

In any case, this is what I wish to call to your notice: the frightening displacement of serious, intelligent public discourse in American culture by the imagery and triviality of what may be called show business. I do not see the decline of intelligent discourse in America leading to the barbarisms that flourished in Germany, of course. No scholars, I believe, will ever need to flee America. There will be no bonfires to burn books. And I cannot imagine any proclamations forbidding once and for all art criticism, or any other kind of criticism. But this is not a cause for complacency, let alone celebration. A culture does not have to force scholars to flee to render them impotent. A culture does not have to burn books to assure that they will not be read. And a culture does not need a Minister of Propaganda issuing proclamations to silence criticism. There are other ways to achieve stupidity, and it appears that, as in so many other things, there is a distinctly America way.

5   To explain what I am getting at, I find it helpful to refer to two films, which taken together embody the main lines of my argument. The first film is of recent vintage and is called *The Gods Must Be Crazy*. It is about a tribal people who live in the Kalahari Desert plains of southern Africa, and what happens to their culture when it is invaded by an empty Coca-Cola bottle tossed from the window of a small plane passing overhead. The bottle lands in the middle of the village and is construed by these gentle people to be a gift from the gods, for they not only have never seen a bottle before but have never seen glass either. The people are almost immediately charmed by the gift, and not only because of its novelty. The bottle, it turns out, has multiple uses, chief among them the intriguing music it makes when one blows into it.

But gradually a change takes place in the tribe. The bottle becomes an irresistible preoccupation. Looking at it, holding it, thinking of things to do with it displace other activities once thought essential. But more than this, the Coke bottle is the only thing these people have ever seen of which there is only one of its kind. And so those who do not have it try to get it from the one who does. And the one who does refuses to give it up. Jealousy, greed, and even violence enter the scene, and come very close to destroying the harmony that has characterized their culture for a thousand years. The people begin to love their bottle more than they love themselves, and are saved only when the leader of the tribe, convinced that the gods must be crazy, returns the bottle to the gods by throwing it off the top of a mountain.

The film is great fun and it is also wise, mainly because it is about a subject as relevant to people in Chicago or Los Angeles or New York as it is to those of the Kalahari Desert. It raises two questions of extreme importance to our situation: How does a culture change when new technologies are introduced to it? And is it always desirable for a culture to accommodate itself to the demands of new technologies? The leader of the Kalahari tribe is forced to confront these questions in a way that Americans have refused to do. And because his vision is not obstructed by a belief in what Americans call "technological progress," he is able with minimal discomfort to decide that the songs of the Coke bottle are not so alluring that they are worth admitting envy, egotism, and greed to a serene culture.

The second film relevant to my argument was made in 1967. It is Mel Brooks's first film, *The Producers*. *The Producers* is a rather raucous comedy that has at its center a painful joke: An unscrupulous theatrical producer has figured out that it is relatively easy to turn a buck by producing a play that fails. All one has to do is induce dozens of backers to invest in the play by promising them exorbitant percentages of its profits. When the play fails, there being no profits to disperse, the producer walks away with thousands of dollars that can never be claimed. Of course, the central problem he must solve is to make sure that his play is a disastrous failure. And so he hits upon an excellent idea: he will take the most tragic and grotesque story of our century—the rise of Adolf Hitler—and make it into a musical.

Because the producer is only a crook and not a fool, he assumes that the stupidity of making a musical on this theme will be immediately grasped by audiences and that they will leave the theater in dumbfounded rage. So he calls his play *Springtime for Hitler,* which is also the name of its most important song. The song begins with the words:

Springtime for Hitler and Germany;
Winter for Poland and France.

10   The melody is catchy, and when the song is sung it is accompa-   10
nied by a happy chorus line. (One must understand, of course, that
Springtime for Hitler is no spoof of Hitler, as was, for example, Charlie
Chaplin's *The Great Dictator*. The play is instead a kind of denial of
Hitler in song and dance; as if to say, it was all in fun.)

The ending of the movie is predictable. The audience loves the play
and leaves the theater humming *Springtime for Hitler*. The musical
becomes a great hit. The producer ends up in jail, his joke having turned
back on him. But Brooks's point is that the joke is on us. Although the
film was made years before a movie actor became President of the
United States, Brooks was making a kind of prophecy about that—
namely, that the producers of American culture will increasingly turn
our history, politics, religion, commerce, and education into forms of
entertainment, and that we will become as a result a trivial people, incapable of coping with complexity, ambiguity, uncertainty, perhaps even
reality. We will become, in a phrase, a people amused into stupidity.

For those readers who are not inclined to take Mel Brooks as seriously as I do, let me remind you that the prophecy I attribute here to
Brooks was, in fact, made many years before by a more formidable
social critic than he. I refer to Aldous Huxley, who wrote *Brave New
World* at the time that the modern monuments to intellectual stupidity
were taking shape: Nazism in Germany, fascism in Italy, communism in
Russia. But Huxley was not concerned in his book with such naked and
crude forms of intellectual suicide. He saw beyond them, and mostly,
I must add, he saw America. To be more specific he foresaw that the
greatest threat to the intelligence and humane creativity of our culture
would not come from Big Brother and Ministries of Propaganda, or
gulags and concentration camps. He prophesied, if I may put it this
way, that there is tyranny lurking lurking in a Coca-Cola bottle; that we
could be ruined not by what we fear and hate but by what we welcome
and love, by what we construe to be a gift from the gods.

And in case anyone missed his point in 1932, Huxley wrote *Brave
New World Revisited* twenty years later. By then, George Orwell's *1984*
has been published, and it was inevitable that Huxley would compare
Orwell's book with his own. The difference, he said, is that in Orwell's
book people are controlled by inflicting pain. In *Brave New World,*
they are controlled by inflicting pleasure.

The Coke bottle that has fallen in our midst is a corporation of
dazzling technologies whose forms turn all serious public business into

527

a kind of *Springtime for Hitler* musical. Television is the principal instrument of this disaster, in part because it is the medium Americans most dearly love, and in part because it has become the command center of our culture. Americans turn to television not only for their light entertainment but for their news, their weather, their politics, their religion, their history—all of which may be said to be their serious entertainment. The light entertainment is not the problem. The least dangerous things on television are its junk. What I am talking about is television's preemption of our culture's most serious business. It would be merely banal to say that television presents us with entertaining subject matter. It is quite another thing to say that on television all subject matter is presented as entertaining. And that is how television brings ruin to any intelligent understanding of public affairs.

15   Political campaigns, for example, are now conducted largely in the form of television commercials. Candidates forgo precision, complexity, substance—in some cases, language itself—for the arts of show business: music, imagery, celebrities, theatrics. Indeed, political figures have become so good at this, and so accustomed to it, that they do television commercials even when they are not campaigning, as, for example, Geraldine Ferraro for Diet Pepsi and former vice-presidential candidate William Miller and the late Senator Sam Ervin for American Express. Even worse, political figures appear on variety shows, soap operas, and sitcoms. George McGovern, Ralph Nader, Ed Koch, and Jesse Jackson have all hosted "Saturday Night Live." Henry Kissinger and former President Gerald Ford have done cameo roles on "Dynasty." Tip O'Neill and Governor Michael Dukakis have appeared on "Cheers." Richard Nixon did a short stint on "Laugh-In." The late Senator from Illinois, Everett Dirksen, was on "What's My Line?" a prophetic question if ever there was one. What *is* the line of these people? Or, more precisely, *where* is the line that one ought to be able to draw between politics and entertainment? I would suggest that television has annihilated it.

It is significant, I think, that although our current President, a former Hollywood movie actor, rarely speaks accurately and never precisely, he is known as the Great Communicator; his telegenic charm appears to be his major asset, and that seems to be quite good enough in an entertainment-oriented politics. But lest you think his election to two terms is a mere aberration, I must remind you that, as I write [1988], Charlton Heston is being mentioned as a possible candidate for the

Republican nomination in 1988. Should this happen, what alternative would the Democrats have but to nominate Gregory Peck? Two idols of the silver screen going one on one. Could even the fertile imagination of Mel Brooks have foreseen this? Heston giving us intimations of Moses as he accepts the nomination; Peck re-creating the courage of his biblical David as he accepts the challenge of running against a modern Goliath. Heston going on the stump as Michelangelo; Peck countering with Doughas MacArthur. Heston accusing Peck of insanity because of *The Boys From Brazil.* Peck replying with the charge that Heston blew the world up in *Return to Planet of the Apes. Springtime for Hitler* could be closer than you think.

But politics is only one arena in which serious language has been displaced by the arts of show business. We have all seen how religion is packaged on television, as a kind of Las Vegas stage show, devoid of ritual, sacrality, and tradition. Today's electronic preachers are in no way like America's evangelicals of the past. Men like Jonathan Edwards, Charles Finney, and George Whitefield were preachers of theological depth, authentic learning, and great expository power. Electronic preachers such as Jimmy Swaggart, Jim Bakker, and Jerry Falwell are merely performers who exploit television's visual power and their own charisma for the greater glory of themselves.

We have also seen "Sesame Street" and other educational shows in which the demands of entertainment take precedence over the rigors of learning. And we well know how American businessmen, working under the assumption that potential customers require amusement rather than facts, use music, dance, comedy, cartoons, and celebrities to sell their products.

Even our daily news, which for most Americans means television news, is packaged as a kind of show, featuring handsome news readers, exciting music, and dynamic film footage. Most especially, film footage. When there is no film footage, there is no story. Stranger still, commercials may appear anywhere in a news story—before, after, or in the middle. This reduces all events to trivialities, sources of public entertainment and little more. After all, how serious can a bombing in Lebanon be if it is shown to us prefaced by a happy United Airlines commercial and summarized by a Calvin Klein jeans commercial? Indeed, television newscasters have added to our grammar a new part of speech—what may be called the "Now . . . this" conjunction, a conjunction that does not connect two things, but disconnects them.

When newscasters say, "Now . . . this," they mean to indicate that what you have just heard or seen has no relevance to what you are about to hear or see. There is no murder so brutal, no political blunder so costly, no bombing so devastating that it cannot be erased from our minds by a newscaster saying, "Now . . . this." He means that you have thought long enough on the matter (let us say, for forty seconds) and you must now give your attention to a commercial. Such a situation is not "the news." It is merely a daily version of *Springtime for Hitler*, and in my opinion accounts for the fact that Americans are among the most ill-informed people in the world. To be sure, we know *of* many things; but we know *about* very little.

20   To provide some verification of this, I conducted a survey a few   20
years back on the subject of the Iranian hostage crisis. I chose this subject because it was alluded to on television *every day for more than a year*. I did not ask my subjects for their opinions about the hostage situation. I am not interested in opinion polls; I am interested in knowledge polls. The questions I asked were simple and did not require deep knowledge. For example, Where is Iran? What language do the Iranians speak? Where did the Shah come from? What religion do the Iranians practice, and what are its basic tenets? What does "Ayatollah" mean? I found that almost everybody knew practically nothing about Iran. And those who did know something said they had learned it from *Newsweek* or *Time* or the *New York Times*. Television, in other words, is not the great information machine. It is the great disinformation machine. A most nerve-wracking confirmation of this came some time ago during an interview with the producer and the writer of the TV mini-series *Peter the Great*. Defending the historical inaccuracies in the drama—which included a fabricated meeting between Peter and Sir Isaac Newton—the producer said that no one would watch a dry, historically faithful biography. The writer added that it is better for audiences to learn something that is untrue, if it is entertaining, than not to learn anything at all. And just to put some icing on the cake, the actor who played Peter, Maximilian Schell, remarked that he does not believe in historical truth and therefore sees no reason to pursue it.

I do not mean to say that the trivialization of American public discourse is all accomplished on television. Rather, television is the paradigm for all our attempts at public communication. It conditions our minds to apprehend the world through fragmented pictures and forces other media to orient themselves in that direction. You know the standard question we put to people who have difficulty understanding even simple language: we ask them impatiently, "Do I have to draw a picture for you?" Well, it appears that, like it or not, our culture will draw pictures for us, will explain the world to us in pictures. As a medium for conducting public business, language has receded in importance; it has been moved to the periphery of culture and has been replaced at the center by the entertaining visual image.

Please understand that I am making no criticism of the visual arts in general. That criticism is made by God, not by me. You will remember that in His Second Commandment, God explicitly states that "Thou shalt not make unto thee any graven image, nor any likeness of anything that is in Heaven above, or that is in the earth beneath, or the waters beneath the earth." I have always felt that God was taking a rather extreme postion on this, as is His way. As for myself, I am arguing from the standpoint of a symbolic relativist. Forms of communication are neither good nor bad in themselves. They become good or bad depending on their relationship to other symbols and on the functions they are made to serve within a social order. When a culture becomes overloaded with pictures; when logic and rhetoric lose their binding authority; when historical truth becomes irrelevant; when the spoken or written word is distrusted or makes demands on our attention that we are incapable of giving; when our politics, history, education, religion, public information, and commerce are expressed largely in visual imagery rather than words, then a culture is in serious jeopardy.

Neither do I make a complaint against entertainment. As an old song has it, life is not a highway strewn with flowers. The sight of a few blossoms here and there may make our journey a trifle more endurable. But in America, the least amusing people are our professional entertainers. In our present situation, our preachers, entrepreneurs, politicians, teachers, and journalists are committed to entertaining us through media that do not lend themselves to serious, complex discourse. But these producers of our culture are not to be blamed. They, like the rest of us, believe in the supremacy of technological progress. It has never occurred to us that the gods might be crazy. And even if it did, there is no mountaintop from which we can return what is dangerous to us.

We would do well to keep in mind that there are two ways in which the spirit of a culture may be degraded. In the first—the Orwellian— culture becomes a prison. This was the way of the Nazis, and it appears to be the way of the Russians. In the Second—the Huxleyan—culture becomes a burlesque. This appears to be the way of the Americans. What Huxley teaches is that in the Age of Advanced Technology, spiritual devastation is more likely to come from an enemy with a smiling countenance than from one whose face exudes suspicion and hate. In the Huxleyan prophecy, Big Brother does not watch us, by his choice; we watch him, by ours. When a culture becomes distracted by trivia; when political and social life are redefined as a perpetual round of entertainments; when public conversation becomes a from of baby talk; when a people become, in short, an audience and their public business a vaudeville act, then—Huxley argued—a nation finds itself at risk and culture-death is a clear possibility. I agree.

Questions on Meaning

1. Why does Postman believe that human intelligence is so fragile? What can damage or destroy it? What example does he provide to show the quick destruction of an intelligent society?
2. Explain why the two films Postman describes—*The Gods Must Be Crazy* and *The Producers*— "embody" his argument. What did the tribal leader in the first film do that Postman states Americans have refused to do? What was the "prophecy" of the second film that will, in Postman's words, turn Americans into "a people amused into stupidity"?
3. Why does Postman single out television as the root of the problem?

Questions on Rhetorical Strategy and Style

1. What is the primary rhetorical strategy of this essay? Show where Postman supports it with example, narration, and cause and effect.
2. How does Postman compare and contrast Huxley's *Brave New World* and Orwell's *1984*? What is the major difference between Huxley's future society and the society described by Orwell? During the 20th century, what has been the fate of well-known Orwellian societies, such as Nazi Germany and communist Russia? Why does Postman characterize American society as becoming Huxleyan?
3. How does Postman compare and contrast the cultures of pre-World War II Germany with the United States? Why does he state that scholars will not have to flee America and books will not need to be burned for the American culture to become "stupid"?

Writing Assignments

1. Postman criticizes the presentation and format of television news—show business—as trivializing what should be serious, blurring the lines between what is important (a bombing in Lebanon) to what isn't (Calvin Klein jeans). Study the evening news for a few nights. Determine how much time is spent on serious news, human interest, and advertising. Note the transitions from the serious to the trivial. Write down your reactions to the studio newsreaders and the reporters in the field—how do their

mannerisms and delivery affect the meaning of the news? Do you agree with Postman's criticisms?

2. Much to the amazement and dismay of many thinking people—such as Postman—former President Ronald Reagan was often called "The Great Communicator." Read something about Reagan's legendary communications skills. How did Reagan, who often bungled facts and could discuss few topics without cue cards, earn such a reputation? What other important elected position did Reagan hold?

3. Write an essay about the trend today to make history alive and real through theme parks, documentaries, and other forms of dramatization. Where must we draw the line between entertainment and distortion? Is it possible for most consumers to be sufficiently discerning to know what to believe and what to question? Is there value in giving half-accurate information versus no information at all?

Sex, Lies, and Advertising

Gloria Steinem

Gloria Steinem (1934-) was born in Toledo, Ohio, and, after graduating from Smith College, went on to further studies at the University of Delhi and the University of Calcutta. She began a career in political journalism with her column for New York *magazine in the late 1960s. In 1971, she cofounded* Ms. *magazine and became its editor, a position she held until 1987. Steinem has been a key figure in the feminist movement and has worked with the National Women's Political Caucus and the Women's Action Alliance. She published her first collection of essays and columns,* Outrageous Acts and Everyday Rebellions, *in 1983, followed by* Revolution from Within *(1992) and* Moving Beyond Words *(1994). The following essay, first published in* Ms. *in 1990, is about Steinem's experience dealing with magazine advertisers when she was founder and editor of that magazine. From this experience we gain an insight not only into the worlds of magazines and advertising but also into how business is conducted in America.*

1   About three years ago, as *glasnost* was beginning and *Ms.* seemed to be ending, I was invited to a press lunch for a Soviet official. He entertained us with anecdotes about new problems of democracy in his country. Local Communist leaders were being criticized in their media for the first time, he explained, and they were angry.

"So I'll have to ask my American friends," he finished pointedly, "how more *subtly* to control the press." In the silence that followed, I said, "Advertising."

The reporters laughed, but later, one of them took me aside: How *dare* I suggest that freedom of the press was limited? How dare I imply his newsweekly could be influenced by ads?

I explained that I was thinking of advertising's media-wide influence on most of what we read. Even newsmagazines use "soft" cover stories to sell ads, confuse readers with "advertorials," and occasionally self-censor on subjects known to be a problem with big advertisers.

5 But, I also explained, I was thinking especially of women's magazines. There, it isn't just a little content that's devoted to attracting ads, it's almost all of it. That's why advertisers—not readers—have always been a problem for *Ms.* As the only women's magazine that didn't supply what the ad world euphemistically describes as "supportive editorial atmosphere" or "complementary copy" (for instance, articles that praise food/fashion/beauty subjects to "support" and "complement" food/fashion/beauty ads), *Ms.* could never attract enough advertising to break even.

"Oh, *women's* magazines," the journalist said with contempt. "Everybody knows they're just catalogs—but who cares? They have nothing to do with journalism."

I can't tell you how many times I've had this argument in 25 years of working for many kinds of publications. Except as moneymaking machines—"cash cows" as they are so elegantly called in the trade—women's magazines are rarely taken seriously. Though changes being made by women have been called more far-reaching than the industrial revolution—and though many editors try hard to reflect some of them in the few pages left to them after all the ad-related subjects have been covered—the magazines serving the female half of this country are still far below the journalistic and ethical standards of news and general interest publications. Most depressing of all, this doesn't even rate an exposé.

If *Time* and *Newsweek* had to lavish praise on cars in general and credit General Motors in particular to get GM ads, there would be a scandal—maybe a criminal investigation. When women's magazines from *Seventeen* to *Lear's* praise beauty products in general and credit Revlon in particular to get ads, it's just business as usual.

I.

When *Ms.* began, we didn't consider *not* taking ads. The most important reason was keeping the price of a feminist magazine low enough for most women to afford. But the second and almost equal reason was providing a forum where women and advertisers could talk to each other and improve advertising itself. After all, it was (and still is) as potent a source of information in this country as news or TV and movie dramas.

10   We decided to proceed in two stages. First, we would convince makers of "people products" used by both men and women but advertised mostly to men—cars, credit cards, insurance, sound equipment, financial services, and the like—that their ads should be placed in a women's magazine. Since they were accustomed to the division between editorial and advertising in news and general interest magazines, this would allow our editorial content to be free and diverse. Second, we would add the best ads for whatever traditional "women's products" (clothes, shampoo, fragrance, food, and so on) that surveys showed *Ms.* readers used. But we would ask them to come in *without* the usual quid pro quo of "complementary copy."

We knew the second step might be harder. Food advertisers have always demanded that women's magazines publish recipes and articles on entertaining (preferably ones that name their products) in return for their ads; clothing advertisers expect to be surrounded by fashion spreads (especially ones that credit their designers); and shampoo, fragrance, and beauty products in general usually insist on positive editorial coverage of beauty subjects, plus photo credits besides. That's why women's magazines look the way they do. But if we could break this link between ads and editorial content, then we wanted good ads for "women's products," too.

By playing their part in this unprecedented mix of *all* the things our readers need and use, advertisers also would be rewarded: ads for products like cars and mutual funds would find a new growth market; the best ads for women's products would no longer be lost in oceans of ads for the same category; and both would have access to a laboratory of smart and caring readers whose response would help create effective ads for other media as well.

I thought then that our main problem would be the imagery in ads themselves. Carmakers were still draping blondes in evening gowns over the hoods like ornaments. Authority figures were almost always male, even in ads for products that only women used. Sadistic, he-man campaigns even won industry praise. (For instance, *Advertising Age* had hailed the infamous Silva Thin cigarette theme, "How to Get a Woman's Attention: Ignore Her," as "brilliant.") Even in medical journals, tranquilizer ads showed depressed housewives standing beside piles of dirty dishes and promised to get them back to work.

Obviously, *Ms.* would have to avoid such ads and seek out the best ones—but this didn't seem impossible. *The New Yorker* had been selecting ads for aesthetic reasons for years, a practice that only seemed to make advertisers more eager to be in its pages. *Ebony* and *Essence* were asking for ads with positive black images, and though their struggle was hard, they weren't being called unreasonable.

15 Clearly, what *Ms.* needed was a very special publisher and ad sales 15 staff. I could think of only one woman with experience on the business side of magazines—Patricia Carbine, who recently had become a vice president of *McCall's* as well as its editor in chief—and the reason I knew her name was a good omen. She had been managing editor at *Look* (really *the* editor, but its owner refused to put a female name at the top of his masthead) when I was writing a column there. After I did an early interview with Cesar Chavez, then just emerging as a leader of migrant labor, and the publisher turned it down because he was worried about ads from Sunkist, Pat was the one who intervened. As I learned later, she told the publisher she would resign if the interview wasn't published. Mainly because *Look* couldn't afford to lose Pat, it *was* published (and the ads from Sunkist never arrived).

Though I barely knew this woman, she had done two things I always remembered: put her job on the line in a way that editors often talk about but rarely do, and been so loyal to her colleagues that she never told me or anyone outside *Look* that she had done so.

Fortunately, Pat did agree to leave *McCall's* and take a huge cut in salary to become publisher of *Ms.* She became responsible for training and inspiring generations of young women who joined the *Ms.* ad sales force, many of whom went on to become "firsts" at the top of publishing. When *Ms.* first started, however, there were so few women with experience selling space that Pat and I made the rounds of ad agencies ourselves. Later the fact that *Ms.* was asking companies to do business in a different way meant our saleswomen had to make many times the usual number of calls—first to convince agencies and then client companies besides—and to present endless amounts of research. I was often asked to do a final ad presentation, or see some higher decision-maker, or speak to women employees so executives could see the interest of women they worked with. That's why I spent more time persuading advertisers than editing or writing for *Ms.* and why I ended up with an unsentimental education in the seamy underside of publishing that few writers see (and even fewer magazines can publish).

Let me take you with us through some experiences, just as they happened:

• Cheered on by early support from Volkswagen and one or two other car companies, we scrape together time and money to put on a major reception in Detroit. We know U.S. carmakers firmly believe that women choose the upholstery, not the car, but we are armed with statistics and reader mail to prove the contrary: a car is an important purchase for women, one that symbolizes mobility and freedom.

20 But almost nobody comes. We are left with many pounds of 20 shrimp on the table, and quite a lot of egg on our face. We blame ourselves for not guessing that there would be a baseball pennant play-off on the same day, but executives go out of their way to explain they wouldn't have come anyway. Thus begins ten years of knocking on hostile doors, presenting endless documentation, and hiring a full-time saleswoman in Detroit; all necessary before *Ms.* gets any real results.

This long saga has a semihappy ending: foreign and, later, domestic carmakers eventually provided *Ms.* with enough advertising to make cars one of our top sources of ad revenue. Slowly, Detroit began to take the women's market seriously enough to put car ads in other women's magazines, too, thus freeing a few pages from the hothouse of fashion-beauty-food ads.

But long after figures showed a third, even a half, of many car models being bought by women, U.S. makers continued to be uncomfortable addressing women. Unlike foreign carmakers, Detroit never quite learned the secret of creating intelligent ads that exclude no one, and then placing them in women's magazines to overcome past exclusion. (*Ms.* readers were so grateful for a routine Honda ad featuring rack and pinion steering, for instance, that they sent fan mail.) Even now, Detroit continues to ask, "Should we make special ads for women?" Perhaps that's why some foreign cars still have a disproportionate share of the U.S. women's market.

• In the *Ms.* Gazette, we do a brief report on a congressional hearing into chemicals used in hair dyes that are absorbed through the skin and may be carcinogenic. Newspapers report this too, but Clairol, a Bristol-Myers subsidiary that makes dozens of products—a few of which have just begun to advertise in *Ms.*—is outraged. Not at newspapers or newsmagazines, just at us. It's bad enough that *Ms.* is the only women's magazine refusing to provide the usual "complementary" articles and beauty photos, but to criticize one of their categories—*that* is going too far.

We offer to publish a letter from Clairol telling its side of the story. In an excess of solicitousness, we even put this letter in the Gazette, not in Letters to the Editors where it belongs. Nonetheless—and in spite of surveys that show *Ms.* readers are active women who use more of almost everything Clairol makes than do the readers of any other women's magazine—*Ms.* gets almost none of these ads for the rest of its natural life.

25   Meanwhile, Clairol changes its hair coloring formula, apparently   25
in response to the hearings we reported.

• Our saleswomen set out early to attract ads for consumer electronics: sound equipment, calculators, computers, VCRs, and the like. We know that our readers are determined to be included in the technological revolution. We know from reader surveys that *Ms.* readers are buying this stuff in numbers as high as those of magazines like *Playboy,* or "men 18 to 34," the prime targets of the consumer electronics industry. Moreover, unlike traditional women's products that our readers buy but don't need to read articles about, these are subjects they want covered in our pages. There actually *is* a supportive editorial atmosphere.

"But women don't understand technology," say executives at the end of ad presentations. "Maybe not," we respond, "but neither do men—and we all buy it."

"If women *do* buy it," say the decision-makers, "they're asking their husbands and boyfriends what to buy first." We produce letters from *Ms.* readers saying how turned off they are when salesmen say things like "Let me know when your husband can come in."

After several years of this, we get a few ads for compact sound systems. Some of them come from JVC, whose vice president, Harry Elias, is trying to convince his Japanese bosses that there is something called a women's market. At his invitation, I find myself speaking at huge trade shows in Chicago and Las Vegas, trying to persuade JVC dealers that showrooms don't have to be locker rooms where women are made to feel unwelcome. But as it turns out, the shows themselves are part of the problem. In Las Vegas, the only women around the technology displays are seminude models serving champagne. In Chicago, the big attraction is Marilyn Chambers, who followed Linda Lovelace of *Deep Throat* fame as Chuck Traynor's captive and/or employee. VCRs are being demonstrated with her porn videos.

30   In the end, we get ads for a car stereo now and then, but no VCRs;   30 some IBM personal computers, but no Apple or Japanese ones. We notice that office magazines like *Working Woman* and *Savvy* don't benefit as much as they should from office equipment ads either. In the electronics world, women and technology seem mutually exclusive. It remains a decade behind even Detroit.

• Because we get letters from little girls who love toy trains, and who ask our help in changing ads and box-top photos that feature little boys only, we try to get toy-train ads from Lionel. It turns out that Lionel executives *have* been concerned about little girls. They made a pink train, and were surprised when it didn't sell.

Lionel bows to consumer pressure with a photograph of a boy *and* a girl—but only on some of their boxes. They fear that, if trains are associated with girls, they will be devalued in the minds of boys. Needless to say, *Ms.* gets no train ads, and little girls remain a mostly unexplored market. By 1986, Lionel is put up for sale.

But for different reasons, we haven't had much luck with other kinds of toys either. In spite of many articles on child-rearing; an annual listing of nonsexist, multiracial toys by Letty Cottin Pogrebin; Stories for Free Children, a regular feature also edited by Letty; and other prizewinning features for or about children, we get virtually no toy ads. Generations of *Ms.* saleswomen explain to toy manufacturers that a larger proportion of *Ms.* readers have preschool children than do the readers of other women's magazines, but this industry can't believe feminists have or care about children.

• When *Ms.* begins, the staff decides not to accept ads for feminine hygiene sprays or cigarettes; they are damaging and carry no appropriate health warnings. Though we don't think we should tell our readers what to do, we do think we should provide facts so they can decide for themselves. Since the antismoking lobby had been pressing for healthy warnings on cigarette ads, we decide to take them only as they comply.

35   Philip Morris is among the first to do so. One of its brands, Virginia Slims, is also sponsoring women's tennis and the first national polls of women's opinions. On the other hand, the Virginia Slims theme, "You've come a long way, baby," had more than a "baby" problem. It makes smoking a symbol of progress for women.

We explain to Philip Morris that this slogan won't do well in our pages, but they are convinced its success with some women means it will work with *all* women. Finally, we agree to publish an ad for a Virginia Slims calendar as a test. The letters from readers are critical—and smart. For instance: Would you show a black man picking cotton, the same man in a Cardin suit, and symbolize the antislavery and civil rights movements by smoking? Of course not. But instead of honoring the tests results, the Philip Morris people seem angry to be proven wrong. They take away ads for *all* their many brands.

This costs *Ms.* about $250,000 the first year. After five years, we can no longer keep track. Occasionally, a new set of executives listen to *Ms.* saleswomen, but because we won't take Virginia Slims, not one Philip Morris product returns to our pages for the next 16 years.

Gradually, we also realize our naiveté in thinking we *could* decide against taking cigarette ads. They became a disproportionate support of magazines the moment they were banned on television, and few magazines could compete and survive without them; certainly not *Ms.,* which lacks so many other categories. By the time statistics in the 1980s showed that women's rate of lung cancer was approaching men's, the necessity of taking cigarette ads has become a kind of prison.

• General Mills, Pillsbury, Carnation, DelMonte, Dole, Kraft, Stouffer, Hormel, Nabisco: you name the food giant, we try it. But no matter how desirable the *Ms.* readership, our lack of recipes is lethal.

40   We explain to them that placing food ads *only* next to recipes associates food with work. For many women, it is a negative that works *against* the ads. Why not place food ads in diverse media without recipes (thus reaching more men, who are now a third of the shoppers in supermarkets anyway), and leave the recipes to specialty magazines like *Gourmet* (a third of whose readers are also men)?

These arguments elicit interest, but except for an occasional ad for a convenience food, instant coffee, diet drinks, yogurt, or such extras as avocados and almonds, this mainstay of the publishing industry stays closed to us. Period.

• Traditionally, wines and liquors didn't advertise to women: men were thought to make the brand decisions, even if women did the buying. But after endless presentations, we begin to make a dent in this category. Thanks to the unconventional Michel Roux of Carillon Importers (distributors of Grand Marnier, Absolut Vodka, and others), who assumes that food and drink have no gender, some ads are leaving their men's club.

Beermakers are still selling masculinity. It takes *Ms.* fully eight years to get its first beer ad (Michelob). In general, however, liquor ads are less stereotyped in their imagery—and far less controlling of the editorial content around them—than are women's products. But given the underrepresentation of other categories, these very facts tend to create a disproportionate number of alcohol ads in the pages of *Ms.* This in turn dismays readers worried about women and alcoholism.

• We hear in 1980 that women in the Soviet Union have been producing feminist *samizdat* (underground, self-published books) and circulating them throughout the country. As punishment, four of the leaders have been exiled. Though we are operating on our usual shoestring, we solicit individual contributions to send Robin Morgan to interview these women in Vienna.

The result is an exclusive cover story that includes the first news of a populist peace movement against the Afghanistan occupation, a prediction of *glasnost* to come, and a grass-roots, intimate view of Soviet women's lives. From the popular press to women's studies courses, the response is great. The story wins a Front Page award.

Nonetheless, this journalistic coup undoes years of efforts to get an ad schedule from Revlon. Why? Because the Soviet women on our cover *are not wearing makeup.*

• Four years of research and presentations go into convincing airlines that women now make travel choices and business trips. United, the first airline to advertise in *Ms.,* is so impressed with the response from our readers that one of its executives appears in a film for our ad presentations. As usual, good ads get good results.

But we have problems unrelated to such results. For instance: because American Airlines flight attendants include among their labor demands the stipulation they could choose to have their last names preceded by "Ms." on their name tags—in a long-delayed revolt against the standard, "I am your pilot, Captain Rothgart, and this is your flight attendant, Cindy Sue"—American officials seem to hold the magazine responsible. We get no ads.

There is still a different problem at Eastern. A vice president cancels a subscription for thousands of copies on Eastern flights. Why? Because he is offended by ads for lesbian poetry journals in the *Ms.* Classifieds. A "family airline," as he explains to me coldly on the phone, has to "draw the line somewhere."

50 It's obvious that *Ms.* can't exclude lesbians and serve women. 50
We've been trying to make that point since our first issue included an article by and about lesbians, and both Suzanne Levine, our managing editor, and I were lectured by such heavy hitters as Ed Kosner, then editor of *Newsweek* (and now of *New York Magazine*), who insisted that *Ms.* should "position" itself *against* lesbians. But our advertisers have paid to reach a guaranteed number of readers, and soliciting new subscriptions to compensate for Eastern would cost $150,000, plus rebating money in the meantime.

Like almost everything ad-related, this presents an elaborate organizing problem. After days of searching for sympathetic members of the Eastern board, Frank Thomas, president of the Ford Foundation, kindly offers to call Roswell Gilpatrick, a director of Eastern. I talk with Mr. Gilpatrick, who calls Frank Borman, then the president of Eastern. Frank Borman calls me to say that his airline is not in the business of censoring magazines: *Ms.* will be returned to Eastern flights.

• Women's access to insurance and credit is vital, but with the exception of Equitable and a few other ad pioneers, such financial services address men. For almost a decade after the Equal Credit Opportunity Act passes in 1974, we try to convince American Express that women are a growth market—but nothing works.

Finally, a former professor of Russian named Jerry Welsh becomes head of marketing. He assumes that women should be cardholders, and persuades his colleagues to feature women in a campaign. Thanks to this 1980s series, the growth rate for female cardholders surpasses that for men.

For this article, I asked Jerry Welsh if he would explain why American Express waited so long. "Sure," he said, "they were afraid of having a 'pink' card."

55 • Women of color read *Ms.* in disproportionate numbers. This is a source of pride to *Ms.* staffers, who are also more racially representative than the editors of other women's magazines. But this reality is obscured by ads filled with enough white women to make a reader snowblind.

Pat Carbine remembers mostly "astonishment" when she requested African American, Hispanic, Asian and other diverse images. Marcia Ann Gillespie, a *Ms.* editor who was previously the editor in chief of *Essence,* witnesses ad bias a second time: having tried for *Essence* to get white advertisers to use black images (Revlon did so eventually, but L'Oréal, Lauder, Chanel, and other companies never did), she sees similar problems getting integrated ads for an integrated magazine. Indeed, the ad world often creates black and Hispanic ads only for black and Hispanic media. In an exact parallel of the fear that marketing a product to women will endanger its appeal to men, the response is usually, "But your [white] readers won't identify."

In fact, those we are able to get—for instance, a Max Factor ad made for *Essence* that Linda Wachner gives us after she becomes president—are praised by white readers, too. But there are pathetically few such images.

• By the end of 1986, production and mailing costs have risen astronomically, ad income is flat, and competition for ads is stiffer than ever. The 60/40 preponderance of edit over ads that we promised to readers becomes 50/50; children's stories, most poetry, and some fiction are casualties of less space; in order to get variety into limited pages, the length (and sometimes the depth) of articles suffers; and, though we do refuse most of the ads that would look like a parody in our pages, we get so worn down that some slip through. Still, readers perform miracles. Though we haven't been able to afford a subscription mailing in two years, they maintain our guaranteed circulation of 450,000.

Nonetheless, media reports on *Ms.* often insist that our unprofitability must be due to reader disinterest. The myth that advertisers simply follow readers is very strong. Not one reporter notes that other comparable magazines our size (say, *Vanity Fair* or *The Atlantic*) have been losing more money in one year than *Ms.* has lost in 16 years. No matter how much never-to-be-recovered cost is poured into starting a magazine or keeping one going, appearances seem to be all that matter. (Which is why we haven't been able to explain our fragile state in public. Nothing causes ad-flight like the smell of nonsuccess.)

60   My healthy response is anger. My not-so-healthy response is constant worry. Also an obsession with finding one more rescue. There is hardly a night when I don't wake up with sweaty palms and pounding heart, scared that we won't be able to pay the printer or the post office; scared most of all that closing our doors will hurt the women's movement.

Out of chutzpah and desperation, I arrange a lunch with Leonard Lauder, president of Estée Lauder. With the exception of Clinique (the brainchild of Carol Phillips), none of Lauder's hundreds of products has been advertised in *Ms.* A year's schedule of ads for just three or four of them could save us. Indeed, as the scion of a family-owned company whose ad practices are followed by the beauty industry, he is one of the few men who could liberate many pages in all women's magazines just by changing his mind about "complementary copy."

Over a lunch that costs more than we can pay for some articles, I explain the need for his leadership. I also lay out the record of *Ms:* more literary and journalistic prizes won, more new issues introduced into the mainstream, new writers discovered, and impact on society than any other magazine; more articles that became books, stories that became movies, ideas that became television series, and newly advertised products that became profitable; and, most important for him, a place for his ads to reach women who aren't reachable through any other women's magazine. Indeed, if there is one constant characteristic of the ever-changing *Ms.* readership, it is their impact as leaders. Whether it's waiting until later to have first babies, or pioneering PABA as sun protection in cosmetics, *whatever* they are doing today, a third to a half of American women will be doing three to five years from now. It's never failed.

But, he says, *Ms.* readers are not *our* women. They're not interested in things like fragrance and blush-on. If they were, *Ms.* would write articles about them.

On the contrary, I explain, surveys show they are more likely to buy such things than the readers of, say, *Cosmopolitan* or *Vogue.*

They're good customers because they're out in the world enough to need several sets of everything: home, work, purse, travel, gym, and so on. They just don't need to read articles about these things. Would he ask a men's magazine to publish monthly columns on how to shave before he advertised Aramis products (his line for men)?

65   He concedes that beauty features are often concocted more for advertisers than readers. But *Ms.* isn't appropriate for his ads anyway, he explains. Why? Because Estée Lauder is selling "a kept-woman mentality."

I can't quite believe this. Sixty percent of the users of his products are salaried, and generally resemble *Ms.* readers. Besides, his company had the appeal of having been started by a creative and hardworking woman, his mother, Estée Lauder.

That doesn't matter, he says. He knows his customers, and they would *like* to be kept women. That's why he will never advertise in *Ms.*

In November 1987, by vote of the Ms. Foundation for Education and Communication (*Ms.*'s owner and publisher, the media subsidiary of the Ms. Foundation for Women), *Ms.* was sold to a company whose officers, Australian feminists Sandra Yates and Anne Summers, raised the investment money in their country that *Ms.* couldn't find in its own. They also started *Sassy* for teenage women.

In their two-year tenure, circulation was raised to 550,000 by investment in circulation mailings, and, to the dismay of some readers, editorial features on clothes and new products made a more traditional bid for ads. Nonetheless, ad pages fell below previous levels. In addition, *Sassy*, whose fresh voice and sexual frankness were an unprecedented success with young readers, was targeted by two mothers from Indiana who began, as one of them put it, "calling every Christian organization I could think of." In response to this controversy, several crucial advertisers pulled out.

70   Such links between ads and editorial content was a problem in Australia, too, but to a lesser degree. "Our readers pay two times more for their magazines," Anne explained, "so advertisers have less power to threaten a magazine's viability."

"I was shocked," said Sandra Yates with characteristic directness. "In Australia, we think you have freedom of the press—but you don't."

Since Anne and Sandra had not met their budget's projections for ad revenue, their investors forced a sale. In October 1989, *Ms.* and *Sassy* were bought by Dale Lange, owner of *Working Mother, Working Woman,* and one of the few independent publishing companies left among the conglomerates. In response to a request from the original *Ms.* staff—as well as to reader letters urging that *Ms.* continue, plus his own belief that *Ms.* would benefit his other magazines by blazing a trail—he agreed to try the ad-free, reader-supported *Ms.* you hold now and to give us complete editorial control.

II.

Do you think, as I once did, that advertisers make decisions based on solid research? Well, think again. "Broadly speaking," says Joseph Smith of Oxtoby-Smith, Inc., a consumer research firm, "there is no persuasive evidence that the editorial context of an ad matters."

Advertisers who demand such "complementary copy," even in the absence of respectable studies, clearly are operating under a double standard. The same food companies place ads in *People* with no recipes. Cosmetic companies support *The New Yorker* with no regular beauty columns. So where does this habit of controlling the content of women's magazines come from?

75 Tradition. Ever since *Ladies Magazine* debuted in Boston in 1828, 75 editorial copy directed to women has been informed by something other than its readers' wishes. There were no ads then, but in an age when married women were legal minors with no right to their own money, there was another revenue source to be kept in mind: husbands. "Husbands may rest assured," wrote editor Sarah Josepha Hale, "that nothing found in these pages shall cause her [his wife] to be less assiduous in preparing for his reception or encourage her to 'usurp station' or encroach upon prerogatives of men."

Hale went on to become the editor of *Godey's Lady's Book,* a magazine featuring "fashion plates": engravings of dresses for readers to take to their seamstresses or copy themselves. Hale added "how to" articles, which set the tone for women's service magazines for years to come: how to write politely, avoid sunburn, and—in no fewer than 1,200 words—how to maintain a goose quill pen. She advocated education for women but avoided controversy. Just as most women's magazines now avoid politics, poll their readers on issues like abortion but rarely take a stand, and praise socially approved lifestyles, Hale saw to it that *Godey's* avoided the hot topics of its day: slavery, abolition, and women's suffrage.

What definitively turned women's magazines into catalogs, however, were two events: Ellen Butterick's invention of the clothing pattern in 1863 and the mass manufacture of patent medicines containing everything from colored water to cocaine. For the first time, readers could purchase what magazines encouraged them to want. As such magazines became more profitable, they also began to attract men as editors. (Most women's magazines continued to have men as top editors until the feminist 1970s.) Edward Bok, who became editor of *The Ladies' Home Journal* in 1889, discovered the power of advertisers when he rejected ads for patent medicines and found that other advertisers canceled in retribution. In the early 20th century, *Good Housekeeping* started its Institute to "test and approve" products. Its Seal of Approval became the grandfather of current "value added" programs that offer advertisers such bonuses as product sampling and department store promotions.

By the time suffragists finally won the vote in 1920, women's magazines had become too entrenched as catalogs to help women learn how to use it. The main function was to create a desire for products, teach how to use products, and make products a crucial part of gaining social approval, pleasing a husband, and performing as a homemaker. Some unrelated articles and short stories were included to persuade women to pay for these catalogs. But articles were neither consumerist nor rebellious. Even fiction was usually subject to formula: if a woman had any sexual life outside marriage, she was supposed to come to a bad end.

In 1965, Helen Gurley Brown began to change part of that formula by bringing "the sexual revolution" to women's magazines—but in an ad-oriented way. Attracting multiple men required even more consumerism, as the Cosmo Girl made clear, than finding one husband.

80 In response to the workplace revolution of the 1970s, traditional 80 women's magazines—that is, "trade books" for women working at home—were joined by *Savvy, Working Woman,* and other trade books for women working in offices. But by keeping the fashion/beauty/entertaining articles necessary to get traditional ads and then adding career articles besides, they inadvertently produced the antifeminist stereotype of Super Woman. The male-imitative, dress-for-success woman carrying a briefcase became the media image of a woman worker, even though a blue-collar woman's salary was often higher

than her glorified secretarial sister's, and though women at a real briefcase level are statistically rare. Needless to say, these dress-for-success women were also thin, white, and beautiful.

In recent years, advertisers' control over the editorial content of women's magazines has become so institutionalized that it is written into "insertion orders" or dictated to ad salespeople as an official policy. The following are recent typical orders to women's magazines:

• Dow's Cleaning Products stipulates that ads for its Vivid and Spray 'n Wash products should be adjacent to "children or fashion editorial"; ads for Bathroom Cleaner should be next to "home furnishing/family" features; and so on for other brands. "If a magazine fails for 1/2 the brands or more," the Dow order warns, "it will be omitted from further consideration."

• Bristol-Myers, the parent of Clairol, Windex, Drano, Bufferin, and much more, stipulates that ads be placed next to "a full page of compatible editorial."

• S.C. Johnson & Son, makers of Johnson Wax, lawn and laundry products, insect sprays, hair sprays, and so on, orders that its ads *"should not be opposite extremely controversial features or material antithetical to the nature/copy of the advertised product."* (Italics theirs.)

85 • Maidenform, manufacturer of bras and other apparel, leaves a   85
blank for the particular product and states: "The creative concept of the _____ campaign, and the very nature of the product itself appeal to the positive emotions of the reader/consumer. Therefore, it is imperative that all editorial adjacencies reflect that same positive tone. The editorial must not be negative in content or lend itself contrary to the _____ product imagery/message (e.g., *editorial relating to illness, disillusionment, large size fashions, etc.*)" (Italics mine.)

• The De Beers diamond company, a big seller of engagement rings, prohibits magazines from placing its ads with "adjacencies to hard news or anti/love-romance themed editorial."

• Procter & Gamble, one of this country's most powerful and diversified advertisers, stands out in the memory of Anne Summers and Sandra Yates (no mean feat in this context): its products were not to be placed in *any* issue that included *any* material on gun control, abortion, the occult, cults, or the disparagement of religion. Caution was also demanded in any issue covering sex or drugs, even for educational purposes.

Those are the most obvious chains around women's magazines. There are also rules so clear they needn't be written down: for instance, an overall "look" compatible with beauty and fashion ads. Even "real" nonmodel women photographed for a women's magazine are usually made up, dressed in credited clothes, and retouched out of all reality. When editors do include articles on less-than-cheerful subjects (for instance, domestic violence), they tend to keep them short and unillustrated. The point is to be "upbeat." Just as women in the street are asked, "Why don't you smile, honey?" women's magazines acquire an institutional smile.

Within the text itself, praise for advertisers' products has become so ritualized that fields like "beauty writing" have been invented. One of its frequent practitioners explained seriously that "It's a difficult art. How many new adjectives can you find? How much greater can you make a lipstick sound? The FDA restricts what companies can say on labels, but we create illusion. And ad agencies are on the phone all the time pushing you to get their product in. A lot of them keep the business based on how many editorial clippings they produce every month. The worst are products," like Lauder's as the writer confirmed, "with their own name involved. It's all ego."

90 Often, editorial becomes one giant ad. Last November, for instance, *Lear's* featured an elegant woman executive on the cover. On the contents page, we learned she was wearing Guerlain makeup and Samsara, a new fragrance by Guerlain. Inside were full-page ads for Samsara and Guerlain antiwrinkle cream. In the cover profile, we learned that this executive was responsible for launching Samsara and is Guerlain's director of public relations. When the *Columbia Journalism Review* did one of the few articles to include women's magazines in coverage of the influence of ads, editor Frances Lear was quoted as defending her magazine because "this kind of thing is done all the time." 90

Often, advertisers also plunge odd-shaped ads into the text, no matter what the cost to the readers. At *Women's Day*, a magazine originally founded by a supermarket chain, editor in chief Ellen Levine said, "The day the copy had to rag around a chicken leg was not a happy one."

Advertisers are also adamant about where in a magazine their ads appear. When Revlon was not placed as the first beauty ad in one Hearst magazine, for instance, Revlon pulled its ads from *all* Hearst magazines. Ruth Whitney, editor in chief of *Glamour*, attributes some of these demands to "ad agencies wanting to prove to a client that they've squeezed the last drop of blood out of a magazine." She also is, she says, "sick and tired of hearing that women's magazines are controlled by cigarette ads." Relatively speaking, she's right. To be as censoring as are many advertisers for women's products, tobacco companies would have to demand articles in praise of smoking and expect glamorous photos of beautiful women smoking their brands.

I don't mean to imply that the editors I quote here share my objections to ads: most assume that women's magazines have to be the way they are. But it's also true that only former editors can be completely honest. "Most of the pressure came in the form of direct product mentions," explains Sey Chassler, who was editor in chief of *Redbook* from the sixties to the eighties. "We got threats from the big guys, the Revlons, blackmail threats. They wouldn't run ads unless we credited them.

"But it's not fair to single out the beauty advertisers because these pressures came from everybody. Advertisers want to know two things: What are you going to charge me? What *else* are you going to do for me? It's a holdup. For instance, management felt that fiction took up too much space. They couldn't put any advertising in that. For the last ten years, the number of fiction entries into the National Magazine Awards has declined.

95 "And pressures are getting worse. More magazines are more 95 bottom-line oriented because they have been taken over by companies with no interest in publishing.

"I also think advertisers do this to women's magazines especially," he concluded, "because of the general disrespect they have for women."

Even media experts who don't give a damn about women's magazines are alarmed by the spread of this ad-edit linkage. In a climate *The Wall Street Journal* describes as an unacknowledged Depression for media, women's products are increasingly able to take their low standards wherever they go. For instance: newsweeklies publish uncritical stories on fashion and fitness. *The New York Times Magazine* recently ran an article on "firming creams," complete with mentions of advertisers. *Vanity Fair* published a profile of one major advertiser, Ralph Lauren, illustrated by the same photographer who does his ads, and turned the lifestyle of another, Calvin Klein, into a cover story. Even the outrageous *Spy* has toned down since it began to go after fashion ads.

And just to make us really worry, films and books, the last media that go directly to the public without having to attract ads first, are in danger, too. Producers are beginning to depend on payments for displaying products in movies, and books are now being commissioned by companies like Federal Express.

But the truth is that women's products—like women's magazines—have never been the subjects of much serious reporting anyway. News and general interest publications, including the "style" or "living" sections of newspapers, write about food and clothing as cooking and fashion, and almost never evaluate such products by brand name. Though chemical additives, pesticides, and animal fats are major health risks in the United States, and clothes, shoddy or not, absorb more consumer dollars than cars, this lack of information is serious. So is ignoring the contents of beauty products that are absorbed into our bodies through our skins, and that have profit margins so big they would make a loan shark blush.

III.

100 What could women's magazines be like if they were as free as books? 100 as realistic as newspapers? as creative as films? as diverse as women's lives? We don't know.

But we'll only find out if we take women's magazines seriously. If readers were to act in a concerted way to change traditional practices of *all* women's magazines and the marketing of *all* women's products, we could do it. After all, they are operating on our consumer dollars; money that we now control. You and I could:

- write to editors and publishers (with copies to advertisers) that we're willing to pay *more* for magazines with editorial independence, but will *not* continue to pay for those that are just editorial extensions of ads;
- write to advertisers (with copies to editors and publishers) that we want fiction, political reporting, consumer reporting—whatever is, or is not, supported by their ads;
- put as much energy into breaking advertising's control over content as into changing the images in ads, or protesting ads for harmful products like cigarettes;
- support only those women's magazines and products that take *us* seriously as readers and consumers.

Those of us in the magazine world can also use the carrot-and-stick technique. For instance: pointing out that, if magazines were a regulated medium like television, the demands of advertisers would be against FCC rules. Payola and extortion could be punished. As it is, there are probably illegalities. A magazine's postal rates are determined by the ratio of ad to edit pages, and the former costs more than the latter. So much for the stick.

The carrot means appealing to enlightened self-interest. For instance: there are many studies showing that the greatest factor in determining an ad's effectiveness is the credibility of its surroundings. The "higher the rating of editorial believability," concluded a 1987 survey by the *Journal of Advertising Research,* "the higher the rating of the advertising." Thus, an impenetrable wall between edit and ads would also be in the best interest of advertisers.

Unfortunately, few agencies or clients hear such arguments. Editors often maintain the false purity of refusing to talk to them at all. Instead, they see ad salespeople who know little about editorial, are trained in business as usual, and are usually paid by commission. Editors might also band together to take on controversy. That happened once when all the major women's magazines did articles in the same month on the Equal Rights Amendment. It could happen again.

105   It's almost three years away from life between the grindstones of 105
advertising pressures and readers' needs. I'm just beginning to realize how edges got smoothed down—in spite of all our resistance.

I remember feeling put upon when I changed "Porsche" to "car" in a piece about Nazi imagery in German pornography by Andrea Dworkin—feeling sure Andrea would understand that Volkswagen, the distributor of Porsche and one of our few supportive advertisers, asked only to be far away from Nazi subjects. It's taken me all this time to realize that Andrea was the one with a right to feel put upon.

Even as I write this, I get a call from a writer for *Elle,* who is doing a whole article on where women part their hair. Why, she wants to know, do I part mine in the middle?

It's all so familiar. A writer trying to make something of a nothing assignment; an editor laboring to think of new ways to attract ads; readers assuming that other women must want this ridiculous stuff; more women suffering for lack of information, insight, creativity, and laughter that could be on these same pages.

I ask you: Can't we do better than this?

Questions on Meaning

1. What does Steinem mean when she refers to most women's magazines as "catalogs"?
2. In this relatively long essay Steinem has a number of major points to communicate. What are the most important ones?
3. Why do magazine advertisers persist in their discriminatory habits about where and how they place their ads, even when the evidence suggests they are making foolish business decisions?

Questions on Rhetorical Strategy and Style

1. This essay uses examples to show the sexism prevalent in the world of magazine publishing. What two or three specific examples stick in your mind from your reading? Reread those sections of the essay to determine why they have such an impact on our reading.
2. Steinem tells the story of *Ms.* magazine as she explains the problem of advertising in women's magazines and argues for change. Comment on how (and how well) she balances these different elements through the essay.
3. Near the end of the essay Steinem attempts to persuade you (or female readers) to take specific actions to help improve the situation with women's magazines. Are you moved to action? Why or why not? To what extent is the essay successful in convincing you of the importance of this action? Why or why not?

Writing Assignments

1. Get a copy of a magazine that seems to be a "men's magazine" in the same sense that Steinem refers to women's magazines. Study its ads and editorial content: do these demonstrate a harmonious relationship in the same way Steinem shows occurs with women's magazines? Do similar or different factors seem to be at work in men's and women's magazines?
2. Steinem points out that the major advertisers in women's magazines seem to discriminate against people of color in the same way they discriminate against women. Think about this association in our society in general. Do you think there is a sociological or psychological relationship among different types of discrimination?

Write an essay in which you explain your ideas about the causes and targets of discrimination.

3. What is the status of the Feminist movement today? Is there still so much discrimination against women that such a movement is needed? What are, or should be, its most important concerns? Indeed, what is the exact nature of this concern as a "movement"? Write an essay explaining your opinion about the feminist movement.

Sex, Lies, and Conversation

Deborah Tannen

Deborah Tannen (1945–), born in Brooklyn, New York, received her Ph.D. in linguistics from the University of California, Berkeley and teaches at Georgetown University. Her research into how people communicate has brought her critical and popular acclaim, and she has appeared on several television programs and has written for The New York Times, *the* Washington Post, *and* Vogue. *Her book* That's Not What I Meant *(1987) analyzes the effects of conversational styles on relationships.* You Just Don't Understand *(1990), in which the following selection was included, examines differences in how men and women converse.* Talking From 9 to 5 *(1994) resulted from her research into conversational styles in work settings and their impact on how work is performed and who gets ahead. The following essay, which first appeared in* The New York Times, *is based on her scientific study of the conversational patterns of men and women and how differences in these styles lead to misinterpretation, tension, and sometimes divorce.*

1   I was addressing a small gathering in a suburban Virginia living room—a women's group that had invited men to join them. Throughout the evening, one man had been particularly talkative, frequently offering ideas and anecdotes, while his wife sat silently beside him on the couch. Toward the end of the evening, I commented that women frequently complain that their husbands don't talk to them. This man quickly concurred. He gestured toward his wife and said, "She's the talker in our family." The room burst into laughter;

the man looked puzzled and hurt. "It's true," he explained. "When I come home from work I have nothing to say. If she didn't keep the conversation going, we'd spend the whole evening in silence."

This episode crystallizes the irony that although American men tend to talk more than women in public situations, they often talk less at home. And this pattern is wreaking havoc with marriage.

The pattern was observed by political scientist Andrew Hacker in the late '70s. Sociologist Catherine Kohler Riessman reports in her new book *Divorce Talk* that most of the women she interviewed—but only a few of the men—gave lack of communication as the reason for their divorces. Given the current divorce rate of nearly 50 percent, that amounts to millions of cases in the United States every year—a virtual epidemic of failed conversation.

In my own research, complaints from women about their husbands most often focused not on tangible inequities such as having given up the chance for a career to accompany a husband to his, or doing far more than their share of daily life-support work like cleaning, cooking, social arrangements and errands. Instead, they focused on communication: "He doesn't listen to me," "He doesn't talk to me." I found, as Hacker observed years before, that most wives want their husbands to be, first and foremost, conversational partners, but few husbands share this expectation of their wives.

5   In short, the image that best represents the current crisis is the stereotypical cartoon scene of a man sitting at the breakfast table with a newspaper held up in front of his face, while a woman glares at the back of it, wanting to talk.

Linguistic Battle of the Sexes

How can women and men have such different impressions of communication in marriage? Why the widespread imbalance in their interests and expectations?

In the April [1990] issue of *American Psychologist,* Stanford University's Eleanor Maccoby reports the results of her own and others' research showing that children's development is most influenced by the social structure of peer interactions. Boys and girls tend to play with children of their own gender, and their sex-separate groups have different organizational structures and interactive norms.

I believe these systematic differences in childhood socialization make talk between women and men like cross-cultural communication, heir to all the attraction and pitfalls of that enticing but difficult enterprise. My research on men's and women's conversations uncovered patterns similar to those described for children's groups.

For women, as for girls, intimacy is the fabric of relationships, and talk is the thread from which it is woven. Little girls create and maintain friendships by exchanging secrets; similarly, women regard conversation as the cornerstone of friendship. So a woman expects her husband to be a new and improved version of a best friend. What is important is not the individual subjects that are discussed but the sense of closeness, of a life shared, that emerges when people tell their thoughts, feelings, and impressions.

10 Bonds between boys can be as intense as girls', but they are based 10 less on talking, more on doing things together. Since they don't assume talk is the cement that binds a relationship, men don't know what kind of talk women want, and they don't miss it when it isn't there.

Boys' groups are larger, more inclusive, and more hierarchical, so boys must struggle to avoid the subordinate position in the group. This may play a role in women's complaints that men don't listen to them. Some men really don't like to listen, because being the listener makes them feel one-down, like a child listening to adults or an employee to a boss.

But often when women tell men, "You aren't listening," and the men protest, "I am," the men are right. The impression of not listening results from misalignments in the mechanics of conversation. The misalignment begins as soon as a man and a woman take physical positions. This became clear when I studied videotapes made by psychologist Paul Dorval of children and adults talking to their same-sex best friends. I found that at every age, the girls and women faced each other directly, their eyes anchored on each other's faces. At every age, the boys and men sat at angles to each other and looked elsewhere in the room, periodically glancing at each other. They were obviously attuned to each other, often mirroring each other's movements. But the tendency of men to face away can give women the impression they aren't listening even when they are. A young woman in college was frustrated: Whenever she told her boyfriend she wanted to talk to him, he would lie down on the floor, close his eyes, and put his arm over his face. This signaled to her, "He's taking a nap." But he insisted he was listening extra hard. Normally, he looks around the room, so he is easily distracted. Lying down and covering his eyes helped him concentrate on what she was saying.

Analogous to the physical alignment that women and men take in conversation is their topical alignment. The girls in my study tended to talk at length about one topic, but the boys tended to jump from topic to topic. The second-grade girls exchanged stories about people they knew. The second-grade boys teased, told jokes, noticed things in the room and talked about finding games to play. The sixth-grade girls talked about problems with a mutual friend. The sixth-grade boys talked about fifty-five different topics, none of which extended over more than a few turns.

Listening to Body Language

Switching topics is another habit that gives women the impression men aren't listening, especially if they switch to a topic about themselves. But the evidence of the tenth-grade boys in my study indicates otherwise. The tenth-grade boys sprawled across their chairs with bodies parallel and eyes straight ahead, rarely looking at each other. They looked as if they were riding in a car, staring out the windshield. But they were talking about their feelings. One boy was upset because a girl had told him he had a drinking problem, and the other was feeling alienated from all his friends.

15 Now, when a girl told a friend about a problem, the friend responded by asking probing questions and expressing agreement and understanding. But the boys dismissed each other's problems. Todd assured Richard that his drinking was "no big problem" because "sometimes you're funny when you're off your butt." And when Todd said he felt left out, Richard responded, "Why should you? You know more people than me."

Women perceive such responses as belittling and unsupportive. But the boys seemed satisfied with them. Whereas women reassure each other by implying, "You shouldn't feel bad because I've had similar experiences," men do so by implying, "You shouldn't feel bad because your problems aren't so bad."

There are even simpler reasons for women's impression that men don't listen. Linguist Lynette Hirschman found that women make more listener-noise, such as "mhm," "uhuh," and "yeah," to show "I'm with you." Men, she found, more often give silent attention. Women who expect a stream of listener-noise interpret silent attention as no attention at all.

Women's conversational habits are as frustrating to men as men's are to women. Men who expect silent attention interpret a stream of listener-noise as overreaction or impatience. Also, when women talk to each other in a close, comfortable setting, they often overlap, finish each other's sentences and anticipate what the other is about to say. This practice, which I call "participatory listenership," is often perceived by men as interruption, intrusion, and lack of attention.

A parallel difference caused a man to complain about his wife, "She just wants to talk about her own point of view. If I show her another view, she gets mad at me." When most women talk to each other, they assume a conversationalist's job is to express agreement and support. But many men see their conversational duty as pointing out the other side of an argument. This is heard as disloyalty by women, and refusal to offer the requisite support. It is not that women don't want to see other points of view, but that they prefer them phrased as suggestions and inquiries rather than as direct challenges.

20 In his book *Fighting for Life,* Walter Ong points out that men use "agonistic," or warlike, oppositional formats to do almost anything; thus discussion becomes debate, and conversation becomes a competitive sport. In contrast, women see conversation as a ritual means of establishing rapport. If Jane tells a problem and June says she has a similar one, they walk away feeling closer to each other. But this attempt at establishing rapport can backfire when used with men. Men take too literally women's ritual "troubles talk," just as women mistake men's ritual challenges for real attack.

The Sounds of Silence

These differences begin to clarify why women and men have such different expectations about communication in marriage. For women, talk creates intimacy. Marriage is an orgy of closeness: you can tell your feelings and thoughts, and still be loved. Their greatest fear is being pushed away. But men live in a hierarchical world, where talk maintains independence and status. They are on guard to protect themselves from being put down and pushed around.

This explains the paradox of the talkative man who said of his silent wife, "She's the talker." In the public setting of a guest lecture, he felt challenged to show his intelligence and display his understanding of the lecture. But at home, where he has nothing to prove and no one to defend against, he is free to remain silent. For his wife, being home means she is free from the worry that something she says might offend someone, or spark disagreement, or appear to be showing off; at home she is free to talk.

The communication problems that endanger marriage can't be fixed by mechanical engineering. They require a new conceptual framework about the role of talk in human relationships. Many of the psychological explanations that have become second nature may not be helpful, because they tend to blame either women (for not being assertive enough) or men (for not being in touch with their feelings). A sociolinguistic approach by which male-female conversation is seen as cross-cultural communication allows us to understand the problem and forge solutions without blaming either party.

Once the problem is understood, improvement comes naturally, as it did to the young woman and her boyfriend who seemed to go to sleep when she wanted to talk. Previously, she had accused him of not listening, and he had refused to change his behavior, since that would be admitting fault. But then she learned about and explained to him the differences in women's and men's habitual ways of aligning themselves in conversation. The next time she told him she wanted to talk, he began, as usual, by lying down and covering his eyes. When the familiar negative reaction bubbled up, she reassured herself that he really was listening. But then he sat up and looked at her. Thrilled, she asked why. He said, "You like me to look at you when we talk, so I'll try to do it." Once he saw their differences as cross-cultural rather than right and wrong, he independently altered his behavior.

25   Women who feel abandoned and deprived when their husbands   25
won't listen to or report daily news may be happy to discover their husbands trying to adapt once they understand the place of small talk in women's relationships. But if their husbands don't adapt, the women may still be comforted that for men, this is not a failure of intimacy. Accepting the difference, the wives may look to their friends or family for that kind of talk. And husbands who can't provide it shouldn't feel their wives have made unreasonable demands. Some couples will still decide to divorce, but at least their decisions will be based on realistic expectations.

In these times of resurgent ethnic conflicts, the world desperately needs cross-cultural understanding. Like charity, successful cross-cultural communication should begin at home.

Questions on Meaning

1. What do men generally want out of conversation? What do women want?
2. Describe the differences between men and women in physical position and behavior during conversation with others of the same sex. What are the differences in how men and women speak?
3. Does Tannen argue that men and women should both try to change so that there are no differences anymore in conversational styles? If so, why? If not, what is her solution?

Questions on Rhetorical Strategy and Style

1. Examine how Tannen uses the rhetorical strategy of comparison and contrast to describe and explain the differences between men and women. How balanced is her analysis?
2. Tannen also uses examples to support and develop her points about how men and women communicate differently. Without rereading, how many different examples can you recall about such differences?
3. At the end of the essay Tannen switches from an emphasis that has been mostly descriptive to one that briefly argues a position. Evaluate the effectiveness of her concluding argument about how men and women should try to understand each other and adapt. What might make her argument stronger?

Writing Assignments

1. Tannen writes of couples who have apparently been married at least a little while, but whose problems are moving them toward divorce. Speculate about a topic she does not discuss: how couples might act and converse differently when they are first dating and forming a relationship. If their conversational styles are the same even early on, enough to cause divorce later on, how do they overcome these problems at first and get married? Or if you think people's conversational styles change after they have been married a while, what causes that change?
2. Tannen generalizes about communication differences between all males and females, even though she writes primarily about married couples. How much do you think her observations apply to single people in your own age group? Go to a place where you can

easily observe apparently single people near your age. Observe at least three conversations: one between two males, one between two females, and one between a male and a female. Take note of behaviors such as physical position, the amount of eye contact, how long each person seems to speak, and so on. Then write an essay presenting your findings.

From the Margins to Mainstream: The Political Power of Hip-Hop

Katina R. Stapleton

Katina R. Stapleton was born in Baltimore, Maryland in 1973. She was graduated in 1995 from the University of Maryland at College Park with a BA in print journalism and entered Duke University's political science department, where she is currently working on a dissertation that examines the role of the media in the urban education policy process. She writes and teaches on the politics of music. In this 1998 article, she describes the musical phenomenon called hip-hop in relation to African-American and youth culture, demonstrating the relationship between music and political action.

1   'They didn't know what they were playing with, look what they got', spoke Jungle Brothers rapper Mike G from the floor of a conference on the state of hip-hop in the late 1990s. In the 20-plus years since it emerged in inner-city New York as an alternative to violence and a way to escape harsh urban realities, hip-hop has become a worldwide musical and cultural force. But the widespread popularity of rap music and hip-hop culture among youth has caught many outside the hip-hop community by surprise. Once considered 'black noise', hip-hop has claimed for itself the role of cultural and political voice of an entire generation of youth.

     When hip-hop emerged in New York City in the 1970s, its primary sphere of influence was the youth in the neighborhoods where it evolved. In areas like the Bronx, breakdancers, graffiti artists, MCs (rappers), DJs and fans formed the hip-hop community. Hip-hop scholar Tricia Rose argues that 'alternative local identities were forged in fashions and language, street names, and most important, in establishing neighborhood crews or posses' (Rose, 1994: 34). Crews provided an opportunity for youth to form family-like bonds similar to, but not based on, gang affiliation. Instead of always fighting with fists, hip-hop gave youth the option of fighting with words, art, dance or the ability to produce good beats (Fernando, 1994).

Hip-hop emerged at a time of crisis for youth in urban communities. The situation was no less than a 'deindustrialized meltdown where social alienation, prophetic imagination, and yearning intersect' (Rose, 1994: 21). Hip-hop enabled youth to create their own cultural space within the city that countered the poverty and alienation that surrounded them on a day-to-day basis. As a type of genuine street culture, hip-hop evolved for several years before being discovered by the mass media (Shomari, 1995).

As scholars began to research hip-hop, it became clear that while it developed as an alternative youth culture, hip-hop incorporated many elements of the larger African-American and African cultures (DeMott, 1988; Floyd, 1995; Remes, 1991; Stephens, 1991). One such element is 'playing the dozens', a time-honored tradition in the African-American community. Also known as bragging, boasting, toasting or signifying, the process includes 'ritual insults' in which the speakers test their verbal prowess by seeing who can form the best taunt. Dozens-playing was an integral part of the early rap competitions and has remained a significant element of rap music today.

5   Hip-hop's use of the spoken or sung word to tell stories and teach   5
'life-lessons' is also part of a tradition among African peoples that goes back to the *griots*, African storytellers who played the important role of oral historians. The griots' role in African communities was to pass down the stories of each generation in song, while imparting knowledge about society. 'Endowed with this much prized oral skill, the griot enjoyed a very respected position within his community, just like many modern-day microphone personalities' (Fernando, 1994: 255). Rappers have become urban griots, using their lyrics to disperse social commentary about what it means to be young and black in the late 20th century (Kuwahara, 1992).

Like more traditional griots, what makes hip-hop artists such successful purveyors of cultural and political information is that they relay messages of importance to youth in a form that they enjoy. Rap music, currently the most visible element of hip-hop, has proven its ability to both capture the ear of those who listen to it for aesthetic reasons and those who look to the genre for deeper meaning. From its rough and tumble forms to the most commercial jams, hip-hop has been able to raise awareness among African-Americans and the general public about the issues that face black youth on a day-to-day basis.

Another strong tradition in African-American music that hip-hop has followed is the use of song to 'tell it like it is' and protest against social injustice (Nelson, 1992; Remes, 1991). In the early 1900s an examination of Negro spirituals as folksongs noted that folksongs were developed out of experience (Krehbiel, 1914). The pathos of what it meant to be a slave was reflected in music of the times. Krehbiel writes, 'as a rule the finest songs are the fruits of suffering undergone and the hope of deliverance from bondage' (Krehbiel, 1914: 26–7). Rochelle Larking (1972) argues that the historic conditions of black Americans will always serve as a basis for protest music. Her 1970s examination of soul music as a form of protest noted that beginning with the blues, black popular music has joined church songs as calls to freedom.

African-Americans, according to the musicologist Jon Spencer, have used secular music such as the blues to reflect the 'hell on earth' which they have been subjected to throughout the ages. These songs, claims Spencer, are no less profound than Old Testament psalms and lamentations. Like these biblical tales of woe, the blues are songs 'that reveal the nitty-gritty details of life as it is lived at the underside of society and the underbelly of history' (Spencer, 1996: xiv). Black music from the blues to funk, soul, jazz and now to hip-hop often shares the hope for deliverance found in Negro folksongs. As noted by Henry Charles (1990), the concept of deliverance is found in many aspects of African-American culture.

The central purpose of this article is to examine how hip-hop culture and music are uniquely situated among youth as a means of political action. While the most obvious means is through lyrical protest, Mark Mattern (1997) provides a larger framework for political action that includes music and the culture in which it develops. In his examination of Cajun music, Mattern suggests three categories of political action that will also form the basis of my analysis: confrontational (protest), deliberative and pragmatic.

Hidden transcripts and confrontational lyrics

10   Creating culture is not easy. . . . There is a politically   10
conscious, culturally aware, liberated, Black survival kit side to rap music that is being seriously overlooked. (Jackson, 1994)

One of the greatest contributions of hip-hop artists to the political landscape is one of protest. Mattern (1997) argues that the use of music to provide protest is a clear example of confrontational political action. Protest music is characterized by objections to injustices and oppressions inflicted on certain individuals and groups. Resistance is key and so are clear distinctions between those being subjugated and those perpetrating the injustice. 'Typically, the intent of protest musicians is to oppose the exploitation and oppression exercised by dominant elites and members of dominant groups' (Mattern, 1997: 2). Mattern finds similar elements of resistance in Cajun music that had been previously found in rap music.

In her seminal study of hip-hop, Tricia Rose (1994) provides an examination of rap music and hip-hop culture as a means to resist the dominant social order. Drawing on the work of James Scott (1990), Rose makes the critical distinction between the means by which those in dominant versus marginalized groups are able to get their messages across. Those in power are represented by dominant public transcripts, which are 'maintained through a wide range of social practices', such as setting the terms of public debate (Rose, 1994: 100). Cut out of the public debate, marginalized groups develop their own resistive or hidden transcripts. These communications take place in disguised form and tend to include critiques of the predominant culture. As one of the most marginalized groups in American history, African-Americans have long fought to be included in public debate. Since its inception, one of the areas found to be most problematic for the expression of African-American culture has been television. While there has been more of an influx of television shows and films that feature African-Americans in recent years, critics argue that blacks are mostly portrayed as comedic objects or criminals (Dates and Barlow, 1990; Greenberg and Brand, 1990). Black youths in particular have looked to the media to find representations of their own lives. Rap music and rap music videos gained in popularity among black youth as they recognized rap as their voice. Rap veteran Chuck D of Public Enemy has been widely quoted as calling rap music the 'Black man's CNN'. In the face of under- and/or misrepresentation in traditional media, black youths have turned to hip-hop as a means to define themselves. In terms of resistance, hip-hop provided a forum from which black youth can portray what it means to be young and black in America and protest against it. In its musical form, hip-hop has been able to form what are termed 'hidden transcripts'. While those from dominant cultural groups have public transcripts, those from marginalized groups often must create their own forum from which they can communicate with each other and transmit messages to the dominant culture. The use of resistive transcripts in rap music serves the dual purpose of using symbolism to critique power holders (Rose, 1994) and providing a dialogic arena in which rappers shape the terms of entry (Skeggs, 1993).

The transcripts found in rap music, while often protesting the treatment of all African-Americans, find black youth, not adults, as their primary audience. Dates and Barlow (1990) suggest that this age division among African-Americans over rap is based in part on perceived class consciousness. They argue that this can be seen in radio programming. Many radio formats reflect a class style, with stations wooing urban contemporary listeners with jazz, soul and traditional R&B while other stations woo black youth with hip-hop influenced R&B and rap music (Dates and Barlow, 1990; Jackson, 1994). In terms of political action, this means that black youth and black adults are finding that they have differing ideas of what protest music should sound like. While 'Say it Loud, I'm Black and I'm Proud' by James Brown and 'Respect' by Aretha Franklin were anthems for blacks who came of age in the 1960s, rap is providing new anthems for black youth of the 1990s.

One of the earliest raps credited with going beyond the boast/party elements of rap music to provide a protest anthem was simply called 'The Message'. Released by Grandmaster Flash and the Furious Five in the early 1980s, 'The Message' captured the angst of black youth growing up in the inner city and lent its name to a type of rap music that would follow.

15   Flash's message that society shouldn't push him because he was   15 close to the edge was something that anyone who had grown up in the ghetto could understand. According to Flash, being raised in the impoverished 'second rate' conditions is what often causes young blacks to harbor deep feelings of anger towards society.

While raps like 'The Message' may have started with GrandMaster Flash in 1982, over the years, the group Public Enemy has brought hard-hitting societal critiques to the forefront of hip-hop. Public Enemy has brought hard-hitting societal critiques to the forefront of hip-hop. Public Enemy's founder and lead rapper Chuck D, writes how PE decided to use their music for social purposes:

> The sociopolitical meaning of Public Enemy came after we decided the group would be called that, because the meaning and the connection of what we were about fit right in. The Black man and woman was considered three-fifths of human being in the Constitution of the United States. Since the government and the general public follow the Constitution, then we must be the enemy. (Chuck D, 1997: 86)

Public Enemy credit their strong commitment to protest to the influences of the Black Panther Party and the Nation of Islam. The combination of PE's political background and their ability to create strong musical and video images allowed them to use their songs to provide powerful statements. Two of the most remembered rap commentaries from PE are '911 is a Joke' and 'Fight the Power'. Even before newspaper and television reporters started telling the general public about the problems inner-city residents had with receiving prompt ambulance service, Public Enemy detailed the situation in rhyme. The raps of nationalist groups such as Public Enemy serve as direct examples of confrontational political action. One criterion of this type of political action is the placement of the group, which is perceived as being oppressed in direct opposition to the oppressors (Mattern, 1997). The resistive transcripts of Public Enemy's song 'Hitler Day', locate people of color in direct opposition to white America.

'Hitler Day' is a critique of America's celebration of Columbus Day. According to the rap, a holiday which celebrates the 'discovery' of America at the expense of its native inhabitants is inherently offensive to people of color.

Chuck D explains that asking native and African-American people to celebrate Columbus Day is analogous to asking Jews to celebrate Adolf Hitler Day. 'For me, that's what Christopher Columbus represents to Black, Brown, and Red nations in North America and throughout the world because he opened the gates for five hundred years of mayhem' (Chuck D, 1997: 198). Other more well known confrontational songs by the group include 'Shut 'Em Down', which encouraged the boycotting of businesses that take from the black community without giving back, and the self-explanatory rap 'Fight the Power'.

Other nation-conscious rappers like Brand-Nubian, X-Clan, Poor Righteous Teachers and KRS-One have provided either direct indictments of the dominant social structure or more hidden critiques (Decker, 1993; Eurie and Spady, 1991; Henderson, 1996). But nation-consciousness in rap music also includes messages of empowerment. Next to Public Enemy, Kris Parker is one of the most well known deliverers of political and social messages to the hip-hop community. Ironically, Kris Parker (KRS-One) began his career as part of Boogie Down Productions (BDP) with the late Scott LaRock. Posing on the cover of 'Criminal Minded with Guns', BDP produced some of the earliest music with a gangster ethic, while at the same time promoting messages of black nationalism, safe sex and the rejection of the drug trade. As a solo artist, KRS-One has cemented his role as a teacher among the hip-hop community. From his 1997 album *I Got Next* KRS-One urges the hip-hop nation to shed what he calls ghetto mentality for one of success. Both Public Enemy and KRS-One represent nation-consciousness based in the 1960s black power movement. Jeffery Decker contends that hip-hop nationalists:

> . . . are most effective when they appropriate popular knowledge from within the black community and exploit its most progressive elements in the process of envisioning a new society. At these moments rappers function in a manner resembling what Antonio Gramsci calls 'organic intellectuals'. (Decker, 1993: 59)

Much of the literature on the presence of confrontational political action in music is implicitly or explicitly indebted to Gramscian Marxism. Organic intellectuals are individuals who hold close ties to their class of origin and whose function is to express class identity and goals (Mattern, 1997). The relationship of the hip-hop artist to a class identity has been clear since hip-hop began. Early hip-hop artists came directly from specific inner-city communities and represented a class of youth facing economic deprivation along with social and political marginalization. Even though the hip-hop community has expanded beyond its core to include youth of all classes, races and cultures, hip-hop artists are expected to remain true to their positions as the representative of black youth. 'Hip-hop nationalists are organic cultural intellectuals to the degree that their activities are directly linked to the everyday struggles of black folk and that their music critically engages the popular knowledge of which they have a part' (Decker, 1993: 59). Henderson (1996) and Decker (1993) note that many prominent examples of hip-hop nationalists are not explicitly linked to 1960s nationalism. The Fugees are among rappers whose vision of nationhood is bounded not by geography, but rather one's link to the African or Afro-Hispanic diaspora. Referring to black youth as black diamonds and pearls, Fugees vocalist Lauren Hill raps, 'If I ruled the world, I'd free all my sons'. This type of nationalism is Afrocentric in nature. Rappers like Queen Latifah look to Mother Africa for inspiration in forming their hip-hop identity.

Gangster rap is another prominent source of confrontational nationalist rap (Decker, 1993). Known for their universal distrust of the police, gangster rappers often use their music to provide graphic indictments of the police and the government interspersed with tales of gangster living. Many gangster rappers prefer to be called realists, because they feel their rap describes what is really going on in the 'hood. With black on black violence being the leading source of death for black youth since 1969, it doesn't seem wrong to many rappers to reflect that in their music (Kitwana, 1994: 41). King George, a member of TRU, contends that this type of realism is more than just talk about killing. 'I'm just relating to what's going on and keeping everybody aware at the same time' (Davis, 1996: 63).

Gender and gangsta-rap

Claims to realism aside, however, there has been widespread debate about whether or not songs that call black women 'bitches' and 'hoes' (whores) as well as songs which detail sex acts, drug sales and extreme violence are negative influences of youth. The portrayal of women and whites in hip-hop music have been special sources of concern (Allison, 1994; Hansen, 1995; Johnson et al., 1995). It would seem obvious that no woman would want to be called a female dog on tape, or have their boyfriends 'Treat 'em like a prostitute'. But while female rappers like M.C. Lyte, Queen Latifah, Yo-Yo and Salt 'n' Pepa began to challenge the conception that only males could rap and shape perceptions of women in the urban community, some female rappers responded by becoming hard-core rappers themselves (Rose, 1994; Skeggs, 1993)

In the late 1990s female rappers have emerged as a force equal to male rappers. Skeggs (1993) argues that if rap in general is used to combat racism and oppression, female artists use rap to battle sexism. While many female hip-hop artists rap about female solidarity, others provide images of women being in control of their sexuality. Skeggs theorizes that for black women, 'sexuality is one of the few cultural resources that they can use for the construction of embodied self worth' (Skeggs, 1993: 310). This notion has not gone unchallenged. Female rappers like Lil' Kim and Foxy Brown have been both vilified and held up for praise for their hard-core attitude and blatantly sexy style. The question 'harlots or heroines?' has followed them since they came on the scene. While supporters celebrate the two female rappers' ability to take charge and proclaim their sexuality, critics challenge their claim to feminism. The Lady of Rage, like many other female rappers, holds conflicting views of artists like Kim and Foxy. "I like Little Kim because she sounds so hard. At first I thought what she was saying was not good because we already got problems as far as women getting recognition and being accepted. I felt that might hinder it a little bit.' But, as Rage notes, 'Sex sells and she's good' (Williams, 1997:63).

25 Many in the hip-hop community contend that while there are 25 valid concerns about the level of sexual and violent content in hip-hop music, the concern from the media and politicians is not genuine. In stead, negative sentiments towards hip-hop are considered to have racial overtones. Hip-hop artists in attendance at the 1997 Life After Death conference contended that the media and politicians are down

on hip-hop because it is a black art from that is being consumed by white youth. The consumption of hip-hop by young whites allows them to become 'ghetto chic' without actually having to live in ghetto conditions (Allison, 1994). Though much of the criticism of hip-hop comes from those outside of the black community, there is a large concern about the tone of rap music within African-American discourse. Rose, who applauds rap for its ability to provide resistive transcripts, lambasts rappers for their sexism. 'I am thoroughly frustrated but not surprised by the apparent need for some rappers to craft elaborate and creative stories about the abuse and domination of young black women' (Rose, 1994: 15).

Likewise, trends toward the inclusion of sex, drugs, violence and, most recently, materialism in rap music have not gone unnoticed or unchallenged by member s of the hip-hop community itself (Life After Death, 1997). Hip-hop conferences held in the aftermath of the violent deaths of favorite sons, Tupac Shakur and the Notorious B.I.G. have looked at whether hip-hop has a social responsibility to the youth that listen to the music. Participants at Life After Death (1997) asked serious questions about the role of violence in the genre. The consensus among panel and audience members seemed to be that in many ways hip-hop is out of control. However, they note—and I agree—that rappers who talk about sex and violence should not be expected to take all the blame. Equal shares of blame should lie with record companies and managers who promote violent/sexual rappers, with the youth who buy these records, and with parents who do not take the time to listen to what their children are listening to. Blame also lies with American society itself, which criticizes rappers for talking about ideals that are in fact embedded in the American way of life, as well as the media who often blow up the violence in hip-hop out of context. A sampling of newspaper articles following the shooting death of Biggie Smalls seems to support claims that in a society where black men are killed in record numbers the media still insist on implying that the rap industry, not guns, kills people (Patillo, 1997).

The fact that rappers reflect aspects of American society and the pursuit of the American dream is important in a political context. Rap has many elements in common with country and hard rock music, but receives more critical attention. 'Rap and country lyrics implicate underclass reality, that the alternative symbol systems have a parallel socio-economic provenience' (Armstrong, 1993: 69). Though both genres are based on somewhat different social realities, they both share a rhetoric of violence. Analyses of press coverage of country and rap have found that while the genres share a tendency towards machismo, they are not treated the same way by the press. The difference, as found by Noe, lies not in the song lyrics, but in the racial lenses through which the songs are interpreted.

> When Ice Cube says, 'Let the suburbs see a nigga invasion', many whites interpret that as an incitement to violence. But when Johnny Cash sings, 'Shot a man in Reno/just to watch him die', the public taps its feet and hums. (Noe, 1995: 20)

The irony, says Noe, is that rap is no more amoral than other musical genres, but rappers are being punished for catering to prevalent American themes: sex, violence and materialism.

Setting the boundaries of hip-hop

30 Hip-hop is bigger than any one person's opinion of what it should be, said Chuck D of Public Enemy, now a reporter for the Fox News Channel (Chuck D, 1997: 152). The process of establishing where the boundaries of hip-hop should stand is one of deliberation. Mattern (1997) elaborates on this type of political action. He writes, 'Deliberation is a political process and a form of political action in its own right, as well as a necessary preliminary step in forging agreement on common interests and goals for action in other political arenas to address them' (Mattern, 1997: 7). Mattern uses rap and Cajun music as examples of how differing visions of what a genre should stand for are deliberated within a community. The main point of deliberation within the hip-hop community revolves around the question: 'Has hip-hop gone too far?' Related questions include, but are not limited to: 'Has rap music become too sexual, too violent, and too materialistic?' 'Has hip-hop sold its soul for commercial success?' 'Has hip-hop crossed too far into the territory of other music forms?' 'As a community, has hip-hop become more suburban and white than black and urban?'

The answers to all these questions are not clear-cut. The very nature of hip-hop culture has been one that accommodated many types of people, many types of subject matter, and many types of music. The underlying question, then, is whether or not hip-hop can accommodate varying interests, while still retaining its distinctive urban identity. The presence of intra-group differences and disagreements, and of border zones between different groups, suggests that we consider, at least in some instances, a framework for understanding and action of negotiation, rather than an either-or struggle between opposing forces. Popular music would be viewed in these cases as a site and a medium for disagreement and debate over both intra- and inter-group identity and commitments. This takes shape in a deliberative form of political action (Mattern, 1997:6).

Hip-hop's identity as form of resistance among black youth lies at the heart of deliberation in the hip-hop community. Part of hip-hop's credibility among young blacks lies in its ability to claim that it is an authentic street culture (Powell, 1991). But if hip-hop is 'by the ghetto, for the ghetto', how is the community changed by the fact that it is being played on college campuses across the nation and in the homes of suburban whites? When hip-hop style is being used to sell movies, breath mints, sodas, make-up, fast food, alcohol, clothing, shoes and various other products, one knows that this is a valid concern (Blair, 1993). Similar feelings have been reported from England's hip-hop community. 'Hip-hop's integrity has been prostituted in the pursuit of financial gain', writes a columnist in *Hip-Hop Connection*, one of Britain's hip-hop magazines (Salsa, 1997: 5). Though the author was from England, she accurately summed up concerns that are held across the hip-hop community. Salsa charges that hip-hop is at its best in its resistive mode, but that it has lost its subversiveness due to mainstreaming and commercialization. Bernard-Donais (1994: 133) shares this opinion. 'The very fact that it is covered by an institution like the [*New York*] *Times* suggests that rap has found its way into the canon, and that it has ceased to be the subversive (or in other terms, marginal) form that it had been at one time.'

In the case of hip-hop, the transference from subculture to mainstream has been driven by technological advances. As long as artists performed rap in venues limited to neighborhoods, its marginal status was assured. But as rap music expanded to being mass produced hip-hop spread across the nation (Blair, 1993; Kuwahara, 1992). Hip-hop's influence has not been limited to America. Fans from across the world are able to buy rap music both from traditional record stores and from mail order distribution. The worldwide audience for hip-hop should not be underestimated (Toop, 1991). Hip-hop artists regularly perform to international audiences. Wu Tang Clan and the Fugees are just two examples of what is called global hip-hop. The appeal of hip-hop around the world is based in part on the fact that marginalization, oppression and struggle can be understood by many youth. The love of hip-hop has a universal appeal, agrees Chuck D (1997). He believes that one of the reasons that rap crosses over successfully into mainstream culture is that young whites are able to gain an African-American perspective through the music.

The character of deliberation within the hip-hop community is necessarily shaped by its widespread audience. Stephens (1991) contends that rap provides a 'double-voiced discourse' in which rap crosses racial and geographic boundaries. Hip-hop, writes Stephens, provides a point of intersection where blacks and whites can have a dialogue. Though not always acknowledge in the media, the members of the Hispanic community have also been involved in hip-hop since its inception. In this case, it is urbanity and similar social situations that guide Hispanic contributions to hip-hop (Fernando, 1994; Stephens, 1991). As Rose notes, 'Rap's black cultural address and its focus on marginal identities may appear to be in opposition to its crossover appeal for people from different racial or ethnic groups and social positions', but in reality it suggests 'that rap is a black idiom that prioritizes black culture and that articulates the problems of black urban life in the face of such diverse constituencies' (Rose, 1994: 4).

35 Discussions of hip-hop as a street culture sometimes overlook 35 contributions of college students who have since become hip-hop artists and the strong identification of many black college students with hip-hop culture. Music, if not social class, draws young African-Americans of differing socioeconomic status to hip-hop.

Zillman et al. have looked at the effects of popular rock, non-political rap and radical political rap on African-American and white high-school students. They found that while radical political rap seemed to motivate white students to be more supportive of racial harmony, there was no positive link between political rap and ethnic consciousness or ethnic solidarity among the black students (Zillman et al., 1995). The authors note that this does not imply that message rap does not have an effect on black students. In fact the opposite could be true.

> It can be argued that African-American students, in contrast to white students, are massively exposed to rap and that any effect of rap may have manifested itself already prior to exposure. Several additional exposures thus could have influenced white students, especially those who are relatively unfamiliar with radical rap, but not African-American students—because of the informational saturation and its perceptual and evaluative consequences. (Zillman et al., 1995: 21)

Debate about the relative effects of hip-hop on youth is a major area of discussion within the academic community. Instead of concentrating on consciousness, researchers Johnson et al. looked at the effects of violent rap on youth. They found that there was greater acceptance of dating violence among youth exposed to violent rap videos than those exposed to non-violent rap videos or no video at all. In a slightly different experiment they also found that youth exposed to either type of rap video expressed greater desire to be like the materialistic youth portrayed in a scenario than his college-bound friend (Johnson et al., 1995).

Materialism, sexism and violence are points of deliberation among hip-hop artists and fans. Chuck D (1997) recounts the extremely negative reactions he got from African hip-hop fans to the newest incarnations of hip-hop. But as he also notes, the more negative aspects of rap are the easiest to market. 'If you give a fourteen-year-old a choice between a positive video, and a video with tits and ass, or guns and violence, he's going to choose the tits and ass, guns and violence almost every time' (Chuck D, 1997: 33). Researchers have shown that white youth who listen to rap are particularly attracted to its most violent elements. 'The more rappers are packaged as violent black criminals, the bigger their audiences become', writes Ewan Allison (1994: 449).

40   Is this preoccupation with ghetto culture detrimental to youth,   40 black or white? In some ways it is positive, according to Rose, because the ghetto provides a source of social identity for the millions of youth who call it home. Other positive interpretations include the fact that rap has values both because of its brutal honesty and as a point of deliberation. Freestyle rapper Supernatural feels that gangster rap gives other types of rappers more incentive to present the hip-hop experi-

ence from all points of view. Looking at the situation from a slightly different perspective, KRS-One notes that the existence of more than one type of rap exposes the tendency for the public to choose negative over positive. Among participants at Life After Death (1997), the origins of hip-hop were seen as being positive in contrast to more recent developments. Old-school hip-hop artists stressed that hip-hop has strayed too far from its original intentions of combating gang activity to promoting gangster ethics; from promoting black unity to encouraging east coast-west coast feuds; from MC'ing, DJ'ing, breaking, and painting graffiti to simply rapping; from performing for the love of it to performing for money; and from simple boasting to gross exaggerations of one's sexual prowess (Life After Death, 1997; Nia, 1997). Though each of these issues is important to the future of hip-hop, the charge that there has been a dilution of hip-hop as a distinct, protest-based culture and music form is the most political.

Actions speak louder than words

Though the previous discussion in this article has concentrated on both the resistive and deliberative aspects of hip-hop, Mattern suggests music and its related culture also can be used as a basis for pragmatic political action. This type of action, says Mattern, 'begins from the premise of shared political interests. Pragmatic political action occurs when individuals and groups use music to promote awareness of shared interests and to organize collaborative action to address them' (Mattern, 1997: 7). In the past, hip-hop artists have come together for many causes. One prominent example, though considered ill-fated, was the Stop the Violence movement (STV), an attempt to discourage black-on-black crime. Other movements include HEAL (Human Education Against Lies) and the current Rap the Vote project.

Currently there seems to be a resurgence of hip-hop artists attempting to form groups to further the common interests of African-diasporic peoples and/or members of the hip-hop nation. KRS-One, whose song 'Stop the Violence' typified the spirit of the STV movement, has recently started the Temple of Hip-Hop, a non-profit cultural center with the purpose of preserving hip-hop culture. The Zulu nation remains a long-standing conduit of nationalism within the hip-hop community. Many other rap groups and individual artists have taken on specific service projects in order to give back to the community. Perhaps some of the most interesting projects are coming from the ground up. One such project is the Wiseguys, led by Raymond 'Ray Benzino' Scott, president of Boston-based Surrender Records. Using a similar concept to the one of trading a gang for a team, Scott and three friends encouraged former gang rivals to 'trade their hardware for mics'. The project, called Wiseguys, resulted in former gang members coming together to record an album now distributed nationally. Says Scott, 'It becomes a political platform of hypocrisy when you're scared to actually go in and touch the people who are going through the problems' (Walker, 1997: 30–1).

Whether initiated by artists, producers or fans, it is clear that hip-hop has great potential for becoming a major agent of change. All hip-hop needs, according to Chuck D and others, is organization. 'We have to really tie up some areas in the hip-hop Nation: the Zulu Nation, the Rhyme Syndicate, any organization is good. It's just that we have to drop these badges when we come down to dialogue and figure out how to help our people . . .' (Chuck D, 1997: 181). Robert Jackson, author of the *The Last Black Mecca*, believes that an organized hip-hop nation has the potential to be a powerful social and political base within the African-American community: 'The next revolution should be more than televised—it should be political' (Jackson, 1994: 99). The next level for hip-hop, says Jackson, is to organize around a progressive political agenda which would include housing, education and health reform as well as affirmative action and employment.

Music has always been a major source of cultural identity within the African-American community. Rap music is no exception. As part of the larger hip-hop culture, rap music has served to form a cohesive bond among urban youth. Through the mass distribution of hip-hop records and videos, hip-hop has also been able to at least partially erase lines between young people of different socioeconomic backgrounds and vastly different geographic locations. Equally important, hip-hop culture has established itself as a powerful informational tool and means of resistance. It is not an overstatement to say that despite its faults, hip-hop has provided America with one of its only hard-hitting indictments of the social conditions that continue to be a harsh reality for African-American young people.

45 Hip-hop has shown itself to be both the site of political controversy and a means of more than one type of political action. As Mattern notes, confrontational, deliberative and pragmatic political action 45

can occur 'whenever music is produced and consumed', and thus, '[they] should not be viewed as mutually exclusive of each other' (Mattern, 1997: 8). In the case of hip-hop, this is especially true. Rap music, while a significant source of political action within hip-hop, should not be considered its only source. It is its presence within hip-hop community that lends it the context in which resistance emerges. As the hip-hop community looks towards the 21st century, it will be the challenge of hip-hop to define how hip-hop will continue to evolve as a culture and as genuine political force.

References

Allison, E. (1994) 'It's a Black Thing: Hearing How Whites Can't', *Cultural Studies* 8(3): 438–56.

Armstrong, E.G. (1993) 'The Rhetoric of Violence in Rap and Country Music', *Sociological Inquiry* 63(1): 64–83.

Bernard-Donais, M. (1994) 'Jazz, Rock 'n' Roll, Rap and Politics', *Journal of Popular Culture* 28(2): 127–38.

Blair, M.E. (1993) 'The Commercialization of the Rap Music Youth Subculture', *Journal of Popular Culture* 27(3): 21–32.

Charles, H. (1990) *Culture and African American Politics*. Bloomington: Indiana University Press.

Craddock-Willis, A. (1989) 'Rap Music and the Black Musical Tradition', *Radical America* 23(4): 29–38.

D. Chuck (1997) *Fight the Power: Rap, Race and Reality*. New York: Delacorte Press.

Dates, J.L. and W. Barlow (1990) *Split Image: African Americans in the Mass Media*. Washington, DC: Howard University Press.

Davis, T. (1996) 'King George: Tru Royalty', *4080* 35: 63.

Decker, J. (1993) 'The State of Rap: Time and Place in Hip Hop Nationalism', *Social Text* 34: 53–84.

DeMott, D. (1988) 'The Future is Unwritten: Working-Class Youth Cultures in England and America', *Critical Text* 5(1): 42–56.

Eurie, J.D. and J.G. Spady (eds) (1991) *Nation Conscious Rap*. New York: PC International Press.

Fernando, S.H. (1994) *The New Beats: Exploring the Music, Culture, and Attitudes of Hip-Hop Culture*. New York: Harmony Books.

Floyd, S.A. (1995) *The Power of Black Music: Interpreting its History from Africa to the United States.* New York: Oxford University Press.

Greenberg, B. and J. Brand (1994) 'Minorities and the Mass Media: 1970s to 1990s', pp. 273–314 in J. Bryant and D. Zillman (eds) *Media Effects: Advances in Theory and Research.* Hillsdale, NJ: Lawrence Erlbaum Associates.

Hansen, C.H. (1995) 'Predicting Cognitive and Behavioral Effects of Gangsta Rap,' *Basic and Applied Social Psychology* 16(1–2): 43–52.

Henderson, E.A. (1996) 'Black Nationalism and Rap Music', *Journal of Black Studies* 26(3): 308–39.

Jackson, R. (1994) *The Last Black Mecca: Hip-Hop.* Chicago, IL: Research Associates and Frontline Distribution International Inc.

Johnson, J.D., et al. (1995) 'Violent Attitudes and Deferred Academic Aspirations: Deleterious Effects of Exposure to Rap Music', *Basic and Applied Social Psychology* 16(1–2): 27–41.

Kitwana, B. (1994) *The Rap on Gangsta Rap.* Chicago, IL: Third World Press.

Krehbiel, H.E. (1914) *Afro-American Folksongs: A Study in Racial and National Music.* New York and London: G. Shirmer.

Kuwahara, Y. (1992) 'Power to the People Y'all', *Humanity and Society* 16(1): 54–73.

Larking, R. (1972) 'The Soul Message', pp. 92–104 in R. Serge Denisoff and R. Peterson (eds) *The Sounds of Social Change.* Chicago: Rand McNally.

Life After Death: Rap, Reality and Social Responsibility (1997) Harvard University, Cambridge, MA. 3 May.

Mattern, M. (1997) 'Cajun Music, Cultural Revival: Theorizing Political Action in Popular Music', paper prepared for delivery at the 1997 Annual Meeting of the American Political Science Association, Washington, DC.

Nelson, A. (1992) 'The Persistence of Ethnicity in African American Popular Music', *Explorations in Ethnic Studies* 15(1): 47–57.

Nia, M. (1997) 'From God's to Niggas, From Queens to Bitch's: Do Rappers Have An Identity Crisis?', *Beat Down* 5(5): 20.

Noe, D. (1995) 'Parallel Worlds', *Humanist* 55(4): 20–2.

Patillo, M. (1997) 'The Public Eulogy of a Slain Rapper', *The Source* 92: 83.

Powell, C. (1991) 'Rap Music: An Education with a Beat from the Street', *Journal of Negro Education* 60(3): 245–59.

Remes, P. (1991) 'Rapping: A Sociolinguistic Study of Oral Tradition', *Anthropological Society of Oxford* 22(2): 129–49.

Rose, T. (1994) *Black Noise: Rap and Black Culture in Contemporary America*. Hanover, NH: Wesleyan University Press.

Salsa, M. (1997) 'Hard Lines', *Hip Hop Connection* 104:5.

Scott, J.C. (1990) *Domination and the Arts of Resistance: Hidden Transcripts*. New Haven, CT: Yale University Press.

Shomari, H. (1995) *From the Underground: Hip Hop Culture As An Agent of Social Change*. Fairwood, NJ: X-Factor Publications.

Skeggs, B. (1993) 'Two Minute Brother: Contestation Through Gender, "Race" and Sexuality', *Innovation* 6(3): 299–322.

Spencer, J.M. (1996) *Re-searching Black Music*. Knoxville: University of Tennessee Press.

Stephens, G. (1991) 'Rap Music's Double-Voiced Discourse', *Journal of Communication Inquiry* 15(2): 70–91.

Toop, D. (1991) *Rap Attack 2: African Rap to Global Hip Hop*. London: Serpent's Tail.

Walker, S. (1997) 'Glocks Down', *The Source* 98: 30–1.

Williams, F. (1997) 'Rage against the Machine', *The Source* 94: 63–6.

Zillman, D., et al. (1995) 'Radical Rap: Does it Further Ethnic Division?', *Basic and Applied Social Psychology* 16(1–2): 1–25.

Questions on Meaning

1. Explain the function of the griot in African culture.
2. What are the main goals of the hip-hop culture? How does it accomplish those goals? In what direction is its development taking it, according to Stapleton's sources?
3. Listen to some blues recordings by artists such as Muddy Waters or Aretha Franklin and compare their lyrics to those of hip-hop artists. Do they have common themes? similar language? How do they differ?

Questions on Rhetorical Strategy and Style

1. Stapleton's article is persuasive that mainstream and intellectual cultures should respect hip-hop. Identify passages that would tend to influence an audience that does not already listen to hip-hop.
2. Stapleton describes the sexism and violence in hip-hop in the same context as her description of hip-hop's positive social protest. What is Stapleton's point in creating the comparison? Does she mean to show the shortcomings of hip-hop artists? Is she arguing that the ghetto conditions justify the sexism and violence?

Writing Assignments

1. Find recordings or videos by one of the hip-hop artists Stapleton names. After you have reviewed the materials, write an essay that explains the artist's political position.
2. Social and political protest were an important part of pop music during the 60s in the work of folk artists such as Joan Baez and Pete Seeger, as well as rock groups such as the Beatles, Jefferson Airplane, and Country Joe and the Fish. Listen to some of those recordings and write an essay that identifies the themes of social protest in the pop mainstream then and now.
3. Poets have often spoken out against injustice. Study some of the rap artists that Stapleton cites and then read some of the works of Robert Bly, Robinson Jeffers, Denise Levertov, Allen Ginsberg, or a comparable white poet writing out of the American experience. Does race matter to white protest poets? If not, what does?

Pornography

Margaret Atwood

Margaret Atwood (1939–), born in Ottawa, Canada, attended the University of Toronto, Radcliffe, and Harvard. At a young age she decided to become a writer, and she has published a remarkable list of novels, poetry, and essays, along with forays into other genres such as children's stories and television scripts. She is best known, however, for her novels: The Edible Women *(1969),* Surfacing *(1972),* Lady Oracle *(1976),* Life Before Man *(1979),* Bodily Harm *(1982),* The Handmaid's Tale *(1985),* Cat's Eye *(1989),* The Robber Bride *(1994),* Alias Grace *(1996),* The Blind Assassin *(2000),* Oryx and Crake *(2003), which was shortlisted for the Giller Prize, and the Man Booker Prize,* The Penelopiad *(2005), and* The Tent *(2006). In the following selection, first published in 1988, she explores a topic she first became involved in when doing research for a novel. As a gifted stylist, Atwood is well aware of the power of language—which she uses in this essay to describe vividly the violence of pornography.*

1   When I was in Finland a few years ago for an international writers' conference, I had occasion to say a few paragraphs in public on the subject of pornography. The context was a discussion of political repression, and I was suggesting the possibility of a link between the two. The immediate result was that a male journalist took several large bites out of me. Prudery and pornography are two halves of the same coin, said he, and I was clearly a prude. What could you expect from an Anglo-Canadian? Afterward,

a couple of pleasant Scandinavian men asked me what I had been so worked up about. All "pornography" means, they said, is graphic depictions of whores, and what was the harm in that?

Not until then did it strike me that the male journalist and I had two entirely different things in mind. By "pornography," he meant naked bodies and sex. I, on the other hand, had recently been doing the research for my novel *Bodily Harm,* and was still in a state of shock from some of the material I had seen, including the Ontario Board of Film Censors' "outtakes." By "pornography," I meant women getting their nipples snipped off with garden shears, having meat hooks stuck into their vaginas, being disemboweled; little girls being raped; men (yes, there are some men) being smashed to a pulp and forcibly sodomized. The cutting edge of pornography, as far as I could see, was no longer simple old copulation, hanging from the chandelier or otherwise: it was death, messy, explicit and highly sadistic. I explained this to the nice Scandinavian men. "Oh, but that's just the United States," they said. "Everyone knows they're sick." In their country, they said, violent "pornography" of that kind was not permitted on television or in movies; indeed, excessive violence of any kind was not permitted. They had drawn a clear line between erotica, which earlier studies had shown did not incite men to more aggressive and brutal behavior toward women, and violence, which later studies indicated did.

Some time after that I was in Saskatchewan, where, because of the scenes in *Bodily Harm,* I found myself on an open-line radio show answering questions about "pornography." Almost no one who phoned in was in favor of it, but again they weren't talking about the same stuff I was, because they hadn't seen it. Some of them were all set to stamp out bathing suits and negligees, and, if possible, any depictions of the female body whatsoever. God, it was implied, did not approve of female bodies, and sex of any kind, including that practised by bumblebees, should be shoved back into the dark, where it belonged. I had more than a suspicion that *Lady Chatterley's Lover,* Margaret Laurence's *The Diviners,* and indeed most books by most serious modern authors would have ended up as confetti if left in the hands of these callers.

For me, these two experiences illustrate the two poles of the emotionally heated debate that is now thundering around this issue. They also underline the desirability and even the necessity of defining the terms. "Pornography" is now one of those catchalls, like "Marxism" and "feminism," that have become so broad they can mean almost anything, ranging from certain verses in the Bible, ads for skin lotion and sex texts for children to the contents of Penthouse, Naughty '90s postcards and films with titles containing the word *Nazi* that show vicious scenes of torture and killing. It's easy to say that sensible people can tell the difference. Unfortunately, opinions on what constitutes a sensible person vary.

5   But even sensible people tend to lose their cool when they start talking about this subject. They soon stop talking and start yelling, and the name-calling begins. Those in favor of censorship (which may include groups not noticeably in agreement on other issues, such as some feminists and religious fundamentalists) accuse the others of exploiting women through the use of degrading images, contributing to the corruption of children, and adding to the general climate of violence and threat in which both women and children live in this society; or, though they may not give much of a hoot about actual women and children, they invoke moral standards and God's supposed aversion to "filth," "smut" and deviated *perversion,* which may mean ankles.

The camp in favor of total "freedom of expression" often comes out howling as loud as the Romans would have if told they could no longer have innocent fun watching the lions eat up Christians. It too may include segments of the population who are not natural bedfellows: those who proclaim their God-given right to freedom, including the freedom to tote guns, drive when drunk, drool over chicken porn and get off on videotapes of women being raped and beaten, may be waving the same anticensorship banner as responsible liberals who fear the return of Mrs. Grundy, or gay groups for whom sexual emancipation involves the concept of "sexual theatre." *Whatever turns you on* is a handy motto, as is *A man's home is his castle* (and if it includes a dungeon with beautiful maidens strung up in chains and bleeding from every pore, that's his business).

Meanwhile, theoreticians theorize and speculators speculate. Is today's pornography yet another indication of the hatred of the body, the deep mind-body split, which is supposed to pervade Western Christian society? Is it a backlash against the women's movement by men who are threatened by uppity female behavior in real life, so like to fantasize about women done up like outsize parcels, being turned into hamburger, kneeling at their feet in slavelike adoration or sucking off guns? Is it a sign of collective impotence, of a generation of men who can't relate to real women at all but have to make do with bits of celluloid and paper? Is the current flood just a result of smart marketing and aggressive promotion by the money men in what has now become a multibillion-dollar industry? If they were selling movies about men getting their testicles stuck full of knitting needles by women with swastikas on their sleeves, would they do as well, or is this penchant somehow peculiarly male? If so, why? Is pornography a power trip rather than a sex one? Some say that those ropes, chains, muzzles and other restraining devices are an argument for the immense power female sexuality still wields in the male imagination: you don't put these things on dogs unless you're afraid of them. Others, more literary, wonder about the shift from the 19th-century Magic Women or Femme Fatale image to the lollipop-licker, airhead or turkey-carcass treatment of women in porn today. The proporners don't care much about theory: they merely demand product. The antiporners don't care about it in the final analysis either: there's dirt on the street, and they want it cleaned up, now.

It seems to me that this conversation, with its *You're-a-prude/ You're-a-pervert* dialectic, will never get anywhere as long as we continue to think of this material as just "entertainment." Possibly we're deluded by the packaging, the format: magazine, book, movie, theatrical presentation. We're used to thinking of these things as part of the "entertainment industry," and we're used to thinking of ourselves as free adult people who ought to be able to see any kind of "entertainment" we want to. That was what the First Choice pay-TV debate was all about. After all, it's only entertainment, right? Entertainment means fun, and only a killjoy would be antifun. What's the harm?

This is obviously the central question: *What's the harm?* If there isn't any real harm to any real people, then the antiporners can tsk-tsk and/or throw up as much as they like, but they can't rightfully expect more legal controls or sanctions. However, the no-harm position is far from being proven.

10 (For instance, there's a clear-cut case for banning—as the federal 10 government has proposed—movies, photos and videos that depict children engaging in sex with adults: real children are used to make the movies, and hardly anybody thinks this is ethical. The possibilities for coercion are too great.)

To shift the viewpoint, I'd like to suggest three other models for looking at "pornography"—and here I mean the violent kind.

Those who find the idea of regulating pornographic materials repugnant because they think it's Fascist or Communist or otherwise not in accordance with the principles of an open democratic society should consider that Canada has made it illegal to disseminate material that may lead to hatred toward any group because of race or religion. I suggest that if pornography of the violent kind depicted these acts being done predominantly to Chinese, to blacks, to Catholics, it would be off the market immediately, under the present laws. Why is hate literature illegal? Because whoever made the law thought that such material might incite real people to do real awful things to other real people. The human brain is to a certain extent a computer: garbage in, garbage out. We only hear about the extreme cases (like that of American multimurderer Ted Bundy) in which pornography has contributed to the death and/or mutilation of women and/or men. Although pornography is not the only factor involved in the creation of such deviance, it certainly has upped the ante by suggesting both a variety of techniques and the social acceptability of such actions. Nobody knows yet what effect this stuff is having on the less psychotic.

Studies have shown that a large part of the market for all kinds of porn, soft and hard, is drawn from the 16-to-21-year-old population of young men. Boys used to learn about sex on the street, or (in Italy, according to Fellini movies) from friendly whores, or, in more genteel surroundings, from girls, their parents, or, once upon a time, in school, more or less. Now porn has been added, and sex education in the schools is rapidly being phased out. The buck has been passed, and boys are being taught that all women secretly like to be raped and that real men get high on scooping out women's digestive tracts.

Boys learn their concept of masculinity from other men: is this what most men want them to be learning? If word gets around that rapists are "normal" and even admirable men, will boys feel that in order to be normal, admirable and masculine they will have to be rapists? Human beings are enormously flexible, and how they turn out depends a lot on how they're educated, by the society in which they're immersed as well as by their teachers. In a society that advertises and glorifies rape or even implicitly condones it, more women get raped. It becomes socially acceptable. And at a time when men and the traditional male role have taken a lot of flak and men are confused and casting around for an acceptable way of being male (and, in some cases, not getting much comfort from women on that score), this must be at times a pleasing thought.

15   It would be naïve to think of violent pornography as just harmless entertainment. It's also an educational tool and a powerful propaganda device. What happens when boy educated on porn meets girl brought up on Harlequin romances? The clash of expectations can be heard around the block. She wants him to get down on his knees with a ring, he wants her to get down on all fours with a ring in her nose. Can this marriage be saved?

Pornography has certain things in common with such addictive substances as alcohol and drugs: for some, though by no means for all, it induces chemical changes in the body, which the user finds exciting and pleasurable. It also appears to attract a "hard core" of habitual users and a penumbra of those who use it occasionally but aren't dependent on it in any way. There are also significant numbers of men who aren't much interested in it, not because they're undersexed but because real life is satisfying their needs, which may not require as many appliances as those of users.

For the "hard core," pornography may function as alcohol does for the alcoholic: tolerance develops, and a little is no longer enough. This may account for the short viewing time and fast turnover in porn theatres. Mary Brown, chairwoman of the Ontario Board of Film Censors, estimates that for every one mainstream movie requesting entrance to Ontario, there is one porno flick. Not only the quantity consumed but the quality of explicitness must escalate, which may account for the growing violence: once the big deal was breasts, then it was genitals, then copulation, then that was no longer enough and the hard users had to have more. The ultimate kick is death, and after that, as the Marquis de Sade so boringly demonstrated, multiple death.

The existence of alcoholism has not led us to ban social drinking. On the other hand, we do have laws about drinking and driving, excessive drunkenness and other abuses of alcohol that may result in injury or death to others.

This leads us back to the key question: what's the harm? Nobody knows, but this society should find out fast, before the saturation point is reached. The Scandinavian studies that showed a connection between depictions of sexual violence and increased impulse toward it on the part of male viewers would be a starting point, but many more questions remain to be raised as well as answered. What, for instance, is the crucial difference between men who are users and men who are not? Does using affect a man's relationship with actual women, and, if so, adversely? Is there a clear line between erotica and violent pornography, or are they on an escalating continuum? Is this a "men versus women" issue, with all men secretly siding with the proporners and all women secretly siding against? (I think not; there *are* lots of men who don't think that running their true love through the Cuisinart is the best way they can think of to spend a Saturday night, and they're just as nauseated by films of someone else doing it as women are.) Is pornography merely an expression of the sexual confusion of this age or an active contributor to it?

20   Nobody wants to go back to the age of official repression, when even piano legs were referred to as "limbs" and had to wear pantaloons to be decent. Neither do we want to end up in George Orwell's *1984,* in which pornography is turned out by the State to keep the proles in a state of torpor, sex itself is considered dirty and the approved practise is only for reproduction. But Rome under the emperors isn't such a good model either.

If all men and women respected each other, if sex were considered joyful and life-enhancing instead of a wallow in germ-filled glop, if everyone were in love all the time, if, in other words, many people's lives were more satisfactory for them than they appear to be now, pornography might just go away on its own. But since this is obviously not happening, we as a society are going to have to make some informed and responsible decisions about how to deal with it.

Questions on Meaning

1. What does Atwood mean when she says violent pornography is "an educational tool and a powerful propaganda device"?
2. Atwood speculates about the possible causes for what she sees as an explosion of pornography in modern times. List some of these causes. Does she argue for one cause rather than another? Explain why or why not.
3. The essay asks far more questions about pornography than it attempts to answer, but Atwood still has a clear point to make. State her primary theme in your own words.

Questions on Rhetorical Strategy and Style

1. Atwood's style is quite graphic in some places in this essay, such as in the second paragraph where she describes violent details of the pornographic film out-takes she saw from the Ontario Board of Film Censors. What effect did such descriptions have on you as you read the essay? Explain how this style is appropriate for what she has to say about her subject.
2. One goal of this essay is simply to define pornography. After establishing that different people mean very different things by the word, Atwood does attempt to define it. What writing techniques does she use to define what she means by pornography?
3. To explain the argument that pornography should be regulated by laws, Atwood compares it to hate literature. Examine how she uses this strategy of comparison and contrast explicitly in that part of the essay but also implicitly throughout by associating the concepts of hatred and pornography.

Writing Assignments

1. The term "date rape" has arisen in the last decade to describe a specific kind of sexual coercion. Date rape has become so common on most college campuses that colleges and universities have developed programs for purposes of education and prevention. Research what is being done on your own campus to help overcome this problem.
2. Atwood comments that when discussing pornography, people "soon stop talking and start yelling." Think of other social issues about which people become highly emotional. Without getting

into a debate on the issue itself, write an essay exploring why you think it is so difficult for people on both sides of such issues to calmly and rationally debate the question.

3. Atwood mentions how much better it would be "if sex were considered joyful and life-enhancing." Consider all the different ways you have seen sex portrayed in reality and in the media. Write an essay in which you compare and contrast different representations of sex.

Erotica and Pornography

Gloria Steinem

Gloria Steinem (1934–) was born in Toledo, Ohio, and after graduating from Smith College went on to further studies at the University of Delhi and the University of Calcutta. She began a career in political journalism with her column for New York *magazine in the late 1960s. In 1971 she cofounded* Ms. *magazine and became its editor, a position she held until 1987. Steinem has been a key figure in the feminist movement and has worked with the National Women's Political Caucus and the Women's Action Alliance. She published her first collection of essays and columns,* Outrageous Acts and Everyday Rebellions, *in 1983, followed by* Revolution from Within *(1992) and* Moving Beyond Words *(1994). Her concern for women's rights and equality can be seen in the following essay, which explores one of the ways women's bodies have been exploited.*

1   Human beings are the only animals that experience the same sex drive at times when we can—and cannot—conceive.

Just as we developed uniquely human capacities for language, planning, memory, and invention along our evolutionary path, we also developed sexuality as a form of expression; a way of communicating that is separable from our need for sex as a way of perpetuating ourselves. For humans alone, sexuality can be and often is primarily a way of bonding, of giving and receiving pleasure, bridging differentness, discovering sameness, and communicating emotion.

Reprinted from *Outrageous Acts and Everyday Rebellions* (1983), by permission of East Toledo Productions. Published by Henry Holt and Company, Inc. Copyright © 1983 by Gloria Steinem. Copyright © 1984 by East Toledo Productions, Inc. Gloria Steinem is a feminist activist and writer.

We developed this and other human gifts through our ability to change our environment, adapt physically, and in the long run, to affect our own evolution. But as an emotional result of this spiraling path away from other animals, we seem to alternate between periods of exploring our unique abilities to change new boundaries, and feelings of loneliness in the unknown that we ourselves have created; a fear that sometimes sends us back to the comfort of the animal world by encouraging us to exaggerate our sameness.

The separation of "play" from "work," for instance, is a problem only in the human world. So is the difference between art and nature, or an intellectual accomplishment and a physical one. As a result, we celebrate play, art, and invention as leaps into the unknown; but any imbalance can send us back to nostalgia for our primate past and the conviction that the basics of work, nature, and physical labor are somehow more worthwhile or even moral.

5   In the same way, we have explored our sexuality as separable from conception: a pleasurable, empathetic bridge to strangers of the same species. We have even invented contraception—a skill that has probably existed in some form since our ancestors figured out the process of birth—in order to extend this uniquely human difference. Yet we also have times of atavistic suspicion that sex is not complete—or even legal or intended-by-god—if it cannot end in conception.

No wonder the concepts of "erotica" and "pornography" can be so crucially different, and yet so confused. Both assume that sexuality can be separated from conception, and therefore can be used to carry a personal message. That's a major reason why, even in our current culture, both may be called equally "shocking" or legally "obscene," a word whose Latin derivative means "dirty, containing filth." This gross condemnation of all sexuality that isn't harnessed to childbirth and marriage has been increased by the current backlash against women's progress. Out of fear that the whole patriarchal structure might be upset if women really had the autonomous power to decide our reproductive futures (that is, if we controlled the most basic means of production), right-wing groups are not only denouncing prochoice abortion literature as "pornographic," but are trying to stop the sending of all contraceptive information through the mails by invoking obscenity laws. In fact, Phyllis Schlafly recently denounced the entire Women's Movement as "obscene."

Not surprisingly, this religious, visceral backlash has a secular, intellectual counterpart that relies heavily on applying the "natural" behavior of the animal world to humans. That is questionable in it-self, but these Lionel Tiger-ish studies make their political purpose even more clear in the particular animals they select and the habits they choose to emphasize. The message is that females should accept their "destiny" of being sexually dependent and devote themselves to bearing and rearing their young.

Defending against such reaction in turn leads to another tempta-tion: to merely reverse the terms, and declare that *all* nonprocreative sex is good. In fact, however, this human activity can be as constructive or destructive, moral or immoral, as any other. Sex as communication can send messages as different as life and death; even the origins of "erot-ica" and "pornography" reflect that fact. After all, "erotica" is rooted in *eros* or passionate love, and thus in the idea of positive choice, free will, the yearning for a particular person. (Interestingly, the definition of erotica leaves open the question of gender.) "Pornography" begins with a root meaning "prostitution" or "female captives," thus letting us know that the subject is not mutual love, or love at all, but domination and violence against women. (Though, of course, homosexual pornography may imitate this violence by putting a man in the "feminine" role of victim.) It ends with a root meaning "writing about" or "description of" which puts still more distance between subject and object, and replaces a spontaneous yearning for closeness with objectification and a voyeur.

The difference is clear in the words. It becomes even more so by example.

10   Look at any photo or film of people making love; really making   10
love. The images may be diverse, but there is usually a sensuality and touch and warmth, an acceptance of bodies and nerve endings. There is always a spontaneous sense of people who are there because they *want* to be, out of shared pleasure.

Now look at any depiction of sex in which there is clear force, or an unequal power that spells coercion. It may be very blatant, with weapons or torture or bondage, wounds and bruises, some clear humil-iation, or an adult's sexual power being used over a child. It may be much more subtle: a physical attitude of conqueror and victim, the use of race or class difference to imply the same thing, perhaps a very un-equal nudity, with one person exposed and vulnerable while the other is clothed. In either case, there is no sense of equal choice or equal power.

The first is erotic: a mutually pleasurable, sexual expression be-tween people who have enough power to be there by positive choice.

It may or may not strike a sense-memory in the viewer, or be creative enough to make the unknown seem real; but it doesn't require us to identify with a conqueror or a victim. It is truly sensuous, and may give us a contagion of pleasure.

The second is pornographic: its message is violence, dominance, and conquest. It is sex being used to reinforce some inequality, or to create one, or to tell us the lie that pain and humiliation (ours or someone else's) are really the same as pleasure. If we are to feel anything, we must identify with conqueror or victim. That means we can only experience pleasure through the adoption of some degree of sadism or masochism. It also means that we may feel diminished by the role of conqueror, or enraged, humiliated, and vengeful by sharing identity with the victim.

Perhaps one could simply say that erotica is about sexuality, but pornography is about power and sex-as-weapon—in the same way we have come to understand that rape is about violence, and not really about sexuality at all.

15   Yes, it's true that there are women who have been forced by violent families and dominating men to confuse love with pain; so much so that they have become masochists. (A fact that in no way excuses those who administer such pain.) But the truth is that, for most women—and for men with enough humanity to imagine themselves into the predicament of women—true pornography could serve as aversion therapy for sex.

Of course, there will always be personal differences about what is and is not erotic, and there may be cultural differences for a long time to come. Many women feel that sex makes them vulnerable and therefore may continue to need more sense of personal connection and safety before allowing any erotic feelings. We now find competence and expertise erotic in men, but that may pass as we develop those qualities in ourselves. Men, on the other hand, may continue to feel less vulnerable, and therefore more open to such potential danger as sex with strangers. As some men replace the need for submission from childlike women with the pleasure of cooperation from equals, they may find a partner's competence to be erotic, too.

Such group changes plus individual differences will continue to be reflected in sexual love between people of the same gender, as well as between women and men. The point is not to dictate sameness, but to discover ourselves and each other through sexuality that is an exploring, pleasurable, empathetic part of our lives; a human sexuality that is unchained both from unwanted pregnancies and from violence.

But that is a hope, not a reality. At the moment, fear of change is increasing both the indiscriminate repression of all nonprocreative sex in the religious and "conservative" male world, and the pornographic vengeance against women's sexuality in the secular world of "liberal" and "radical" men. It's almost futuristic to debate what is and is not truly erotic, when many women are again being forced into compulsory motherhood, and the number of pornographic murders, tortures, and woman-hating images are on the increase in both popular culture and real life.

It's a familiar division: wife or whore, "good" woman who is constantly vulnerable to pregnancy or "bad" woman who is unprotected from violence. *Both* roles would be upset if we were to control our own sexuality. And that's exactly what we must do.

20 In spite of all our atavistic suspicions and training for the "natural" role of motherhood, we took up the complicated battle for reproductive freedom. Our bodies had borne the health burden of endless births and poor abortions, and we had a greater motive for separating sexuality and conception.

Now we have to take up the equally complex burden of explaining that all nonprocreative sex is *not* alike. We have a motive: our right to a uniquely human sexuality, and sometimes even to survival. As it is, our bodies have too rarely been enough our own to develop erotica in our own lives, much less in art and literature. And our bodies have too often been the objects of pornography and the woman-hating, violent practice that it preaches. Consider also our spirits that break a little each time we see ourselves in chains or full labial display for the conquering male viewer, bruised or on our knees, screaming a real or pretended pain to delight the sadist, pretending to enjoy what we don't enjoy, to be blind to the images of our sisters that really haunt us—humiliated often enough ourselves by the truly obscene idea that sex and the domination of women must be combined.

Sexuality *is* human, free, separate—and so are we.

But until we untangle the lethal confusion of sex with violence, there will be more pornography and less erotica. There will be little murders in our beds—and very little love.

Questions on Meaning

1. How does Steinem define "erotica"? What is her definition for "pornography"?
2. Why does Steinem discuss contraception and abortion rights in this essay? How do they fit into the larger context in which she discusses erotica?
3. What does she mean by the "little murders in our beds" in the final sentence? How is this related to a key theme throughout the essay?

Questions on Rhetorical Strategy and Style

1. For whom is Steinem writing? Identify the "we" of the essay. How does this identification between the writer and reader strengthen her message in the essay?
2. Make a list of adjectives that describe Steinem's sentence-level style. How vivid and persuasive is she in her writing? Compare her style with that of other feminist writers you have read.
3. Some men (and women) have found Steinem's style polarizing and confrontational. Are there any points in this essay at which she seems to lose objectivity or go too far in her generalizations about men and women—to the point of unjustifiably criticizing all men? If so, what is her point in doing so?

Writing Assignments

1. Steinem makes it seem a simple process to distinguish between erotica and pornography, since her definitions and examples are so clear-cut. Courts have had great difficulties, however, in applying antipornography laws, because sometimes the difference is not so clear. Using a hypothetical example or a real example from a case you may know of, explain how in some cases there may seem to be an overlap between erotica and pornography.
2. Steinem writes that most pornography involves images of men in domination over women— showing women in vulnerable, power-less roles—with women's bodies "the objects of pornography." Erotica, on the other hand, is "mutually pleasurable" and "truly sensuous" and not degrading to women. Interestingly, however, most erotic literature and art has been produced by men, with women's bodies the object. One need only consider the long art

tradition of female "nudes." Should there be a balance of the sexes for erotica to exist in the positive way in which Steinem defines it? Would she seem to be arguing for artistic display of men and women making love? Do some research about what is usually meant by "erotica" and write an essay in which you describe (or argue for or against) a feminist version of erotica.

Why Are We Dressing Our Daughters Like This?

Lianne George

Lianne George has written for New York *magazine and* Metro TV, *and served as a reporter on the arts for the* National Post. *At present George is a senior editor for* Macleans, *Canada's national weekly current affairs magazine.* Macleans *covers not only national and world political news, but also social issues of concern to the average family in Canada and the United States. Among those issues is what many consider the disturbing trend of marketing sexualized fashion and toys to younger and younger girls. Beginning with the emergence of Barbie dolls in the late 1950s, girls have been exposed to toys that celebrate an unrealistic—and some contend eroticized—image of the mature female form. But in more recent years, dolls have become far more overtly sexual, and the clothing found in shops catering to young girls has followed suit. In this article, originally published in* Macleans, *George explores this phenomenon, focusing on both the marketing of the clothing and its potential impact on little girls.*

1   In his most recent visual tome, *Katlick School*, the famed American   1
fashion photographer Sante D'Orazio examines the titillating power of the Catholic schoolgirl uniform—a fetish, his publishers write, "as psycho-sexually resonant as the black motorcycle jacket or the nurse's uniform." The book chronicles the coming of age of Kat, a "beautiful Latina schoolgirl," whose sexual curiosity grows increasingly outsized for her pleated skirt and bobby socks. (It's not the most

601

original idea, maybe, but it's a crowd-pleaser.) Kat's unravelling begins with flashes of Snoopy underwear. In a matter of pages, she's traded in her pressed plaid uniform for nothing but a pair of thigh-high spike-heeled boots. "I was experimenting with a symbol of virginity, the untouched, the ideal, the romantic notion of the pure," says D'Orazio, who famously enshrined Pamela Anderson in the canon of erotic coffee-table literature in 2005 with *Pam: American Icon*. "That is what the uniform signifies."

The book also signifies something rather less high-minded—it's a lascivious ode to the cultural muse of the moment, the Lolita. Shortly after it was launched last month, the Catholic League for Religious and Civil Rights registered its disgust in the *New York Post* (after which, not coincidentally, sales of *Katlick School* spiked). And yet, the response was not entirely honest. Because if there is one iconic symbol of the girl-about-to-go-wild, it's the schoolgirl uniform—and the Catholic community is well aware of it.

Even before Britney Spears paired a kilt with pigtails and a midriff-baring blouse in the 1998 video that launched her career, the kilt was a source of deep discomfort for Catholic schoolteachers, administrators and parents. Rules evolved to control its power: it should be three inches from the knee—no higher—and one Canadian uniform manufacturer even patented the X-Kilt, with built-in shorts to prevent girls from transforming them into miniskirts. So far, in Ontario alone, at least seven Catholic schools have voted to phase out the garment altogether. "It always has been an issue," says Ron Crocco, principal of St. Augustine Catholic High School in Markham, Ont., where the kilt was banned in 2003. "As a male, it's difficult to enforce, to say: your kilt is too short. Because then, why am I looking there?" In a post-Britney era, it seems, the kilt is just too sexy for school.

How, then, to explain the low-slung jeans, sequined halter tops and lacy miniskirts that so many young girls are wearing to class? In fact, in the broader universe of children's clothing, "Why am I looking there?" has become an increasingly pressing question. Streetwear for little girls has never been more overtly provocative. Girls as young as 6 are adopting the external cues of womanhood, adorning themselves not only with lip gloss and nail polish, but also body sprays, skin glitters and spa lotions. Club Libby Lu, a Saks Fifth Avenue spinoff with 62 outlets across the United States, invites "super fabulous girls" ages 6 and up to book "sparkle spa" makeover parties for their friends.

5   North American retailers like La Senza Girl, Abercrombie & Fitch   5
and Limited Too sell fishnet stockings, skinny jeans, message panties
and padded "bralettes" in micro-sizes. In 2002, Abercrombie & Fitch
launched its infamous kiddie thong collection, arguing that girls as
young as 10 "are style-conscious and want underwear that doesn't
produce a Visible Panty Line." (They have since dropped the line.)
Earlier this month, the New York designer Marc Jacobs, having his
pick of every grown-up bombshell in Hollywood, tapped 12-year-old
Dakota Fanning, star of the newly released *Charlotte's Web*, to be the
face of his latest womenswear collection.

Meanwhile, in an odd inversion of the Lolita trend, women old
enough to vote are embracing the trappings of girlhood, with varying
degrees of tongue-in-cheek. Victoria's Secret's lingerie collections have
innocent, girlie names like "Angels" and "Pink." Starlets such as Paris
Hilton and Britney Spears tote around miniature dogs in tutus—
called Tinkerbell and Bit Bit—as though they were cuddly stuffed
animals. In her latest video, *Fergalicious*, the musician Fergie is dressed
in a sexed-up Brownie uniform, surrounded by a troupe of bootie-
popping Brownie dancers. Last month, the British retailer Tesco
landed in hot water over a pole-dancing kit for sale on its website.
The kit, packaged in a pink plastic tube, featured an illustrated
Barbie-type character and bubble letters that read: "Unleash the sex
kitten inside." It was inadvertently placed on the site's children's toy
section, where it looked so entirely at home that none of the Web
designers questioned it. Perhaps most creepily, we're in a moment
when one of the latest celebrity "trends"—exemplified by Spears and
Lindsay Lohan—is to expose one's privates, completely waxed to look
like a 10-year-old's, from the backseat of a car.

The eroticization of girlhood—once the stuff of Russian literature,
Atom Egoyan films, Japanese comic books and good old-fashioned
American porn—has been seeping ever more into the larger culture.
Now it is one of our dominant aesthetics. In a Lolita-tinged culture,
whether the sell is "my body is underdeveloped, but I am precocious"
or "my brain is underdeveloped, but I am stacked," the message is the
same: exploit me. "For adult women, that notion of being kind of
girlie and innocent and sexually pure, as well as very sexy, has been in
men's magazines forever," says Lyn Mikel Brown, co-author of *Packaging Girlhood: Rescuing Our Daughters from Marketers' Schemes*. But
whether it's because of the pornification of culture or the extreme

worship of youth, the trend has migrated to ever younger age groups. Add this to the fact that the physiological onset of puberty itself keeps inching downward, and the definitions of "girl" and "women" have become moving targets. Which raises the question: what does it mean for little girls when the very things of their lives—kilts, puppies, angels, pink, princesses—become fetishized to the point of rendering them obscene?

In stores marketing to young girls, a phenomenon that the authors of *Packaging Girlhood* have termed "the pink wars" is easy to discern. There's the sweet, innocent "princess" girl (baby pink) and the saucy, naughty "diva" girl (hot pink). The two aesthetics are clearly delineated in the selection of novelty T-shirts on offer. A "princess," for instance, would wear one of these scrawled across her chest: *Sweet Treats, Angel, Daddy's Girl, Official Cheer Bunny*. While a "diva" would gravitate toward: *Trouble-maker, Drama Queen, You Will Do What I Say*, and of course, Paris Hilton's idiotic tag line, *That's Hot*. But T-shirts are just the beginning. It is the "total girl" marketers are after, write Brown and Sharon Lamb in *Packaging Girlhood*. "'Total girl' to marketers means finding every inch of their body to adorn," they write. "Expanding one's market means not just reaching down to the lower ages for products introduced to the older ages, but finding new parts of their bodies to colonize or own. The tiniest parts, the forgotten parts, such as nails, which should be dirty after a day of play." Implicit in the various products available is a sexy wink that has never before been associated with children so young.

Or so we think. The idea of children as innocent is a relatively modern one. "Children are the great vessels of fantasy," says Anne Hollander, a New York-based clothing historian and author of the classic 1978 text *Seeing Through Clothes*. Historically, a mother saw a little girl as a smaller, unspoiled version of herself, and so a daughter should be formed in her mother's image—and through most of history, she was. Up until the late 18th century, children, both male and female, were outfitted like little adults. Labourers' children dressed like labourers, and society children dressed like their elders, in garments designed for their pomp and rigidity to encourage socially appropriate behaviour. Moreover, says Hollander, royal children were dressed to look sexually attractive so that heads of state in other countries might look at their portraits and think, hmm, maybe I'd like to marry that sweet thing. "Girls of 6 wore low-cut dresses and very fetching hairdos," she says. "You can see it in the paintings, all meant to be sent off to Louis XV or some such. They don't have any breasts yet, but never mind."

10 It was only with the advent of the Romantic period in the late 10 1700s that modern notions of childhood arose, inspired largely by the sentimental writings of the Swiss-born philosopher Jean-Jacques Rousseau. "As the 18th century took on its second half," says Hollander, "you have an idea that children are a separate marvellous, terribly fragile, impressionable, innocent kind of creature that needs freedom and liberty of all kinds. There was the sense of nature infusing everything. They get to play and have a wonderful time and move all of their parts." And so, for the first time, girls were dressed differently from their adult counterparts—in a simple chemise with a sash.

As the Victorian age crept in, there was a stiffening of everybody's clothing, but girls and women remained sartorially distinct. "It was very, very important that the girls wore short dresses and the ladies wore long dresses," says Hollander. "Girls wore their hair down in curls or braids and put their hair up at the time they got long dresses—whenever they were supposed to be marriageable. The idea was that children are innocent. They don't have any sexuality, so don't worry."

What we're seeing now, she says, is a reversion to pre-Enlightenment days, a time before children were innocent, when they were nothing but smaller versions of ourselves in every way. "We are back in the 17th century," she says. "We're dressing little kids like adults and adults are dressing like little children. There is no distinction once again. A girl is a woman by the time she's 8 and a woman remains a girl until she's 80."

For many parents, there's nothing wrong with this. Kids are always trying to be more like teenagers, and the precocious fashions are kind of sweet and funny in the way those Anne Geddes photos of kids kissing are. "There is a mistaken sense that kids don't get the joke or the meaning so it's okay for them to wear sexualized slogans," says Susan Linn, an instructor in psychiatry at Harvard Medical School and a co-founder of the coalition Campaign for a Commercial-Free Childhood.

But even for parents who do have a problem with these off-the-rack identities, there is tremendous pressure to buy in. For one thing, they are susceptible to the "everyone is doing it" argument, and they don't want their kid to be ostracized. For another, it's often the least of their concerns. "They are in the middle of numerous commercially created battles with their children," says Linn. "Battles about junk food, violent media, expensive brands and all sorts of things. It's hard, if not impossible, to say no all of the time."

15   The popular marketing spin—which, incidentally, is supposed to reassure parents in some way—is that it is *kids* who are "getting older younger," a theory called age compression, brought on by the fact that young people have never had access to so much information. But what we're really seeing, says Linn, is marketers exploiting the natural tendency of young girls to want to emulate older girls, who appear to them to have more independence and social prestige.

In the end, then, it's not really a kid problem, but a grown-up problem. Because girls, looking the way they look, are only aping grown women, which serves to remind us of the turmoil and confusion surrounding what we currently believe a woman should be. The New York-based writer Ariel Levy documented this phenomenon, which she dubbed "raunch culture," in her 2006 book *Female Chauvinist Pigs*. The idea is that, in a post-feminist universe, a woman can be the agent of her own objectification and still be empowered. And so we see a boom in trends inspired by porn culture: pole-dancing and striptease lessons, boob jobs and Brazilian waxes. "A tawdry, tarty, cartoonlike version of female sexuality has become so ubiquitous, it no longer seems particular," writes Levy. "What we once regarded as a kind of sexual expression, we now view as sexuality." More recently, the *New York Times* columnist Bob Herbert, inspired by an Abercrombie & Fitch T-shirt he came across that read *Who Needs A Brain When I Have These?*, addressed what he calls a "disrespectful, degrading, contemptuous treatment of women" that has become "so pervasive and so mainstream that it has just about lost its ability to shock."

"This is some sort of response to the feminist movement," says Hollander. In fact, it's part of a trial-and-error continuum. In the '70s, as women prepared to invade the workplace en masse, the most overt manifestation of this new societal phase was sartorial. "It meant throwing out the skirts and certainly girdles and dressing so that you couldn't tell the difference between a man and a woman, except very small things," she says. "The masculine wardrobe was entirely co-opted by women. Suits and shoulder pads denied curves. Breasts and behinds and hips were not in fashion."

The current hyper-feminine aesthetic, one could argue, is an over-correction of this correction—an almost fanatical reclaiming of pink and frilly. But what may have been born of a spirit of defiance has lost its revolutionary edge, and now young girls are learning the not-so-progressive lesson that their primary value lies in their worth as sex objects. "Just because we are post doesn't mean we are feminists," writes Levy. "There is a widespread assumption that simply because my generation of women has the good fortune to live in a world touched by the feminist movement, that means everything we do is magically imbued with its agenda."

The trickle-down effect we're now seeing among very young girls has resulted in a Junior Miss version of raunch culture. Watching kids adopt these same behaviours is like looking at the larger culture through a fun-house mirror. On the body of a six-year-old, the diminishing aspect of an *Eye Candy* T-shirt is amplified and twisted— and entirely devoid of any of the irony that makes it pseudo-radical coming from a twentysomething pop star. "The problem is that girls are acquiring the trappings of maturity," Linn says, "but there's no indication that their social or emotional development is keeping pace." In fact, the aspiring-up trend preys upon and heightens the particular insecurities of kids in this age group. "Will she be popular? Will she be invited somewhere? With what group does she belong?" write Brown and Lamb. "Before a girl has half a chance to reflect on issues of belonging and desirability, she is being confronted with a market that tells her she should be concerned about this—even when she's as young as 8."

20 We tell girls that, in wearing these things, they are somehow 20 expressing themselves in an essential way. "If Ts expressed who a girl is," write Brown and Sharon Lamb, "you'd think she'd be wearing the T she got at the summer camp she went to, the music festival she attended or the Humane Society where she volunteers to walk the dogs. But instead they express 'attitude' rather than interests, skills, concerns, and hobbies." Worse still, in their very construction, these clothes prescribe behaviours that are hard to describe as empowering. A micromini, for instance, is a great disincentive to playing on the monkey bars. A halter top and tight, low-rise jeans make it rather more challenging to run and jump. "Every message to a preteen girl," write Brown and Lamb, "says that it's preferable to pose on the beach rather than surf, to shop rather than play, to decorate rather than invent."

But for marketers, it's not about grooming girls to be the next generation's cast of *Girls Gone Wild*. It has much more to do with grooming them to be promiscuous consumers. "Marketers are not setting out to sexualize little girls," says Susan Linn. "They are setting out to make a profit selling clothes to and for children and don't care what the consequences are." Girls themselves don't necessarily understand the clothing as sexual, she says, but "what they do comprehend is that they get a lot of attention by dressing in a particular way."

Female power has always been inextricably linked to ornamentation. When a woman comes of age, the convention is that she takes on a series of external cues to indicate sexual readiness: bright red lips that signal arousal, high heels that show off shapely legs, clothing that hugs fertile curves. This is what it means to be a sophisticated, mature and, to some extent, a powerful woman. But these things no longer correspond to any sort of biological turning point. Instead, they signify a claiming of personal economic autonomy. Call it consumer readiness. And as far as marketers are concerned, girls are never too young to be ready.

In fact, the most important identity of all for girls to cultivate is their identity as shoppers. For example, the educational toy brand International Playthings has a product called My First Purse, marketed to girls two years old and up. It's pink, purple and plush, and it includes play accessories, among them a wallet, debit card, lipstick, keys, mirror, and cellphone. (No, they don't make oversized baby-blue billfolds for boys to wedge in the back of their diapers.)Likewise, Mattel's Barbie Bank-with-ME ATM machine for girls 3 and up that takes bills and coins and displays their balance on the screen. The debit card activates sound effects and banking commands from Barbie. Anyone for a game of "Transfer funds"?

Ultimately, it is the "play" aspect of aspirational products that seems to have evaporated. Young girls have always loved to play dress-up—to trip around the house in their mother's heels and pearls. Playing mom, playing house, playing glamour girl or doctor was about little girls creating safe spaces for themselves in which to experiment with grown-up female identities. The difference is you can turn play off. Play time is confined and varied. Whereas now, taking on a womanly identity is incorporated into girls' everyday lives. They don't see it as a pretend purse, it's *their* purse. Wearing a halter top is not for dress-up, it's for show. "There's a seriousness to it that there wasn't," says Brown. "Now, it's really not about fantasy play. It's about adopting something that's out there for them. It's like practice for something very specific, to be like Jessica Simpson."

25   The latest dolls for girls offer not-so-subtle reinforcement of the   25
same ideas. Twenty years ago, popular collections including Cabbage
Patch Kids and Strawberry Shortcake had big floppy hats, pudgy
limbs, and silly clothing. They were cartoonish—with bright colours
and scents created to appeal to kids' imaginations. In 2001, MGA
Entertainment launched the Bratz dolls with the tag line: "The girls
with a passion for fashion." These toys, says Linn, are a "ratcheted up
male fantasy of what women should look like—big eyes, big lips, big
breasts, an anorexic waistline and very long legs." Soon, the Bratz
dolls—who do nothing but shop and socialize—were outselling even
Barbie, grossing roughly US$2 billion per year. Mattel fought back
with a sluttier, more urban line of Barbie dolls called the My Scene
collection. "That kind of plastic sexuality seems to be normalized for
younger and younger kids," says Linn. We used to worry about Barbie, with her improbable proportions and dismal math skills. Now we
long for Barbie. Not the new Bling Bling Barbie, but the old one with
the job. At least she *tried* to do math.

     It is no coincidence that the Lolita moment is surfacing now, at a
time when boys are supposedly in crisis, says Brown. "Twenty years
ago, we were talking about girls and loss of voice and self-esteem and
there were all these empowerment programs," says Brown. "Now we
have girls and women more likely to go to college, getting better
grades, being really out there and claiming more power. What women
are doing is challenging the status quo, and when that happens,
things tighten up. It's an anxiety, a collective response."

     And so, while adults try to navigate all of these complicated, frag-
mented ideals about gender, childhood, empowerment and sexuality,
girls have become our ideological guinea pigs. And they're being
taught some pretty unappealing lessons. "You can learn a whole lot of
very serious narcissism by being brought up to be looked at constantly," says Hollander. "That was Marie Antoinette's upbringing,
who was scheduled to be the queen of France since she was born."
And we all know how that one turned out.

     Unless we are prepared to see six-year-olds in garters, then it
would seem we're ready for another backlash. Already, the boundaries
of what the public will put up with are beginning to constrict. Religious and family groups, media critics, feminists and other concerned
citizens have teamed up to halt production of certain products
deemed too outrageous—including a line of Bratz bras for little girls,

and a line of Hasbro dolls aimed at six-year-olds based on the Pussycat Dolls, a burlesque troupe turned singing group. Now, advocacy groups have their sights set on a new line of clothing for babies called Pimpfants. "It's a kid thang," the company's slogan says. But when you see a six-month-old child in a *M.I.L.F.* onesie, even the most permissive grown-up has to stop and ask herself, whom is this really about?

Questions on Meaning

1. How does George distinguish between little girls playing dress-up and wearing provocative clothing designed for them? Why does she present one as innocent and the other as dangerous? Do you agree with this assessment? Why, or why not?

2. According to the article, how does the pervasiveness of child-oriented advertising make it more difficult for parents to say no to provocative clothing for their daughters? Based on your experience, is this a valid argument? Explain your response.

3. The authors of *Packaging Girlhood* argue that in selling sexualized clothing to young girls, marketers are "finding new parts of their bodies to colonize or own." What is your understanding of the concept of colonizing countries, and how does it apply to human bodies?

Questions on Rhetorical Strategy and Style

1. George quotes a number of experts in support of her conclusions. List the names and credentials of each of those experts, and explain their impact on the article. In what ways do they lend credibility to George's position?

2. Example is often used to illustrate abstract concepts. Select several examples used in this article and explain how they illustrate the points that George is making.

3. Cause-and-effect reasoning seeks to answer the question "why" about a given phenomenon. The phenomenon in this article is the increasingly sexualized nature of girls' clothing. What causes does George offer for this phenomenon? Which ones do you find most persuasive, and why?

Writing Assignments

1. Write a letter to *Macleans* in agreement or disagreement with this article. Use specific examples from your own experience to support your position.

2. Visit a shopping mall with a number of children's shops and department stores with children's sections, and note the slogans and images on T-shirts for little girls. Write an essay describing

your overall impression of the message that the T-shirts send and offering your position on their appropriateness for young girls.

3. Research the history of childhood from the Renaissance to the present. Write a report categorizing the different characterizations of children featured in different time periods. Based on your research, do you agree with Anne Hollander that "we're back in the 17th century"? Explain your response.

Girl

Jamaica Kincaid

Born Elaine Potter Richardson in St. John's, Antigua, in the West Indies, Jamaica Kincaid (1949-) left Antigua for New York when she was seventeen, took classes at a community college, studied photography at the New School for Social Research, and attended Franconia College. She has been a staff writer for The New Yorker *and has published her work in* Rolling Stone, The Village Voice, *and* The Paris Review. *Her first book,* At the Bottom of the River *(1983) won an award from the American Academy and Institute of Arts and Letters. Her more recent works include* The Autobiography of My Mother *(1996) and* My Brother *(1997). The following selection originally appeared in* The New Yorker *and was included in* At the Bottom of the River. *It vividly narrates a relationship between a powerful mother and her young daughter and confronts us with the advice the daughter must listen to.*

1   Wash the white clothes on Monday and put them on the stone heap; wash the color clothes on Tuesday and put them on the clothesline to dry; don't walk barehead in the hot sun; cook pumpkin fritters in very hot sweet oil; soak your little clothes right after you take them off; when buying cotton to make yourself a nice blouse, be sure that it doesn't have gum on it, because that way it won't hold up well after a wash; soak salt fish overnight before you cook it; is it true that you sing benna in Sunday school?; always eat your food in such a way that it won't turn someone else's stomach; on Sundays try to walk like a lady and not like the slut you are so bent on becoming; don't sing benna in Sunday school; you

mustn't speak to wharf-rat boys, not even to give directions; don't eat fruits on the street—flies will follow you; *but I don't sing benna on Sundays at all and never in Sunday school*; this is how to sew on a button; this is how to make a buttonhole for the button you have just sewed on; this is how to hem a dress when you see the hem coming down and so to prevent yourself from looking like the slut I know you are so bent on becoming; this is how you iron your father's khaki shirt so that it doesn't have a crease; this is how you iron your father's khaki pants so that they don't have a crease; this is how you grow okra—far from the house, because okra tree harbors red ants; when you are growing dasheen, make sure it gets plenty of water or else it makes your throat itch when you are eating it; this is how you sweep a corner; this is how you sweep a whole house; this is how you sweep a yard; this is how you smile to someone you don't like too much; this how you smile to someone you don't like at all; this is how you smile to someone you like completely; this is how you set a table for tea; this is how you set a table for dinner; this is how you set a table for dinner with an important guest; this is how you set a table for lunch; this is how you set a table for breakfast; this is how to behave in the presence of men who don't know you very well, and this way they won't recognize immediately the slut I have warned you against becoming; be sure to wash every day, even if it is with your own spit; don't squat down to play marbles—you are not a boy, you know; don't pick people's flowers—you might catch something; don't throw stones at blackbirds, because it might not be a blackbird at all; this is how to make a bread pudding; this is how to make doukona; this is how to make pepper pot; this is how to make a good medicine for a cold; this is how to make a good medicine to throw away a child before it even becomes a child; this is how to catch a fish; this is how to throw back a fish you don't like, and that way something bad won't fall on you; this is how to bully a man; this is how a man bullies you; this is how to love a man, and if this doesn't work there are other ways, and if they don't work don't feel too bad about giving up; this is how to spit up in the air if you feel like it and this is how to move quick so that it doesn't fall on you; this is how to make ends meet; always squeeze bread to make sure it's fresh; *but what if the baker won't let me feel the bread?*; you mean to say that after all you are really going to be the kind of woman who the baker won't let near the bread?

Questions on Meaning

1. In this short piece, Kincaid gives us a glimpse into the relationship between a mother and daughter. How would you describe that relationship?
2. How would you characterize the advice offered by the mother in this story? What information about her community and its assumptions regarding gender roles can you infer from it?

Questions on Rhetorical Strategy and Style

1. What is this story's texture? How does it make you feel? Why do you think Kincaid chose to present it as a brief monologue?
2. Kincaid doesn't describe the physical setting of "Girl" directly, but provides clues in the content of the mother's advice. Go through the story and find as many details about place as you can, then write a description of the characters' home and neighborhood.
3. "Girl" makes an interesting use of example: Kincaid strings together a barrage of examples to tell her reader something about the characters, but doesn't explain precisely what they're meant to illustrate. What point do you think she is trying to make with them?

Writing Assignments

1. Write a short narrative piece about a time when someone with authority over you gave you advice. What kind of advice was it? How did you feel about receiving it? What was your response? In your narrative, try to convey a sense of the mood surrounding the exchange by the way you describe the things around you.
2. Write an essay about your relationship with one of your parents. Recount in detail significant moments you spent together. Your purpose is to convey something about the understandings you share.

The Gender Blur

Deborah Blum

Deborah Blum (1954–   ) was born in Urbana, Illinois to an entomologist and a legal scholar. Educated in journalism at the University of Georgia (B.A.) and the University of Wisconsin (M.A.), she has worked as a reporter for several newspapers in Georgia and Florida, and as a science writer for the Sacramento, California Bee. *Currently, Blum is professor of journalism at the University of Wisconsin. Her first book,* The Monkey Wars, *explored the issue of medical and psychological experimentation on primates. Lauded for its balanced approach, the book grew out of a Pulitzer Prize-winning series she had written on the subject in 1992. Her work has also earned her other awards, among them a Westinghouse Award from the American Academy of Arts and Sciences and a Clarion Award for Investigative Reporting, both in 1992; and a National Award for Non-Deadline Reporting from the Society of Professional Journalists in 1996. In 1997 she co-edited* A Field Guide for Science Writers. *Her most recent book,* Sex on the Brain: The Biological Differences Between Men and Women *(1997), explores the roles of biology and environment in determining gender. In this selection, based on that book, Blum describes how imprecise biological determiners of sex can be. Using extensive examples of indeterminate sexual identity, Blum raises questions about the rigid classification of male and female in the human race.*

1   I was raised in one of those university-based, liberal elite families
that politicians like to ridicule. In my childhood, every human
being—regardless of gender—was exactly alike under the skin,
and I mean exactly, barring his or her different opportunities. My parents wasted no opportunity to bring this point home. One Christmas,
I received a Barbie doll and a softball glove. Another brought a green
enamel stove, which baked tiny cakes by the heat of a lightbulb, and
also a set of steel-tipped darts and competition-quality dartboard. Did
I mention the year of the chemistry set and the ballerina doll?

It wasn't until I became a parent—I should say, a parent of two
boys—that I realized I had been fed a line and swallowed it like a
sucker (barring the part about opportunities, which I still believe).
This dawned on me during my older son's dinosaur phase, which
began when he was about 2 1/2. Oh, he loved dinosaurs, all right, but
only the blood-swilling carnivores. Plant-eaters were wimps and
losers, and he refused to wear a T-shirt marred by a picture of a
stegosaur. I looked down at him one day, as he was snarling around
my feet and doing his toddler best to gnaw off my right leg, and I
thought: This goes a lot deeper than culture.

Raising children tends to bring on this kind of politically incorrect reaction. Another friend came to the same conclusion watching a
son determinedly bite his breakfast toast into the shape of a pistol he
hoped would blow away—or at least terrify—his younger brother.
Once you get past the guilt part—Did I do this? Should I have bought
him that plastic allosaur with the oversized teeth?—such revelations
can lead you to consider the far more interesting field of gender biology, where the questions take a different shape: Does love of carnage
begin in culture or genetics, and which drives which? Do the gender
roles of our culture reflect an underlying biology, and, in turn, does
the way we behave influence that biology?

The point I'm leading up to—through the example of my son's
innocent love of predatory dinosaurs—is actually one of the most
straightforward in this debate. One of the reasons we're so fascinated
by childhood behaviors is that, as the old saying goes, the child becomes the man (or woman, of course.) Most girls don't spend their
preschool years snarling around the house and pretending to chew
off their companion's legs. And they—mostly—don't grow up to be
as aggressive as men. Do the ways that we amplify those early differences in childhood shape the adults we become? Absolutely. But

it's worth exploring the starting place—the faint signal that somehow gets amplified.

"There's plenty of room in society to influence sex differences," says Marc Breedlove, a behavioral endocrinologist at the University of California at Berkeley and a pioneer in defining how hormones can help build sexually different nervous systems. "Yes, we're born with predispositions, but it's society that amplifies them, exaggerates them. I believe that—except for the sex differences in aggression. Those [differences] are too massive to be explained simply by society."

Aggression does allow a straightforward look at the issue. Consider the following statistics: Crime reports in both the United States and Europe record between 10 and 15 robberies committed by men for every one by a woman. At one point, people argued that this was explained by size difference. Women weren't big enough to intimidate, but that would change, they predicted, with the availability of compact weapons. But just as little girls don't routinely make weapons out of toast, women—even criminal ones—don't seem drawn to weaponry in the same way that men are. Almost twice as many male thieves and robbers use guns as their female counterparts do.

Or you can look at more personal crimes: domestic partner murders. Three-fourths of men use guns in those killings; 50 percent of women do. Here's more from the domestic front: In conflicts in which a woman killed a man, he tended to be the one who had started the fight—in 51.8 percent of the cases, to be exact. When the man was the killer, he again was the likely first aggressor, and by an even more dramatic margin. In fights in which women died, they had started the argument only 12.5 percent of the time.

Enough. You can parade endless similar statistics but the point is this: Males are more aggressive, not just among humans but among almost all species on earth. Male chimpanzees, for instance, declare war on neighboring troops, and one of their strategies is a warning strike: They kill females and infants to terrorize and intimidate. In terms of simple, reproductive genetics, it's an advantage of males to be aggressive: You can muscle you way into dominance, winning more sexual encounters, more offspring, more genetic future. For the female—especially in a species like ours, with time for just one successful pregnancy a year—what's the genetic advantage in brawling?

Thus the issue becomes not whether there is a biologically influenced sex difference in aggression—the answer being a solid, technical

"You betcha"—but rather how rigid that difference is. The best science, in my opinion, tends to align with basic common sense. We all know that there are extraordinarily gentle men and murderous women. Sex differences are always generalizations: They refer to a behavior, with some evolutionary rationale behind it. They never define, entirely, an individual. And that fact alone should tell us that there's always—even in the most biologically dominated traits—some flexibility, an instinctive ability to respond, for better and worse, to the world around us.

10 This is true even with physical characteristics that we've often assumed are nailed down by genetics. Scientists now believe height, for instance, is only about 90 percent heritable. A person's genes might code for a six-foot-tall body, but malnutrition could literally cut that short. And there's also some evidence, in girls anyway, that children with stressful childhoods tend to become shorter adults. So while some factors are predetermined, there's evidence that the prototypical male/female body design can be readily altered. 10

It's a given that humans, like most other species—bananas, spiders, sharks, ducks, any rabbit you pull out of a hat—rely on two sexes for reproduction. So basic is that requirement that we have chromosomes whose primary purpose is to deliver the genes that order up a male or a female. All other chromosomes are numbered, but we label the sex chromosomes with the letters X and Y. We get one each from our mother and our father, and the basic combinations are these: XX makes female, XY makes male.

There are two important—and little known—points about these chromosomal matches. One is that even with this apparently precise system, there's nothing precise—or guaranteed—about the physical construction of male and female. The other point makes that possible. It appears that sex doesn't matter in the early stages of embryonic development. We are unisex at the point of conception.

If you examine an embryo at about six weeks, you see that it has the ability to develop in either direction. The fledgling embryo has two sets of ducts—Wolffian for male, Muellerian for female—an either/or structure, held in readiness for further development. If testosterone and other androgens are released by hormone-producing cells, then the Wolffian ducts develop into the channel that connects penis to testes, and the female ducts wither away.

Without testosterone, the embryo takes on a female form; the male ducts vanish and the Muellerian ducts expand into oviducts, uterus, and vagina. In other words, in humans, anyway (the opposite is true in birds), the female is the default sex. Back in the 1950s, the famed biologist Alfred Jost showed that if you castrate a male rabbit fetus, choking off testosterone, you produce a completely feminized rabbit.

15   We don't do these experiments in humans—for obvious reasons—but there are naturally occurring instances that prove the same point. For instance: In the fetal testes are a group of cells called Leydig cells, that make testosterone. In rare cases, the fetus doesn't make enough of these cells (a defect known as Leydig cell hypoplasia). In this circumstance we see the limited power of the XY chromosome. These boys have the right chromosomes and the right genes to be boys; they just don't grow a penis. Obstetricians and parents often think they see a baby girl, and these children are routinely raised as daughters. Usually, the "mistake" is caught about the time of puberty, when menstruation doesn't start. A doctor's examination shows the child to be internally male; there are usually small testes, often tucked with the abdomen. As the researchers put it, if the condition had been known from the beginning, "the sisters would have been born as brothers."

Just to emphasize how tricky all this body-building can get, there's a peculiar genetic defect that seems to be clustered by heredity in a small group of villages in the Dominican Republic. The result of the defect is a failure to produce an enzyme that concentrates testosterone, specifically for building genitals. One obscure little enzyme only, but here's what happens without it: You get a boy with undescended testes and a penis so short and stubby that it resembles an oversized clitoris.

In the mountain villages of this Caribbean nation, people are used to it. The children are usually raised as "conditional" girls. At puberty, the secondary tide of androgens rises and is apparently enough to finish the construction project. The scrotum suddenly descends, the phallus grows, and the child develops a distinctly male body—narrow hips, muscular build, and even slight beard growth. At that point, the family shifts the child over from daughter to son. The dresses are thrown out. He begins to wear male clothes and starts dating girls. People in the Dominican Republic are so familiar with this condition that there's a colloquial name for it: *guevedoces*, meaning "eggs (or testes) at 12."

It's the comfort level with this slip-slide of sexual identity that's so remarkable and, I imagine, so comforting to the children involved. I'm positive that the sexual transition of these children is less traumatic than the abrupt awareness of the "sisters who would have been brothers." There's a message of tolerance there, well worth repeating, and there are some other key lessons too.

These defects are rare and don't alter the basic male-female division of our species. They do emphasize how fragile those divisions can be. Biology allows flexibility, room to change, to vary and grow. With that comes room for error as well. That it's possible to live with these genetic defects, that they don't merely kill us off, is a reminder that we, male and female alike, exist on a continuum of biological possibilities that can overlap and sustain either sex.

20   Marc Breedlove points out that the most difficult task may be separating how the brain responds to hormones from how the brain responds to the *results* of hormones. Which brings us back, briefly, below the belt: In this context, the penis is just a result, the product of androgens at work before birth. "And after birth," says Breedlove, "virtually everyone who interacts with that individual will note that he has a penis, and will, in many instances, behave differently than if the individual was a female."   20

Do the ways that we amplify physical and behavioral differences in childhood shape who we become as adults? Absolutely. But to understand that, you have to understand the differences themselves— their beginning and the very real biochemistry that may lie behind them.

Here is a good place to focus on testosterone—a hormone that is both well-studied and generally underrated. First, however, I want to acknowledge that there are many other hormones and neurotransmitters that appear to influence behavior. Preliminary work shows that fetal boys are a little more active than fetal girls. It's pretty difficult to argue socialization at that point. There's a strong suspicion that testosterone may create the difference.

And there are a couple of relevant animal models to emphasize the point. Back in the 1960s, Robert Goy, a psychologist at the University of Wisconsin at Madison, first documented that young male monkeys play much more roughly than young females. Goy went on to show that if you manipulate testosterone level—raising it in females, damping it down in males—you can reverse those effects, creating sweet little male monkeys and rowdy young females.

Is testosterone the only factor at work here? I don't think so. But clearly we can argue a strong influence, and, interestingly, studies have found that girls with congenital adrenal hypoplasia—who run high in testosterone—tend to be far more fascinated by trucks and toy weaponry than most little girls are. They lean toward rough-and-tumble play, too. As it turns out, the strongest influence on this "abnormal" behavior is not parental disapproval, but the company of other little girls, who tone them down and direct them toward more routine girl games.

25   And that reinforces an early point: If there is indeed a biology to sex differences, we amplify it. At some point—when it is still up for debate—we gain a sense of our gender, and with it a sense of "gender-appropriate" behavior.

Some scientists argue for some evidence of gender awareness in infancy, perhaps by the age of 12 months. The consensus seems to be that full-blown "I'm a girl" or "I'm a boy" instincts arrive between the ages of 2 and 3. Research shows that if a family operates in a very traditional, Beaver Cleaver kind of environment, filled with awareness of and association with "proper" gender behaviors, the "boys do trucks, girls do dolls" attitude seems to come very early. If a child grows up in a less traditional family, with an emphasis on partnership and sharing—"We all do the dishes, Joshua"—children maintain a more flexible sense of gender roles until about age 6.

In this period, too, relationships between boys and girls tend to fall into remarkably strict lines. Interviews with children find that 3-year-olds say that about half their friendships are with the opposite sex. By the age of 5, that drops to 20 percent. By 7, almost no boys or girls have, or will admit to having, best friends of the opposite sex. They still hang out on the same playground, play on the same soccer teams. They may be friendly, but the real friendships tend to be boy-to-boy or girl-to-girl.

There's some interesting science that suggests that the space between boys and girls is a normal part of development; there are periods during which children may thrive and learn from hanging out with peers of the same sex. Do we, as parents, as a culture at large, reinforce such separations? Is the pope Catholic? One of my favorite studies looked at little boys who asked for toys. If they asked for a heavily armed action figure, they got the soldier about 70 percent of the time. If they asked for a "girl" toy, like a baby doll or a Barbie, their parents purchased it maybe 40 percent of the time. Name a child who won't figure out to work *that* system.

How does all this fit together—toys and testosterone, biology and behavior, the development of the child into the adult, the way that men and women relate to one another?

30   Let me make a cautious statement about testosterone: It not only has some body-building functions, it influences some behaviors as well. Let's make that a little less cautious: These behaviors include rowdy play, sex drive, competitiveness, and an in-your-face attitude. Males tend to have a higher baseline of testosterone than females—in our species, about seven to ten times as much—and therefore you would predict (correctly, I think) that all of those behaviors would be more generally found in men than in women.   30

But testosterone is also one of my favorite examples of how responsive biology is, how attuned it is to the way we live our lives. Testosterone, it turns out, rises in response to competition and threat. In the days of our ancestors, this might have been hand-to-hand combat or high-risk hunting endeavors. Today, scientists have measured testosterone rise in athletes preparing for a game, in chess players awaiting a match, in spectators following a soccer competition.

If a person—or even just a person's favored team—wins, testosterone continues to rise. It falls with a loss. (This also makes sense in an evolutionary perspective. If one was being clobbered with a club, it would be extremely unhelpful to have a hormone urging one to battle on.) Testosterone also rises in the competitive world of dating, settles down with a stable and supportive relationship, climbs again if the relationship starts to falter.

It's been known for years that men in high-stress professions—say, police work or corporate law—have higher testosterone levels than men in the ministry. It turns out that women in the same kind of strong-attitude professions have higher testosterone than women who choose to stay home. What I like about this is the chicken-or-egg aspect. If you argue that testosterone influenced the behavior of those women, which came first? Did they have high testosterone and choose the law? Or did they choose the law, and the competitive environment ratcheted them up on the androgen scale? Or could both be at work?

And, returning to children for a moment, there's an ongoing study by Pennsylvania researchers, tracking that question in adolescent girls, who are being encouraged by their parents to engage in competitive activities that were once for boys only. As they do so, the researchers are monitoring, regularly, two hormones: testosterone and cortisol, a stress hormone. Will these hormones rise in response to this new, more traditionally male environment? What if more girls choose the competitive path; more boys choose the other? Will female testosterone levels rise, male levels fall? Will that wonderful, unpredictable, flexible biology that we've been given allow a shift, so that one day, we will literally be far more alike?

35   We may not have answers to all those questions, but we can ask 35 them, and we can expect that the answers will come someday, because science clearly shows us that such possibilities exist. In this most important sense, sex differences offer us a paradox. It is only through exploring and understanding what makes us different that we can begin to understand what binds us together.

Questions on Meaning

1. According to Blum, why are males naturally more aggressive than females? What evidence does she offer to support this conclusion?
2. What does Blum mean when she says that "the female is the default sex" in humans? How do the examples she provides explain the importance of understanding this biological fact?
3. Blum and the experts she cites emphasize the significance of culture and environment "amplifying" biological differences. What biologically determined behaviors are often amplified in male and female children? How are those behaviors amplified?

Questions on Rhetorical Strategy and Style

1. Effective classification demands that each part of an identified group share the same features. How does Blum's analysis call into question the classifications "male" and "female"? What generally accepted features of each group does she question?
2. Blum employs several examples to illustrate her point. Choose two of those examples and explain how they work with the scientific data to underscore the imprecision of sex determiners in humans.
3. What is the impact of Blum's opening her essay with the story of her own childhood and her son's? How do you react as a reader to those stories? What would be the effect on the essay by beginning with a more scientific discussion?

Writing Assignments

1. Think about your own childhood: In what ways did your family reinforce traditionally accepted sex roles? To what extent were you free to exhibit behaviors of the opposite sex? Write an essay in which you use these examples to support or challenge Blum's conclusions.
2. Although Blum does not discuss the political implications of her work, it is clear that sex roles are important to many political discussions. Find articles in magazines and newspapers on sex-discrimination, "family values," the feminist movement, the promise-keepers movement, and other sex-related issues. What groups are more likely to embrace a biological explanation of sex roles? What groups emphasize cultural influences? To what extent do any of these groups use scientific evidence to support their positions?

Femininity

Susan Brownmiller

Susan Brownmiller (1935-) graduated from Cornell University and has worked as a journalist and researcher for The Village Voice, Newsweek *and the ABC television network. An active feminist, she founded the organization Women Against Pornography and has written a number of pieces about pornography. Her most well-known book is* Against Our Will: Men, Women, and Rape *(1975). The following selection is excerpted from her book* Femininity *(1984), which looks at female/male issues from a variety of perspectives: historical, social, societal, psychological. In this excerpt you will note how she fluidly moves in and out of these different dimensions as she develops her thesis.*

1 Femininity, in essence, is a romantic sentiment, a nostalgic tradition of imposed limitations. Even as it hurries forward in the 1980s, putting on lipstick and high heels to appear well dressed, it trips on the ruffled petticoats and hoopskirts of an era gone by. Invariably and necessarily, femininity is something that women had more of in the past, not only in the historic past of prior generations, but in each woman's personal past as well—in the virginal innocence that is replaced by knowledge, in the dewy cheek that is coarsened by age, in the "inherent nature" that a woman seems to misplace so forgetfully whenever she steps out of bounds. Why should this be so? The XX chromosomal message has not been scrambled, the estrogen-dominated hormonal balance is generally as biology intended, the reproductive organs, whatever use one has made of them, are usually in

place, the breasts of whatever size are most often where they should be. But clearly, biological femaleness is not enough.

Femininity always demands more. It must constantly reassure its audience by a willing demonstration of difference, even when one does not exist in nature, or it must seize and embrace a natural variation and compose a rhapsodic symphony upon the notes. Suppose one doesn't care to, has other things on her mind, is clumsy or tone-deaf despite the best instruction and training? To fail at the feminine difference is to appear not to care about men, and to risk the loss of their attention and approval. To be insufficiently feminine is viewed as a failure in core sexual identity, or as a failure to care sufficiently about oneself, for a woman found wanting will be appraised (and will appraise herself) as mannish or neutered or simply unattractive, as men have defined these terms.

It is fashionable in some quarters to describe the feminine and masculine principles as polar ends of the human continuum, and to sagely profess that both polarities exist in all people. Sun and moon, yin and yang, soft and hard, active and passive, etcetera, may indeed be opposites, but a linear continuum does not illuminate the problem. (Femininity, in all its contrivances, is a very active endeavor.) What, then, is the basic distinction? The masculine principle is better understood as a driving ethos of superiority designed to inspire straightforward, confident success, while the feminine principle is composed of vulnerability, the need for protection, the formalities of compliance and the avoidance of conflict—in short, an appeal of dependence and good will that gives the masculine principle its romantic validity and its admiring applause.

Questions on Meaning

1. Brownmiller refers negatively to femininity as a "romantic senti-ment." What does "romantic" mean in this usage? Why is this negative?
2. How does the essay distinguish between biological "femaleness" and femininity?
3. In your own words, compare and contrast femininity and mas-culinity as Brownmiller delineates the differences.

Questions on Rhetorical Strategy and Style

1. Analyze the examples of femininity described in the essay. Are they sufficient to clarify Brownmiller's point? (Remember that this is only a short excerpt from a book on the same topic.)
2. The key rhetorical strategy here is definition. Analyze how Brownmiller uses this strategy paragraph by paragraph.

Writing Assignments

1. This essay was written in 1984. Is society still as insistent on fem-ininity as when this was written, or have things changed? If so, how? Have the specific manifestations of femininity changed? Write an essay that defines and compares and contrasts femininity and masculinity using contemporary examples.
2. Brownmiller seems to argue that women strive for femininity for the sake of men. Some manifestations of femininity she cites in-clude clothing and makeup. Some social observers, including some women writers, have argued that women actually dress and modify their appearance more for other women than for men— that women are their own harshest judges. What are your thoughts on this based on your own observations and experience? If it is true that women dress for other women, is this inconsis-tent with Brownmiller's perspective? Explain.

Beauty

Susan Sontag

Susan Sontag (1933–2004) was born in New York City and reared in Arizona and California. She attended the University of California at Berkeley, the University of Chicago (from which she graduated at age 18), received a graduate degree from Harvard University, and served as an instructor and writer-in-residence at several colleges. Accomplished as both a fiction and nonfiction writer, Sontag was best known for her social commentary, which often focused on trends in literature, art, and film. Her books include Against Interpretation and Other Essays *(1966),* Death Kit *(1967),* Trip to Hanoi *(1968),* The Style of Radical Will *(1969),* On Photography *(1976),* Illness as a Metaphor *(1978),* AIDS and Its Metaphors *(1989),* The Volcano Lover *(1992), and* Alice in Bed *(1993). She won the National Book Award for* In America *in 2004. She also wrote and directed four movies:* Duet for Cannibals *(1969),* Brother Carl *(1971),* Promised Lands *(1974), and* Unguided Tour *(1975). In this 1975 essay, Sontag argued that our society traps women into an endless preoccupation with outward appearance by associating beauty with femininity.*

1   For the Greeks, beauty was a virtue: a kind of excellence. Persons then were assumed to be what we now have to call—lamely, enviously—whole persons. If it did occur to the Greeks to distinguish between a person's "inside" and "outside," they still expected that inner beauty would be matched by beauty of the other kind. The well-born young Athenians who gathered around Socrates found it quite paradoxical that their hero was so intelligent, so brave, so honorable,

so seductive—and so ugly. One of Socrates' main pedagogical acts was to be ugly—and teach those innocent, no doubt splendid-looking disciples of his how full of paradoxes life really was.

They may have resisted Socrates' lesson. We do not. Several thousand years later, we are more wary of the enchantments of beauty. We not only split off—with the greatest facility—the "inside" (character, intellect) from the "outside" (looks); but we are actually surprised when someone who is beautiful is also intelligent, talented, good.

It was principally the influence of Christianity that deprived beauty of the central place it had in classical ideals of human excellence. By limiting excellence (*virtus* in Latin) to *moral* virtue only, Christianity set beauty adrift—as an alienated, arbitrary, superficial enchantment. And beauty has continued to lose prestige. For close to two centuries it has become a convention to attribute beauty to only one of the two sexes: the sex which, however Fair, is always Second. Associating beauty with women has put beauty even further on the defensive, morally.

A beautiful woman, we say in English. But a handsome man. "Handsome" is the masculine equivalent of—and refusal of—a compliment which has accumulated certain demeaning overtones, by being reserved for women only. That one can call a man "beautiful" in French and in Italian suggests that Catholic countries—unlike those countries shaped by the Protestant version of Christianity—still retain some vestiges of the pagan admiration for beauty. But the difference, if one exists, is of degree only. In every modern country that is Christian or post-Christian, women *are* the beautiful sex—to the detriment of the notion of beauty as well as of women.

5   To be called beautiful is thought to name something essential to   5
women's character and concerns. (In contrast to men—whose essence is to be strong, or effective, or competent.) It does not take someone in the throes of advanced feminist awareness to perceive that the way women are taught to be involved with beauty encourages narcissism, reinforces dependence and immaturity. Everybody (women and men) knows that. For it is "everybody," a whole society, that has identified being feminine with caring about how one *looks*. (In contrast to being masculine—which is identified with caring about what one *is* and *does* and only secondarily, if at all, about how one looks.) Given these stereotypes, it is no wonder that beauty enjoys, at best, a rather mixed reputation.

It is not, of course, the desire to be beautiful that is wrong but the obligation to be—or to try. What is accepted by most women as a flattering idealization of their sex is a way of making women feel inferior to what they actually are—or normally grow to be. For the ideal of beauty is administered as a form of self-oppression. Women are taught to see their bodies in *parts,* and to evaluate each part separately. Breasts, feet, hips, waistline, neck, eyes, nose, complexion, hair, and so on—each in turn is submitted to an anxious, fretful, often despairing scrutiny. Even if some pass muster, some will always be found wanting. Nothing less than perfection will do.

In men, good looks is a whole, something taken in at a glance. It does not need to be confirmed by giving measurements of different regions of the body, nobody encourages a man to dissect his appearance, feature by feature. As for perfection, that is considered trivial—almost unmanly. Indeed, in the ideally good-looking man a small imperfection or blemish is considered positively desirable. According to one movie critic (a woman) who is a declared Robert Redford fan, it is having that cluster of skin-colored moles on one cheek that saves Redford from being merely a "pretty face." Think of the depreciation of women—as well as of beauty—that is implied in that judgment.

"The privileges of beauty are immense," said Cocteau. To be sure, beauty is a form of power. And deservedly so. What is lamentable is that it is the only form of power that most women are encouraged to seek. This power is always conceived in relation to men; it is not the power to do but the power to attract. It is a power that negates itself. For this power is not one that can be chosen freely—at least, not by women—or renounced without social censure.

To preen, for a woman, can never be just a pleasure. It is also a duty. It is her work. If a woman does real work—and even if she has clambered up to a leading position in politics, law, medicine, business, or whatever—she is always under pressure to confess that she still works at being attractive. But in so far as she is keeping up as one of the Fair Sex, she brings under suspicion her very capacity to be objective, professional, authoritative, thoughtful. Damned if they do—women are. And damned if they don't.

10   One could hardly ask for more important evidence of the dangers   10 of considering persons as split between what is "inside" and what is "outside" than that interminable half-comic half-tragic tale, the oppression of women. How easy it is to start off by defining women as caretakers of their surfaces, and then to disparage them (or find them adorable) for being "superficial." It is a crude trap, and it has worked

for too long. But to get out of the trap requires that women get some critical distance from that excellence and privilege which is beauty, enough distance to see how much beauty itself has been abridged in order to prop up the mythology of the "feminine." There should be a way of saving beauty *from* women—and *for* them.

Questions on Meaning

1. Why does Sontag say that beauty carries "demeaning overtones"? Was this always so throughout history?
2. Sontag points out that beauty is a form of power. Why does she feel that this power can work against women? How can beauty be detrimental to a woman in the workplace?
3. What does Sontag say that Socrates tried to teach his students about beauty, ugliness, and life's paradoxes? If Socrates' beauty was not physical, where did it lie?

Questions on Rhetorical Strategy and Style

1. In explaining why beauty is a form of self-oppression for women, Sontag compares and contrasts how women and men are seen and see themselves. What major differences does she expose in terms of the quest for perfection?
2. Find where Sontag uses cause and effect to describe the impact of Christianity on perceptions of beauty. How does she compare the *virtue* of beauty of the ancient Greeks with the Christian view?

Writing Assignments

1. How does Sontag relate the perceptions of beauty to women's character? How does this compare with perceptions associated with the term *masculine*?
2. What role does physical beauty play in your life? How much time and money do you spend on your appearance—clothes, makeup, hair styling, etc.? How does your interest in your appearance compare with your friends' interest in their appearance? What is your motivation (or lack thereof) for your attention (inattention) to your appearance?
3. When Sontag wrote this essay in 1975, feminists such as Sontag were alerting Americans to the stigmas and stereotypes in society that harmed women. How is the concept of "femininity" attached to perceptions of "beauty" today? Have things changed? How do advertising and the media affect women's ability to be seen as a "whole" person in the classical Greek sense of the word?
4. Choose a person you admire greatly—a parent, teacher, neighbor, friend, politician, or friend—and write an essay describing the elements that make him or her a "whole" person. Why are you

attracted to this person? Do you aspire to be like him or her? What characteristics of this person reflect his or her "inner beauty"?

Virtual Sex, Lies and Cyberspace

Amy Harmon

Amy Harmon (1968–) has an undergraduate degree in American culture from the University of Michigan. She now works as a reporter for the New York Times, *after having been a staff reporter for seven years at the* Los Angeles Times. *In this selection, Harmon writes about the world of online junkies and the fantasies that feed their addictions.*

1 The first time Donna Tancordo "cybered," she switched off her computer midway through the typed seduction, shocked and scared at the power of the words scrolling down her screen.

"I've never described what I was feeling like that before," she said. "I freaked out."

But Tancordo, a happily married New Jersey housewife with three kids, soon logged back onto America Online. In a chat room called "Married and Flirting," she met another man. For days, they whispered the details of their lives into the ether. When he asked her if he could take her on a virtual trip to the mountains, she agreed.

This time her computer stayed on.

5 All hours of the day and night, America Online's chat rooms teem with people seeking something missing in their lives—like Jay, a successful business consultant in Boston, who says he logs on to fill "the void of passionate emotion."

The blurted confidences and anonymous yearning scrolling through AOL's frames reveal a rare picture of the American psyche unshackled from social convention.

In the vacuum of cyberspace, self-exploration is secret and strangely safe. Much has been made lately of how cults may find fertile recruiting ground among online seekers. A vast range of support groups—for pregnant mothers, cancer patients, substance abusers—also flourish. Unlikely friendships are struck and sometimes sustained.

But in an age when sex is scary and intimacy scarce, the keyboard and modem perhaps most often serve a pressing quest for romantic connection and sexual discovery.

Eric lives in a small California farming town: "I'm pretty much a straight kind of dude." When he flips on the computer at 4:30 a.m. to check the weather, he is drawn to rooms where San Franciscans recount stories of sexual bondage.

10 Eleanor, 13, is 5-foot-1, with dark brown hair. When she surfs the "Teen Chat" rooms after school, she looks for kicks as a tall strawberry blond.

Peter, a 45-year-old professional in Manhattan, spent his first weekend on AOL posing as a 26-year-old woman while his wife was away on business. Enthralled with the ease of uninhibited communion, he cycled through a whirl of identities. He disguised himself as a gay man, a lesbian and a young girl. But eventually he settled on a more mundane form of seduction.

"What I really wanted was to have sexual conversations with women," Peter said. "Kind of garden variety, but that's who I am, and what made it such a fever for me—that's not too strong a word—was the flirtation aspect of it."

The ritual of pursuing secret desires from behind a facade is as old as the masquerade. But perhaps because it has never been so easy, the compulsion has never seemed so strong.

"Leave the Meat Behind"

The free computer disks that arrive unbidden in the mail offer not only a mask, but an escape from the body—the ability, as cyberpunk author William Gibson puts it, to "leave the meat behind."

15 It is an offer with remarkable mass appeal. As AOLs subscriber count doubled over the last year to 8 million, the number of chat rooms on busy nights tripled to 15,000. And the recent, much-publicized agitation over the service's busy signals was due

largely to people chatting longer, now that a new pricing plan means they do not have to pay by the minute.

AOL is by far the most popular gathering spot on the Internet, in part because its culture of anonymity—members can choose up to five fictional screen names—promotes what one observer calls "the online equivalent of getting drunk and making a fool of yourself." Although it is possible to chat on the World Wide Web and other areas of the Internet, the technology doesn't work nearly as well.

Largely because of the unabashed sexual character of many of its chat rooms, AOL executives traditionally have downplayed their importance to the company's bottom line. "What we're offering at AOL is convenience in a box," said AOL Network's President Robert Pittman. "If you use AOL it will save you time. People aren't buying it for chat."

Perhaps. The service offers e-mail, Internet access and information and entertainment features. Many of its customers never venture near the chat rooms, and most usage of the Internet is unrelated to chat.

But according to America Online statistics, more than three-quarters of its subscribers use chat rooms at least once a month, the equivalent of 1 million hours a day

20   "If AOL eliminated chat you'd see the subscriber base go from 8   20 million to 1 million faster than you could spit," said Alan Weiner, an analyst at Dataquest, a consulting firm.

Not all chat is laden with sexual innuendo. "I can say I'm a voluptuous teen and I still don't get attention when I go into the sports and finance rooms," quipped one frequent female chatter.

Some chat rooms emerge as genuine communities where the same group gathers regularly. The "SoCalifover30" room even holds regular "fleshmeets" at restaurants or members' homes. A core group keeps up on one another's romantic exploits online and offline.

"Ladykuu," a San Diego bus driver trainer and the mother of twins, says she has become close friends with another mother of twins in Boston, with whom she shares life's tribulations.

But even Ladykuu enjoys "lurking" and listening to others tell secrets to which she ordinarily would not be privy:

25   "It's just fascinating to me to see, what is that deep dark fantasy   25 what is the naughty thing you're thinking about and—oh my gosh, I've been thinking about that too."

Some sexual-oriented chat is basic singles bar sleaze—and some is mainly an excuse to swap pornographic pictures. But much more prevalent is the search for genuine connection, and perhaps seduction.

Some chatters seek a companion to meet in person. Others, who shun the idea of a real-life affair, seize on the opportunity to engage in the thrill of a new seduction over the computer from the comfort of home—often while their spouses sleep in the next room.

Whether the demi-realities of chat can fulfill real world needs or only add to their urgency is a subject of much debate among online seekers. Some discover hidden pieces of themselves that lead to significant changes in what, in a telling delineation, is called RL— real life.

Others grow sickened by the relentless layering of illusion, where friends and lovers appear suddenly, and then melt into air, or morph into aliens. For there is in all this a bitter irony: That a search for intimacy brings people to pose as airbrushed versions of themselves, so that they may share their inner fantasies with strangers.

30 "It's not healthy for people to pretend to be someone they're not 30 and fantasize about that constantly," said Nancy Wesson, a psychologist in Mountain View, California. She has seen marriages break up in part because of one partner's online activities. "It allows you to perpetually live in a fantasy instead of living in real life."

Ultimately, marriage may be the institution most rocked by the new technology. Although cyberspace obviously doesn't invent secret longings, it does provide a way to uncover and exploit them that has never been so available to so many

Cheating Without Really Cheating

Some flirters say the ability to cheat without really cheating, to voice fantasies somehow too personal to share even with spouses, has invigorated them.

Donna and Ralph Tancordo, high school sweethearts who have been married for 17 years, sign onto AOL and "cyber" with other married people—with each other's consent.

"My cheekbones hurt I've been smiling so much lately," said Donna, who opened her account a month ago. "I think it's the flattery. It's like, 'Wow, somebody else is attracted to me other than my husband.' And it's improved our sex life 150%."

35   In the case of Peter, the Manhattan professional, the online habit   35
nearly broke up his marriage. Finding a woman that he would care to
talk to and who would talk to him could take hours on any given
night. He would stay up after his wife, Janet, went to bed, and look
forward to when she would leave him alone at home.

In the end, Janet became too distraught over his regular online
meetings with a woman who lived thousands of miles away. Peter
agreed to cancel his AOL account. Both say the experience has opened
up a productive, if painful, period of exploration for them.

"I was bored and I lied about it to myself," Peter said. "I had a sex
life, but it didn't have passion. At some level, that's what I was seeking,
and it's hard to find. There may not be an answer."

For Janet, the hardest part has been trying to sift out what may
be her husband's harmless fantasy life from what to her is hurtful
reality.

"Everyone knows someone who has had an affair," Janet said. "If
your husband's having an affair and you tell your girlfriend, you're
going to have instant sympathy. But do I have a right to be pissed
about this? I don't know."

40   She has not talked to any of her friends about it: "It's   40
embarrassing. I don't know anyone else who has gone through this."

A lot of people have. The online consensus is that, as Tiffany
Cook of the SoCalifover30 chat room puts it, "if you're talking to a
married man often enough, that's an affair even if you never meet."

But in the 1990s, when interest in family values is on the rise and
the ethic of safe sex prevails, AOL offers 1960s-style free love from
behind the safety of the screen. The medium offers a sense of physical
and psychological safety that strips away taboos faster than the sexual
revolution ever did.

Many married people—they constitute two-thirds of AOL
subscribers—comb chat rooms, scope the profiles and send private
instant messages (IMs) to prospective romantic partners.

The flirtation medium of choice, IMs pop up on-screen as soon
as they are sent, heedless of whatever the recipient may be doing.
More insistent and perhaps more intimate than e-mail, they solicit an
immediate response.

45   "I've tried erotic e-mail. It's like bad D. H. Lawrence," said an   45
artist who prefers the edge of IMs.

Three million IM sessions are opened every day. They are by nature fleeting and the exchange is rapid-fire, lessening the risk and increasing the nerve.

"I make advances to men the same age group as I am to start flirting and sometimes it goes a lot further than flirt," said Donna. "I read their profile first. If I like it, I'll IM them by saying . . . 'BUSY?'"

In the curious state of disembodiment, where the body is nonetheless very much the point, the typed words come as stream of consciousness, and then, with the click of a mouse, they disappear.

"I'm sorry I can't talk right now," one woman tells a reporter. "I'm getting nine IMs as we speak."

50 Often, IM exchanges begin between people in the same chat room. At any given moment, subscribers fill rooms of varying salaciousness—"Hot and Ready Female," "Discreet in Illinois," "CA Cops Who Flirt," "BiCuriousM4M." Many of the chat rooms created by subscribers—as opposed to those established by AOL—have overtly sexual themes and many others draw people interested in romance.

"There's a lot more diversity out there than I would have given people credit for," said Jenny, a 27-year-old lesbian from Manhattan who roams the chat rooms when she is not using the service to check stock quotes.

"Wanna cyber?" comes the standard query, proffering the on-line equivalent of a one-night stand. "M/F?" "What are you wearing?"

"On AOL you could be talking about sex within three minutes of meeting someone," said a 28-year-old male marketing consultant who goes by the handle "MindUnit."

Many simply want to experiment in the intricate art of flirtation, sometimes behind a guise, sometimes as themselves.

55 "It's the only place you can throw yourself at someone and not care if you get rejected," said Jenny.

Women especially say the ability to both be more aggressive than they would in real life and to hit "cancel" or "ignore" if a flirtation gets out of control is liberating—and perhaps good practice.

For many, the point is not cybersex per se, but delving into the forbidden realm of sexuality. Says one online explorer on the East Coast: "We live in a world and particularly this culture that seeks to, on the surface, completely repress our sexuality. I think for many people, AOL represents a safe and healthy expression, although, like all pleasures, from fatty foods to erotic pleasure, there is probably a price to pay."

After empty nights of chat room prowling for the ideal cybermate, many end up being as disappointing as such searches often are in real life.

"All I can tell you is that there are thousands of searching people out there . . . and AOL has become a vehicle to meet others . . . affairs, etc. . . . ." types a Southern California man to a reporter one Saturday night. "But it doesn't solve the problems of real life."

60   Sometimes connections that seem solid suddenly fade away. Even   60
carefree Donna was thrown off-balance recently when her AOL lover sent a cryptic message saying he wouldn't be spending as much time online.

"He was basically blowing me off and I was really upset," she said. "I was sitting in the dentist's chair and I couldn't get him out of my head. I've gotten too emotional about this. I really need to handle it better."

Psychologists caution against getting wrapped up in a reality that is not, in fact, real. And online junkies acknowledge that it can be hard to pull out of what one calls "AOL's sticky web," which can become an addictive escape from three-dimensional existence.

Psychologist Kimberly Young, who has studied online addiction, says it's comparable to compulsive gambling in its mood-altering appeal—and is just as dangerous.

Sherry Turkle, a professor of the sociology of science at the Massachusetts Institute of Technology, draws a more optimistic conclusion. In her recent book, *Life on the Screen,* she argues that online technology is enabling a new, decentered sense of identity to emerge, and that the practice of trying on different personalities could be a useful way to work through real-life issues.

65   Swapping genders is a popular activity among both sexes, but   65
since (real) men outnumber women by about 2 to 1, the likelihood of talking to a man claiming to be a woman is fairly high.

MindUnit has devised an only-sort-of tongue-in-cheek "Rules to Establish Gender," testament that even in a world without gender, well-socialized roles remain largely intact.

They state, in part: "If she sounds 'too good to be true,' that is One Strike. If she has no profile, that is One Strike. If she seems preoccupied with sex, or starts the sex talk herself, that is One Strike.

If she volunteers exact statistics about herself, especially measurements or bra size, that is One Strike. If the statistics are really hot, that is Two Strikes." By MindUnit's trauma-tested logic, three strikes means the woman you're chatting with is a man.

Little in the AOL chat world is as it appears to be. But, for many, the chance to honestly express their desires and be privy to those of others outweighs the veil of lies that seems somehow necessary to make it possible. "Let me find someone with an open mind, good intentions, and sincerity," reads MindUnit's profile. "Failing that, I'll take a nymphomaniac."

Few know better than Tiffany Cook the perils of confusing online illusions with real-life truths. First, the 30-year-old Santa Monica interior designer hit it off with a man who flew to visit her from New York. The chemistry didn't translate in person.

70 But then for three months she spent hours a day chatting with a man from Northern California. He said he was 33. Then he confessed to being 43, and then to his actual age: 71. He had sent her a picture—it turned out to be of his son.

"It was terrible," she said. "I felt so deceived."

Still, Tiffany, who changed her screen name after learning the truth about her most passionate correspondence, still spends part of almost every day online.

"You know what? It's expanded my world," she said. "I've laughed really hard and I've learned a lot, and no matter what I might think of [him] now, the fact is we had a huge amount to talk about.

"Besides, your chances of meeting someone who's hiding behind something online and someone who's hiding behind something in real life [are] about the same."

Questions on Meaning

1. Harmon's piece deals with a growing trend: online addiction. According to Harmon, what has led to this development? What are some of its consequences of it? Are there any positive aspects to online culture? If so, what are they?
2. How are online conversations different from face-to-face exchanges? What changes in social habits and arrangements do they cause?
3. Does Harmon suggest that women are more likely to become online junkies than men? If so, do you agree or disagree? Is the same true for teen girls and boys? If so, what does this imply about gender or other identity issues?

Questions on Rhetorical Strategy and Style

1. Most of the information in this report comes from personal accounts. Do you see these accounts as representative of people in general? Why or why not? How effective are these accounts, in your view? What do you find most convincing about the selection? What makes you skeptical?
2. Any piece of writing has an angle and reflects the writer's attitude. Demonstrate how Harmon tries to remain unbiased in the selection. What overall point of view emerges from what she presents and how she presents it?

Writing Assignments

1. Visit a popular online chat room and analyze it the way a cultural anthropologist might. That is, try to understand how that "society" is arranged. Which members get to nominate topics, and what do they talk about? If so, what appears to be important to the participants? Are there any power struggles? If so, how would you characterize them? What kinds of identities are members presenting online?
2. Write an opinion piece about online culture. Explore questions such as the following: Why are online relationships so popular today? How has human interaction changed because of this technology? What have we gained? What have we lost?

Filling the Open Mind in the Information Age

Wiley Miller

Wiley Miller was born in California and raised in Maclean, Virginia, a suburb of Washington, D.C. Interested in cartooning since high school, he spent a good deal of his career as an editorial cartoonist for several newspapers, among them the Greensboro, North Carolina, News and Record, *the* Santa Rosa Press Democrat, *and the* San Francisco Examiner. *While living in California, he also perfected the art of drawing "Bartoons," cartoons on cocktail napkins. His career received a boost when* Playboy *magazine published several of his Bartoons. In the early 1980s, Wiley produced a strip called* Fenton, *but it was not until 1991 that* Non Sequitur, *considered his masterpiece, debuted. Since then, the strip has won an unprecedented four Reuben Awards (considered the Oscars of the cartoon industry) from the National Cartoonists Society. Wiley has also produced three books of cartoons:* Dead Lawyers and Other Pleasant Thoughts *(1993),* The Non Sequitur Survival Guide for the Nineties *(1995), and* Beastly Things *(1999).* Non Sequitur *is currently published in more than 400 newspapers in 20 countries. Wiley himself considers cartooning equivalent to writing a newspaper column: "Cartoonists are essentially columnists," he claims. "We perform exactly the same function; we just work in a different format." The parallel is evident in the following strip, in which Wiley criticizes Americans' desire for only news that reinforces their own narrow view of the world.*

Questions on Meaning

1. How does this cartoon characterize the average citizen? Describe the features highlighted in the strip.
2. What should news do for readers, according to Wiley? What do you look for in newspapers? Confirmation of your views? Challenges? Alternative views?

Questions on Rhetorical Strategy and Style

1. The way in which Wiley presents this story suggests a journey or quest. Describe that quest and explain how the graphics in the cartoon emphasize that theme.
2. What is an appropriate definition of news, according to Wiley? What does the term "information age" mean to him?
3. This cartoon suggests an implicit contrast between real news and the kind of news the couple is seeking. How do the two kinds of news differ?

Writing Assignments

1. Write an essay describing the newspaper you read most often. Does the paper have a clearly recognizable perspective of its own? If so, what is that perspective? Does the paper reflect diverse views and perspectives? If so, how?
2. Radio talk shows such as *Imus*, *Howard Stern*, and *Rush Limbaugh* often represent one narrow perspective. Listen to one of these programs and write an analysis of the host's perspective and that of his viewers. Comment on how callers with differing perspectives are treated. Conclude with your own assessment of the value of such shows.

Is Google Making Us Stupid?

Nicholas Carr

Nicholas Carr (1959–), a graduate of Dartmouth College, earned his MA at Harvard before beginning a distinguished career as a writer. His central focus on technology and economics has produced books translated into twenty languages. His latest book, The Shallows: What the Internet Is Doing to Our Brains *(2011), was named a Pulitzer Prize finalist. He has published in the* New York Times, *the* Wall Street Journal, Wired, *the* Financial Times, *and the* London Times, *among others. The following article from* The Atlantic *investigates the effects of easy access to information. Carr asks what it means to the human mind to read in sound bites and to have everything at our immediate call.*

1   "Dave, stop. stop, will you? Stop, Dave. Will you stop, Dave?" So the supercomputer HAL pleads with the implacable astronaut Dave Bowman in a famous and weirdly poignant scene toward the end of Stanley Kubrick's *2001: A Space Odyssey.* Bowman, having nearly been sent to a deep-space death by the malfunctioning machine, is calmly, coldly disconnecting the memory circuits that control its artificial "brain." "Dave, my mind is going," HAL says, forlornly. "I can feel it. I can feel it."

I can feel it, too. Over the past few years I've had an uncomfortable sense that someone, or something, has been tinkering with my brain, remapping the neural circuitry, reprogramming the memory. My mind isn't going—so far as I can tell—but it's changing. I'm not thinking the way I used to think. I can feel it most strongly when I'm reading. Immersing myself in a book or a lengthy article used to be easy. My mind would get caught up in the narrative or the turns of the argument, and I'd spend hours strolling through long stretches of prose. That's rarely the case anymore. Now my concentration often

Reprinted from the *Atlantic Monthly*, July 2008, by permission of the author.

starts to drift after two or three pages. I get fidgety, lose the thread, begin looking for something else to do. I feel as if I'm always dragging my wayward brain back to the text. The deep reading that used to come naturally has become a struggle.

I think I know what's going on. For more than a decade now, I've been spending a lot of time online, searching and surfing and sometimes adding to the great databases of the Internet. The Web has been a godsend to me as a writer. Research that once required days in the stacks or periodical rooms of libraries can now be done in minutes. A few Google searches, some quick clicks on hyperlinks, and I've got the telltale fact or pithy quote I was after. Even when I'm not working, I'm as likely as not to be foraging in the Web's info-thickets' reading and writing e-mails, scanning headlines and blog posts, watching videos and listening to podcasts, or just tripping from link to link to link. (Unlike footnotes, to which they're sometimes likened, hyperlinks don't merely point to related works; they propel you toward them.)

For me, as for others, the Net is becoming a universal medium, the conduit for most of the information that flows through my eyes and ears and into my mind. The advantages of having immediate access to such an incredibly rich store of information are many, and they've been widely described and duly applauded. "The perfect recall of silicon memory," *Wired's* Clive Thompson has written, "can be an enormous boon to thinking." But that boon comes at a price. As the media theorist Marshall McLuhan pointed out in the 1960s, media are not just passive channels of information. They supply the stuff of thought, but they also shape the process of thought. And what the Net seems to be doing is chipping away my capacity for concentration and contemplation. My mind now expects to take in information the way the Net distributes it: in a swiftly moving stream of particles. Once I was a scuba diver in the sea of words. Now I zip along the surface like a guy on a Jet Ski.

5   I'm not the only one. When I mention my troubles with reading to friends and acquaintances—literary types, most of them—many say they're having similar experiences. The more they use the Web, the more they have to fight to stay focused on long pieces of writing. Some of the bloggers I follow have also begun mentioning the phenomenon. Scott Karp, who writes a blog about online media, recently confessed that he has stopped reading books altogether. "I was a lit major in college, and used to be [a] voracious book reader," he wrote.

"What happened?" He speculates on the answer: "What if I do all my reading on the web not so much because the way I read has changed, i.e. I'm just seeking convenience, but because the way I THINK has changed?"

Bruce Friedman, who blogs regularly about the use of computers in medicine, also has described how the Internet has altered his mental habits. "I now have almost totally lost the ability to read and absorb a longish article on the web or in print," he wrote earlier this year. A pathologist who has long been on the faculty of the University of Michigan Medical School, Friedman elaborated on his comment in a telephone conversation with me. His thinking, he said, has taken on a "staccato" quality, reflecting the way he quickly scans short passages of text from many sources online. "I can't read *War and Peace* anymore," he admitted. "I've lost the ability to do that. Even a blog post of more than three or four paragraphs is too much to absorb. I skim it."

Anecdotes alone don't prove much. And we still await the long-term neurological and psychological experiments that will provide a definitive picture of how Internet use affects cognition. But a recently published study of online research habits, conducted by scholars from University College London, suggests that we may well be in the midst of a sea change in the way we read and think. As part of the five-year research program, the scholars examined computer logs documenting the behavior of visitors to two popular research sites, one operated by the British Library and one by a U.K. educational consortium, that provide access to journal articles, e-books, and other sources of written information. They found that people using the sites exhibited "a form of skimming activity," hopping from one source to another and rarely returning to any source they'd already visited. They typically read no more than one or two pages of an article or book before they would "bounce" out to another site. Sometimes they'd save a long article, but there's no evidence that they ever went back and actually read it. The authors of the study report:

> It is clear that users are not reading online in the traditional sense; indeed there are signs that new forms of "reading" are emerging as users "power browse" horizontally through titles, contents pages and abstracts going for quick wins. It almost seems that they go online to avoid reading in the traditional sense.

Thanks to the ubiquity of text on the Internet, not to mention the popularity of text-messaging on cell phones, we may well be reading more today than we did in the 1970s or 1980s, when television was our medium of choice. But it's a different kind of reading, and behind it lies a different kind of thinking—perhaps even a new sense of the self. "We are not only what we read," says Maryanne Wolf, a developmental psychologist at Tufts University and the author of *Proust and the Squid: The Story and Science of the Reading Brain.* "We are *how* we read." Wolf worries that the style of reading promoted by the Net, a style that puts "efficiency" and "immediacy" above all else, may be weakening our capacity for the kind of deep reading that emerged when an earlier technology, the printing press, made long and complex works of prose commonplace. When we read online, she says, we tend to become "mere decoders of information." Our ability to interpret text, to make the rich mental connections that form when we read deeply and without distraction, remains largely disengaged.

Reading, explains Wolf, is not an instinctive skill for human beings. It's not etched into our genes the way speech is. We have to teach our minds how to translate the symbolic characters we see into the language we understand. And the media or other technologies we use in learning and practicing the craft of reading play an important part in shaping the neural circuits inside our brains. Experiments demonstrate that readers of ideograms, such as the Chinese, develop a mental circuitry for reading that is very different from the circuitry found in those of us whose written language employs an alphabet. The variations extend across many regions of the brain, including those that govern such essential cognitive functions as memory and the interpretation of visual and auditory stimuli. We can expect as well that the circuits woven by our use of the Net will be different from those woven by our reading of books and other printed works.

10   Sometime in 1882, Friedrich Nietzsche bought a typewriter—a Malling-Hansen Writing Ball, to be precise. His vision was failing, and keeping his eyes focused on a page had become exhausting and painful, often bringing on crushing headaches. He had been forced to curtail his writing, and he feared that he would soon have to give it up. The typewriter rescued him, at least for a time. Once he had mastered touch-typing, he was able to write with his eyes closed, using only the tips of his fingers. Words could once again flow from his mind to the page.

But the machine had a subtler effect on his work. One of Nietzsche's friends, a composer, noticed a change in the style of his writing. His already terse prose had become even tighter, more telegraphic. "Perhaps you will through this instrument even take to a new idiom," the friend wrote in a letter, noting that, in his own work, his "'thoughts' in music and language often depend on the quality of pen and paper."

"You are right," Nietzsche replied, "our writing equipment takes part in the forming of our thoughts." Under the sway of the machine, writes the German media scholar Friedrich A. Kittler, Nietzsche's prose "changed from arguments to aphorisms, from thoughts to puns, from rhetoric to telegram style."

The human brain is almost infinitely malleable. People used to think that our mental meshwork, the dense connections formed among the 100 billion or so neurons inside our skulls, was largely fixed by the time we reached adulthood. But brain researchers have discovered that that's not the case. James Olds, a professor of neuroscience who directs the Krasnow Institute for Advanced Study at George Mason University, says that even the adult mind "is very plastic." Nerve cells routinely break old connections and form new ones. "The brain," according to Olds, "has the ability to reprogram itself on the fly, altering the way it functions."

As we use what the sociologist Daniel Bell has called our "intellectual technologies"—the tools that extend our mental rather than our physical capacities—we inevitably begin to take on the qualities of those technologies. The mechanical clock, which came into common use in the 14th century, provides a compelling example. In *Technics and Civilization*, the historian and cultural critic Lewis Mumford described how the clock "disassociated time from human events and helped create the belief in an independent world of mathematically measurable sequences." The "abstract framework of divided time" became "the point of reference for both action and thought."

15 The clock's methodical ticking helped bring into being the scientific mind and the scientific man. But it also took something away. As the late MIT computer scientist Joseph Weizenbaum observed in his 1976 book, *Computer Power and Human Reason: From Judgment to Calculation*, the conception of the world that emerged from the widespread use of timekeeping instruments "remains an impoverished version of the older one, for it rests on a rejection of those direct experiences that formed the basis for, and indeed constituted, the old reality." In deciding when to eat, to work, to sleep, to rise, we stopped listening to our senses and started obeying the clock.

The process of adapting to new intellectual technologies is reflected in the changing metaphors we use to explain ourselves to ourselves. When the mechanical clock arrived, people began thinking of their brains as operating "like clockwork." Today, in the age of software, we have come to think of them as operating "like computers." But the changes, neuroscience tells us, go much deeper than metaphor. Thanks to our brain's plasticity, the adaptation occurs also at a biological level.

The Internet promises to have particularly far-reaching effects on cognition. In a paper published in 1936, the British mathematician Alan Turing proved that a digital computer, which at the time existed only as a theoretical machine, could be programmed to perform the function of any other information-processing device. And that's what we're seeing today. The Internet, an immeasurably powerful computing system, is subsuming most of our other intellectual technologies. It's becoming our map and our clock, our printing press and our typewriter, our calculator and our telephone, and our radio and TV.

When the Net absorbs a medium, that medium is re-created in the Net's image. It injects the medium's content with hyperlinks, blinking ads, and other digital gewgaws, and it surrounds the content with the content of all the other media it has absorbed. A new e-mail message, for instance, may announce its arrival as we're glancing over the latest headlines at a newspaper's site. The result is to scatter our attention and diffuse our concentration.

The Net's influence doesn't end at the edges of a computer screen, either. As people's minds become attuned to the crazy quilt of Internet media, traditional media have to adapt to the audience's new expectations. Television programs add text crawls and pop-up ads, and magazines and newspapers shorten their articles, introduce capsule summaries, and crowd their pages with easy-to-browse info-snippets. When, in March of this year, *The New York Times* decided to devote the second and third pages of every edition to article abstracts, its design director, Tom Bodkin, explained that the "shortcuts" would give harried readers a quick "taste" of the day's news, sparing them the "less efficient" method of actually turning the pages and reading the articles. Old media have little choice but to play by the new-media rules.

20   Never has a communications system played so many roles in our   20
lives—or exerted such broad influence over our thoughts—as the Internet does today. Yet, for all that's been written about the Net,

there's been little consideration of how, exactly, it's reprogramming us. The Net's intellectual ethic remains obscure.

About the same time that Nietzsche started using his typewriter, an earnest young man named Frederick Winslow Taylor carried a stopwatch into the Midvale Steel plant in Philadelphia and began a historic series of experiments aimed at improving the efficiency of the plant's machinists. With the approval of Midvale's owners, he recruited a group of factory hands, set them to work on various metalworking machines, and recorded and timed their every movement as well as the operations of the machines. By breaking down every job into a sequence of small, discrete steps and then testing different ways of performing each one, Taylor created a set of precise instructions—an "algorithm," we might say today—for how each worker should work. Midvale's employees grumbled about the strict new regime, claiming that it turned them into little more than automatons, but the factory's productivity soared.

More than a hundred years after the invention of the steam engine, the Industrial Revolution had at last found its philosophy and its philosopher. Taylor's tight industrial choreography—his "system," as he liked to call it—was embraced by manufacturers throughout the country and, in time, around the world. Seeking maximum speed, maximum efficiency, and maximum output, factory owners used time-and-motion studies to organize their work and configure the jobs of their workers. The goal, as Taylor defined it in his celebrated 1911 treatise, *The Principles of Scientific Management*, was to identify and adopt, for every job, the "one best method" of work and thereby to effect "the gradual substitution of science for rule of thumb throughout the mechanic arts." Once his system was applied to all acts of manual labor, Taylor assured his followers, it would bring about a restructuring not only of industry but of society, creating a utopia of perfect efficiency. "In the past the man has been first," he declared; "in the future the system must be first."

Taylor's system is still very much with us; it remains the ethic of industrial manufacturing. And now, thanks to the growing power that computer engineers and software coders wield over our intellectual lives, Taylor's ethic is beginning to govern the realm of the mind as well. The Internet is a machine designed for the efficient and automated collection, transmission, and manipulation of information, and its legions of programmers are intent on finding the "one best method"—the perfect algorithm—to carry out every mental movement of what we've come to describe as "knowledge work."

Google's headquarters, in Mountain View, California—the Googleplex—is the Internet's high church, and the religion practiced inside its walls is Taylorism. Google, says its chief executive, Eric Schmidt, is "a company that's founded around the science of measurement," and it is striving to "systematize everything" it does. Drawing on the terabytes of behavioral data it collects through its search engine and other sites, it carries out thousands of experiments a day, according to the *Harvard Business Review*, and it uses the results to refine the algorithms that increasingly control how people find information and extract meaning from it. What Taylor did for the work of the hand, Google is doing for the work of the mind.

25   The company has declared that its mission is "to organize the   25
world's information and make it universally accessible and useful." It seeks to develop "the perfect search engine," which it defines as something that "understands exactly what you mean and gives you back exactly what you want." In Google's view, information is a kind of commodity, a utilitarian resource that can be mined and processed with industrial efficiency. The more pieces of information we can "access" and the faster we can extract their gist, the more productive we become as thinkers.

Where does it end? Sergey Brin and Larry Page, the gifted young men who founded Google while pursuing doctoral degrees in computer science at Stanford, speak frequently of their desire to turn their search engine into an artificial intelligence, a HAL-like machine that might be connected directly to our brains. "The ultimate search engine is something as smart as people—or smarter," Page said in a speech a few years back. "For us, working on search is a way to work on artificial intelligence." In a 2004 interview with *Newsweek*, Brin said, "Certainly if you had all the world's information directly attached to your brain, or an artificial brain that was smarter than your brain, you'd be better off." Last year, Page told a convention of scientists that Google is "really trying to build artificial intelligence and to do it on a large scale."

Such an ambition is a natural one, even an admirable one, for a pair of math whizzes with vast quantities of cash at their disposal and a small army of computer scientists in their employ. A fundamentally scientific enterprise, Google is motivated by a desire to use technology, in Eric Schmidt's words, "to solve problems that have never been solved before," and artificial intelligence is the hardest problem out there. Why wouldn't Brin and Page want to be the ones to crack it?

Still, their easy assumption that we'd all "be better off" if our brains were supplemented, or even replaced, by an artificial intelligence is unsettling. It suggests a belief that intelligence is the output of a mechanical process, a series of discrete steps that can be isolated, measured, and optimized. In Google's world, the world we enter when we go online, there's little place for the fuzziness of contemplation. Ambiguity is not an opening for insight but a bug to be fixed. The human brain is just an outdated computer that needs a faster processor and a bigger hard drive.

The idea that our minds should operate as high-speed data-processing machines is not only built into the workings of the Internet, it is the network's reigning business model as well. The faster we surf across the Web—the more links we click and pages we view—the more opportunities Google and other companies gain to collect information about us and to feed us advertisements. Most of the proprietors of the commercial Internet have a financial stake in collecting the crumbs of data we leave behind as we flit from link to link—the more crumbs, the better. The last thing these companies want is to encourage leisurely reading or slow, concentrated thought. It's in their economic interest to drive us to distraction.

30   Maybe I'm just a worrywart. Just as there's a tendency to glorify   30
technological progress, there's a countertendency to expect the worst of every new tool or machine. In Plato's *Phaedrus*, Socrates bemoaned the development of writing. He feared that, as people came to rely on the written word as a substitute for the knowledge they used to carry inside their heads, they would, in the words of one of the dialogue's characters, "cease to exercise their memory and become forgetful." And because they would be able to "receive a quantity of information without proper instruction," they would "be thought very knowledgeable when they are for the most part quite ignorant." They would be "filled with the conceit of wisdom instead of real wisdom." Socrates wasn't wrong—the new technology did often have the effects he feared—but he was shortsighted. He couldn't foresee the many ways that writing and reading would serve to spread information, spur fresh ideas, and expand human knowledge (if not wisdom).

The arrival of Gutenberg's printing press, in the 15th century, set off another round of teeth gnashing. The Italian humanist Hieronimo Squarciafico worried that the easy availability of books would lead to intellectual laziness, making men "less studious" and weakening their minds. Others argued that cheaply printed books and broadsheets would undermine religious authority, demean the work of scholars and scribes, and spread sedition and debauchery. As New York University professor Clay Shirky notes, "Most of the arguments made against the printing press were correct, even prescient." But, again, the doomsayers were unable to imagine the myriad blessings that the printed word would deliver.

So, yes, you should be skeptical of my skepticism. Perhaps those who dismiss critics of the Internet as Luddites or nostalgists will be proved correct, and from our hyperactive, data-stoked minds will spring a golden age of intellectual discovery and universal wisdom. Then again, the Net isn't the alphabet, and although it may replace the printing press, it produces something altogether different. The kind of deep reading that a sequence of printed pages promotes is valuable not just for the knowledge we acquire from the author's words but for the intellectual vibrations those words set off within our own minds. In the quiet spaces opened up by the sustained, undistracted reading of a book, or by any other act of contemplation, for that matter, we make our own associations, draw our own inferences and analogies, foster our own ideas. Deep reading, as Maryanne Wolf argues, is indistinguishable from deep thinking.

If we lose those quiet spaces, or fill them up with "content," we will sacrifice something important not only in our selves but in our culture. In a recent essay, the playwright Richard Foreman eloquently described what's at stake:

> I come from a tradition of Western culture, in which the ideal (my ideal) was the complex, dense and "cathedral-like" structure of the highly educated and articulate personality—a man or woman who carried inside themselves a personally constructed and unique version of the entire heritage of the West. [But now] I see within us all (myself included) the replacement of complex inner density with a new kind of self—evolving under the pressure of information overload and the technology of the "instantly available."

As we are drained of our "inner repertory of dense cultural inheritance," Foreman concluded, we risk turning into "'pancake people'—spread wide and thin as we connect with that vast network of information accessed by the mere touch of a button."

35   I'm haunted by that scene in *2001*. What makes it so poignant, and so weird, is the computer's emotional response to the disassembly of its mind: its despair as one circuit after another goes dark, its childlike pleading with the astronaut—"I can feel it. I can feel it. I'm afraid"—and its final reversion to what can only be called a state of innocence. HAL's outpouring of feeling contrasts with the emotionlessness that characterizes the human figures in the film, who go about their business with an almost robotic efficiency. Their thoughts and actions feel scripted, as if they're following the steps of an algorithm. In the world of *2001*, people have become so machinelike that the most human character turns out to be a machine. That's the essence of Kubrick's dark prophecy: as we come to rely on computers to mediate our understanding of the world, it is our own intelligence that flattens into artificial intelligence.

Questions on Meaning

1. Carr gives many examples of people who used to read long and dense texts and now cannot concentrate for more than a paragraph or two. Why does he blame this phenomenon on the Internet?

2. Carr tells of the philosopher who stopped writing long essays when he got a typewriter and started writing short notes and comments. What point does Carr make about typing and its effect on thinking?

3. Finally, Carr suggests that the assembly line, invented by a time-management specialist named Taylor, led to the end of specialized work. He goes on to suggest that the Google team would also like to end deep reading and research. Does this example seem likely to work out the way that Carr predicts? What arguments does he give for the likelihood of his predictions?

4. The essay notes that all great advances in writing have been questioned, including writing itself, which Aristotle argued might weaken memory. What does Carr admit about Aristotle's argument, but what advantage does he also note?

Questions on Rhetorical Strategy and Style

1. This essay provides deep evidence for the arguments that it makes. What is ironic in the contention that deep reading is disappearing when the essay that makes the argument demands deep reading?

2. The essay begins and ends with a reference to Hal, the computer in Kubrick's *Space Odyssey*. How does this reference emphasize the doubts Carr expresses about computers?

3. Carr assumes that his reader will stay with him through the complexities of his argument. How does he organize the essay and use examples to continue to hold the reader's attention? What is the effect of the examples he chooses?

Writing Assignments

1. List the kinds of reading you do in a week during the school year. How much time do you spend doing "deep reading"? When is the last time you read a long novel for fun? Write about your

reading habits, and explain whether you would confirm or deny Carr's contentions.

2. Look up one of the famous people Carr uses in his examples: Aristotle, Taylor, Gutenberg, or Nietzsche. Write about the person's life and thinking and their influence on reading and writing.

3. Trace your own research practices. How often do you look up information? What do you use the information for in your schoolwork? Have your patterns changed as technology has advanced? How? Write about the changes.

How Computers Change the Way We Think

Sherry Turkle

Sherry Turkle (1948–), Abby Rockefeller Mauzé Professor of the Social Studies of Science and Technology in the Program in Science, Technology, and Society at MIT, founded (2001) and directs the MIT Initiative on Technology and Self. A Harvard doctoral graduate in sociology and personality, Professor Turkle practices as a clinical psychologist. Her books include Psychoanalytic Politics *(1978),* The Second Self *(1984),* Life on the Screen *(1995),* Evocative Objects *(2007),* Falling for Science (2008), The Inner History of Devices *(2008),* Simulation and Its Discontents *(2009), and* Alone Together: Why We Expect More from Technology and Less from Each Other *(2011). She is among the most noted experts on the effects of technology on the human psyche.*

1   The tools we use to think change the ways in which we think. The invention of written language brought about a radical shift in how we process, organize, store, and transmit representations of the world. Although writing remains our primary information technology, today when we think about the impact of technology on our habits of mind, we think primarily of the computer.

    My first encounters with how computers change the way we think came soon after I joined the faculty at the Massachusetts

Reprinted from the *Chronicle of Higher Education*, January 30, 2004, by permission of the author.

Institute of Technology in the late 1970s, at the end of the era of the slide rule and the beginning of the era of the personal computer. At a lunch for new faculty members, several senior professors in engineering complained that the transition from slide rules to calculators had affected their students' ability to deal with issues of scale. When students used slide rules, they had to insert decimal points themselves. The professors insisted that that required students to maintain a mental sense of scale, whereas those who relied on calculators made frequent errors in orders of magnitude. Additionally, the students with calculators had lost their ability to do "back of the envelope" calculations, and with that, an intuitive feel for the material.

That same semester, I taught a course in the history of psychology. There, I experienced the impact of computational objects on students' ideas about their emotional lives. My class had read Freud's essay on slips of the tongue, with its famous first example: The chairman of a parliamentary session opens a meeting by declaring it closed. The students discussed how Freud interpreted such errors as revealing a person's mixed emotions. A computer-science major disagreed with Freud's approach. The mind, she argued, is a computer. And in a computational dictionary—like we have in the human mind—"closed" and "open" are designated by the same symbol, separated by a sign for opposition. "Closed" equals "minus open." To substitute "closed" for "open" does not require the notion of ambivalence or conflict.

"When the chairman made that substitution," she declared, "a bit was dropped; a minus sign was lost. There was a power surge. No problem."

5   The young woman turned a Freudian slip into an information-processing error. An explanation in terms of meaning had become an explanation in terms of mechanism.

Such encounters turned me to the study of both the instrumental and the subjective sides of the nascent computer culture. As an ethnographer and psychologist, I began to study not only what the computer was doing for us, but what it was doing to us, including how it was changing the way we see ourselves, our sense of human identity.

In the 1980s, I surveyed the psychological effects of computational objects in everyday life—largely the unintended side effects of people's tendency to project thoughts and feelings onto their machines. In the 20 years since, computational objects have become more explicitly designed to have emotional and cognitive effects. And those "effects by design" will become even stronger in the decade to come. Machines are being designed to serve explicitly as companions, pets, and tutors. And they are introduced in school settings for the youngest children.

Today, starting in elementary school, students use e-mail, word processing, computer simulations, virtual communities, and Power-Point software. In the process, they are absorbing more than the content of what appears on their screens. They are learning new ways to think about what it means to know and understand.

What follows is a short and certainly not comprehensive list of areas where I see information technology encouraging changes in thinking. There can be no simple way of cataloging whether any particular change is good or bad. That is contested terrain. At every step we have to ask, as educators and citizens, whether current technology is leading us in directions that serve our human purposes. Such questions are not technical; they are social, moral, and political. For me, addressing that subjective side of computation is one of the more significant challenges for the next decade of information technology in higher education. Technology does not determine change, but it encourages us to take certain directions. If we make those directions clear, we can more easily exert human choice.

Thinking About Privacy

10 Today's college students are habituated to a world of online blogging, instant messaging, and Web browsing that leaves electronic traces. Yet they have had little experience with the right to privacy. Unlike past generations of Americans, who grew up with the notion that the privacy of their mail was sacrosanct, our children are accustomed to electronic surveillance as part of their daily lives.

I have colleagues who feel that the increased incursions on privacy have put the topic more in the news, and that this is a positive change. But middle-school and high-school students tend to be willing to provide personal information online with no safeguards, and college students seem uninterested in violations of privacy and in increased governmental and commercial surveillance. Professors find that students do not understand that in a democracy, privacy is a right, not merely a privilege. In 10 years, ideas about the relationship of privacy and government will require even more active pedagogy. (One might also hope that increased education about the kinds of silent surveillance that technology makes possible may inspire more active political engagement with the issue.)

Avatars or a Self?

Chat rooms, role-playing games, and other technological venues offer us many different contexts for presenting ourselves online. Those possibilities are particularly important for adolescents because they offer what Erik Erikson described as a moratorium, a time out or safe space for the personal experimentation that is so crucial for adolescent development. Our dangerous world—with crime, terrorism, drugs, and AIDS—offers little in the way of safe spaces. Online worlds can provide valuable spaces for identity play.

But some people who gain fluency in expressing multiple aspects of self may find it harder to develop authentic selves. Some children who write narratives for their screen avatars may grow up with too little experience of how to share their real feelings with other people. For those who are lonely yet afraid of intimacy, information technology has made it possible to have the illusion of companionship without the demands of friendship.

From Powerful Ideas to PowerPoint

In the 1970s and early 1980s, some educators wanted to make programming part of the regular curriculum for K-12 education. They argued that because information technology carries ideas, it might as well carry the most powerful ideas that computer science has to offer. It is ironic that in most elementary schools today, the ideas being carried by information technology are not ideas from computer science like procedural thinking, but more likely to be those embedded in productivity tools like PowerPoint presentation software.

15   PowerPoint does more than provide a way of transmitting content. It carries its own way of thinking, its own aesthetic—which not surprisingly shows up in the aesthetic of college freshmen. In that aesthetic, presentation becomes its own powerful idea.

To be sure, the software cannot be blamed for lower intellectual standards. Misuse of the former is as much a symptom as a cause of the latter. Indeed, the culture in which our children are raised is increasingly a culture of presentation, a corporate culture in which appearance is often more important than reality. In contemporary political discourse, the bar has also been lowered. Use of rhetorical devices at the expense of cogent argument regularly goes without notice. But it is precisely because standards of intellectual rigor outside the educational sphere have fallen that educators must attend to how we use, and when we introduce, software that has been designed to simplify the organization and processing of information.

In "The Cognitive Style of PowerPoint" (Graphics Press, 2003), Edward R. Tufte suggests that PowerPoint equates bulleting with clear thinking. It does not teach students to begin a discussion or construct a narrative. It encourages presentation, not conversation. Of course, in the hands of a master teacher, a PowerPoint presentation with few words and powerful images can serve as the jumping-off point for a brilliant lecture. But in the hands of elementary-school students, often introduced to PowerPoint in the third grade, and often infatuated with its swooshing sounds, animated icons, and flashing text, a slide show is more likely to close down debate than open it up.

Developed to serve the needs of the corporate boardroom, the software is designed to convey absolute authority. Teachers used to tell students that clear exposition depended on clear outlining, but presentation software has fetishized the outline at the expense of the content.

20   Narrative, the exposition of content, takes time. PowerPoint, like   20
so much in the computer culture, speeds up the pace.

Word Processing Verses Thinking

The catalog for the Vermont Country Store advertises a manual typewriter, which the advertising copy says "moves at a pace that allows time to compose your thoughts." As many of us know, it is possible to manipulate text on a computer screen and see how it looks faster than we can think about what the words mean.

Word processing has its own complex psychology. From a pedagogical point of view, it can make dedicated students into better writers because it allows them to revise text, rearrange paragraphs, and experiment with the tone and shape of an essay. Few professional writers would part with their computers; some claim that they simply cannot think without their hands on the keyboard. Yet the ability to quickly fill the page, to see it before you can think it, can make bad writers even worse.

A seventh grader once told me that the typewriter she found in her mother's attic is "cool because you have to type each letter by itself. You have to know what you are doing in advance or it comes out a mess." The idea of thinking ahead has become exotic.

Taking Things at Interface Value

We expect software to be easy to use, and we assume that we don't have to know how a computer works. In the early 1980s, most computer users who spoke of transparency meant that, as with any other machine, you could "open the hood" and poke around. But only a few years later, Macintosh users began to use the term when they talked about seeing their documents and programs represented by attractive and easy-to-interpret icons. They were referring to an ability to make things work without needing to go below the screen surface. Paradoxically, it was the screen's opacity that permitted that kind of transparency. Today, when people say that something is transparent, they mean that they can see how to make it work, not that they know how it works. In other words, transparency means epistemic opacity.

25   The people who built or bought the first generation of personal computers understood them down to the bits and bytes. The next generation of operating systems were more complex, but they still invited that old-time reductive understanding. Contemporary information technology encourages different habits of mind. Today's college students are already used to taking things at (inter)face value; their successors in 2014 will be even less accustomed to probing below the surface.

Simulation and its Discontents

Some thinkers argue that the new opacity is empowering, enabling anyone to use the most sophisticated technological tools and to experiment with simulation in complex and creative ways. But it is also true that our tools carry the message that they are beyond our understanding. It is possible that in daily life, epistemic opacity can lead to passivity.

I first became aware of that possibility in the early 1990s, when the first generation of complex simulation games were introduced and immediately became popular for home as well as school use. SimLife teaches the principles of evolution by getting children involved in the development of complex ecosystems; in that sense it is an extraordinary learning tool. During one session in which I played SimLife with Tim, a 13-year-old, the screen before us flashed a message: "Your orgot is being eaten up." "What's an orgot?" I asked. Tim didn't know. "I just ignore that," he said confidently. "You don't need to know that kind of stuff to play."

For me, that story serves as a cautionary tale. Computer simulations enable their users to think about complex phenomena as dynamic, evolving systems. But they also accustom us to manipulating systems whose core assumptions we may not understand and that may not be true.

We live in a culture of simulation. Our games, our economic and political systems, and the ways architects design buildings, chemists envisage molecules, and surgeons perform operations all use simulation technology. In 10 years the degree to which simulations are embedded in every area of life will have increased exponentially. We need to develop a new form of media literacy: readership skills for the culture of simulation.

30   We come to written text with habits of readership based on centuries of civilization. At the very least, we have learned to begin with the journalist's traditional questions: who, what, when, where, why, and how. Who wrote these words, what is their message, why were they written, and how are they situated in time and place, politically and socially? A central project for higher education during the next 10 years should be creating programs in information-technology literacy, with the goal of teaching students to interrogate simulations in much the same spirit, challenging their built-in assumptions.   30

Despite the ever-increasing complexity of software, most computer environments put users in worlds based on constrained choices. In other words, immersion in programmed worlds puts us in reassuring environments where the rules are clear. For example, when you play a video game, you often go through a series of frightening situations that you escape by mastering the rules—you experience life as a reassuring dichotomy of scary and safe. Children grow up in a culture of video games, action films, fantasy epics, and computer programs that all rely on that familiar scenario of almost losing but then regaining total mastery: There is danger. It is mastered. A still-more-powerful monster appears. It is subdued. Scary. Safe.

Yet in the real world, we have never had a greater need to work our way out of binary assumptions. In the decade ahead, we need to rebuild the culture around information technology. In that new sociotechnical culture, assumptions about the nature of mastery would be less absolute. The new culture would make it easier, not more difficult, to consider life in shades of gray, to see moral dilemmas in terms other than a battle between Good and Evil. For never has our world been more complex, hybridized, and global. Never have we so needed to have many contradictory thoughts and feelings at the same time. Our tools must help us accomplish that, not fight against us.

Information technology is identity technology. Embedding it in a culture that supports democracy, freedom of expression, tolerance, diversity, and complexity of opinion is one of the next decade's greatest challenges. We cannot afford to fail.

When I first began studying the computer culture, a small breed of highly trained technologists thought of themselves as "computer people." That is no longer the case. If we take the computer as a carrier of a way of knowing, a way of seeing the world and our place in it, we are all computer people now.

Questions on Meaning

1. Turkle begins by asking whether technology actually changes the ways that the mind perceives reality. How does she use the example of slide rule versus calculator to illustrate this idea?
2. Why does the young woman who encodes computers find a new explanation for the concept of Freudian slip? What does her explanation say about her worldview?
3. When computers first appeared, most users understood the machines they were using. What does Turkle say about our current comprehension of the machines we use today?
4. Turkle fears that the younger generation no longer understands the dangers of invasion of privacy. How does she explain her fears?

Questions on Rhetorical Strategy and Style

1. This essay appeared in a publication meant for college faculty and administrators. How do the examples Turkle chooses fit her audience? In what ways will they share her concerns?
2. Is it likely the concern for student originality and privacy greater with the audience of college faculty and administrators than with students themselves? What is the difference between the point of view of teachers and university leaders from the students in their charge?
3. The essay ends with a proclamation that "we" (Turkle's readers) are all computer people. How does that rhetorical move appeal to the readers to accept her other arguments?

Writing Assignments

1. Are you on Facebook? What warnings have you received about the content and privacy of your page? Write about how you choose what to put up and what to keep private.
2. Talk about the format differences between the Mac and PC. Turkle argues that the Mac format hides the workings of the program and has led to less knowledge of how a computer works. Agree or disagree with her argument.

3. Write about how you use technology in your writing. What resources do you use (PowerPoint, Google, etc.)? How do you use them?

Always On

Sherry Turkle

Sherry Turkle (1948–) was born in New York City. She is a Professor of the Social Studies of Science and Technology at MIT and is the founder and director of the MIT Initiative on Technology and Self. The goal of this Initiative "is to be a center for research and reflection on the subjective side of technology and to raise the level of public discourse on the social and psychological dimensions of technological change." Turkle holds a doctorate in sociology and personality psychology from Harvard and is also a licensed clinical psychologist. Her most recent publications are Simulation and Its Discontents *(2009) and* Alone Together: Why We Expect More from Technology and Less from Each Other *(2011). As the latter title suggests, it analyzes how technology has the power to shape social lives, to connect us or isolate us from each other. In this chapter from* Alone Together *Turkle questions whether being connected as much as we are these days is actually harming our ability to communicate with each other.*

1   Pia Lindman walked the halls of MIT with cyborg dreams. She was not the first. In the summer of 1996. I met with seven young researchers at the MIT Media Lab who carried computers and radio transmitters in their backpacks and keyboards in their pockets. Digital displays were clipped onto eyeglass frames. Thus provisioned, they called themselves "cyborgs" and were always wirelessly connected to the Internet, always online, free from desks and cables. The group was about to release three new 'borgs into the world, three more who would live simultaneously in the physical and virtual.

Reprinted from *Alone Together: Why We Expect More from Technology and Less from Each Other* (2011), by permission of Basic Books, an imprint of the Perseus Books Group.

I felt moved by the cyborgs as I had been by Lindman: I saw a bravery, a willingness to sacrifice for a vision of being one with technology. When their burdensome technology cut into their skin, causing lesions and then scars, the cyborgs learned to be indifferent. When their encumbrances caused them to be taken as physically disabled, they learned to be patient and provide explanations.

At MIT, there was much talk about what the cyborgs were trying to accomplish. Faculty supporters stressed how continual connectivity could increase productivity and memory. The cyborgs, it was said, might seem exotic, but this technology should inspire no fear. It was "just a tool" for being better prepared and organized in an increasingly complex information environment. The brain needed help.

From the cyborgs, however, I heard another story. They felt like new selves. One, in his mid-twenties, said he had "become" his device. Shy, with a memory that seemed limited by anxiety, he felt better able to function when he could literally be "looking up" previous encounters with someone as he began a new conversation. "With it," he said, referring to his collection of connectivity devices, "it's not just that I remember people or know more. I feel invincible, sociable, better prepared. I am naked without it. With it, I'm a better person." But with a sense of enhancement came feelings of diffusion. The cyborgs were a new kind of nomad, wandering in and out of the physical real. For the physical real was only one of the many things in their field of vision. Even in the mid-1990s, as they walked around Kendall Square in Cambridge, the cyborgs could not only search the Web but had mobile e-mail, instant messaging, and remote access to desktop computing. The multiplicity of worlds before them set them apart: they could be with you, but they were always somewhere else as well.

Within a decade, what had seemed alien was close to becoming everyone's way of life, as compact smartphones replaced the cyborgs' more elaborate accoutrements. This is the experience of living full-time on the Net, newly free in some ways, newly yoked in others. We are all cyborgs now.

5   People love their new technologies of connection. They have made parents and children feel more secure and have revolutionized business, education, scholarship, and medicine. It is no accident that corporate America has chosen to name cell phones after candies and ice cream flavors: chocolate, strawberry, vanilla. There is a sweetness to them. They have changed how we date and how we travel. The

global reach of connectivity can make the most isolated outpost into a center of learning and economic activity. The word "apps" summons the pleasure of tasks accomplished on mobile devices, some of which, only recently, we would not have dreamed possible (for me, personally, it is an iPhone app that can "listen" to a song, identify it, and cue it up for purchase).

Beyond all of this, connectivity offers new possibilities for experimenting with identity and, particularly in adolescence, the sense of a free space, what Erik Erikson called the *moratorium*. This is a time, relatively consequence free, for doing what adolescents need to do: fall in and out of love with people and ideas. Real life does not always provide this kind of space, but the Internet does.

No handle cranks, no gear turns to move us from one stage of life to another. We don't get all developmental tasks done at age-appropriate times—or even necessarily get them done at all. We move on and use the materials we have to do the best we can at each point in our lives. We rework unresolved issues and seek out missed experiences. The Internet provides new spaces in which we can do this, no matter how imperfectly, throughout our lives. So, adults as well as adolescents use it to explore identity.

When part of your life is lived in virtual places—it can be Second Life, a computer game, a social networking site—a vexed relationship develops between what is true and what is "true here," true in simulation. In games where we expect to play an avatar, we end up being ourselves in the most revealing ways; on social-networking sites such as Facebook, we think we will be presenting ourselves, but our profile ends up as somebody else—often the fantasy of who we want to be. Distinctions blur. Virtual places offer connection with uncertain claims to commitment. We don't count on cyberfriends to come by if we are ill, to celebrate our children's successes, or help us mourn the death of our parents. People know this, and yet the emotional charge on cyberspace is high. People talk about digital life as the "place for hope," the place where something new will come to them. In the past, one waited for the sound of the post—by carriage, by foot, by truck. Now, when there is a lull, we check our e-mail, texts, and messages.

The story of my own hesitant steps toward a cyborg life is banal, an example of the near universality of what was so recently exotic. I carry a mobile device with me at all times. I held out for years. I don't like attempting to speak to people who are moving in and out of contact as they pass through tunnels, come to dangerous intersections, or otherwise approach dead zones. I worry about them. The clarity and fidelity of sound on my landline telephone seems to me a technical advance over what I can hear on my mobile. And I don't like the feeling of always being on call. But now, with a daughter studying abroad who expects to reach me when she wants to reach me, I am grateful to be tethered to her through the Net. In deference to a generation that sees my phone calls as constraining because they take place in real time and are not suitable for multitasking, I text. Awkwardly.

10   But even these small things allow me to identify with the cyborgs claims of an enhanced experience. Tethered to the Internet, the cyborgs felt like more than they could be without it. Like most people, I experience a pint-sized version of such pleasures. I like to look at the list of "favorites" on my iPhone contact list and see everyone I cherish. Each is just a tap away. If someone doesn't have time to talk to me, I can text a greeting, and they will know I am thinking of them, caring about them. Looking over recent text exchanges with my friends and family reliably puts me in a good mood. I keep all the texts my daughter sent me during her last year of high school. They always warm me: "Forgot my green sweater, bring please." "Can you pick me up at boathouse, 6?" "Please tell nurse I'm sick. Class boring. Want to come home." And of course, there are the photos, so many photos on my phone, more photos than I would ever take with a camera, always with me.

Yet, even such simple pleasures bring compulsions that take me by surprise. I check my e-mail first thing in the morning and before going to bed at night. I have come to learn that informing myself about new professional problems and demands is not a good way to start or end my day, but my practice unhappily continues. I admitted my ongoing irritation with myself to a friend, a woman in her seventies who has meditated on a biblical reading every morning since she was in her teens. She confessed that it is ever more difficult to begin her spiritual exercises before she checks her e-mail; the discipline to defer opening her inbox is now part of her devotional gesture. And she, too, invites insomnia by checking her e-mail every night before turning in.

Nurturance was the killer app for robotics. Tending the robots incited our engagement. There is a parallel for the networked life. Always on and (now) always with us, we tend the Net, and the Net teaches us to need it.

Online, like MIT's cyborgs, we feel enhanced; there is a parallel with the robotic moment of more. But in both cases, moments of more may leave us with lives of less. Robotics and connectivity call each other up in tentative symbiosis, parallel pathways to relational retreat. With sociable robots we are alone but receive the signals that tell us we are together. Networked, we are together, but so lessened are our expectations of each other that we can feel utterly alone. And there is the risk that we come to see others as objects to be accessed—and only for the parts we find useful, comforting, or amusing.

Once we remove ourselves from the flow of physical, messy, untidy life—and both robotics and networked life do that—we become less willing to get out there and take a chance. A song that became popular on YouTube in 2010, "Do You Want to Date My Avatar?" ends with the lyrics "And if you think I'm not the one, log off, log off and we'll be done."

15   Our attraction to even the prospect of sociable robots affords a   15
new view of our networked life. In Part One we saw that when children grow up with fond feelings for sociable robots, they are prepared for the "relationships with less" that the network provides. Now I turn to how the network prepares us for the "relationships with less" that robots provide. These are the unsettling isolations of the tethered self. I have said that tethered to the network through our mobile devices, we approach a new state of the self, itself. For a start, it presumes certain entitlements: It can absent itself from its physical surround—including the people in it. It can experience the physical and virtual in near simultaneity. And it is able to make more time by multitasking, our twenty-first-century alchemy.

THE NEW STATE OF THE SELF: TETHERED AND MARKED ABSENT

These days, being connected depends not on our distance from each other but from available communications technology. Most of the time, we carry that technology with us. In fact, being alone can start to seem like a precondition for being together because it is easier to communicate if you can focus, without interruption, on your screen. In this new regime, a train station (like an airport, a café, or a park) is no longer a communal space but a place of social collection: people come together but do not speak to each other. Each is tethered to a mobile device and to the people and places to which that device serves as a portal. I grew up in Brooklyn where sidewalks had a special look. In every season—even in winter, when snow was scraped away—there were chalk-drawn hopscotch boxes. I speak with a colleague who lives in my old neighborhood. The hopscotch boxes are gone. The kids are out, but they are on their phones.

When people have phone conversations in public spaces, their sense of privacy is sustained by the presumption that those around them will treat them not only as anonymous but as if absent. On a recent train trip from Boston to New York, I sat next to a man talking to his girlfriend about his problems. Here is what I learned by trying not to listen: He's had a recent bout of heavy drinking, and his father is no longer willing to supplement his income. He thinks his girlfriend spends too much money and he dislikes her teenage daughter. Embarrassed, I walked up and down the aisles to find another seat, but the train was full. Resigned, I returned to my seat next to the complainer. There was some comfort in the fact that he was not complaining to me, but I did wish I could disappear. Perhaps there was no need. I was already being treated as though I were not there.

Or perhaps it makes more sense to think of things the other way around: it is those on the phone who mark themselves as absent. Sometimes people signal their departure by putting a phone to their ear, but it often happens in more subtle ways—there may be a glance down at a mobile device during dinner or a meeting. A "place" used to comprise a physical space and the people within it. What is a place if those who are physically present have their attention on the absent? At a café a block from my home, almost everyone is on a computer or smartphone as they drink their coffee. These people are not my friends, yet somehow I miss their presence.

Our new experience of place is apparent as we travel. Leaving home has always been a way to see one's own culture anew. But what if, tethered, we bring our homes with us? The director of a program that places American students in Spanish universities once complained to me that her students were not "experiencing Spain." They spent their free time on Facebook, chatting with their friends from home. I was sympathetic, thinking of the hours I had spent walking with my teenage daughter on a visit to Paris the summer after she first got her mobile phone. As we sat in a café, waiting for a friend to join us for dinner, Rebecca received a call from a schoolmate who asked her to lunch in Boston, six hours behind us in time. My daughter said simply, "Not possible, but how about Friday?" Her friend didn't even know she was out of town. When I grew up, the idea of the "global village" was an abstraction. My daughter lives something concrete. Emotionally, socially, wherever she goes, she never leaves home. I asked her if she wouldn't rather experience Paris without continual reminders of Boston. (I left aside the matter that I was a reminder of Boston and she, mercifully, did not raise it.) She told me she was happy; she liked being in touch with her friends. She seemed to barely understand my question. I was wistful, worried that Rebecca was missing an experience I cherished in my youth: an undiluted Paris. My Paris came with the thrill of disconnection from everything I knew. My daughter's Paris did not include this displacement.

20   When Rebecca and I returned home from France, I talked about the trip with a close friend, a psychoanalyst. Our discussion led her to reminisce about her first visit to Paris. She was sixteen, travelling with her parents. But while they went sightseeing with her younger brother, she insisted on staying in her hotel room, writing long letters to her boyfriend. Adolescents have always balanced connection and disconnection; we need to acknowledge the familiarity of our needs and the novelty of our circumstances. The Internet is more than old wine in new bottles; now we can always be elsewhere.

In the month after Rebecca and I returned from Paris, I noted how often I was with colleagues who were elsewhere as well: a board meeting where members rebelled when asked to turn off their mobile devices; a faculty meeting where attendees did their e-mail until it was their turn to speak; a conference at which audience members set up Internet back channels in order to chat about speakers' presentations during the presentations themselves.

Since I teach in a university, I find examples of distracted academics of particular interest. But it is the more mundane examples of attention sharing that change the fabric of daily life. Parents check e-mail as they push strollers. Children and parents text during family dinners. As I watched the annual marathon in Florence, Italy, in November 2009, a runner passed me, texting. Of course, I tried to take her picture on my cell phone. After five years, my level of connectivity had finally caught up with my daughter's. Now when I travel, my access to the Net stays constant. There is security and pleasure in a good hotel on the other side of the world, but it cannot compare to the constancy of online connections.

Research portrays Americans as increasingly insecure, isolated, and lonely. We work more hours than ever before, often at several jobs. Even high school and college students, during seasons of life when time should be most abundant, say that they don't date but "hook up" because "who has the time?" We have moved away, often far away, from the communities of our birth. We struggle to raise children without the support of extended families. Many have left behind the religious and civic associations that once bound us together. To those who have lost a sense of physical connection, connectivity suggests that you make your own page, your own place. When you are there, you are by definition where you belong, among officially friended friends. To those who feel they have no time, connectivity, like robotics, tempts by proposing substitutions through which you can have companionship with convenience. A robot will always be there, amusing and compliant. On the Net, you can always find someone. "I never want to be far from my BlackBerry," a colleague told me. "That is where my games are. That is where my sites are. Without it, I'm too anxious."

Today, our machine dream is to be never alone but always in control. This can't happen when one is face-to-face with a person. But it can be accomplished with a robot or . . . by slipping through the portals of a digital life.

Questions on Meaning

1. How does the concept of the cyborg—a term from science fiction—apply to Turkle's essay? Why does she characterize the young MIT researchers as cyborgs?

2. Respond to the statement that "connectivity offers new possibilities for experimenting with identity." Explain how that idea applies to you.

3. The author refers to the notion of a "Second Life," a life one lives in a virtual world. This concept, then, draws a distinction "between what is true and what is 'true here,' true in simulation." How do you interpret this idea?

4. Explain why the author asserts that "We are all cyborgs now." Do you agree or disagree?

Questions on Rhetorical Strategy and Style

1. Why does the author include the passage in which she describes her own process of becoming a cyborg? What discoveries does she make?

2. What argument is the author attempting to make about the effect of technology on our lives? How would you describe her means of persuasion?

3. Why is her essay structured in two distinct parts? How does the argument in the second part shift the tone established in the first?

Writing Assignments

1. Considering the meaning of the title of Turkle's essay, write a narrative of your life in relation to technology. How much of your daily life is spent "on" in the sense the author uses the concept?

2. Interview a few people who are old enough to have entered adulthood before the age of the screen. Write an essay that recounts their experience of making the transition to life with technology. What were the challenges or struggles they encountered? How do they feel about technology now? How has it changed their lives?

Predictable Crises of Adulthood

Gail Sheehy

*Gail Sheehy (1937–) attended the University of Vermont
and Columbia School of Journalism. She has pursued a
writing career as a contributing editor for* New York Magazine *and as a writer for* Esquire, McCall's, Ms., *and*
Rolling Stone. *She has written popular books on sociological
and psychological phenomena such as race*—Panthermania:
The Clash of Black Against Black in One American City
(1971); prostitution—Prostitution in Our Wide Open
Society *(1973); and about life transitions*—Passages: Predictable Crises of Adult Life *(1976),* The Silent Passage
(1992), and New Passages *(1995). Her books about life
transitions have won her fame, as she has kept pace with the
changing lives of the Baby Boom generation, a group preoccupied with change and self-improvement. In this article
from her original* Passages *she lays out the major points of
change, called crises, which the Boomers had experienced up
to the point of her book's publication.*

1   We are not unlike a particularly hardy crustacean. The lob-
ster grows by developing and shedding a series of hard,
protective shells. Each time it expands from within, the
confining shell must be sloughed off. It is left exposed and vulnerable
until, in time, a new covering grows to replace the old.

   With each passage from one stage of human growth to the next
we, too, must shed a protective structure. We are left exposed and vulnerable—but also yeasty and embryonic again, capable of stretching
in ways we hadn't known before. These sheddings may take several

years or more. Coming out of each passage, though, we enter a longer and more stable period in which we can expect relative tranquillity and a sense of equilibrium regained. . . .

As we shall see, each person engages the steps of development in his or her own characteristic *step-style*. Some people never complete the whole sequence. And none of us "solves" with one step—by jumping out of the parental home into a job or marriage, for example—the problems in separating from the caregivers of childhood. Nor do we "achieve" autonomy once and for all by converting our dreams into concrete goals, even when we attain those goals. The central issues or tasks of one period are never fully completed, tied up, and cast aside. But when they lose their primacy and the current life structure has served its purpose, we are ready to move on to the next period.

Can one catch up? What might look to others like listlessness, contrariness, a maddening refusal to face up to an obvious task may be a person's own unique detour that will bring him out later on the other side. Developmental gains won can later be lost—and rewon. It's plausible, though it can't be proven, that the mastery of one set of tasks fortifies us for the next period and the next set of challenges. But it's important not to think too mechanistically. Machines work by units. The bureaucracy (supposedly) works step by step. Human beings, thank God, have an individual inner dynamic that can never be precisely coded.

5   Although I have indicated the ages when Americans are likely to   5 go through each stage, and the differences between men and women where they are striking, do not take the ages too seriously. The stages are the thing, and most particularly the sequence.

Here is the briefest outline of the developmental ladder.

Pulling Up Roots

Before 18, the motto is loud and clear: "I have to get away from my parents." But the words are seldom connected to action. Generally still safely part of our families, even if away at school, we feel our autonomy to be subject to erosion from moment to moment.

After 18, we begin Pulling Up Roots in earnest. College, military service, and short-term travels are all customary vehicles our society provides for the first round trips between family and a base of one's own. In the attempt to separate our view of the world from our family's view, despite vigorous protestations to the contrary—"I know exactly what I want!"—we cast about for any beliefs we can call our own. And in the process of testing those beliefs we are often drawn to fads, preferably those most mysterious and inaccessible to our parents.

Whatever tentative memberships we try out in the world, the fear haunts us that we are really kids who cannot take care of ourselves. We cover that fear with acts of defiance and mimicked confidence. For allies to replace our parents, we turn to our contemporaries. They become conspirators. So long as their perspective meshes with our own, they are able to substitute for the sanctuary of the family. But that doesn't last very long. And the instant they diverge from the shaky ideals of "our group," they are seen as betrayers. Rebounds to the family are common between the ages of 18 and 22.

10 The tasks of this passage are to locate ourselves in a peer group 10 role, a sex role, an anticipated occupation, an ideology or world view. As a result, we gather the impetus to leave home physically and the identity to *begin* leaving home emotionally.

Even as one part of us seeks to be an individual, another part longs to restore the safety and comfort of merging with another. Thus one of the most popular myths of this passage is: We can piggyback our development by attaching to a Stronger One. But people who marry during this time often prolong financial and emotional ties to the family and relatives that impede them from becoming self-sufficient.

A stormy passage through the Pulling Up Roots years will probably facilitate the normal progression of the adult life cycle. If one doesn't have an identity crisis at this point, it will erupt during a later transition, when the penalties may be harder to bear.

The Trying Twenties

The Trying Twenties confront us with the question of how to take hold in the adult world. Our focus shifts from the interior turmoils of late adolescence—"Who am I?" "What is truth?"—and we become almost totally preoccupied with working out the externals. "How do I put my aspirations into effect?" "What is the best way to start?" "Where do I go?" "Who can help me?" "How did *you* do it?"

In this period, which is longer and more stable compared with the passage that leads to it, the tasks are as enormous as they are exhilarating: To shape a Dream, that vision of ourselves which will generate energy, aliveness, and hope. To prepare for a lifework. To find a mentor if possible. And to form the capacity for intimacy, without losing in the process whatever consistency of self we have thus far mustered. The first test structure must be erected around the life we choose to try.

15   Doing what we "should" is the most pervasive theme of the twenties. The "shoulds" are largely defined by family models, the press of the culture, or the prejudices of our peers. If the prevailing cultural instructions are that one should get married and settle down behind one's own door, a nuclear family is born. If instead the peers insist that one should do one's own thing, the 25-year-old is likely to harness himself onto a Harley-Davidson and burn up Route 66 in the commitment to have no commitments.

One of the terrifying aspects of the twenties is the inner conviction that the choices we make are irrevocable. It is largely a false fear. Change is quite possible, and some alteration of our original choices is probably inevitable.

Two impulses, as always, are at work. One is to build a firm, safe structure for the future by making strong commitments, to "be set." Yet people who slip into a ready-made form without much self-examination are likely to find themselves *locked in.* The other urge is to explore and experiment, keeping any structure tentative and therefore easily reversible. Taken to the extreme, these are people who skip from one trial job and one limited personal encounter to another, spending their twenties in the *transient* state.

Although the choices of our twenties are not irrevocable, they do set in motion a Life Pattern. Some of us follow the locked-in pattern, others the transient pattern, the wunderkind pattern, the caregiver pattern, and there are a number of others. Such patterns strongly influence the particular questions raised for each person during each passage. . . .

20   Buoyed by powerful illusions and belief in the power of the will, we commonly insist in our twenties that what we have chosen to do is the one true course in life. Our backs go up at the merest hint that we are like our parents, that two decades of parental training might be reflected in our current actions and attitudes.

"Not me," is the motto, "I'm different."

Catch-30

Impatient with devoting ourselves to the "shoulds," a new vitality springs from within as we approach 30. Men and women alike speak of feeling too narrow and restricted. They blame all sorts of things, but what the restrictions boil down to are the outgrowth of career and personal choices of the twenties. They may have been choices perfectly suited to that stage. But now the fit feels different. Some inner aspect that was left out is striving to be taken into account. Important new choices must be made, and commitments altered or deepened. The work involves great change, turmoil, and often crisis—a simultaneous feeling of rock bottom and the urge to bust out.

One common response is the tearing up of the life we spent most of our twenties putting together. It may mean striking out on a secondary road toward a new vision or converting a dream of "running for president" into a more realistic goal. The single person feels a push to find a partner. The woman who was previously content at home with children chafes to venture into the world. The childless couple reconsiders children. And almost everyone who is married, especially those married for seven years, feels a discontent.

If the discontent doesn't lead to a divorce, it will, or should, call for a serious review of the marriage and of each partner's aspirations in their Catch-30 condition. The gist of that condition was expressed by a 29-year-old associate with a Wall Street law firm:

25 "I'm considering leaving the firm. I've been there four years now; 25 I'm getting good feedback, but I have no clients of my own. I feel weak. If I wait much longer, it will be too late, too close to that fateful time of decision on whether or not to become a partner. I'm success-oriented. But the concept of being 55 years old and stuck in a monotonous job drives me wild. It drives me crazy now, just a little bit. I'd say that 85 percent of the time I thoroughly enjoy my work. But when I get a screwball case, I come away from court saying, 'What am I doing here?' It's a *visceral* reaction that I'm wasting my time. I'm trying to find some way to make a social contribution or a slot in city government. I keep saying, 'There's something more.' "

Besides the push to broaden himself professionally, there is a wish to expand his personal life. He wants two or three more children. "The concept of a home has become very meaningful to me, a place to get away from troubles and relax. I love my son in a way I could not have anticipated. I never could live alone."

Consumed with the work of making his own critical life-steering decisions, he demonstrates the essential shift at this age: an absolute requirement to be more self-concerned. The self has new value now that his competency has been proved.

His wife is struggling with her own age-30 priorities. She wants to go to law school, but he wants more children. If she is going to stay home, she wants him to make more time for the family instead of taking on even wider professional commitments. His view of the bind, of what he would most like from his wife, is this:

"I'd like not to be bothered. It sounds cruel, but I'd like not to have to worry about what she's going to do next week. Which is why I've told her several times that I think she should do something. Go back to school and get a degree in social work or geography or whatever. Hopefully that would fulfill her, and then I wouldn't have to worry about her line of problems. I want her to be decisive about herself."

30   The trouble with his advice to his wife is that it comes out of concern with *his* convenience, rather than with *her* development. She quickly picks up on this lack of goodwill: He is trying to dispose of her. At the same time, he refuses her the same latitude to be "selfish" in making an independent decision to broaden her own horizons. Both perceive a lack of mutuality. And that is what Catch-30 is all about for the couple.

Rooting and Extending

Life becomes less provisional, more rational and orderly in the early thirties. We begin to settle down in the full sense. Most of us begin putting down roots and sending out new shoots. People buy houses and become very earnest about climbing career ladders. Men in particular concern themselves with "making it." Satisfaction with marriage generally goes downhill in the thirties (for those who have remained together) compared with the highly valued, vision-supporting marriage of the twenties. This coincides with the couple's reduced social life outside the family and the inturned focus on raising their children.

The Deadline Decade

In the middle of the thirties we come upon a crossroads. We have reached the halfway mark. Yet even as we are reaching our prime, we begin to see there is a place where it finishes. Time starts to squeeze.

The loss of youth, the faltering of physical powers we have always taken for granted, the fading purpose of stereotyped roles by which we have thus far identified ourselves, the spiritual dilemma of having no absolute answers—any or all of these shocks can give this passage the character of crisis. Such thoughts usher in a decade between 35 and

45 that can be called the Deadline Decade. It is a time of both danger and opportunity. All of us have the chance to rework the narrow identity by which we defined ourselves in the first half of life. And those of us who make the most of the opportunity will have a full-out authenticity crisis.

To come through this authenticity crisis, we must reexamine our purposes and reevaluate how to spend our resources from now on. "Why am I doing all this? What do I really believe in?" No matter what we have been doing, there will be parts of ourselves that have been suppressed and now need to find expression. "Bad" feelings will demand acknowledgment along with the good.

35   It is frightening to step off onto the treacherous footbridge lead- 35
ing to the second half of life. We can't take everything with us on this journey through uncertainty. Along the way, we discover that we are alone. We no longer have to ask permission because we are the providers of our own safety. We must learn to give ourselves permission. We stumble upon feminine or masculine aspects of our natures that up to this time have usually been masked. There is grieving to be done because an old self is dying. By taking in our suppressed and even our unwanted parts, we prepare at the gut level for the reintegration of an identity that is ours and ours alone—not some artificial form put together to please the culture or our mates. It is a dark passage at the beginning. But by disassembling ourselves, we can glimpse the light and gather our parts into a renewal.

Women sense this inner crossroads earlier than men do. The time pinch often prompts a woman to stop and take an allpoints survey at age 35. Whatever options she has already played out, she feels a "my last chance" urgency to review those options she has set aside and those that aging and biology will close off in the *now foreseeable* future. For all her qualms and confusion about where to start looking for a new future, she usually enjoys an exhilaration of release. Assertiveness begins rising. There are so many firsts ahead.

Men, too, feel the time push in the mid-thirties. Most men respond by pressing down harder on the career accelerator. It's "my last chance" to pull away from the pack. It is no longer enough to be the loyal junior executive, the promising young novelist, the lawyer who does a little *pro bono* work on the side. He wants now to become part of top management, to be recognized as an established writer, or an active politician with his own legislative program. With some chagrin, he discovers that he has been too anxious to please and too vulnerable to criticism. He wants to put together his own ship.

During this period of intense concentration on external advancement, it is common for men to be unaware of the more difficult, gut issues that are propelling them forward. The survey that was neglected at 35 becomes a crucible at 40. Whatever rung of achievement he has reached, the man of 40 usually feels stale, restless, burdened, and unappreciated. He worries about his health. He wonders, "Is this all there is?" He may make a series of departures from well established lifelong base lines, including marriage. More and more men are seeking second careers in midlife. Some become self-destructive. And many men in their forties experience a major shift of emphasis away from pouring all their energies into their own advancement. A more tender, feeling side comes into play. They become interested in developing an ethical self

Renewal or Resignation

Somewhere in the mid-forties, equilibrium is regained. A new stability is achieved, which may be more or less satisfying.

40   If one has refused to budge through the midlife transition, the   40
sense of staleness will calcify into resignation. One by one, the safety and supports will be withdrawn from the person who is standing still. Parents will become children; children will become strangers; a mate will grow away or go away; the career will become just a job—and each of these events will be felt as an abandonment. The crisis will probably emerge again around 50. And although its wallop will be greater, the jolt may be just what is needed to prod the resigned middle-ager toward seeking revitalization.

On the other hand . . .

If we have confronted ourselves in the middle passage and found a renewal of purpose around which we are eager to build a more authentic life structure, these may well be the best years. Personal happiness takes a sharp turn upward for partners who can now accept the fact: "I cannot expect *anyone* to fully understand me." Parents can be forgiven for the burdens of our childhood. Children can be let go without leaving us in collapsed silence. At 50, there is a new warmth and mellowing. Friends become more important than ever, but so does privacy. Since it is so often proclaimed by people past midlife, the motto of this stage might be "No more bullshit."

Questions on Meaning

1. Explain why the phrase "Pulling Up Roots" is an appropriate way to describe the mindset of someone in the period between the late teens and early twenties.
2. What, according to Sheehy, is the problem with getting married during the "pulling up roots" period? Explain in as much detail as you can.
3. What are the primary developmental tasks of the Trying Twenties, Catch-30, and the Deadline Decade?

Questions on Rhetorical Strategy and Style

1. During the twenties, according to Sheehy, "Two impulses are always at work." Do the impulses she describes—to build a safe structure or to explore and experiment—explain the behavior of twenty somethings you know? Clarify the definition of that class of people.
2. Does Sheehy's explanation of adult "crises" seem persuasive to you? If so, identify points that seem especially telling. If her explanations don't persuade you, explain where and why they fail. In particular, how well do the age boundaries work to define the groups?
3. How do relationships with others (parents, friends, mates) affect the choices people make at each of the stages Sheehy describes?

Writing Assignments

1. Find the last novel you read and skim it, noting the ages of the important characters. Do you see signs in the characters of the motivations and behavior Sheehy describes? Write an essay that interprets the novel from the standpoint of crises of adulthood.
2. Tell the story of a transition you have observed or experienced. How did the changes affect the person and those close to him or her? How did the passage begin? How was it resolved?

On the Fear of Death

Elisabeth Kübler-Ross

Elisabeth Kübler-Ross (1926–2004) was born in Zurich, Switzerland. She received an M.D. from the University of Zurich (1957); served residencies in psychiatry at Manhattan State, Montefiore, and Colorado General hospitals; taught at the University of Chicago; and directed a center for terminal patients in rural Virginia. Her pivotal book, On Death and Dying *(1969), changed the manner in which the medical profession views terminally ill patients and prompted medical schools to add courses on death. Other books by Kübler-Ross include* Questions and Answers on Death and Dying *(1974),* Death: The Final Stage of Growth *(1975),* To Live Until We Say Goodbye *(1978),* Working it Through *(1982),* On Childhood and Death *(1985),* AIDS: The Ultimate Challenge *(1987), and* Death Is of Vital Importance: On Life, Death, and Life After Death *(1995). Kübler-Ross has been a leader in the hospice movement. In this essay, she argues that advances in science and the mindset of today's civilized society combine to make natural death something to be shunned and feared.*

> *Let me not pray to be sheltered from dangers but to be fearless in facing them.*
> *Let me not beg for the stilling of my pain but for the heart to conquer it.*
> *Let me not look for allies in life's battlefield but to my own strength.*
> *Let me not crave in anxious fear to be saved but hope for the patience to win my freedom.*

Grant me that I may not be a coward, feeling your mercy in my success alone; but let me find the grasp of your hand in my failure.

Rabindranath Tagore,
Fruit-Gathering

1   Epidemics have taken a great toll of lives in past generations. Death in infancy and early childhood was frequent and there were few families who didn't lose a member of the family at an early age. Medicine has changed greatly in the last decades. Widespread vaccinations have practically eradicated many illnesses, at least in western Europe and the United States. The use of chemotherapy, especially the antibiotics, has contributed to an ever decreasing number of fatalities in infectious diseases. Better child care and education have effected a low morbidity and mortality among children. The many diseases that have taken an impressive toll among the young and middle-aged have been conquered. The number of old people is on the rise, and with this fact come the number of people with malignancies and chronic diseases associated more with old age.

Pediatricians have less work with acute and life-threatening situations as they have an ever increasing number of patients with psychosomatic disturbances and adjustment and behavior problems. Physicians have more people in their waiting rooms with emotional problems than they have ever had before, but they also have more elderly patients who not only try to live with their decreased physical abilities and limitations but who also face loneliness and isolation with all its pains and anguish. The majority of these people are not seen by a psychiatrist. Their needs have to be elicited and gratified by other professional people, for instance, chaplains and social workers. It is for them that I am trying to outline the changes that have taken place in the last few decades, changes that are ultimately responsible for the increased fear of death, the rising number of emotional problems, and the greater need for understanding of and coping with the problems of death and dying.

When we look back in time and study old cultures and people, we are impressed that death has always been distasteful to man and will probably always be. From a psychiatrist's point of view this is very understandable and can perhaps best be explained by our basic knowledge that, in our unconscious, death is never possible in regard to ourselves. It is inconceivable for our unconscious to imagine an actual ending of our own life here on earth, and if this life of ours had to end, the ending is always attributed to a malicious intervention from the outside by someone else. In simple terms, in our unconscious mind we can only be killed; it is inconceivable to die of a natural cause or of old age. Therefore death in itself is associated with a bad act, a frightening happening, something that in itself calls for retribution and punishment.

One is wise to remember these fundamental facts as they are essential in understanding some of the most important, otherwise unintelligible communications of our patients.

5   The second fact that we have to comprehend is that in our unconscious mind we cannot distinguish between a wish and a deed. We are all aware of some of our illogical dreams in which two completely opposite statements can exist side by side—very acceptable in our dreams but unthinkable and illogical in our wakening state. Just as our unconscious mind cannot differentiate between the wish to kill somebody in anger and the act of having done so, the young child is unable to make this distinction. The child who angrily wishes his mother to drop dead for not having gratified his needs will be traumatized greatly by the actual death of his mother—even if this event is not linked closely in time with his destructive wishes. He will always take part or the whole blame for the loss of his mother. He will always say to himself—rarely to others—"I did it, I am responsible, I was bad, therefore Mommy left me." It is well to remember that the child will react in the same manner if he loses a parent by divorce, separation, or desertion. Death is often seen by a child as an impermanent thing and has therefore little distinction from a divorce in which he may have an opportunity to see a parent again.

Many a parent will remember remarks of their children such as, "I will bury my doggy now and next spring when the flowers come up again, he will get up." Maybe it was the same wish that motivated the ancient Egyptians to supply their dead with food and goods to keep them happy and the old American Indians to bury their relatives with their belongings.

When we grow older and begin to realize that our omnipotence is really not so omnipotent, that our strongest wishes are not powerful enough to make the impossible possible, the fear that we have contributed to the death of a loved one diminishes—and with it the guilt.

The fear remains diminished, however, only so long as it is not challenged too strongly. Its vestiges can be seen daily in hospital corridors and in people associated with the bereaved.

A husband and wife may have been fighting for years, but when the partner dies, the survivor will pull his hair, whine and cry louder and beat his chest in regret, fear and anguish, and will hence fear his own death more than before, still believing in the law of talion—an eye for an eye, a tooth for a tooth—"I am responsible for her death, I will have to die a pitiful death in retribution."

Maybe this knowledge will help us understand many of the old customs and rituals which have lasted over the centuries and whose purpose is to diminish the anger of the gods or the people as the case may be, thus decreasing the anticipated punishment. I am thinking of the ashes, the torn clothes, the veil, the *Klage Weiber* of the old days— they are all means to ask you to take pity on them, the mourners, and are expressions of sorrow, grief, and shame. If someone grieves, beats his chest, tears his hair, or refuses to eat, it is an attempt at self-punishment to avoid or reduce the anticipated punishment for the blame that he takes on the death of a loved one.

10   This grief, shame, and guilt are not very far removed from feelings of anger and rage. The process of grief always includes some qualities of anger. Since none of us likes to admit anger at a deceased person, these emotions are often disguised or repressed and prolong the period of grief or show up in other ways. It is well to remember that it is not up to us to judge such feelings as bad or shameful but to understand their true meaning and origin as something very human. In order to illustrate this I will again use the example of the child— and the child in us. The five-year-old who loses his mother is both blaming himself for her disappearance and being angry at her for having deserted him and for no longer gratifying his needs. The dead person then turns into something the child loves and wants very much but also hates with equal intensity for this severe deprivation.   10

The ancient Hebrews regarded the body of a dead person as something unclean and not to be touched. The early American Indians talked about the evil spirits and shot arrows in the air to drive the spirits away. Many other cultures have rituals to take care of the "bad" dead person, and they all originate in this feeling of anger which still exists in all of us, though we dislike admitting it. The tradition of the tombstone may originate in this wish to keep the bad spirits deep down in the ground, and the pebbles that many mourners put on the grave are left-over symbols of the same wish. Though we call the firing of guns at military funerals a last salute, it is the same symbolic ritual as the Indian used when he shot his spears and arrows into the skies.

I give these examples to emphasize that man has not basically changed. Death is still a fearful, frightening happening, and the fear of death is a universal fear even if we think we have mastered it on many levels.

What has changed is our way of coping and dealing with death and dying and our dying patients.

Having been raised in a country in Europe where science is not so advanced, where modern techniques have just started to find their way into medicine, and where people still live as they did in this country half a century ago, I may have had an opportunity to study a part of the evolution of mankind in a shorter period.

15   I remember as a child the death of a farmer. He fell from a tree   15
and was not expected to live. He asked simply to die at home, a wish that was granted without questioning. He called his daughters into the bedroom and spoke with each one of them alone for a few moments. He arranged his affairs quietly, though he was in great pain, and distributed his belongings and his land, none of which was to be split until his wife should follow him in death. He also asked each of his children to share in the work, duties, and tasks that he had carried on until the time of the accident. He asked his friends to visit him once more, to bid good-bye to them. Although I was a small child at the time, he did not exclude me or my siblings. We were allowed to share in the preparations of the family just as we were permitted to grieve with them until he died. When he did die, he was left at home, in his own beloved home which he had built, and among his friends and neighbors who went to take a last look at him where he lay in the midst of flowers in the place he had lived in and loved so much. In that country today there is still no make-believe slumber room, no embalming, no false makeup to pretend sleep. Only the signs of very disfiguring illnesses are covered up with bandages and only infectious cases are removed from the home prior to the burial.

Why do I describe such "old-fashioned" customs? I think they are an indication of our acceptance of a fatal outcome, and they help the dying patient as well as his family to accept the loss of a loved one. If a patient is allowed to terminate his life in the familiar and beloved environment, it requires less adjustment for him. His own family knows him well enough to replace a sedative with a glass of his favorite wine; or the smell of a home-cooked soup may give him the appetite to sip a few spoons of fluid which, I think, is still more enjoyable than an infusion. I will not minimize the need for sedatives and infusions and realize full well from my own experience as a country doctor that they are sometimes life-saving and often unavoidable. But I also know that patience and familiar people and foods could replace many a bottle of intravenous fluids given for the simple reason that it fulfills the physiological need without involving too many people and/or individual nursing care.

The fact that children are allowed to stay at home where a fatality has stricken and are included in the talk, discussions, and fears gives them the feeling that they are not alone in the grief and gives them the comfort of shared responsibility and shared mourning. It prepares them gradually and helps them view death as part of life, an experience which may help them grow and mature.

This is in great contrast to a society in which death is viewed as taboo, discussion of it is regarded as morbid, and children are excluded with the presumption and pretext that it would be "too much" for them. They are then sent off to relatives, often accompanied with some unconvincing lies of "Mother has gone on a long trip" or other unbelievable stories. The child senses that something is wrong, and his distrust in adults will only multiply if other relatives add new variations of the story, avoid his questions or suspicions, shower him with gifts as a meager substitute for a loss he is not permitted to deal with. Sooner or later the child will become aware of the changed family situation and, depending on the age and personality of the child, will have an unresolved grief and regard this incident as a frightening, mysterious, in any case very traumatic experience with untrustworthy grownups, which he has no way to cope with.

It is equally unwise to tell a little child who lost her brother that God loved little boys so much that he took little Johnny to heaven. When this little girl grew up to be a woman she never solved her anger at God, which resulted in a psychotic depression when she lost her own little son three decades later.

20   We would think that our great emancipation, our knowledge of science and of man, has given us better ways and means to prepare ourselves and our families for this inevitable happening. Instead the   20

days are gone when a man was allowed to die in peace and dignity in his own home.

The more we are making advancements in science, the more we seem to fear and deny the reality of death. How is this possible?

We use euphemisms, we make the dead look as if they were asleep, we ship the children off to protect them from the anxiety and turmoil around the house if the patient is fortunate enough to die at home, we don't allow children to visit their dying parents in the hospitals, we have long and controversial discussions about whether patients should be told the truth—a question that rarely arises when the dying person is tended by the family physician who has known him from delivery to death and who knows the weaknesses and strengths of each member of the family.

I think there are many reasons for this flight away from facing death calmly. One of the most important facts is that dying nowadays is more gruesome in many ways, namely, more lonely, mechanical, and dehumanized; at times it is even difficult to determine technically when the time of death has occurred.

Dying becomes lonely and impersonal because the patient is often taken out of his familiar environment and rushed to an emergency room. Whoever has been very sick and has required rest and comfort especially may recall his experience of being put on a stretcher and enduring the noise of the ambulance siren and hectic rush until the hospital gates open. Only those who have lived through this may appreciate the discomfort and cold necessity of such transportation which is only the beginning of a long order—hard to endure when you are well, difficult to express in words when noise, light, pumps, and voices are all too much to put up with. It may well be that we might consider more the patient under the sheets and blankets and perhaps stop our well-meant efficiency and rush in order to hold the patient's hand, to smile, or to listen to a question. I include the trip to the hospital as the first episode in dying, as it is for many. I am putting it exaggeratedly in contrast to the sick man who is left at home—not to say that lives should not be saved if they can be saved by a hospitalization but to keep the focus on the patient's experience, his needs and his reactions.

25 When a patient is severely ill, he is often treated like a person 25 with no right to an opinion. It is often someone else who makes the decision if and when and where a patient should be hospitalized. It would take so little to remember that the sick person too has feelings,

has wishes and opinions, and has—most important of all—the right to be heard.

Well, our presumed patient has now reached the emergency room. He will be surrounded by busy nurses, orderlies, interns, residents, a lab technician perhaps who will take some blood, an electrocardiogram technician who takes the cardiogram. He may be moved to X-ray and he will overhear opinions of his condition and discussions and questions to members of the family. He slowly but surely is beginning to be treated like a thing. He is no longer a person. Decisions are made often without his opinion. If he tries to rebel he will be sedated and after hours of waiting and wondering whether he has the strength, he will be wheeled into the operating room or intensive treatment unit and become an object of great concern and great financial investment.

He may cry for rest, peace, and dignity, but he will get infusions, transfusions, a heart machine, or tracheotomy if necessary. He may want one single person to stop for one single minute so that he can ask one single question—but he will get a dozen people around the clock, all busily preoccupied with his heart rate, pulse, electrocardiogram or pulmonary functions, his secretions or excretions but not with him as a human being. He may wish to fight it all but it is going to be a useless fight since all this is done in the fight for his life, and if they can save his life they can consider the person afterwards. Those who consider the person first may lose precious time to save his life! At least this seems to be the rationale or justification behind all this—or is it? Is the reason for this increasingly mechanical, depersonalized approach our own defensiveness? Is this approach our own way to cope with and repress the anxieties that a terminally or critically ill patient evokes in us? Is our concentration on equipment, on blood pressure, our desperate attempt to deny the impending death which is so frightening and discomforting to us that we displace all our knowledge onto machines, since they are less close to us than the suffering face of another human being which would remind us once more of our lack of omnipotence, our own limits and failures, and last but not least perhaps our own mortality?

Maybe the question has to be raised: Are we becoming less human or more human? . . . [I]t is clear that whatever the answer may be, the patient is suffering more—not physically, perhaps, but emotionally. And his needs have not changed over the centuries, only our ability to gratify them.

Questions on Meaning

1. What is Kübler-Ross's thesis? Restate it in your own words.
2. Kübler-Ross states in the first paragraph of this 1969 essay that "the many diseases that have taken an impressive toll among the young and middle-aged have been conquered." Do you agree? What medical conditions do young and middle-aged people face today that Kübler-Ross was unaware of? What does this suggest to you about the occasional wide-ranging claim from some expert that "all disease will be eliminated" in the future?
3. Why does Kübler-Ross believe that children should be exposed to death and dying? What does she argue happens when adults attempt to insulate children from dying?

Questions on Rhetorical Strategy and Style

1. Kübler-Ross compares and contrasts the "old-fashioned" customs related to illness and death with more modern customs. How does she use description to support her argument that some of the former customs (or customs in countries where science is "not so advanced") may be more desirable than today's practices? What role does she believe the home environment should play in dying?
2. How does Kübler-Ross use examples to persuade the reader that young children cannot tell the distinction between a desire for someone to be dead and that person's actual death? How does the belief that one might have contributed to a death diminish as one grows older?
3. What examples does Kübler-Ross provide to argue that advancements in science have caused us to "fear and deny the reality of death" more than we used to? Why does she contend that death today is "more gruesome"?

Writing Assignments

1. Reread the last five paragraphs. How does Kübler-Ross's description of medical care compare and contrast with your experiences? Explain why you feel you have been treated like a person or a thing. What do you feel doctors and nurses and other medical professionals should do differently in their patient treatment?
2. What role did death and dying play in your family when you were a child? Was death discussed openly? If you asked questions about

death and dying, were they answered? Explain why you viewed death as scary or a normal part of life. How do you feel death and dying should be explained to children?

3. Kübler-Ross comments that in our dreams, "two completely opposite statements can exist side by side." Write an essay about a dream you had in which reality was turned upside down—or sideways, or reversed. What elements of the dream made it real? What made it profoundly absurd? Describe whether the dream lingered with you long after you awoke or whether its imagery was ephemeral. What experiences or mood might have caused you to have such a strange dream?

The Cosmic Calendar

Carl Sagan

Carl Sagan (1934–1996) wrote many bestselling scientific books, especially Cosmos, *the bestselling science book in English. The book became the basis for the Emmy and Peabody award-winning television series. His novel,* Contact, *was made into a major motion picture. Having taught at Stanford and Harvard, he became the David Duncan Professor of Astronomy and Space Sciences and Director of the Laboratory for Planetary Studies at Cornell University. His role in the American space program included consulting with and advising NASA, briefing the Apollo astronauts on their flights to the Moon, and work on the Mariner, Viking, Voyager, and Galileo planetary expeditions. Among many awards, Sagan received the NASA medals for Exceptional Scientific Achievement and (twice) for Distinguished Public Service, as well as the NASA Apollo Achievement Award. This set of charts and explanations is taken from his 1977 Pulitzer Prize winning book* The Dragons of Eden: Speculations of the Evolution of Human Intelligence.

1   The world is very old, and human beings are very young. Significant events in our personal lives are measured in years or less; our lifetimes in decades; our family genealogies in centuries; and all of recorded history in millennia. But we have been preceded by an awesome vista of time, extending for prodigious periods into the past, about which we know little—both because there are no written records and because we have real difficulty in grasping the immensity of the intervals involved.

Reprinted from *The Dragons of Eden* (1977), by permission of the Estate of Dr. Carl Sagan and Democritis Properties LLC. As with so many of Dr. Sagan's other predictions, his warning in the fourth paragraph of this piece turned out to be correct. The current scientific consensus on the age of the universe is 13.7 billion years old. Even so, this chapter remains an exemplar of science writing, conveying a difficult concept so that all of us can understand it.

Yet we are able to date events in the remote past. Geological stratification and radioactive dating provide information on archaeological, paleontological and geological events; and astrophysical theory provides data on the ages of planetary surfaces, stars, and the Milky Way Galaxy, as well as an estimate of the time that has elapsed since that extraordinary event called the Big Bang—an explosion that involved all of the matter and energy in the present universe. The Big Bang may be the beginning of the universe, or it may be a discontinuity in which information about the earlier history of the universe was destroyed. But it is certainly the earliest event about which we have any record.

The most instructive way I know to express this cosmic chronology is to imagine the fifteen-billion-year lifetime of the universe (or at least its present incarnation since the Big Bang) compressed into the span of a single year. Then every billion years of Earth history would correspond to about twenty-four days of our cosmic year, and one second of that year to 475 real revolutions of the Earth about the sun. [In Figures 1, 2, and 3] I present the cosmic chronology in three forms: a list of some representative pre-December dates; a calendar for the month of December; and a closer look at the late evening of New Year's Eve. On this scale, the events of our history books—even books that make significant efforts to deprovincialize the present—are so compressed that it is necessary to give a second-by-second recounting of the last seconds of the cosmic year. Even then, we find events listed as contemporary that we have been taught to consider as widely separated in time. In the history of life, an equally rich tapestry must have been woven in other periods—for example, between 10:02 and 10:03 on the morning of April 6th or September 16th. But we have detailed records only for the very end of the cosmic year.

The chronology corresponds to the best evidence now available. But some of it is rather shaky. No one would be astounded if, for example, it turns out that plants colonized the land in the Ordovician rather than the Silurian Period; or that segmented worms appeared earlier in the Precambrian Period than indicated. Also, in the chronology of the last ten seconds of the cosmic year, it was obviously impossible for me to include all significant events; I hope I may be excused for not having explicitly mentioned advances in art, music and literature or the historically significant American, French, Russian and Chinese revolutions.

5 The construction of such tables and calendars is inevitably 5 humbling. It is disconcerting to find that in such a cosmic year the

Pre-December Dates

Big Bang	January 1
Origin of Milky Way Galaxy	May 1
Origin of the solar system	September 9
Formation of the Earth	September 14
Origin of life on Earth	~ September 25
Formation of the oldest rocks known on Earth	October 2
Date of oldest fossils (bacteria and blue-green algae)	October 9
Invention of sex (by microorganisms)	~ November 1
Oldest fossil photosynthetic plants	November 12
Eukaryotes (first cells with nuclei) flourish	November 15

~ = approximately.

Figure 1

Cosmic Calender
DECEMBER

Sunday	Monday	Tuesday	Wednesday	Thursday	Friday	Saturday
	1 Significant oxygen atmosphere begins to develop on Earth.	**2**	**3**	**4**	**5** Extensive vulcanism and channel formation on Mars.	**6**
7	**8**	**9**	**10**	**11**	**12**	**13**
14	**15**	**16** First worms.	**17** Precambrian ends. Paleozoic Era and Cambrian Period begin. Invertebrates flourish.	**18** First oceanic plankton. Trilobites flourish.	**19** Ordovician Period. First Fish. First vertebrates.	**20** Silurian Period. First vascular plants. Plants begin colonization of land.
21 Devonian Period begins, First insects. Animals begin colonization of land.	**22** First amphibians. First winged insects.	**23** Carboniferous Period. First trees. First reptiles.	**24** Permian Period begins. First dinosaurs.	**25** Paleozoic Era ends. Mesozoic Era Begins.	**26** Triassic Period. First mammals.	**27** Jurassic Period. First birds.
28 Cretaceous Period. First flowers. Dinosaurs become extinct.	**29** Mesozoic Era ends. Cenozoic Era and Tertiary Period begin. First cetaceans. First primates.	**30** Early evolution of frontal lobes in the brains of primates. First hominids. Giant mammals flourish.	**31** End of the Pliocene Period. Quaternary (Pleistocene and Holocene) Period. First humans.			

Figure 2

Earth does not condense out of interstellar matter until early September; dinosaurs emerge on Christmas Eve; flowers arise on December 28th; and men and women originate at 10:30 P.M. on New Year's Eve. All of recorded history occupies the last ten seconds of

December 31	
Origin of *Proconsul and Ramapithecus*, probable ancestors of apes and men	~ 1:30 P.M.
First humans	~ 10:30 P.M.
Widespread use of stone tools	11:00 P.M.
Domestication of fire by Peking man	11:46 P.M.
Beginning of most recent glacial period	11:56 P.M.
Seafarers settle Australia	11:58 P.M.
Extensive cave painting in Europe	11:59 P.M.
Invention of agriculture	11:59:20 P.M.
Neolithic civilization; first cities	11:59:35 P.M.
First dynasties in Sumer, Ebla and Egypt; development of astronomy	11:59:50 P.M.
Invention of the alphabet; Akkadian Empire	11:59:51 P.M.
Hammurabic legal codes in Babylon; Middle Kingdom in Egypt	11:59:52 P.M.
Bronze metallurgy; Mycenaean culture; Trojan War; Olmec culture; invention of the compass	11:59:53 P.M.
Iron metallurgy; First Assyrian Empire; Kingdom of Israel; founding of Carthage by Phoenicia	11:59:54 P.M.
Asokan India; Ch'in Dynasty China; Periclean Athens; birth of Buddha	11:59:55 P.M.
Euclidean geometry; Archimedean physics; Ptolemaic astronomy; Roman Empire; birth of Christ	11:59:56 P.M.
Zero and decimals invented in Indian arithmetic; Rome falls; Moslem conquests	11:59:57 P.M.
Mayan civilization; Sung Dynasty China; Byzantine empire; Mongol invasion; Crusades	11:59:58 P.M.
Renaissance in Europe; voyages of discovery from Europe and from Ming Dynasty China; emergence of the experimental method in science	11:59:59 P.M.
Widespread development of science and technology; emergence of global culture; acquisition of the means of self-destruction of the human species; first steps in spacecraft planetary exploration and the search of extraterrestrial intelligence	Now: The first second of New Year's Day

Figure 3

December 31; and the time from the waning of the Middle Ages to the present occupies little more than one second. But because I have arranged it that way, the first cosmic year has just ended. And despite the insignificance of the instant we have so far occupied in cosmic time, it is clear that what happens on and near Earth at the beginning of the second cosmic year will depend very much on the scientific wisdom and the distinctly human sensitivity of mankind.

Questions on Meaning

1. How old is the universe by scientific reasoning? What happened over the course of the "universal year" in Sagan's analysis?
2. When did the earth began to develop an atmosphere? How long did it take humans to emerge?
3. How do scientists come up with these figures? What dating do they use, and how do they analyze the data they find from carbon dating?

Questions on Rhetorical Strategy and Style

1. Scientists and science teachers have often used Sagan's cosmic calendar to explain the history of the universe. Why is the graphic image more effective than an explanation in words?
2. Why is the graph divided into three forms? What do we learn by breaking December out into specific days?
3. What do we learn from the minute-to-minute elaboration? How does that illustrate Sagan's statement that humans are very young?

Writing Assignments

1. Look carefully at the chart of December 31. Write about the history of humans as illustrated in this graph. What does our technological era mean to the whole history? What might that suggest about our world?
2. Sagan concludes by saying that these charts are humbling. Another younger scientist has suggested that recent research suggests that we are not made merely of dust but rather of stardust. What does understanding the universe tell us about the importance of being able to investigate our world?
3. Sagan appreciated the achievements of human investigators. Read about the trips to the moon and the more recent Mars probe. What human efforts are involved in such research and exploration?

Why Vampires Never Die

Guillermo del Toro and Chuck Hogan

Coauthors of The Strain *(2009), a vampire novel, these two writers bring together several threads of current cinema and fiction motifs. Best known as the writer and director of* Pan's Labyrinth *(2006) and* Hellboy *(2004), Mexican born Guillermo del Toro (1964–) was reared by his devout Catholic grandmother. His fascination with evil monstrous creatures may be traced to various causes, but his reading of fantasy writer Jorge Luis Borges and science fiction writer H. P. Lovecraft provided imagery for his work. He portrays the evils of fascist power while evoking sympathy for the young and defenseless. His earlier works include* The Devil's Backbone *(2001) and* Chronos *(1993). Chuck Hogan (ca. 1968–), on the other hand, creates romances entwined with science and politics. His hovel* The Killing Moon *(2008) demonstrates the complexity of his work. Earlier novels include* Prince of Thieves *(2005),* The Blood Artists *(1999), and* The Standoff *(1995). This article from* The New York Times *demonstrates the effectiveness of their teamed composition.*

1   Tonight, you or someone you love will likely be visited by a   1
vampire—on cable television or the big screen, or in the
bookstore. Our own novel describes a modern-day epidemic
that spreads across New York City.

    It all started nearly 200 years ago. It was the "Year Without a Summer" of 1816, when ash from volcanic eruptions lowered temperatures around the globe, giving rise to widespread famine. A few friends gathered at the Villa Diodati on Lake Geneva and decided to engage in a small competition to see who could come up with the most terrifying tale—and the two great monsters of the modern age were born.

One was created by Mary Godwin, soon to become Mary Shelley, whose Dr. Frankenstein gave life to a desolate creature. The other monster was less created than fused. John William Polidori stitched together folklore, personal resentment and erotic anxieties into "The Vampyre," a story that is the basis for vampires as they are understood today.

With "The Vampyre," Polidori gave birth to the two main branches of vampiric fiction: the vampire as romantic hero, and the vampire as undead monster. This ambivalence may reflect Polidori's own, as it is widely accepted that Lord Ruthven, the titular creature, was based upon Lord Byron—literary superstar of the era and another resident of the lakeside villa that fateful summer. Polidori tended to Byron day and night, both as his doctor and most devoted groupie. But Polidori resented him as well: Byron was dashing and brilliant, while the poor doctor had a rather drab talent and unremarkable physique.

5   But this was just a new twist to a very old idea. The myth, established well before the invention of the word "vampire," seems to cross every culture, language and era. The Indian Baital, the Ch'ing Shin in China, and the Romanian Strigoi are but a few of its names. The creature seems to be as old as Babylonia and Sumer. Or even older.

The vampire may originate from a repressed memory we had as primates. Perhaps at some point we were—out of necessity—cannibalistic. As soon as we became sedentary, agricultural tribes with social boundaries, one seminal myth might have featured our ancestors as primitive beasts who slept in the cold loam of the earth and fed off the salty blood of the living.

Monsters, like angels, are invoked by our individual and collective needs. Today, much as during that gloomy summer in 1816, we feel the need to seek their cold embrace.

Herein lies an important clue: in contrast to timeless creatures like the dragon, the vampire does not seek to obliterate us, but instead offers a peculiar brand of blood alchemy. For as his contagion bestows its nocturnal gift, the vampire transforms our vile, mortal selves into the gold of eternal youth, and instills in us something that every social construct seeks to quash: primal lust. If youth is desire married with unending possibility, then vampire lust creates within us a delicious void, one we long to fulfill.

In other words, whereas other monsters emphasize what is mortal in us, the vampire emphasizes the eternal in us. Through the panacea of its blood it turns the lead of our toxic flesh into golden matter.

10   In a society that moves as fast as ours, where every week a new   10
"blockbuster" must be enthroned at the box office, or where idols are fabricated by consensus every new television season, the promise of something everlasting, something truly eternal, holds a special allure. As a seductive figure, the vampire is as flexible and polyvalent as ever. Witness its slow mutation from the pansexual, decadent Anne Rice creatures to the current permutations—promising anything from chaste eternal love to wild nocturnal escapades—and there you will find the true essence of immortality: adaptability.

Vampires find their niche and mutate at an accelerated rate now—in the past one would see, for decades, the same variety of fiend, repeated in multiple storylines. Now, vampires simultaneously occur in all forms and tap into our every need: soap opera storylines, sexual liberation, noir detective fiction, etc. The myth seems to be twittering promiscuously to serve all avenues of life, from cereal boxes to romantic fiction. The fast pace of technology accelerates its viral dispersion in our culture.

But if Polidori remains the roots in the genealogy of our creature, the most widely known vampire was birthed by Bram Stoker in 1897.

Part of the reason for the great success of his "Dracula" is generally acknowledged to be its appearance at a time of great technological revolution. The narrative is full of new gadgets (telegraphs, typing machines), various forms of communication (diaries, ship logs), and cutting-edge science (blood transfusions)—a mash-up of ancient myth in conflict with the world of the present.

Today as well, we stand at the rich uncertain dawn of a new level of scientific innovation. The wireless technology we carry in our pockets today was the stuff of the science fiction in our youth. Our technological arrogance mirrors more and more the Wellsian dystopia of dissatisfaction, while allowing us to feel safe and connected at all times. We can call, see or hear almost anything and anyone no matter where we are. For most people then, the only remote place remains within. "Know thyself" we do not.

15   Despite our obsessive harnessing of information, we are still ulti-   15
mately vulnerable to our fates and our nightmares. We enthrone the

deadly virus in the very same way that "Dracula" allowed the British public to believe in monsters: through science. Science becomes the modern man's superstition. It allows him to experience fear and awe again, and to believe in the things he cannot see.

And through awe, we once again regain spiritual humility. The current vampire pandemic serves to remind us that we have no true jurisdiction over our bodies, our climate or our very souls. Monsters will always provide the possibility of mystery in our mundane "reality show" lives, hinting at a larger spiritual world; for if there are demons in our midst, there surely must be angels lurking nearby as well. In the vampire we find Eros and Thanatos fused together in archetypal embrace, spiraling through the ages, undying.

Forever.

Questions on Meaning

1. Where and when did the modern vampire story begin? What qualities did the first vampire have?
2. On whom was the Bram Stoker vampire modeled, and what do we know about the poet who provided the image?
3. What human qualities are blended in the vampire? Why does the idea of the vampire evoke eternal youth?
4. How is sexuality and lust incorporated into the vampire image? Has this aspect of the vampire developed in most recent vampire fiction?

Questions on Rhetorical Strategy and Style

1. The essay begins by evoking an almost fictional time when a volcano stopped a summer from happening and sent a group of writers to a villa to compose. How does this intro catch the interest of the reader and reflect the romantic tone of the essay?
2. The writing in this essay partakes of the poetic as the authors evoke a kind of religious and spiritual feeling about vampires. How does this mood help the reader to understand the point of the essay?
3. The essay ends with a hopeful promise that vampire stories will become better and better as they reflect the technological togetherness and the psychological aloneness of our era. How does that rhetorical move help the reader to feel the power of the argument?

Writing Assignments

1. Consider the power of the technology that you carry in your pocket. How long has this technology been available? Ask older people you know about communication twenty or forty years ago, and watch a movie from the sixties. Then write about how the electronic devices affect the people and the plot of the film.
2. Pick your favorite vampire in modern film or fiction, then write a character analysis of that creature. What good traits does the creature have? What are its flaws or weaknesses?

3. Why does society suppress the desires of young people? What are the dangers in those desires? What freedom does the idea of eternal youth at the cost of vampirism promise? Write about why this concept continues to appeal to youthful readers.

Fairy Tales and Modern Stories

Bruno Bettelheim

Bruno Bettelheim (1903–90), a noted psychotherapist, was born in Vienna, Austria. He graduated from the University of Vienna (1938), where he studied with Sigmund Freud. Bettelheim was imprisoned by the Nazis at Dachau and Buchenwald from 1938 to 1939. After his release from prison, Bettelheim emigrated to the United States, where he went to work at the University of Chicago. In 1944, he became director of the University's Sonia Shankman Orthogenic School, a treatment facility for severely disturbed children. Bettelheim gained international recognition for his work with autistic children, although not without some controversy over his methods. He published many books on psychotherapy, including Love Is Not Enough: The Treatment of Emotionally Disturbed Children *(1950),* The Children of the Dream *(1969),* The Uses of Enchantment *(1976), and* Freud and Man's Soul *(1982). He also wrote articles on rearing normal children for lay audiences. In addition to a well-known article on his experiences in Nazi concentration camps (1943), Bettelheim published two books on the death camps,* The Informed Heart: Autonomy in a Mass Age *(1960) and* Surviving and Other Essays *(1979), reprinted as* Surviving the Holocaust *(1986). In this essay, taken from* The Uses of Enchantment, *Bettelheim argues that fairy tales can provide children more comfort than "sensible" stories.*

The shortcomings of the realistic stories with which many parents have replaced fairy tales is suggested by a comparison of two such stories—"The Little Engine That Could" and "The Swiss Family Robinson"—with the fairy tale of "Rapunzel." "The Little Engine That Could" encourages the child to believe that if he tries hard and does not give up, he will finally succeed. A young adult has recalled how much impressed she was at the age of seven when her mother read her this story. She became convinced that one's attitude indeed affects one's achievements—that if she would now approach a task with the conviction that she could conquer it, she would succeed. A few days later, this child encountered in first grade a challenging situation: she was trying to make a house out of paper, gluing various sheets together. But her house continually collapsed. Frustrated, she began to seriously doubt whether her idea of building such a paper house could be realized. But then the story of "The Little Engine That Could" came to her mind; twenty years later, she recalled how at that moment she began to sing to herself the magic formula "I think I can, I think I can, I think I can . . . " So she continued to work on her paper house, and it continued to collapse. The project ended in complete defeat, with this little girl convinced that she had failed where anybody else could have succeeded, as the Little Engine had. Since "The Little Engine That Could" was a story set in the present, using such common props as engines that pulled trains, this girl had tried to apply its lesson directly in her daily life, without any fantasy elaboration, and had experienced a defeat that still rankled twenty years later.

Very different was the impact of "The Swiss Family Robinson" on another little girl. The story tells how a shipwrecked family manages to live an adventurous, idyllic, constructive, and pleasurable life—a life very different from this child's own existence. Her father had to be away from home a great deal, and her mother was mentally ill and spent protracted periods in institutions. So the girl was shuttled from her home to that of an aunt, then to that of a grandmother, and back home again, as the need arose. During these years, the girl read over and over again the story of this happy family who lived on a desert island, where no member could be away from the rest of the family. Many years later, she recalled what a warm, cozy feeling she had when, propped up by a few large pillows, she forgot all about her present predicament as she read this story. As soon as she had finished it, she started to read it over again. The happy hours she spent with the

Family Robinson in that fantasy land permitted her not to be defeated by the difficulties that reality presented to her. She was able to counteract the impact of harsh reality by imaginary gratifications. But since the story was not a fairy tale, it merely gave her a temporary escape from her problems; it did not hold out any promise to her that her life would take a turn for the better.

Consider the effect that "Rapunzel" had on a third girl. This girl's mother had died in a car accident. The girl's father, deeply upset by what had happened to his wife (he had been driving the car), withdrew entirely into himself and handed the care of his daughter over to a nursemaid, who was little interested in the girl and gave her complete freedom to do as she liked. When the girl was seven, her father remarried, and, as she recalled it, it was around that time that "Rapunzel" became so important to her. Her stepmother was clearly the witch of the story, and she was the girl locked away in the tower. The girl recalled that she felt akin to Rapunzel because the witch had "forcibly" taken possession of her, as her stepmother had forcibly worked her way into the girl's life. The girl felt imprisoned in her new home, in contrast to her life of freedom with the nursemaid. She felt as victimized as Rapunzel, who, in her tower, had so little control over her life. Rapunzel's long hair was the key to the story. The girl wanted her hair to grow long, but her stepmother cut it short; long hair in itself became the symbol of freedom and happiness to her. The story convinced her that a prince (her father) would come someday and rescue her, and this conviction sustained her. If life became too difficult, all she needed was to imagine herself as Rapunzel, her hair grown long, and the prince loving and rescuing her.

"Rapunzel" suggests why fairy tales can offer more to the child than even such a very nice children's story as "The Swiss Family Robinson." In "The Swiss Family Robinson," there is no witch against whom the child can discharge her anger in fantasy and on whom she can blame the father's lack of interest. "The Swiss Family Robinson" offers escape fantasies, and it did help the girl who read it over and over to forget temporarily how difficult life was for her. But it offered no specific hope for the future. "Rapunzel," on the other hand, offered the girl a chance to see the witch of the story as so evil that by comparison even the "witch" stepmother at home was not really so bad. "Rapunzel" also promised the girl that her rescue would be effected by her own body, when her hair grew long. Most important of all, it promised that the "prince" was only temporarily blinded—that he would regain his sight and rescue his princess. This fantasy continued to sustain the girl, though to a less intense degree, until she fell in love and married, and then she no longer needed it. We can understand why at first glance the stepmother, if she had known the meaning of "Rapunzel" to her stepdaughter, would have felt that fairy tales are bad for children. What she would not have known was that unless the stepdaughter had been able to find that fantasy satisfaction through "Rapunzel," she would have tried to break up her father's marriage and that without the hope for the future which the story gave her she might have gone badly astray in life.

5   It seems quite understandable that when children are asked to name their favorite fairy tales, hardly any modern tales are among their choices. Many of the new tales have sad endings, which fail to provide the escape and consolation that the fearsome events in the fairy tale require if the child is to be strengthened for meeting the vagaries of his life. Without such encouraging conclusions, the child, after listening to the story, feels that there is indeed no hope for extricating himself from his despairs. In the traditional fairy tale, the hero is rewarded and the evil person meets his well-deserved fate, thus satisfying the child's deep need for justice to prevail. How else can a child hope that justice will be done to him, who so often feels unfairly treated? And how else can he convince himself that he must act correctly, when he is so sorely tempted to give in to the asocial proddings of his desires?

Questions on Meaning

1. Describe why Bettelheim feels that traditional fairy tales are more comforting to children than more realistic stories.
2. What did long hair in the fairy tale *Rapunzel* symbolize to the third subject described by Bettelheim?
3. What does the fairy tale *Rapunzel* offer a child (because of the witch) that *The Swiss Family Robinson* lacks?

Questions on Rhetorical Strategy and Style

1. Find where Bettelheim uses comparison and contrast to argue what he feels are "shortcomings" of the realistic stories he discusses, *The Little Engine That Could* and *The Swiss Family Robinson.*
2. What rhetorical strategy does Bettelheim use in the final paragraph? Identify the elements of the strategy.

Writing Assignments

1. Name your favorite fairy tale. Write an essay explaining its importance to you as a child. Explain how you adapted the fantasy to your own life. Describe how it affected you as an adolescent and how it affects you now.
2. Losing oneself in fantasy is a common and—as Bettelheim might advise—healthy reaction to some aspects of life. Write an essay in which you describe a current fantasy in your life—such as winning a sports contest, buying a car, or dating a special someone. How did the fantasy develop? Are you able to keep it in check as a fantasy?

Index